A Companion to Cognitive Anthropology

The *Blackwell Companions to Anthropology* offers a series of comprehensive syntheses of the traditional subdisciplines, primary subjects, and geographic areas of inquiry for the field. Taken together, the series represents both a contemporary survey of anthropology and a cutting edge guide to the emerging research and intellectual trends in the field as a whole.

1. *A Companion to Linguistic Anthropology*, edited by Alessandro Duranti
2. *A Companion to the Anthropology of Politics*, edited by David Nugent and Joan Vincent
3. *A Companion to the Anthropology of American Indians*, edited by Thomas Biolsi
4. *A Companion to Psychological Anthropology*, edited by Conerly Casey and Robert B. Edgerton
5. *A Companion to the Anthropology of Japan*, edited by Jennifer Robertson
6. *A Companion to Latin American Anthropology*, edited by Deborah Poole
7. *A Companion to Biological Anthropology*, edited by Clark Larsen
8. *A Companion to the Anthropology of India*, edited by Isabelle Clark-Decès
9. *A Companion to Medical Anthropology*, edited by Merrill Singer and Pamela I. Erickson
10. *A Companion to Cognitive Anthropology*, edited by David B. Kronenfeld, Giovanni Bennardo, Victor C. de Munck, and Michael D. Fischer
11. *A Companion to Cultural Resource Management*, edited by Thomas King
12. *A Companion to the Anthropology of Education*, edited by Bradley A. Levinson and Mica Pollock
13. *A Companion to the Anthropology of the Body and Embodiment*, edited by Frances E. Mascia-Lees
14. *A Companion to Paleopathology*, edited by Anne L. Grauer
15. *A Companion to Folklore*, edited by Regina F. Bendix and Galit Hasan-Rokem
16. *A Companion to Forensic Anthropology*, edited by Dennis Dirkmaat
17. *A Companion to the Anthropology of Europe*, edited by Ullrich Kockel, Máiréad Nic Craith, and Jonas Frykman
18. *A Companion to Border Studies*, edited by Thomas M. Wilson and Hastings Donnan
19. *A Companion to Rock Art*, edited by Jo McDonald and Peter Veth
20. *A Companion to Moral Anthropology*, edited by Didier Fassin
21. *A Companion to Gender Prehistory*, edited by Diane Bolger
22. *A Companion to Organizational Anthropology*, edited by D. Douglas Caulkins and Ann T. Jordan
23. *A Companion to Paleoanthropology*, edited by David R. Begun
24. *A Companion to Chinese Archaeology*, edited by Anne P. Underhill
25. *A Companion to the Anthropology of Religion*, edited by Janice Boddy and Michael Lambek
26. *A Companion to Urban Anthropology*, edited by Donald M. Nonini
27. *A Companion to the Anthropology of the Middle East*, edited by Soraya Altorki
28. *A Companion to Heritage Studies*, edited by William Logan, Máiréad Nic Craith and Ullrich Kockel
29. *A Companion to Dental Anthropology*, edited by Joel D. Irish and G. Richard Scott

Forthcoming

A Companion to Witchcraft and Sorcery, edited by Bruce Kapferer
A Companion to Anthropological Genetics, edited by Dennis H. O'Rourke
A Companion to Anthropology and Environmental Health, edited by Merrill Singer
A Companion to South Asia in the Past, edited by Gwen Robbins Schug and S. R. Walimbe
A Companion to Oral History, edited by Mark Tebeau

A Companion to Cognitive Anthropology

Edited by
David B. Kronenfeld,
Giovanni Bennardo,
Victor C. de Munck,
and Michael D. Fischer

WILEY Blackwell

This paperback edition first published 2016

Edition history: Blackwell Publishing Ltd (hardback, 2011)

Registered Office
John Wiley & Sons Ltd, The Atrium, Southern Gate, Chichester, West Sussex, PO19 8SQ, UK

Editorial Offices
350 Main Street, Malden, MA 02148-5020, USA
9600 Garsington Road, Oxford, OX4 2DQ, UK
The Atrium, Southern Gate, Chichester, West Sussex, PO19 8SQ, UK

For details of our global editorial offices, for customer services, and for information about how to apply for permission to reuse the copyright material in this book please see our website at www.wiley.com/wiley-blackwell.

Library of Congress Cataloging-in-Publication Data applied for

Hardback 9781405187787
Paperback 9781119111658

A catalogue record for this book is available from the British Library.

Cover image: From top: Brain scan, photo ©Mehau Kulyk / Science Photo Library; African drumming, photo ©Tracey Fahy / Alamy; Storytelling session, photo ©Image Source / Alamy

Set in 10/12.5pt ITC Galliard by SPi Global, Pondicherry, India
Printed and bound in Malaysia by Vivar Printing Sdn Bhd

1 2016

Contents

Notes on Contributors

Dominik Albrecht is a medical doctor at the Department of Psychiatry at the University of Magdeburg. He holds an additional master's degree in neuroscience involving research performed at the Leibniz Institute for Neurobiology. His scientific interests range from the neurobiology of psychiatric disorders to cognitive and social neuroscience.

E. N. Anderson is professor of anthropology, emeritus, at the University of California, Riverside. He received his Ph.D. from the University of California, Berkeley, in 1967. He has done research on human ecology in several countries, with most time spent in Hong Kong, British Columbia, and Quintana Roo (Mexico), focusing on how people think about and manage plants and animals. He has published several books, including *The Food of China* (1988), *Ecologies of the Heart* (1996), *Everyone Eats* (2005), and *The Pursuit of Ecotopia* (2010).

Sieghard Beller is research fellow at the University of Freiburg, Germany, where he received his doctorate and habilitation in psychology. His research covers reasoning processes and language effects in a broad range of domains and from a cross-cultural perspective. He is the author of a textbook on empirical research methods and coauthor of textbooks on thinking and language and on culture and cognition. His most relevant publications are "The Limits of Counting: Numerical Cognition between Evolution and Culture" (together with Andrea Bender, *Science*, 2008), "Weighing Up Physical Causes: Effects of Culture, Linguistic Cues and Content" (together with Andrea Bender and Jie Song, *Journal of Cognition and Culture*, 2009), and "Deontic Reasoning Reviewed: Psychological Questions, Empirical Findings, and Current Theories" (*Cognitive Processing*, 2010).

Andrea Bender is Heisenberg Fellow at the University of Freiburg. She received her doctorate in cultural anthropology, completed her habilitation in psychology, and has carried out repeated fieldwork in the Pacific, particularly in Tonga. She is coauthor of textbooks on thinking and language and on culture and cognition; her most relevant publications are "The Limits of Counting: Numerical Cognition between Evolution and Culture" (together with Sieghard Beller, *Science*, 2008) and "Anthropology in Cognitive Science" (together with Edwin Hutchins and Douglas L. Medin, *Topics in Cognitive Science*, 2010).

Giovanni Bennardo is an associate professor in linguistic and cognitive anthropology and founding member of the Cognitive Studies Initiative at Northern Illinois University. His primary geographic focus is Oceania, in particular, western Polynesia, the Kingdom of Tonga, where he has conducted extensive fieldwork. His research and publications examine the relationship between language, cognition, and cross-modular and cross-domain interactions. In his recent book *Language, Space, and Social Relationships: A Foundational Cultural Model in Polynesia* he investigated features of the mental representations of space instantiated in various cultural realms such as exchange, navigation, kinship, land distribution, social networks, and politics. His current research interest is on the conceptualization (cultural models) of nature and the environment across cultures.

B. G. Blount retired from the University of Georgia and the University of Texas and is currently a consultant and owner of SocioEcological Informatics, consulting on NOAA-funded research on the resilience and vulnerability of fishing communities on the US Gulf Coast. Recent publications include "Responses to Globalization," in *MAST (Maritime Studies)*, and "An Anthropological Research Protocol for Marine Protected Areas: Creating a Niche in a Multi-Disciplinary Cultural Hierarchy," with Ariana Pitchon, in *Human Organization*.

Stephen P. Borgatti is the Paul Chellgren Endowed Chair of Management at the University of Kentucky, where he is affiliated with the LINKS Center for Organizational Social Network Analysis. He is the author of Anthropac, a software package for cultural domain analysis, and a coauthor of UCINET, a software package for social network analysis. He is a past director of the NSF Summer Institute for Ethnographic Research Methods.

James Boster is a professor of cognitive, psychological, and linguistic anthropology at the University of Connecticut. His earlier work concerned how patterns of intracultural variation reflect the ways in which culture is learned and transmitted, and how the patterns of correspondence between different systems of biological classification reflect pan-human perceptual strategies drawing common inferences from similar experience. His current research focuses on how people understand themselves and each other, and in how intra- and intercultural variation in emotions, personality, and values is patterned.

F. K. L. Chit Hlaing (F. K. Lehman) has engaged in fieldwork largely in Burma and Southeast Asia, where he grew up. His BA was in mathematics, his Ph.D. in anthropology and linguistics. He has applied mathematics in his ethnographic and linguistic work, beginning with his dissertation, which was on the cultural history of India. This led him early into cognitive science and generative linguistics from the end of the

1950s. He is a specialist in Southeast Asian ethnology, history, and languages, and in formal theoretical analysis. He is emeritus professor of anthropology and linguistics and in the program for cognitive science in the University of Illinois at Urbana–Champaign. Recent publications include "Formalism and Empiricism: On the Value of Thinking Mathematically about Social Grouping and Corporateness" in *Structure and Dynamics* (e-journal), and "The Central Position Of Shan/Tai Buddhism for the Sociopolitical Development of the Wa and Kayah Peoples" in *Journal of Contemporary Buddhism.*

Benjamin N. Colby is emeritus professor of anthropology at University of California, Irvine and a member of the social dynamics and complexity group at the Institute for Mathematical Behavioral Sciences at UC Irvine. He is editor of the University of California electronic journal, *Structure and Dynamics.* His current research involves the development of new tests for a theory of adaptive potential and related variables such as health, nutrition, and new indicators of cultural well-being. Additionally he is doing an ethnography of agricultural practices, carbon sequestration, and other responses to climate change in Sonoma County, California.

Roy D'Andrade is emeritus professor of anthropology at the University of California, San Diego and the University of Connecticut. His research interests focus on culture and cognition, social theory, and quantitative methods. He has recently completed a study of values among Americans, Japanese, and Vietnamese (*A Study of Values: American, Vietnamese and Japanese*) and is currently working on a theory of cultural life worlds within modern societies.

Victor C. de Munck is an associate professor at SUNY New Paltz. His specialty is cognitive anthropology and his cultural areas of specialization are Sri Lanka, Macedonia, Lithuania, Russia, and the USA. He is the author of five books – two on methods, an urban ethnography on Vilnius (with three co authors), an ethnography of a Sri Lankan village, and a book entitled *Culture, Self and Meaning* – and of over 50 articles in academic journals. His areas of research are cross-cultural research, cultural models, self and identity, romantic love, and the synthesis of qualitative and quantitative methods. Two recent areas of research are a focus on psychic unity or sameness across people and cultures, and processes of the development of intimate dyads versus public identities.

Roy Ellen is professor of anthropology and human ecology at the University of Kent and director of its Centre for Biocultural Diversity. He received his anthropological training at the London School of Economics and has worked largely on issues relating to the environment and knowledge systems in the Moluccas. His recent publications include a monograph, *On the Edge of the Banda Zone: Past and Present in the Social Organization of a Moluccan Trading Network* (2003); a collection of essays, *The Categorical Impulse: Essays in the Anthropology of Classifying Behaviour* (2006); and two edited works, *Ethnobiology and the Science of Humankind* (2006) and *Modern Crises and Traditional Strategies: Local Ecological Knowledge in Island Southeast Asia* (2007). He is a Fellow of the British Academy and President of the Royal Anthropological Institute between 2007 and 2011.

Michael D. Fischer is professor of anthropological sciences at the University of Kent and has written *Applications in Computing for Social Anthropologists* (1994).

Linda C. Garro holds doctorates in social sciences (anthropology) and cognitive psychology and is professor of anthropology at the University of California, Los Angeles. Her research activities are in the areas of medical and psychological anthropology and include representing cultural knowledge about illness; variability in cultural knowledge; health care decision-making; health and everyday family life; illness narratives; and remembering as a social, cultural, and cognitive process. Her articles have appeared in *American Anthropologist*, *American Ethnologist*, *Culture, Medicine and Psychiatry*, *Ethos*, *Medical Anthropology Quarterly*, *Social Science and Medicine*, *Transcultural Psychiatry*, and other journals. In 1999 she received the Stirling Award from the Society for Psychological Anthropology.

John B. Gatewood is a cognitive anthropologist at Lehigh University in Bethlehem, Pennsylvania. His principal research interest is the social organization of knowledge or socially distributed cognition, which he has studied in a variety of contexts, such as commercial fishing boats, university admissions, credit unions, and tourism sites. His recent research focuses on conjoining the cultural models approach with cultural consensus analysis, as well as methodological refinements to cultural consensus analysis.

Miriam Noël Haidle received her doctoral and habilitation degrees in prehistory and paleoanthropology from the University of Tübingen, Germany, in 1996 and 2006. She is the coordinator of "The Role of Culture in Early Expansions of Humans" Research Center of the Heidelberg Academy of Sciences and Humanities. Current work about her special focus on tool behavior and the evolution of mind has been published in "Working Memory Capacity and the Evolution of Modern Cognitive Capacities – Implications from Animal and Early Human Tool Use" (*Current Anthropology* 51/S1, 2010, S149–S166).

Daniel S. Halgin is a visiting assistant professor of management at the University of Kentucky. He is also affiliated with the LINKS Center for Organizational Social Network Analysis. His program of research focuses on social network theory, identity dynamics, and research methodologies.

W. Penn Handwerker was trained as a general anthropologist with an emphasis on the intersection of biological and cultural anthropology, and has published in all four fields of the discipline. His book *The Origin of Cultures* (2009) develops the idea that the shared assumptions, norms, and patterns of behavior that constitute cultures originate unexpectedly and are subject to selective processes that optimize a cultural participant's ability to survive and eat well reliably. He is currently developing the implication that cultures shaped our cognitive abilities in ways that improved how cultures worked, in a forthcoming book *The Evolution of Teamwork*.

Brian Hazlehurst is a senior investigator at Kaiser Permanente's Center for Health Research where he studies how clinicians think, make decisions, and use technology such as electronic medical records. He believes that these technologies shape cognitive performance in specific ways, which can affect patient safety, efficiency, and the quality of care. He has a Ph.D. in cognitive science and anthropology from the University of California, San Diego and was formerly Chief Scientist and Director of Research and Informatics at WebMD, Inc. Recent publications include "Distributed Cognition: An Alternative Model of Cognition for Medical Informatics," coauthored with P. N. Gorman and C. K. McMullen in the *International Journal of Medical Informatics*, "Distributed Cognition in the Heart Room: How Situation Awareness Arises from Coordinated Communications During Cardiac Surgery," coauthored with P. N. Gorman and C. K. McMullen, in the *Journal of Biomedical Informatics*, and "Orienting Frames and Private Routines: The Role of Cultural Process in Critical Care Safety," coauthored with C. K. McMullen in the *International Journal of Medical Informatics.*

Madelyn Iris, director of the Leonard Schanfield Research Institute, CJE SeniorLife, has worked for over 20 years studying topics related to Alzheimer's disease and diagnosis-seeking, protective services for older adults, and social service program evaluation. She is an adjunct associate professor in the departments of Psychiatry and Preventive Medicine, Feinberg School of Medicine and the Department of Anthropology, Northwestern University. Her current research focuses on factors related to time to diagnosis of AD, how family caregivers make decisions about AD diagnosis seeking, cultural and social factors related to beliefs about AD, as well as elder abuse and self-neglect. She has recently published "The Development of a Conceptual Model for Understanding Elder Self-Neglect" with John Ridings and Kendon Conrad in the *Gerontologist* (2010).

Janet Dixon Keller is professor of anthropology and associate dean of the Graduate College at University of Illinois, Urbana–Champaign. Past editor-in-chief of *American Anthropologist*, she currently edits *Ethos: Journal of the Society for Psychological Anthropology*. She coedited *Symbolism and Cognition* (1981–82), edited *Directions in Cognitive Anthropology* (1985), and is author or coauthor of *Cognition and Tool Use* (1996), "Human Cognitive Ecology: An Instructive Paradigm for Comparative Primatology" (*American Journal of Primatology*, 2004), and "Geographies of Memory and Identity in Oceania" (in *Intangible Heritage Embodied*, 2009).

Christian Kluge is a medical doctor at the Department of Neurology at the University of Magdeburg, Germany. He also holds an honorary research fellowship at the Institute of Cognitive Neuroscience, University College London. Besides medicine, his background covers empirical neuroscience, especially emotional memory and attention, as well as philosophy, particularly philosophy of neuroscience. He has published research articles ranging from cellular physiology to cognitive science.

David B. Kronenfeld, an emeritus professor of anthropology, has spent his professional career at University of California, Riverside. His major fieldwork was in Ghana; other fieldwork has been in Mexico and in the United States. His major substantive research topic has been kinship and more broadly the semantics and pragmatics of ordinary words; he has used that and other work to explore and develop a theory of culture as a differentially shared system of distributed cognition. Other interests include stranger communities, ethnicity, and formal methods.

Kateryna Maltseva earned her Ph.D. degree in anthropology from the University of Connecticut where she currently teaches. She is interested in the use of multi-item scales to research complex cultural dimensions (such as values, norms, attitudes, etc.) and in quantitative methods to address conceptual problems in social sciences. She has done fieldwork in Sweden, the Ukraine, and the United States.

Douglas L. Medin is Louis Menk Professor of Psychology at Northwestern University, with a joint appointment in the School of Education and Social Policy. His research interests include science learning in and out of the classroom, decision-making, categorization and reasoning, and culture and cognition. He is a coauthor of *Culture and Resource Conflict: Why Meanings Matter* (2006) and *The Native Mind and the Cultural Construction of Nature* (2008).

Carol C. Mukhopadhyay, professor of anthropology, San Jose State University, specializes in gender, sexuality, race/ethnicity, and education, with field research in India and the United States, primarily on gendered activities in domestic and public life. Recent publications include *How Real is Race? A Sourcebook on Race, Culture and Biology* (with R. Henze and Y. Moses, 2007), "A Feminist Cognitive Anthropology: The Case of Women and Mathematics" (*Ethos*, 2004), "How Exportable are Western Theories of Gendered Science?" (in N. Kumar, ed., *Women and Science in India*, 2009), "Getting Rid of the Word 'Caucasian'" (in M. Pollock, ed., *Everyday Antiracism*, 2008).

Naomi Quinn is professor emerita of cultural anthropology at Duke University. She is a psychological anthropologist whose career-long interest has been in the nature of culture, understood as shared cognitive schemas. Her most extended research has been on Americans' cultural schema for marriage. She is coauthor, with Claudia Strauss, of *A Cognitive Theory of Cultural Meaning* (1997) and editor of *Finding Culture in Discourse: A Collection of Methods* (2005). Major essays include "Universals of Child Rearing" (*Anthropological Theory*, 2005) and "The Self" (*Anthropological Theory*, 2006).

Dwight W. Read received his Ph.D. at the University of California, Los Angeles in mathematics, with focus on abstract algebras. He is a professor of anthropology and of statistics at UCLA and publishes in all the sub-disciplines of anthropology (transition from biological to cultural evolution, theory and method of artifact classification, mathematical representation of cultural constructs, especially kinship terminologies). His current research focuses on the interrelationship between the material and the ideational domains in human societies. He had a visiting scientist affiliation with the IBM Los Angeles Research Center from 1986 to 1989. He has edited two special issues of the *Journal of Quantitative Anthropology* and a special issue of the *Journal of Artificial Societies and Social Simulation.* He has developed a major computer program (Kinship Algebraic Expert System, or KAES) which constructs a formal (algebraic) model for the logic underlying the structure of a kinship terminology.

Norbert Ross is associate professor in anthropology and psychology at Vanderbilt University. His interests focus on the relation of culture and cognition with a special focus on categories, concepts, and decision-making. He has conducted research on folk biology and folk medicine, incorporating developmental studies with research among adults. His work focuses on Maya people in Mexico and Guatemala, as well as Native Americans in the USA. He has published several books, including *Culture and Cognition* (2004) and *Culture and Resource Conflict* (with D. L. Medin and D. G. Cox, 2006).

Robert W. Schrauf is associate professor of applied linguistics at Pennsylvania State University in the United States. His background is in medical anthropology and cognitive psychology, and he conducts research in three areas: cross-cultural gerontology; cognitive aging and cognitive impairment; and multilingualism and aging. Recent publications include *Language Development across the Lifespan* (2009), coedited with Kees de Bot, and "Using Freelisting to Identify, Assess, and Characterize Age-Differences in Cultural Domains" (with Julia Sanchez) in *Journal of Gerontology: Social Sciences* (2008).

Hidetada Shimizu is a psychological anthropologist at Northern Illinois University. His research interests are acculturation of individuals, cultural influence on personality and behavioral development, cultural phenomenology of self, and multivocal visual ethnography. His publications include *Japanese Frames of Mind: Cultural Perspectives on Human Development* (coedited with Robert LeVine, 2001) and "Japanese Cultural Psychology and Empathic Understanding: Implications for Academic and Cultural Psychology" (*Ethos*, 2000).

Lynn Thomas works at a small liberal arts college in Claremont, California. He has done work on kinship as practiced in West Sumatra, Indonesia and on political ideologies, mainly justificatory ones, in the United States.

Halvard Vike is professor of anthropology at the University of Oslo. He has carried out extensive research on local politics, planning, public organizations, history, gender, and cultural heritage in Norway, and is currently working on issues relating to comparative political culture. His previous publications include *Maktens Samvittighet* (The Conscience of Power, 2002), *Culminations of Complexity* (2002), *L'État de la morale et la morale de l'État* (2009), and "Utopian and Contemporary Time: Temporal Dimensions of Planning and Reform in the Norwegian Welfare State" (in Simone Abram and Gisa Weszkalnys, eds., *Elusive Promises: Planning in the Contemporary World*).

Jürg Wassmann is professor emeritus and founding professor of the Institute of Anthropology, University of Heidelberg. His field area is Papua New Guinea, where he has carried out fieldwork among the Iatmul and the Yupno, and Bali, Indonesia. His main research interests are culture and cognition, memory, and concepts of personhood, space, and time. He is the author of *The Song to the Flying Fox* (1991), "The Yupno as Post-Newtonian Scientists: The Question of What is Natural in Spatial Descriptions" (1993), "Balinese Spatial Orientation" (with P. Dasen, *Journal of the Royal Anthropological Society*, 1998), "The Politics of Religious Secrecy" (in A. Rumsey and J. Weiner, eds., *Emplaced Myth*, 2001), has edited *Pacific Answers to Western*

Hegemony (1998), and is editor of the series Person, Space and Memory in the Contemporary Pacific.

Douglas R. White is professor of anthropology and chair of social dynamics and complexity at the Institute of Mathematical Behavioral Sciences at the University of California, Irvine; editor-in-chief of *Structure and Dynamics*; recipient of the Alexander von Humboldt Distinguished Senior Scientist award; and serves on the external faculty at the Santa Fe Institute (complexity sciences). He does social network analysis, ethnosociology, long-term field site and historical analysis, as in his book *Network Analysis and Ethnographic Problems: Process Models of a Turkish Nomad Clan* (2005), with Ulla Johansen. His coauthored paper "Economic Networks: The New Challenges" appeared in *Science* (2009), and his *Kinship, Class, and Community* is forthcoming.

Acknowledgments

We would like to acknowledge with thanks the help, support, and patience provided by Rosalie Robertson, Julia Kirk, Sarah Dancy, and Jacqueline Harvey from the Wiley-Blackwell team. We are also grateful to our contributors – and for the patience that many of them have shown. Thanks also to J. Scott Bentley who first suggested the idea of this collection.

Acknowledgment is made for permission to reproduce the following:

Figures 10.1 and 15.3, reprinted by permission of Sage Publications.
Figures 15.4 and 15.8, copyright © Taylor & Francis LLC.
Figure 15.5, copyright © 2004, The American Association for the Advancement of Science.

Introduction

This Companion volume is aimed at providing an overview of where cognitive anthropology is today and at giving a sense of where the field is going. The overview necessarily entails some attention to what in the past shaped the field's current nature. Cognitive anthropology, while clearly a sub-field of cultural anthropology, is and has been closely related to linguistics and linguistic anthropology. Additionally cognitive anthropology was one of the important early constituents of cognitive sciences – a connection that we aim at revivifying. Thus we see this volume as speaking importantly to elements of mainstream anthropology, linguistics, and cognitive sciences, as well as more narrowly to the intersection of the three.

Cognitive anthropology is a diverse field, and that diversity is well reflected in this volume – as one can see both from the range of topics and from the range of citations in the various contributions. To give a fuller range of this diversity, later on in this introduction I will talk a little about what we were *not* able to include in the volume. But under this diversity lie some consistent elements: a concern with culturally shared and variable distributed complex cognitive systems, including how such systems work, how they are structured, how they differ from one culture to another, how they are learned and passed on, and how they are adapted by people to contexts. As we shall see, different researchers concentrate more on some of these concerns than on others. The focus on cultural (or collective) vs. individual knowledge distinguishes cognitive anthropology from cognitive psychology, though, obviously, the one builds on the other and the line between the two can be subtle.

The stuff of cognitive anthropology is the stuff of human societies and cultures, and thus ultimately entails all the complexity that human groups can embody. And, to remind us of the obvious academic disciplines are human groups with specific social organizations and with specific shared and distributed cognitive systems. As anthropologists

A Companion to Cognitive Anthropology, First Edition. Edited by David B. Kronenfeld, Giovanni Bennardo, Victor C. de Munck, and Michael D. Fischer.

(or linguists or cognitive scientists) we are no different from the people we study or model; we have no privileged position beyond the power of the theories and models that we create to account for target phenomena. At the same time, as maybe particularly curious and rigorous people, we are in a position to call on all of the folk wisdom and folk insights that have been produced by our various cultural histories and by our interpersonal experience. Thus, at one extreme, anthropology includes the interpretative approach that Thomas treats (Chapter 22), while, at the other, we get the complex models such as that of Schank and Abelson (1977; see discussion in Chapter 12). In another direction, we get the kind of careful delineation of cognitive differences across cultures (Ross and Medin, Chapter 19).

The Companion is organized in parts. Part I – a "how we got here and where we are" section – treats the history of cognitive anthropology, the role of cognition and linguistic thought in cognitive anthropology, and the nature and types of collective cognitive structures. In Chapter 1 Benjamin Blount provides a broad and insightful overview of the history of cognitive anthropology. Naomi Quinn, in Chapter 2, provides a more personal perspective on the history of the important strand to which she has been central. Chapter 3, by Jürg Wassmann and his colleagues, describes – in a rich analytic overview – the cognitive context of cognitive anthropology. Janet Keller (Chapter 4) provides an extensive coverage of scholarship in anthropology and related fields pertaining to the relationship, in a cultural context, between language and thought. In Chapter 5 Giovanni Bennardo and David Kronenfeld discuss the types and range of collective representations that are important to cognitive anthropology and related parts of linguistics. Part I concludes with Chapter 6, John Gatewood's use of three relatively prosaic topics to provide clear and insightful explication of what we mean by collective representations, and how these relate to personal knowledge.

Part II covers methodologies. In Chapter 7 Penn Handwerker leads off with data collection – not just the methods but also how to approach the enterprise. James Boster (Chapter 8) carefully examines the interpretation of data in cognitive anthropology, especially in contrast with cognitive psychology. Kateryna Maltseva and Roy D'Andrade, in Chapter 9, explore in depth the uses of one form of data (multi-item scales) and its analysis. Chapter 10, by Stephen Borgatti and Daniel Halgin, provides a very clear and understandable explanation of how consensus analysis works and what it can be used for. In Chapter 11 Benjamin Colby uses a discussion of narrative structures and their analysis to offer us, also, a neuroscience-based approach to mind and culture, including the role of narrative in these. And, finally, in Chapter 12 Michael Fischer and David Kronenfeld offer characterizations of a wide range of simulations, models, and simulation studies, with a view to showing the usefulness of these for enabling an experimental approach to the study of collective cognitive systems.

In Part III we turn to the cognitive structures of various specific domains. In Chapter 13 Dwight Read looks at the role of mathematic structure in the organization of cultural domains including Zapotec wedding ritual, kinship terminologies, "sidedness" in moiety systems, and so forth. F. K. L. Chit Hlaing focuses on the formal, mathematical analysis of kinterm systems in Chapter 14, relating the attributes of kinterms to the system by which they are defined, and while doing so provides a history of relevant kinship studies. Andrea Bender and Sieghard Beller (Chapter 15) tell us about the cognition of number systems, including their cognitive architecture, the mental and material tools needed of number representation and numerical operations, and the implications those tools have for cognitive processes in general. Roy Ellen, in Chapter 16 gives us a rich and full treatment of indigenous knowledge systems, including work on ethnobiological systems, on taxonomies and taxonomic thinking including universals, on technology and its products, and on the psychology that underlies these (along with related questions of intracultural variation and transmission). In Chapter 17 E. N. Anderson provides a timely and insightful discussion of the role played by emotion in cognition; his discussion includes the role of emotions in motivation and the universality of emotions. In Chapter 18 Douglas White offers a network perspective on cognition and culture; he provides some key network definitions, illustrates how social groups and associated cognitive sharing (consensus) emerge from this perspective, and offers a way of discerning implicit social structures as well as stability and instability.

Part IV's chapters explore the relationship – both as it is and as it might become – of cognitive anthropology to other, neighboring disciplines. In Chapter 19 Norbert Ross and Douglas Medin offer an extensive and insightful discussion of the role of cognitive anthropology in cultural anthropology and cognitive science – both what the relationship has been and what it should be in the future, including what cognitive anthropology has to do, including both methods, concepts, and perspectives. Halvard Vike's Chapter 20 looks at the way in which cognitive approaches can contribute to our understanding of how power works in society, and considers how individual actors draw on their cultural knowledge in negotiating their lives and understanding the forces that impinge on them. In a related vein, Carol Mukhopadhyay (Chapter 21) uses a relatively personal perspective to look at cognitive anthropology's interactions with feminist theory. She looks at what that interaction has been (and has not been, given some substantial overlap of personnel), and explores what it might become. Next, in Chapter 22, Lynn Thomas considers the relationship between mainstream contemporary cultural anthropology (with its strong interpretivist orientation) and cognitive anthropology, especially as the field is evolving. Thomas notes significant, if under-recognized, relevance, but goes on to suggest ways of improving both relevance and salience. With Hidetada Shimizu's Chapter 23, we shift gears a bit and go on to a new format. Shimizu uses a particular set of interrelated research projects (with findings) to exemplify how cognitive anthropology can serve important educational purposes – and how work on education might help the rest of us out. Completing Part IV, Miriam Haidle in Chapter 24 considers the relationship between archaeology and cognitive studies, especially in regard to cultural issues. She looks at the history of cognitively oriented approaches and at core themes. Her coverage includes archaeological perspectives and insights regarding human cognitive evolution.

Our final section, Part V, consists of some extended examples of contemporary empirical research. We lead with Brian Hazlehurst's account in Chapter 25 of the distributed cognition that is involved in Swedish fishermen's understanding of sonar pictures; he frames that account in a comparison of two contrasting approaches to cognitive architecture: the Turing machine mind (TMM) and the distributed cognition mind (DCM), which latter, unlike the former, takes account of information embedded in their environments and of people's use of that information. Next, in Chapter 26, comes Giovanni Bennardo's explication of a Tongan foundational cultural model (radiality). His explication includes both a detailing of how the model works and an indication of the rich array of empirical work across a number of domains on which his account is based; he explicitly roots his account in a particular modular view of human cognition. Victor de Munck (Chapter 27) describes the variety of methods and analytic perspectives he used to try to get at the contrasting understandings of romantic love in US and Lithuanian communities. These ranged from ethnographic interviews to a variety of insightful cognitive experiments. Linda Garro in Chapter 28 looks at the cognitive framework within which people process illness. She considers the role of narrative for understanding life in time, for ordering experience and constructing reality (including interpretations of illness events and their treatment), and does this via a small number of specific cases from a couple of different cultural communities. Finally, Robert Schrauf and Madelyn Iris (Chapter 29) offer us a description of whether older members of several contrasting ethnic communities have a coherent model (embodying a useful understanding) of Alzheimer's disease and contrastingly of non-Alzheimers's "age-associated memory impairment." They take us through the phases of their study and the methods used.

In any collection such as this numerous relevant topics are necessarily omitted. In the interest of giving readers a more complete and filled-out picture of cognitive anthropology it seems useful to briefly review some of what we were not able to include.

First are a variety of topics and approaches which are discussed in various chapters, but which get no full explication or separate treatment. Theories and assumptions concerning modularity of mind are treated extensively from one perspective by Giovanni Bennardo in Chapter 26, and more thinly elsewhere. But we were not able to include a focused consideration of the fuller range of modularity versions that one sees in the discipline.

Similarly, cultural models show up throughout the volume, but we were not able to have the overview of the history and range of cultural model treatments that we would have liked. And the same holds for systems of orientation, specifically Frames of Reference (FoR), that represent one of the most fertile and groundbreaking research areas in contemporary cognitive anthropology (see Senft 1997; Bennardo 2002; Levinson 2003; Levinson and Wilkins 2006). Closely intertwined with it is the cross-cultural research on gesture (McNeill 2000; Kita 2003; Kendon 2004).

Second, there are a variety of approaches that have not been covered, to which it's worth calling attention. These include:

- the classic ethnoscience approach of Goodenough, Lounsbury, Conklin, Frake, Metzger and Williams, and Wallace and Atkins;
- the psychological version of ethnoscience and early cognitive anthropology of Romney, D'Andrade, and their students;
- the decision-making approach developed by Christina Gladwin, Hugh Gladwin, Robert Randall, James Young, and Carol Mukhopadhyay;
- the study of indigenous knowledge systems, as exemplified in the work of Jean Lave;
- the interpretative version, as seen in the work, for example, of Maurice Block and Pascal Boyer.

Finally, there is kinship, a conceptual system that has been of great importance in the development of cognitive anthropology, and whose importance continues. Kinship is brilliantly treated in Chapter 15 by F. K. L. Chit Hlaing from one perspective. But there exist several other important perspectives that are well worth mentioning:

- Sydney H. Gould's (2000) formal algebraic system, similar in some ways to the system of Dwight Read (discussed by Chit Hlaing), but based directly on the Ms and Fs that Chit Hlaing speaks of;
- Ian Keen's (1985) direct use of natural language categories and native speaker calculations;
- the Marking Theory approach of Per Hage (see 1997, 1999, 2001) based on the work of Joseph Greenberg and subsequently elaborated by Doug Jones (in press);
- the set of socially and linguistically oriented approaches brought together in Trautmann and Whiteley (in press), including Allen (1998).

Next, there exist several important topics and issues that we could not get this time, but might aim for in future editions. Theories of mind loom large in much cognitive work, whether cognitive anthropology, cognitive psychology, or cognitive science. The topic is alluded to in several of our chapters, but not ever focally addressed.

A related topic is the evolution of the capacity for culture. How did the human ability (and then propensity) to develop systems of collective knowledge emerge? What other species are relevant, and how? Are both language and culture products of the same evolutionary process or do they – and to what degree – represent separate developments?

Given that humans have the propensity to create and learn systems of collective knowledge, how does the propensity evince itself in the cognitive development of human children, and how does that propensity, combined with the experience of communities using such systems, show itself in the child's learning – construction or reconstruction – of the systems of culture and language. That is, some sense of the processes of child development seems important for cognitive anthropology.

A different kind of topical issue which we see running through our chapters but which is nowhere foregrounded is the contrast between top-down vs. bottom-up approaches to understanding cultural cognitive systems. The contrast is, in one sense, that between (1) creating models of whole systems or sub-systems and then assessing how well these account for observed empirical regularities (see Chapter 13 for examples) and (2) working up to a broader understanding through a cumulation of observed empirical findings in theoretically guided studies. The former approach can be seen in Edwin Hutchins's (1980, 1995; see Chapter 25) pathbreaking work while the latter can be seen in the careful and insightful studies of Douglas Medin and his colleagues (see Chapter 19). In a sense this contrast can be seen as one between a focus on systems themselves vs. a focus on attributes of pertinent systems (though nothing is ever quite that neat!).

We have not been able to include all of the sub-disciplinary interactions with cognitive anthropology that we would have liked. In particular, one important omission is applied anthropology. Important here is the effective, practical use that is made in it of methods, analytic tools, and theories from cognitive anthropology, as well as cognitive science and cognitive psychology. Important also are the insights that cognitive anthropology has gained from practical, applied work such as that in, for example, John Gatewood et al.'s (2006 and 2008) study of credit unions and Gatewood and Cameron's (2009) study of tourism in the Turks and Caicos Islands.

Similarly, it would have been useful to have a full and focused discussion of the relationship between cognitive anthropology and work in humanistic branches of anthropology. It seems that there exists a potential usefulness of both cognitive methods and theories for a number of kinds of humanistic studies, while well-drawn subjective or interpretative portrayals have always provided an important stimulus to the anthropological imagination. Lynn Thomas (Chapter 22) hints at what might be there, but his focus is elsewhere.

I began by saying that cognitive anthropology is a diverse field. The diversity can be seen in specific research goals, in theoretical perspectives and modes of attack, in data collection and analytic methods, and in the kinds of conclusions that are reached. It follows that there can exist no overview that will simply summarize it, or pull it all together. At the same time I suggested that behind this diversity are some consistent elements – including the idea that culture exists in minds and a concern with culturally shared and variable distributed complex cognitive systems. In the Afterword at the end of this collection I offer one particular view of how culture might look from a dynamic, distributed cognitive perspective. The Afterword represents no consensual bottom line, but it does represent the kind of perspective that we think can rejoin anthropology and cognitive studies, and make both better than they have been.

REFERENCES

Allen, N. J.

1998 The Prehistory of Dravidian-Type Terminologies. *In* Transformations of Kinship. Maurice Godelier, Thomas R. Trautmann, and Franklin F. Tjon Sie Fat, eds. Pp. 324–331. Washington, DC and London: Smithsonian Institution Press.

Bennardo, G., ed.

2002 Representing Space in Oceania: Culture in Language and Mind. Canberra: Pacific Linguistics, Research School of Pacific and Asian Studies, Australian National University.

Gatewood, John B., and Catherine M. Cameron

2009 Belonger Perceptions of Tourism and Its Impacts in the Turks and Caicos Islands. Final report to the Turks and Caicos Islands Ministry of Tourism. http://www.lehigh.edu/~jbg1/Perceptions-of-Tourism.pdf.

Gatewood, John B., and John W. Lowe

2008 Employee Perceptions of Credit Unions: Implications for Member Profitability. Madison, WI: Filene Research Institute. http://www.lehigh.edu/~jbg1/credit_unions_2008.pdf.

Gatewood, John B., and John W. Lowe, with Carolyn E. Kelly

2006 Employee Perceptions of Credit Unions: A Pilot Study. Madison, WI: Filene Research Institute.

Gould, Sydney H.

2000 A New System for the Formal Analysis of Kinship. David B. Kronenfeld, ed. Lanham, MD: University Press of America.

Hage, Per

1997 Unthinkable Categories and the Fundamental Laws of Kinship. American Ethnologist 24:652–667.

1999 Marking Universals and the Structure and Evolution of Kinship Terminologies: Evidence from Salish. Journal of the Royal Anthropological Institute 5:423–441.

2001 Marking Theory and Kinship Analysis: Cross-Cultural and Historical Applications. Special issue, "Kinship," Anthropological Theory 1:197–211.

Hutchins, Edwin
1980 Culture and Inference: A Trobriand Case Study. Cambridge, MA: Harvard University Press.
1995 Cognition in the Wild. Cambridge, MA: MIT Press.
Jones, Doug
In press Human Kinship, from Conceptual Structure to Grammar. Behavioral and Brain Sciences.
Keen, Ian
1985 Definitions of Kin. Journal of Anthropological Research 41:62–90.
Kendon, A.
2004 Gesture: Visible Action as Utterance. Cambridge: Cambridge University Press.
Kita, S., ed.
2003 Pointing: Where Language, Culture, and Cognition Meet. Mahwah, NJ: Lawrence Erlbaum.
Levinson, S. C.
2003 Space in Language and Cognition. Cambridge: Cambridge University Press.
Levinson, S. C., and David Wilkins, eds.
2006 Grammars of Space: Explorations in Cognitive Diversity. Cambridge: Cambridge University Press.
McNeill, D.
2000 Language and Gesture. Cambridge: Cambridge University Press.
Schank, Roger, and R. P. Abelson
1977 Scripts, Plans, Goals and Understanding: An Inquiry into Human Knowledge Structures. Hillsdale, NJ: Lawrence Erlbaum.
Senft, G., ed.
1997 Referring to Space: Studies in Austronesian and Papuan Languages. Oxford: Oxford University Press.
Trautmann, Thomas R., and Peter M. Whiteley
In press Crow–Omaha: New Light on a Classic Problem of Kinship Analysis. Tucson: University of Arizona Press.

PART I

History of Cognitive Anthropology; Nature and Types of Cultural Knowledge Structures

CHAPTER 1

A History of Cognitive Anthropology

B. G. Blount

Cognitive anthropology as a distinct area of inquiry is a relatively recent one, dating from the early 1960s. Antecedents exist, of course, even from the beginnings of anthropology in the mid-19th century, but focal questions on mental constructs and their underlying principles have appeared systematically only during the past 50 or so years. Aspects of the early history relevant to cognitive anthropology will be traced below, but some introductory comments are in order. An initial concern is to locate cognitive anthropology within the discipline of anthropology.

Introduction

Although cognitive anthropology is typically seen as one of the sub-fields of cultural anthropology, that placement has always been problematic. There are two related issues. One is the identification of cognitive anthropology as psychology. While there is a Society for Psychological Anthropology section of the American Anthropological Association, it is relatively small, reflecting the general disinterest or even antipathy of many cultural anthropologists to the discipline of psychology. There are historical grounds for those sentiments. In the late 19th century, anthropology was struggling to become an academic discipline in its own right, which meant independence from an already established psychology. Anthropology needed a perspective or orientation definitive of the discipline and differentiating it from psychology. The concept of culture emerged to play that role. It became the key concept of the discipline, and many, but certainly not all, anthropologists continue to see it in that way.

In addition to competition for departmental independence, anthropologists in the late 19th century were opposed to psychological theory as it was then practiced. Psychologists tended to view the mind as consisting of innate properties. Levels and types

A Companion to Cognitive Anthropology, First Edition. Edited by David B. Kronenfeld, Giovanni Bennardo, Victor C. de Munck, and Michael D. Fischer.

of mental activity were to be explained, through reductionism, as properties of the brain. By contrast, anthropologists saw knowledge as cultural, as socially based, and as mutable. From the beginnings of the discipline, cultural anthropologists were opposed to reductionism, opting instead for radical relativity and for societies with unique sets of traits, to be described ethnographically. The perspective came to be known as historical particularism. While that perspective is no longer in vogue, at least in those terms, opposition to reductionism has remained, and in fact appears to have become more steadfast.

Cognitive anthropologists have also been concerned with accurate ethnographic description, but in addition they have sought principles that underlie behavior. A search for underlying order within kinship systems has been a prime example. Cognitive anthropology is, in fact, reductionist in the sense that observable behavioral phenomena are recognized as expressions of more basic and fundamental underlying organizational order and principles. Differences in perspective between cultural anthropologists and cognitive anthropologists still center on reductionism, but that difference is emblematic of a broader academic issue, humanities versus science. Anthropologists sometimes claim that anthropology is both a humanity and a science (a classic statement is by Wolf 1964), but the two approaches are not equally weighted and valued within the discipline. A good argument can be made that, in terms of number of practitioners and dominant theoretical perspectives, anthropology has always been much more a humanistic than a scientific discipline. Historical factors drive much of the character of the discipline, especially through the idea that ethnography must be qualitative, but cultural relativism plays an even more significant role. At issue is how ethnographic data are to be interpreted, as will be discussed below. The pursuit of explanatory principles in cognitive anthropology differentiates it from cultural anthropology.

The place of cognitive anthropology within the discipline of anthropology, then, has been and remains problematic. The "fit" within cultural anthropology is forced, at best. Given its history and problem of "disciplinary place," it is perhaps not surprising that claims are sometimes heard that cognitive anthropology is moribund or even dead. An aim of the discussion here will be to present the counterclaim that cognitive anthropology is alive and well and that its place within anthropology lies within scientific anthropology, not within fine gradations of cultural anthropology.

A Brief History of the Culture Concept: Cognitive from the Outset

Given that cognition has not been a central topic of inquiry in anthropology, it is perhaps ironic that the first anthropological definition of culture was fundamentally cognitive. That definition was provided by E. B. Tylor, the first academic anthropologist, who was engaged in an intellectual competition for several decades in the 19th century to account for the "place" among humankind of recently "discovered" people of Africa, Asia, and the Americas (1865, 1871). Rather than viewing the people as sinners degraded from a state of grace, he argued that they had not advanced as far comparatively as European folk toward civilization. The concept of culture was a centerpiece of his argument. Culture, in his view, was an intellectual capacity of humankind, a capacity that allowed all people to become more advanced, eventually to civilization. Tylor's definition of culture was the predominant view of culture for several decades in the early history of anthropology: "Culture … is that complex whole which includes knowledge, belief, art, law, morals, custom, and any other capabilities and habits acquired by man as a member of society" (1871:1). The operant concept is "capabilities," referring to the ability of people to acquire and produce knowledge, beliefs, etc. In contemporary terms, ability would include cognition.

Concerns with definitions of culture reappeared in the 1930s. Cognitive capacity continued to be a central aspect of definitions, expressed typically as "ideas" or "knowledge." In an effort to bring clarity to the abundance of definitions, two leading anthropologists of the time, Alfred Kroeber and Clyde Kluckhohn, produced a book based on extant definitions (1952). They identified 164 complete definitions and 300 partial ones, which they collapsed into a synthetic definition. The definition was too complex and cumbersome to be very useful (Marvin Harris [1968:10] referred to it as a theory), but it is noteworthy that their proposal contained the statement "the essential core of culture consists of traditional (i.e., historically derived and selected) ideas and especially their attached values" (1952:357). As was the case for Tylor, knowledge was at the core. The book, incidentally, provides an excellent and detailed discussion of the history of the culture concept during the 18th and 19th centuries.

Not until 1957 did a definition of culture appear that was intended to support research toward cognitive ends, provided by Ward Goodenough. Anthropology at the time was heavily influenced by structural linguistics, which was often seen as the most scientific of the sub-fields within anthropology. Goodenough saw the structural and taxonomic approaches in linguistics as applicable to cultural phenomena and proposed a definition of culture accordingly: "A society's culture consists of whatever one has to know or believe in order to operate in a manner acceptable to its members, and do so in any role that they accept for any one of themselves" (1957:167). The definition placed culture squarely within knowledge and belief systems but without an iteration of kinds of knowledge or their application. The intent was to encourage anthropologists to produce classification and nomenclature systems to replace the simple iteration of traits. His definition required discovery procedures to identify domains and their content, organization, and underlying features.

The Emergence of Cognitive Anthropology

The decade of the 1960s was one of change in the linguistic sciences. Linguistics was revolutionized by the work of Noam Chomsky (1965), who redirected linguistic theory from surface descriptions to an underlying, generative, and transformational basis. Sociolinguistics began to be developed as a new sub-field of linguistics and linguistic anthropology (Gumperz and Hymes 1964, 1972; Labov 1972; Blount 1974), searching for social and cultural factors that structured discourse. At the same time, taxonomic linguistic principles were being applied innovatively in anthropology. The intellectual center of the new perspective was at Stanford University, developed in the early 1960s by Kim Romney, Roy D'Andrade, Charles Frake, and their students, including Brent Berlin, David Kronenfeld, and Naomi Quinn, among others.

A second locus later in the 1960s was at the University of California at Berkeley, led by Brent Berlin and Paul Kay. The theoretical perspective was first labeled as "ethnoscience," the study of the ways in which domains of knowledge in traditional societies were distinguished and organized. In time, a number of other labels were applied, including "ethnosemantics," "componential analysis," "lexical semantic analysis," and eventually "ethnographic semantics." A research procedure was established, in which the anthropologist began with a domain such as kinship or color, then elicited exhaustively the terms for the types of objects (kin types, color types) within the domain, followed by an analysis of the components (semantic features) from which the objects are uniquely constructed. Lastly, the psychological reality of the analysis could be demonstrated, through feedback from the folk whose domain was under description. Descriptions of the procedure can be found in the now classic articles by Frake (1962), "The Ethnographic Study of Cognitive Systems" and Conklin (1962), "Lexicographical Treatment of Folk Taxonomies."

A particular interest within ethnographic semantics, perhaps not surprisingly, was in kinship. Kinterms and their determinants has been a dominant theme in anthropology, since L. H. Morgan's monumental work in 1871, to G. P. Murdock's lineage-based account (1949) and sociological approaches in British social anthropology (Radcliffe-Brown and Forde 1950). To touch on only two prominent areas of inquiry within ethnographic semantics, Floyd Lounsbury proposed a formal procedure for kinship analysis (1964b), "The Structural Analysis of Kinship Semantics," and he also carried out a reanalysis of Crow and Omaha kinship systems (1964a), "A Formal Account of the Crow- and Omaha-Type Kinship Terminologies," showing how generational skewing rules clarified some of the terminological challenges of the two systems. In each system, some kinterms are applied to individuals (kin types) in generational levels both above and below ego, a seeming anomaly in kinship systems.

The second arena of lexical semantic analyses of kinship was in a series of publications on American English kinship, providing different outcomes and sharp intellectual debates about relevance. The first publication was by Wallace and Atkins (1960), "The Meaning of Kinship Terms," in which a componential paradigm was presented as evidence of the psychological relevance of the terminological system. Their publication was followed, however, by a publication by Romney and D'Andrade (1964), "Cognitive Aspects of English Kin Terms," presenting a different analysis and an argument for its psychological validity, based on the typological representation of the results and on a series of confirmatory tests given to native speakers. A second discussion on American English kinship was between Ward Goodenough (1965), "Yankee Kinship Terminology: A Problem in Componential Analysis," and David Schneider (1965), "American Kin Terms and Terms for Kinsmen: A Critique of Goodenough's Componential Analysis of Yankee Kinship Terminology." Schneider's criticism was essentially against the formalism of componential analysis, bringing to bear various types of sociological and psychological variables external to a domain-based analysis.

Each of the two sets of discussions is important in the history of cognitive anthropology for the focus of analytic attention to the psychological reality of the native speakers who utilize the terminological systems. Accurate representation of informant knowledge continued to be a central concern in subsequent research, including major advances in color terminology at the end of the decade and in later developments in ethnobiology. The paper by Schneider is important on different grounds, as it illustrates the types of criticisms that cultural anthropologists tended to make of lexical semantic analysis. Critics argued that the research was focused much too narrowly on single or isolated domains, thereby missing even broader traditional domain based knowledge (see Burling 1964), much less the larger picture and broader concerns of cultural anthropology (Geertz 1973). The core of the latter type of criticism was that formal analysis could never provide overarching cultural descriptions of individual societies of the types expected in information-rich ethnographies. Formal analysis was perceived by critics as too narrow and piecemeal for holistic ethnographic descriptions. The response of cognitive anthropologists was that their method of representing informant knowledge was more principled and thus more accurate, in contrast to impressionistic, non-replicable ethnography.

There were three signal publications in the 1960s. A special publication in 1964 of the *American Anthropologist*, entitled "Transcultural Studies in Cognition," edited by A. Kimball Romney and Roy Goodwin D'Andrade, contained papers on linguistic, anthropological, and psychological approaches to cognition, reflecting the cross-field nature of the field from the outset. The first reader, *Cognitive Anthropology*, edited by Stephen A. Tyler (1969), included many of the classic papers in the emergence of cognitive anthropology. *Basic Color Terms* (1969), was based on the groundbreaking work by Brent Berlin and Paul Kay on color terminology. Their work spawned interest in color terms that continues to the present, and their research helped to usher in prototype theory cognitive anthropology. In 1972 Harold Conklin published a topically arranged bibliography with over 5,000 entries in eight sections, including kinship, ethnobotany, ethnozoology, ethnomedicine, orientation, color, and sensation.

By the 1970s, however, cognitive anthropology had moved away from componential analysis, mainly from their recognition that the results of their research could be seen as enriched lexical semantics but not necessarily of features that actually reflected informant knowledge. A goal of lexical semantics research was to produce an analysis in which each term within a domain could be defined by a unique set of semantic features. In English kinterms, for example, the semantic description of father as "male, generation +1, lineal," mother as "female, generation +1," uncle as "male, generation +1, collateral," et cetera for all of the kinterms, allowed for a taxonomic display of lexical features. There was no assurance, however, that the kinterms were processed cognitively by native speakers in those forms. It seemed unlikely that native speakers relied on sets of lexical features in their mental computation – perception and production – of kinterms. Lexical semantic analyses provided a set of possibilities that might be used for cognitive computation, but there were no principled ways in which one possibility among others could be clearly demonstrated as the most fundamental. Classificational and nomenclatural systems based on feature distributions of lexical items were increasingly called into question, not only in ethnographic semantics but also in linguistics (Fillmore 1975).

By the end of the 1960s, a newer theoretical approach held greater promise for studies of cognition, specifically prototype theory. Cognitive anthropologists began to use the new perspective with the objective, as before, to provide an accurate description of native knowledge. The central aim of the domain-based research remained in place, to characterize knowledge of the types of objects belonging to a domain, including their relationships to each other, but to make the results more psychologically real.

PROTOTYPES

Anthropologists have long recognized that people in different societies do not have the same array of color terms to partition the color spectrum, but until the research by Berlin and Kay (1969), there was no sound basis for understanding the distribution of color terms. The prevailing view for much of the 20th century was cultural relativism, which in circular fashion, merely noted that the array of terms within a particular society was due to cultural factors, generally unspecified. Berlin and Kay began their work utilizing a procedure consistent with the lexical semantic approach used in the 1960s, using hue, brilliance, and saturation as the features of color underlying terminology and classification. They also elicited information directly from speakers of different languages, initially 20 languages. The elicitation techniques, however, were innovative. Each individual was shown the color spectrum as illustrated on a chart containing "chips" (small squares), and was asked to draw on an acetate overlay a line around the range of the chips for each color term in their language, thereby illustrating a boundary. In addition, they were asked to identify the chip that was the best representative of the color indicated by the term, giving a focal point. The results were interesting. Individuals speaking the same language did not draw boundary lines consistently, and across time the same individual did not replicate accurately their original boundary line. By contrast, the agreement on the focal color was much more consistent, both across individuals and by the same individual at different times. Cultural influence was on focal salience to a considerably greater extent than on boundaries.

The result of immediate interest here is that the reliance of speakers on focal salience raises questions about how domains and their classification are to be characterized. If they are not defined by boundaries, then what is the basis or bases for domain identification? Focal salience indicates that the color domain is partitioned not by subsets of boundaries, as thought to be the case in kinship systems, but by focality, a relationship to centrally representative "objects," in this case focal color. This type of object and domain relationship eventually came to be called prototypes, in which a prototypical object becomes the focal point for domain membership of other, related objects.

The results of the color-term study created additional interest in explaining cultural variation. Berlin and Kay initially viewed the distribution of basic color terms across languages and societies as reflecting an evolution toward a larger number of basic terms, fueled by the need for more generic terms as a consequence of societal complexity. They eventually rejected that proposal and turned to questions of neural correlates as constraining the most basic of the terms (Kay et al. 1991). Neural bases, however, did not explain all of the distribution of basic color terms. Extra-biological features are involved, as explored by MacLaury (1991a), who identified a complex of factors that may have influence on the culturally driven aspects of terminology. These include societal complexity, harsh environmental conditions, and abrupt and intense cultural contact. The underlying hypothesis is that a differentiation and expansion of basic color terms will occur when environmental conditions require necessary and close attention for an extended period of time. The hypothesis is not as yet fully tested, leaving the question of cultural relativity not fully answered.

Like color-term studies, research in ethnobiology has a long and productive history in cognitive anthropology, often on the basis of collaborative work between anthropologists, botanists, and zoologists. Similarly, ethnobiological researchers have been concerned with the classificational and nomenclatural distinctions that members of traditional societies make. In addition, ethnobiology addresses questions of constraints on cultural relativity, asking why societies make the distinctions that they do among plants and animals. As in color-term studies, answers required comparative research, but a framework for comparison was less readily available than the physiological and neural bases of color-term perception. Ethnobiological studies of traditional societies have spanned several decades, expanding in the 1970s. By 1980, descriptions were available from a number of traditional societies throughout the world. The most complete were accounts of the Tzeltal Maya of Chiapas, Mexico, from the work of Berlin and associates, especially Breedlove and Raven (Berlin et al. 1966). One of Berlin's graduate students, Eugene Hunn, carried out research on Tzeltal ethnozoology (1977), complementing earlier research on ethnobotany. Particularly detailed studies were also conducted among Jivaro groups in the Peruvian Amazon by Berlin and Berlin (1983) and with the assistance of another then graduate student, James Boster (Berlin et al. 1981).

Aside from descriptions of ethnobiological systems on the basis of intellectual curiosity, one central question was the extent to which traditional systems were similar to the Linneaus system followed in botany and zoology. A simple answer is that native systems were largely similar to the one developed by Linneaus (1735), which is not surprising given that his system was based on European folk models (Atran 1990). A related but more fundamental question was the identification of a system characteristic of folk societies in general. Aspects of an overarching system were identified in publications during the 1970s by Berlin and associates (Berlin 1972), but a full, synthetic picture was not available until the appearance of his book in 1992, *Ethnobiological Classification*. As background on theory, Berlin's major claim is, to quote: "that the observed structural and substantive typological regularities found among systems of ethnobiological classification of traditional peoples ... can best be explained in terms of human beings' similar perceptual and largely unconscious appreciation of the natural affinities among groupings of plants and animals in their environment – groupings that are recognized and named quite independently of their actual or potential usefulness or symbolic importance to humans" (1992:xi).

Berlin's claim is still often not understood and is confused with cultural factors specific to individual societies. Individuals, independent of cultural factors, perceive distinctive morphological features of plants and animals and the discontinuities between them, and they perceive them in highly similar ways. As Atran (1990) and others have indicated, people "carve nature at its joints," that is, they superimpose their perceptual system over the morphological discontinuities seen in nature. The ways in which people in traditional societies superimpose their perspectives are sufficiently similar that Berlin was able to identify and establish seven principles of categorization and five of nomenclature from his review of the extant ethnobiological literature. These principles are definitive of the classification of taxa, that is, kinds of plants and animals, allowing recognition of hierarchically arranged ranks, each of which exhibits systematic similarities in their relative numbers and biological content across all folk systems of classification. Berlin labels the ranks as kingdom, life form, intermediate, generic, specific, and varietal. The rank *generic* is roughly equivalent to the concept of species within the Linnaean system and contains approximately 80 percent of the approximately 500 taxa in folk traditional systems. The ranks above generic are increasingly inclusive, whereas those below are differentiated. Interested readers should consult Berlin's book and a brief summary is available in an account of cultural bases of folk classification systems by Blount and Schwanenflugel (1993).

Berlin refers to his ethnobiological classification and nomenclature system as intellectualist, to distinguish it from special purpose, cultural-based, or utilitarian classifications. In one sense the distinction is clear. The same objects can be classified in a number of ways, as for example, fish can be a life form, but they can also be classified as a type of food, as an animal to be caught for recreation, and likely in other ways. Classifications of fish other than life form, however, tend to be specific to individual societies, or in other words, cultural. Even more clearly, culture is present in Berlin's categorization at the specific and varietal levels, in part due to the research of Boster (1986). Specifics and varietals are likely to be cultivars, thus receiving special, that is, cultural attention.

The importance of culture, however, continues to be problematic, at least for some ethnobiologists. Confusion arises relative to the defining morphological characteristics of given plants or animals. A utilitarian perspective points to cultural selection of those characteristics among other possible ones that could be chosen. The intellectualist response would be that if the preponderance of folk societies identify the same characteristics, then the selection is unlikely to be cultural. They would ask, in addition, what a given classification is for, noting that if the categorization is not special purpose and if it is part of the categorization of local flora and fauna, it is unlikely to be cultural. While the weight of evidence appears to be on the side of the intellectualist position, culture can still be seen as a possible confound. Not all of the flora and fauna in any traditional society are recognized as taxa (Hunn 1999), raising the question as to why only some are selected, in much the case as why only some basic color terms are present in given societies. Another, in-depth discussion can be found in Atran and Medin (2008).

Although prototype theory as such may not have been central to the development of Berlin's ethnobiological work, his perspective was akin to prototype theory, and in later work (1992), perception of biological taxa were described specifically in terms of prototypes. However Berlin's and Kay's work contributed directly to the development of prototype theory. Eleanor Rosch, initially at the University of California, Berkeley, and then at Stanford University, was a major player in the development of the new theoretical perspective. She defined the concept "psychologically basic level objects," by which she meant objects within a domain that appeared to provide maximum information with the least perceptual effort (1978). Moreover, the objects were perceived not as a list or a bundle of features but as a configurational whole. To test for the reality of basic-level objects, Rosch asked undergraduate students to consider nine three-level taxonomies and for each level to identify features that characterized the objects at each level, for example "tree," "oak, maple, birch," and then types of oak, maple, et cetera. She found that, in general, the basic-level objects, oak, maple, and birch, contained more information than in the other levels. Pursuing the work further, Rosch redefined basic-level objects as prototypes and conducted a second set of experiments in which students rated items within a domain list in terms of their prototypicality. That led to the now well-known results of passerine birds being judged as the most typical within the domain of birds and of robins and sparrows heading the list of most prototypical (Rosch 1978).

Prototypes replaced clusters of features as the psychological basis for the definition of categories (domains) and their membership. Individuals appear to use a focal representative, a prototype, to define a category and to identify other members of the category according to the degree of similarity to the prototype. As Roy D'Andrade noted in his excellent discussion of Rosch's prototype concept, "it is as if the human cognitive system were a structure seeking device … [finding] … which attributes of a class of instances are most strongly correlated and creates generic or basic-level objects by forming a gestalt configuration of these attributes" (1995:120). A consequence of that system is greater cognitive efficiency in categorization. The prototype concept enables cognitive scientists to think in new ways about category construction and membership (D'Andrade 1995:121).

The prototype concept has been utilized constructively in cognitive science fields, especially in anthropology, linguistics, and psychology. Discussions of prototype theory itself have continued. Their role in cultural construction of work meaning can be found in Schwanenflugel et al. (1991), and a broader discussion is provided by MacLaury (1991b).

Cultural Models

The seminal publication on cultural models appeared in 1987, *Cultural Models in Language & Thought*, edited by Dorothy Holland and Naomi Quinn. As they noted in the preface, earlier versions of the papers had been presented at a conference in 1983, held at the Institute for Advanced Study in Princeton, New Jersey. The edited book contains 15 chapters, including an introduction ("Culture and Cognition") by Quinn and Holland (1987) and a concluding Appraisal by the late Roger M. Keesing (1987). Collectively the chapters have been instrumental in the emergence of widespread interest in cultural models within cognitive anthropology. Cultural models are defined in the introduction as "presupposed, taken-for-granted models of the world that are widely shared (although not necessarily to the exclusion of other, alternative models) by the members of a society and that play an enormous role in their understanding of the world and their behavior in it" (1987:4). The goal of cultural model research is ambitious, no less than a description of the organization of knowledge and its link to what is known about how humans think. Much of the introduction is devoted to an account of what cultural models might be and of how one goes about identifying and constructing them. Multiple topics are discussed in relation to current concerns and issues in anthropology and the cognitive sciences, including research methodology, directive force (cognitive structure and content as motivating behavior), discourse analysis, artificial intelligence and scripts, prototype theory, schemas, and metaphor and metonymy. Each of the topics presaged research emergent in the late 1980s and beyond. The introduction is a tour de force, situating cultural model research within the extant anthropology and cognitive science concerns and projecting future research.

Naomi Quinn, associates, and students have continued their research on cultural models during the past two decades, responding also to criticisms of the original work. One of the criticisms was that it was not clear how the models, however elegant, could be drivers of behavior. The problem came to be called directive force. To address that problem, a second book was published in 1992, *Human Motives and Cultural Models* (D'Andrade and Strauss 1992). A summary of the findings of the individual case studies by D'Andrade points to two major conclusions. First, directive force can be identified but additional ethnography must be devoted to a demonstration of the linkages between the ideational models and behavior (1992:225). Second, that motivational force is only one of the psychological forces that can be associated with a model. A given model may have also an orientational force, thereby redirecting meanings of events, and evaluative force, providing assessment of qualities such as good or bad. In addition, a given model may have more than one force associated with it, leading D'Andrade to speculate that "as models become more deeply internalized, they tend to include more functions" (1992:226).

A Cognitive Theory of Cultural Meaning appeared five years later (Strauss and Quinn 1997). The book takes aim at the dichotomy in anthropology between meaning as interpretation of behavior in public and culture as organized, structured information in the brain. The dichotomy is clearly false, reflective of the history of anthropology and of the rejection of culture as a meaningful concept. A dismissal of the concept of culture is essentially a denial of the reality of mental concepts and processes, relegating meaning only to what can be perceived in the external world, which clearly is untenable. In fact, Strauss and Quinn demonstrate that leading anthropologists who argue against the utility of the culture concept actually incorporate it into their perspectives and analyses (1997:4). The first two chapters are devoted to the developments in anthropology in the 1960s and 1970s that led to the rejection within cultural anthropology of formal cognitive approaches. Strauss and Quinn, rightly, are especially critical of the role played by Clifford Geertz in the isolation of cognitive anthropology from departments of anthropology. They note that a turning point in the dichotomization of the field was Geertz's criticism of Goodenough's definition of culture, a criticism that erroneously conflated the claim of internalized knowledge with lexical formalism (Strauss and Quinn 1997:254–255). In a direct sense, the formalism of lexical semantic analysis was taken as representative of all cognitive research, and the aim was to dismiss all of it.

The overall aim of the book, however, is neither to be polemic nor to argue for superiority of public or private (mental) approaches to the study of human society. Far from it, the book is an interesting and extensive effort to show that cognitive anthropology is not what its critics have claimed but that centripetal (external) effects of culture, which the critics champion, are a product of interaction between minds and an external world. Strauss and Quinn develop a model based on connectionism, using it effectively to show that human knowledge is constructed from information "in the head" – cultural models – in interaction with the contingent environment. Paraphrasing Strauss and Quinn liberally and referring to the section above on the culture concept, an anthropology that rejects meaning as an interaction between the mind and contingent environment can be seen as a culmination of the distrust against psychology, again apparent from the beginnings of academic anthropology. It is also a political stance taken against anthropological perspectives that attempt to be scientific (reductionist), again, as an aspect of the history of the discipline.

To touch only briefly on the cultural theory of meaning based on connectionism, Strauss and Quinn provided a strong, rationalized account of connectionist perspectives.

Their aim was not to expand or refine connectionism but to use prototypical connectionist models of cognition, in which the building blocks in the model are "units," activated by the environment (or other units), and which are connected to "weights"; numeric values give differential association between units. Concepts that are learned in the interaction of units are said to be "distributed," in the sense that the information does not reside in symbols but in patterns of activity (over units). Information processing is seen as occurring both serially and in simultaneous multiple actions ("in parallel"). Lastly the system builds up knowledge by learning associations between the features of a number of specific cases, not by being "taught" specific rules. As Strauss and Quinn note, the approach has been called the "new connectionism" (Quinlan 1991), and it follows the classic work of Rumelhart and McClelland (1986) on parallel distributed processing. The heart of the content of the book is a demonstration of how connectionism can be used to produce models of culture from specific case studies in linguistics, psychology, and anthropology.

A fourth volume, *Finding Culture in Talk: A Collection of Methods*, was edited by Naomi Quinn (2005). The first one-third of the book, approximately 80 pages, is by Quinn and devoted to an expansion of concepts and methods from the 1987 volume, including further explication and development of her cultural model of marriage, likely the most described and elaborated of all cultural models. A chapter by D'Andrade, "Some Methods for Studying Cultural Cognitive Structures," provides an explicit account of how he sets about methodologically to conduct the research. The focus is on what he calls "contexts of discovery" and "contexts of verification," following a philosopher of science, Reichenbach (1938). Both are necessary steps in scientific research, though not always necessarily followed. D'Andrade points out that philosophers of science attend more to verification than to discovery, and departments of social science typically have methods courses that do likewise. D'Andrade presents the discovery procedures that he has developed in his long experience in cognitive research. They are presented step-wise and illustrated with a project studying people's knowledge of the concept of "social equality." The result is an excellent demonstration of how to pursue "contexts of discovery" and to study cultural cognitive structures.

Cultural model research has developed in several directions. In the cultural model research described thus far, the research procedure is to analyze discourse and search for underlying organizational structure, that is, models. Differences exist, however, in the orientation and scale of the research. Quinn, associates, and students have continued to develop and refine a theoretical perspective and rationale for "finding talk in culture," resulting in more and more refined and detailed knowledge that allows for identification of very specific models within discourse. In almost completely separate endeavors, environmental and medical anthropologists have used cultural models in their research, largely as methodological tools. This approach aims to mine discourse for shared knowledge within specific domains, particularly knowledge about aspects of the local environment such as the classic study on American environmental values by Kempton et al. (1995). The aim is more extensional than intensional. These two related approaches can be labeled, respectively, discourse-internal and discourse-external.

Model construction has proven useful in ecological and environmental research largely as a way to describe traditional or local ecological knowledge, also called ethnoecology (Gragson and Blount 1999). For example, work by Michael Paolisso, colleagues, and students at the University of Maryland (Paolisso et al. 2000; Paolisso 2002) uses cultural models as core components of ethnographic content focusing on local knowledge in the Chesapeake Bay relating to fishermen, pollution, and resource management. Linda Garro has used cultural models productively in her research on medical topics (1986), relating these in a methodological paper comparing the utility of cultural models with cultural consensus analysis in her field research (Garro 2000). The use of cultural models has appeared also in agricultural research (Silvasti 2003), mining (Horowitz 2008), fisheries (Blount and Kitner 2007), and a number of studies concerning infancy, childhood, and child-rearing.

When the Department of Anthropology at the University of Georgia created a new doctoral program in ecological anthropology in the early 1990s, cognitive anthropology became the specialization most pursued by graduate students. Whatever their topical specialization (forests, agriculture, fisheries, aid and development programs, ethnobiology, etc.), students realized that they need a principled way to conduct background ethnography in the communities in which they were working. The demand for cognitive training and of how to construct cultural models prompted the author to prepare a working paper on the subject, widely distributed among the students (Blount 2002). An innovative aspect of the methods was to use "keywords" in the search for and construction of models. Keywords are labels commonly used by community members to name and refer to "packets" or "chunks" of knowledge. Keywords serve as pivotal points in construction of discourse, by focusing on topics of the moment, but they also are shorthand for subsumed informational content, information constructed from the encyclopedic knowledge held by individuals. In a direct sense, they name cultural models. Several dissertations were produced by doctoral students at Georgia using keyword analysis to construct cultural models (Dailey 1999; Cooley 2003; Garcia-Quijano 2006).

These approaches based on discourse analysis differ considerably from another type of cultural model research we might denote as elicitation-analytical. Lexical items are elicited from respondents, typically through word listing, and analyses are conducted to determine amount or degree of sharing, through consensus analysis (see Romney et al. 1986; Weller and Romney 1988; Weller 2007). Discourse analysis is seen within this perspective as expensive in terms of time and energy and is thus eschewed.

Following this approach, William Dressler, colleagues, and students at the University of Alabama developed an innovative way to use cultural models in medical anthropology (Dressler et al. 2005). Dressler constructs community cultural models through elicitation and consensus analysis, and then compares the models of individuals against the community norm or standard. As a result, he has measures of what he calls cultural consonance, a quantitative score of how well individual knowledge matches the community pattern. He can then predict that individuals who match least well are the most likely members of a community to suffer from stress and related medical problems.

John Gatewood has developed a set of procedures that he refers to as "cognitive ethnography" (2008). Ethnographic research is conducted in a community, from which cultural models are constructed. The models are tested for "cultural validity," using cultural consensus analysis. The results are used to inform the construction of questionnaire surveys, which are administered to community members following standard sampling procedures. The idea is to have ethnographically informed surveys.

As an aside, the author developed independently an almost identical set of procedures to construct culturally informed survey questionnaires (Blount and Gezon 2003; Blount 2004). A cognitive ethnography serves as background from which survey questions can be generated. Results from the surveys can be analyzed for clusters of similar or identical responses. The clusters can be seen as packets of shared or common perspectives within communities, thereby constituting approximate cultural models. The distribution of the models reflects degree of similarity, which can then be related to historic and sociodemographic considerations within communities.

Current and Future Directions

Cognitive anthropology has a relatively brief history in anthropology as a focused and named area of inquiry. Throughout the paradigms of research, the overall aim has remained constant, the search for principles that underlie and give order to higher-level observations and behavior. That procedure is inherently scientific, a search for patterns in perceived phenomena and underlying "drivers" that help to account for and explain the patterns. The place of cognitive anthropology within the broader discipline lies within scientific anthropology. If it is forced to be located within the traditional sub-fields of anthropology, the place would be cultural anthropology, but the accommodation has always been strained. The perception of cognitive anthropology as psychology has worked against its standing within anthropology, as has the insistence that cognitive anthropology be scientific. Two ironies present themselves, both in relation to definitions of culture, which have always played a role in the conceptualization of cultural anthropology and its future directions. The first irony is that the first definition that was intended to be directly supportive of cognitive studies, Goodenough's definition, also served as the means for efforts to disenfranchise cognitive anthropology. The second, broader irony is that from the very beginning of anthropology culture has been seen in its core as ideational. Culture was defined by Tylor as knowledge, shared by individuals, a perspective that has continued to the present day. Cognitive anthropology can be touted as the approach within contemporary anthropology that has made the original and persistent aims of the field its own. Moreover, the current acceleration of interest in the brain sciences has fueled research in linguistics, psychology, cognitive science, and neuroscience, providing an abundance of research questions and possibilities for cognitive anthropology. Opportunities abound for innovative, contributory research.

This historical sketch has not included many recent and current contributions, due in part to space but also due to the coverage of those topics in other sections of this Companion. Particularly constructive contributions have been made in research methods, notably in cultural consensus analysis, often used to test the cultural validity of cultural models, as cited above. A full array of research methods can be found in Bernard (2006), and a recent discussion of cognitive theory and methods can be found in Ross (2004). New, computer-based approaches have been developed to address issues in kinship, in particular the Kinship Algebra Expert System (Fischer and Read 2005; Fischer 2009; Read 2009). Several publications have addressed interesting new questions in cognition and religion (Boyer 2001; Atran 2002; Whitehouse and Laidlaw 2007), and recent work has raised new issues in ethnobiology

(Medin and Atran 1999) and in the cultural construction of nature (Sanga and Ortalli 2003; Atran and Medin 2008). Cognitive linguistics and cognitive anthropology have a deep history on mutual influence. Major works that one may want to consult are Lakoff 1987; Langacker 1987, 1990, 2008; Taylor 1989, 2002; Taylor and MacLaury 1995; Boden 2006; Feldman 2006.

Lastly, several publications beyond those already noted provide in-depth overviews of cognitive anthropology at different stages of its development: Casson's *Language, Culture, and Cognition* (1981), Dougherty's *Directions in Cognitive Anthropology* (1985), D'Andrade's *The Development of Cognitive Anthropology* (1995), Kronenfeld's *Plastic Glasses and Church Fathers* (1996), Shore's *Culture in Mind* (1996), and, more recently, Kronenfeld's *Language, Culture, and Cognition* (2008) and Bennardo's *Language, Space, and Social Relationships* (2009). Mention should also be made of E. N. Anderson's book *Ecologies of the Heart* (1996), in which salient and fundamental elements of culture are identified. They are similar to cultural models, although the terminology differs.

Cognitive anthropology has made significant advances during the past several decades, methodologically and theoretically. While remaining focused throughout on lexical items and how they convey shared meanings, cognitive anthropologists have become more proficient and accurate in the description of those features and processes. The direction of advance is toward better science, in alliance with sister disciplines of linguistics, psychology, and computer science. While better science may not be a premium in contemporary anthropology, the contribution to the discipline is nonetheless noteworthy, especially in the long run.

REFERENCES

Anderson, E. N.

1996 Ecologies of the Heart: Emotion, Belief, and the Environment. New York: Oxford University Press.

Atran, S.

1990 Cognitive Foundations of Natural History. Cambridge: Cambridge University Press.

2002 In Gods We Trust: The Evolutionary Landscape of Religion. New York: Oxford University Press.

Atran, S., and D. Medin

2008 The Native Mind and the Cultural Construction of Nature. Cambridge, MA: MIT Press.

Bennardo, Giovanni

2009 Language, Space, and Social Relationships: A Foundational Cultural Model in Polynesia. Cambridge: Cambridge University Press.

Berlin, B. O.

1972 Speculations on the Growth of Ethnobiological Nomenclature. Language in Society 1:63–98.

1992 Ethnobiological Classification: Principles of Categorization of Plants and Animals in Traditional Societies. Princeton: Princeton University Press.

Berlin, B. O., and E. A. Berlin

1983 Adaptation and Ethnozoological Classification: Theoretical Implications of Animal Resources and Diet of the Aguaruna and Huambisa. *In* Adaptive Responses of Native Amazonians. R. B. Hames and W. T. Vickers, eds. New York: Academic Press.

Berlin, B. O., and P. D. Kay
1969 Basic Color Terms: Their Universality and Evolution. Berkeley: University of California Press.
Berlin, B. O., J. Boster, and J. P. O'Neill
1981 The Perceptual Bases of Ethnobiological Classification: Evidence from Aguaruna Folk Ornithology. Journal of Ethnobiology 1:95–108.
Berlin, B. O., D. E. Breedlove, and P. H. Raven.
1966 Folk Taxonomies and Biological Classification. Science 154:273–275.
Bernard, H. R.
2006 Research Methods in Anthropology. 4th edition. Lanham, MD: AltaMira.
Blount, B. G.
2002 Keywords, Cultural Models, and Representation of Knowledge: A Case Study from the Georgia Coast (USA). Occasional Publication no. 3. Athens: Coastal Anthropology Resources Laboratory, Department of Anthropology, University of Georgia.
2004 Public Perceptions Concerning Water Use and Planning in Georgia Coastal Counties: Final Report to the Coastal Resources Division of the Department of Natural Resources, Brunswick, GA.
Blount, B. G., ed.
1974 Language, Culture, and Society: A Book of Readings. Cambridge, MA: Winthrop. Reissued 1985 by Waveland.
Blount, B. G., and L. Gezon
2003 Cultural Models of Water Issues on the Georgia Coast: Proceedings of the 2003 Georgia Water Resources Conference. K. Hatcher, ed. Athens: Institute of Ecology, University of Georgia.
Blount, B. G., and K. Kitner
2007 Life on the Water: A Historical-Cultural Model of African American Fishermen on the Georgia Coast (USA). NAPA Bulletin (National Association of Practicing Anthropologists) 28:109–122.
Blount, B. G., and P. J. Schwanenflugel
1993 Cultural Bases of Folk Classification Systems. *In* Cognition and Culture: A Cross-Cultural Approach to Cognitive Psychology. J. Altarriba, ed. Advances in Psychology 103. Amsterdam: North-Holland.
Boden, M. A.
2006 Mind as Machine: A History of Cognitive Science. Oxford: Oxford University Press.
Boster, J.
1986 Exchange of Varieties and Information between Aguaruna Manioc Cultivators. American Anthropologist 3:381–399.
Boyer, P.
2001 Religion Explained: The Human Instincts that Fashion Gods. London: Heinemann.
Burling, R.
1964 Cognition and Componential Analysis: God's Truth or Hocus-Pocus. Special issue. American Anthropologist 66:20–28.
Casson, R. W., ed.
1981 Language, Culture, and Cognition: Anthropological Perspectives. New York: Macmillan.
Chomsky, N.
1965 Aspects of the Theory of Syntax. Cambridge, MA: MIT Press.
Conklin, H. C.
1962 Lexicographical Treatment of Folk Taxonomies. *In* Problems in Lexicography. F. W. Householder and S. Saporta, eds. Bloomington: Indiana University Research Center in Anthropology, Folklore, and Linguistics.
1972 Folk Classification: A Topically Arranged Bibliography of Contemporary and Background References through 1971. New Haven, CT: Department of Anthropology, Yale University.

Cooley, D. R.
2003 Cultural Models and Fishing Knowledge: A Case Study of Commercial Blue Crab Fishermen in Georgia, USA. Unpublished doctoral dissertation, University of Georgia.
Dailey, M.
1999 The Mind's Eye: Cultural Models, Forests, and Environmental History of the Northern Allegheny Plateau, 1750–1860. Unpublished doctoral dissertation, University of Georgia.
D'Andrade, R. G.
1992 Schemas and Motivation. *In* Human Motives and Cultural Models. R. G. D'Andrade and C. Strauss, eds. Cambridge: Cambridge University Press.
1995 The Development of Cognitive Anthropology. Cambridge: Cambridge University Press.
2005 Some Methods for Studying Cultural Cognitive Structures. *In* Finding Talk in Culture: A Collection of Methods. N. Quinn, ed. New York: Palgrave Macmillan.
D'Andrade, R. G., and C. Strauss, eds.
1992 Human Motives and Cultural Models. Cambridge: Cambridge University Press.
Dougherty, J. W. D., ed.
1985 Directions in Cognitive Anthropology. Urbana: University of Illinois Press.
Dressler, W., C. D. Borges, M. C. Balieiro, and J. E.Dos Santos
2005 Measuring Cultural Consonance: Examples with Special Reference to Measurement Theory in Anthropology. Field Methods 17:331–355.
Feldman, J. A.
2006 From Molecule to Metaphor: A Neural Theory of Language. Cambridge, MA: MIT Press.
Fillmore, C.
1975 An Alternative to Checklist Theories of Meaning. *In* First Annual Meeting of the Berkeley Linguistics Society. C. Cogen, H. Thompson, G. Thurgood, K. Whistler, and J. Wright, eds. Berkeley: University of California Press.
Fischer, M.
2009 Computer Modeling of Kinship. Presentation at the 5th Annual Meeting of the Society for Anthropological Sciences, Las Vegas, Nevada.
Fischer, M., and D. Read
2005 Kinship Algebra Expert System (KAES). http://kaes.anthrosciences.net.
Frake, C. O.
1962 The Ethnographic Study of Cognitive Systems. *In* Anthropology and Human Behavior. T. Gladwin and W. C. Sturtevant, eds. Washington, DC: Anthropological Society of Washington.
Garcia-Quijano, C. G.
2006 Resisting Extinction: The Value of Ecological Knowledge for Small-Scale Fishers in Southeastern Puerto Rico. Unpublished doctoral dissertation, University of Georgia.
Garro, L. C.
1986 Intracultural Variation in Folk Medical Knowledge: A Comparison between Curers and Non-Curers. American Anthropologist 88:351–370.
2000 Remembering What One Knows and the Construction of the Past: A Comparison of Cultural Consensus Theory and Cultural Schema Theory. Ethos 28:275–319.
Gatewood, J.
2008 Conjoining Cultural Models and Consensus Analysis: Variations in Residents' Understandings of Tourism in the Turks & Caicos Islands. Presentation at the 4th Annual Meeting of the Society for Anthropological Sciences, New Orleans, Louisiana.
Geertz, C.
1973 The Interpretation of Cultures: Selected Essays. New York: Basic Books.

Goodenough, W. H.
1957 Cultural Anthropology and Linguistics. *In* Report of the Seventh Annual Round Table on Linguistics and Language Study. P. Garvin, ed. Georgetown University Monograph Series on Language and Linguistics 9. Washington, DC: Georgetown University.
1965 Yankee Kinship Terminology: A Problem in Componential Analysis. Special issue. American Anthropologist 67(5.2):259–287.
Gragson, T., and B. G. Blount, eds.
1999 Ethnoecology: Knowledge, Resources, and Rights. Athens: University of Georgia Press.
Gumperz, J. J., and D. H. Hymes, eds.
1964 The Ethnography of Communication. Special issue, American Anthropologist 66(6.2).
1972 Directions in Sociolinguistics: The Ethnography of Communication. New York: Holt, Rinehart, and Winston.
Harris, M.
1968 The Rise of Anthropological Theory: A History of Theories of Culture. New York: HarperCollins.
Holland, D., and N. Quinn, eds.
1987 Cultural Models in Language & Thought. Cambridge: Cambridge University Press.
Horowitz, L. S.
2008 Destroying God's Creation or Using What He Provided? Cultural Models of a Mining Project in New Caledonia. Human Organization 67:292–306.
Hunn, E.
1977 Tzeltal Folk Zoology. New York: Academic Press.
1999 Size as Limiting the Recognition of Biodiversity in Folkbiological Classifications: One of Four Factors Governing the Cultural Recognition of Biological Taxa. *In* Folkbiology. D. Medin and S. Atran, eds. Cambridge, MA: MIT Press.
Kay, P. D., B. O. Berlin, and W. Merrifield
1991 Biocultural Implications of Systems of Color Naming. Journal of Linguistic Anthropology 1:12–25.
Keesing, R. M.
1987 Models, "Folk" and "Cultural": Paradigms Regained? *In* Cultural Models in Language and Thought. D. Holland and N. Quinn, eds. Cambridge: Cambridge University Press.
Kempton, W., J. Boster, and J. Hartley
1995 Environmental Values in American Culture. Cambridge, MA: MIT Press.
Kroeber, A. L., and C. Kluckhohn
1952 Culture: A Critical Review of Concepts and Definitions. New York: Vintage.
Kronenfeld, D.
1996 Plastic Glasses and Church Fathers: Semantic Extension from the Ethnoscience Tradition. New York: Oxford University Press.
2008 Language, Culture, and Cognition: Collective Goals, Values, Actions, and Knowledge. Berlin: Mouton de Gruyter.
Labov, W.
1972 Sociolinguistic Patterns. Philadelphia: University of Pennsylvania Press.
Lakoff, G.
1987 Women, Fire, and Dangerous Things: What Categories Reveal about the Mind. Chicago: University of Chicago Press.
Langacker, R. W.
1987 Foundations of Cognitive Grammar, vol. 1. Stanford: Stanford University Press.
1990 Concept, Image, and Symbol: The Cognitive Basis of Grammar. Berlin: Mouton de Gruyter.

2008 Cognitive Grammar: A Basic Introduction. Oxford: Oxford University Press.
Linneaus, C.
1735 Systema Naturae. Leiden: Haak.
Lounsbury, F. G.
1964a A Formal Account of the Crow- and Omaha-Type Kinship Terminologies. *In* Explorations in Cultural Anthropology. W. H. Goodenough, ed. New York: McGraw-Hill.
1964b The Structural Analysis of Kinship Semantics: Proceedings of the Ninth International Congress of Linguists. The Hague: Mouton.
MacLaury, R. E.
1991a Exotic Color Categories: Linguistic Relativity to What Extent? Journal of Linguistic Anthropology 1:26–51.
1991b Prototypes Revisited. Annual Review of Anthropology 20:55–74.
Medin, Douglas M., and Scott Atran, eds.
1999 Folkbiology. Cambridge, MA: MIT Press.
Morgan, L. H.
1871 Systems of Consanguinity and Affinity of the Human Family. Smithsonian Contributions to Knowledge 17. Washington, DC: Smithsonian Institution.
Murdock, G. P.
1949 Social Structure. New York: Macmillan.
Paolisso, M.
2002 Blue Crabs and Controversy on the Chesapeake Bay: A Cultural Model for Understanding Watermen's Reasoning about Blue Crab Management. Human Organization 61:226–239.
Paolisso, M., R. S. Maloney, and E. Chambers
2000 Cultural Models of Environment and Pollution. Anthropology News 41:48–49.
Quinlan, P. T.
1991 Connectionism and Psychology. Chicago: University of Chicago Press.
Quinn, N., ed.
2005 Finding Culture in Talk: A Collection of Methods. New York: Palgrave Macmillan.
Quinn, N., and D. Holland
1987 Culture and Cognition. *In* Cultural Models in Language and Thought. D. Holland and N. Quinn, eds. Cambridge: Cambridge University Press.
Radcliffe-Browne, A. R., and C. D. Forde, eds.
1950 African Systems of Kinship and Marriage. London: Oxford University Press.
Read, D.
2009 Computer Modeling of Kinship. Presentation at the 5th Annual Meeting of the Society for Anthropological Sciences, Las Vegas, Nevada.
Reichenbach, H.
1938 Experience and Prediction. Chicago: University of Chicago Press.
Romney, A. K., and R. G. D'Andrade
1964 Cognitive Aspects of English Kin Terms. Special issue, American Anthropologist 66(3.2):146–170.
Romney, A. K., and R. G. D'Andrade, eds.
1964 Transcultural Studies in Cognition. Special issue, American Anthropologist 66(3.2).
Romney, A. K., W. Batchelder, and S. Weller
1986 Culture as Consensus: A Theory of Culture and Informant Accuracy. American Anthropologist 88:313–338.
Rosch, E.
1978 Principles of Categorization. *In* Cognition and Categorization. E. Rosch and B. Lloyd, eds. Hillsdale, NJ: Lawrence Erlbaum.
Ross, N.
2004 Culture and Cognition: Implications for Theory and Method. Thousand Oaks, CA: Sage.

Rumelhart, D. E., and J. L. McClelland
1986 An Interactive Activation Model of Context Efforts in Letter Perspective. Part 1: An Account of Basic Findings. *In* Parallel Distributed Processing, vol. 2. J. L. McClelland, ed. Cambridge, MA: MIT Press.
Sanga, G., and G. Ortalli, eds.
2003 Nature Knowledge: Ethnoscience, Cognition, and Utility. New York: Berghan.
Schneider, David M.
1965 American Kin Terms for Kinsmen: A Critique of Goodenough's Componential Analysis of Yankee Kinship Terminology. Special issue, American Anthropologist 67(5.2):288–308.
Schwanenflugel, P. J., B. G. Blount, and P. J. Lin
1991 Cross-Cultural Aspects of Word Meaning. *In* The Psychology of Word Meanings. P. J. Schwanenflugel, ed. Hillsdale, NJ: Lawrence Erlbaum.
Shore, B.
1996 Culture in Mind: Cognition, Culture, and the Problem of Meaning. Oxford: Oxford University Press.
Silvasti, T.
2003 The Cultural Model of "The Good Farmer" and the Environmental Question in Finland. Agriculture and Human Values 20:143–150.
Strauss, C., and N. Quinn
1997 A Cognitive Theory of Cultural Meaning. Cambridge: Cambridge University Press.
Taylor, J. R.
1989 Linguistic Categorization: Prototypes in Linguistic Theory. Oxford: Clarendon.
2002 Cognitive Grammar. Oxford: Oxford University Press.
Taylor, J. R., and R. E. MacLaury, eds.
1995 Language and the Cognitive Construal of the World. Trends in Linguistics, Studies and Monographs 82. Berlin: Mouton de Gruyter.
Tyler, S. A., ed.
1969 Cognitive Anthropology. New York: Holt, Rinehart, and Winston.
Tylor, E. B.
1865 Early Researches into the History of Mankind and the Development of Civilization. London: John Morrow.
1871 Primitive Culture: Researches into the Development of Mythology, Philosophy, Religion, Language, Art, and Custom. London: John Morrow.
Wallace, A. F. C., and J. Atkins
1960 The Meaning of Kinship Terms. American Anthropologist 62:58–80.
Weller, S. C.
2007 Cultural Consensus Theory: Applications and Frequently Asked Questions. Field Methods 19:339–368.
Weller, S. C., and A. K. Romney
1988 Systematic Data Collection. Newbury Park, CA: Sage.
Whitehouse, H., and J. Laidlaw, eds.
2007 Religion, Anthropology, and Cognitive Science. Durham, NC: Carolina Academic Press.
Wolf, E.
1964 Anthropology. Englewood Cliffs, NJ: Prentice Hall.

CHAPTER 2

The History of the Cultural Models School Reconsidered: A Paradigm Shift in Cognitive Anthropology

Naomi Quinn

Amidst the hoopla and hyper-positioning that characterize academic politics in every discipline, and that flourish in contemporary cultural anthropology, it is easy for more subterranean, if sometimes significant, theoretical developments to go unnoticed. The history of one such development, a paradigm shift that occurred over the course of the second half of the 20th century within what is now commonly referred to as the "cultural models school," a sub-field of cognitive anthropology, is worth recounting because it will help us understand the current direction this sub-field is taking. I will first briefly explain how my account of this history is revisionist in positing a heretofore unidentified paradigm shift within this school, then describe the intellectual state of affairs that led up to this shift, and finally demonstrate how it unfolded in two distinguishable stages.

The Motivation for a New Account

There have been previous historical treatments of cognitive anthropology, the fullest and most useful being Roy D'Andrade's 1995 book, *The Development of Cognitive Anthropology*. D'Andrade's separate chapter discussions of advances in this sub-field,

A Companion to Cognitive Anthropology, First Edition. Edited by David B. Kronenfeld, Giovanni Bennardo, Victor C. de Munck, and Michael D. Fischer.

from its beginnings in studies of the meaning of kinterms, to its contemporary focus on emotion and other psychological processes, remain unparalleled. I always consult this book for its scholarly reach and powerful syntheses whenever, in the course of my own work, I return to one or another of the topics it treats. D'Andrade's account of the field of cognitive anthropology is full of insights into the history of this subdiscipline. However, in this chapter I will depart from D'Andrade at one significant point in this overarching narrative.

He begins his book by reviewing the mid-20th-century paradigm shift that was signaled by the collapse of behaviorism and became known as the "cognitive revolution," first in psychology and linguistics and spreading to other fields including anthropology, where it was reflected in the "move towards more ideational, mental, and cognitive concerns – the study of ideas, beliefs, values, and cosmologies" (D'Andrade 1995:12). The account of cognitive anthropological research that follows seems to me to be first and foremost an unapologetic effort to persuade readers of the unquestionable value of the work that has been done in our field. To this end, D'Andrade's story highlights a series of progressive advances, each chapter in this story adding further weight to this record of accomplishment.

I will complicate the account. I argue that somewhere in the middle of the story, there was a decided rupture, in the form of a theoretical dead end that demanded a drastic change in approach. This is the story I want to tell. My revision of D'Andrade's history might be viewed as a metaphorical inset to the map he provides. He himself is a central actor in this story, and, certainly, in his account, he provides some broad hints to what I will be describing. Nevertheless, I feel that this rupture deserves to be highlighted, and recognized for the paradigm shift that it was. I was a part of the story, too, and in telling it I will be foregrounding certain intellectual developments that were especially salient to me at the time, and that, in retrospect, seem especially diagnostic of the paradigm shift that I am describing.[1]

I should note parenthetically that D'Andrade defends the use of Kuhn's concept of a "paradigm shift" to describe the mid-20th-century cognitive revolution that fueled developments in several social sciences, even though the "paradigms" that characterize these disciplines may be less well formed than those that typify the natural sciences.[2] I conceive of the rupture I will be describing as a theoretical paradigm shift as well. It was a shift subsequent to the cognitive revolution, and can be understood as a further outgrowth of that revolution. While the development I will describe had, and continues to have, wide-ranging effects on the several cognitive sciences, its influence on cognitive anthropology has been especially profound. For this development provided a compelling basis for a theory of culture, the project at the heart of the sub-field and, indeed, critical to its parent field of cultural anthropology.

There were two distinct moments in the paradigm shift I am describing. The first was marked by a radical change in the way we thought about what in earlier terms would have been designated something like "the organization of cultural knowledge," but which became known as *cultural models*, and, ultimately, *cultural schemas*.[3] This development was associated with a relatively small intellectual school within cognitive anthropology, one that came to be called the "cultural models" school. The second moment in the shift involved a levels reduction. What had come to be understood as cultural schemas were reconceptualized in terms of a new theory of brain processing from artificial intelligence, known as *connectionism*. In D'Andrade's aforementioned account, these two moments in the history of the cultural models school are elided. But, significantly, there was a gap of well over a decade between them, and I think it is instructive to distinguish the two developments analytically, examining how the second came to fill a theoretical need that had been created by the first.

The Felt Inadequacy of Existing Theory

To start at the beginning, the cultural models school was the direct heir of another tightly knit and highly identifiable school of anthropological research that flourished in the United States in the 1960s and 1970s, called *ethnoscience* (a label switched later, and tellingly, to *ethnographic semantics* and still later and more expansively, to *cognitive anthropology*).[4] Bradd Shore (1996:316) has characterized ethnoscience as having lost its appeal in the 1980s and just faded away, to be replaced by ethnopsychology. This characterization misses the important fact that, as I will go on to describe, ethnoscience was the site of the theoretical crisis that occasioned the emergence of the cultural models approach. It must be added that the cultural models school was not the only enduring offshoot of ethnoscience. The emergence of ethnopsychology, mentioned by Shore, was another such development, pursued by a different group of psychological anthropologists (see White 1992:22).[5] Still another branching was cultural consensus theory, developed by A. Kimball Romney and his colleagues.[6] These other schools fall outside the scope of my account.

The cultural models approach grew, in the way new theory often does, out of the felt inadequacy of existing theory. In this case the existing theory concerned the nature of cultural meaning. Ethnoscience had begun with a grand quest for a theory of cultural knowledge, articulated first in Ward Goodenough's (1957:167) expansive and thereafter widely quoted assertion that "a society's culture consists of whatever it is one has to know or believe in order to operate in a manner acceptable to its members" (see Keesing 1972:300, 302 and D'Andrade 1995:xiii for critiques of Goodenough's definition). While this dictum was thereafter widely quoted and paraphrased, and often coupled with calls for an eventual "cultural grammar" or "cultural code" (see Keesing 1972:306), this linguistic analogy remained an abstraction, and this theory of culture went undeveloped – presumably because none of those who subscribed to it could figure out how to realize it.

Instead, and understandably, most ethnoscientists settled for a much more restricted but manageable definition of cultural meaning, one that lent itself to formal, replicable methods of analysis. The meanings of objects and events were equated with the meanings of the words that label them, and then, following the treatment of linguistic features in the then regnant school of structural linguistics, word meaning was reduced to just those features that define the differences between words in a lexical contrast set. Within this minimalist theory of word meaning, kinship terms and other terminological systems such as ethnobotanical terms were favorite domains for analysis, and such analyses proliferated. Kinship terminologies were found to be organized by a small number of cross-cutting dimensions such as gender, generation, seniority, and so forth, and their investigation came to be known as *componential analysis*, while ethnobotanical terms and some other terminological domains were found to have a taxonomic structure. It was as if the human head were stuffed with taxonomies and paradigms, and not much else.

A number of practitioners of ethnoscience, no less than its many vocal external critics, became increasingly dissatisfied with this older theory. Early signs of this mounting dissatisfaction within the school itself were separate attempts to rethink the organization of cultural knowledge. A study of disease categories by Roy D'Andrade and co-workers concluded from a cluster analysis of these categories "that the defining properties of a set of terms are not always the properties which determine how people categorize or react to those terms. Thus, the categories discovered by the analysis of how disease terms distribute across beliefs do not seem to be related to the features which define these disease terms" (D'Andrade et al. 1972:50). Instead, American beliefs about illness were grouped on the basis of salient but non-defining features: bad weather illnesses, childhood diseases, other contagious diseases, and serious non-contagious ones. D'Andrade et al. added that "the model of lexical domains as organized into taxonomic and paradigmatic relations is not always useful" (1972:51).

Others experimented with extending the possibilities for how cultural knowledge was organized beyond taxonomies and paradigms – and domains such as ethnobotany and kinship – to other types of relation in other domains. Charles Frake (1977:373), for instance, explained that "some of my work has been guided by an image of a society as an organization for the production of social occasions, or 'scenes,' as I have called them, and of a culture as a script for planning, staging and performing scenes." Within this framework, he had produced earlier descriptions of, for instance, the ceremonial performance of Subanun (a Philippine group) religious offerings (1964) – delineating settings, provisions, and paraphernalia for such offerings, and the ceremonial routines that comprised them – and the intricate interplay of etiquette between Yakan (another Philippine group) host and visitor that led to the visitor being invited into the host's residence (1975). Paul Kay (1973) suggested, instead, the centrality of propositions to the organization of knowledge. Benjamin N. Colby (1975) recommended starting with highly routinized or stereotyped cultural productions – such as folk narratives, or rituals – and working out the "culture grammars," or heuristics used to produce these. Ward Goodenough (1971) made perhaps the most expansive proposal, considering the "content of culture" to include not just *forms* (by which he meant categories), but also *propositions, beliefs, values, rules, recipes, routines and customs*, and *systems of customs.*

Around the same time, too, my graduate school cohort and I experimented with decision models of various domains – for example, of residence (Geoghegan 1969; Quinn 1973), fishing crew composition (Quinn 1971), and fish marketing (Gladwin and Gladwin 1971; Quinn 1978). Tellingly, later efforts in this direction pushed the limits of decision-modeling, reconstructing the shared heuristic "systems" that people used in making these decisions (Quinn 1976 on Mfantse litigation settlement), or identifying the life goals and imagined future "scenarios" that informed them (Nardi 1983 on Samoan fertility decision-making). What these later attempts reflect is that we were coming to see the inadequacy of a decision-making approach – that the nodes on a decision tree did not capture the complex mental representations that lay behind, and influenced, decisions.

All these efforts signaled the impending collapse of the regnant word-based theory of cultural meaning. The number and variety of proposals to rethink how cultural knowledge is organized, and the two decades-long period over which these proposals kept appearing, indicated that the existing paradigm was in trouble. Over this period as well, even advocates of the componential analysis of kinterms, the classic domain for application of lexical semantics, had begun to develop doubts about their approach. Analysts debated the "psychological reality" of competing analyses, with increasing confusion over what was meant by such "reality" in the context of terminological contrast sets.[7] Did it even make sense to speak of a psychological reality underlying kinterms or their usage, and, if so, did one or another componential analysis capture it?[8]

To cap my argument for this period of "felt inadequacy," I turn to the explicit accounts of this dissatisfaction from two contemporaneous participant observers of the school. Roger Keesing put the onset of grave doubts about "the new ethnography" (as the enterprise was initially dubbed) at five years previous to his writing. He wrote, tartly:

> For almost 15 years cognitive anthropologists have pursued "the new ethnography" for as far as it would lead them. For the last five, at least, it has been obvious that this would not be very far – that the messianic promises of the early polemic were not to be realized. "The new ethnographers" have been unable to move beyond the analysis of artificially simplified and delineated (and usually trivial) semantic domains, and this has discouraged many of the originally faithful. Ethnoscience has almost bored itself to death. [Keesing 1972:307–308]

Keesing rightly identified the school's decline as due not only to the realization of its severe analytic limitations, but also to the collapse of the theoretical paradigm on which analysis was founded. Within linguistics, from which the theory had been borrowed, it had been destroyed by the transformational revolution. Keesing was dubious that the new linguistics could guide the investigation of (non-linguistic) cultural knowledge. Benjamin N. Colby (1975), like Keesing, distinguished two phases in the enterprise. He noted that in the first, ethnoscience phase, beginning at the end of the 1950s, the new field gained great visibility for its methodological emphasis on validity. In the second phase, however, ongoing as he wrote, interest in ethnoscience was waning due to what he saw as the evident lack of an underlying theory. Practitioners had begun calling themselves cognitive anthropologists and orienting themselves toward cognitive studies, taking an interest in universal cognitive categories, and concerning themselves with cultural context and with cultural learning. Colby's contemporaneous view was more optimistic than Keesing's, or than retrospect supports, about the promise of some of the efforts then underway.

The First Moment: Cultural Schemas

The various separate and typically fragmentary proposals I have listed remained isolated from one another, failing to gel into a comprehensive, agreed upon new theory of cultural meaning. Agreement around such a new theory came only as the eighties advanced, and what follows is my story of how it happened. The neighboring field of cognitive linguistics, a growing branch of the discipline from which ethnoscience had borrowed its problematic theory of word meaning in the first place, now decisively recanted it (Fillmore 1975; Langacker 1979; see, for an excellent account, Casson 1983; see also Quinn and Holland 1987). Cognitive linguists' new theory about the "prototype worlds" or "functional assemblages" that underlay words and gave them their meaning belonged to a family of new proposals from cognitive science, variously called *frames*, *scenes*, *scenarios*, and *scripts* (D'Andrade 1995:122), that were soon to be subsumed under the idea of the *schema*, changing the way almost everyone in several disciplines thought about cognition.

In my own case, I turned away from my brief fling with decision-modeling, because I began to see that, as I thought of it, the decisions people made were the tip of an iceberg. I wanted to investigate the iceberg. All of us cognitive anthropologists became as fully immersed in all the debates and developments surrounding the schema concept as everyone else in the cognitive sciences. I was much influenced at the time by Charles Fillmore's 1975 paper, "An Alternative to Checklist Theories of Meaning," which was very widely circulated informally, in spite of having been originally tucked away in the *Proceedings* of the first annual meeting of the Berkeley Linguistic Society. The broad influence of that paper is remarked on by D'Andrade (1995:123). Fillmore there argued that a word like *bachelor* did more than merely designate an "unmarried man"; the word posited a simplified world in which (back in the day when people were more concerned about such matters) a man was expected to marry at a certain age, and *bachelor* designated those men who remained unmarried beyond that expected age. While Fillmore and other linguists were intent on solving the problem of word meaning by referencing such background knowledge, to my mind it was that simplified world itself – or, as we began calling them by the mid-1980s (Holland and Quinn 1987), cultural models – that I and other cultural anthropologists ought to be addressing.

I also remember being much taken at first with Roger Schank and Robert Abelson's *Scripts, Plans, Goals and Understanding* (1977). But even this novel and comprehensive proposal for the organization of shared knowledge I eventually found too limiting as an account of culture. Like other proposals arising from artificial intelligence (D'Andrade 1995:125–126), theirs was unable to handle the vast extent and variety of cultural meanings that people of any group had at their disposal. Indeed, it became clear that Schank and Abelson had left culture out of their theory. They conceptualized higher-level knowledge or beliefs as deriving from undifferentiated bundles of goals, rather than from culturally distinctive representations in which goals are embedded and from which these beliefs and goals draw their emotional and motivational force – which force they had no way of explaining. In their examples of goals, too, they fell back overly exclusively on assumptions either about human needs and drives they (often erroneously) assumed to be universal, or about rational action based on assessment of rewards and costs, again assumed to be universal. My struggle to figure out what was lacking in Schank and Abelson's scheme helped me to see what was needed in an adequate account of culture.

Ultimately, cultural models theorists such as myself gravitated toward the more culture compatible concept of the schema. Schemas organize and process experience. Summarizing D'Andrade (1995:122) and Mandler (1984:55–56), whom he quotes, a schema is a "bounded, distinct, and unitary representation," and the activation of any part activates the whole. Schemas are built up out of experience – experience to which we attend consciously or unconsciously, including experience of both the outer world and the inner world of bodily sensation, mental representations, and emotions. Once existing, they structure our memories of the past, our perceptions, and our expectations of the future – though new experience, if it is salient enough, can also modify them; schemas are not set in stone.

What anthropologists borrowed from the schema concept was the deceptively simple realization that this concept could be applied to cultural as well as individual meanings: When a group of individuals have, and attend to, generally similar experiences, they end up sharing schemas, which are generic representations of that common experience. Such a shared schema can be said to be a *cultural schema*. Of course experience is never perfectly shared, but to the extent that it overlaps – whether for siblings growing up in the same household, say, or for members of the same organization, or for residents of the same region – those people will come to share cultural schemas.[9]

This reconceptualization of culture in schema theoretic terms was a deceptively simple move. In actuality, it introduced a whole new theory of culture. It gave anthropologists a basis for beginning to think about cultural knowledge in cognitive terms – in terms of what might actually be going on in their brains when individuals learned and used this shared knowledge. And it seems to be the nature of the human adaptation to our environment that many, many of our schemas are cultural ones.

To my knowledge, the first to use the actual term *cultural schema* was Ronald Casson in the introduction to his 1981 edited volume. Gradually, this term began to supplant *cultural model*, though both are still used, sometimes interchangeably. (Some authors today prefer to use *cultural schema* generically and to reserve *cultural model* for only those cultural schemas of some size [D'Andrade 1995:152–153] or complexity [Quinn 1997:139]).[10]

The application of the schema concept to culture had been cooking for a while. In a 1971 paper entitled "Semantics, Schemata, and Kinship," which was widely circulated among his friends and came to be known by the color of the paper it was mimeographed on, as "the yellow paper," Hugh Gladwin advocated rethinking the meanings attached to kinship in terms of schemas. He argued, for example, that it made better sense of how small children learned kinterms – say, learning to distinguish between *father* and *uncle* – to assume a gestalt-like *household* schema (which a child might then connect to other like household schemas), rather than to assume that such knowledge was entirely built up from combinations of kinterm features.[11]

The yellow paper was never published and, at the time of its circulation, I do not think that those of us who read it were ready to appreciate fully the breadth of applicability of the schema concept to culture beyond the limited domain of kinship, or the theoretical implications of so applying it. Yet, a number of cognitive anthropologists at that time were busy describing cultural schema-like entities and calling them by various names. Some of us wrote simply of "systems" of thought – "cultural belief systems" (D'Andrade 1972), for example, or "cultural meaning systems" (D'Andrade 1984), or "natural systems" of decision-making (Quinn 1976). One anthropologist, Edwin Hutchins, in his 1978 dissertation (and resulting 1980 book) on Trobriand land litigation, wrote explicitly of *schemata* that were the templates for land transactions; he characterized the set of such schemata as a *cultural code*.[12] By the mid-1980s we were mostly all talking about schemas.

I think my own epiphany about cultural schemas came while trying to describe and animate such shared "systems" as the one described in my 1976 article on Mfantse litigation settlement, cited earlier. This was a template that panels of elders used to set fines in litigation cases that arose over ordinary disputes such as domestic quarrels or petty theft, in the coastal Ghanaian town where I was conducting my field research. The template allowed the panel to adjust fines upwards or downwards on an ordinal scale for a variety of attenuating circumstances.

By the late 1970s and early 1980s, I was moved not only to abandon the study of decision-making altogether, but to fashion my own entirely new approach to the investigation of cultural representations. In a move that was to radically influence the subsequent trajectory of my work and thinking, I collected an entirely new kind of data, extended discourse from interviews, on a topic – American marriage – that I rightly surmised would result in a rich body of material for analysis. Then I spent some years figuring out how to analyze this discourse for the underlying cultural representations or schemas that, as I thought of it, interviewees must have had in mind to say the things they did. At first my stabs at new methods were tentative and undirected, but eventually they led to the discovery of reliable patterns across speakers, in the metaphors for, and reasoning about, marriage that they shared (Quinn 2005). From these and other discourse patterns I reconstructed what I thought of as a cultural model or cultural schema of marriage.

Others, I am sure, experienced similar periods of bafflement, culminating in their own eureka moments and other new departures – a sequence characteristic of paradigm shift. D'Andrade (1995:126) summarizes how his turn to schemas grew out of his inability to produce the same kind of defining feature analysis of beliefs about illness that had worked for kinship terms:

> In my own work in the early 1970s I had begun to encounter difficulty with further analyses of American beliefs about illness. Consideration of these difficulties led me to the conclusion that something like schema theory was necessary for an adequate description of cultural knowledge.

The fuller account that follows, of his own unsuccessful efforts to fit the results of his cluster analyses of Americans' illness beliefs into the older, distinctive feature way of thinking about the semantic properties of terms such as those for illness, is telling. His problem stemmed from the fact that he was working, not with the limited data provided by sets of illness terms and informant's comparisons or sortings of these, but from richer, more unruly data he had elicited from informants on what they *believed* about these illnesses – what they themselves thought was important to know about them. He was able to reduce these beliefs about illness to a smallish number of properties, and to diagram the inferential links that informants must be making between specific illnesses and their properties in order to answer questions about illness (D'Andrade 1995:128). But, he concluded, the links between diseases and their properties did not amount to "anything like a representation of the way Americans actually understand illness" (D'Andrade 1995:129). He went on to say that the kind of analysis he had conducted in the 1970s

> fails to give an adequate representation of American beliefs about illness because it does not explicate the *schemas* Americans use to understand illness. To understand American beliefs about *colds, measles, polio, et cetera*, requires an understanding of the *germ* schema and this cannot be obtained from an analysis of the properties of diseases alone. The answer to the question about how respondents were able to answer novel questions appears to be that they made use of complex schemas to compute their way through new terrain.

D'Andrade appears to have experienced a very similar frustration with his attempt to cast cultural meaning in terms of the inferences people made from the properties of things, to that I had experienced when I tried to do the same in terms of the decisions people made. These outputs of cognitive processes were, as I have said, the tip of the iceberg, and schemas, we came to think, were the iceberg. And, as I have tried to indicate (and to switch metaphors), schemas were already in the air, and available to think with.

The Second Moment: Connectionism

While the idea of the schema had been around at least since Kant, and has drawn interest from psychologists beginning with Bartlett, the way in which schemas actually did what they did – for example, filling in missing information, connecting to other schemas, changing over time – was not well understood. Moreover, anthropologists' earliest attempts to think of cultural schemas in cognitive terms were often somewhat clunky, borrowing notions from prototype theory[13] about "slots" to be filled in with "default values," and relying on a computer analogy that had these values "stored" in memory.

Then came the second moment in the paradigm shift I am describing, the appearance on the scene of connectionism (also known, in its latest version, as parallel distributed processing) with the publication and widespread influence of the two volume treatment of this approach and its applications by the PDP (Parallel Distributed Processing) Research Group led by James McClelland and David Rumelhart (Rumelhart et al. 1986a; McClelland et al. 1986). Of course, connectionism had a broad and significant influence on multiple disciplines at this moment in time (Boden 2006:945–948). For cognitive anthropologists in the cultural models school, it was a second stage in our own local paradigm shift, providing an explanation for how schemas worked. For us, perhaps the most important chapter in this two volume publication was chapter 14 in volume 2, "Schemata and Sequential Thought Processes in PDP Models" (Rumelhart et al. 1986b; see also Rumelhart 1980). Here the schema was given a new and more neurally convincing realization as a cluster of strong neural associations (which could include inhibitions).[14]

Remember that, within cognitive anthropology, the shift to thinking about culture in terms of shared schemas was occurring in the 1970s, while it was a full decade and a half later, at the beginning of the nineties, that these cognitive anthropologists began to acquaint themselves with connectionism and to think about its application to cultural schemas. That these two developments were far from instantaneous suggests that the recruitment of connectionism to explain properties of cultural schemas was the result of an intellectually effortful search for better ways to conceptualize these entities. On the other hand, that connectionism was picked up as rapidly as it was by this group of cognitive anthropologists was probably due to the path already worn to cognitive science. In the same way that we had been tracking the developments in linguistics that led us to schema theory, we were now tracking developments in schema theory.

To my awareness, the first ones to recognize the power of connectionism to more satisfactorily render cultural schemas were Maurice Bloch in England, in a

1992 article, and, simultaneously on the other side of the Atlantic, Claudia Strauss and Roy D'Andrade, as reflected in their separate contributions to the 1992 volume they jointly edited, *Human Motives and Cultural Models* (D'Andrade 1992:28–29; Strauss 1992:11–12). D'Andrade had also given a paper on this topic, "PDP and Culture, or Some Implications of a New Model of Cognition with Respect to Anthropological Theory," at the October 1991 biennial meeting of the Society for Psychological Anthropology in Chicago. D'Andrade and Strauss each subsequently further developed these ideas about the connectionist basis for cultural schemas (D'Andrade 1995:136–149; Strauss and Quinn 1994, 1997:48–84). Edwin Hutchins, an anthropologist who worked closely with the PDP Group, was also clearly using connectionist ideas in a sophisticated way at the same time or even earlier. In a 1995 book about ship navigation, Hutchins extended connectionist modeling to encompass distributed cognition – conceptualizing the schemas held by individuals as separate neural networks, and the communication links between individuals as the connections between these networks that formed a "community of networks" (Hutchins 1995:247–248). Another who had been thinking perceptively about culture and connectionism around that same time was the psychologist Drew Westen (2001).

As Strauss (1992:11–12) wrote in her chapter in the 1992 volume:

> Some of the most interesting work in the cognitive sciences at present comes from new ways of thinking about the mind – approaches inspired more by the workings of the brain than by the specifications of the digital serial computer. One particularly important feature of these new "connectionist" models for our purposes is that knowledge need not be learned or retained as explicit generalizations or formulae; instead regularities in behavior reflect cognitive patterns unconsciously extracted from repeated experience.

With regard to culture, as I have already explained, this way of building up cognitive associations from recurrent experience meant that, to the extent that members of any group shared like experiences, they would share similar schemas. Of course, since no two individuals ever shared identical experiences, the extent to which people shared meanings was only ever partial. Indeed, throughout her own work (e.g., Strauss 1990, 1997), Strauss has explored the ways in which individuals import cultural meanings into distinctive schemas that they share only partially with only some others; she has called these "personal semantic networks." On the other hand, as Strauss and Quinn (1997:123–124), among others, have pointed out, experience is often substantially shared, not the least because the environment in which a given group of individuals lives – including their institutions, practices, and responses to these – is already extensively culturally shaped.

Update and Conclusion

To circle back to the beginning of the story, the original theory of cultural meaning as lexical contrast did not support a very rich examination of cognitive processes – beyond the narrow (and exceedingly difficult to research) question of how such lexical contrast sets had evolved,[15] and the muddled question I have already mentioned of what might be their "psychological reality." In 1995, D'Andrade concluded:

> Schema theory and connectionist networks created a new class of mental entities. Prior to the development of schema theory, the major things in the mind, at least in anthropology, were symbols – words or other kinds of signifiers – and features, which are the perceptual qualities that connect linguistic forms to the world. With schemas and connectionist networks, the strong dependence of thought upon language was broken. Connectionist networks put together schematic clusters of features into complex objects without any necessary linguistic base. Along with this divorce from strict semantic analysis went an increase in interest in mental processes such as reasoning, metaphor, and memory. In anthropology this period was marked by a focus on cultural models and their function in inference and metaphor, as exemplified by Holland and Quinn's volume, *Cultural Models in Language and Thought*, and George Lakoff's *Women, Fire, and Dangerous Things*, both published in 1987.

With hindsight, it can be argued that the second moment in the paradigm shift I have described opened up the exploration of cognitive processes even further. If schema theory created "mental entities," deserving of investigation in their own right, connectionism set these entities in motion. For instance, connectionist modeling could explain how one cultural schema might bring to mind others, on which it might, for example, lean metaphorically, or draw upon for culture-wide themes, or gain more or less powerful emotional and motivational resonance. Furthermore, connectionist modeling could account for dynamic properties of culture, not only the tendencies of cultural understandings to become shared across populations and endure over time, but their equally characteristic tendencies to vary across populations and change over time. A connectionist view of cultural schemas could also treat individual variation in a new way, positing that individuals incorporate cultural schemas into their distinctive understandings of themselves and their worlds (see the reference to Strauss's "personal semantic networks" in the previous section). Within a connectionist framework, as well, schemas could readily be understood as a blend of experience, cognition, emotion, and motivation, giving cultural schema theorists a way to think about these "mental entities" as inherently motivating, including psychodynamic motivation. An interest in motivation has also opened up exploration of the interaction between culture and biology, and with this effort, new questions about the universality of some schemas and their role in human evolutionary adaptation. Again, thinking about cultural schemas in connectionist terms leads cognitive anthropologists to be alert to emerging neurobiological findings and models, and to ask new questions about how culture is internalized. In our 1997 book, *A Cognitive Theory of Cultural Meaning*, Claudia Strauss and I began the task of addressing some of these properties of culture within a connectionist framework. Whether or not connectionism turns out to be the ultimate model of how the brain works, this second moment in the new paradigm has underwritten a new and extremely productive theory of culture.

I read Kuhn's *The Structure of Scientific Revolutions* in graduate school, when it first came out in the early sixties. Ironically, this was at the very onset of the theoretical difficulties in my chosen sub-field that precipitated the paradigm shift I have described here. It was not until much later that I realized that I myself had been confronted in my own thinking and in that of those around me, with the kind of intellectual crisis about which I had been simultaneously reading. I recall only my own dissatisfaction and perplexity as I tried to work out for myself the cognitive implications of the semantic theory I was being taught. Just so, paradigm shifts like this one are likely to be invisible to those who are working in their midst – and, apparently, even after they have transpired, to those who have lived through them. It follows that there is nothing much one can do to prepare for or to circumvent a paradigm shift. The best one can do is to read widely, attend conferences, and converse frequently with colleagues in related disciplines, with an eye alert and a mind open to other contemporary theoretical approaches that may augment or advance or transform one's own. And hope to be lucky.

Even if one is open to other approaches in this way, and even if one is lucky, immersed in an ongoing project one cannot hope to avoid the successive periods of false confidence and theoretical flailing that inevitably precede a paradigm shift. These prior stages are as intrinsic to science and as necessary to theoretical advance as they are inevitable. Those who participate in the unsettling developments leading up to such a shift, frustrating as their efforts may be at the time, or misdirected as they may sometimes seem in retrospect, are contributing to a larger, longer-term collective project. The hard-thought contributions of everyone who participated in this particular development in the history of cognitive anthropology are to be acknowledged and appreciated as crucial moments in the larger enterprise.

ACKNOWLEDGMENTS

Final revision of this chapter has benefited from the helpful suggestions of Roy D'Andrade and Victor de Munck, and especially from the close reading and astute observations of Holly Mathews.

NOTES

1 My own occasional memories of what it was like to be smack dab in the middle of a moment of intellectual ferment will hopefully enhance my telling. I do not intend, by relating these memories, in any way to exaggerate my own modest role in the story. Because I am telling the story from my perspective, too, I may overcite the work known to me – my own and that of close colleagues – while overlooking some contributions, especially those that were published in obscure places or never published at all – that should rightly be included in an account of these developments, but of which I am simply not aware. Short of conducting a full-blown research project, I have tried to be inclusive.

2 As D'Andrade puts it, "the physical and natural science paradigms are *better* than the paradigms in psychology and anthropology" in the sense that "the paradigms in physics, chemistry, and biology fit a broader range of facts, are more precisely stated, and give more effective predictions than the paradigms in the social sciences and psychology" (1995:11).

3 Some have preferred to retain the Greek number, singular *schema*, plural *schemata*. I join those others who have caved in to the Anglicization of the plural, *schemas*. Annoyingly but predictably, many who write about schemas make the mistake of treating the singular, *schema*, as if it were the plural – based on the Latin template for pluralizing collective nouns such as *memorabilia* and *fauna*.

4 Name changes that earned Clifford Geertz's (1973:11) unkind gibe about "a terminological wavering which reflects a deeper uncertainty."

5 Even more inaccurate than this idea that ethnopsychology *replaced* ethnoscience is Richard Shweder's (1990) rendition of this history – that ethnopsychology was a *subdiscipline* of ethnoscience (see White 1992:22 on this point). Instead, it was an outgrowth of ethnoscience parallel to the cultural models approach, and appears to have been fueled by some of the same dissatisfactions (see Kirkpatrick and White 1984:14–18). There was some overlap in approach between the two newer schools, but little overlap in personnel (though, of course, we knew one another).

6 Cultural consensus theorists are concerned with the distribution of cultural knowledge across individuals, rather than the organization of this knowledge. However, their underlying, if implicit, assumption about how cultural knowledge is organized is quite different than that of cultural models theorists (see Garro 2000 for this comparison, and a critique of the cultural consensus theory view).

7 Some critics took the position in this debate that "the psychological reality of an individual is the world as he perceives and knows it, in his own terms; it is his world of meanings. A 'psychologically real' description of a culture thus is a description which approximately reproduces in an observer the world of meanings of the native users of that culture" (Wallace and Atkins 1960:75, quoted in D'Andrade 1995:51). This requirement for kinterm analyses was hardly consistent with the spirit of the componential analysis enterprise, which sought specifiable, replicable operations by which cultural meaning could be identified. Wallace and Atkins, in their reference to the native's "world of meanings," were falling back on a definition of culture as general and underspecified as Ward Goodenough's (1957:167), quoted earlier. In fact, it lacked Goodenough's emphasis on the connection between cultural meaning and action.

8 Raymond Fogelson subsequently observed that kinship had become a dead topic, venturing that "its demise can be accounted for by a variety of overdetermined factors, including changes in the scale and scope of contemporary anthropology, the decline of fieldwork, critical views of scientific understanding, and the emergence of postmodern multiculturalism" (2001:41). To this extensive list he added one more item, saying that David Schneider's (1984) critique of the field "was an influential, if not decisive, factor in the death of kinship studies." My argument here would suggest that, to the contrary, the main reason for the decline in kinship studies (whether permanent or temporary) was internal – that it was due to the collapse of the broader paradigm of which the domain of kinship was such a representative illustration.

9 On the other hand, people of entirely different cultural backgrounds viewing the same film, say (or hearing the same story, as in Laura Bohannan's famous 1966 example of a Tiv audience's response to her telling of the story of *Hamlet*) can be expected to interpret it very differently because they assimilate it to very different pre-existing cultural schemas.

10 Increasingly I am coming to view cultural schemas from an evolutionary perspective, as *cultural task solutions*, but that is another story altogether.

11 Gladwin supposed that words, rather than being incorporated directly into schemas as we would be inclined to argue today (Strauss and Quinn 1997:53), contained "pointers" to schemas.

12 Subsequently, Hutchins's (1983) stunning description of Micronesian navigation was published in a book on "mental models" edited by psychologists.

13 Eleanor Rosch's prototype theory was of great interest to cognitive anthropologists at the time, and prototypes might be said to have provided us with a bridge from the older theory of cultural meaning based on lexical semantics to the newer theory of cultural meaning organized by schemas. D'Andrade (1995:115–122) describes the influence of prototype theory in cognitive anthropology, and its ultimate limitations. As he points out, a prototype turns out to be just one specialized type of schema (1995:124).

14 The authors of the 1986 book were always careful to treat theirs as an "as if" model "inspired" by neural processes rather than a direct rendition of these processes. However, the model was clearly useful, long before neurobiologists would be able to provide such an account, for theorizing about the development and operation of schema-like entities in the brain (see, e.g., O'Reilly and Munakata 2000); connectionism's third name, after all, was neural networks. Indeed, the very limitations of connectionist models of neural processing could provide clues to how the actual brain worked differently (see McClelland et al. 1995).

15 Answered most successfully in the domain of color terms.

REFERENCES

Bloch, Maurice

1992 Language, Anthropology, and Cognitive Science. Man 26:183–198.

Boden, Margaret

2006 Mind as Machine: A History of Cognitive Science. 2 vols. Oxford: Clarendon.

Bohannan, Laura

1966 Shakespeare in the Bush. Natural History 75:28–33.

Casson, Ronald

1981 Language, Culture, and Cognition. *In* Language, Culture, and Cognition. R. Casson, ed. Pp. 11–22. New York: Macmillan.

1983 Schemata in Cognitive Anthropology. Annual Review of Anthropology 12:439–462.

Colby, Benjamin N.

1975 Cultural Grammars. Science 187:913–919.

D'Andrade, Roy G.

1972 Cultural Belief Systems. Report to the National Institute of Mental Health Committee on Social and Cultural Processes, November.

1984 Cultural Meaning Systems. *In* Culture Theory: Essays on Mind, Self, and Emotion. R. A. Shweder and R. A. LeVine, eds. Cambridge: Cambridge University Press.

1991 PDP and Culture, or Some Implications of a New Model of Cognition with Respect to Anthropological Theory. Paper delivered at the biennial meeting of the Society for Psychological Anthropology, Chicago, October.

1992 Schemas and Motivation. *In* Human Motives and Cultural Models. R. G. D'Andrade and C. Strauss, eds. Pp. 23–44. Cambridge: Cambridge University Press.

1995 The Development of Cognitive Anthropology. Cambridge: Cambridge University Press.

D'Andrade, Roy G., and Claudia Strauss, eds.

1992 Human Motives and Cultural Models. Cambridge: Cambridge University Press.

D'Andrade, Roy G., Naomi Quinn, A. Kimball Romney, and Sara Nerlove

1972 Categories of Disease in American-English and Mexican-Spanish. *In* Multidimensional Scaling: Theory and Applications in the Behavioral Sciences, vol. 2: Applications. A. K. Romney, R. N. Shepard, and S. B. Nerlove, eds. Pp. 9–54. New York: Seminar.

Fillmore, Charles

1975 An Alternative to Checklist Theories of Meaning. *In* Proceedings of the First Annual Meeting of the Berkeley Linguistics Society. C. Cogen, H. Thompson, G. Thurgood, K. Whister, and J. Wright, eds. Pp. 123–131. Berkeley: University of California Press.

Fogelson, Raymond D.

2001 Schneider Confronts Componential Analysis. *In* The Cultural Analysis of Kinship: The Legacy of David M. Schneider. R. Feinberg and M. Ottenheimer, eds. Pp. 33–45. Urbana: University of Illinois Press.

Frake, Charles

1964 A Structural Description of Subanun "Religious Behavior." *In* Explorations in Cultural Anthropology. W. Goodenough, ed. Pp. 111–129. New York: McGraw-Hill.

1975 How to Enter a Yakan House. *In* Sociocultural Dimensions of Language Use. Pp. 25–40. New York: Academic Press.

1977 Plying Frames Can Be Dangerous: Some Reflections on Methodology in Cognitive Anthropology. Quarterly Newsletter of the Institute for Comparative Human Development 1(3):1–7.

Garro, L. C.

2000 Remembering What One Knows and the Construction of the Past: A Comparison of Cultural Consensus Theory and Cultural Schema Theory. *Ethos* 28(3):275–319.

Geertz, Clifford

1973 Thick Description: Toward an Interpretive Theory of Culture. *In* The Interpretation of Cultures: Selected Essays by Clifford Geertz. Pp. 3–30. New York: Basic Books.

Geoghegan, William

1969 Decision-Making and Residence on Tagtabon Island. Working Paper no. 17, Language-Behavior Research Laboratory, University of California, Berkeley.

Gladwin, Hugh

1971 Semantics, Schemata, and Kinship. Paper delivered at the 70th Annual Meeting of the American Anthropological Association, New York, November.

Gladwin, Hugh, and Christina Gladwin

1971 Estimating Market Conditions and Profit Expectations of Fish Sellers at Cape Coast, Ghana. *In* Studies in Economic Anthropology. G. Dalton, ed. Pp. 122–142. Anthropological Studies 7. Washington, DC: American Anthropological Association.

Goodenough, Ward

1957 Cultural Anthropology and Linguistics. *In* Report of the Seventh Annual Round Table Meeting on Linguistics and Language Study. Pp. 167–173. Washington, DC: Georgetown University.

1971 Culture, Language, and Society. McCaleb Module in Anthropology. Reading, MA: Addison-Wesley.

Holland, Dorothy, and Naomi Quinn

1987 Cultural Models in Language and Thought. Cambridge: Cambridge University Press.

Hutchins, Edwin

1978 Reasoning in Discourse: An Analysis of Trobriand Island Land Litigation. Unpublished Ph.D. dissertation, University of California, San Diego.

1980 Culture and Inference: A Trobriand Case Study. Cambridge, MA: Harvard University Press.

1983 Understanding Micronesian Navigation. *In* Mental Models. D. Gentner and A. L. Stevens, eds. Pp. 191–225. Hillsdale, NJ: Lawrence Erlbaum.

1995 Cognition in the Wild. Cambridge, MA: MIT Press.

Kay, Paul

1973 Ethnography and Cultural Theory. *In* Drinking Patterns in Highland Chiapas. H. Siverts, ed. Pp. 59–64. Bergen: Universitetsforlaget.

Keesing, Roger

1972 Paradigms Lost: The New Ethnography and the New Linguistics. Southwestern Journal of Anthropology 28(4):299–332.

Kirkpatrick, John, and Geoffrey M. White

1984 Exploring Ethnopsychologies. *In* Person, Self, and Experience: Exploring Pacific Ethnopsychologies. G. M. White and J. Kirkpatrick, eds. Pp. 3–32. Berkeley: University of California Press.

Kuhn, Thomas

1962 The Structure of Scientific Revolutions. Chicago: University of Chicago Press.

Lakoff, George

1987 Women, Fire, and Dangerous Things: What Categories Reveal About the Mind. Chicago: University of Chicago Press.

Langacker, Ronald
1979 Grammar as Image. Paper delivered at the conference on Neurolinguistics and Cognition, Program in Cognitive Science, University of California, San Diego, March.
Mandler, George
1984 Mind and Body: The Psychology of Emotion and Stress. New York: W. W. Norton.
McClelland, James L., David E. Rumelhart, and the PDP Research Group, eds.
1986 Parallel Distributed Processing: Explorations in the Microstructure of Cognition, vol. 2: Psychological and Biological Models. Cambridge, MA: MIT Press.
McClelland, James L., Bruce L. McNaughton, and Randall C. O'Reilly
1995 Why There are Complementary Learning Systems in the Hippocampus and Neocortex: Insights from the Successes and Failures of Connectionist Models of Learning and Memory. Psychological Review 102:419–459.
Nardi, Bonnie A.
1983 Goals in Reproductive Decision Making. American Ethnologist 10(4):697–714.
O'Reilly, Randall C., and Yuko Munakata
2000 Computational Explorations in Cognitive Neuroscience: Understanding the Mind by Simulating the Brain. Cambridge, MA: MIT Press.
Quinn, Naomi
1971 Mfantse Fishing Crew Composition: A Decision-Making Analysis. Unpublished Ph.D. dissertation, Stanford University.
1973 Asking the Right Question: A Reexamination of Akan Residence. *In* Solving Problems of Survey Research in Africa. W. O'Barr, D. Spain, and M. Tessler, eds. Pp. 168– 183. Chicago: Northwestern University Press.
1976 A Natural System for Settling Mfantse Litigation. American Ethnologist 3:331–351.
1978 Do Mfantse Fish Sellers Estimate Probabilities in Their Heads? American Ethnologist 5:2:206–226.
1997 Research on Shared Task Solutions. *In* A Cognitive Theory of Cultural Meaning. C. Strauss and N. Quinn. Pp. 137–188. Cambridge: Cambridge University Press.
2005 How to Reconstruct Schemas People Share, from What They Say. *In* Finding Culture in Talk: A Collection of Methods. N. Quinn, ed. Pp. 35–81. New York: Palgrave Macmillan.
Quinn, Naomi, and Dorothy Holland
1987 Culture and Cognition. *In* Cultural Models in Language and Thought. D. Holland and N. Quinn, eds. Pp. 3–40. Cambridge: Cambridge University Press.
Rumelhart, David E.
1980 Schemata: The Building Blocks of Cognition. *In* Theoretical Issues in Reading Comprehension: Perspectives from Cognitive Psychology, Linguistics, Artificial Intelligence, and Education. R. J. Spiro, B. C. Bruce, and W. F. Brewer, eds. Pp. 33–58. Hillsdale, NJ: Lawrence Erlbaum.
Rumelhart, David E., James L. McClelland, and PDP Research Group
1986a Parallel Distributed Processing: Exploration in the Microstructure of Cognition, vol. 1: Foundations. Cambridge, MA: MIT Press.
Rumelhart, David E., P. Smolensky, J. L. McClelland, and G. E. Hinton
1986b Schemata and Sequential Thought Processes in PDP Models. *In* Parallel Distributed Processing: Explorations in the Microstructure of Cognition, vol. 2: Psychological and Biological Models. James L. McClelland, David E. Rumelhart, and the PDP Research Group, eds. Pp. 7–57. Cambridge, MA: MIT Press.
Schank, Roger, and Robert Abelson
1977 Scripts, Plans, Goals and Understanding: An Inquiry into Human Knowledge Structures. Hillsdale, NJ: Lawrence Erlbaum.
Schneider, David M.
1984 A Critique of the Study of Kinship. Ann Arbor: University of Michigan Press.

Shore, Bradd

1996 Culture in Mind: Meaning Construction and Cultural Cognition. Oxford: Oxford University Press.

Shweder, Richard

1990 Cultural Psychology: What Is It? *In* Cultural Psychology: Essays on Comparative Human Development. J. Stigler, R. Shweder, and G. Herdt, eds. Pp. 1–43. Cambridge: Cambridge University Press.

Strauss, Claudia

1990 Who Gets Ahead? Cognitive Responses to Heteroglossia in American Political Culture. American Ethnologist 17(2):312–328.

1992 Models and Motives. *In* Human Motives and Cultural Models. R. G. D'Andrade and C. Strauss, eds. Pp. 1–20. Cambridge: Cambridge University Press.

1997 Research on Cultural Discontinuities. *In* A Cognitive Theory of Cultural Meaning. C. Strauss and N. Quinn. Pp. 210–251. Cambridge: Cambridge University Press.

Strauss, Claudia, and Naomi Quinn

1994 A Cognitive/Cultural Anthropology. *In* Assessing Cultural Anthropology. R. Borofsky, ed. Pp. 284–297. New York: McGraw-Hill.

1997 A Cognitive Theory of Cultural Meaning. Cambridge: Cambridge University Press.

Wallace, Anthony F. C., and John Atkins

1960 The Meaning of Kinship Terms. American Anthropologist 62:58–80.

Westen, Drew

2001 Beyond the Binary Opposition in Psychological Anthropology: Integrating Contemporary Psychoanalysis and Cognitive Science. *In* The Psychology of Cultural Experience. C. C. Moore and H. F. Mathews, eds. Pp. 21–47. Cambridge: Cambridge University Press.

White, Geoffrey M.

1992 Ethnopsychology. *In* New Directions in Psychological Anthropology. T. Schwartz, G. M. White, and C. A. Lutz, eds. Pp. 21–46. Cambridge: Cambridge University Press.

CHAPTER 3

The Cognitive Context of Cognitive Anthropology

Jürg Wassmann, Christian Kluge, and Dominik Albrecht

As its title suggests, this chapter focuses on quite a formal issue, namely what the "cognitive" in "Cognitive Anthropology" is all about. It aims to connect some of the recent advances of cognitive sciences proper to ongoing debates in the field of cognitive anthropology and it will also try to demonstrate how these connections can be put into a wider systematic context. As an exemplary application, then, results from anthropological fieldwork are discussed to further elucidate the relations present, and to demonstrate the advantages brought about by an even more cognitive approach to cognitive anthropology.

This seems worthwhile given the fact that the definitions of cognition (and many related concepts) used by mainstream anthropologists are often so sociological that agreement across disciplines cannot be reached. It is striking how frequently anthropologists' theories of thinking, meaning, memory, and the like are not compatible with those of cognitive scientists. This seems an unfortunate deficit since, obviously, there is a lot of overlap between the two disciplines. Given that ultimately both disciplines are concerned with very related aspects of human nature it is not surprising that there are many topics and questions shared here, for example:

- How do individuals relate to and interact with the physical world? In other words, how does the world enter our head? (PERCEPTION)
- Once information is mentally accessible to us, how do we structure and manipulate it? (CATEGORIZATION)
- What are thoughts? How are they brought about, structured, organized? What does this uncoupling of perception and reasoning imply with respect to our nature, our abilities, our interactions? (REASON)

A Companion to Cognitive Anthropology, First Edition. Edited by David B. Kronenfeld, Giovanni Bennardo, Victor C. de Munck, and Michael D. Fischer.

- How can our capacity to store and retrieve information on demand be explained? In what way are we as individuals shaped by such a capacity? (MEMORY)
- It is clear that our elaborate form of communicating is a uniquely human trait. How is it brought about and what can be learned from studying it? (LANGUAGE)
- Humans do not act as isolated individuals. What is the basis of cooperative behavior and which factors shape these processes? (CULTURE)
- Why do the representations of the world in our heads seem to take a particular form? What brings about these distortions? (CULTURAL MODELS)

There are, however, significant differences in *how* these issues are addressed in the respective academic branches. It is clear, for instance, that knowledge can be attributed to individuals as well as to cultural systems as a whole. Disciplines such as psychology, neuroscience, and psychiatry are more concerned with the individual, while cultural anthropology focuses on interindividual phenomena from which inferences about individual life forms are then made. Therefore, besides the conceptual incompatibilities, there are, naturally, methodological and technical differences, and the full consequences of these particular perspectives have been debated actively in both domains.

Within cognitive anthropology, for instance, Rogoff and Lave (1984), realizing the limitations of the purely cultural focus, proposed a shift away from the "représentations collectives" toward a more central role for the single individual. On the other hand, they also pointed out the limitations of relying on single individuals in special social roles (e.g., village principals) when seen as omniscient informants. As a sole source of information they are not sufficient and research should more frequently turn to single individuals in non-exposed roles or, as they put it, to "just plain folks." Along the same lines, Bloch (1991) criticized the prominent anthropological concept of the individuum as "over-socialized," and Keck (1998) further expanded the discussion by pointing to the fact that "single lives in common worlds differ." In other words, the idea of *one homogeneous culture* (at any scale, applied to an individual or the society) can be seen as quite inadequate, given the tremendous variability of individual biographies.

However, when driven to extremes, the isolated "plain folk" individual, completely stripped of any cultural ties, is a limited model system too. Nevertheless, in agreement with the general aims and practices sketched above, for neuroscientists, exactly this view has been (and to some extent still is) the most prevalent. Apart from some socio-psychological strands, experimental work is often carried out on individuals in isolation and in highly non-natural (but carefully controlled) environments. This holds true especially for more biological fields, such as the domain of neuroimaging.

Within the psychological roots of modern neuroscience, on the other hand, the work of Piaget dealt with the expansion of cognitive abilities in children as a function of biological maturation and constant interaction with the world, a process which leads to continuous modification and refinement of worldviews. Although focused on individuals, this now classic work therefore also had a strong interindividual and contextual aspect. The question as to whether the results obtained by Piaget and others were generalizable soon sparked the need for cross-cultural comparisons, leading to the advent of cross-cultural psychology. Prominent researchers in this field such as Dasen and Segall later concluded that certain information processing mechanisms per se show very little variance across individuals:

> We found evidence of differences across cultural groups, differences in habitual strategies for classifying and for solving problems, differences in cognitive style, and differences in rates of progression through developmental stages ... these differences, however, are in performance rather than in competence. They are differences in the way basic cognitive processes are applied to particular contexts, rather than in presence or absence of the processes. Despite these differences, then, there is an underlying universality of cognitive processes. [Segall et al. 1990:184; cf. Berry et al. 2002]

In this, Segall sees early generalizations by Franz Boas (1927[1911]) confirmed, according to which there is a certain "psychic unity" of all human agents. Along the same lines, Cole and Scribner, in agreement with Boas and Segall, explicitly named certain basic capacities that seemed to prove invariant in their empirical research sampling different cultural contexts. Among others, these were "the capacity to remember, generalize, form concepts, operate with abstractions, and [to] reason logically" (Cole and Scribner 1974). Since these early empirical investigations, however, little work has been done in this field and almost none of it explicitly addressed the biological basis of these modules. It also seems somewhat enigmatic how it is possible that a common set of basic functions brings about such enormously variable results both across individuals as well as in comparisons between sets of individuals. In other words, it is clear that cognitive styles *across* cultural borders differ enormously (see Berry et al. 2002, ch. 5 for an extensive overview) but there is also no doubt that the spectrum of individual cognitive capacities is extremely broad *within* a given culture, that is, that individual abilities are highly variant.

Obviously precise knowledge of and about such general cognitive base modules would be most important for any field dealing with human biology, psychology, human nature, or culture. It would also potentially provide guidelines for finding the right balance between individual and cultural perspectives on cognition and culture – and this, in turn, would have highly relevant implications for the fieldworking anthropologist as well as the brain scanning neurobiologist. In actually assessing the invariants in human cognition *themselves*, however, cognitive neuroscience is the discipline to ask. It is exactly *because* individual minds have been the focus of studies dealing with perception, attention, memory, and related capacities that here the base modules are most directly assessed. Hence, it shall be outlined now how, from a neurobiological perspective, using neurobiological terminology, such invariant modules can be proposed and where this kind of heuristic reasoning leads.

While Cole and Scribner mentioned some examples in their original publications (memory, generalization, conceptualization, abstraction, logical reasoning: see citation above), here, three slightly different candidate faculties shall be considered as possible basic invariants in human cognition:

1 concept formation
2 working memory
3 theory of mind

Needless to say, any language-using individual must necessarily make distinctions of the kind we make when we decide whether something actually is water, or a brick building, or a valid argument or not. This ability is generally defined as possession of a concept. This is a uniquely human faculty only insofar as humans can make very sophisticated distinctions, communicate them, and are able to cognitively reflect on their distinctions. Even very simple organisms, for instance, can distinguish a medium high in carbohydrates from one of lower sugar concentrations (in such cases, we would not speak of the organism having concepts the way human beings have them).

Then, in order to put systems of concepts to use, an organism must be able to dynamically operate with and on them. The cognitive module allowing for this is the capacity of working memory (WM). Working memory enables us to manipulate information, allowing for the integrating percept and memory on the one hand and for the uncoupling of thought and percept on the other. It has been called "the blackboard of the mind" by Goldman-Rakic (e.g., in Goldman-Rakic 1996) and this expression well captures its nature as a buffer holding the current content of a cognitive operation. WM is therefore critical for any animal that is not solely stimulus driven in its behaviour. Content that is in the WM space can – depending on the individual's intentions, the salience or relevance of the information, and many other factors – be consolidated into long-term memory. The buffer function WM brings about is therefore essential for many ways of information processing. Crucially however, whereas the content of WM for non-human animals is usually exclusively related to some form of sensory percept, humans are able to reason offline, decoupled from direct perception.

The relation between concept formation and WM is clearly interdependent: without content, WM would be empty, and without WM, concepts could not be abstracted (or constructed) from recurring sensory input. Furthermore, memory in general allows taxonomies to become wider and more elaborated over time. Together, both allow for rule and regularity learning (both in explicit as well as in implicit memory forms) and form an absolute *sine qua non* for interindividual communication.

Individuals without a fully developed WM, such as young children, act as if "out of sight" is "out of mind" and Jean Piaget fittingly coined the term *sensomotoric stadium* for this stage in human ontogenesis (cf. Gazzaniga et al. 2008). The number of items humans can keep in WM depends on the type of item (e.g., numbers, letters, words, visual images) but varies only little for a given category of items. This would well fit into the view of WM as one of principles of human cognition showing little interindividual variability.

With a functional WM, operating on an elaborate taxonomic system, another characteristically human faculty becomes possible: theory of mind (TOM). TOM means the capacity and tendency of individuals to impute mental states not only to themselves but also to fellow human beings. Thereby, the subject, on a cognitive level, puts herself into the other's shoes in a way much alike to projection, bringing about a reconstruction of the other's thoughts and percepts.

In summa, already these very rudimentary base modules, together with the ability to transform selected WM content into long-term memories, allow for a surprising complexity in human interaction. Let us examine, how, with the combination of these faculties, a range of further refinements become possible.

An organism with WM capacities is, as mentioned above, capable of integrating over longer periods of sensory stimulation, and is therefore able to recognize regularities, which can then be abstracted and employed as a concept. The connection of WM to long-term implicit and explicit memory (Tulving 1985) extends this window even more. Furthermore, building on TOM capacities, an individual does not even have to observe the regularities leading to certain concepts himself. He can learn from the experience of others. In the long run, these processes allow for intricate systems of knowledge to be transmitted and shared across large numbers of individuals, which, in turn, leads to the plethora of striking phenomena of cooperative behavior that we call culture. Specifically, knowledge is not only present in individuals, but can be externally "outsourced" in systems of notations such as knotted chords, churingas, or in buildings, objects, and – of course – in writings. These are the "external dimensions" (Assmann 1999[1992]) that support our cultural memories. The notion of "cultural memory" goes beyond the notation of tradition, belonging to an external dimension of human memory which Assmann subsumed in four categories: (1) mimetic memory (e.g., daily activities), (2) memory of objects (e.g., cities, trees), (3) communicative memory (e.g., language), and (4) cultural memory (e.g., the transmission of sense).

However, it is clear that this use of "memory" and "knowledge" differs from our everyday use. "Knowledge" usually refers to the content of memories, and memories are formed by individuals with certain capacities. In the above – *cultural* – sense, however, it is not the individual subject who is able to form memories but this capability is ascribed to *a set of individuals* (as a whole) in a given cultural context. The content of these memories, that is the cultural knowledge, is then ascribed to the abstract community and it is in some way thought to be present in the individual minds that constitute members of that cultural context or society. However, no individual member has *all* the cultural knowledge present in herself. Furthermore, cultural knowledge is not only evident in individuals but it also shows in artifacts they produce (books, knotted chords, folk songs).

Highlighting these differences is important because they can easily lead to confusions and invalid generalizations when we talk about cultural memory formation and cultural knowledge and in doing so simply use the grammar of the day-to-day meaning of "memory." When we talk of cultural knowledge, we usually mean a kind of *potential* knowledge that becomes available to individuals because they are embedded in a certain cultural context. We would, for instance, readily agree that "we know today" what the 26th digit of pi is, but surely few readers of this text will actually *know*. However, a few clicks on the internet, a calculator, or a piece of paper and a pencil will enable most of us to quickly find out – because our cultural context puts us in a position to do that. Therefore, it might be best to think of cultural knowledge as information, which, given certain abilities to interact with other individuals (either directly or through artifacts), can be assimilated by a subject, thereby becoming knowledge. The process of transferring information from individual minds to the public domain in the first place is what could be called cultural memory formation.

In this light, then, cultural knowledge is an emergent phenomenon and it is obvious that certain cooperative abilities of individuals are indispensable for its generation. Usually, we are not aware of these interactive processes. They have become perfectly natural to us. Even more, these processes do not only occur in the declarative domain. Implicit forms of memory are shared just as much as explicit content. We all have an idea of what a chair or a book or a tree looks like, what freedom or a good life or laziness is, whether a given song is typical of the eighties, or how we should behave in front of children as opposed to at a pub with old friends. However, we rarely talk about these things and we are usually not aware of them being used or shared.

Crucially, however, *we not only share these concepts but we also agree on the rules for their use.* Given especially the latter aspect, we are able to combine them in new and useful ways without rendering ourselves unintelligible. This agreement, in the special case of its application to language, is well captured by Ludwig Wittgenstein:

> "So you are saying that human agreement decides what is true and what is false?" – It is what human beings *say* that is true and false; and they agree in the language they use. That is not agreement in opinions but in form of life. [Wittgenstein 1953:§ 241]

How, then, can we assess this "agreement in form of life"? Obviously content and form of this agreement are not constant across cultures. So, which parts of the consensus are due to invariant aspects, that is general *human nature*, and what can be seen as dependent on external factors such as contextual requirements?

One way of addressing these questions is the study of *schemata* or *cultural models*. In the 1930s, Bartlett's research was concerned with how people's understanding and remembrance of events were shaped by their expectations. He suggested that these expectations were mentally represented by the individuals in a schematic form. In one famous experiment, he gave English subjects a Native American folktale to memorize and recall later at different time intervals. The folktale had many attributions and causal structures that were contrary to Western expectations. He found that subjects *reconstructed* the story rather than remembering it verbatim, and that this reconstruction was consistent with a Western worldview (Bartlett 1932). In a similar sense, Piaget has also used the schema idea to capture cognitive development and maturation of children. Later, schema theories re-emerged as a dominant interest in the 1970s: for concepts very similar to the original term Schank and Abelson (1977) introduced the term *script* while Minsky coined the term *frame* (1975).

In all of the above uses, schemata are defined as mental models, which organize our knowledge and our knowing in stereotypical and prototypical sequences of actions and thoughts. They are often described as *simplified worlds* from which the complex and holistic knowledge can be reconstructed on the spot. It is important to note that these models are not directly observable. They do not *exist* in the way that stones or other material objects exist. They are constructs that the observing researcher develops in an abstracting process: on the basis of observed behavior she makes inferences about general (prototypical) underlying views and representations. Therefore, they are not directly presented, but rather represented in observable behavior. Across individuals, these learned representations (models) of the world can differ, of course, and it can generally not be ruled out that the observed behavior could be described more fittingly with different models. In other words, it does not make sense to speak of these models being right or wrong, but rather to query their *usefulness*, that is, can they coherently capture and explain the observed behavior? Is it possible to make predictions on their basis? Or, how fruitful, or *pragmatic*, is a given model?

It is clear that research employing such schemata or cultural models can lead to considerable improvements in our attempts to coherently understand cultures (see, for instance, Holland and Quinn 1987; Kronenfeld 2008) because it aims at reconstructing worldviews. This, in turn, is the basis for any comparison across cultures, which, then, enables us to readdress the question "what are the invariant aspects of human cognition?"

Therefore, let us now examine the properties of mental models in more detail. First, since the proposed models necessarily employ concepts, there is a relation to the external world, that is objects, events. What the structure of the model now provides on top of that are "slots" into which, depending on context and available information, a given item can be sorted into. In other words, the concepts employed in the formulation of a model are generally wider and more abstract than the ones used in day-to-day life of the individual and thus, in a cultural model, the concepts used in everyday situations are *categorized*. Since this happens not only with respect to their content (meaning) but also with respect to the rules for their use (grammar), in addition, the *relations* between groups of concepts (slots) are *systematized*. In summa, this leads to a more broadly encompassing representation of the individual's knowledge and cognitive style and such representations are greatly advantageous: they are robust, accessible templates which can be related to individual instantiations of cognitive activity. Because of their prototypical nature, they can also be employed for cross-cultural comparisons.

Applying a classification of Lakoff (1987), the form of mental schemata can now be either of the *visual image*, or *propositional* form. The former is a somewhat classic notion, but the reference to vision must be seen as a modality placeholder, since mental schemata, of course, can also be based on other modalities (auditory, olfactory, tactile) or on combinations of these. These mental images are the individual, internalized, cognitive representations of, for example the external world (in a physical or geographical sense). They are not static images, but "the symbolic and internalized mental reflection of spatial action" (Piaget and Inhelder 1967:454). Sometimes they are analog representations of the environment but usually they are incomplete, distorted, and reduced to a sketch-like quality (rather than a photographic image). Their principle of organization is the *metaphor*: information – both content and relations – is transformed from the physical to a non-physical, mental, domain.

On the other hand, *propositional representations* are more abstract, more language-like (although they are not words). They are meant to capture the conceptual content of *situations*, that is, of relations between concepts. The form they take is, for example, "on" (as in "on the table" or "on the bookshelf") and their principle of organization is that of metonymy. Here, a whole is represented by one of its parts. Whereas in the metaphor, the substitution of one form for another is based on similarity, the metonymic substitution is based on contiguity.

The researcher chooses the form (purely image-like, purely propositional, or any combination) with respect to the phenomena he wants to capture. In a pure form, each has advantages and disadvantages and usually one proves of little use without the other.

Initially the model is derived from individuals. Then, through highlighting what is common across individuals and disregarding interindividual differences, the model is abstracted and generalized so it also applies to groups of individuals, in the process of which it acquires its prototypic character. In the end, what is aimed for is *what it is like to be a so and so*, an example application for this being the reconstruction of the world-view of the Yupno of Papua New Guinea (see below), or the analysis of kinship networks provided by Kronenfeld (2008), the former of which will be outlined below. So, the relevance and the implications of the above considerations will, hopefully, become more concrete and their usefulness obvious.

The Yupno Valley, in the Finisterre Mountains of Papua New Guinea, is of a roughly elongated oval shape. It is oriented approximately west to east, with a slight downward inclination, whilst high mountains on all sides separate it from neighboring regions. From a source at about 3,000 meters, the Yupno River traverses the entire valley along the long axis of the oval. It flows through steep gorges and along rock faces, some of which are up to 700 meters high, all the way through the valley until it finally disembogues into Astrolabe Bay. The seaside in the east is the only side of the valley not cut off from the rest of the world by the fence-like mountains. Unsurprisingly, these physical circumstances lead to a worldview different from the one we are used to. The Yupno see the world as oriented along the course of the river which itself is seen as *Morap*, the creator, or literally "the one who dwells in abundance." Above, upriver, is the source from which humanity originated, and originally, humans were washed ashore in bamboo pipes (*teet*, a term which also stands for "right body part"). Literally, the Yupno River is "the one who washes everything ashore and deposits it on the banks." Its source is Morap's head and the estuary forms his feet. Morap is looking downstream, just as for the individual Yupno the canonical orientation is the one downstream.

In this unique setting, the complex mutual interactions between context and culture are strikingly obvious on many levels. Firstly, the *Yupno concept of "the world"* is clearly influenced by the geographical circumstances: As is evident in dirt drawings, the world has the shape of a closed oval with a line along the long axis, symbolizing the river.

This worldview is also replicated in the structure of the *Yupno house*, which is also oval, oriented downriver, with a single opening at the front (toward the estuary of the river in the east). In the middle of the house there is a long fireplace, which extends through the full length of the dwelling. Men sit on the right (which is active and hot) while women and children sit on the left (passive and cold). The side the Yupno sits on is signified with the same words that are used for "this side of the river" and the converse holds for the other side of the fire and the river, respectively. The spatial analogies evident in the concepts of world and house are dynamic and generalizable insofar as they are readily applied to new contexts and spatial circumstances. When a Yupno, for instance, visits the coastal town of Madang for the first time, he will apply the canonical spatial reference frame to the new situation: the city's main street "becomes" the Yupno river and the direction toward the sea will be "downriver," the opposite "upriver." However, in absolute terms, this miniature river system is rotated by roughly 90° with respect to the original river which, naturally, is present in the scene too.

The *Yupno human being* itself consists of several parts: (1) *the body itself*, (2) *a free soul*, also referred to as "image" or "shadow," (3) *a body soul*, signified as "the steam appearing in the morning when the sun shines on the ground wet from the dew," and (4) *kongap*, "the voice of the dead spirit," which is an integral part of the individual's personality and is expressed as a short sequence of three to five sounds which was found in a dream. The latter sequence, together with a personal name, is used as an individual identification call. Everybody also possesses "vital energy," a kind of impersonal energy contained in the body soul, the amount of which fluctuates and determines whether an individual is considered metaphorically "hot" (a dangerous, non-controllable state; the same word also signifies illness), "cold" (associated with immobility and speechlessness), or "cool." Only the *cool* state is desirable since exclusively then the individual takes on the ideal stance: a slightly bent posture. In this position, he can actively listen to others and thereby become a "knowing human being" – "hearing" and "knowing" are signified by the same word.

Just like the world in general and the house, the *body of the Yupno* is divided into two unequal parts by an imaginary line leading from the nose to the penis. The left side (in analogy to the house) is considered to be female, passive and "cold," that is with little vital energy in the body – the left hand only assists by holding the bow. The right side, in contrast, is considered male, active and "hot," that is with much vital energy – the right hand pulls the bowstring.

Very strikingly, the geographical references do not only take the form of spatial analogies applied to concrete physical entities of central cultural importance (house, body), but they also show in the *Yupno concepts of completely abstract relata*. The Yupno word for "upriver," for instance, is also used for the general relation "up" or "above" and, coherently, the word for "downriver" is also used to express "below" and "to the front."

Even the *Yupno concept of time* is often couched in spatial metaphors. In the Western world, the so-called ego-moving metaphor is dominant, wherein the observer's context progresses along the time line toward the future. The Yupno, however, conceptualize time in a different metaphor: time is a river or conveyor belt on which items are moving from the future to the past (time-moving metaphor). The (known) past therefore lies in front, or downstream, of the individual. In this way, the past is visually accessible, whereas the future lies behind the observer's back, upstream, and cannot be seen. The Yupno's gestures are coherent with this conceptual framework: a hand extended to the front symbolizes the past, a hand close to the body points to the present, and a movement over the shoulder, towards the back, alludes to the future (cf. Boroditsky 2000; Gentner et al. 2002; compare also Núñez and Sweetser 2006; Núñez et al. n.d.).

In summa, the Yupno utilize a conceptual framework that is radically different from the one we are used to within the Western world. The most obvious and stark differences are apparent in their views of space and time. Both seem – *from our perspective* – unusually interrelated. Just think of the fact, that, given the concept of time sketched above, it becomes clear that the dirt drawings created by individuals to illustrate their view of the world capture both spatial and temporal aspects. Whatever a Western individual would produce upon such a query, it would certainly be a view of the world at a snapshot in time – since our conceptualization of time is orthogonal to the concept of space.

When we, with our fixed conceptual framework try to capture the views of the Yupno, we cannot help but compare our view to theirs, and we will see their views through our biased eyes. Our own conceptual frameworks are like a pair of glasses that produce distortions but that we cannot take off. This thought is well captured by Bloch:

> If an anthropologist is attempting to give an account of chunked and non-sentential knowledge in a linguistic medium (writing) he or she must be aware that in so doing he or she is not representing the organisation of the knowledge of the people he or she studies but is transmuting it into an entirely different logical form. [Bloch 1998: 15]

In that sense, the Yupno agree on a different form of life, to speak in Wittgenstein's terms, and they do so at a very basic level. However, some of the general ways of workings, some of the basic logical forms are shared across all human beings. These are the cognitive base modules: category formation, working memory and theory of mind. From and with these, all individuals start out. They are probably hard-wired into our biological nature. In an iterative process, then, the individual interacts with her worldly context on the one hand, and with her fellow human beings, that is with her cultural context, on the other hand. Here, on two levels, variability, selection, and – ultimately – adaptation come into play. Concepts and ways of working that prove useful are consolidated in the individual. Then, they are, through social interactions, proposed to others and if they prove useful to them too they will most probably be adopted by them. This shows the relevance of another aspect: what works for one individual is of little use to others if it is very hard to communicate. This calls for conceptual content and forms to be not only as powerful as possible, but also as obvious and accessible as possible. Taking into account these two needs, it is comprehensible why the Yupno have agreed on concepts which employ analogies that are the way they are. Having an oval shaped world template is perfectly sufficient if the physical form of your worldly context is of that shape and it never changes. Such an analogy is – in the Yupno's context – not one bit less powerful than ours. It is pragmatic and in many ways optimized. From our, Western, point of view, the relatively straightforward relationship between the geographical situation, combined with a stark local concentration and the almost complete lack of interaction with individuals socialized under different circumstances, makes the causal relationship reconstructable (for us as outside observers). It seems peculiar, however, since within our own complex and vastly interconnected social setting (just think of the term *globalization*) we face much greater difficulties to reconstruct causal interrelations and mutual dependencies between context and cultural characteristics. Therefore, straightforward spatial analogies would not be flexible enough, and we agree on concepts, cultural models, and, in the end, on life forms that are of a more abstract nature.

Also, the fact that the Yupno world drawings vary greatly, depending on whether or not the subject has left the valley before, further illustrate the role of experience and memory in individual concept formation processes. This intra-individual variation might have been limited in the past (since few Yupno actually left the valley), but, naturally, in the 21st century, the fence-like and isolating nature of the mountains becomes less and less absolute. So, as the proportion of individuals with an outside experience steadily increases, the general Yupno concept of "the world" gradually changes. New experiences can no longer be incorporated into the traditional view. Therefore the spatial analogies have to be modified in order to render the entire system pragmatic again. In other words, the worldview, the life form agreed upon, is *dynamic*. If the Yupno, as a society, were to be placed in a totally different context, the life forms and worldviews they agree upon would necessarily change. The mechanisms involved in their generation, however, will stay the same.

Since a given individual, from birth on, interacts with a society that already has established a worldview, a form of life the members agree on, naturally, the consensus is not built up from scratch for each generation. What the maturing individual benefits from is exactly what we have referred to as "cultural knowledge" above. In this sense, human ontogenesis is best captured by connectionist frameworks, which see information processing as an emergent, parallel processing of interconnected units. In such systems, learning is brought about by modifications of the connection weights (or transmission efficiencies) assigned to a given connection. During development, social interaction and learning from peers will now, in a given individual, modify the weights (on the neural networks level) to produce a result optimally coherent with the rest of the cultural context. Thus, importantly, a given individual does not have to learn everything from experience but can learn without actually going through the trial and error loops herself (obviously few of us will actually have developed the concept of pi ourselves). This is in stark contrast to classical reinforcement learning theories that would have to attribute such a behavior to genetic influences or would not be able to capture this characteristically human interindividual perspective at all. From the frequency of such encounters of individuals with certain culturally preserved values, norms, and practices, further links to the psychological and neurobiological levels can be established. Following Whitehouse (2001), variations in the frequency with which social practices are enacted result in the use of distinct memory systems. Very frequent rituals (e.g., Christian services) attract plenty of widely known and stable exegesis and very little spontaneous exegetical reflection. In contrast, very rare or climactic rituals (e.g., male initiations) tend to be accompanied by little official exegesis and explanation but a great amount of independently generated interpretation, reflection, and overall cognitive involvement. These circumstances lead to an organization of knowledge concerning frequent practices in the implicit memory in many individuals. Rare rituals, with intense cognitive involvement, however, require explicit memory systems. Therefore, this type of cultural knowledge is "stored" in mnemonic devices (artifacts) and by experts (see Wassmann, in press). This is universal and does not apply only to rituals and the like: the latter case holds true for members of Western societies, for example with respect to the above question what the 26th digit of pi is (and we would use artifacts such as a calculator or the internet to answer the question). This, again, highlights the importance of the psychological capacity of memory formation and renders relevant a thought that is more than half a century old: W. Goodenough (1956) defined culture as what people have to *know* in order to be able to act in a socially acceptable way in their given environment.

Returning to the above example, on a fundamental level, the Yupno worldview, although it is in many ways radically different from what we are used to, is not brought about using cognitive faculties that differ from the ones employed in the Western or any other cultural sphere. Of course the Yupno form concepts in the same way that we do. They systematize their perceptive inputs, relate them to the conceptual framework they already operate in, and come up with distinctions that are coherent (as a whole), while allowing for the optimum of specificity needed in day-to-day life. For this process, obviously, working memory is crucial and for the interindividual transmission of these conceptual systems theory of mind is a necessary precondition. These three examples for invariant base modules of human cognition prove valid here and it is hard to see how they could not in any other cross-cultural comparison.

Research on the neurophysiological basis of these fundamental cognitive capacities has been extensive and productive. For concept formation, various biological mechanisms have been demonstrated (reviewed in Smith 2008; Mahon and Caramazza 2009). Specifically, depending on whether the processes involved rely on rule-based or similarity-based reasoning, the network implicated comprises different sub-regions of the frontal lobe as well as the thalamus and parietal cortical regions (Grossman et al. 2002; Koenig et al. 2005).

Also, working memory has been studied in great detail, both in the perceptive as well as in the cognitive domain. Networks implicated in these processes involve low-level sensory circuits as well as the parietal cortex and certain frontal regions (reviewed in Goldman-Rakic 1996; Baddeley 2003; Pasternak and Greenlee 2005; Linden 2007). Apart from these localizationistic approaches, actual mechanistic explanations have also been proposed. The biological correlates of ongoing working memory activity, for instance, have been shown to vary systematically with individual memory load capacity (Vogel and Machizawa 2004), when assessed via the electroencephalogram.

For theory of mind, neurobiological correlates have also been demonstrated. There seems to be a functional specialization in parts of the prefrontal cortex and inferior parietal areas, and, together with other parts of the brain, these regions seem to form a network, which is selectively activated in psychological processes we subsume as theory of mind (reviewed in Carrington and Bailey 2009). During different kinds of social reasoning, distinct parts of the network have been shown to be involved. This was shown, for example by Lissek et al. (2008), who demonstrated selective differences in the spatio-temporal patterns of brain metabolism during tasks involving cooperation and deception.

This short and superficial survey is meant to show that the biological branch of the cognitive sciences is well equipped to assess the cognitive base modules mechanistically. In fact, much detail has already been revealed about their nature and the physiology behind them. The motivation to propose concept formation (CF), WM, and TOM as invariants in human cognition came from theoretical reasoning on the one hand, and from early empirical cross-cultural research on the other. In the discussion of the Yupno worldview per se, as well as in comparison with the classical Western frameworks, it became evident that these base modules constitute necessary preconditions for any cultural model formation whatsoever, independent of the cultural context. Thus, a strong prediction can be derived from this line of reasoning: If CF, WM, and TOM really do form invariant base modules of human cognition, their neurophysiological correlates should not differ across cultures. This is a highly interesting task, especially given that today, neurobiological processes can be assessed with great objectivity, reproducibility, and with incredible precision. Such cross-cultural research has been done. One very interesting example is the study by Carreiras and colleagues (2005), who demonstrated that Silbo Gomero, a whistled language used by shepherds on the island of La Gomera (Canary Islands), is processed differently by proficient whistlers when compared to control subjects. It is only in proficient whistlers that listening to sequences of Silbo Gomero activated the classical language processing networks, not in control subjects. However, this work, like most other cross-cultural studies in neurobiology, obviously focused on very high level cognitive processes. What should be attempted now is a systematic inquiry into the very basic processes named above. Assessing the proposed invariants in human cognition using neurobiological techniques will not only shed light on anthropological matters, it will also point to potential distortions that Western ways of thinking, cultural models, and worldviews bring about in the design, conduction, and interpretation of experiments in cognitive neuroscience. Working with individuals from different cultural backgrounds will therefore provide a chance to assess what is due to the glasses we cannot take off and what other pairs of glasses there are to choose from. Ultimately, this will help illuminate central aspects of human nature – and this is the common goal of both biology and anthropology. That is why anthropology needs biology, and biology has much to learn from anthropology.

REFERENCES

Assmann, Jan
1999[1992] Das kulturelle Gedächtnis. Munich: Beck.
Baddeley, Alan
2003 Working Memory: Looking Back and Looking Forward. Nature Reviews Neuroscience 4(10):829–839.
Bartlett, Frederic C.
1932 Remembering. Cambridge: Cambridge University Press.
Berry, John, Ype Poortinga, Marshall Segall, and Pierre R. Dasen, eds.
2002 Cross Cultural Psychology. Cambridge: Cambridge University Press.
Bloch, Maurice
1991 Language, Anthropology, and Cognitive Science. Man 26:183–198.
1998. How We Think They Think. Oxford: Westview.
Boas, Franz
1927[1911] The Mind of Primitive Man. New York: Macmillan.
Boroditsky, Lera
2000 Metaphoric Structuring: Understanding Time through Spatial Metaphors. Cognition 75:1–28.
Carreiras, Manuel, Jorge Lopez, Rivero Francisco, and Corina David
2005 Linguistic Perception: Neural Processing of a Whistled Language. Nature 433(7021):31–32.
Carrington, Sarah J., and Anthony J. Bailey
2009 Are There Theory of Mind Regions in the Brain? A Review of the Neuroimaging Literature. Human Brain Mapping 30(8):2315–2335.
Cole, Michel, and Sylvia Scribner
1974 Culture and Thought: A Psychological Introduction. New York: John Wiley.
Gazzaniga, Michael S., Richard B. Irvy, and George R. Mangun
2008 Cognitive Neuroscience: The Biology of the Mind. 3rd edition. New York: W. W. Norton.
Gentner, Dedre, Imai Mutsumi, and Lera Boroditsky
2002 As Time Goes By: Evidence for Two Systems in Processing Space-Time Metaphors. Language and Cognitive Processes 17(5):537–565.
Goldman-Rakic, Patricia
1996 Regional and Cellular Fractionation of Working Memory. Proceedings of the National Academy of Sciences of the United States of America 93(24):13473–13480.
Goodenough, Ward
1956 Componential Analysis and the Study of Meaning. Language 32:195–216.
Grossman, Murray, Phillis Koenig, Chris DeVita, Guila Glosser, David Alsop, John Detre, and James Gee
2002 The Neural Basis for Category-Specific Knowledge: An fMRI Study. Neuroimage 15(4):936–948.
Holland, Dorothy, and Naomi Quinn, eds.
1987 Cultural Models in Language and Thought. Cambridge: Cambridge University Press.
Keck, Verena, ed.
1998 Common Worlds and Single Lives: Constituting Knowledge in Pacific Societies. Oxford: Berg.
Koenig, Phyllis, Edward E. Smith, Guila Glosser, Chris DeVita, Peachie Moore, Corey McMillan, Jim Gee, and Murray Grossman
2005 The Neural Basis for Novel Semantic Categorization. Neuroimage 24(2):369–383.

Kronenfeld, David
2008 Culture, Society, and Cognition: Collective Goals, Values, Action, and Knowledge. Berlin: Mouton de Gruyter.
Lakoff, George
1987 Woman, Fire and Dangerous Things: What Categories Reveal about the Mind. Chicago: University of Chicago Press.
Linden, David E. J.
2007 Working Memory Networks of the Human Brain. Neuroscientist 13(3):257–267.
Lissek, Silke, Soren Peters, Nina Fuchs, Henning Witthaus, Volkmar Nicholas, Martin Tegenthoff, Georg Juckel, and Martin Brüne
2008 Cooperation and Deception Recruit Different Subsets of the Theory-of-Mind Network. PLoS ONE 3(4):e2023.
Mahon, Bradford Z., and Alfonso Caramazza
2009 Concepts and Categories: A Cognitive Neuropsychological Perspective. Annual Review of Psycholoy 60:27–51.
Minsky, Marvin
1975 A Framework for Representing Knowledge. *In* The Psychology of Computer Vision. P. Winston, ed. New York: McGraw Hill. Pp. 211–277.
Núñez, Rafael, and Eve Sweetser
2006 With the Future behind Them: Convergent Evidence from Aymara Language and Gesture in the Crosslinguistic Comparison of Spatial Construals of Time. Cognitive Science: A Multidisciplinary Journal 30(3):401–450.
Núñez, Rafael, Kensy Cooperrider, and Jürg Wassmann
n.d. Tomorrow, Uphill. Topographic Construals of Past, Present, and Future Time in the Finisterre Range in Papua New Guinea. (Manuscript)
Pasternak, Tatiana, and Mark W. Greenlee
2005 Working Memory in Primate Sensory Systems. Nature Reviews Neuroscience 6(2):97–107.
Piaget, Jean, and Bärbel Inhelder
1967 Child's Conception of Space. New York: W. W. Norton.
Rogoff, Barbara, and Jean Lave, eds.
1984 Everyday Cognition: Its Development in Social Context. Cambridge, MA: Harvard University Press.
Schank, Roger, and Robert Abelson
1977 Scripts, Plans, Goals, and Understanding: An Inquiry into Human Knowledge Structure. Hillsdale, NJ: Lawrence Erlbaum.
Segall, Marshall, Pierre R. Dasen, John Berry, and Ype Poortinga, eds.
1990 Human Behavior in Global Perspective: An Introduction to Cross-Cultural Psychology. New York: Pergamon.
Smith, Edward E.
2008 The Case for Implicit Category Learning: Cognitive, Affective & Behavioral. Neuroscience 8(1):3–16.
Tulving, Endel
1985 How Many Memory Systems Are There? American Psychologist 40:385–398.
Vogel, Edward K., and Maro G. Machizawa
2004 Neural Activity Predicts Individual Differences in Visual Working Memory Capacity. Nature 428(6984):748–751.
Wassmann, Jürg
In press Person, Space and Memory. *In* Cultural Memories: The Geographical Point of View. P. Meusburger, M. Heffernan, and E. Wunder, eds. Dordrecht: Springer.
Whitehouse, Harvey, ed.
2001 The Debated Mind. Oxford: Oxford University Press.
Wittgenstein, Ludwig
1953 Philosophical Investigations. Oxford: Blackwell.

CHAPTER 4

The Limits of the Habitual: Shifting Paradigms for Language and Thought

Janet Dixon Keller

Most readers of this chapter will be familiar with the popular notion that people see the world differently through the lenses of different languages. This idea lies at the heart of what has been known in Western scholarly circles as linguistic relativity: the hypothesis that the language one speaks shapes habitual ways of thinking and by extension shapes ties of belonging. The scholarly argument asserts the influence of lexico-grammatical properties of language on sensory experience and non-verbal, cognitive, and conceptual constructions of a worldview; a habitual, linguistically governed relation between modes of mental activity results. Implicit in most scholarly (and popular) understandings is the further assumption that individuals more easily achieve "intersubjective coherence" with those others who coinhabit shared habitual orientations to the world (see Sapir 1949[1933]:15; Pratt 1987; Anderson 1991[1983]; Silverstein 2000, 2004).

Scholarly arguments for linguistic relativity grew out of research by Benjamin Lee Whorf and Edward Sapir who, building on the insights of Franz Boas (e.g., 1889), investigated cognitive and cultural consequences of structural diversity between languages (Mandelbaum 1949; Whorf 1956[1936], 1956[1941]; Hill and Mannheim 1992; Lucy 1992b; Bennardo 2003). Emphasizing the importance of linguistics to the human sciences, Sapir argued that "Language is a guide to 'social reality'" (1949[1929]:162).

> Human beings do not live in the objective world alone, nor alone in the world of social activity as ordinarily understood, but are very much at the mercy of the particular

A Companion to Cognitive Anthropology, First Edition. Edited by David B. Kronenfeld, Giovanni Bennardo, Victor C. de Munck, and Michael D. Fischer.

> language which has become the medium of expression for their society … the "real world" is to a large extent unconsciously built up on the language habits of the group [such that] … We see and hear and otherwise experience very largely as we do because the language habits of our community predispose certain choices of interpretation … [Sapir 1949[1929]:162]

As if in illustration, Whorf compares linguistic encodings of action in English and Hopi demonstrating "how language produces an organization of experience" (Whorf 1956[1936]:55).

> We are inclined to think of language simply as a technique of expression, and not to realize that language first of all is a classification and arrangement of the stream of sensory experience which results in a certain world order, a certain segment of the world that is easily expressible by the type of symbolic means that language employs. [Whorf 1956[1936]:55]

Mid-20th-century anthropologists and psychologists, often without discussion of broader intellectual considerations that informed Whorf and Sapir, represented these ideas as the linguistic relativity hypothesis positing a habitual influence of language on thought (Hill and Mannheim 1992; Lucy 1992b). On analogy with the sound contrasts constituting a phonological system, scholars accepted a system of meaningful relations constituted by *langue* as the conceptual foundation for a particular sociocultural world (see Pratt 1987; Bennardo 2003). This mid-20th-century intellectual platform generated considerable research, but inconsistent problem foci and findings failed to decide the relativity issue (Lucy 1992b). Recently scholars have reformulated the relativity hypothesis generating multiple, more tractable questions (Hill and Mannheim 1992; Bennardo 2003; Gentner and Goldin-Meadow 2003; Pinker 2007). The reformulations are not unified as a single perspective. Instead scholars are selectively guided by increasingly sophisticated understandings of dialogic and dialectic properties of situated, social action in which language is embedded and by increasingly sophisticated understanding of the architecture of the mind–brain in which language functions with other cognitive capacities.

In the present article I review recent research touching on issues originally framed as linguistic relativity to integrate the present intellectual diversity within larger, ongoing paradigm shifts for understanding relations of linguistic expression, modes of thinking, and social action. I argue that the plausibility of non-directed and many-to-many relations between language and other modes of cognition can be coupled with a focus on emergent social action to reveal flexible interrelations between diverse modes of thinking and between modalities of thinking and acting. This intellectual synthesis requires a rethinking of the *habitual* so crucial to relativity and refocuses debate away from a presumption of linguistic influence to address versatile and situated cognition.

Going Beyond Relativity Debates

In independent reviews, John Lucy (1992b), Giovanni Bennardo (2003), Steven Pinker (2007:124–151), Jane Hill and Bruce Mannheim (1992), and Stephen Levinson (2003a) critically assess cognitive and linguistic contributions to research on linguistic relativity. Their reviews simultaneously acknowledge achievements and recognize sites of incoherence in the mid-20th-century paradigm. I briefly examine these reviews to outline points of debate and reframe questions of language and thought.

Lucy (1992b) addresses 20th-century inconsistencies in research designs and results, noting a pervasive emphasis on biopsychology rather than language (Hill and Mannheim 1992). He proposes that comparative investigation of language and thought start from linguistic structures constituting fashions of speaking to ask whether other modes of experience converge with lexico-grammatical patterns. In studies now considered classic Lucy himself administers a variety of linguistic and non-linguistic tasks in two language communities to speakers of Yucatec Maya and American English (1992a). His results demonstrate correlations between linguistic structures and non-verbal task performances where ontological orientations to number, form, and substance are at issue. Such co-variation, he argues, provides evidence of habitual relations between language and thought supporting the relativity hypothesis.

At the same time, Lucy himself recognizes challenges that remain. Patterns of co-variation identified in his experiments fall short of providing causal accounts. A residue of non-correlated relations between language and other modes of thought or action raise the question of how subjects attend to or perhaps decide salient features of experience in a moment. Lucy identifies a focus on causal relations as critical for future investigations of the role of language in cognition (1992a:158–161).[1]

Based on extensive research into spatial cognition represented in language and in non-verbal task performances, Stephen Levinson and colleagues find linguistic preferences for object-centric, egocentric, or absolute modes of spatial reckoning correlate with visuo-motor spatial conceptions and actions (2001, 2003a, 2003b; Levinson and Wilkins 2006). Levinson accounts for the patterns of co-variation within a theory of mind emphasizing layers of mental processing. Like Whorf, he contends that human psychic unity is basic to cognition. Yet, again in Whorfian fashion, he argues that universal possibilities for orienting in space while shared as *potential* dispositions of mind are selectively shaped at higher levels of conceptualization by lexico-grammatical choices for spatial reference. This account integrates universalist biopsychological capacities with an argument for selective linguistic classification that shapes habitual modes of reason (see also Shore 1996:7–8; Kay and Regier 2007).

Bennardo and Pinker argue against relativity as an explanatory component for a theory of cognition, taking instead positions that simultaneously account for observations of researchers like Levinson and Lucy but also predict greater cognitive flexibility than the relativity hypothesis allows (Bennardo 2003; Pinker 2007). On one hand, Pinker emphasizes flexibility characteristic of peoples' mental attitudes as they engage with the world, noting variation within as well as across communities. Countering relativist claims, he explicitly remarks on the diversity in propositional form and structure correlated with subjective vantage points.[2] Pinker also draws attention to imprecise discriminations encoded by language for domains such as spatiality that are more finely partitioned in visual and kinesthetic modes. Bennardo (1996, 2009), on the other hand, notes that fundamentally similar models of experience may be represented across cognitive modes: language, spatial reckoning, and social relations, within a community without requiring the causal force attributed to language by relativity.

These arguments invoke a functional architecture for a theory of a mind in which information is discretely processed. Verbal, visual, spatial, motor, and emotional cognition exemplify distinct, more or less modular systems (Jackendoff 1992, 2007). The right and left hemispheres of the brain function semi-autonomously as well. Conceptual dispositions for organizing predication, space, time, substance, causality, number, logic, living things, and a folk theory of mind are among universal possibilities for organizing modes of information processing yet these systems are not redundant (see Pinker 2007:160). How the output of modular processing systems are integrated in higher-level conceptual thought remains an open question.

In this view, scholars entertain many-to-many possible relations between cognitive structures and processes. In principle non-redundant relations such as parallel processing, non-comparability, contradiction, and complementarity are as feasible as structural homology or co-variation across information modes. Bateson's double bind is a well-known example of parallel and contradictory modes of simultaneous cognitive processing (Bateson 1972; see also Strauss 1992; Strauss and Quinn 1997; Jackendoff 2007). This framework for a theory of mind transcends the dichotomy posed by relativity's focus on language and thought and offers the possibility for generating research questions regarding relations between *multiple* modalities of mental activity (see also Gentner and Goldin-Meadow 2003; Enfield and Levinson 2006; Gardner 2006). Resituating linguistic relativity within this poststructualist theory of mind creates possibilities for many-to-many intercognitive relations but leaves open the question of the place of language in thinking in any given instance. Investigating particular cognitive dynamics is advanced by synthesizing this perspective on mind with a theory of social action.

It is in social action centered on *empty drums*, as a mode of linguistic reference with hazardous implications for industrial fire, that Whorf initially observed "linguistic conditioning" of thought and resulting behaviors (Whorf 1956[1941]:135). In the context of a review of anthropological investigations relevant to issues of language and worldview Hill and Mannheim (1992) take social action as their point of departure. They fragment ideas of both language and worldview much as the poststructuralist theory of mind fragments thought. Hill and Mannheim point to the increasing recognition in Western scholarship of the distributed and contingent nature of social lives. They argue, "where 'world view' would once have served, 'ideology' is often heard, suggesting representations that are contestable, socially positioned, … laden with political interest" and structurally diverse (1992:382). Where language was once the focus of study, interanimating processes embed language in multimodal social activities. From this vantage point issues of cognitive complexity, situation, and interest destabilize the basic terms of the traditional relativity hypothesis: *language*, *thought*, and their proposed *habitual* relation.

In the following sections on experimental evidence, situated discourse, and multi-dimensional cognition in social action, I reconsider recent research typically framed in terms of relativity in light of the possibilities for non-directed and variable relations between modes of thought emergent within social action. I suggest that a paradigm shift is well underway that will advance understanding of intercognitive dynamics through a synthesis of the functional architecture of the mind–brain with dialogic and dialectic accounts of social action. In this theoretical framework the question of what might constitute habitual relations cannot be assumed but lies at the crux of reimagining research endeavors.

Experimental Evidence

Cognitive anthropology's investigations of language and thought center on meticulously designed experimental and linguistic studies of color, space, quantification, form, and substance. Research is often augmented by ethnography. These investigations turn on the question of language dominance and two additional issues emerge as directly relevant to the debates above. The first is a tension between relativity and universalism in cognition (Berlin and Kay 1969; Garro 1988; Lucy 1992a; Bennardo 1996, 2002; Bowerman and Levinson 2001; Palmer 2002; Gentner and Goldin-Meadow 2003; Levinson 2003a, 2003b; Gilbert et al. 2005). The second is the question of what counts as habitual (Lucy 1992a; Bennardo 1996, 2009).

Research on color perception and classification over 50 years demonstrates "non-trivial universal tendencies in cross-language color naming" derived from universally perceived foci of the visual spectrum (Kay and Regier 2007). The universal foci, red, yellow, green, and blue as well as white and black, are identified in the interactions of human neurophysiology with hue, saturation, and brightness (Kay and McDaniel 1978). Where color is the basis for lexical elaboration, these perceptions provide foci and limits constraining the organization of the full range of color distinctions into basic categories.[3] In addition, however, when languages vary in the number of basic color terms encoded in their lexicons, these differences can have relative effects on memory and communication (Lucy and Shweder 1979; Lucy 1992b; Gilbert et al. 2005). As Kay and Reiger (2007) note, accounts of the language and cognition of color require both universal constraints on color naming and evidence for color naming effects on memory and discrimination. However, this picture is incomplete. Perceptual and linguistic modes of engagement with the visual world of color are independent (as well as interdependent) and may distinctively influence task performances. Thus perceptual foci and labels as well as mixed strategies combining imagery with descriptive phrases can affect cognitive processes like memory (Garro 1988). In addition Gilbert et al. (2005) demonstrate that naming effects impact activities of the right, but not the left, visual field, thus tying influences from color naming to the functional organization of the brain. These findings in combination make sense within an increasingly complex functional architecture for the mind–brain that permits many-to-many relations between verbal and non-verbal cognitive systems.

Investigations of spatial orientations in language and mind move along a different path but also toward novel possibilities for understanding language within complex cognitive and social fields. Stephen Levinson argues that "the language one happens to speak affords, or conversely, makes less accessible, certain complex concepts" (2003a:33) and that while there surely exists a broad-based "psychic unity" rooted in perception, more abstract representations closer to language vary (2003a:35). Coordinating detailed study of numerous languages, Levinson demonstrates that universal possibilities for orienting in space are differentially emphasized in linguistic systems. Experimental research reveals correlations of particular language structures with non-linguistic preferences for establishing environmental order, positioning self, other, or objects; and reckoning movement (Bennardo 1996, 2002; Levinson 1996, 2001, 2003b; Brown 2001; Palmer 2002; Bowerman and Choi 2003). Echoing Whorf in two distinct respects, this work shows that even while a set of universal dimensions for spatial order are accessible to all human beings, spatial categories and their interrelations are almost never encoded in the same manner across languages. Experimental results demonstrate that particular linguistic variants facilitate correlated structures of reasoning in other cognitive modalities (Palmer 2002; Levinson 2003a:31; 2003b; Levinson and Wilkins 2006).

Building on this, Melissa Bowerman and colleagues (Bowerman 1996; Bowerman and Choi 2001, 2003) address developmental processes. Among their linguistically marked spatial distinctions, for example, Korean children acquire a lexicon differentiating tightly versus loosely fitting relations of contact (*kkita* vs. *nehta*) while English-speaking children attend more globally to contact lexicalized as *in* or *on*. Children highlight particular conceptual distinctions for spatial relations as they acquire the particular distinctions encoded in their language while they may also lose ready access, at least verbally, to the full range of possibilities (Bowerman and Choi 2003).[4]

Such research demonstrates a tendency for language to shape non-verbal cognition, but the role of language in the experimental designs themselves and limitations on generalizations derived from experimental conditions, leave open questions of what might constitute habitual correlations of language with non-verbal processes of spatial cognition and reckoning in a broader range of tasks. Levinson and colleagues move beyond these limitations in research linking gesture and gestural components of deixis to lexico-grammatical reference in spatial reckoning where again co-variation appears the rule (Levinson 2003b; Levinson and Wilkins 2006). However, going still further, Enfield and Levinson (2006) have begun an inquiry into the roots of human sociality, positioning language within multiply constructed interactions. In this work these authors and their colleagues recognize interanimating dynamics between social and cognitive processes. The issue of language dominance becomes problematic. The new turn to sociality in this research offers the possibility for contextualizing experimental results and constitutes a foundation for reassessing Whorfian as well as potentially non-Whorfian situated and emergent relations of language with diverse modes of thought and action.

Other experimental research has focused on the expression and manipulation of number among human and non-human primates. Number emerges in languages at a variety of points: individuating objects (one and another), marking plurality, distinguishing count versus mass nouns, indicating agreement between nouns and verbs, and in quantification. Yet these distinctions build on numerical concepts available to children prior to language (Carey 2001). The simple distinctions made in language between small numbers; between singular and plural, countability and extended substance; and between categories such as "one," "another," "few," and "many" reflect conceptual foundations of the primate brain incorporated differently into particular linguistic grammars (Carey 2001:210; Pinker 2007:138–141). At the same time the grammatical alternatives respect non-linguistic continua of experience. Grammatical plurality, for example, is correlated with count–mass distinctions and these distinctions reflect non-linguistic properties such as animacy and motion. Languages differ with respect to where they draw count–mass and plural marking lines but do so against universally accessible ranges of experience (Gentner and Boroditsky 2001:229–230). Within investigations of number, non-linguistic cognitive capacities support particular linguistic formulations. Strategies for numerical reasoning draw on diverse cognitive modalities: language, gesture, visual assessment, informed by conceptual dispositions of the primate brain. These findings complicate issues of language dominance and distribute thought over multiple activities of the human mind–brain.

In some societies innate numerical concepts provide a basis for counting algorithms and more complex mathematics that are culturally constructed and linguistically encoded. Individuals learn these mathematical processes explicitly and their applications develop in formal training and practice. Availability of culturally constructed and linguistically encoded modes of numerical reasoning, however, does not replace the use of heuristics for numerical reasoning derived from the more basic distinctions and applied in social action. Individuals often eschew formal mathematics in everyday numerical reasoning. Instead mixed strategies such as weight-watchers' variable use of measures, visual estimations, substitutions, and embodied partitioning of substances complementing linguistically represented heuristics for reckoning quantity emerge in personal styles for cooking (Lave 1988:127–131; Pinker 2007). Such research suggests mixed and non-redundant reasoning processes co-occurring in social action.

In other research, Lucy specifically tests for the role of grammar on cognitive discriminations of number. His work, experimental in design, demonstrates that English speakers rely more frequently on number as a feature of experience than Yucatec Maya-speaking counterparts. This discrepancy is more robust for certain categories of objects than for others (1992a). These effects correlate with grammatical pluralization and count–mass distinctions in the two languages. In line with their respective grammatical systems, Yucatec Maya speakers also show a strong tendency to group objects in perceptual or visuo-motor tasks on the basis of material composition while US English speakers are more likely to attend to characteristics of shape again as language structure predicts. However, as with mixed strategies identified above, Lucy's experiments show that speakers of both languages sometimes ignore linguistically salient grammatical features in favor of non-linguistic discriminable properties. Lucy himself in yet another context is unsurprised at such cognitive diversity and remarks that "obligatory linguistic categories are only one source of effects on behavior" (Lucy 1992b:201).

This discussion introduces the question central to linguistic relativity: what counts as *habitual*. Perhaps Whorf's initial pointer to habitual modes of thought "easily expressible" in language (Whorf 1956[1936]:55; Lucy 1992a:158) hobbled research on language and cognition while also potentially offering new direction. Whorf's reliance on "language" and "habits" as the basis for relativity presumes a typical mode for cognitive engagement with the world. The assumption of experimentalists is that results obtained in research will reflect this presumably "habitual" mode of reason.

Yet this supposition denies the multiple grounds informing social action and the potential for mixed reasoning strategies. In human action, "all things are never equal." Habermas (1971) articulates this with respect to human interests, but it applies equally to the diversity of influences entailed by intersubjective encounters. Color, ripeness, texture or smell may be attended to as features of the "same" object depending on the goals for social action with or without linguistic direction. Individuals manipulate verbal expression with other modes of thought and attention according to situated dimensions of encounters. For example, small-scale or large-scale environmental concerns may trigger alternative forms of spatial reckoning simultaneously available in language. Or closeness of fit, lexicalized in Korean spatial terms but not in basic

English prepositions, can nonetheless be critical to the English-speaking blacksmith forging a pin for a hole or the carpenter making sliding drawers for both of whom action directs attention to closeness of fit and facilitates talk of "slop," "tolerance," and "goodness of fit" as needed (see Keller and Keller 1996a).

How does such versatility (Bourdieu 1977; Hallam and Ingold 2007) alter ideas of the habitual as employed in linguistic relativity? In a series of experiments and ethnographic observations over more than a decade conducted in the Kingdom of Tonga, Bennardo (1996, 2002, 2003, 2009) explored cognitive orientations to space revealed in linguistic, psychological, and behavioral practices of social exchange, networking, kinship, drawing, offering directions, telling stories, positioning objects, and ascribing spatial orientations to them. In this work he identified several linguistic systems of spatial reckoning including object intrinsic, ego relative, and absolute frameworks used differentially in small-scale and large-scale space. In fact the Tongan language, he argues, provides a variety of linguistic means for realizing any of the frames of reference that have been recognized in research on spatial cognition (2000:537). Linguistic spatial descriptions in Tongan use these diverse resources in correlation with scale, visibility of the environment at issue, and visibility of an interlocutor creating a set of patterns that require at the least recognizing contextually specific versions of *the habitual*.

Bennardo does go on to identify a further sense of the *habitual* in a preference for representing spatial relations in what he calls radial terms for a range of activities from map drawing to visuo-motor strategies, to the logic of kin reckoning, to organizing narrative, to depicting and remembering social relations, and to the interpretation and generation of social exchange (2001, 2008b, 2009). The radial model makes three primary distinctions: (1) direction or movement toward a center, (2) movement or direction away from such a center, and (3) direction or movement away from a specific center identified as speaker and hearer. Bennardo finds radiality sufficiently widespread in experiments (object manipulations, depictions of social relations), interviews, and naturalistic tasks (offering directions, mapping, and social exchange) to serve as a candidate for a habitual way of thinking among Tongans living in Tonga. Yet he contends that this patterning is not relativist. He finds no evidence to support a Whorfian effect from language (2003:50).[5] Instead, Bennardo's research (2009) shows multiple cognitive modalities taking advantage of radial conceptual relations. Bennardo argues that this is evidence of homologous structures of the mind reflecting cultural priorities (2003).

Further, Bennardo does not claim that what he calls foundational cultural modeling is the only possible relation between cognitive modalities or an exclusive cognitive perspective motivating action. The rich options noted above for spatial representation as encoded in the Tongan language itself attest, in fact, to diverse instantiations of ways of thinking about space than either habitual relativity or foundational cultural modeling would suggest. In the process of this research and his analyses, Bennardo raises new questions, crucially shifting the paradigm for framing investigations of intercognitive relations to one of multimodal interactions open to both habitual covariation and to other dynamics (see also Hill and Mannheim 1992).

The preceding discussion of experimental research in cognitive anthropology suggests multiple possibilities for intercognitive relations and the mix of cognitive underpinnings contributing to social action. This framework leaves open the possibility of relations of language dominance, but does not restrict investigators to this influence. Hill and Mannheim, for example, while arguing for complex dialogic and dialectic grounds of human engagements, remark on the existence of Whorfian effects among others (1992:387–388). Pinker acknowledges that having a word (or perhaps a grammatical distinction) may provide a "dollop of additional retrievability and manipulability" that is cognitively helpful (2007:129), while he also emphasizes that language is neither a unitary nor necessarily a habitually dominant mode of thought. Pursuing this further, Gentner and Boroditsky (2001) suggest a division of dominance between non-linguistic cognition and linguistic structure during language acquisition. They show how relational terms such as conjunctions and determiners are linguistically embedded, their meanings acquired only with linguistic direction, while with respect to object naming, they demonstrate the substantial role of non-linguistic cognition in facilitating language learning. Verbs, they reason, fall in between these extremes and their acquisition is guided by language-specific configurational properties and non-verbal cognition.

Such expansions of the questions relevant to intercognitive dynamics should embolden researchers in cognitive anthropology to shift toward investigating diverse relations between modalities of thought emergent in situated activities. Construing situations multiply, innovating, improvising, and manipulating structural constraints, and bricoleurishly adapting one conceptual ground to another exemplify typical human proclivities (Bourdieu 1977; Lave 1988; Hutchins 1995; Keller and Keller 1996b, 1999; Strauss and Quinn 1997; West 1999; Hallam and Ingold 2007; Pinker 2007; Keller 2009). New understanding of the functional diversity of the mind lays the groundwork for investigating versatility and cognitive flexibility inherent in social action. Such a framework replaces traditional questions of linguistic relativity with questions of how and when particular cognitive and conceptual modes of organizing experience interanimate one another. The focus on social action also raises questions of the complex and mutually influential relations between modes of cognition and behavior.

Situated Discourse

In his volume *Culture in Mind*, Bradd Shore argues that meaning can "only be understood as an ongoing process, an active construction by people with the help of cultural resources" (Shore 1996:7). He goes on to contend, however, that "variations in cultural cognition can be traced to important local differences in the specific models and general schemes that constrain ordinary perception and understanding." Bennardo's research also documents the culturally specific foundations of emergent properties of meaning. Yet both scholars also recognize more general constraints derived from the functional organization of the mind–brain. This conjunction of emergence, cultural constraint, and mental architecture offers a foundation for addressing questions raised above and leads to further considerations of cognitive and social dynamics.

With this in mind I turn to research by scholars (e.g., Strauss 1992; Duranti 1994; Slobin 1996, 2003; Bennardo 2008a; Urciuoli 2008) who independently investigate cognition in social action. I start with research closely in tune with the experimental traditions discussed in the preceding section and move on to consider discursive patterns in context.

Psychologist Dan Slobin (2003) hypothesizes that mental representations governing language use in communicative or interpretive modes encode those distinctions essential for linguistic practices. For instance, in listening to oral texts or reading for comprehension, in experiencing events with an anticipation of talking about them, in translating, or in imagery associated with verbal descriptions, representations bear traces of articulated or anticipated linguistic structures (2003:177–178). To test this hypothesis, Slobin designed a range of experiments and directed observations to assess cognitive accompaniments of verbalized manners of motion. He distinguishes language-particular expressions of path and manner of motion and investigates nonlinguistic consequences and correlates of two primary patterns.

Slobin finds that manner of motion may be obligatorily encoded in main clausal verbs, as is frequently the case in English, German, Polish, Russian, Finnish, and Mandarin Chinese or may be expressed optionally in adjunct phrases modifying a main verb as is typical in French, Spanish, Moroccan Arabic, Hebrew, Turkish, Japanese, and American Sign.

For speakers of languages emphasizing obligatory encoding of manner, manner verbs are of relatively high salience as determined quantitatively from free listings and frequency of use in verbal descriptions. Children acquire competence in the use of these verbs early in their development. Speakers evidence attention to manner in oral, written, and translated texts, metaphorical extension, and mental imagery associated with linguistic data. By contrast, speakers of languages that encode manner in adjunct phrases show less attention to differentiations between ways of performing actions in all of the areas noted above (2003:161–176).

Slobin coins the phrase "thinking for speaking" (1996, 2003) to capture this patterning. He argues that language structures influence mental representations constructed with a view to continuing language-based practices. In defining the properties of thinking for speaking, Slobin also provides an operational measure of what Whorf may have meant by *habitual*: that is, the relatively frequent use of a linguistic distinction across various domains of activity (2003:161). Slobin suggests that the co-variation constituting thinking for speaking illustrates this sense of the habitual.[6]

Yet Slobin's move to a focus on thinking for speaking also reconceptualizes Whorf by highlighting linguistic expression as only one form of mental-cum-behavioral activity; that is thinking and acting in language (Tomasello 2003:56). Slobin argues that as people think with language their thoughts and practice manifest distinctions marked obligatorily or by special grammatical constructions in their verbal resources (2003:161). This version of relativity associates language dominance with language-based modes of thought and action, while simultaneously leaving open possibilities for other cognitive patterns when activities do not center on language.

Turning to additional conceptualizations of social action in which language is embedded pushes the process of rethinking relativity further: first, by demonstrating the significance of human interests and situated encounters for emergent intercognitive dynamics; and secondly, by emphasizing the interplay between multiple cognitive modes engaged in social action.

The work I discuss builds on an insight articulated by Sapir (1949[1933]:15–16) who remarks on language practices as correlated with shared interests:

> In between the recognized dialect or language as a whole and the … speech of a given individual lies a kind of linguistic unit which is not often discussed by the linguist but which is of the greatest importance to social psychology. This is the sub-form of a language current within a group of people who are held together by ties of common interest. Such a group may be a family, the undergraduates of a college, a labor union, the underworld in a large city, the members of a club, a group of four or five friends who hold together through life in spite of differences of professional interest, and untold thousands of other kinds of groups.

Sapir's remark directs us today to studies of discourse. In a recent article in the *American Ethnologist*, Bonnie Urciuoli (2008) analyzes the language of "internet sites marketing skills-related services." She investigates the semiotics of discourses that shape the corporate world within which workers must position themselves when seeking, and perhaps performing, their jobs (2008:211). The discourse she focuses on is characterized by a cluster of key terms: *skills*, *communication*, *team*, *leadership*. Skills at issue are quantified. They are rhetorically constructed as segmentable, testable, rankable, measurable, subject to rating, and grammatically countable, most frequently presented in the plural (2008:215, 217). The discourse renders diverse skills commensurable, subject similarly to assessment and transaction "making it unproblematic to talk about" market value of one's own self or other selves as desirable members of a frontline workforce, management team, or leadership cohort. It is in such terms that one evaluates oneself as ready to go on the market. In short, one *thinks about* labor and employment within capitalist economic production with the discursive structures. Urciuoli understands this process as one of giving "linguistic form to the inchoate … through what Whorf called 'fashions of speaking' " (224). Using language outside the normative rhetoric is likely to be effortful, and when achieved such talk positions interlocutors outside core productive segments of the market.

These observations might at first glance appear to exemplify thinking for speaking. Yet if Urciuoli's observations constitute a Whorfian effect, this effect arises not from linguistic relativity conceived broadly as extending across domains, but rather from situated practice. Speakers "enregister" their talk in particular contexts. A discourse associated with certain neoliberal skills is pervasive, read *habitual*, only in discussions of neoliberal employment and job performance. Such fashions of speaking are not obligatory in the sense Whorf or Sapir intended nor in Slobin's full sense of thinking for speaking. Urciuoli mentions that when one steps outside the corporate world of employment, for example, to domains of craft or artisanship, while still speaking the "same" language, the discourse and thinking about skill and its correlates shifts (2008:214). The contribution of Urciuoli's skills register for encoding thoughts is specific to neoliberal interests at stake in professionalization, employment, job performance, and economic personhood.

While Urciuoli claims her research demonstrates Whorfian effects from discursive registers, I read her evidence as more complicated. She investigates linguistic phenomena that are not habitual, obligatory, or ubiquitously manifest in the speech of Americans whose first language is English. Instead she finds these phenomena situated, contextually relevant, and offering one mode of entrée into engagements with a world governed independently by capitalist market forces and corporate production. Her discussion indicates the limits of the concept of the habitual, demonstrating instead an interanimation of linguistic effects and particular properties of the world.

Duranti's ethnographic and linguistic research in Samoa (1994) similarly demands refinement of conventional notions of relativity in light of discursive practices. Duranti's research focuses on specialized and intentional uses of ergative grammatical constructions for assigning social responsibility to transitive agents. Utterances constructed in the Samoan ergative constitute purposeful claims about individuals' actions, claims not lightly made or received in the Samoan cultural context where collaborative processes are central to community maintenance.

Duranti suggests a powerful grammar of responsibility, praising, and blaming is at work (1994:4, 145). Ergativity, sometimes also associated with other forms of linguistic emphasis and contrast, produces and reproduces a culturally viable mode of expressing individual responsibility. Ethnographic evidence for the impact of such utterances is compelling; as indicated by people's reactions, making clear that they have felt an accusation or attribution implied by the use of an ergative construction (e.g., Duranti 1994:4, 130–139, 158). Contrasting patterns of speech avoiding transitive agents offer additional evidence of the special impacts of ergativity (1994:151).

Unlike verbs of motion, however, but like skills discourses, ergativity exemplifies contextual and intentional linguistic usage rather than a ubiquitous or obligatory pattern. Duranti shows this linguistic strategy to be an unusual (in terms of frequency) rather than habitual element of linguistic expression, although when speakers do use ergative constructions issues of responsibility are *habitually* evoked. Indeed ergativity is used at least in public by only a subset of Samoan speakers, typically by Samoan community leaders charged with resolving conflict through the public discourses of the *fono* (village council). Ergativity then constitutes a contextually and agentively restricted grammatical element for particular linguistic interventions. Duranti claims ergativity has a Whorfian effect. The grammatical form impacts, shapes, and in part constitutes the world. Yet the question arises – how to understand this situated and intentional use of language that bears a resemblance to relativity and yet violates notions of habitual and obligatory modes of language influence?

The focus on discourses in the research of Urciuoli and Duranti entails attention to multiply grounded social action in which linguistic structures not only refer to but also index properties of experience accessed by a diversity of non-linguistic modes of thinking (see also Silverstein 2000, 2004). Mutuality rather than dominance captures much of the mix of modes of thinking in action. Language does not stand alone either in mind or in social encounters.[7]

Another aspect of intercognitive dynamics in social action grows out of research in cognitive anthropology, suggesting that even when diverse modes of thinking are correlated with linguistic expression the nature of the linking relation may vary. In research not discussed above, Bennardo (2008b) finds a common verbal refrain, "We are all the same," bears little resemblance to the complexities of actual social experience. In the Tongan context where people mobilize social networks daily for a variety of purposes along a variety of dimensions, hierarchy, family, age, and gender create a lack of sameness among community members. Yet the utterance above fits neatly with a cultural ideology of cooperation and is uttered to draw on this collective (but mostly unrealized) value. Similarily, Strauss (1992) finds that among a group of working-class Americans linguistic utterances express ways of thinking more or less remote from everyday experiences. Subjects' talk slides from ideological clichés to expressions of empirical contingencies of everyday life. The former impact thinking and acting insignificantly, although they may serve as cooperative responses in interactions. In contrast, speakers co-implicate multimodal experience as they speak less glibly about everyday life. And finally, Gatewood (1985), in arguing that "actions speak louder than words," demonstrated that in purse seining, novices may superficially reproduce expert discourses long before these discourses implicate expert thinking.

Like Slobin, Urciuoli, and Duranti, these examples raise questions for traditional linguistic relativity. The idea of a habitual mode of thinking, consistently governed by integrated, unconscious, and habitual linguistic structures, fails to illuminate the evident diversity, drawing instead on a notion of the habitual that makes sense only within a framework essentializing notions of language, thought, and culture.

By contrast, current anthropological emphases on agency, knowledge distribution, interest, and situated practice can be combined with contributions from cognitive science (Jackendoff 1992, 2007; Bennardo 2003; Pinker 2007) to create an opportunity for cognitive anthropologists to reframe questions regarding intercognitive dynamics. Building on further insights in the scholarship reviewed above I turn to a final focus on many-to-many relations between cognitive modalities and social praxis.

Multidimensional Cognition in Social Action

At the same time that Urciuoli and Duranti argue for contextual Whorfian effects, their research transcends the original Whorfian position by drawing attention to the embedding of language in multimodal cognition and practice. When Urciuoli emphasizes indexical processes entailed by fashions of speaking, her discussion offers an example of multidirectional influences between language strategies and lived experience. In this case a language of marketable skills indexes *and* takes its meaning from economic and historical conditions of capitalist and corporate production independent of language. "Meaning proceeds," she argues, "from the system through which it is constituted" (2008:221; see also Keller and Lehman 1991). Neither language nor properties of the social and physical environments take priority in cognizing one's place in the capitalist, neoliberal political economy. Discursive patterns at issue here do not shape a truly inchoate world as Urciuoli suggests, but emerge historically as conditions of the world themselves emerge. The discursive patterns encompassing a range of integrated lexical and grammatical structures find situated relevance with a cultural theory of neoliberal economics and with topics of employment situated within that framework. Discursive structures, cultural knowledge, and world structures are co-referential, have co-evolved, and "habitually" co-implicate one another in multimodal experiences of the "neoliberal utopia" (Bourdieu 1991; Urciuoli 2008).

Duranti (1994) also makes a case for the mutual constitution of events in the Samoan case. Speakers construct culturally meaningful encounters through a give and take between linguistic and non-linguistic modes of thinking and acting. Ergativity is only one feature of conflict resolution. Linguistic utterances are embedded in background knowledge, complemented by spatial positionality, posture and gesture, emotional expression, and interpreted in light of participants' identities (see also Goodwin 2006:97–125). Samoans mutually construct significance in social action by establishing intersubjective and intercognitive resonances between these elements or by failing in that regard.[8] In such emergent dynamics individuals engage from positions of interest drawing on multiple intelligences and multidimensional connections with the world (Norman 1993; Hutchins 1995; Gardner 2006).

Finally, both Urciuoli and Duranti find it necessary to include power in their analysis of linguistic effects. Urciuoli argues that the use of skills discourses is not always persuasive. However, individuals seeking employment are particularly readily convinced to adopt a discourse supported by the weight of the neoliberal economy and corporate employers. Duranti too suggests that the impact of ergative constructions in the Samoan *fono* stems in part from the authority of those who speak. The linguistic expressions at issue gain meaning neither by virtue of their unconscious hold on the mind of community members, nor exclusively by their links to other modes and genres of thinking and acting. They acquire dominance through being authored by individuals and institutions with positions of power. The extent to which language shapes thinking in these settings varies according to what parties have to gain by adhering to particular lines of thought and expression (Bourdieu 1991). Adding power as a factor in linking language to ways of thinking augments the flexibility already introduced. Power relations are essential in accounting for particular intercognitive dynamics and for lines of connection between modes of thought and social action. As Silverstein notes, "specific words and expressions ... gel as text-in-context" only as evoked, validated, and valued in multidimensional interactions framed by wider scale genres and institutional "orders of interactionality" (2004:622–623).

Conclusions

In this chapter I propose that shifting paradigms open the possibilities for moving beyond linguistic relativity to a focus on intercognitive dynamics embedded in social action. In the relativity hypothesis the use of the terms *language* and *thought* hark back to the structural notion of *langue* and the dualistic sign in which phonological strings are irrevocably attached to significances. In the view proposed here, neither language nor thought are monolithic and, as a result, linguistic expressions have no one-to-one relation with other cognitive modalities. Thinking involves interanimation between different linguistic and non-linguistic representations and processes (Boroditsky et al. 2003:76–77; Pinker 2007; Lakoff 2008). This means that the mental lives of individuals within and across language communities may achieve intrapersonal and intersubjective resonance or may differ dramatically in all manner of engagements. Questions of correlations, parallelisms, complementarity, and contradiction can only be empirically resolved.

The potential to synthesize the complexities of social action with the functional diversity of the mind to incorporate many-to-many possible intercognitive relations enriches research possibilities for cognitive anthropology (Jackendoff 1992, 2007; Bennardo 2003; Pinker 2007). The poststructuralist mind allows for multiple dynamics and for distinct human intelligences more or less adept at particular modes of engaging with the world. Social action augments the possibilities for developing accounts of intercognitive dynamics through attention to situated practices organized by participants' intentions, relations of power, a mix of indexicality and reference, cultural frames, and diverse modes of cognition and action. Humans interact using multiple modes of thought and action to achieve their particular ends.[9] Language may play a structuring role in some encounters, may support alternative modes of thought and action in others, or may be sidelined, even contradicted by other modalities such as imagery, emotion, or embodied actions in yet other events. Multiple construals of experience may be interdependently bound or parallel and independent. And in the process of social action commitments to orienting parameters and modes of thought may shift. In short, the *habitual* is problematic ground for a theory of cognition in action.

Anthropological linguistics and cognitive science have come a long way since Whorf claimed that "thinking is most mysterious, and by far the greatest light upon it that we have is thrown by the study of language" (Whorf 1956[1942]:252).[10] Today mysteries of thinking certainly remain but the points of entrée and arrays of variables that can be taken into account in investigations have been greatly expanded. Questions of co-inhabiting shared worlds are greatly complicated by dynamics of mind and interaction. As a result, research on thinking can now be a more robust and interesting arena in which investigations address intercognitive dynamics of multidimensional subjects engaged in negotiated social actions.

ACKNOWLEDGMENTS

I wish to thank Giovanni Bennardo, Stephen Maas, and Wenyi Zhang for their comments on an earlier version of this chapter. I offer special thanks to Elizabeth Spreng who worked through several drafts with me in detail, offering insightful critical commentary and fruitful pointers to literature.

NOTES

1 In subsequent writing on the subject Lucy cautions that scholars must anticipate a potentially confounding effect of "semantic accent." Given the potential for unconscious features of language structure to influence other modes of engaging with the world, researchers can be easily blinded by linguistic-cum-cognitive attitudes encoded in their first language orientations. Research must avoid projecting investigators' dispositions on subjects' modes of reason and action (2005). This is of concern for the argument developed here and should be kept in mind in evaluating research under discussion.

2 This is interestingly a position akin to literary observations of Bakhtin (1981) and the emphasis in recent linguistic anthropology on language and ideology, although Pinker himself does not draw on these precedents for evidence.

3 Rarer but notable scholarship suggests the possibility of more radical incommensurability across linguistic communities. In early research on color Hal Conklin argued that terminological contrasts in the Hanunóo language of the Philippines that encode moisture content of vegetation overlap in typical extensional reference with hue-based distinctions yet do not encode the latter (Conklin 1955). In research on a Polynesian outlier language I found similar overlap among terms for ripeness and dryness among the most conservative and oldest living speakers of the native language (Dougherty 1975). Such extensional overlap, Conklin argues, belies an underlying difference in intensional features of contrast (see also Lucy 1992b). This is not to say that basic focal points or perceptual discriminations of the visual spectrum vary for the Hanunóo from the human norm, they do not. However, at the

time Conklin did his research the "theory" of appearances linguistically expressed in Hanunóo emphasized features of the world other than the nexus of hue, saturation, and brightness that provides a basis for linguistic theories of color in many of the world's other languages (Berlin and Kay 1969). Even such radical distinctions in reference, however, do not preclude shared perception or linguistic reference to color when desired through secondary vocabularies (Dougherty 1975).

4 This research recalls the work of Boas over a century ago as he explored phonological contrasts among languages and suggested that individual development of language-specific phonological contrasts highlights some articulatory distinctions while diminishing perceptual access to others (Boas 1889). Contrasting with such a process are Brown's (2001) arguments that spatial orientations are learned contextually and that language and culturally particular modes of spatial reckoning may not simply reflect universal parameters.

5 Non-experimental data support Bennardo's argument for preferred cultural models distributed in diverse cognitive modalities. Witherspoon (1975), anticipating these directions, identifies philosophical and cosmological principles that govern Navajo grammatical relations, ritual conduct, and artistic composition. Keller and Kuautonga (2007; Keller 2009) identify cosmological principles entailing a particular cultural geography shaping traditional narratives of a Polynesian outlier community in rural Vanuatu. One example notes the tacit extension of this same cultural geography to urban settings inhabited during recent decades of immigration (Keller 2009). Migrants expect particular arrangements of living space that are instead violated by the European-influenced neighborhood designs of colonial origins. As with Bennardo's research, in both these cases homologies reflect and reproduce foundational cultural principles. No evidence suggests that language is the dominant influence on these conceptual strategies.

6 This is a definition of *habitual* that may apply to Bennardo's foundational cultural model as well. In Bennardo's case, however, the similarities in modes of thinking are interpreted as homologies, not linguistically directed "thinking for speaking."

7 We can draw on the history of research in linguistic anthropology to further expand issues of complexity in discourse. Austin (1975[1962]) among many others demonstrated the construction of meaning involving indirection and implicature, nonreferential aspects of the situated use of speech that rely on nonlinguistic contextual cues. Grice (1957, 1975) emphasized the place of nonlinguistic principles of cooperation for scaffolding coherent and meaningful conversation.

8 A similar position is evidenced in Geertz's articulation of webs of significance, and more particularly in his accounting of the meaning of a wink (Geertz 1973, 2002). Hutchins (1995) too, from the perspective of activity theory, finds that, rather than structuring practice and thought in navigation, language is only one of many modes of engagement co-constructing and reflecting thinking in action.

9 Manipulating modes of expression may be tacitly or consciously directed.

10 Perhaps it is because the sounds of speech are readily accessible to conscious reflection (Jackendoff 2007) that attention, both in popular and scholarly circles, has focused on language as the primary mode of structuring experience. It is language one can most easily grasp.

REFERENCES

Anderson, Benedict

1991 [1983] Imagined Communities: Reflections on the Origin and Spread of Nationalism. 2nd edition. London: Verso.

Austin, John L.
1975[1962] How to Do Things with Words. 2nd edition. Cambridge, MA: Harvard University Press.
Bakhtin, M. M.
1981 The Dialogic Imagination. *In* Four Essays by M. M. Bakhtin. Michael Holquist, ed. Caryl Emerson and Michael Holquist, trans. Austin: University of Texas Press.
Bateson, Gregory
1972 Steps to an Ecology of Mind. New York: Ballantine.
Bennardo, Giovanni
1996 A Computational Approach to Spatial Cognition: Representing Spatial Relationships in Tongan Language and Culture. Unpublished Ph.D. dissertation, Department of Anthropology, University of Illinois, Urbana–Champaign.
2000 Language and Space in Tonga: "The Front of the House is where the Chief Sits!" Anthropological Linguistics 42(4):499–544.
2001 A Possible Tongan Cultural Model: Radiality. Paper presented at the 100th Meeting of the American Anthropological Association. Washington DC, November 28.
2003 Language, Mind, and Culture: From Linguistic Relativity to Representational Modularity. *In* Mind, Brain, and Language: Multidisciplinary Perspectives. Marie T. Banich and Molly Mack, eds. Pp. 23–60. Mahwah, NJ: Lawrence Erlbaum.
2008a Familiar Space in Social Memory. Structure and Dynamics: ejournal of Anthropological and Related Sciences. http://escholarship.org/uc/item/19t2623t, accessed September 17, 2010.
2008b Influence Structures in a Tongan Village: "Every Villager Is Not the Same." Structure and Dynamics: ejournal of Anthropological and Related Sciences. http://escholarship.org/uc/item/8mx8t8nx, accessed September 17, 2010.
2009 Language, Space, and Social Relationships: A Foundational Cultural Model in Polynesia. Cambridge: Cambridge University Press.
Bennardo, Giovanni, ed.
2002 Representing Space in Oceania: Culture in Language and Mind. Canberra: Pacific Linguistics.
Berlin, Brent, and Paul Kay
1969 Basic Color Terms: Their Universality and Evolution. Berkeley: University of California Press.
Boas, Franz
1889 On Alternating Sounds. American Anthropologist 2(1):47–54.
Boroditsky, Lera, Laura Schmidt, and Webb Phillips
2003 Sex, Syntax, and Semantics. *In* Language in Mind: Advance Studies in Language and Thought. Dedre Gentner and Susan Goldin-Meadows, eds. Pp. 61–80. Cambridge, MA: MIT Press.
Bourdieu, Pierre
1977 Outline of a Theory of Practice. Richard Nice, trans. Cambridge: Cambridge University Press.
1991 Language and Symbolic Power. Cambridge, MA: Harvard University Press.
Bowerman, Melissa
1996 The Origins of Children's Spatial Semantic Categories: Cognitive versus Linguistic Determinants. *In* Rethinking Linguistic Relativity. John Gumperz and Stephen C. Levinson, eds. Cambridge: Cambridge University Press.
Bowerman, Melissa, and Soonja Choi
2001 Shaping Meanings for Language: Universal and Language-Specific in the Acquisition of Spatial Semantic Categories. *In* Language Acquisition and Conceptual Development. Melissa Bowerman and Stephen C. Levinson, eds. Pp. 475–511. Cambridge: Cambridge University Press.

2003 Space under Construction: Language-Specific Spatial Categorization in First Language Language Acquisition. *In* Language in Mind. Dedre Gentner and Susan Goldin-Meadow, eds. Pp. 387–428. Cambridge, MA: MIT Press.

Bowerman, Melissa, and Stephen Levinson, eds.
2001 Language Acquisition and Conceptual Development. Cambridge: Cambridge University Press.

Brown, Penelope
2001 Learning to Talk about Motion UP and DOWN in Tzeltal: Is There a Language Specific Bias for Verb Learning? *In* Language Acquisition and Conceptual Development. Melissa Bowerman and Stephen C. Levinson, eds. Pp. 512–543. Cambridge: Cambridge University Press.

Carey, Susan
2001 Whorf vs. Continuity Theorists: Bringing Data to Bear on the Debate. *In* Language Acquisition and Conceptual Development. Melissa Bowerman and Stephen C. Levinson, eds. Pp. 185–214. Cambridge: Cambridge University Press.

Conklin, Hal
1955 Hanunóo Color Categories. Southwestern Journal of Anthropology 11(4):339–344.

Dougherty, Janet W. D.
1975 A Universalist Analysis of Variation and Change in Color Semantics. Unpublished thesis, University of California, Berkeley.

Duranti, Allessandro
1994 From Grammar to Politics: Linguistic Anthropology in a Western Samoan Village. Berkeley: University of California Press.

Enfield, N. J., and Stephen C. Levinson
2006 Introduction: Human Sociality as a New Interdisciplinary Field. *In* Roots of Human Sociality: Culture, Cognition and Interaction. N. J. Enfield and Stephen C. Levinson, eds. Pp. 1–38. New York: Berg.

Gardner, Howard
2006 Multiple Intelligences: The Theory in Practice. New York: Basic Books.

Garro, Linda C.
1988 Language, Memory and Focality: A Re-Examination. American Anthropologist 88(1):128–136.

Gatewood, John B.
1985 Actions Speak Louder than Words. *In* Directions in Cognitive Anthropology. Janet W. Dougherty, ed. Pp. 199–220. Urbana: University of Illinois Press.

Geertz, Clifford
1973 The Interpretation of Culture. New York: Basic Books
2002 Religion as Cultural System. *In* A Reader in the Anthropology of Religion. Michael Lambek, ed. Pp. 61–82. Oxford: Blackwell.

Gentner, Dedre, and Lera Boroditsky
2001 Individuation, Relativity, and Early Word Learning. *In* Language Acquisition and Conceptual Development. Melissa Bowerman and Stephen C. Levinson, eds. Pp. 215–256. Cambridge: Cambridge University Press.

Gentner, Dedre, and Susan Goldin-Meadow, eds.
2003 Language in Mind: Advances in the Study of Language and Thought. Cambridge, MA: MIT Press.

Gilbert, Aubrey L., Terry Regier, Paul Kay, and Richard B. Ivry
2005 Whorf Hypothesis Is Supported in the Right Visual Field but Not the Left. Proceedings of the National Academy of Sciences 103:489–494.

Goodwin, Charles
2006 Human Sociality as Mutual Orientation in a Rich Interactive Environment: Multimodal Utterances and Pointing in Aphsia. *In* Roots of Human Sociality: Culture,

Cognition and Interaction. N. J. Enfield and Stephen C. Levinson, eds. Pp. 97–125. New York: Berg.

Grice, H. Paul

1957 Meaning. Philosophical Review 67:377–388.

1975 Logic and Conversation. *In* Syntax and Semantics 3: Speech Acts. P. Cole and J. Morgan, eds. Pp. 41–58. New York: Academic Press.

Gumperz, John, and Stephen Levinson, eds.

1996 Rethinking Linguistic Relativity. Cambridge: Cambridge University Press.

Habermas, Jürgen

1971 Knowledge and Human Interests. Boston, MA: Beacon.

Hallam, Elizabeth, and Tim Ingold, eds.

2007 Creativity and Cultural Improvisation. New York: Berg.

Hill, Jane, and Bruce Mannheim

1992 Language and World View. Annual Review of Anthropology 21:381–406.

Hutchins, Edwin

1995 Cognition in the Wild. Cambridge, MA: MIT Press.

Jackendoff, Ray

1992 Languages of the Mind: Essays on Mental Representation. Cambridge, MA: MIT Press.

2007 Language, Consciousness, Culture: Essays on Mental Structure. Cambridge, MA: MIT Press.

Kay, Paul, and Chad K. McDaniel

1978 The Linguistic Significance of the Meanings of Basic Color Terms. Language 54(3):610–646.

Kay, Paul, and Terry Regier

2007 Color Naming Universals: The Case of Berinmo. Cognition 102(2):289–298.

Keller, Charles M., and Janet Keller

1996a Cognition and Tool Use: The Blacksmith at Work. Cambridge: Cambridge University Press.

1996b Imaging in Iron Is Not Inner Speech. *In* Rethinking Linguistic Relativity. John Gumperz and Stephen Levinson, eds. Pp. 115–132. Cambridge: Cambridge University Press.

1999 Imagery in Cultural Tradition and Innovation. Mind, Culture, and Activity 6(1):3–32.

Keller, Janet

2009 Geographies of Memory and Identity in Oceania. *In* Intangible Heritage. Dede Fairchild Ruggles and Helaine Silverman, eds. Dordrecht: Springer.

Keller, Janet, and Takaronga Kuautonga

2007 Nokonofo Kitea: a hkai ma a tagi i Futuna, Vanuatu [We keep on living this way: Myths and Music of Futuna, Vanuatu]. Honolulu: University of Hawaii Press.

Keller, Janet Dixon, and F. K. Lehman

1991 Complex Concepts. Cognitive Science 15(2):271–292.

Lakoff, George

2008 The Political Mind: Why You Can't Understand 21st-Century American Politics with an 18th-Century Brain. New York: Viking.

Lave, Jean

1988 Cognition in Practice: Mind, Mathematics and Culture in Everyday Life. Cambridge: Cambridge University Press.

Levinson, Stephen

1996 Relativity in Spatial Conception and Description. *In* Rethinking Linguistic Relativity. John Gumperz and Stephen Levinson, eds. Pp. 177–202. Cambridge: Cambridge University Press.

2001 Covariation between Spatial Language and Cognition, and Its Implications for Language Learning. *In* Language Acquisition and Conceptual Development. Melissa

Bowerman and Stephen C. Levinson, eds. Pp. 566–588. Cambridge: Cambridge University Press.
2003a Language in Mind: Let's Get the Issues Straight. *In* Language in Mind. Dedre Gentner and Susan Goldin-Meadow, eds. Pp. 25–46. Cambridge: Cambridge University Press.
2003b Space in Language and Cognition. Cambridge: Cambridge University Press.

Levinson, Stephen, and David Wilkins, eds.
2006 Grammars of Space: Explorations in Cognitive Diversity. Cambridge: Cambridge University Press.

Lucy, John
1992a Grammatical Categories and Cognition: A Case Study of the Linguistic Relativity Hypothesis. Cambridge: Cambridge University Press.
1992b Language Diversity and Thought. Cambridge: Cambridge University Press.
2005 Semantic Accent in the Research Process. Closing address, First Midwest Conference on Culture, Language, and Cognition, Northwestern University, Evanston, IL, USA, May14.

Lucy, John, and Richard Shweder
1979 Whorf and His Critics: Linguistic and Non-Linguistic Influences on Color Memory. American Anthropologist 81:581–615.

Mandelbaum, David G., ed.
1949 Selected Writings of Edward Sapir. Berkeley: University of California Press.

Norman, Donald A.
1993 Things That Make Us Smart: Defending Human Attributes in the Age of the Machine. Reading, MA: Addison-Wesley.

Palmer, William
2002 Absolute Spatial Reference and the Grammaticalisation of Perceptually Salient Phenomena. *In* Representing Space in Oceania: Culture in Language and Mind. Giovanni Bennardo, ed. Pp. 107–157. Canberra: Pacific Linguistics.

Pinker, Steven
2007 The Stuff of Thought: Language as a Window into Human Nature. New York: Penguin.

Pratt, Mary Louise
1987 Linguistic Utopias. *In* The Linguistics of Writing: Arguments between Language and Literature. Nigel Fabb, Derek Attridge, Alan Durant, and Colin MacCabe, eds. New York: Methuen.

Sapir, Edward
1949[1929] The Status of Linguistics as a Science. *In* Selected Writings of Edward Sapir. David G. Mandelbaum, ed. Pp. 160–166. Berkeley: University of California Press.
1949[1933] Language. *In* Selected Writings of Edward Sapir. David G. Mandelbaum, ed. Pp. 7–32. Berkeley: University of California Press.

Shore, Brad
1996 Culture in Mind: Cognition, Culture, and the Problem of Meaning. New York: Oxford University Press.

Silverstein, Michael
2000 Whorfianism and the Linguistic Imagination of Nationality. *In* Regimes of Language. Paul V. Kroskrity, ed. Pp. 85–138. Santa Fe, NM: School of American Research Press.
2004 "Cultural" Concepts and the Language Culture Nexus. Current Anthropology 5(5):621–652.

Slobin, Dan
1996 From "Thought and Language" to "Thinking for Speaking." *In* Rethinking Linguistic Relativity. John Gumperz and Stephen Levinson, eds. Pp. 70–96. Cambridge: Cambridge University Press.

2003 Language and Thought Online: Cognitive Consequences of Linguistic Relativity. *In* Language in Mind: Advances in the Study of Language and Thought. Dedre Gentner and Susan Goldin-Meadow, eds. Pp. 157–192. Cambridge, MA: MIT Press.

Strauss, Claudia

1992 What Makes Tony Run: Schemas as Motives Reconsidered. *In* Human Motives and Cultural Models. Roy D'Andrade and Claudia Strauss, eds. Pp. 191–224. Cambridge: Cambridge University Press.

Strauss, Claudia, and Naomi Quinn

1997 A Cognitive Theory of Cultural Meaning. Cambridge: Cambridge University Press.

Tomasello, Michael A.

2003 The Key is Social Cognition. *In* Language in Mind: Advances in the Study of Language and Thought. Dedre Gentner and Susan Goldin-Meadow, eds. Pp. 47–57. Cambridge, MA: MIT Press.

Urciuoli, Bonnie

2008 Skills and Selves in the New Workplace. American Ethnologist 35(2):211–229.

West, Cornell

1999 The New Cultural Politics of Difference. *In* The Cornell West Reader. Pp. 119–139. New York: Basic *Civitas* Books.

Whorf, Benjamin Lee

1956[1936] The Punctual and Segmentation Aspects of Verbs in Hopi. *In* Language, Thought and Reality: Selected Writings of Benjamin Lee Whorf. John B. Carroll, ed. Pp. 51–56. Cambridge, MA: MIT Press.

1956[1941] The Relation of Habitual Thought and Behavior to Language. *In* Language, Thought and Reality: Selected Writings of Benjamin Lee Whorf. John B. Carroll, ed. Pp. 134–159. Cambridge, MA: MIT Press.

1956[1942] Language, Mind, and Reality. *In* Language, Thought and Reality: Selected Writings of Benjamin Lee Whorf. John B. Carroll, ed. Pp. 246–270. Cambridge, MA: MIT Press.

Witherspoon, Gary

1975 Language and Art in the Navajo Universe. Ann Arbor: University of Michigan Press.

CHAPTER 5

Types of Collective Representations: Cognition, Mental Architecture, and Cultural Knowledge

Giovanni Bennardo and David B. Kronenfeld

Introduction

We offer an overview of the kinds of cultural systems that cognitive anthropologists have described, analyzed, and used. We offer some analytic discussion of both what is at issue in differences between these representations and what are significant common elements among them.

In agreeing with the modularity of mind proposed by a number of authors (e.g., Chomsky 1972; Fodor 1983; Hirschfeld and Gelman 1994), we suggest that culture is rooted in mental modules and is as modular as is the mind, but in its own ways which relate to the differences between individual and collective knowledge.

About modules

We see these various cultural systems as constituting sets of systemic conceptual modules (with no claim about whether or not the modules are hard-wired in or are necessary or probable by-products of biological wiring). We use "modules" to refer to logically independent framing systems with their own sets of axioms and derived abstract forms. Obviously the final concrete behavioral "realizations" (see Trubetzkoy 1969[1939]) of implemented systems from each module involve interaction with the

A Companion to Cognitive Anthropology, First Edition. Edited by David B. Kronenfeld, Giovanni Bennardo, Victor C. de Munck, and Michael D. Fischer.

products of other modules and incidental factors. "Conceptual" refers to the notion that culture is a cognitive system – even if that system often leads to the production of material and social objects.

Some of the modules we discuss below seem clearly unitary and autonomous, while others seem to consist of more or less autonomous sub-modules. For some of them the system which the given module encompasses seems well understood (at least from one or another given theoretical perspective), while our analytic understanding of others is not so clear. For these latter cases it is, then, unclear whether the analytic problem lies with our understanding or with the phenomena in question themselves. That is, we do not yet know whether or not all modules will prove equally amenable to formal modeling, let alone to one or another form of modeling.

It seems likely that some modules directly produce realized observable behavior, while others seem to be more in the nature of meta-programs for producing more specific behavioral models. Such produced models can remain ad hoc constructs or can become more standardized modules. We are talking here of an analog of Schank and Abelson's (1977) "plan" (worked out on the fly from goals, knowledge, and situation) vs. their "script" (pre-scripted set of activities for a commonly recurrent situation), but with the proviso that, in many situations at least, the distinction between "plan" and "script" is more of a continuum than a dichotomous break. The continuum relates to the degree to which there exists a stable experiential basis which people then rely on in producing further elaborations; such a continuum can relate to differing degrees of knowledge within the relevant population. At issue also is the task to which the meta-program is addressed: producing new modular models vs. producing elaborated and/or differentiated applications of pre-existing modules.

The Mind: Its Working and Architecture

It is within the above framework that we talk about "types of cultural knowledge" (by definition "mental"). These structures may at times completely overlap with the content and structure of individual mental modules, and at times diverge from them in significant ways. It is the peculiarities of these "cultural" mental structures that we focus on. Difficult as it is to distinguish these cultural structures from the other mental ones, we think it is imperative to try to do so and in this endeavor we attempt to demonstrate how much culture contributes to the final architecture of human minds.

We are convinced that in order to talk about the role that culture plays in the mind, it is important to think about what types of fundamental computations might contribute to the functioning and development or formation (ontogeny) of the mind as well as what shape a mental architecture might take at the end of its maturation process. First, we conceive of the mind as a computational device whereby axioms generate theorems according to constraining universal logical processes, that is, a "radically intensional" approach (Keller and Lehman 1991; Bennardo 2009) – theorems which may themselves then become axioms for the generation of new theorems. Only the characteristics of the computational, or relational, spaces that make up what we call "cognition" are reiterated in each cognitive module and not the specific characteristics of the substantive content that instantiate these "abstract" relationships.

Second, we subscribe to the modularity of the mind, in other words, we believe that a number of modules are in charge of different types of knowledge, both their processing, generation, and possibly storage (Hirschfeld and Gelman 1994). Each module shares with all the others its fundamental computational nature, thus an exchange of content is always possible. The knowledge that each module produces and processes is generated uniquely, and might exist completely separate from that of any other module – or might be utilized simultaneously in cross-modular events (see Strauss and Quinn 1997:ch. 7).

Third, culture is not only located in mind as knowledge (Goodenough 1964[1957]; Shore 1996), but it contributes substantially, both phylogenetically and ontogenetically (Tomasello 1999; Boyd and Richerson 2005; Richerson and Boyd 2005), to the final form (architecture and substance or content) of the mind. Thus, while acknowledging the difficulty of the task, we are convinced that it is possible to elucidate organizations of knowledge that are specifically and intrinsically cultural against a background of other knowledge that may be considered universal, or simply and inherently mental. In so doing, we want to highlight how intertwined culture is with human cognition and consequently point out how timely and necessary our attempt is regardless of its capacity to achieve its stated general goal (see Kronenfeld 2008).

The two of us have slightly differing views of the relevant mental architecture, and our differences seem worth briefly describing, since they – taken together – encompass the major immediate research issue of how the modules go together.

Bennardo's view of mental architecture

Based on proposals for mental architecture by Levinson (2003), Jackendoff (2007), and Bennardo (2009; Chapter 26 in this volume), among others, GB has suggested that culture in mind capitalizes on Jackendoff-style architecture while at the same time it shapes the mind in its own way (Atran and Medin 2008). In Figure 26.1 in this volume, he introduces Jackendoff's proposal about the architecture of the mind that he calls "Representational Modularity"[1] (1983, 1992, 1997, 2002, 2007). Crucial to this proposal are a number of interface modules that provide a link between major modules by being structurally compatible with the two modules that they unite. This is accomplished by a structural core of the interface module made up of correspondence rules (not directly in contact with other modules to be linked), and two peripheral structures each compatible with the structure of one of the two modules linked (Jackendoff 1997, 2002). The advantage of this proposal is that it allows for major modules to be substantially different in their structures, while information can still move between them. In Figure 26.2 GB offers a version adapted to our cultural concerns.

Kronenfeld's view

DK's sense (see Kronenfeld 2008) is that the architecture of the mind – and thus of culture (and language) which lies within it – is multidimensional and includes a large number of cross-referenced hierarchies of inclusion that in turn link variously to objects in the world of experience, to social groups, to universes of presumed holders, to different conversational perspectives, and so forth. He suggests that the cultural part or set of cognitive structures differs in some basic and important ways from individual structures even though they are represented, and only represented, in individual versions of them. But he doesn't think enough is yet known to propose any precise general architecture.

This view develops out of DK's experience in writing flexible computer programs. You never wanted to write the same code twice, but instead, where a process was repeated, you made the process into a "procedure" where contextually relevant information was passed via parameter values. The cognitive insight is that we humans create potential modules whenever we experience an apparent pattern. If enough of us experience the same pattern and have reason to presume that others share the pattern and the expectation of its sharing, then a cultural module is born. Such a process would seem to result in a kind of willy-nilly architecture.

It is useful – very useful – to have proposed particular structures such as that of GB because they point us to issues and empirical hypotheses, but DK's fear is that our knowledge is still too inadequate for any general research agenda to be based too tightly on any particular hypothesized architecture.

The rest of the story

For each of these modules (however the global architecture pans out) there exist universal structures that, by interacting ontogenetically with both the mental and the cultural milieu, develop into the functioning cultural mental organization that each individual obtains. In other words, culture-specific organizations of knowledge contribute not only to the content but also to the structure of the fully matured mental modules (at least those involving any cultural content). Thus, we firmly believe that culture is clearly located in the minds of individuals and that it gets there by a triadic cross-feeding process between universal mental structures and processes, a cultural milieu, and the ongoing mental representations of this milieu.

As the cultural milieu gets represented (i.e., mentally constructed in interaction with universal and pre-existing properties of the mind) in individuals' minds, it contributes to the establishing of particular computational preferences in the various modules as well as to their specific content. For example, given a number of (pre-existing and universal) spatial axioms and combinatorial processes, frames of reference are built as a partial but substantial content of the spatial relationship module (Lehman and Bennardo 2003; Levinson 2003; Bennardo 2009). Which frames are built first and which are used more often in the matured mind of members of a cultural group is a consequence of their frequency of use and salience in the cultural milieu. A mature individual ends up with a preference for a specific frame of reference that conditions his or her performance in solving spatial cognitive tasks (Levinson 2003). Thus, a mind capable of constructing any frame of reference eventually prefers one or more over other possible ones, thus displaying a specific culturally determined content and processing modality within the Spatial Representation module.

Thus, principles of cognition, the modularity of culture, and specifics of the given culture need to be considered together in describing the "different" ways in which members of cultures think and speak about spatial relationships. A preference for a given frame of reference is a culturally established form of cognition. The various forms these preferences can take are forms of cultural organizations. It is exactly in this way that we mean to examine and highlight cultural forms of mental organizations without negating the necessity of universal aspects of cognition either regarding processes (for example reasoning) and/or content (that is, knowledge).

Types of Cultural and Mental Representations

There exist a number of ways in which types of collective representations might be broken down. An analytically useful approach is to sort these types – modules – by the larger linguistic and cultural systems in which they principally participate – here, language proper, culture, and the interface between the two. We offer such an arrangement, with characterizations of the salient features of each specific module, immediately below. But this functional understanding has only gradually emerged and thus has not been taken into account in much of the existing work in the field. It is therefore useful to characterize what have been seen as the major approaches – methodological and conceptual (often a mix of the two) – of basic work in past cognitive anthropology, and to relate those approaches to our functional arrangement.

We first offer, in "Systems of modules," a kind of typology of collective modules and their groupings and then, taking things from a different angle, a view of what we know about the nature and structure of cultural representations – both in general and for some specific domains.

Systems of modules

Our typology is organized around the collective systems that each belongs to: (1) language proper, (2) the language–culture interface, and (3) culture. Given our focal concern with culture in this chapter, we list but otherwise ignore the major components of language proper. The interface has to do with the ways in which language is used to communicate about the stuff of our lives, including what concepts words refer to, what other concepts are entailed or precluded by the use of a given word, what connotations and situations are evoked by a word's use in some context, and so forth. Culture is that collective system of knowledge, belief, action, values, interactive patterns, and so forth which anthropologists have always understood it to be, but taken from the point of view of the shared mental constructs which underlie and enable it.

Each of the modules and examples represents some interaction of universal mental or experiential givens with more culturally specific adaptations. Where it is useful, and where we have some insights to offer, we will address the specific mix for the given module.

The stuff of language proper: syntax (morphology), phonology, lexicon; the language–culture interface

(1) Semantic systems (SS). These include the "sense" relations of contrast and inclusion by which words (i.e., morphemes, terms, lexemes, or "segregates") relate to words and, as relevant, the distinctive features along which these are organized. They

include also reference, the relations of words to things in the world (including hypothetical posited things and abstract conceptual things); distinctive features can be used to recognize (i.e., define) referents of terms and/or to delineate important aspects of referents. Semantic systems do not directly include, nor do they represent, the processes or understandings by which sets of referents are organized in the physical or biological world or are organized, understood, and sometimes defined in the cultural world of our understood experience. The "directly" hedge is by way of recognizing that semantic attributes are likely to relate to – but not imitate or "mirror" – the physical and cultural attributes which produce and structure our understandings of systems of natural or cultural phenomena.

The above characterization seems universal. What varies are the specifics of the local natural, cultural, and historical context within which and often about which conversations take place.

(2) Language-based modes of reasoning seem also to belong here, though our cross-language, cross-cultural understanding of them is much weaker than our understanding of semantic systems. Here we have in mind the kinds of reasoning issues discussed in Hutchins 1980:46–61. Included are kinds of logical operations and the terms that pertain to other kinds of reasoning and inference. It is possible that this module might relate in some direct manner to "cultural modes of thought" below, but we are still unsure.

Cultural models In this section we describe nine kinds of cultural models, with particular attention to the first three. See Kronenfeld 2008:162–163 for an overview of cultural knowledge systems including cultural models.

(1) Cultural modes of thought (CMT), what Bennardo (2009) speaks of as "foundational cultural models," represent culturally specific presuppositions about how stuff is organized. They can provide the basis for Schank and Abelson (1977) type "plans." Particular exemplification can be seen in Bennardo's discussions of the role of "radiality" in Tongan organization of a wide variety of specific domains, ranging from spatial reference through physical maps, social event structure, kin group organization, to kinterm structure (Bennardo 2009). A simple, but notable, precursor can be seen in Bateson's portrayal of Iatmul *eidos* in *Naven* (1958[1938]:218–256).[2] It is this sort of module that we had in mind when we spoke of "meta-program" modules above. We presume that all cultures have such modules. The degree to which, in general, a culture's ecological or social context shapes such modules is unclear.

This kind of module provides a kind of default conceptual or organizational structure and point of view for situations in which members of a culture confront some situation for which they do not already have culturally standardized means for handling. The idea is that members of the culture in question have some sort of general idea of what a plan should look like along with some generic templates for forming plans. They infer or learn these templates through their experience of the more direct structures that characterize existent specific cultural organizations of phenomena. Thus these meta-structures represent abstract uniformities that run across some range of salient (and relevant) specific structures. As such they reflect something like Bateson's (1972:159–176) idea of "deutero-learning."

(2) Cultural conceptual systems (CCS) provide a kind of reference library of how sets of concepts go together logically and culturally, and thus of how the things that words refer to are organized in the real or putatively real world. They necessarily involve assertions about the world (outside of language). They can involve functional relations and functional knowledge (how tables go with chairs), or cultural constructs (how a high school relates to football), or logical relations (how a "father" relates to a "brother"). Such systems can include sequential knowledge (as the progression through primary and secondary school), parts and wholes (what are the rooms in a house), and so forth. Some of these systems can be logically precise (as kinterm systems), while others can be looser and more incidental (as the relationship of high school to sports); they can be literal (as a map of Los Angeles) or conceptual (one's map of anthropology). But they do not involve any direct implementation of the knowledge. They are, thus, classifications of one sort or another that we draw on for thought and action but which do not themselves model action.

We again presume that all cultures have such systems, but that the content will be dependent on the specifics of the experience and interests of members of the culture. The mechanisms by which these seem to be learned could be, in general, to track common foci of experience. Where such experiential foci are common across some cross-cultural universe we would expect relevant aspects of the resultant systems (whether specifics of content or of structural shape) to be shared – up to the point of being universal.

Within this general class we have some types of structures – or distinctions between structures. One important distinction is between labeled (and hence explicit) and non-labeled (more or less implicit) ones. For instance, the rules of sandlot pick-up soccer games are there, but are simpler and looser than those of organized institutionalized soccer. Another important distinction is that between general, sociocentric categories ("Los Angeles," "schoolteacher") and someone's personal, egocentric ones ("Joe's hometown," "my favorite dessert," "your job"); the former are unary while the latter are binary and always require a reference point – and in this sense are like deictics ("here" vs. "there," "my" vs. "your"). Social groups can be either unary ("the Smith Family") or binary ("my family"). Similarly, social roles can be either ("John is a schoolteacher" vs. "Bill is my teacher"). Some roles, though, are intrinsically binary: as a "friend" always has to be someone's friend; especially salient here are kinterms.

Thus, this kind of module will contain a great many particular systems, and variations of the included systems will interact with one another in a great variety of ways. In many cases the systems will cross-reference each other while still only being loosely related (as in some places "Grade 9" of a grade progression, in a "kind of school" progression, sometimes falls into "high school" while in others into "middle school" or "junior high school"; family TV watching [with its attendant paraphernalia] can go in a "living room" or a "den" or a "family room"). One important aspect of culture is represented by these systems, with their cross-cutting interrelations.

(3) Cultural models of action (CMA) represent game plans or scenarios for doing things (see Kronenfeld 2008:164–188). They relate goals, values, knowledge, available resources (material, social, conceptual, etc.), context, and so forth to action (e.g., running a ranch, building a house, writing a paper, asking a relative for help, etc.). They involve recognition of relevant scenes (e.g., static "snapshots" of healthy vs.

unhealthy range land, shape and make-up of intended house lot, state of the art and state of writer's knowledge, personality and resources of different relatives, etc.). At their most detailed they can be something akin to Schank and Abelson's (1977) scripts, but, more generally, they range along a hierarchy of specificity from script-like detail for specific familiar situations to more plan-like bases of deduction for thinly known or generic situations. They are productive generative action plans that can vary in subtle (or gross) ways across various kinds of subcultural variation. Thus they seem likely to exist as a hierarchy of defaults, where specific instantiations need only specify aspects that differ from the relevant default (this approach is one presciently suggested and illustrated by Robert Randall in his Berkeley Ph.D. dissertation – Randall 1977). The shape and nature of these seem likely to be universal, while the content seems very dependent on the specifics of varyingly shared cultural experience. They can be included within one another ("nested"), can be grouped into sets of similar alternatives, can be opposed to one another (versus, on the one hand, included in one another, or, on the other hand, be simply irrelevant to each other – "ships passing in the night"). And they often reference or evoke other CMAs as well as CCSs.

CMAs are generic – existing for default versions of abstracted situations.[3] When one is applied to a specific situation ("instantiated"), the generic values of its internal variables are replaced by the variables appropriated to that specific situation. This instantiated version is still a mental abstraction – which may or may not be "realized" (see Trubetzkoy 1969[1939]:36) in actual behavior. It is possible for either an actor or an observer to consider instantiated versions of several alternative CMAs (e.g., on a "date," when the possibility of physical action arises, CMAs involving "true love" or "sexual exploitation" or "just following the rules"). At any given moment only one CMA will be seen by a given person as actually realized in the actual behavior of the dating couple, but, in the manner of our perception of optical illusions, different individuals may see different CMAs as being realized in the same given actions, and a given individual may himself or herself flip back and forth between alternatives (e.g., is it "love" or is it "lust"?).

CMAs do not force action but, instead, offer both actors and interpreters or observers storylines in terms of which a given situation may be structured. For an actor, the CMA can provide a basic game plan which she or he can then adapt to the relevant idiosyncrasies of the situation or of her or his aims. Similarly, for an interpreting recipient of actions from another, or for an interpreting observer, CMAs provide the culture's basic repertoire of reasons for doing the observed behavior and of where different interpretations might lead. Actors are not forced to use CMAs unchanged, or to use them at all(!), but the pressure to use them comes from (a) the advantages of having a more or less off the shelf plan available vs. having to create one from scratch, and (b) the desire for one's actions to be meaningful to others in one's desired ways. Similar advantages accrue to recipients (of behavioral gambits) and observers.

The complexity of CMAs lies in the variety and complexity of concerns and knowledge they pull together rather than in the kind of logical or systemic complexity that can characterize some kinds of CCSs. CCSs organize the interrelationships between a set of parallel or similar concepts (Saussure's paradigmatic relations), isolated from all of the exigencies that affect the application of the concepts to concrete, specific situations, while CMAs organize such applications and thus juxtapose concepts drawn from a variety of conceptual sets (Saussure's syntagmatic relations).

The difference can be seen in Dougherty and Keller's pathbreaking 1982 article, "Taskonomy" which looks at the functional organization of tools and spaces in a smithy as compared with the ways in which the tools are organized taxonomically.

(4) Proxemic systems (see Edward Hall 1959, 1966, and others) that structure our interpersonal, loudness and intensity, spacing, and orientation in various kinds of social situations. Hall's treatment considers uniformities and differences across cultures.

(5) Characteristic modes of expression (again, see Bateson 1958[1938]), and issues of interaction management such as those addressed by Goffman (e.g., 1959, 1974) represent another kind (or set of kinds) of cultural knowledge. This clump might also include the kind of sociolinguistic-cum-interactional structures described for Samoa public events by Duranti (1981, 1994) and others.

(6) Perhaps, also, we might want to consider something analogous to Bateson's "ethos" – culturally characteristic modes of emotional response.

(7) And anthropologists might want to consider systems of active, acted out, values (vs. a classification of named values such as one might get in a semantic structure or a cultural conceptual system). A question arises whether these "values in practice" are best treated as separate structures from the structures of overt named values or whether they are best treated as contextual instantiations of the overt named values (see D'Andrade 2008).

(8) Something like culturally characteristic types of organizational structures might also be considered. The question then is whether these are best seen as detailed versions of the kinds of more underlying cultural modes of thought (discussed above) or whether, analogous to (7) above, they might best be seen as a different class of shared cognitive structure.

And there may well exist others. One important task for cognitive anthropology in the near future seems to be the clarification of this list – both what should be on it and how one might best characterize the separate entries.

What we already know about cultural or mental representations

The specific distributed (varyingly shared) cognitive structures previously studied by cognitive anthropologists fall into various of the above types of systems.

Systems of contrast Systems of contrast are mostly semantic classifications, but also involve significant pragmatic knowledge. The basic units of semantic classification seem to be contrast and inclusion. A binary opposition of X vs. Y is the simplest kind of opposition. Making the contrast a multinary such as the basic color set (in one English version: red, orange, yellow, green, blue, purple) is a simple way of expanding the number of included concepts; adding dimensions of contrast (such as classifying lines by color and length) to produce a *paradigm* further expands the number of concepts. But there exists an upper limit on the number of dimensions people can handle, and a decreasing limit on the number of contrasts per dimension as the number of dimensions rises; additionally, such expansion involves heavy learning effort (not necessarily explicit or explicitly recognized). Another way of expanding the number of concepts is by hierarchically including the members of a given contrast set in a superordinate category, and then contrasting that category with other categories. This is the kind of contrast that underlies taxonomic systems. These considerations are treated at more length in Kronenfeld (1996:114–143) where they are related, on the one hand, to general psychological capabilities and constraints and, on the other, to more or less universal attributes of classificatory systems across languages and cultures.

Significant work on *taxonomic* structures include that of Berlin (see Berlin 1992), and Hunn (1976, 1985). Randall (1976) represents a kind of caveat. Attempts to extend and develop Berlin's findings include Cecil Brown (1977, 1979) and Atran (1985, 1990). The work of Berlin and others strongly suggests that all cultures have such structures with great similarity in content and ordering, though with some significant variability regarding their breadth and depth, and with significant variation in some kinds of specific details. Taxonomic structures relate in interesting ways to paradigmatic ones. *Paradigms* (Goodenough 1956; Lounsbury 1956, 1969[1964]; Wallace and Atkins 1962; Romney and D'Andrade 1964) are systems of classification developed as a way of analyzing kinship terminologies (based on insights from phonological analysis). The initial expectation was that the approach would generalize to a kind of broad semantic "space," but developed paradigmatic structures in semantics seem mostly limited to kinterms and pronouns. On the other hand, D'Andrade's applications of the approach to psychologists' analysis of small group behavioral dynamics (1965, 1974) raise the possibility of much greater usefulness. D'Andrade showed that intersecting semantic components were sufficient to predict the judges' ratings of group participants on a behavioral scale – given one actual observation needed to orient the semantic components. That is, a componential analysis composed of intersecting semantic contrasts accounted for how group participants were judged to differ from one another in a supposedly behavioral study.

The reason for the relative rarity of developed paradigmatic or taxonomic structures in human cultures would seem to be a combination of the preponderance of simple binary or trinary contrasts in most of what we talk about and of the ragged incompleteness of most potentially more elaborate structures (such as, for example, car models, price, manufacturer, etc.) whose incompleteness seems to derive from our reliance on patterns of conversational experience in learning concepts and relations between them (see the above Kronenfeld citations for a fuller explanation). The D'Andrade example, just above, suggests that, while few semantic domains are large enough or complex enough to evoke componential structures, other kinds of conceptual structures may have relevant properties – implying a wider relevance for the approach than has recently been acknowledged.

Kinship structures The semantic and pragmatic structures of terminologies in particular, as well as types of groups and types of obligations – vs. the general nexus of behaviors and expectations and motivations that tie it all together – make up the semantic structures of kinship. Thus, the study of kin terminologies has a long history – too long to treat here (see Kronenfeld 2001 for an account, and Kronenfeld 2009 for the application of a wide range of analytic perspectives and questions to a single system, and see Chapters 13 and 14 in this volume by Read and Chit Hlaing respectively). Central aspects of kinship terminologies are universal, while there exists a significant but limited range of variation between systems. This mix of universality and variation has provided one of the tantalizing aspects of kinship terminologies. An important debate has concerned the degree to which kinship terminologies are to be seen as primarily based on some kind of universal genealogical substrate vs. a system of relations between cultural concepts (where something about parents and children explains the universality). That is, while there is something close to a consensus that kinship terminologies are to be seen as conceptual structures (and thus useful to cognitive anthropology), there have existed a number of competing approaches to how to study, represent, and understand kin terminological structures. Since the genealogical substrate can be reduced to conceptual versions of "mother," "father," and their reciprocals, and since it is increasingly recognized within the cultural concept approach that the key universal concepts that make these systems "kinship" systems are based on "mother" and "father" (and what follows from these), the difference between the two approaches would seem to be narrowing. Sometimes buried in the above disputes has been an opposition between a semantic components approach ("componential" – where "uncle" is a first generation, co-lineal, male) and a relative product approach (where "uncle" is a "father's brother" or a "mother's brother"). The latter – obviously – captures how native speakers do their actual assignment of people to kinterm categories. But the former turns out to be very important for understanding how people think with kinterms (such as, why is a parish priest "father" and not "brother" or "uncle," why are members of the feminist movement "sisters" to one another, and so forth).

Kinship terminologies have provided an important arena for exploring the relationship between semantic and pragmatic knowledge (see, for example, Kronenfeld (1996:147–150, 233; 2008:27; 2009), for relating analytic insights to native-speaker definitions and calculations (see, for example, Read 1984, 2001; Keen 1985), for considering the relationship of terminologies to wider social organization (see Kronenfeld 2009:15–29, 181–202, 205–235, 255–277, 301–318), to behavior (see Kronenfeld 2009:15–29, 71–105, 181–202), and to general conceptual models (see Bennardo and Read 2007). The domain is one whose combination of precision and complication has provoked significant algebraic representations (see, most recently, Gould 2000; Lehman 2001; Read 2001).

Space and frames of reference As already presented above, frames of reference constitute an essential part of the spatial representation module (see Levinson 2003; Bennardo 2004; Jackendoff 2007). However, out of the three possible frames of reference (intrinsic, relative, absolute, and their sub-types) proposed by Levinson (2003), there are some cultures whose members prefer one over the other two and so habitually use that preferred one both in their performance in spatial tasks and in their everyday cognition about spatial relationships (for ample demonstrations across a variety of cultures see Senft 1997; Bennardo 2002; Levinson 2003; Levinson and Wilkins 2006). In other words, a universal cognizing about space is constrained by cultural learning into a more limited activity. This well-understood phenomenon constitutes major supporting evidence toward our proposal of a cultural mind – that is, of a shared and distributed cultural conceptual system that helps to shape the individual concepts and conceptual operations of members of the cultural community.

Emotions Potentially universal emotional states (i.e., emotions) have been proposed (Ekman 1972) like fear, anger, hate, disgust, happiness, sadness, anxiety, loneliness, boredom, anguish, shame, envy. At the same time, the way in which emotions are defined and classified is culturally specific. This compromise between universalists and relativists is the only way in which cross-cultural research on emotions is made possible (see Boster 2005). The salient role played by methodology in the cross-cultural investigation of emotions is usefully highlighted by Boster (2005). He points out the shortcomings of the "translation" method (comparing cross-linguistic sets of emotion terms) and the advantages inherent in the adoption of the "mapping" method (exposing individuals from different languages or cultures to the same set of emotionally evocative stimuli).

This latter method allows him to identify fundamentally different way of conceptualizing emotions between a number of cultures. A group (i.e., Spanish, Polish, Italian) focused on the expression of the abstract emotions associated with the stimuli (a number of faces intended to refer to different emotional states), while another (e.g., Shuar or Jivaro, Waorani of eastern Ecuador) focused on the unrepresented context(s) that yielded those emotions. Then, in the cross-cultural and cross-linguistic research about emotions we see again how the universal mind is "made" into a cultural mind. Relevant to the present volume are both the conceptual machinery with which we endeavor to understand culturally standardized emotional categories and states and the cognitive role that many in this volume have seen emotional states as playing (see, e.g., "hot" vs. "cool" cognition).

Reasoning Hutchins (1980), in a classic study of Trobriand reasoning in a moot court farm litigation case, formally models the logical structure of folk reasoning (in Trobriand), including logical deduction, and evaluations of empirical reasonableness. The work is based on careful semantic analysis of several areas of Trobriand terminology (including logical terms, categories of land or farm rights, kinds of "gifts," and so forth). The reasoning formalism is applied to the transcript of an actual litigation event, and formally relates the structure of the litigants' and witness's presentations, the presuppositions made about the limits of the knowledge of each, and the cultural significant of observed acts to the decision reached by the panel of elders who were trying the case.

Interesting is Hutchins's finding that the Trobriand language (and Trobriand usage) codes entail the same logic that has developed in our world. Given the general role of logic, this finding cannot be surprising, but in the face of some anthropological assertions about the cultural specificity of Western logic, his findings are reassuring.

General Attributes of All "Cultural Models"

In this section we offer a brief overview of the conditions that should apply to all cultural concepts (i.e., collective representations). What is a cultural cognitive structure – or "cultural model" in the general sense (vs. the included, and more specific, sense of a "cultural model of action" – or a "cultural conceptual system," etc.)?

First and fundamentally, such a structure is a mental model. A mental model consists of bits of knowledge organized in such a way as to facilitate storage, retrieval, and use of that same knowledge (Craik 1943; Gentner and Stevens 1983; Johnson-Laird

1983). A comparatively similar mental organization of knowledge is also called frame, or script, or schema (Bateson 1972; Minsky 1975; Schank and Abelson 1977; Rumelhart 1980; Fillmore 1982; Brewer and Nakamura 1984; Brewer 1987, 1999; Keller 1992). In Johnson-Laird's words, "A crucial feature [of mental models] is that their structure corresponds to the structure of what they represent" (1999:525). The investigation of mental models, then, is enhanced by a thorough understanding of the context (physical and human, i.e., cultural) in which they are acquired and realized.

Second, a mental model becomes a cultural model when it "is intersubjectively shared by a social group" (D'Andrade 1989:809). That is, a cultural model entails that the knowledge that it organizes is shared between members of a community (Holland and Quinn 1987; Kronenfeld 1996, 2008; Shore 1996; Strauss and Quinn 1997; Quinn 2005). Third, a cultural model is used in reasoning, in planning actions, and it may contribute to the motivation of action as well (D'Andrade and Strauss 1992; Holland 1992). In other words, cultural models construct the mental context, that is, culture in mind, within which and out of which behavior will be generated. Thus, we add that these models are not simply frozen pictures or incidental bits of knowledge, but form productive generative systems.

Cultural models are constructed by each individual while accumulating life's experiences. These individually constructed models are cultural because they are very similar and highly shared. In whatever community they grow and develop, individuals share a human mind and a similar context of experience. For a fuller discussion of cultural models, including levels of modality, degrees of complexity, image schema, and thematic effects see Bennardo (Chapter 26 in this volume).

We label our own conceptual synthesis of the basic underlying cultural cognitive entity (compare Bateson's idea of *eidos*) either a "cultural mode of thought" (Kronenfeld) or a "foundational cultural model" (Bennardo); both locutions speak to the role of this particular kind of model. It is a basic and simple structure, that is, an assemblage of knowledge that can generate other more complex models when used to merge a larger number of units of knowledge. Bennardo (2009) located one of these potential models in the spatial representation module of Tongans. They prefer to organize mentally spatial relationships by using a specific frame of reference, the radial sub-type of the absolute frame of reference. Besides, he found this preference replicated in a variety of other modules and domains. Then, he called this phenomenon a foundational cultural model and labeled it "radiality" (see Chapter 26, this volume).

Radiality is a mental model that is specifically spatial, and since it is shared within a community, that is, Tongans, it is also cultural. Moreover, since it is repeated in other mental modules and domains therein, it becomes a foundational cultural model. Bennardo (2009) conceives of radiality as a fundamental cognitive process that is used to organize knowledge across mental modules. Its intrinsic nature is spatial and as such it belongs to the spatial representations module. Tongans, though, preferably adopt or use radiality in other domains of knowledge – exchanges, political action, social networks, religion, kinship, and social relationships – in other modules, including the action module, the social cognition module, and the conceptual structure module. The existence of radiality does not exclude the presence of other foundational cultural models. On the contrary, it suggests the way in which other foundational cultural models could be potentially present and shared in the mind. It suggests that we should look carefully at other ontological domains and see how they are organized.

It hopefully points the way to a potentially large number of possible discoveries for the overarching cross-modular and cross-domain organizations of cultural minds.

How are these structures created, transmitted (learned), and adapted (changed)? In general, cultural cognitive structures are learned without being explicitly taught. They are learned through the experience that neophytes have of their various realizations; the underlying principles or structure are sometimes highlighted in feedback interactions with "old hands," but mostly such structure is inferred from experienced instances, but not logically induced – the learner's sample of experiences is far too spotty and incomplete for that. Such inferring without inducing implies that we are predisposed to leap to trial hypotheses, and then use feedback to make new (generally, smaller) leaps as we home in on the shared structure.

What is inferred depends a lot on the (relevant) nature and distribution of the instances experienced. A significant shift in the distribution will lead to different inferences – mistakes in terms of any precise replication of the "old hands" (e.g., parents') structure. But, since we do not directly represent our inferences as direct memories, but, instead, use these inferences as the bases for construction of productive systems for generating a range of instances, our resulting learning "mistakes" do not lead to any loss of systematicity, but instead to a changed systematicity. At the same time, the exigencies of communication and interaction keep the various systems (that different ones of us within a given community infer) from diverging too far from one another. Social functioning requires effective communication and interaction, and thus represents a major constraint on how much divergence there can be in transmission before feedback from others contains or limits it. This is one major way in which linguistic drift takes place, and also a mechanism to keep our linguistic resources adapted to our communicative needs.

We note too that cultures are not monolithic, and hence much of what we have said about intercultural variation applies as well to subcultural variation.

A Few Examples of Current Work on Cultural Knowledge

Recently, following the seminal work on cultural models in Holland and Quinn (1987), D'Andrade and Strauss (1992), Kempton et al. (1995), and Strauss and Quinn (1997), a good number of new research findings have been published. In these publications, a variety of cultural models in several cultures around the world, including the USA, are presented. In a volume edited by Quinn (2005), many authors discuss their experiences in discovering cultural models and report on the usefulness of a multiplicity of methods used. For example, Mathews (2005) presents three methodological approaches to the analysis of a Mexican folktale, the story of "La Llorona," used during the long and painstaking process to discover a cultural model for gender.

De Munck et al. (2002) introduce us to different cultural models of gender in a comparison between the USA and Sri Lanka. Lately, de Munck (2008; Chapter 27 in this volume) has added an insightful description of models of love and love relationships in Lithuania. Shimizu (2007; Chapter 23 in this volume) compares American and Japanese construction of one's identity and highlights the sociocentric nature of the cultural model that underlies the latter. He interestingly demonstrates how pervasive this cultural model is in both informal (home) and formal (institutions) educational settings.

Atran and Medin elicited "mental models of ecological relationships among animals, plants, and humans to the realm of spirits" (2008:269) among the Itza' Maya in Guatemala. They also presented a mental model of how the Menominee (a Native American population residing in Wisconsin, USA) "conceive of relations between humans and animal species in reciprocal terms" and how this model affects their decision-making about ecologically related issues.

Gatewood and Lowe (2008) have recently published an investigation into the way in which people who work in credit unions in the United States conceive of the institution they contribute to sustain. The cultural model evinced is articulated and differs fundamentally depending on whether you are a teller or a high-level executive. Similarly, in Kronenfeld and Hedrick (2005), the cultural model of ranching in the American West differs according to the group considered, either ranchers, ecologists, or the general public.

Other examples are offered in Bennardo (2009; Chapter 26, this volume) and Kronenfeld (2008). This clearly non-exhaustive list of contemporary work on cultural models does not do full justice to the effervescence that has characterized this field in the last decade (and before). Nonetheless, and minimally, it has become clear to all of us that the journey into the cultural mind has only just started. Unforeseen vistas are still there to be discovered and they will eventually leave all of us in awe of the unmistakable beauty that lies within the human mind.

Closing Remarks

We have offered an overview of what we see as the major thrusts and topics of anthropological studies of types of collective representation – cultural models. Any such overview is necessarily selective, bound not just by the vision and preferences of the authors but also, here, by the fact that our target is a moving – and still emerging – one. That is, the field is still much defined by the accidents of what one or another scholar has chosen to look at, and we do not yet have a rich enough array of examples or theoretical angles of attack (with their successes or failures) to produce something more abstract and principled. Future studies still hold out the possibility of radically changing today's tentative understandings; and this is the best reason we can imagine for encouraging both studies of new topics and new kinds of studies of old topics by scholars with differing interests, academic backgrounds, and methodological kit bags. At the same time, to have the impact we look toward, such new studies will increasingly have to be systematically related to the theory, definitions, findings, and constraints of the by now substantial body of work on which our overview rests.

NOTES

1 Foundational to this proposal, but not homologous, are Chomsky's (1972) and Fodor's (1983) modularity suggestions (see also Hirschfeld et al. 1994).

2 *Eidos*: "*a standardization of the cognitive aspects of the personality of the individuals.* Such a standardization and its expression in cultural behaviour I shall refer to as the *eidos* of a culture" (Bateson 1958[1938]:220).

3 CMAs are generic because of the concreteness of their actual use ("Do this, this way, here"), and thus need to have their applications tuned to the specifics of an actual application. CSSs, on the other hand, by representing abstract knowledge, can be very specific and precise in their actual form.

REFERENCES

Atran, S.
1985 The Nature of Folkbotanical Life-Forms. American Anthropologist 87:298–315.
1990 Cognitive Foundations of Natural History: Towards an Anthropology of Science. Cambridge: Cambridge University Press.
Atran, S., and D. Medin
2008 The Native Mind and the Cultural Construction of Nature. Cambridge, MA: MIT Press.
Bateson, Gregory
1958[1938] Naven. Palo Alto, CA: Stanford University Press.
1972 Steps to an Ecology of Mind. New York: Ballantine.
Bennardo, G.
2004 Linguistic Untranslatability vs. Conceptual Nesting of Frames of Reference. *In* Proceedings of the 26th Annual Conference of the Cognitive Science Society. Kenneth Forbus, Dedre Gentner, and Terry Regier, eds. Pp. 102–107. New York: Lawrence Erlbaum.
2009 Language, Space, and Social Relationships: A Foundational Cultural Model in Polynesia. Cambridge: Cambridge University Press.
Bennardo, G., ed.
2002 Representing Space in Oceania: Culture in Language and Mind. Canberra: Pacific Linguistics, Research School of Pacific and Asian Studies, Australian National University.
Bennardo, G., and Dwight Read
2007 Cognition, Algebra, and Culture in the Tongan Kinship Terminology. Journal of Cognition and Culture 7(2):49–88.
Berlin, O. Brent
1992 Ethnobiological Classification. Princeton: Princeton University Press.
Boster, J. S.
2005 Emotion Categories across Languages. *In* Handbook of Categorization in Cognitive Science. H. Cohen and C. Lefebvre, eds. Pp.187–222). Amsterdam: Elsevier.
Boyd, R., and P. Richerson
2005 Not by Genes Alone: How Culture Transformed Human Evolution. Chicago: University of Chicago Press.
Brewer, William F.
1987 Schemas Versus Mental Models in Human Memory. *In* Modelling Cognition. P. Morris, ed. Pp. 187–197. Chichester: John Wiley.
1999 Scientific Theories and Naive Theories as Forms of Mental Representation: Psychologism Revived. Science and Education 8:489–505.
Brewer, William F., and G. V. Nakamura
1984 The Nature and Functions of Schemas. *In* Handbook of Social Cognition, vol. 1. R. S. Wyer and T. K. Srull, eds. Pp. 119–160. Hillsdale, NJ: Lawrence Erlbaum.
Brown, Cecil
1977 Folk Botanical Life-Forms: Their Universality and Growth. American Anthropologist 79:317–334.
1979 Growth and Development of Folk Botanical Life Forms in the Mayan Language Family. American Ethnologist 6:366–385.

Chomsky, N.
1972 Language and Mind. New York: Harcourt Brace Jovanovich.
Craik, K. J. W.
1943 The Nature of Explanation. Cambridge: Cambridge University Press.
D'Andrade, Roy G.
1965 Trait Psychology and Componential Analysis. American Anthropologist 67(5.2): 215–228.
1974 Memory and the Assessment of Behavior. *In* Measurement in the Social Sciences. T. Blalock, ed. Chicago: Aldine-Atherton.
1989 Cultural Cognition. *In* Foundations of Cognitive Science. M. I. Posner, ed. Pp. 795–830. Cambridge, MA: MIT Press.
2008 A Study of Personal and Cultural Values: American, Japanese, and Vietnamese. New York: Palgrave Macmillan.
D'Andrade, Roy, and Claudia Strauss
1992 Human Motives and Cultural Models. Cambridge: Cambridge University Press.
de Munck, Victor
2008 Self, Other and the Love Dyad in Lithuania: Romantic Love as Fantasy and Reality (or, When Culture Matters and Doesn't Matter). *In* Intimacy. W. Jankowiak, ed. Pp. 65–95. New York: Columbia University Press.
de Munck, Victor, Nicole Dudley, and Joseph Cardinale
2002 Cultural Models of Gender in Sri Lanka and the United States. Ethnology 41(3): 225–261.
Dougherty, Janet W. D., and Charles M. Keller
1982 Taskonomy: A Practical Approach to Knowledge Structures. American Ethnologist 9:763–774.
Duranti, Alessandro
1981 The Samoan *fono*: A Sociolinguistic Study. Pacific Linguistics Monographs, series B, vol. 80. Canberra: Department of Linguistics, Australian National University.
1994 From Grammar to Politics: Linguistic Anthropology in a Western Samoa Village. Los Angeles: University of California Press.
Ekman, P.
1972 Universals and Cultural Differences in Facial Expressions of Emotions. *In* Nebraska Symposium on Motivation. J. Cole, ed. Pp. 207–283. Lincoln: University of Nebraska Press.
Fillmore, Charles J.
1982 Frame Semantics. *In* Linguistics in the Morning Calm. Pp. 111–137. Seoul: Hanshin.
Fodor, J.
1983 Modularity of Mind. Cambridge, MA: MIT Press.
Gatewood, John B., and John W. Lowe
2008 Employee Perceptions of Credit Unions: Implications for Member Profitability. Madison, WI: Filene Research Institute.
Gentner, D., and A. L. Stevens, eds.
1983 Mental Models. Hillsdale, NJ: Lawrence Erlbaum.
Goffman, Erving
1959 The Presentation of Self in Everyday Life. Garden City, NY: Doubleday.
1974 Frame Analysis: An Essay on the Organization of Experience. New York: Harper & Row.
Goodenough, W.
1956 Componential Analysis and the Study of Meaning. Language 32: 195–216.
1964[1957] Cultural Anthropology and Linguistics. *In* Language in Culture and Society: A Reader in Linguistic Anthropology. Dell Hymes, ed. Pp. 36–39. New York: Harper & Row.
Gould, Sydney H.
2000 A New System for the Formal Analysis of Kinship. David B. Kronenfeld, ed., annot., intro. Lanham, MD: University Press of America.

Hall, Edward
1959 The Silent Language. New York: Doubleday and Co., Inc.
1966 The Hidden Dimension. Anchor Books ed. Garden City, NY: Anchor Books.
Hirschfeld, Lawrence A., and Susan A. Gelman, eds.
1994 Mapping the Mind: Domain Specificity in Cognition and Culture. Cambridge: Cambridge University Press.
Holland, Dorothy
1992 The Woman Who Climbed Up the House: Some Limitations of Schema Theory. *In* New Directions in Psychological Anthropology. T. Schwartz, G. White, and C. Lutz, eds. Pp. 68–79. Cambridge: Cambridge University Press.
Holland, Dorothy, and Naomi Quinn
1987 Cultural Models in Language and Thought. Cambridge: Cambridge University Press.
Hunn, Eugene
1976 Toward a Perceptual Model of Folk Biological Classification. American Ethnologist 3:508–524.
1985 The Utilitarian Factor in Folk Biological Classification. *In* Directions in Cognitive Anthropology. Janet W. D. Dougherty, ed. Pp. 117–140. Urbana: University of Illinois Press.
Hutchins, Edwin
1980 Culture and Inference: A Trobriand Case Study. Cambridge, MA: Harvard University Press.
Jackendoff, R.
1983 Semantics and Cognition. Cambridge, MA: MIT Press.
1992 Language of the Mind: Essays on Mental Representation. Cambridge, MA: MIT Press.
1997 The Architecture of the Language Faculty. Cambridge, MA: MIT Press.
2002 Foundations of Language: Brain, Meaning, Grammar, and Evolution. Oxford: Oxford University Press.
2007 Language, Consciousness, Culture: Essays on Mental Structure. Cambridge, MA: MIT Press.
Johnson-Laird, Philip N.
1983 Mental Models: Towards a Cognitive Science of Language, Inference, and Consciousness. Cambridge, MA: Harvard University Press.
1999 Mental Models. *In* Encyclopedia of the Cognitive Sciences. R. A. Wilson and F. C. Keil, eds. Pp. 525–527. Cambridge, MA: MIT Press.
Keen, Ian
1985 Definitions of Kin. Journal of Anthropological Research 41:62–90.
Keller, J. D.
1992 Schemas for Schemata. *In* New Directions in Psychological Anthropology. Theodore Schwartz, G. M. White, and Catherine A. Lutz, eds. Pp. 59–67. Cambridge: Cambridge University Press.
Keller, J. D., and Lehman, F. K.
1991 Complex Concepts. Cognitive Science 15(2): 271–292.
Kempton, Willett, James S. Boster, and Jennifer A. Hartley
1995 Environmental Values in American Culture. Cambridge, MA: MIT Press.
Kronenfeld, D.
1996 Plastic Glasses and Church Fathers. New York: Oxford University Press.
2008 Culture, Society, and Cognition: Collective Goals, Values, Action, and Knowledge. Berlin: Mouton de Gruyter.
2009 Fanti Kinship and the Analysis of Kinship Terminologies. Urbana: University of Illinois Press.
Kronenfeld, David, and Kimberly Hedrick
2005 Culture, Cultural Models, and the Division of Labor. Cybernetics and Systems: An International Journal 36:817–845.

Lehman, F. K. (F. K. L. Chit Hlaing)
2001 Aspects of a Formalist Theory of Kinship: The Functional Basis of Its Genealogical Roots and Some Extensions in Generalized Alliance Theory. Anthropological Theory 1:212–238.
Lehman, F. K., and G. Bennardo
2003 A Computational Approach to the Cognition of Space and Its Linguistic Expression. Mathematical Anthropology and Cultural Theory 1(2):1–83.
Levinson, S. C.
2003 Space in Language and Cognition. Cambridge: Cambridge University Press.
Levinson, S. C., and David Wilkins, eds.
2006 Grammars of Space: Explorations in Cognitive Diversity. Cambridge: Cambridge University Press.
Lounsbury, Floyd G.
1956 A Semantic Analysis of the Pawnee Kinship Usage. Language 32(1):158–194.
1969[1964] The Structural Analysis of Kinship Semantics. Proceedings of the Ninth International Congress of Linguists, The Hague, Mouton. Repr. in Cognitive Anthropology. Stephen A. Tyler, ed. Pp. 193–212. New York: Holt, Rinehart and Winston.
Mathews, Holly F.
2005 Uncovering Cultural Models of Gender from Accounts of Folktales. *In* Finding Culture in Talk: A Collection of Methods. Naomi Quinn, ed. Pp. 105–156. New York: Palgrave Macmillan.
Minsky, Marvin
1975 A Framework for Representing Knowledge. *In* The Psychology of Computer Vision. P. H. Winston, ed. New York: McGraw-Hill.
Quinn, Naomi, ed.
2005 Finding Culture in Talk: A Collection of Methods. New York: Palgrave Macmillan.
Randall, Robert
1976 How Tall is a Taxonomic Tree? Some Evidence for Dwarfism. American Ethnologist 3:543–553.
1977 Change and Variation in Samal Fishing: Making Plans to "Make a Living" in the Southern Philippines. Unpublished Ph.D. dissertation, University of California, Berkeley.
Read, Dwight
1984 An Algebraic Account of the American Kinship Terminology. Current Anthropology 25:417–440.
2001 Formal Analysis of Kinship Terminologies and Its Relationship to What Constitutes Kinship. Anthropological Theory 1:239–267.
Richerson, P., and R. Boyd
2005 The Origin and Evolution of Cultures. Oxford: Oxford University Press.
Romney, A. Kimball, and Roy G. D'Andrade
1964 Cognitive Aspects of English Kin Terms. American Anthropologist 66(3):146–170 (special issue).
Rumelhart, David E.
1980 Schemata: The Building Blocks of Cognition. *In* Theoretical Issues in Reading Comprehension: Perspectives from Cognitive Psychology, Linguistics, Artificial Intelligence, and Education. Rand J. Spiro, Bertram C. Bruce, and William F. Brewer, eds. Pp. 33–58. Hillsdale, NJ: Lawrence Erlbaum.
Schank, Roger, and Robert Abelson
1977 Scripts, Plans, Goals, and Understanding: An Inquiry into Human Knowledge Structures. Hillsdale, NJ: Lawrence Erlbaum.
Senft, G., ed.
1997 Referring to Space: Studies in Austronesian and Papuan Languages. Oxford: Oxford University Press.

Shimizu, H.
2007 Cultural Models of Self-Presentations in Japan and the United States: A Multivocal Videography Study. Paper presented at the Annual Meeting of the Society for Anthropological Sciences, San Antonio, Texas.
Shore, Bradd
1996 Culture in Mind: Cognition, Culture, and the Problem of Meaning. Oxford: Oxford University Press.
Strauss, Claudia, and Naomi Quinn
1997 A Cognitive Theory of Cultural Meaning. Cambridge: Cambridge University Press.
Tomasello, M.
1999 The Cultural Origins of Human Cognition. Cambridge, MA: Harvard University Press.
Trubetzkoy, N. S.
1969[1939] Fundamentals of Phonology [Grundzüge der Phonologie]. Christine A. M. Baltaxe, trans. Berkeley: University of California Press.
Wallace, Anthony. F. C., and John Atkins
1960 The Meaning of Kin Terms. American Anthropologist 62:58–80.

CHAPTER 6

Personal Knowledge and Collective Representations

John B. Gatewood

Introduction

Thinking about intracultural variation and cultural models is a bit like the old chicken and egg problem.[1] Both notions make sense, but people seem to differ on which they regard as given and which needs explication. If you start with faith in the notion of cultural models, you're likely to feel intracultural variation is odd, perhaps even contradictory. On the other hand, if you're confident about interindividual differences, then speaking of cultural models may be disconcerting and confusing. I tend to be in this latter camp.

It strikes me as obvious that individuals differ from one another with respect to their accumulated personal knowledge. This much is true whether comparing individuals who live next door to one another or on opposite sides of the world. Further, interindividual differences make sense insofar as all people have to learn things for themselves during their, perhaps unique, life histories. Try as we may to teach our sons and daughters, we cannot learn anything *for* them – life is a lab course. From this viewpoint, then, the fact that everyone resembles some folks more than others is what I find puzzling and interesting. And, this is where cultural models become relevant.

By definition, cultural models are supposed to be shared or held in common by groups of individuals whilst not being shared by other groups. Yet, if individuals within a group hold cultural models in common, how can these same people also differ from one another in terms of their socially transmitted, learned behaviors? That is, if culture entails sharing, how can there be intracultural diversity?

Working toward a solution to this quasi-paradox, I'd like to focus on situations in which individuals of the same cultural tradition differ substantially in their private understandings of the supposedly common culture. That is, I'll concentrate on some

A Companion to Cognitive Anthropology, First Edition. Edited by David B. Kronenfeld, Giovanni Bennardo, Victor C. de Munck, and Michael D. Fischer.

situations in which there are discrepancies between people's personal knowledge (manifest as interindividual differences) despite shared collective representations (minimally, similar ways of talking about things). The general question I would ask goes something like this:

> When can we appropriately say of individuals, who know different things about the world, that they "share a common culture," and what might it mean to say such a thing?

The examples I've selected concern differential knowledge with respect to trees, alcoholic beverages, and salmon fishing among a most mysterious tribe, the Nacirema.

Nacirema Understandings of Trees

My grandfather used to sell insurance to farmers in southern Illinois. As a young child, I often accompanied him on his house calls to clients. Grandfather was born in 1876 and never got the hang of driving faster than 30 miles per hour (hence, his nickname "Speedy," given by the local teenagers). Thus, driving with him along the dirt and gravel country roads, you could actually see the scenery.

To pass the time, Grandfather would point to the various crops, weeds, and trees growing along the roadside and tell me their common names as well as their uses or nuisances, as the case may be. Indeed, Grandfather knew quite a bit about "folk botany." (The local Boy Scouts used to come to his home to work on their "nature" merit badges, because he had about 30 species of trees planted around it and would teach them identifications as well as uses of the different plants.)

Despite this rather ideal learning context, I did not learn much of what Grandfather tried to teach me about the native plants. Oh, the names still swirl around in my head, as do images of the plants themselves, but I was never interested in connecting names with particular kinds of plants – why bother? So, to this day, I know oodles of names for plants I cannot recognize, and I am familiar with oodles of plants that I cannot name. I know the names are supposed to refer to different plants, but the relation between plant names and the plants themselves is precisely what I failed to learn. Thus, when I hear many plant names, I know what sort of landscape the referent plants inhabit, human attitudes about them, and perhaps some of their uses. But, when I walk in the Illinois countryside, all I can say by way of commenting on the familiar plant life is: "Yep, there's one of *those* thingies ... and there's one of *those*."

Given my own mix of knowledge and ignorance with respect to Nacirema plant classification, I was quite taken by anthropological accounts of the extensive ethnobiological knowledge common among various exotic cultures. Those natives sounded a great deal like my grandfather and very little like me. Just like grandfather, they know "names *for* things," whereas I just know "names *and* things." This contrast is what prompted me to collect some data on other Naciremas' knowledge of trees and write a couple of papers on the topic (Gatewood 1983, 1984; Gretz 1987).

People like me engage in "loose talk" when the topic is trees. For the most part, ours is a purely semantic knowledge of tree names. For instance, we know that an "oak" is supposed to be a large deciduous tree whose wood is good for rustic furniture, hardwood flooring, and fuel in fireplaces and stoves. As a metaphor of someone's character, oak is durable, sturdy, and honest (as opposed to fancy and deceitful). I even know there are several kinds of oak trees, and I've been told I have some variety of oak growing in my backyard. But, I wouldn't wager $5 on a one-time chance that I can identify an oak tree growing wild in a mixed deciduous forest.

For people like me, and most Nacirema are, tree names such as "oak," "cherry," and "maple" are collective representations that do not re-present much to us. We've learned *of* these categories by learning their names, but we learn *about* the categories on a need to know basis. Our personal knowledge concerning the collective representation remains partial, incomplete – especially in comparison to truly knowledgeable folks like Grandfather. Nonetheless, partial knowledge is sufficient for our needs. For example, a few years ago I spent $2,000 on "red oak" flooring in our family room because I was convinced by people I regarded as experts that red oak flooring is a good quality material and its graining would complement the graining and hues of our new cherry cabinets. From my level of ignorance, this was $2,000 of "trust the experts" money, because I'd never even heard of "red oak" until then.

In sum, relatively few Nacirema know as much about trees as my grandfather did. For most of us, tree names are *place-holding concepts*. We know of trees, but not necessarily much about them. Simply by knowing the names, however, we are able to talk with experts well enough to get what they tell us we want with respect to important stuff like furniture, landscaping, and firewood. Likewise, we often know enough about the referent trees – their habitats and social associations – to wield tree names appropriately in figurative language. The names, as such, frame our thinking and enable communication, but we are quite variable when it comes to the substantive knowledge we have of the trees we talk about. Although park rangers, carpenters, kitchen designers, and landscape architects are supposed to have substantial personal knowledge underlying these particular collective representations, most of us get by just fine with loose talk when discussing trees.

Synopsis

John knows of Tree X. John talks about Tree X. But, John may or may not know much about Tree X. The degree to which John's knowledge about Tree X is "filled in" depends on his motivations for learning about Tree X. Yet, John's very incomplete personal knowledge doesn't seem to matter, so long as he can talk with experts as the need arises.

Bartender versus Customer Understandings of Mixed Drinks

The domain of names for alcoholic beverages is exceedingly large and diverse; the collective representations are legion. The *Mr. Boston Deluxe Official Bartender's Guide* (Anon. 1974), for example, has a 23-page index of names for "mixed" alcoholic drinks. The entire set of drink names would include all of these *and* a long list of unmixed alcoholic beverages as well as their brand name varieties. A very small sample of drink names is provided in Table 6.1.

An important feature of drink nomenclature, obscured by such listings, is that the drink names do *not* form a closed set. New names are being coined all the time, most

Table 6.1 A sample list of "drink names"

port	sidecar	Ouzo
Stroh's	apple cooler	martini
daiquiri	rob roy	gin and tonic
cuba libre	brandy presbyterian	Drambuie
manhattan	screwdriver	vodka
scotch	Budweiser	old fashioned
harvey wallbanger	bourbon	Campari
Wild Turkey	lager	vodka tonic
stinger	singapore sling	gin
Pernod	scotch and soda	salty dog
triple sec	Grand Marnier	gimlet
tom collins	bloody mary	brandy alexander
black russian	mai tai	seven and seven
champagne	Bombay	perfect manhattan
Galliano	tequila sunrise	margarita
creme de cacao	stout	zombie
pink lady	white russian	sherry
Absolut	vodka martini	bacardi cocktail
between the sheets	frozen daiquiri	brandy sour
ale	rosé	pousse-café

commonly for brand names and new mixed drinks, but occasionally for new "pure" (or "straight") beverages. Creativity is ongoing, and the lexicon allows for this. Lehrer (1983) notes that wine descriptors have this same property of open-endedness.

Lexical analysis of drink names reveals a shallow taxonomy. An ethnoscientist would rapidly discover that "brand names" refer to particular realizations of more basic, generic beverage types. Johnnie Walker Black, J&B, Chivas Regal, Pinch, Cutty Sark are kinds of *scotch*; Tanqueray, Beefeater, Bombay, Gordon's are kinds of *gin*; Hennessy, Martell, Courvoisier are kinds of *cognac*; Budweiser, Moose Head, Beck's, Heineken are kinds of *beer*; and so forth. Set inclusion of this sort might fascinate a Martian, but it is obvious and boring to earthling lounge lizards.

A more interesting aspect of the classificatory system is the distinction between "pure" ("straight") drinks and "mixed drinks." Of course, no alcoholic beverage is pure from a chemical perspective: scotch, gin, bourbon are complex chemical compounds that vary from year to year and month to month, even in products from the same distillery. Yet, it is customary to think these categories refer to stable, homogeneous substances that are, in some sense, fundamental for the domain as a whole – rather like the periodic chart of the elements. They constitute what Rosch (1973; Rosch et al. 1976) would call the *basic object level*. Scotch, gin, bourbon, vodka, and so forth occupy a privileged level in the classificatory system: they are the basic ingredients from which other drinks – "mixed drinks" – are made. Table 6.2 shows the drink names from Table 6.1 sorted into the three major categories recognized so far.

Today, there is very little change in the basic beverage types from one year to the next. By contrast, there is sustained growth in the number of brand name varieties. The area of greatest productivity, however, is clearly in the inventory of named mixed

Table 6.2 "Drink names" by major categories

Brand name	*Basic beverage type*	*Mixed drink*
Absolut (vodka)	ale	apple cooler
Bombay (gin)	bourbon	bacardi cocktail
Budweiser (lager beer)	champagne	between the sheets
Campari	creme de cacao	black russian
Drambuie	gin	bloody mary
Galliano	lager	brandy alexander
Grand Marnier	port	brandy presbyterian
Ouzo	rosé	brandy sour
Pernod	scotch	cuba libre
Stroh's (lager beer)	sherry	daiquiri
Wild Turkey (whiskey)	stout	frozen daiquiri
	triple sec	gimlet
	vodka	gin and tonic
		harvey wallbanger
		mai tai
		manhattan
		margarita
		martini
		old fashioned
		perfect manhattan
		pink lady
		pousse-café
		rob roy
		salty dog
		scotch and soda
		screwdriver
		seven and seven
		sidecar
		singapore sling
		stinger
		tequila sunrise
		tom collins
		vodka martini
		vodka tonic
		white russian
		zombie

drinks. Indeed, every self-respecting, pretentious bar will try to come up with its own specialty concoctions. Creative efforts of this sort justify higher prices all around.

Focusing on the segregate labels for mixed drinks, we see several lexical forms in use. These differ along two dimensions of contrast: (1) morphological complexity of the name, and (2) whether the name gives a clue as to the ingredients or not. Table 6.3 shows the previous sample data analyzed in this way (for definitions of lexeme types, see Frake 1962; Berlin et al. 1973; Casson 1981:79–80).

Although it might be entertaining to continue analyzing drink names as if we didn't know anything about them, I'd like to jump to some observations on the social functions of drink names. For present purposes, there are five relevant points.

Table 6.3 Lexemic analysis of names for "mixed drinks"

	Referentially opaque	*Referentially indicative*
Unanalyzable primary lexemes	daiquiri gimlet mai tai manhattan margarita martini pousse-café stinger zombie	
Analyzable primary lexemes	between the sheets black russian bloody mary cuba libre harvey wallbanger old fashioned pink lady rob roy salty dog screwdriver sidecar singapore sling white russian	brandy alexander brandy presbyterian tequila sunrise
Productive primary lexemes	frozen daiquiri perfect manhattan tom collins[1]	apple cooler bacardi cocktail gin collins[1] brandy sour vodka martini
Secondary lexemes		
Polylexemes	seven and seven[2]	gin and tonic scotch and soda vodka (and) tonic

[1] The alternate name for "tom collins" is "gin collins," which makes the contrast with "vodka collins" much more obvious. "Gin collins" is referentially indicative, whereas "tom collins" is referentially opaque.

[2] A "seven and seven" means a highball composed of Seagram's 7 whiskey and 7-Up. If one knows these brand name products, then the segregate label would be referentially indicative, otherwise not.

(1) The primary function of drink names, independent of their linguistic form, is to establish an unambiguous, one-to-one referential relation – a publicly known semiotic code – whereby customers can ask for a particular potent potable and be reasonably assured of getting what they asked for.

(2) The public code, the system of collective representations, bridges over very asymmetrical knowledge boundaries. When placing an order, all the customer needs to know about a drink is its name. The bartender is supposed to supply all the other knowledge. Thus, so long as the customer and bartender share the same public code, they can interact successfully despite substantial differences in their knowledge of drinks.

(3) Drink names serve an important, though latent, social function. They are used to signal in-group boundaries. People in the know can wield this lexical set to accomplish a variety of face-work (Goffman 1958) vis-à-vis bartenders, cocktail waitresses, and other customers (see Spradley and Mann 1975). This latent function probably accounts for the lexical irregularities and idiosyncrasies of drink names, as well as their referential opacity.

(4) The referential focus of drink names is the ingredients that make up the drinks, including their relative proportions. Other aspects of the actual drink – what is called the drink's full "presentation" – are usually left unsaid. There are, however, a few expressions whereby customers can emphasize, or deviate from, their drink's standard presentation. These utterances are generally linguistic tag-ons to the drink name, for example:

scotch	neat
Wild Turkey	on the rocks
whiskey sour	up
Campari and soda	with a twist
vodka martini	shaken not stirred (à la James Bond)

Correct usage of these auxiliary expressions signifies that one knows the unsaid standard or norm that is being modified. Hence, correct talk of this sort conveys the meta-message that the customer is both discriminating in taste and knowledgeable as regards customary bartending procedures.

(5) Finally, most customers think bartending expertise is pretty much a matter of rote memorization, of simply associating recipes with drink names. Not only does this impression ignore the kinesthetic aspects of bartending knowledge, but it grossly oversimplifies bartenders' mixology or recipe knowledge. Skilled bartenders organize the incredible number of drink names and corresponding recipes into a surprisingly small number of "recipe templates" that define similar families of drinks. For example, a martini, a gibson, a manhattan, and a rob roy all derive from the same deep structure:

Template	= *Booze* (1.5 oz.)	+ *Vermouth*	+ *Garnish* (0.75 oz.)
martini	gin	dry	olives
gibson	gin	dry	onions
manhattan	whiskey	sweet	orange or cherry
rob roy	scotch	sweet	orange or cherry

Similarly, a daiquiri, whiskey sour, tom collins, and bacardi cocktail are all variants of the basic "sour" template: 1 oz. of booze plus 2 oz. of sour mix, then shake or blend to a froth, pour, and add garnish.

Drink varieties within a given family arise by altering the main booze ingredient and by slight "bendings" from the basic structure in terms of glassware, additional (spice) ingredients, and garnishes. Some recipe templates are named, some are not; but most customers aren't even aware such templates exist.

In summary, minor miracles of social organization occur thousands of times per hour at bars across the land. Speaking as a former bartender, I find it simply amazing how little customers need to know in order to get the drinks they want. Minimal similarities in collective representations enable successful social interaction despite large differences in personal knowledge. So long as the customer can talk the talk – *knows of* a drink and asks for it by name – he or she can happily get inebriated. The bartender, whose knowledge of drinks is generally both more extensive and differently organized, stands ready to "fill in" whatever gaps may exist in the customer's knowledge.

Synopsis
The only thing customers need to know to get a mixed drink from a bartender is the drink's name. Customers and bartenders must share these collective representations, but their personal understandings of the mutually identified drinks are generally quite different. What bartenders know about drinks is very "filled in" in comparison with the customers' very partial knowledge.

Salmon Seining in Alaska

My third and final example of differential personal knowledge despite a common core of collective representations comes from purse seining in Alaska. As the reader may not know what purse seining is, let me attempt an explanation.

> Purse seining is a kind of net fishing. The seine is a big net about a quarter-mile long and 90 feet deep, with corks on the top and weights on the bottom. The seine is manipulated in the water by two boats working in tandem: the main boat and a smaller diesel-powered skiff.
>
> Six people do all the work. The skipper stays on the main boat and runs the show, the skiff driver maneuvers the power skiff around, and the other guys are deck hands.
>
> Putting the seine in the water, closing the net to entrap the fish, and retrieving the catch is called "making a set." A "set" begins when the skipper gives the order. The skiff driver and a deck hand take off with one end of the seine in the opposite direction of the main boat. They go out and hold the net open so fish swim into it. When the skipper thinks it is time (after about 15–30 minutes of "holding the set"), he signals for the skiff to return.
>
> Now, the seine is in a big circle with both ends tied to the main boat. Two deck hands start "pursing" the bottom of the net by wrapping a line, which is run through rings attached to the bottom of the seine, around the drums of a winch on the main boat. This slowly closes the bottom of the seine, rather like pulling the purse strings of a lady's purse, and keeps the fish from diving out of the net. While two deck hands are pursing, the other two are running around doing assorted things to keep the seine from getting tangled. When the pursing is finished, the crew hoist up the bottom of the net and drop it on deck. Now, the fish are trapped.
>
> All that is left to do is "haul gear" until there is just a bag of fish in the water. How you get the fish on board depends on how many you've caught – either hoist up the whole bag with a block and tackle or "brail" the fish with a dip net. When

all the fish have been brought aboard, the deck hands haul in the bag-end of the seine, pitch the fish into the hold, then get everything cleaned up and ready for the next set.

This description of purse seining is what I'd call a *narrator's account*. The story is told from the posture of an informed observer of the operation as a whole, and it is a very abbreviated description, almost a distortion, of the personal knowledge required to accomplish seining. Still, it works well enough as an overview. It's the sort of story my brother told me before I went to Alaska, what experienced seiners tell rookies before they go out the first time, what we used to tell tourists back in port, and what I tell students, friends, and relatives who want to know something about purse seining.

Generally, rookies (novices) have heard a couple of narrators' accounts before they actually go fishing. The differences between these narrators' accounts – these ways of representing seining in public discourse – and the personal knowledge required to do seining become painfully clear when rookies participate in their first set. It is well and good to know seining jargon and enough about the referent actions to tell a story, but reciting a narrator's account doesn't get the work done. Speech acts catch no fish. *Knowing about* seining is not the same as *knowing how* to seine.

The collective representations embedded in a narrator's account do provide a somewhat useful, if vague, comprehension of the group's overall efforts. Still, each fisherman must master his own job routine by himself. Getting all his own tasks done properly and on time is what dominates the seiner's thinking and constitutes the immediate reality while fishing. And, most of these "little tasks" aren't even named.

Thus, despite having heard several explanations of purse seining, it took me about a month of fishing before I could connect the little tasks in my job routine with the "big picture" provided in the collective representations. Further, even when crew members do use collective representations to define segments of their private action routines – for example, thinking to themselves, "We are now 'hauling gear' " – crew members vary widely in the personal knowledge mobilized during that time segment (Gatewood 1978, 1985).

Synopsis

Being a competent salmon seiner involves many layers of knowledge: knowing of, talking about, knowing about, and knowing how. Competent seiners can indeed re-present seining to others, but it is their private "know how" that catches fish. Each seiner develops these tacit skills for himself or herself which are only marginally related to the level of public discourse.

Conclusion

Although my examples come from rather trivial Nacirema activities, I think the general points bear on some very general topics within anthropology.

First, I hope the examples have shown that sharing collective representations does *not* necessarily mean people share a great deal of personal knowledge. Second, whereas collective representations generally underlie talk (public discourse), personal knowledge underlies human action.

So, what good are collective representations? Why do they exist at all? Are modern humans just pretentious by nature, do we just enjoy talking about things we don't know much about, or is there some deeper, adaptive rationale for our proclivity to indulge in loose talk? Let me offer some speculative answers to these questions in the guise of an origin myth.

An Origin Myth for Collective Representations

Once upon a time, long, long ago … in the small-scale, face to face societies of proto-human primates, each individual did pretty much the same thing as every other individual, at least those of the same age and sex group. Because everybody was doing pretty much the same things in the same environment while watching each other, individuals developed very similar understandings of their very similar life experiences. But each proto-human could only guess what the others were thinking and feeling, inferring their psychic states from context, non-verbal cues, and occasional emotive vocalizations.

One day, folks began mumbling and grunting to each other as a regular accompaniment to action. The co-presence of speaker, hearer, and referent enabled other folks to associate various "human vocal sounds" with "things in the world." Talk was invented. Before long, folks could talk about things even when they weren't doing them and, through talk, conjure word-pictures in their own as well as their fellows' minds. "Collective representations" were born – ways of communicating about activities and surroundings, ways of making explicit previously implicit understandings. With talk, Garr found out she knew pretty much the same things as Thag, Gwan, and Blodnar (her reference group). She felt less isolated. Talk was comforting, fun, and useful. Unfortunately, babies didn't know how to talk the group's talk at birth. New kids had to learn the talk forms for themselves, but they picked it up fairly quickly with only intermittent coaching and corrections.

Generations passed …

As groups spread out across the Earth, they unconsciously developed distinctive ways of talking, each requiring a period of learning.

More generations …

In some groups, social roles began to proliferate in conjunction with complex divisions of labor. Individuals in these societies depended more and more on other members of their society for things they could not make or do themselves. Each individual talked about more and more things, but knew less and less about most of them. Many aspects of the collective representations became "empty categories" for most of the society – they knew of the categories but very little else. Still, because they shared the same collective representations, individuals with increasingly divergent personal knowledge could interact successfully, learning what the others knew on a "need to know" basis.

And, that is how we got to be the ultra-social creatures we are today … interdependent and reciprocally ignorant.

The evolutionary significance of collective representations is that they dramatically reduce what each of us *must* learn while at the same time providing access to a much greater store of wisdom than we possibly *can* learn. So long as interindividual differences with respect to what *is* learned include a core of shared collective representations, the ensuing intracultural variation is very adaptive.

Returning to my initial question, then, I would suggest it is appropriate to say a group of individuals "share a common culture" if by this we mean simply they have learned similar ways of talking about – of re-presenting – things to one another. But, sharing collective representations does not imply homogeneity as regards substantive knowledge. Personal knowledge concerning the collective representations is highly variable, grading from *knowing of* to *knowing about* to *knowing how*.

NOTE

1 A shorter version of this paper was presented at the 93rd Annual Meeting of the American Anthropological Association in Atlanta, Georgia (Nov. 30–Dec. 4, 1994), in a session entitled "Intracultural Variation and Cultural Models" (organizer Morris Freilich; discussant David M. Schneider).

REFERENCES

Anon.
1974 Mr. Boston Deluxe Official Bartender's Guide. Boston: Mr. Boston Distiller.

Berlin, Brent, Dennis E. Breedlove, and Peter H. Raven
1973 General Principles of Classification and Nomenclature in Folk Biology. American Anthropologist 75:214–242.

Casson, Ronald W.
1981 Folk Classification: Relativity and Universality. *In* Language, Culture, and Cognition: Anthropological Perspectives. R. W. Casson, ed. Pp. 72–91. New York: Macmillan.

Frake, Charles O.
1962 The Ethnographic Study of Cognitive Systems. *In* Anthropology and Human Behavior. Thomas Gladwin and William Sturtevant, eds. Pp. 72–85. Washington, DC: Anthropological Society of Washington.

Gatewood, John B.
1978 Fishing, Memory, and the Stability of Culture Complexes. Unpublished doctoral dissertation, Department of Anthropology, University of Illinois at Urbana–Champaign.

1983 Loose Talk: Linguistic Competence and Recognition Ability. American Anthropologist 85(2):378–387.

1984 Familiarity, Vocabulary Size, and Recognition Ability in Four Semantic Domains. American Ethnologist 11(3):507–527.

1985 Actions Speak Louder Than Words. *In* Directions in Cognitive Anthropology. Janet Dougherty, ed. Pp. 199–219. Urbana: University of Illinois Press.

Goffman, Erving
1958 The Presentation of Self in Everyday Life. Garden City, NY: Doubleday.

Gretz, Jane
1987 Typicality and Its Correlates: A Whorfian View. Unpublished master's thesis, Department of Social Relations, Lehigh University, Bethlehem, Pennsylvania.

Lehrer, Adrienne
1983 Wine and Conversation. Bloomington: Indiana University Press.

Rosch, Eleanor
1973 Natural Categories. Cognitive Psychology 4:328–350.

Rosch, Eleanor, Carolyn B. Mervis, Wayne D. Gray, David M. Johnson, and Penny Boyes-Braem
1976 Basic Objects in Natural Categories. Cognitive Psychology 8:382–439.
Spradley, James P., and Brenda J. Mann
1975 The Cocktail Waitress: Woman's Work in a Man's World. New York: John Wiley.

FURTHER READING

Bohannan, Paul
1964[1960] Conscience Collective and Culture. *In* Essays on Sociology and Philosophy. Kurt H. Wolff, ed. Pp. 77–96. New York: Harper Torchbooks.
Boster, James S.
1985 "Requiem for the Omniscient Informant": There's Life in the Old Girl Yet. *In* Directions in Cognitive Anthropology. Janet Dougherty, ed. Pp. 177–197. Urbana: University of Illinois Press.
D'Andrade, Roy
1995 The Development of Cognitive Anthropology. New York: Cambridge University Press.
2008 A Study of Personal and Cultural Values: American, Japanese, and Vietnamese. New York: Palgrave Macmillan.
Durkheim, Émile
1933[1893] The Division of Labor in Society. George Simpson, trans. New York: Macmillan.
1938[1895] Rules of the Sociological Method. George Catlin, trans. Chicago: University of Chicago Press.
1963[1909] Primitive Classification. Rodney Needham, trans. and ed. Chicago: University of Chicago Press.
Hutchins, Edwin
1995 Cognition in the Wild. Cambridge, MA: MIT Press.
Kronenfeld, David B.
2008 Culture, Society, and Cognition: Collective Goals, Values, Action, and Knowledge. New York: Mouton de Gruyter.
Moscovici, Serge
2001 Social Representations: Explorations in Social Psychology. New York: New York University Press.
Polanyi, Michael
1958 Personal Knowledge: Towards a Post-Critical Philosophy. Chicago: University of Chicago Press.
Roberts, John M.
1964 The Self-Management of Cultures. *In* Explorations in Cultural Anthropology: Essays in Honor of George Peter Murdock. Ward Goodenough, ed. Pp. 433–454. New York: McGraw-Hill.
Romney, A. Kimball, Susan C. Weller, and William H. Batchelder
1986 Culture as Consensus: A Theory of Culture and Informant Accuracy. American Anthropologist 88:313–338.
Schwartz, Theodore
1978 Where Is the Culture? Personality as the Distributive Locus of Culture. *In* The Making of Psychological Anthropology. George Spindler, ed. Pp. 419–441. Berkeley: University of California Press.
Spiro, Melford E.
1951 Culture and Personality: The Natural History of a False Dichotomy. Psychiatry 14:19–46.

Strauss, Claudia
2005 Analyzing Discourses for Cultural Complexity. *In* Finding Culture in Talk: A Collection of Methods. Naomi Quinn, ed. Pp. 203–242. New York: Palgrave Macmillan.
Strauss, Claudia, and Naomi Quinn
1997 A Cognitive Theory of Cultural Meaning. New York: Cambridge University Press.
Wallace, Anthony F. C.
1961 Culture and Personality. New York: Random House.

PART II Methodologies

CHAPTER 7

How to Collect Data that Warrant Analysis

W. Penn Handwerker

We analyze data to answer a research question. It wastes everyone's time, however, to analyze data that don't meet minimal standards of construct validity. This chapter reviews data collection methods that meet these standards. These entail, as Donald Campbell (1970) pointed out many years ago, assembling information one step at a time with multiple, overlapping methods.

How Do We Know?

In his 1932 book *Remembering*, F. C. Bartlett made the observation that each of us constructs our understanding of the world by combining things we perceive with things we remember. In his 1953 book *Innovation*, Homer Barnett added that this constructive process necessarily created new things, qualitatively different from other things, and he exhaustively reviewed the ways in which new things came into being. In his 1996 book *The Cerebral Code*, William Calvin explains how the operation of Hebbian cell assemblies produces these effects.

The processes by which we construct our understanding of the world thus integrate sensory information with information from various forms of memory and, necessarily, create new things (Handwerker 2009). Because the process means, at the level of consciousness, making guesses, we can't help but make mistakes. We look at but do not see the bottle we know should be on the top shelf of the refrigerator. We write an equation incorrectly, as was true in Einstein's 1905 article that introduced the world to special relativity. The most notoriously unreliable evidence consists of eyewitness testimony. We can't see clearly, so we argue over whether or not the world's climate is undergoing a gradual warming – or, perhaps, a new ice age. Because each of us can draw only on our own limited prior experience, we don't see the world perfectly; we

A Companion to Cognitive Anthropology, First Edition. Edited by David B. Kronenfeld, Giovanni Bennardo, Victor C. de Munck, and Michael D. Fischer.

rely heavily on others to find our errors. But even when we have excellent advice and all the information necessary to see clearly, we make silly decisions, as Barbara Tuchman documented in her 1987 book *The March of Folly,* beginning with the prototype decision by the Trojans to accept a gift horse filled with Greek warriors. When we don't make silly decisions, we consistently fail to make rational choices – real world choices depend heavily on availability heuristics, confirmation biases, evaluations based on likeness rather than likelihood, overestimates of the likelihood of rare events, and many forms of "irrelevant" information.

Our evolved central nervous system thus presents us a central dilemma: why we should assume a particular way of thinking about the world of experience is not merely a figment of one's imagination, that a label defined in a particular way, that means used to distinguish one phenomenon from another (i.e., measurement), and that claimed relationships between one phenomenon and any other(s), correspond with the world of experience in some meaningful way.

Comparisons Provide the Solution

As Campbell (1970) observed, research thus consists of a search for ways to distinguish mental constructions that consist largely of fantasy from constructions that consist of less. Data collection boils down to an active search for the errors that must pervade the constructs you use to formulate questions and make observations, the observations you make, and the error or bias attached to the times and places and people from whom you collected those data. *Iterative* data collection distinguishes good research from bad. Design each observation and question to test at least one part of your growing theoretical understanding. Note errors. Ask for clarification. Rethink the theory. Link micro-level observations and interviews with historical records and macro-level trends that only time-series data can reveal. Try again.

All this assumes familiarity with many data collection and analysis tools. The application of a judiciously selected set of tools applied in distinctive ways produces the best research results, so the more tools from which you can draw the better. Bernard's comprehensive introduction to research methods (2005) makes an excellent starting point. Bernard's (1998) edited handbook and writings by Weller (1987, 1998) and Weller and Romney (1988) will establish a baseline which you may expand by consulting the journal *Field Methods* as well as more specialized methods texts. A well-constructed toolkit works best under two conditions. First, explicitly state the assumptions on which you frame your research and their relationship to methods and goals. Second, ask other people to help you find your errors. Table 7.1 shows a generic set of comparisons that will help you and others find remaining flaws in your research question and methods.

Comparison by Means

Different means of data collection yield qualitatively different kinds of information. Informal data collection immerses you (and thus allows greater depth of insight) into the lives of the people you seek to understand. Semi-structured data collection expands the scope of your study in ways that allow you to identify cultural themes and variability.

Table 7.1 Comparative dimensions of data collection

		Interview and observation means						
			Semi-structured		*Structured*			
		Informal	*Variation*	*Depth*	*Categorical (incl. binary)*	*Ratings*	*Ratio scales*	*Similarities*
	Cross-section							
	Measurements							
	Sample design							
	Short-term history							
Times and places	Measurements							
	Sample design							
	Long-term history							
	Measurements							
	Sample design							

Structured data collection makes possible the explicit comparisons necessary for valid and reliable inferences about cultures and cultural variation. Comparisons by means applied to the same question and measurement issue thus provide a primary source of triangulating to the truth.

Informal interviews and observations

Text data collected through informal observations and interviews, for example, give you insight into the assumptions that your informants use to understand and respond to the world of experience, the components of that world, and how those components are organized to form social and behavioral ecosystems. Informal conversations (which will range from chaotic to reasonably controlled interchanges) help you create and build personal relationships. In the process, you will learn how informants feel, think about the world, make decisions, act, see some new alternatives, fail to see other alternatives, and identify and evaluate the pragmatic and moral dimensions of relationships, behavior, knowledge, feelings, and options. Informal interviews make ideal circumstances for asking informants to free-list components of specific cultural domains. This highly flexible interview format lends itself to highly personal one-on-one interviews. But this interview format also yields valuable data when applied to focus groups, where it opens the possibility for a wide-ranging discussion that may bring to light clashing cultural assumptions. Informal interviews and observations also yield excellent information on the key social relations and social actors in a person's life. Observation makes it possible for you to evaluate what people claim they and other people believe, feel, and do, to discover what they may know but take for granted, and to provide data for an independent evaluation of what people do, or say they do. Explicit apprenticeships allow quick cultural immersion. Informal interviews and observations thus help you identify life history events and processes that people find significant, as well as the nature of their significance.

For example, to explore the roots of recidivism among women incarcerated for prostitution or drug use, ask informants to tell you about a typical day, from beginning to end. Make a list of the events, activities, locations, and participants. Identify participants by pertinent social labels. Ethnicity, gender, and age make good starting points, but make sure you find out if and how your informants find these labels pertinent. Ask about others you should know about, like boss, neighbor, friend, husband, daughter, and stranger. Ask how this typical day changes over the course of the week, month, and year. Ask about wonderful days, weeks, and months. Ask about disastrous days, weeks, and months. Ask about particularly wonderful events, activities, and interactions, and about particularly traumatic events, activities, and interactions. Make sure you record specific details, including words, behavior, and social actors. Clearly identify the criteria people use to discriminate wonderful from disastrous. Fill in the gradations between the two. Once you can paint a picture of one person's life, actively search for variation so your picture includes, at least in broad outlines, the complexity found in your study community. While you paint your word picture, add details from your observations of specific events, activities, locations, and participants. Ask how what you see compares to what you hear. Where are the discrepancies? What do those discrepancies tell you?

Can you describe clearly how and under what circumstances cultural norms correspond closely with the activities in which people engage? How, precisely, do those norms force consistency in behavioral compliance? Can you describe the cultural syllogism precisely, so you understand the assumption(s) on which these cultural norms rest? Might recidivism among women jailed for prostitution, for example, reflect a cultural premise that men are rutting beasts who cannot act as responsible adults and, thus, should never be trusted? A responsible adult takes care of herself. Granting a man respect, and acting in ways that place a man's emotional and material welfare on a par with one's own emotional and material welfare, thus count as irresponsible adult behavior. Instead, a woman should make money off men's rutting propensity, because that counts as responsible adult behavior.

Informal interviews grade into semi-structured interviews. The first step in this shift occurs when you write down *and use* a series of questions to guide your interview about specific topics. This step usually makes informal interviews more efficient because writing forces you to think out cultural content and interdependencies. Use the findings of informal interviews to correct your initial guesses, to elaborate them, and to restructure your understanding. In the process, draw up additional lists of questions. Once informal interviews fail to turn up new questions, corrections to old questions, or domain boundaries that had remained hidden, shift to a semi-structured interview format.

Semi-structured interviews and observations

The "structure" in semi-structured interviews comes from asking many people the same questions. *Don't confuse semi-structured interviews with structured interviews.* Structured interviews aim to elicit a specific set of information from everyone interviewed. Semi-structured interviews aim to elicit specific forms of information for many people, just not the same information from everyone interviewed. Semi-structured interviews carried out face to face or in focus groups thus allow you to escape the resource limitations (your time, money, and energy) that restrict the number of informal interviews carried out to a small number. Because they greatly extend the number and variety of people you talk with, semi-structured interviews help especially to identify the range of variation in perceptions, feelings, and understandings about experiences of various kinds. Collect data from focus groups and focused interviews of a large set of informants selected for their diversity to find the limits of variation for specific cultures or cultural domains.

Alternatively, use semi-structured interviews with highly knowledgeable informants to provide the materials for detailed case studies with which to illustrate important general findings. In the hypothetical recidivism study, for example, what set of shared assumptions and cultural norms distinguish repeat offenders from non-recidivists? How do these assumptions and norms appear in the activities released women carry out? How far back in a woman's history can you trace these assumptions and norms? Can you link them to plausible origins in specific events, times, and places?

Structured interviews and observations

By virtue of the interview and observation formats through which you collect such data, informal and semi-structured interviews provide no basis for comparison between informants. They give you only the barest hints about what's common and what's not, what's unusual and what's not, and they leave you guessing about what goes with what. Ethnography rarely lends itself to the application of experimental designs, which would rule out internal validity confounds. You can't eliminate the internal validity confounds in your data until you measure them explicitly. Anticipate data analysis in which you will seek to discriminate sets of data with structure from sets of data with none. The more subtle the variation, the harder you will find it to distinguish structure from randomness (e.g., Handwerker and Borgatti 1998:563–574). Explicit numerical analysis helps you see what you otherwise might miss. Use structured interviews (e.g., Weller 1998) to collect the data necessary for making comparisons between informants, and so to address the analytical tasks of explicitly identifying cultures, cultural variation, and cultural change (see Weller and Romney 1988; Bernard 2005).

Structured interview formats like yes or no, true or false, questions elicit information on the properties of cultural domain items. Rating scales elicit information on their relative importance by one or another criterion. Pile sorts or triads yield data on the relative similarity of domain items and so provide information about the structure of meaning and the organization of activities in particular cultural domains. Keep survey questionnaires or question schedules to a length that can be completed within about 30 minutes, on average. Trim questionnaires or interview schedules to their *absolute essentials.* Don't begin to formulate questions until analysis of informal and semi-structured interviews yields clear ideas about the assumptions that your informants used to understand and respond to the world of experience, the variables that comprise the cultural domains you study, and ways you might best measure them. Once you do, state questions simply and clearly. Make clear transitions between survey sections, if you integrate several structured interview components into a single survey, so the *order* of your questions makes sense to your informants. Don't confuse structured interviews with semi-structured interviews and *do not* put questions that explore unknown domains on structured interviews.

Don't be dismayed if your informants find quantitative scales irrelevant. Ask why they don't bother to pay attention to distinctions like these. Rephrase questions with sensible distinctions. Often, this means binary variables. Is something important or not? Yes or no? Most commonly, perhaps, we ignore fine but spuriously precise measurements to phrase our findings more crudely but more accurately. Structured interviews formulated with crude but accurate phrasing do not lose important forms of precision.

Create a time line for documented historical changes to anticipate potentially important experiences and life events. For example, plot age and date to keep in focus the maturational and historical influences on different cohorts of informants. If your informal interviews produced life history events and processes that people find significant, as well as the nature of their significance, collect documents, written by informants, elicited by you or not (e.g., letters), or assembled by governments or other organizations. Supplement these materials with person- or family-centered case studies, which make great stories that personalize and highlight key findings.

Collect pertinent aggregated databases, construct appropriate variables, and use scatterplots for time-series data to acquaint yourself with important historical trends in macro-level phenomena.

Documenting and determining why, exactly, changes like these occur is one of the biggest challenges facing the social sciences. Many if not most phenomena arise from complexly related sets of variables at multiple scale levels, and exhibit important non-linearities. For example, the properties of gender categories may reflect local and micro-level power relationships. West Indian data consistently show (e.g., Handwerker 1993, 1998, 2003) that power inequalities between domestic partners (e.g., where women have little income, no significant income generating skills, and few or no relatives or friends to help them) elicit violence toward women and their children; conversely, power equalities between partners elicit affectionate and supportive behavior for women and their children, irrespective of class, education, or the presence of stepfathers in the home. The 1998 study pointed out further that, as gender power inequalities decrease, the chances that even rotten men act affectionately grows by a factor of 9 (from 0.057 to 0.512) and the chances that they act violently falls by more than 50 percent (from 0.889 to 0.412). Moreover, power corrupts even good men. As gender power inequalities grow, the chances that even good men act affectionately falls 75 percent (from 0.813 to 0.200), and the chances that they act violently grows by a factor of 4.6 (from 0.145 to 0.660). Similarly, people subject to violence, particularly during childhood, evolve behavioral patterns that reduce their chances of becoming subject to violence as adults. One – the assumption that "men are rutting beasts" – may contribute to recidivism rates in the contemporary United States. Globalization characterized by increasing local and regional economic competition, by contrast, eliminated the cultures of violence that had evolved in non-competitive economies of the early 20th century.

These complexities pose new methods problems. Significant historical or regional change, for example, suggests not only that social relations and cultural categories and meanings may have changed dramatically over the last half century or so; it also suggests sample stratification criteria – who you should talk with to understand retrospectively the processes of cultural change. People who grew up in the 1950s may provide first-hand accounts of one historical period, how their world changed, and how they experienced those changes. People who grew up during the 1970s and 1980s, by contrast, may provide first-hand accounts of transition years, the conflicts that arose and how they came to be resolved (if they were). People who grew up during the 1990s may provide first-hand accounts of what life is like now that the structural changes have clarified themselves, and how they see themselves differ from people in the older cohorts. What cultural boundaries, if any, separate these cohorts? If the cohorts exhibit distinct cultures, are these cohort agreements a function of aging, of historical change, or both?

Documenting and testing explanations for historical changes such as these can be done best with historical, macro-level time-series. One reason ethnographers rarely use time-series is that those available through official sources rarely include the variables that most interest us. When you can't find what you want in conventional databases, create your own. Generate time-series data for variables in which you are specifically interested for historical periods of up to 30 or 40 years from survey data. But to do so you must plan ahead and incorporate important structured interview design features. Do it like this:

1 Plan to estimate parameters for age cohorts, so stratify your sample by age. Randomly sample five-year cohorts, for example. A total sample of around 400 cases can yield acceptably good estimates for many variables for a time span

of up to 40 years, including retrospective estimates of period age-specific fertility. But samples of as few as 200 total cases may suffice, or samples of more than 1,000 may be necessary, depending on the rarity of the event that you want to estimate (e.g., large samples will be necessary for reasonable estimates of infant mortality).

2 Identify age cohorts clearly. In the best of all possible worlds, be able to discriminate people by age precisely, by birthday, so that someone who was born on October 3 is known to be older than someone who was born on October 4 of the same year. For many problems, however, less precise age measurements will suffice.
3 Measure prospective time-series variables for clearly identifiable developmental reference points. For example, measure the number of years of formal schooling completed *by age 20*, or jobs held *at age 25*, or cumulative number of births *by age 30*. You can measure changes in the class composition of a society by estimating the proportion of people who were raised in lower class homes. To create a historical time series, however, you have to relate this variable to a developmental reference point. For example, the time-series variable might be "the proportion of people who were aged 20 in 1950, 1951, 1952, ..., 1980 who were raised in a lower class home."
4 Sort your cases from the youngest to the oldest.
5 Generate LOWESS smoothed values of the time-series variable or variables. A variable like education, which is recorded as the "number of years of completed schooling" can be smoothed in its original measurements. If you are interested in the proportion of women who completed secondary school, you will have to create an appropriate dummy variable first.
6 Equate pertinent developmental ages with years (e.g., assign people who were age 20 in 1950 to the year 1950).
7 The LOWESS smoothed values of "number of years of formal schooling by age 20" can then be used as estimates of the mean years of schooling at age 20 among women who, for example, were 20 in 1950, 1951, ..., 1980. If your statistical software cannot produce LOWESS smoothing, you might compute means for five-year cohorts, assign the means to the year that corresponds to the middle of the age cohort, and assign missing values on the assumption of constant growth rates between existing values. Smooth the resulting series as appropriate.

Comparison by Times and Places

Cultural differences reflect variation in internal processes of development and maturation, the time in human history people live, the region(s) in which life stories take place, and the details of the gender, intergenerational, and intra- and inter-group relationships in which they take part. This calls for the construction of a comprehensive sample design that allows for the historical (time-series) and cross-sectional analyses you need to contextualize your cultural data with pertinent macro- and micro-level historical and regional antecedent experiences and events. Search for concrete events and circumstances in people's lives that may shape the understandings they now work with. What people think and do must reflect not only their individual life history, but broader regional and global histories of people, events, and social interaction into which they were born and in which they grew up. Aim to identify events, circumstances, and processes that provide one set of choices to some people and a different set of choices to others. Ask individuals to identify life experiences that were significant to them, and to help you understand why those experiences were significant. In the process, keep track of life experience markers that people identify as important, as well as those that might be important.

The impact of any one experience (its explanatory power) may vary with when during a life trajectory it was experienced as well as with characteristics of the experience (e.g., duration, intensity). Similarly, different realms of experience mean that choices available to one generation or one part of a population may differ significantly from the choices available to another. Aim to identify events, circumstances, and processes that provide one set of choices to some people and a different set of choices to others. Look at how people identify better ways to act and think. What criteria do they use to discriminate options from non-options, and between different options?

Sample design

Effective identification of cultural variation sources calls for stratified sample designs. *Sample design* refers to the means by which you select the primary units for data collection and analysis appropriate for a specific research question (Handwerker 2005). These units may consist of states, cities, census enumeration districts, court records, cohorts, or – in nearly all our research – individuals. Irrespective of the kind of unit, we always collect data at specific times and places about a specific set of cases (a *sample*) which comprises a selected subset of a larger set of cases, times, and places (a *population*). Answers to research questions thus take the form of inferences from samples to populations. A useful sample design warrants the conclusion that your inferences are both accurate and appropriately precise. Box 7.1 lays out the conventional components of sampling and inference.

Except by contrast, however, don't obsess about conventional sampling procedures. By definition, many people share cultures. Any one participant will do and say things that correspond closely to what other cultural participants do and say. The errors you make in predicting what one cultural participant will do or say will correspond closely to the errors you make predicting what another cultural participant will do or say. When your research question calls for an answer in the form of a construct that summarizes behavioral and cognitive similarities among a set of people, accurate and precise answers depend on samples designed to actively search for cultural variation that comes from specific forms of variation in life experiences. In seeking to understand people from the inside, looking out, we thus aim to accurately characterize spatial and temporal autocorrelation, not correct for it.

When generalizing about cases rather than variables, the meaning of power changes, and sample size depends on the degree of similarity among cases. For example, in ethnographic analyses, power refers to the reliability and validity of inferences about the content of the behavioral and cognitive similarities among cases (the culture or cultures they share). Important work by Susan Weller (1987) has shown that estimates of both the reliability and validity of those inferences come from the application of the Spearman-Brown prophesy formula to the average level of similarity among cases. If the average level of similarity is 0.50, nine cases will

Box 7.1 Conventional basics of sampling and inference

1 Parameters and populations define each other. All the following constitute parameters and their associated populations, for example:
- the *percentage* of students at a university who believe we need to preserve wilderness areas;
- the *incidence* of child abuse in Barbados;
- the *average* number of children born to women in England by age 50;
- the *degree* to which US couples share child care and household responsibilities equally;
- the *proportion* of women employed in the professions in the USA.

2 We identify parameters with Greek letters like *b* (beta), *a* (alpha), *ε* (epsilon), *r* (rho), and *s* (sigma).
3 Samples, by contrast, yield statistics, which we identify with Latin letters and words (like b, *median*, *percentage*, *mean*).
4 Each statistic constitutes a *point estimate* of a parameter – your single best guess about the value of the parameter.
5 Large samples estimate parameters very *precisely* because they contain little sampling error; small samples contain large amounts of sampling error because randomly selected extreme values exert greater effects.
6 Sample precision is measured by the size of *confidence intervals*. Confidence intervals contain the parameter a given proportion (ordinarily 95%) of the time.
7 Statistical test findings apply to samples of all sizes because they incorporate into their results the degree of sampling error contained in samples of different sizes.
8 Statistics from both large and small samples thus estimate parameters equally accurately, but only if the sample from which it comes is reasonably *unbiased*.
9 *Unbiased* samples are those in which all members of the population had an equal chance for sample inclusion.

yield a reliability coefficient of 0.90 and a validity coefficient of 0.95 Only 18 cases will yield a reliability coefficient of 0.95 and a validity coefficient of 0.97. If the average level of agreement is 0.60, only 12 cases are needed for the same level of reliability and validity. As the level of similarity rises to 0.70, 0.80, and 0.90, the number of cases (sample size, n) falls to eight, six, and three cases respectively. At an average level of agreement of 0.90, three cases yield a reliability coefficient of 0.96 and a validity coefficient of 0.99.

Sample designs for ethnographic analysis thus differ in important respects from conventional sample designs. They don't require large sample sizes and they don't depend on random selection. Useful sample designs for the study of cultures stratify the population by contrasting life experiences that may produce cultural differences, employ judgmental selection of key informants and critical cases, and select other cases based on their availability, either out of availability (convenience) or through a snowball procedure. Set sample size for specific strata by quota, depending on the average level of agreement. Efficient sample designs track levels of agreement, and expand sample sizes and change stratification criteria consistent with levels of agreement and identified cultural boundaries.

Pay close attention to your sampling criteria. *They determine to whom you can validly generalize.* The sample you actually select may allow generalization only to a population that differs considerably from the one you originally targeted. For example, if you want to identify and infer critical differences in the cultural models employed by recidivist prostitutes and drug users, a sample drawn from the prison population will exclude a large subset of informants. Where are the non-recidivists? Have you talked with women who haven't (yet?) been incarcerated? How do they differ from women who, later in life, leave the business? The absence of people with these life experiences introduces sample selection bias into your study. If you want to study prostitution and entrepreneurship, don't forget to interview *former* prostitutes about their business experiences – or point out the sample selection bias to your readers and amend your interpretation of findings accordingly. Ask yourself how your chosen sampling method might unintentionally exclude an important subset of informants, and how that exclusion may affect your findings. Health studies that draw clinic samples miss all the informants who don't attend the clinic in question or, more generally, don't seek care during the study. A clinic-based study of women's breast cancer and mammography concerns may help the clinic improve its service delivery to existing patients. But it misses women who don't have mammograms, so it can't give much insight into how the clinic can extend services to people who need them but don't currently use them.

Measurement errors

Measurement error pervades all forms of data collection. Box 7.2 lists some common sources. Before you can avoid or eliminate error, you have to see it. Make sources of measurement error part of your consciousness and take them into all interview and observation situations. Ask your informants to elaborate with examples from both past and present circumstances. Ask for clarification. Summarize your understanding and ask if you got it right. Check regularly with your informant, and cross-check for variability between informants.

But remember that the errors we make apply also to our informants. Your field notes will contain random error merely because you asked a specific informant a specific question at a specific time and place. People lie, sometimes reflexively rather than intentionally. People forget. People rationalize what they do. People do things for many reasons. People aren't aware of all, or even most of the influences on what they do. People may be completely *unaware* of the most important influences on what they do, particularly when those influences are historical, macro-level phenomena which can't be perceived clearly in the minutiae of day-to-day living. What they make conscious varies from one time and place to another. People misjudge the relative importance of their reasons, intentions, or motivations. They change their evaluations. The constantly changing context of fieldwork and social interaction bring into play all of these possibilities. They thus introduce random error – the kind (by definition) that we cannot predict. Random error makes it hard to see nuanced error and exacerbates the problem of distinguishing what's there from what you put there.

Box 7.2 Common sources of measurement error

Reactivity

- informant–investigator (status, gender, race, ethnicity)
- context (e.g., public, private)

Questions

- ambiguity
- offensiveness
- biased phrasing
- make no sense to informants
- mean something different to different informants
- inaccurate translation

Interview format

- overly long
- confusing

Respondent

- disinterest
- fatigue
- lack of time
- etiquette, embarrassment
- traumatic topic or experience
- memory (bias, confusion, decay)
- threatened
- ignorance, lack of awareness or insight
- no common reference standard among informants

Ethnographer

- perceptual biases and filters from prior experience
- memory (confusion, decay)
- perceptual errors of observation or recording of data
- electronic file coding errors
- absence of empathy, active engagement with informants
- failure to speak the same language

Informant analyses and descriptions, and elicited "reasons," intentions, or motivations constitute empirical claims with the same logical status as all hypotheses. Both arise from people's imagination. Both may be figments of someone's imagination with no empirical validity.

You must interact intensively and create personal relationships with the people you want to understand. Spending time getting to know someone opens the only door available for you to learn what that person sees, and what it means, when he or she looks out at the world. This calls for the personal sensitivity and creativity to allow people to feel comfortable with you, to communicate clearly to people whom you ask for assistance that you are non-threatening. Communicate empathy. Share personal experiences when appropriate. If you want to see what it looks like through another person's eyes, let them see what it looks like through your eyes. Being open, making yourself vulnerable, elicits the same from others.

Being a good listener helps. This means to listen *actively*. Intersperse silent probes with both verbal ("yes!") and non-verbal (smiles, questioning expressions) forms of encouragement and acknowledgment. To repeat: Ask for clarification. Summarize your understanding and ask if you got it right. Don't, for example, assume that you speak the same language as your informant, *particularly* if you both speak French, English, Chinese, or Swahili. All speech reflects individually variable life experiences, as well as local and time-specific cultures. What warrant do you have for thinking that the meaning your informant attributes to a word or phrase matches yours? Anticipate getting your best data by appearing a little stupid.

Base Final Judgments on Consistency

Because our minds invariably generate novelty, consistency reliably distinguishes mental constructions that consist largely of fantasy from those that consist of less. For each important finding, assess finding consistency across data collection means for the cross-sectional, short-term historical, and long-term historical distinctions that you incorporated into your sample design. Adjust for potential sources of measurement error, including random error. This chapter would help you immensely if it told you exactly how to carry out this analysis explicitly, with explicit measurements of consistency. It doesn't because we have no such method. Development of such a method for meta-analysis of internal consistency should count as one of cognitive anthropology's important research goals.

REFERENCES

Barnett, H. G.
1953 Innovation: The Basis of Cultural Change. New York: McGraw-Hill.
Bartlett, F. C.
1932 Remembering. Cambridge: Cambridge University Press.
Bernard, H. R.
2005 Research Methods in Anthropology. 4th edition. Walnut Creek, CA: AltaMira.
Bernard, H. R., ed.
1998 Handbook of Methods in Cultural Anthropology. Walnut Creek, CA: AltaMira.
Calvin, W. H.
1996 The Cerebral Code: Thinking a Thought in the Mosaics of the Mind. Cambridge, MA: MIT Press.

Campbell, D. T.
1970 Natural Selection as an Epistemological Model. *In* A Handbook of Methods in Cultural Anthropology. Raoul Naroll and Ronald Cohen, eds. Pp. 51–85. Garden City, NY: Natural History Press.
Handwerker, W. P.
1993 Gender Power Differences between Parents and High Risk Sexual Behavior: AIDS/STD Risk Factors Extend to a Prior Generation. Journal of Women's Health 2:301–316.
1998 Why Violence? Human Organization 57:200–208.
2003 Traumatic Stress, Ecological Contingency, and Sexual Behavior: Antecedents and Consequences of Sexual Precociousness, Sexual Mobility, and Childbearing in Adolescence. Ethos 31:385–411.
2005 Sample Design. *In* Encyclopedia of Social Measurement. Kimberly Kempf-Leonard, ed. New York: Elsevier.
2009 The Origin of Cultures. Walnut Creek, CA: Left Coast.
Handwerker, W. P., and S. P. Borgatti
1998 Reasoning with Numbers. *In* Handbook of Methods in Cultural Anthropology. H. R. Bernard, ed. Pp. 549–587. Walnut Creek, CA: AltaMira.
Tuchman, B.
1987 The March of Folly. New York: Random House.
Weller, S. C.
1987 Shared Knowledge, Intracultural Variation, and Knowledge Aggregation. American Behavioral Scientist 31:178–193.
1998 Structured Interviewing and Questionnaire Construction. *In* Handbook of Methods in Cultural Anthropology. H. R. Bernard, ed. Pp. 365–409. Walnut Creek, CA: AltaMira.
Weller, S. C., and A. K. Romney
1988 Systematic Data Collection. Qualitative Research Methods Series 10. Newbury Park, CA: Sage.

CHAPTER 8

Data, Method, and Interpretation in Cognitive Anthropology

James Boster

If cognitive psychology is prototypically the study of the process of thought in individuals as observed in experimental settings, then cognitive anthropology is prototypically the study of the content of thought, or knowledge, as distributed through communities of individuals and observed in natural settings. This contrast highlights the ways in which they are complementary inquiries into the nature of thought and knowledge. Cognitive anthropologists are more scruffy than neat; find pattern in complexity; trust qualitative data but verify quantitatively; focus on the forest not the trees; often doubt whether data mean what one expected them to mean; and balance an appreciation of the common humanity of individuals with an awareness of the historical uniqueness of the cultural environments in which they develop. They are poised between psychology and anthropology – seeing the hearts and minds of individuals as the loci where culture is generated and seeking to explain how collective representations of the world emerge out of individual efforts to understand. The differences between the ways cognitive anthropologists and cognitive psychologists interpret data follows from these differences between the fields.

Cognitive psychology and cognitive anthropology are complementary inquiries into the nature of thought and knowledge. Cognitive psychology is prototypically the study of the *process* of thought in *individuals* as observed in *experimental settings*, while cognitive anthropology is prototypically the study of the *content* of thought, or knowledge, as distributed through *communities* of individuals and observed in *natural settings*.[1] The differences in the way cognitive anthropologists and cognitive psychologists interpret data follow from these differences in the goals and methods of the fields. Table 8.1 summarizes how the fields complement each other. It also outlines the topics addressed in this essay.

A Companion to Cognitive Anthropology, First Edition. Edited by David B. Kronenfeld, Giovanni Bennardo, Victor C. de Munck, and Michael D. Fischer.

Table 8.1 Cognitive anthropology and cognitive psychology

Cognitive anthropology	*Cognitive psychology*
Studies contents of thought (knowledge)	Studies processes of thought
Studies communities in natural settings	Studies individuals in laboratories
Scruffy	Neat
Ethnographic, descriptive, exploratory	Experimental
Discovers pattern in complexity	Controls experimental parameters
Discovers questions	Tests hypotheses
Derives instrument from people studied	Designs instrument in advance
Strives for ecological validity	Strives for reliability

Content and Process

We humans are united by our common humanity: humans are profoundly biologically similar; they share the same cognitive and emotional capacities; the same physiological systems of hormones and neurons, blood and breath. Yet everywhere, in each of us, that common humanity is instantiated in a culturally specific way. Each of us is born into and learns about a world at a particular place and time, surrounded by speakers of particular languages, who believe in particular interpretations of the world and of each other, and who behave guided by particular sets of cultural rules. A child's acquisition of language provides a good example of a biologically based developmental process that unfolds in a universally similar fashion but with culturally specific results: French babies learn French while Dutch babies learn Dutch. The processes of thought are shared by humans in general; the contents of thought are often shared only within specific cultural communities.

If one is studying universal cognitive processes, almost any individual human is as good an exemplar of the species as any other. (Hence the common use of university undergraduates as research subjects in psychology experiments.) It is a nice paradox that because psychology studies processes shared by the species as a whole, it can use the smallest unit of analysis, the individual. In contrast, because cognitive anthropology studies cultural contents which vary greatly, it must use a larger unit of analysis, a whole community, because a single individual cannot be expected to be able to report on the entire information pool maintained by the group as a whole. Perhaps only universes can be understood in a grain of sand.

Because cognitive psychologists can treat an individual human as a unit of study, they usually bring that individual into a laboratory where they establish clear experimental controls on the particular features of the cognitive processes they want to study. For example, they are able to shine light of a precise wavelength and intensity or images for a precise number of milliseconds into a human eye and measure the responses. Many of the mental processes studied by cognitive psychologists are so general that animal models can be used; much of our understanding of human color vision is derived from DeValois's work with rhesus macaques in which he threaded micro-electrodes into individual neurons of their lateral geniculate nuclei (DeValois et al. 1966). Cognitive anthropologists do not have the luxury of being able to bring their unit of analysis, an entire human community, into a laboratory and establish clear experimental controls over the parameters they would like to study. There are also no good animal models for most of the phenomena they are interested in.

The contrast of psychologists as experimentalists with anthropologists as natural historians may be partly due to the amount of progress that each has made toward being a mature science with well-defined standards for the rigor and reliability of its observations. Psychology is an older discipline than anthropology, staffed throughout its history by a much larger number of investigators, and long ago left behind the natural historical phase that most sciences begin with. Comparatively speaking, anthropology is still in its adolescence and its theories are more like descriptive generalizations than the mathematical models to be found in physics, biology, psychology, and other "harder" sciences. Absent clear models to test, observation and description are the only routes toward understanding.

More Scruffy than Neat

However, it is doubtful that many cognitive anthropologists would move their investigations into laboratories even if they could, except for the most specific questions (e.g., Kay and Kempton 1984). The difference is partly a cultural or aesthetic one: cognitive anthropologists share the ethnographic orientation of other cultural anthropologists. Cognitive anthropologists are generally more scruffy than neat, preferring to study complex social realities as opposed to the simpler ones that can be created in laboratories. Rather than establishing order in the very design of the investigation, as an experimentalist does, they tend to prefer to discover the order or pattern in the messy natural settings where culture is found. Their propensity to orderliness is manifested in their choice of clear, explicit, and systematic methods of data collection and analysis, rather than in their choice of what to study.

This aesthetic of seeking to discover pattern and using systematic methods to do so can clearly be seen in the origin of the field of cognitive anthropology. In the late 1940s and 1950s, many of the graduate students and junior faculty members at Yale joined in a sharp critique of the coding categories used by G. P. Murdoch to make cross-cultural comparisons (Murdoch 1949, 1957). They felt that codes were assigned in ways that did little justice to how members of the society understood themselves. They wanted to develop methods that would allow the native's point of view to emerge intact, without subjecting the description of a society to the procrustean violence of artificial coding categories: They sought descriptions that were free from the interpretive categories of the investigator. Their critique produced something that would seem very strange in later decades: a fierce devotion to the possibility of extreme cultural relativism coupled with as fierce a faith in the power of the right formal methods of systematic data collection and analysis to deliver the native models intact. Thus, even while criticizing his methods, these early cognitive anthropologists bore the imprint of their association with Murdoch. Although they rejected many of Murdoch's assumptions, they embraced the rigor that characterized his systematic approach to cultural materials. The commitment to recovering native understandings of the world intact without imposing on it the investigators' own categories and to systematic methods of investigation continues to characterize the field of cognitive anthropology. It is distinguished from cognitive psychology principally by the first of these commitments and from most other cultural anthropology principally by the second.[2]

Finding Pattern in Ever Increasing Complexity

Although the methods employed by cognitive anthropologists have been explicit and systematic throughout the 50-year history of the discipline, the tool chest and the favored tools have changed markedly over time as have the sorts of the domains explored. Over time, the number of tools in the tool chest grew, enabling the exploration of increasingly complex domains. In the following pages, I trace the history of growth of the tool chest and the complexity of domains studied. I cover much of the same ground as D'Andrade (1995), but with a narrower emphasis on the interrelationships between the types of methods of data collection and analysis used, the sorts of domains studied, and the modes of interpreting the results. At the time the discipline was founded, investigations focused on "the study of the referential use of standard, readily elicitable linguistic responses – or *terms*" (Frake 1962:74) and examined the organization of sets of terms or *lexicons.* The lexicons studied tended to be narrow in scope.

The principal tool used by these early cognitive anthropologists was componential analysis. This is a procedure for discovering the criterial feature dimensions underlying a domain and for mapping feature values of the dimensions onto terms in a lexicon. ("Sex" is an example of a feature dimension, while "male" and "female" are examples of feature values.) The procedure is directly analogous to those which have proved useful to linguists in discovering phonemes and morphemes; one finds pairs or sets of terms that contrast with each other (i.e., are included in the same superordinate category), one attributes everything that is shared in meaning to membership in the superordinate category, and one discovers the attributes that distinguish between the members of the contrast set.[3] Goodenough (1956) and Lounsbury (1956) restricted the application of the method to lexicons that form paradigms, in which every (or nearly every) combination of feature values corresponds to a distinct term.

The most perfect example of the application of componential analysis was probably Conklin's (1962) analysis of Hanunóo pronouns shown in Figure 8.1. The eight pronouns correspond to every possible combination of three binary feature dimensions: inclusion and exclusion of speaker, inclusion and exclusion of hearer, and minimal and non-minimal membership. The whole set of pronouns can be represented as the vertices of a cube, whose depth, width, and height correspond to the three feature dimensions.

The structure reflects the communicative needs of humans to efficiently distinguish who is being referred to in conversation; the pronouns signal whether speaker or hearer are included and whether one or more human is being referred to. Given that English speakers often use awkward formulations like "you all" or "we two," one could argue that Hanunóo pronouns represent a better solution to this universal conversational problem than English pronouns. Unfortunately, examples of such beauty and elegance are rare – there are relatively few domains lexicalized as paradigms.

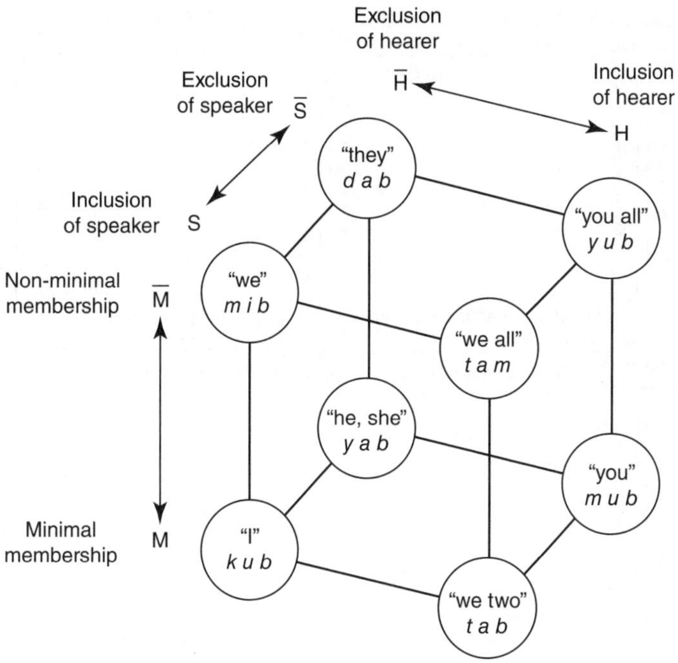

Figure 8.1 Componential analysis of Hanunóo pronouns (adapted from Conklin 1962).

One reason for the rarity of paradigms can be seen by comparing the number of terms required to label the feature values themselves with the number of terms required to label every possible combination of feature values. The number feature values to be labeled go up by a rate of twice the number of feature dimensions (N) while the number of unique combinations of feature values goes up by 2^N. Thus, in a domain in which the features vary independently, it is more efficient to name the feature values themselves, rather than the combinations of features. No wonder paradigms are rare; very frequent reference to the unique combinations of feature values is required to justify the lexical overhead (as is the case in pronominal systems, kinship terminologies, and terms for sex and age classes of humans and other domesticated animals).[4]

Discover the Questions from the People Studied

Metzger and Williams (1966) and Frake (1964) greatly expanded the number and complexity of the domains that could be explored by developing methods that could examine a more general class of semantic relations between terms in a domain.[5] Frake (1964), in particular, advocated discovering the kinds of questions the natives themselves asked about the terms in the domain, rather than going to the field armed with a predetermined set of questions.[6] He used the method to represent the semantic

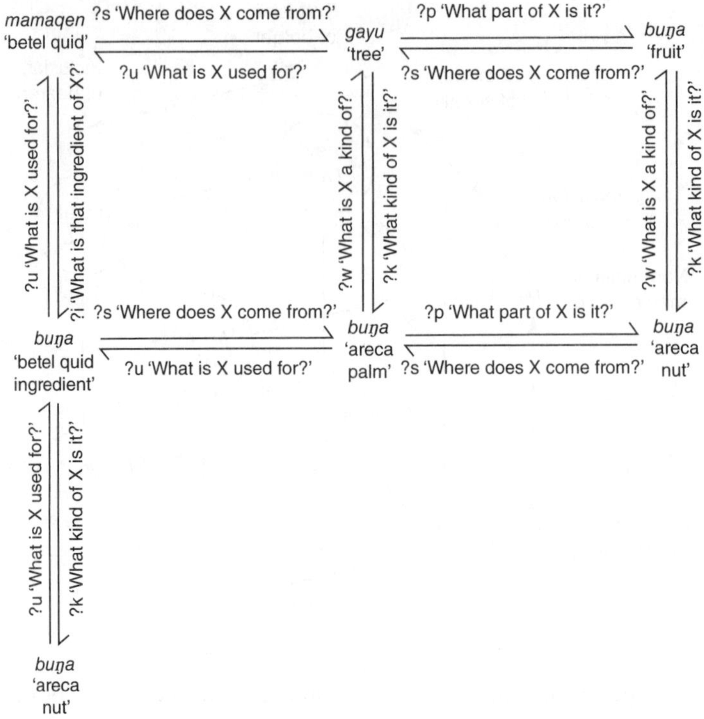

Figure 8.2 A semantic network linked by reciprocal queries (adapted from Frake 1964:fig. 2).

relations between terms used by the Subanun of the southern Philippines to talk about chewing betel nut, shown in Figure 8.2.

The figure also illustrates Frake's sense of humor; he picked an example in which the core term buŋa has five distinct polysemous meanings, so that one can create a series of queries in which the answer is always "buŋa." Starting at the lower left corner of Figure 8.2 where the term buŋa has the sense of areca nut as the raw material for an ingredient of a betel quid and traversing the figure to the upper right corner, where the term buŋa has the sense of fruit, we can ask the question: "What is buŋa used for?" Answer: "For buŋa [betel quid ingredient]." Question: "Where does buŋa come from?" Answer: "From buŋa [areca palm]." Question: "What part of buŋa is it?" Answer: "buŋa [areca nut]." Question: "What is buŋa a kind of?" Answer: "It is a kind of buŋa [fruit]."

Over time, the tool chest expanded to include: using proposition frames to build item-by-attribute matrices (e.g., D'Andrade et al. 1972); methods of eliciting similarity judgments (e.g., Romney et al. 1979); identification tasks (e.g., Berlin and Kay 1969); and propositional analysis (D'Andrade 1976). The expansion of the tool chest allowed a great increase in the lexicon size and complexity in the domains studied. These domains included disease categorization, color classification, folk classification of plants and animals, occupation terms, personality descriptors, et cetera. At the same time, the goals of the analysis shifted from trying to find the criterial features that distinguished the meanings of terms to trying to find the salient features which may characterize an item, but are not part of the definition of the term (D'Andrade 1995:76). For example, "maleness" is a criterial feature of the term *bachelor*, while "possesses wings" may be a salient feature of the term *bird*, but it does not define what a bird is.

Two articles (D'Andrade et al. 1972; D'Andrade 1976) deserve special attention because they show some of the power of the new tools and also continuing adherence to the commitment to assessing native beliefs with instruments drawn from what the natives themselves said, a commitment made both in the foundation of the field and in subsequent works by Metzger and Williams and Frake already mentioned. D'Andrade et al.'s (1972) goal was to produce an item-by-attribute matrix in which the items were diseases and the attributes were the salient characteristics of the diseases. Their first step was to have Americans and Mexicans list all the disease terms they could think of and then select the most common and least ambiguous terms. This was the source of the items for the matrix.

The second step was to interview Americans and Mexicans about the diseases and then select statements that mention properties of particular diseases (e.g., "It is safer to have chicken pox as a child and get it over with"). These propositions were transformed into the slot frame constructions earlier used by Metzger and Williams (1966) in their formal elicitations procedures, yielding frames such as "It is safer to have _____ as a child and get it over with." In other words, both the list of diseases and the queries that were made about them were derived from the natives themselves. Next, Americans and Mexicans were asked to rate the likelihood that a particular disease fit each of the frames.[7] The analysis of the rows and columns of the item-by-attribute matrix with MDSCAL, a multidimensional scaling program, yielded a picture of how the whole set of diseases fit into the entire field of attributes shown in Figure 8.3.

D'Andrade (1976) went on to reason that it was unlikely that either Americans or Mexicans stored a 30 by 30 matrix, or 900 independent propositions about disease, in their heads and so set about to discover the heuristics that must have been employed to generate their answers to the surveys. He did this by examining the 435 contingency tables between all possible pairs of the 30 attributes (29 * 30/2), looking for logical relationships between them. These are signaled by zeros in the two by two contingency tables. The most important and familiar of these logical relationships are implication, mutual implication, and contradiction.[8] Figure 8.4 provides an illustration of the logical relations between attributes that were produced by this propositional analysis.

D'Andrade (1976) represented a turning point in the development of the field of cognitive anthropology. On the one hand, it illustrated the power of the accumulated methods in the tool chest to represent not only how the natives responded to systematic surveys but also what heuristics they must have used to produce their answers. But D'Andrade, although pleased with the number of logical relations that could be generated from an item-by-attribute matrix with his method, was disappointed by the limitations of what the method showed about how Americans actually understand illness (1995:129): treating myself as an informant, I could explicate *why* many of these properties were linked to each other, but nothing in the graph contained this information. He goes on to explain that the graph of logical relations between the properties of disease nowhere represents the germ theory that Americans use to

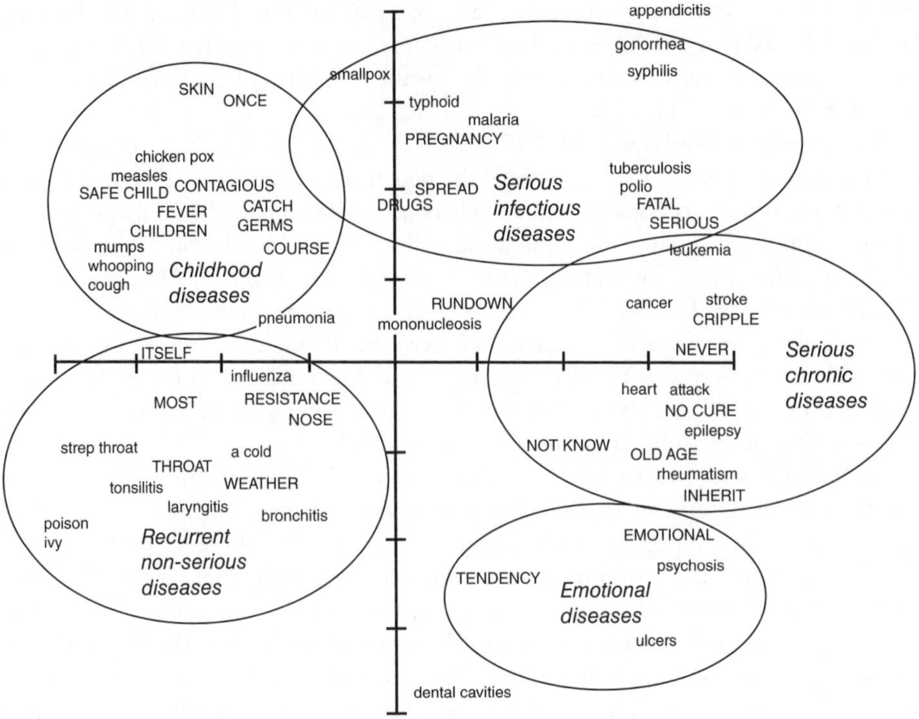

Figure 8.3 Diseases and their attributes. Diseases are shown in lower case, attributes of diseases in upper case, and clusters of diseases in bold italics (adapted from D'Andrade 1995:75, fig. 4.4).

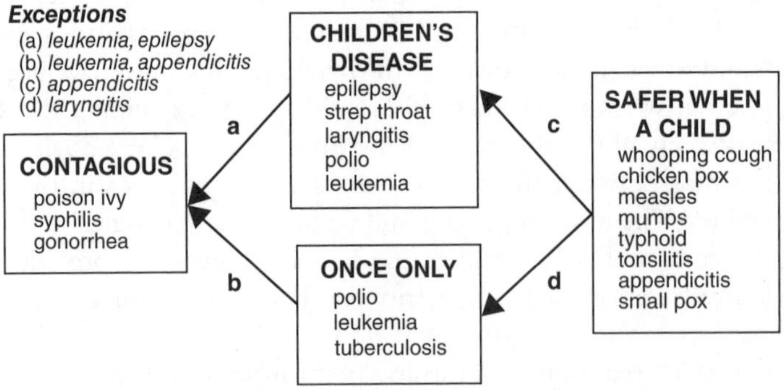

Figure 8.4 Logical relations among a small subset of American disease properties. Attributes of diseases are shown in bold upper case, diseases in lower case, arrows indicate logical implication, and exceptions to the rules are shown in italicized lower case (adapted from part of D'Andrade 1995:128, fig. 6.1).

understand disease. His disappointment initiated a third stage in the expansion of both the number of methods in the cognitive anthropological tool chest and the complexity of the cultural phenomena they could be used to study: it initiated research on cultural models.

Assessing the Validity of Cultural Models: Trust but Verify

At this stage, beginning in the late 1970s, many fine pieces of research were undertaken to explore the mental or cultural models that humans used to guide their understandings of the world, many of which are to be found in Holland and Quinn (1987) and in D'Andrade and Strauss (1992). To tackle these new questions, cognitive anthropologists adopted the methods of open-ended interviewing long used by other cultural anthropologists (and by cognitive anthropologists to generate their instruments), but there remained important differences in how they analyzed the narratives that were generated.

Describing cultural models presents challenges that were not faced by earlier cognitive anthropologists because there is no practical way to use interpretation-free methods to discover and describe them. One must learn them and somehow check to see if one's own understanding matches that of the natives who have the cultural model. One means of testing the adequacy of a cultural model was stated in Goodenough's classic definition of culture:

> A society's culture consists of whatever it is one has to know or believe in order to operate in a manner acceptable to its members, and to do so in any role that they accept for any one of themselves. [Goodenough 1957:36]

This definition of culture was novel in being an operational one. It outlined what a cultural description should look like and described a test for the adequacy of that description. An ethnography, according to Goodenough, should present a theory of the conceptual models people use rather than just a simple description of their behavior. It should be like a grammar or rule book for acting like a native. One tested the adequacy of an ethnography in much the same way that Turing thought we should test for artificial intelligence. If using the ethnography allows us to pass as a native, it is good enough.[9]

This was essentially the method used by Gladwin (1970) in his account of Micronesian navigation (D'Andrade 1995:158). But other investigators of cultural models have used methods of checking the validity of their descriptions of the cultural models more analogous to those adopted by Romney and D'Andrade (1964) in their comparison of the psychological validity of their own model of American kinship with that provided by Wallace and Atkins (1960). One generates a representation of a cultural model using linguistic means and tests the adequacy of the model using data collected independently.

Quinn (1985) studied the different senses of the term *commitment* in marriage in the way a linguist might – she generated a corpus through a long series of open-ended interviews, found all the instances of the use of the term *commitment*, identified the sense of each instance, and then assessed what proportion of her corpus was accounted for by the three senses she identified.

Garro (1988) in her study of Ashinabe cultural models of hypertension, and Kempton et al. (1995) in their study of American environmental beliefs and values, used essentially the same procedure. They first conducted open-ended interviews with a number of informants, extracted salient propositions from the transcripts of the interviews, and then built surveys to test the amount of agreement on each of the propositions and their patterns of social distribution.

Kempton (1987) compared his informants' cultural models of how a thermostat works with their actual patterns of interactions with their thermostats. His open-ended interviews revealed two models of the functioning of a thermostat: the valve model and the switch model. Adherents to the valve model thought of the thermostat dial as a kind of spigot – the further one turned the dial, the faster the house would be heated. Adherents to the switch model conceived of the thermostat dial as controlling a switch that would turn the furnace on and off – the furnace would generate heat at a constant rate no matter how far the dial had been turned above the set point. (The switch model is technically accurate.) Kempton had also installed devices which recorded the history of settings on each of his informants' thermostats. Adherents of the valve model would come home from the cold, turn their thermostats up very high and turn them back down when they were comfortable, while adherents of the switch model would pick a setting and then leave the thermostat alone. Ironically, Kempton discovered that it was the informants with the "incorrect" valve model who produced the greatest human comfort with the least expenditure of BTUs (British Thermal Units), because actual houses differ from ideal ones in being drafty and actual humans differ from ideal ones in experiencing warmth not in absolute but in relative terms.

Mathews's (1992) account of different versions of the "La Llorona" (The Weeping Woman) story comes closest to exemplifying what Goodenough (1957) was asking for: a description of a cultural grammar that would generate the various versions of the story. She interpreted a corpus of stories about "La Llorona." For men this is a story about how women can tempt men and lead them to their deaths while for women it is a story of how a man who wastes his resources on other women rather than devoting them to his own wife and children is responsible for his own demise. Moving beyond simple descriptions of the story and its variants, Mathews constructed a story grammar that generates the various versions of the story she had collected. This is hermeneutical validation – using a generative model that explains the similarity and difference between the various versions of the story to establish the validity of her analysis of them.

Focus on the Forest, Not the Trees

Cognitive anthropologists as natural historians and cognitive psychologists as experimentalists also differ in their preferred tools of data analysis. Because an experimentalist is most interested in whether the parameters that have been manipulated in the experiment make a significant difference, the most important tools are analysis of variance (ANOVA), multivariate analysis of variance (MANOVA), or t-tests. Much more often cognitive anthropologists are not seeking to test a hypothesis as much as map an overall pattern. We have seen one illustration of this in D'Andrade et al.'s (1972) use of MDSCAL to place a set of diseases amid a large field of attributes of the diseases. Instead of ANOVA, cognitive anthropologists have tended to use

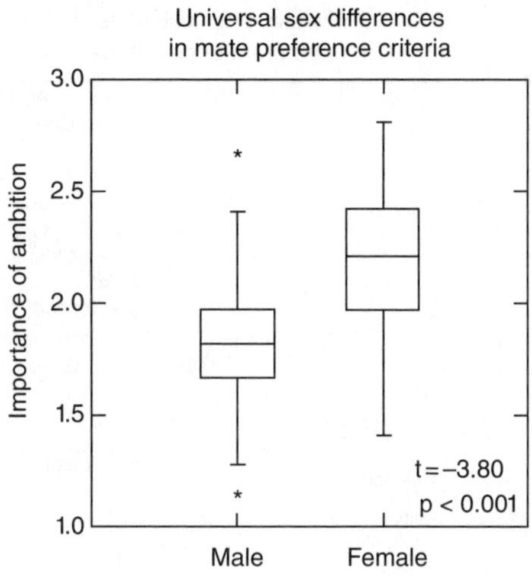

Figure 8.5 Sex differences in the rating of the importance of ambition in a mate (data from Buss 1989).

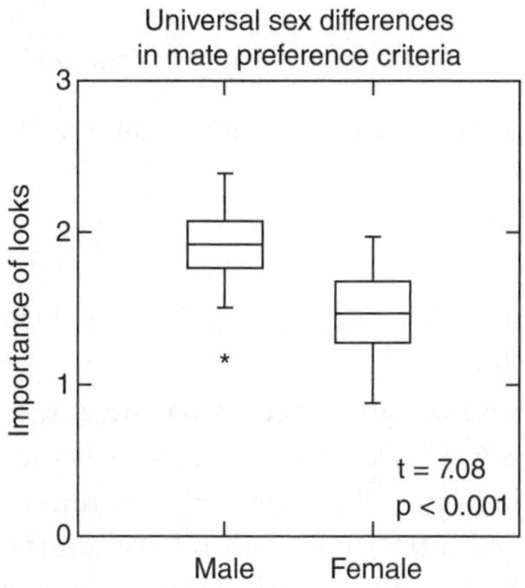

Figure 8.6 Sex differences in the rating of the importance of looks in a mate (data from Buss 1989).

multidimensional scaling (MDS), factor analysis, correspondence analysis, cluster analysis, or simple scatter plots that will show the overall picture of informants' understanding of a domain or the overall picture of the distribution of knowledge through a community.

Figures 8.5, 8.6, and 8.7 illustrate the different things one learns from the tools favored by cognitive psychologists versus cognitive anthropologists, even though my example comes from the social and evolutionary psychologist Buss. Buss (1989) and Buss et al. (1990) argued that men and women systematically differ in their mate preferences: women value signs that their potential mate can provide

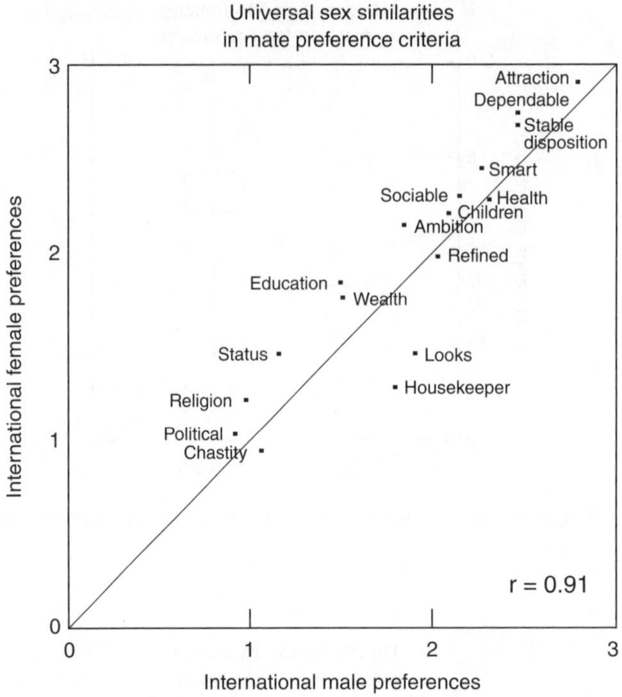

Figure 8.7 Sex similarity in the overall relative importance of characteristics of a mate (data from Buss et al. 1990).

resources (e.g., wealth, ambition) and men value signs that their potential mate is healthy and fertile (e.g., looks).

And significant sex differences are exactly what he and his collaborators found, as shown in Figures 8.5 and 8.6. However, if one uses tools that expose the whole pattern of preferences, as shown in Figure 8.7, one sees that differences emphasized by Buss are actually small residuals on a 0.91 correlation between the mate preferences of men and women. If one tests the hypothesis that men and women differ in their mate preferences in the way predicted by evolutionary theory, there are indeed significant differences. But if one approaches the question by seeking to reveal the overall pattern of similarity and difference in ratings, one discovers that men and women are actually very similar in their judgments. Both rate most important characteristics that would allow one to trust one's partner in making a lifetime commitment that includes shared child-rearing (mutual attraction, dependable, stable, good disposition, smart) and both rate least important characteristics of mates that do not have much to do with that shared enterprise (religion, political beliefs, chastity). The characteristics emphasized by Buss fall in the middle of relative importance, but the statistically significant difference between the sexes is a small one: men and women agree about what is most important and least important and differ only on those traits that both rate as of middling importance. These sorts of representations of overall pattern are essential to the more natural historical and descriptive approach of cognitive anthropologists. It is easy to report the outcomes of t-tests or ANOVA in a sentence or two, but it would take a very long

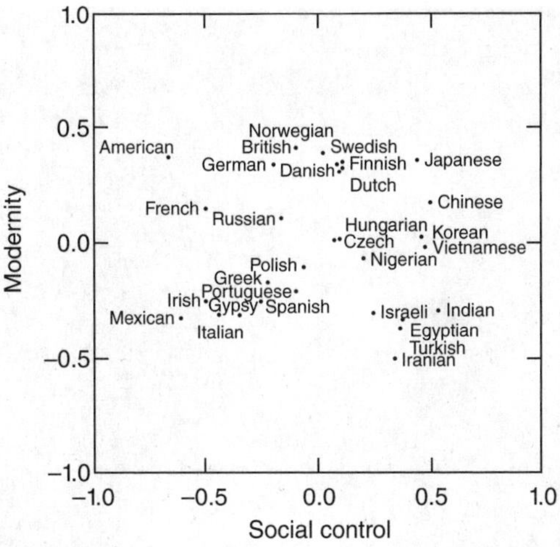

Figure 8.8 Nations plotted on dimensions interpreted as relative social control and modernity (from Boster and Maltseva 2006).

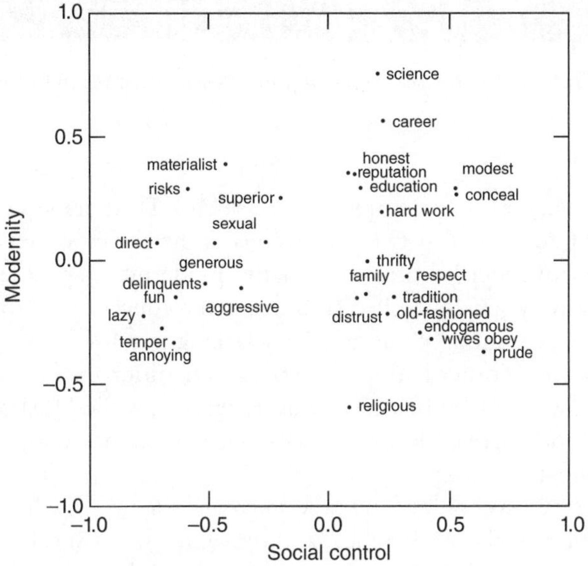

Figure 8.9 Attributes plotted on dimensions interpreted as relative social control and modernity (from Boster and Maltseva 2006).

narrative to describe the overall placement of diseases and attributes of disease shown in Figure 8.3 or the sex differences in the ratings of all the desirable attributes of a mate, shown in Figure 8.7. But pictures allow one to see whole forests at a glance.

These sorts of pictures are especially necessary when one wants to place a collection of items in a field of attributes, as D'Andrade et al. (1972) did. Figures 8.8 and 8.9 show a collection of nations and their attributes as judged by samples of about 70 informants each in 16 locations in Europe (Boster and Maltseva 2006), using

Figure 8.10 *Is This the Mona Lisa?* (original print used by permission of the owner, James Boster).

correspondence analysis to accomplish the task that D'Andrade et al. (1972) had done with MDSCAL. The first two dimensions of the correspondence analysis were interpreted as relative social control and relative modernity: Japanese were judged as modern and relatively self-controlled (modest; value education, hard work, and reputation), Americans as modern and relatively lacking in self-control (materialist, risk taking, feel superior to other nations), Iranians as traditional and relatively self-controlled (prudish, wives obey their husbands, religious), while Mexicans were judged to be traditional and relatively lacking in self-control (lazy, hot-tempered, and annoying in large groups).

In sum, cognitive psychologists as experimentalists focus on whether the parameters they manipulate make a difference, and thus rely on statistical methods that test for differences (such as ANOVA). Cognitive anthropologists as natural historians strive to view the overall picture with less concern for the details, and thus depend on statistical methods that show overall pattern (such as factor analysis). In short, cognitive psychologists examine trees and cognitive anthropologists contemplate forests.

Data Do Not Always Mean What One Expected

In the natural, complex, and sometimes exotic settings where culture is found, cognitive anthropologists often feel lost. They know they are not in Kansas anymore, but they are not certain exactly where they are. In particular, often the humans they are trying to understand are guided by fundamentally different sets of assumptions from their own, yet it is hard to see either one's own or the other's assumptions clearly. Usually, it is one's own blinders that are the hardest to see. Often the totally unexpected offers the best chance to examine one's assumptions.[10] This experience of feeling lost and trying to find one's way in an alien world breeds a certain kind of skepticism about whether things are as they seem – whether the data one collects means what one expected them to mean. This skepticism is most acute among those who try to see the world through the eyes of humans very different from themselves.

An excellent example of the way in which data might mean something different from what it was expected to mean can be found in Scribner (1977). She gave syllogistic reasoning problems to Liberians, some of whom had gone to school while others had not. Those who had gone to school answered much the same way as educated people anywhere, but her unschooled Liberian informants seemed highly illogical – they answered the reasoning problems at only barely better than a chance rate. But there was a pattern in which they deviated from the "correct answers" which she called an *empirical bias*. In some cases, her respondents rejected part of the problem information so that when presented (for example) with the syllogism "All people who live in Monrovia are married; Kemu is not married; Does she live in Monrovia?" they would answer, "Yes. Monrovia is not for any one kind of people, so Kemu came to live there." In other instances, they would import new evidence to respond, so that when presented (for example) with the syllogism "All people who own houses pay house tax; Boima does not pay a house tax; Does he own a house?" they would answer, "Boima has a house but he is exempted from paying house tax. The government appointed Boima to collect house tax so they exempted him from paying house tax." To repeat, this empirical bias was found only among Liberians who had not gone to school; those who gone to school answered similarly to educated people from other places. Instead of interpreting this difference as evidence of a defect in the logic of individuals that schooling can ameliorate, Scribner saw it as her informants' refusal to reason within the narrow and sometimes absurd framework presented by the questioner. Those who had gone to school knew what this game was about; even if the question did not make any sense, one's task was to reason within the false world created by the problem posed by one's questioner. In other words, they had learned to give teachers the response they wanted, because that is the strategy that earns the best grades in school. Those who had never gone to school did not learn the costs of failing to adopt this submissive strategy. In effect, having an empirical bias means not instantly acquiescing to the false world created by a questioner, but answering according to one's own understanding of the world.

I encountered a similar sort of situation as that faced by Scribner (1977) when I asked members of a Shuar community to identify what emotion was being expressed in a series of facial gestures of emotion (Boster 2005b). Even though the same photos had generated "genuine" emotion terms from most of my English-, Spanish-, Italian-, and Polish-speaking informants (that is to say, terms for internally experienced subjective states which usually give rise to particular facial gestures of emotion, the equivalents of English terms such as *angry*, *happy*, and *sad*), only a plurality of my Shuar respondents gave such "genuine" emotion terms. Another set of respondents gave descriptions of other actions by the person photographed (e.g., "He's saying 'Who is there?'" "He's making a joke"); or descriptions of thoughts or beliefs (e.g., "He's thinking of

Table 8.2 Correlations among observed behavior, remembered behavior, and semantic similarity of the coding categories

	Observed behavior	*Remembered behavior*
Remembered behavior	0.34	
Semantic similarity	0.03	0.60

his lover," "He's thinking he will never find a wife"); or descriptions of events that had just happened to the person photographed (e.g., "Her mother just died"). A third set of respondents gave flat descriptions of the facial gestures of emotion themselves (e.g., "She's smiling," "He's laughing," "She is gritting her teeth," "He has his mouth open").

I believe that my Shuar respondents would have been perfectly capable of answering the question "What is this person thinking or feeling?" if they had chosen to, but many of them chose to give me insightful criticism of my research design instead (Boster 2005b).[11] They were telling me that a photograph of an isolated human face lacks the social context that would allow any reasonable inference of what the person photographed is feeling; they were responding with the same kind of empirical bias that Scribner's (1977) respondents had. One can tell from a facial gesture that an individual is "angry," but not whether the person is "jealous," "imposed upon," "insulted," "frustrated," et cetera.[12] This lack of social context gave my Shuar informants three choices: (1) go along and supply the emotion term they believed I wanted (the schooled response); (2) supply a social context in which the gesture makes sense; or (3) give up and flatly describe the facial gesture itself.

An empirical bias is a very general phenomenon in which other humans respond to a scientist's tools of investigation differently from the scientist's expectations. At a first glance, guided by a scientist's starting assumptions, the unexpected responses seem lunatic, deranged, illogical, or idiotic. The judicious application of skepticism reminds one that one is not in Kansas anymore and to look for disparities in cultural starting assumptions.

An early example of this kind of skepticism among cognitive anthropologists was expressed by D'Andrade (1974). For many years previously and since, the social psychologist Bales had been giving classes in the observation of social interaction in which most of the class would be engaged in discussion most of the time, and a few members of the class would slip out of the classroom behind a mirrored window to code what they observed their classmates saying and doing. At the end of the term, all the students would think about the interactions between all the students in the class and report how they remembered each other's behavior. The question is "What behaviors go with which other behaviors?" D'Andrade (1974) showed that the association of behaviors in students' memory of interactions was more similar to the semantic similarity of the codes used than to the actual association of behaviors in the students' observations, as shown in Table 8.2.

In other words, when the students tried to remember each other's behaviors over a term, they assigned positive codes to the students they liked and negative codes to the students they did not like, despite the fact that, in the observed behavior, the various positively coded behaviors and negatively coded behaviors were not strongly associated. (Some individuals tended to be more active in the conversations than others and would receive more positive and more negative codes than other students.) Thus, the pattern in remembered behavior had more to do with the constructive distortions of memory rather than any pattern in the behavior itself.

Randall (1976) exhibited the same skepticism when he doubted whether informants' responses to a series of queries about the inclusion of one category in another really constituted evidence that respondents had taxonomies in their heads (e.g., Question: "What kind of thing is an eastern white pine?" Answer: "A white pine." "What kind of thing is a white pine?" Answer: "A pine." "What kind of thing is a pine?" Answer: "A tree." "What kind of thing is a tree?" Answer: "A plant"). He offered the thought experiment of asking informants about what things eat other things (e.g., Question: "What eats small fish?" Answer: "Bigger fish." Question: "What eats bigger fish?" Answer: "Even bigger fish"; etc.). He doubted whether the answers to such a series of questions constituted evidence that the respondents had a notion of trophic levels.

Similarly, Gatewood (1983) demonstrated that American college students can talk confidently about biological kinds, but the terms used simply served as placeholders without much associated knowledge; students might know that *maple*, *oak*, and *elm* refer to kinds of trees, but often were unable to identify any examples of them.

The message of these examples is that research design in cognitive anthropology does not end with setting research methods – even after one has collected data, one should reverse engineer the procedures to see whether the data mean what one had hoped they would mean. In other words, one should examine whether the questions asked, if understood as intended, could have plausibly produced the responses obtained. If not, one should figure out the question the respondents must have thought they were answering.

The examples tell us we should be especially skeptical when the results indicate either incredible mental limitations of the respondents – unable to reason logically (Scribner 1977); unable to follow simple instructions (Boster 2005b) – or incredible mental prowess – summing and correlating frequencies of behaviors well enough to remember accurately which behaviors go with which over a period of months (D'Andrade 1974); drawing on deeply branched mental representations when they answer a series of questions (Randall 1976); or showing profound biological knowledge when they have had no opportunity to acquire it (Gatewood 1983).

Closing

Cognitive anthropologists explore the substance, organization, and social distribution of human beliefs and knowledge in whatever natural settings they are found. This exploration carries them to the highlands of Chiapas, the lowland rain forests of South America, and islands scattered across the Pacific. It puts them on Alaskan fishing boats and takes them to manioc gardens and blacksmith shops. This essay has emphasized several characteristics: cognitive anthropologists are more scruffy than neat; find pattern in complexity; discover questions to be asked rather than designing all in advance; trust qualitative data but verify quantitatively; focus on the forest not the trees; and often doubt whether data mean what they expected them to mean. They balance an appreciation of our common humanity with one of the historical uniqueness of the cultural environments in which humans develop. Between psychology and anthropology, they see the hearts and minds of individuals as the loci where culture is generated and seek to explain how collective understandings of the world emerge out of individual efforts to understand.

ACKNOWLEDGMENTS

This chapter was first given as a paper at the Annual Meeting of the Society for Scientific Anthropology in Las Vegas, Nevada, February 2009. I would like to thank the organizer of the session, Andrea Bender, and other participants, especially Giovanni Bennardo, John Gatewood, and Doug Medin for their lively presentations and discussion. I also thank my wife for her careful reading and editing of the paper.

NOTES

1 Of course, there are many exceptions to this generalization. There are cognitive psychologists (like Doug Medin) who do fieldwork and cognitive anthropologists who perform experiments. However, the contrast as stated captures the difference in the central tendencies of the two disciplines. The contrasts I draw between cognitive psychology and cognitive anthropology are meant to be between the prototypes of the two fields, not between all of their practitioners.
2 A more complete retelling of this origin story can be found in Boster (2005a).
3 The property of language exploited in these methods is its capacity to make near infinite use of finite means. At every level of the analysis of language (phonology, morphology, semantics, and syntax), one finds a finite set of elements (phonemes, morphemes, etc.) combined through a finite set of rules (phonological, morphological, and syntactic rules) to generate a much greater number of possible forms. Linguists and cognitive anthropologists use this property of language to work backwards, systematically comparing minimally different complex units (sounds, words, meanings) to discover the underlying universe of elements and the rules for combining them.
4 Boster (2005a) offers a more complete explanation of why paradigmatic organizations of domains are rare and taxonomic organizations are common.
5 In the mid-1960s the capacity to make detailed ethnographic descriptions outstripped the theoretical motivations to make them or the analytic capacity to make sense of them. The best example of this problem is probably the "Chiapas drinking project" which produced many cubic yards of printout of detailed ethnographic descriptions of the Tenejapa Tzeltal Maya. Brent Berlin showed me many boxes of these printouts around 1978, when they were mildewing in the basement of the Language Behavior Research Laboratory at the University of California, Berkeley. As far as I know, those boxes continued to mildew until the building was torn down and the massive effort to produce these detailed ethnographic descriptions was largely wasted.
6 The term *natives* in this essay refers to any cultural group whose understanding of the world an anthropologist wants to understand. Both Subanun and Americans count as natives.
7 Americans rated the diseases on a five point scale and Mexicans rated on a three point scale.

8 Table 8.3 shows the contingency matrices of the six kinds of logical relationships between attributes. The most important are types #1, #5, and #6: one-way implication, mutual implication, and contradiction respectively.

Table 8.3

#1		*If a then b*			#2		*If a then not b*		
		b					b		
		0	1				0	1	
a	0	30	30	60	a	0	40	30	70
	1	0	40	40		1	30	0	30
		30	70	100			70	30	100
		If not a then not b					*If not a then b*		
#3		b			#4		b		
		0	1				0	1	
a	0	30	0	30	a	0	0	30	30
	1	30	40	70		1	30	40	70
		60	40	100			30	70	100
		a if and only if b					*a if and only if not b*		
#5		b			#6		b		
		0	1				0	1	
a	0	50	0	50	a	0	0	50	50
	1	0	50	50		1	50	0	50
		50	50	100			50	50	100

9 Goodenough's definition of culture articulated what he thought was important about human understandings of the world and how he thought they should be studied. He joined other anthropologists, each of whom had defined culture in their own way. However, I understand him to say that if one uses his definition, one will find out about a certain kind of aspect of how humans understand the world – the model constructing, rule seeking, grammar building part. He was not saying that culture *must* be understood in his way. He invited other anthropologists to define culture in any way they found useful, as long as it was similar enough to other definitions of culture to insure that one is talking about the same sort of thing. Definitions of culture by other cognitive anthropologists bear a family resemblance to Goodenough's and share the property of articulating what a cultural description is. This is my own definition:

Culture is an information pool that emerges when members of a community attempt to make sense of the world and each other as they struggle and collaborate with each other to get what they want and need (e.g., food, sex, power, acceptance, etc.). Because individuals construct their conceptions of the world from their own experiences and for their own motivations, their understandings vary from one another depending on the characteristics of the individuals, the nature of the domain learned, and the social situations in which learning takes place. [modified from Boster 1986]

The definition shares Goodenough's insistence that culture is learned, but adds that culture is (usually) useful and that individuals vary in their knowledge. It also emphasizes that an ethnography should describe and explain the social distribution of knowledge.

10 One example of violated assumptions signaling a different set of cultural premises occurred when I was irritated that my Awajun guests would repeatedly spit on my floor during my fieldwork with them in the 1970s. The explanation for why their "rude" behavior was actually polite is that spitting is an excellent means to signal non-hostile intent in a very warlike society, because it honestly signals low sympathetic nervous system arousal. In other words, if my guests had come visiting intending to kill me, they would not have been able to spit to save their lives (Boster 2003).

11 The Shuar term *anentaimiawai* refers to both thinking and feeling. Lutz (1985) has described the same sort of single category of thoughts and feelings between the Ifaluk.

12 The lack of social context helps explain why it is that facial gestures of emotions are associated with basic emotion terms and not with secondary terms.

REFERENCES

Berlin, B., and P. Kay

1969 Basic Color Terms: Their Universality and Evolution. Berkeley: University of California Press.

Boster, J. S.

1986 Exchange of Varieties and Information Between Aguaruna Manioc Cultivators. American Anthropologist 88:429–436.

2003 Blood Feud and Table Manners: A Neo-Hobbesian Approach to Jivaroan Warfare. Antropológica 99–100:153–164.

2005a Categories and Cognitive Anthropology. *In* Categorization in the Cognitive Sciences. C. LeFebvre and H. Cohen eds. Amsterdam: Elsevier.

2005b Emotion Categories across Languages. *In* Categorization in the Cognitive Sciences. C. LeFebvre and H. Cohen, eds. Amsterdam: Elsevier.

Boster, J. S., and K. Maltseva

2006 A Crystal Seen from Each of Its Vertices: European Views of European National Characters. Cross-Cultural Research 40(1):47–64.

Buss, D. M.

1989 Sex Differences in Human Mate Preferences: Evolutionary Hypotheses Tested in 37 Cultures. Behavioral and Brain Sciences 12:1–49.

Buss, D. M., et al.

1990 International Preferences in Selecting Mates: A Study of 37 Societies. Journal of Cross Cultural Psychology 21: 5–47.

Conklin, H.

1962 Lexicographical Treatment of Folk Taxonomies. International Journal of American Linguistics 28:119–141.

D'Andrade, R.

1974 Memory and the Assessment of Behavior. *In* Measurement in the Social Sciences. T. Blalock, ed. Pp. 159–186. Chicago: Aldine.

1976 A Propositional Analysis of U.S. American Beliefs about Illness. *In* Meanings in Anthropology. K. Basso and H. Selby, eds. Albuquerque: University of New Mexico Press.

1995 The Development of Cognitive Anthropology. Cambridge: Cambridge University Press.

D'Andrade, R., and C. Strauss

1992 Human Motives and Cultural Models. Cambridge: Cambridge University Press.

D'Andrade, R., N. Quinn, S. Nerlove, and A. K. Romney

1972 Categories of Disease in American-English and Mexican Spanish. *In* Multidimensional Scaling, vol. 2. A. K. Romney, R. Shepard, and S. B. Nerlove, eds. New York: Seminar.

DeValois, R. L., I. Abramov, and G. H. Jacobs

1966 Analysis of the Response Patterns of LGN Cells. Journal of the Optical Society of America 56:966–977.

Frake, C. O.

1962 The Ethnographic Study of Cognitive Systems. *In* Anthropology and Human Behavior. Washington, DC: Anthropological Society of Washington.

1964 Notes on Queries in Ethnography. American Anthropologist 66:132–145.

Garro, L.

1988 Explaining High Blood Pressure: Variation in Knowledge about Illness. American Anthropologist 90:98–119.

Gatewood, J.

1983 Loose Talk: Linguistic Competence and Recognition Ability. American Anthropologist 85:378–387.

Gladwin, T.

1970 East Is a Big Bird. Cambridge, MA: Harvard University Press.

Goodenough, W.

1956 Componential Analysis and the Study of Meaning. Language 32:195–216.

1957 Cultural Anthropology and Linguistics. Georgetown University Monograph Series on Language and Linguistics 3:22–54.

Holland, D., and N. Quinn

1987 Cultural Models of Language and Thought. New York: Cambridge University Press.

Kay, P., and W. Kempton

1984 What is the Sapir Whorf Hypothesis? American Anthropologist 86(1):65–79.

Kempton, W.

1987 Two Theories of Home Heat Control. *In* Cultural Models in Language and Thought. D. Holland and N. Quinn, eds. Cambridge: Cambridge University Press.

Kempton, W., J. S. Boster, and J. A. Hartley

1995 Environmental Values in American Culture. Cambridge, MA: MIT Press.

Lounsbury, F. G.

1956 A Semantic Analysis of the Pawnee Kinship Usage. Language 32:158–194.

Lutz, C.

1985 Ethnopsychology Compared to What? Explaining Behavior and Consciousness among the Ifaluk. *In* Person, Self, and Experience. G. White and J. Kirkpatrick, eds. Berkeley: University of California Press.

Mathews, H.

1992 The Directive Force of Morality Tales in a Mexican Community. *In* Human Motives and Cultural Models. Roy D'Andrade and Claudia Strauss, eds. Cambridge: Cambridge University Press.

Metzger, D., and G. Williams

1966 Some Procedures and Results in the Study of Native Categories: Tzeltal "Firewood." American Anthropologist 65:1076–1101.

Murdoch, G. P.

1949 Social Structure. New York: Macmillan.

1957 World Ethnographic Sample. American Anthropologist 59:664–687.

Quinn, N.
1985 "Commitment" in American Marriage: A Cultural Analysis. *In* Directions in Cognitive Anthropology. J. Dougherty, ed. Urbana: University of Illinois Press.
Randall, R.
1976 How Tall is a Taxonomic Tree? Some Evidence of Dwarfism. American Ethnologist 3(3):545–546.
Romney, A. K., and R. G. D'Andrade
1964 Cognitive Aspects of English Kin Terms. American Anthropologist 68(3.2):146–170.
Romney, A. K., T. Smith, H. E. Freeman, J. Kagan, and R. E. Klein
1979 Concepts of Success and Failure. Social Science Research 8:302–338.
Scribner, S.
1977 Modes of Thinking and Ways of Speaking: Culture and Logic Reconsidered. *In* Thinking: Readings in Cognitive Science. P. N. Johnson-Laird and P. C. Wason, eds. Cambridge: Cambridge University Press.
Wallace, A., and J. Atkins
1960 The Meaning of Kin Terms. American Anthropologist 62:58–80.

CHAPTER 9

Multi-Item Scales and Cognitive Ethnography

Kateryna Maltseva and Roy D'Andrade

In the debate concerning the definition of culture, the terms *custom*, *trait*, *value*, *belief*, *norm*, *institution*, *mazeway*, *worldview*, *meaning*, *ideology*, *model*, *meme*, *practice*, and *discourse* have all been used to refer to the specific content of culture. This chapter introduces another kind of object to the vocabulary of cultural things: *orientations*, or the cognitive-affective objects that can be measured by multi-item scales. The multi-item scale is a well-known social science tool (DeVellis 1991). However, use of such scales in ethnographic description has not been common in anthropology, although multi-item scales are used frequently in psychological studies, usually to test hypotheses.

There have been exceptional psychologists who have used multi-item attitude scales in an ethnographic fashion. For example, Harry Triandis has been a major developer of the use of multi-items scales to measure *collectivism* versus *individualism*, arguing that this is an important descriptive dimension by which cultures differ (Triandis 1994; see also Hofstede 1980). The basic idea – that societies differ in the degree to which people are committed to their own personal welfare (individualism) versus being committed to the welfare of their basic groups (collectivism) – is an active source of exploration, with papers supporting and critiquing the construct, and meta-analyses of the degree to which different investigators agree about which societies are collectivistic and which societies are individualistic (Oyserman et al. 2002). In the field of political science, Ronald Inglehart has developed an impressive data set for a world sample of countries, including not only demographic, political, and economic variables, but also multi-item scales to measure values, subjective well-being, religiosity, national pride, achievement orientation, sexuality, tolerance, and other orientations (Inglehart 1997).

A Companion to Cognitive Anthropology, First Edition. Edited by David B. Kronenfeld, Giovanni Bennardo, Victor C. de Munck, and Michael D. Fischer.

Table 9.1

	How important to you are the following?	*Not at all*	*A little*	*Moderately*	*Quite a bit*	*Extremely*
1	Having strong religious faith	0	1	2	3	4
2	Observing religious holidays	0	1	2	3	4
3	Doing what God wants me to	0	1	2	3	4
4	Being religious	0	1	2	3	4
5	Being guided by religious scriptures	0	1	2	3	4

In the 1960s another pioneer, Milton Rokeach, a psychologist interested in values, developed a list of 36 values and obtained rankings on these values from a large sample of Americans (Rokeach 1967). Adding to the Rokeach items, Scholom Schwartz developed a list of 68 values for which ratings were obtained from over 50 societies, including large representative samples from more than 12 nations. One major finding of Schwartz and his associates (Schwartz and Bardi 2001) is that the variation in values across societies is remarkably small; the average correlation between a society's profile for personal values and the average value profile for all societies is over 0.90. Similarly, D'Andrade (2008) found that for three societies – Americans, Japanese, and Vietnamese – over 49 percent of the co-variation concerning 58 multi-item values scales was common to all three societies, and 39 percent was due to individual variation, while only 12 percent of the variation was unique to each society. These different data sources all indicate that, with respect to personal values, cultures are much more similar than they are different. The large differences in values reported for different cultures appear to rest on institutionalized values, which are the values one is expected to hold as a member of a collective institution, such as the military, or as a student at the University of Connecticut, or as an American, rather than the personal and subjective responses of individuals (see D'Andrade 2008 for a discussion of institutionalized values).

What kinds of things are measured by these multi-items scales? They typically consist of two parts. The first part involves an *evaluation frame*. The second involves the selection of the items to be evaluated. For example, the evaluation frame "How important to you is X?" where X is each of the five items shown in Table 9.1.

There are a variety of evaluation frames; for example, ratings for the degree to which a respondent agrees with the item, or the degree to which a respondent approves of the item, or values the item, or supports the item, or the degree to which the individual feels the item accurately describes somebody or something, or thinks the items is good or important, or has some feeling about the item, et cetera. The source of the rating is usually the personal response of the respondent, but can be modified to be the respondent's idea of how other people would rate the item, or how strongly held the item is by some institution. Not included here are scales like true or false tests used to measure knowledge, such as IQ tests, the Scholastic Aptitude Test (SAT), or the Graduate Record Examination (GRE), since such tests do not try to measure affective or motivational response, and are concerned primarily with affect-free assessment. The distinction here is not a hard and fast one; despite the fact that frames such as "How accurately does … describe you" ask for objective assessments, such ratings typically show evaluative effects.

For lack of a better term, we will call a content of a multi-item rating scale an orientation. Thus an American who rates as important "having strong religious faith," "observing religious holidays," "doing what God wants me to," "being religious," and "being guided by religious scriptures" can be said to have a positive orientation with respect to religion. The degree of commonality between the items can be measured using Conbach's *alpha*, a reliability measure analogous to split-half-scale correlations, or by the relative size of the first component of the scale items in a principal components analysis (Zeller and Carmines 1980). For the six items above, alpha for a University of California sample of 220 students was found to be 0.89. Generally, *alphas* of 0.50 or higher are considered usable, and alphas above 0.60 are considered satisfactory (DeVellis 1991). High reliability can be taken as an indication that the items all measure something (something must have caused the correlations between the items), although reliability does not measure validity (what you have measured may not be what you think you have measured).

While various cognitive models related to religion are implicit in the items above, the score that a person might get from rating these five items is not a purely cognitive measure, but an amalgam of affective response and cognitive characteristics. A culture may have a complex cognitive model of witchcraft, for example, but witchcraft as an orientation would include not just the cognitive model but also measures of the affect – the awe or fear or horror or whatever – that is associated in that culture with witchcraft. Of course, one can distinguish analytically between the affective response and the model which arouses that response, but this distinction does not map well onto how people typically experience the world. For example, in our orientations to people, our experience of others is often so intertwined with both feeling and idea that it is often almost impossible to separate objective characteristics from subjective affective responses (Kenny 1994).

Outside of the usual methods of ethnographic research, such as being present in many cultural settings, asking questions, and observing what people say and do, et cetera, there appear to be no systematic and quantitative methods beside multi-item scales to investigate how people experience their worlds. For example, consider a public university. Ethnographically there are many questions an anthropologist might want to know about the orientations of the students. An anthropologist might wonder what it is that these students value, what it is that they feel is prestigious, what attitudes they have towards their college, the kinds of obligations they experience, et cetera. Moffatt's ethnography of Rutgers, *Coming of Age in New Jersey* (1989) and Rebekah Nathan's *My Freshman Year* (2005) provide qualitative information about student orientations for two different universities at two different points in time. To find the answers to such questions effectively and reliably, a systematic, quantitative method is needed. In this chapter we address the problem of developing such a method. Below, we will explore some of the major evaluation orientation of young adults in the Ukraine and undergraduates at the University of Connecticut using multi-items scales and discuss some of the methodological problems involved.

Personal Values in the Ukraine and the USA

A 68-item value questionnaire was administered to 136 University of Connecticut undergraduates and 40 Ukrainian young adults. The 68 items were taken from the 308 items used in D'Andrade (2008). More than one evaluation frame was used in

Table 9.2 Research design based on the frame "I don't know about others, but for me personally ..."

Individual values	*Is not important at all*	*Is a little important*	*Is somewhat important*	*Is very important*
1 Avoiding war	1	2	3	4
2 Being a leader	1	2	3	4
3 Being a success	1	2	3	4
4 Being able to adjust	1	2	3	4
5 Being ambitious	1	2	3	4

collecting the data, but only one – ratings of importance – is discussed in Table 9.2. The other rating frames will be discussed in forthcoming papers (Maltseva, n.d.).

The frame shown in Table 9.2, which centers on how important something is to the respondent, is frequently used to measure values. Usually the items selected by the investigator are positive in connotation, but this is not necessary, since something bad, like war, can also be very important to someone. For Americans and most Europeans, a semantically similar rating frame, "How much do you value ..." produces results that are nearly identical to the results obtained with the importance frame (D'Andrade 2008). The problem with the term *value* is that it is difficult to find universal translation equivalents; for example, in D'Andrade's study of Americans, Japanese, and Vietnamese, no adequate translation of the word *value* was found in either Japanese or Vietnamese. Interestingly, no translation difficulties have been reported for the importance frame in any of the papers on values. Schwartz, for example, who has collected data from more than 63 societies without frame translation problems, uses a rating frame which asks respondents to rate items on a scale with respect to "importance as a guiding principle in my life" (Schwartz et al. 2001).

The Ukrainian sample was 50 percent female, 50 percent male. Informants ranged in age from 20 to 59 years old, averaging 34 years of age. Most of the informants had one sibling and came from two-child families (which constituted a typical family in the pre-1989 Soviet Union); the majority of informants were eldest children. Half of the informants had children of their own at the moment of taking the survey; three informants (or their spouses) were expecting a baby. In terms of marital status, approximately equal portions of the sample were married and single; four individuals were divorced, there were no widows or widowers in the sample. The majority of the sample was gainfully employed full-time; three individuals did not work, and two individuals were employed on a part-time basis. Most of the informants came either from central or eastern Ukraine; two were from the western Ukraine and one from the south; one informant was originally from Russia. Childhood environment varied from rural areas to big cities such as Kiev, but the majority of people surveyed were small-town people. Ukrainian- and Russian-speaking informants constituted almost equal portions in the sample; there were two bilingual persons.

There was little variation in years of education of the informants in the sample. Most of the informants had completed their higher education by the time of the study; within the education system in the USSR and after its disintegration, higher education was free and hence a college degree was not a rarity – most people went to university after high school. There was considerably more variation in the education level of the informants' parents; on average, informants' mothers were less educated than their fathers. Within the sample there were a variety of majors (music, philosophy, law, physics, anthropology, culture studies), with engineering the most frequent choice. The majority of the informants indicated that they had few economical difficulties; however, self-reports of income are difficult to verify, even when using the descriptive format of what the family can afford, then giving the actual sums per annum. The majority of respondents indicated that their parents spent time with them and invested in them emotionally when they were little; most of the respondents report coming from caring, loving families.

The respondents at the University of Connecticut were 58 percent female, with an average age of 21, ranging from 18 to 32. Most of the informants had one sibling and an average family size of 2.2. Of the two-child families, approximately 50 percent of the respondents were elder children. None of the respondents had children, and fewer than 10 percent were married. Approximately 30 percent were employed part-time or more. Most of the respondents came from suburban Connecticut. Mothers and fathers were approximately equal in level of education, with most respondents having attended or graduated from college. Within the sample there was a wide variety of majors, with communication and psychology the most frequent choice. The majority of the informants indicated that their families did not have financial difficulties. Like the Ukrainians, the majority of informants indicated that their parents spent considerable time with them and invested in them emotionally when they were little; again most of the informants appear to have come from caring, loving families. Overall, outside of language, the biggest difference between the University of Connecticut students and the Ukrainians was in average age, with the Ukrainians a little more than ten years older.

One unusual thing about our data analysis is our winnowing of items. Rather than use all 68 items, we have selected a subset of items which have high absolute correlations. To select items which have high absolute correlations the correlation matrices for the 68 items for each society were computed, and then the sum of the squared correlations for each row of the matrix calculated. For both the Ukrainians and the University of Connecticut students, the top 25 items with the highest sum of squared correlations were selected. The larger the sum, the greater the number of high absolute correlations for that item across the other items.

This selection process is intended to insure that highly meaningful items will be selected for each society. The problem with using all items is that, given reasonable translations, the items in each language will refer to roughly the same things. While the intercorrelations between well-translated items will not be identical across different societies, they will nonetheless be quite similar, since semantically similar things are being rated, and correlations measure how similar things are to each other. In working with correlation matrices from different societies of the same objects, we have found that semantic relations often overwhelm cultural differences (D'Andrade 2008). Some support for this generalization can be found in the differences between correlations for those items which are in the top 25 for both societies (8 items which correlate –0.39) and those items which are not both in the top 25 (60 items which correlate 0.27). Thus the top items, selected to show cultural differences, are negatively correlated across our two societies, while the non-top items are moderately but positively correlated.

Table 9.3 Top 15 of 328 value items: Americans, Japanese, and Vietnamese

	Americans	*Japanese*	*Vietnamese*
1	Enjoying life	Being healthy	Having deep respect for parents and grandparents
2	Being a good person	Avoiding war	Taking care of my parents when they get older
3	Having a personally fulfilling life	Treating human life as precious	Treating human life as precious
4	Having love	Having close supportive friends	Following my conscience and doing right
5	Having someone I can really talk to	Having a world free of war	Not dishonoring my family
6	Choosing my own goals	Making friends	Fulfilling family obligations
7	Being true to myself	Having someone I can really talk to	Being employed
8	Finding a mate with good qualities	Having a positive outlook on life	Being healthy
9	Having wisdom	Enjoying life	Being responsible
10	Being independent and self-reliant	Having love	Having a secure job
11	Having close supportive friends	The future	Respecting superiors and showing kindness to inferiors
12	Being intelligent	Being reliable	Being honest and genuine
13	Being responsible	Showing gratitude	Forgiving others
14	Having a sense of humor	Being relaxed	The future
15	Being honest and genuine	The elimination of racism	Having a close-knit family

When culturally distinct relations between items occur, the orientations involved are generally *connotative* attributions of various kinds – attributions of goodness or badness, or culturally based associations with other things. We assume respondents' ratings are influenced by a variety of unique individual attributions and culturally shared attributions. As a result of the shared cultural attributions, differences in patterns of correlations and also differences in the mean ratings of items will occur. To the extent cultural connotative attributions are strong for a particular item, such an item is also likely to show more extreme ratings than an item whose ratings are based entirely on semantic features, since the culturally shared connotative attributions act as an additional influence on the items' ratings.

A good example of this effect was found in the analyses of the values of Americans, Japanese, and Vietnamese Americans. Three hundred and twenty-eight items were chosen to represent the domain of values. These were translated from English to Japanese and Vietnamese, including the normal back translation procedures. The average correlation between these three societies was 0.63 for the 328 items across societies. Overall, the value profiles were quite similar. But if only the top 20 items for each society are selected – the 20 items with the highest mean ratings of personal importance – these 20 items are almost completely uncorrelated (D'Andrade 2008). Thus, while the overall profiles for each of the three societies were very similar, the very top items for each society displayed differentiated and ethnographically recognizable profiles. Table 9.3 presents the 15 top value items for each of the three societies.

Table 9.4 Top ten of 68 value items for University of Connecticut students and Ukrainians (individual values: "I don't know about others but for me personally X," where X represents the phrase chosen out of the following list: 1 not at all important, 2 of little importance, 3 quite important, 4 very important)

Mean	*University of Connecticut students*	*Mean*	*Ukrainians*
3.71	Being a good person	3.75	Avoiding war
3.67	Enjoying life	3.63	Finding meaning in life
3.65	Having a personally fulfilling life	3.60	Having my own point of view
3.65	Being honest and genuine	3.58	Being competent and effective
3.56	Being intelligent	3.58	Fulfilling my family obligations
3.51	Being healthy	3.53	Being a success
3.50	Having my own point of view	3.53	Being faithful and avoiding temptation
3.49	Being responsible	3.53	Not giving up
3.49	Improving myself	3.50	Improving myself
3.49	Pursuing knowledge	3.48	Being intelligent

While there is some item overlap in items for the three societies, the differences are dramatic. These large cultural differences were found only in the items with extreme averages, where cultural attributions resulted in more extreme ratings, because, given many reasonably translated items, similarities based on purely semantic relations overwhelm differences in culture-based associations. In the limiting case, if translations had *exactly* the same meaning, both denotatively and connotatively, we would expect ratings and correlations to be identical across cultures.

Table 9.4 shows the comparison of the American versus Ukraine top ten mean item ratings. The American results are similar to the data reported above for Americans in Table 9.3. Americans give high importance ratings to "being a good person," "enjoying life," and "having a personally fulfilling life." Health, intelligence, self-determination, and self-improvement are also highly rated. The overall picture is of a particular kind of American individualism – there is a strong focus on self and on being a good person with a fulfilled and enjoyable life. The Ukrainian picture is somewhat different. Not surprisingly in a country that experienced the ravages of World War II and the East–West tensions of the Cold War, avoiding war is a top item. The top Ukrainian items are not without their own kind of rugged individualism: a search for meaning, success, and effectiveness, along with a refusal to give up. In general, the Ukrainians appear to show more concern with the world outside the self as indicated by high ratings on fulfilling family obligations and being faithful and avoiding temptations.

The University of Connecticut

The first step in constructing the multi-item scales was to ipsatize the data by normalizing each person's scores to a mean of 0 and a standard deviation of 1. Ipsatization corrects the effect of raters using different parts of the scale. Ipsatization also often removes the first component of a principal components analysis when the correlation matrix is entirely, or almost entirely, composed of positive correlations (D'Andrade

2008). This first component is often a nonspecific desirability factor which gives little information about the structure of relations between items. Removing it by ipsatization generally results in clearer and more interpretable output.

The next step was to compute the intercorrelation matrices for the 68 ipsatized value items for both the University of Connecticut students and for the Ukrainians. Then the sums of the squared correlation coefficients for each item in each matrix were calculated. The 25 items with the highest sums were selected for each society. These high correlation profile items do not always include the very top rating items, since top rated items are constrained by the ceiling effects which occur when most people make ratings at the very top of the scale, resulting in restricted variance. Because of the restricted variance, correlations to other items are necessarily lowered (Jaeger 1990).

For the Americans, a cluster analysis using the average linkage method produced four distinct clusters. Grouping into scales the items of each cluster resulted in four multi-item scales given in Table 9.5.

The alpha for each scale is given in bold in the first column of the table. The second column gives the mean Pearson correlation coefficient of the item with all the other items in the scale. The figures in bold in the last column, following the summary phrasing for the items, are the mean ratings for the items in the scale. Thus, the items that are listed under the summary phrase "living a good, considerate life" have a total mean rating of 3.3. The means for each of the individual items are presented below the total mean. For example, the item with highest mean (3.7) is "having a personally fulfilling life." The summary phrases "living a good, considerate life", "self-determination," et cetera are attempts to characterize the basic idea common to the items of the scale. For these scales the items are loosely connected semantically, and the characterization of what is common to the all the items in the scale makes, at best, a loose fit.

The University of Connecticut undergraduate results are quite similar to the University of California, San Diego results. The four clusters making up the multi-item scales form the end points of two universal dimensions: altruism vs. self-interest and individualism vs. collectivism. Thus the scale "living a good, considerate life" (altruism) is negatively correlated with "having material success" (self-interest), while "self-determination" (individualism) is negatively correlated with "conservative values" (collectivism). Figure 9.1 (see page 163) presents a plot for a principal components analysis with varimax rotation for these four scales.

It is important to note that opposing scales are not contradictories of each other; for example, the contradictory of "living a good, considerate life" would be "living a bad, inconsiderate life" – for contradictory characterizations cannot both be true. But "living a good, considerate life" (doing good to others) does not mean that one cannot also value "having material success" (doing what is good for oneself). However, it is culturally understood that there is tension between trying to do both that involve various goal conflicts so that a respondent who is high on one scale is likely to be low on the other. The same kind of structure holds for "self-determination" (valuing one's own choice of goals) and "conservative values" (valuing the group's choice of goals).

As shown in Table 9.5, the American sample gives the highest average rating of importance to "living a good, considerate life," followed by "self-determination." "Conservative values" have the lowest average rating (Connecticut is a notably blue,

Table 9.5 US individual value scales

alpha	*mean r*			*mean rating*
0.64		Living a good, considerate life		**3.3**
	0.23		Trying to understand others	**3.3**
	0.23		Being tolerant of different ideas and beliefs	**3.4**
	0.21		Having a personally fulfilling life	**3.7**
	0.19		Being open to new ideas	**3.4**
	0.16		Living in harmony with nature	**2.8**
	0.16		Liking art and literature	**2.8**
	0.13		Helping other people	**3.4**
	0.13		Pursuing knowledge	**3.5**
0.60		Self-determination		**2.7**
	0.24		Resisting authority	**1.9**
	0.22		Going against the crowd	**2.2**
	0.20		Living a life of adventure	**2.9**
	0.19		Avoiding war	**3.1**
	0.18		Being imaginative	**3.3**
	0.17		Being spontaneous and open	**2.9**
0.63		Having material success		**2.6**
	0.34		Having social status	**2.3**
	0.33		Having nice things	**2.5**
	0.30		Having money and being prosperous	**2.6**
	0.17		Being a success	**3.2**
	0.14		Being competitive	**2.5**
0.65		Conservative values		**2.5**
	0.26		Being loyal to my country	**2.6**
	0.25		Doing what others expect of me	**2.3**
	0.24		Respecting authority	**2.7**
	0.24		Being obedient	**2.3**
	0.24		Law and order	**3.0**
	0.20		Having strong religious faith	**2.0**

i.e. Democrat, state). It is worth repeating that the characterizing phrases do not always give an adequate description of the items that make up the scale. If you are an undergraduate at the University of Connecticut, you know what the good way to live is, and for most students this includes understanding others, being tolerant, having a fulfilling life, being open to new ideas, living in harmony with nature, liking art and literature, helping people, and pursuing knowledge. But the people of some other place or time might not think these items are part of the best way to live.

There is a fair amount of variation between the item ratings within the same scale. This would seem to be a result of the fact that different aspects of the same orientation can be evaluated differently. But this raises an important issue: What are these orientations really? They are not what are normally called "attitudes," because unlike an attitude towards the war in Iraq or an attitude towards football, where the orientational object is explicitly known and explicitly understood, and where the orientational object exists whether or not people have any attitude towards it, none of the four multi-item scales refers to an externally defined entity. Gordon Allport (1937), in his classic definition of attitudes, stated: "Both attitude and trait are indispensable concepts ... Ordinarily attitude should be employed when the disposition is bound to an object or value, that is ... when it is aroused by a well-defined class of stimuli, and when the individual feels toward these stimuli a definite attraction." Instead, for these scales, the items appear to have reference to ideals or virtues which are not well defined, and which exist only because people experience them as ideals.

It is odd that if when people are asked to rate what is most important to them, they should organize their ratings around such ineffable things as "self-determination" or "living a good life." These are *ways of living*, not institutional objects like football or money or war (see Searle 1995 on the definition of an institution and its ontologically objective nature). Our argument is that these ways of living, however ineffable, are important cultural things to be investigated through systematic quantitative research. They are shared and pass from generation to generation. They can be *normed* in the sense that in some groups certain ways of living are treated as the ways one *should* value, and if one does not value them one will be sanctioned. Within a group of Quakers in the late 1600s, for example, various benevolent ways of living were normed in that one would be likely to be sanctioned by the community if one showed that one did not want to "help others" or "be tolerant of different ideas and beliefs" (Fischer 1989). But in many cases these ways of living are not normed; in most American urban areas people who do not think it is important to help others and to be tolerant of different ideas and beliefs are not negatively sanctioned.

The dimensions of "altruism" versus "self-interest" and "individualism" versus "collectivism" in Figure 9.1 give an interesting picture of the potential conflicts in ways of living experienced by University of Connecticut undergraduates. While greater importance is placed on "living a good, considerate life" than on "having material success," in fact both are, to some degree, student goals. This results in some motivational conflict or tension, although students feel that at least something of both can be achieved. Similarly, greater importance is given to "self-determination" than to "conservative values," although students do not think respect for authority, patriotism, religion, law and order, et cetera, are without value.

It is not quite right to say that these four scales are particular *values*. Given a value is the experience of the goodness of something (D'Andrade 2008), or a criterion for preferring one thing over another (Schwartz 1993), one would expect these scales to refer to unitary things. But the orientations of these scales are clusters without clear boundaries or single focal centers. Normally one thinks of a value not as a loose bag of things, but as something processed as a unified entity in experience and decision-making. Given the semantic spread of the item, unlike the cultural schemas described by Strauss and Quinn (1998), "living a good, considerate life" is unlikely to be processed as an entity in decision-making. Rather, "living a good life" seems to be a grouping of elements which are related by different kinds of associations. In Strauss and Quinn's terms, these complexes are more like a number of separate schemas where the different schemas have similar features. This heterogeneity helps to explain why "individualism" and "collectivism," ways of life that are found again and again in

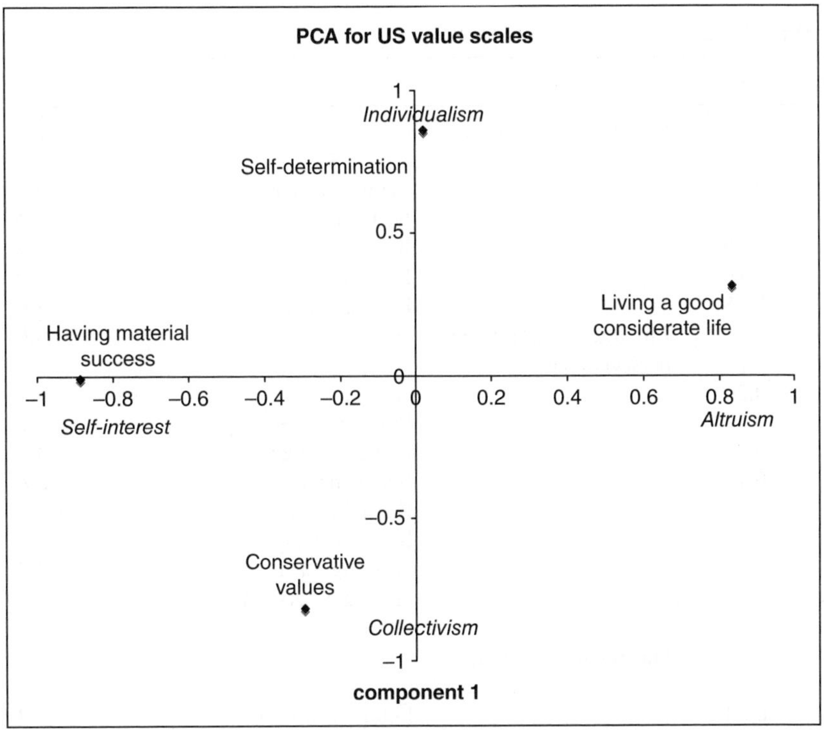

Figure 9.1 Principal components analysis for University of Connecticut (US) value scales.

analyses of importance ratings, are nevertheless so difficult to measure – different investigators use different items, eliciting different responses, with the result that the same society is found to be highly collective in some studies but not in others (Oyserman et al. 2002). Thus a characteristic like "living a good, considerate life" does not obviously apply to all the items in the scale; for example, "liking art and literature" may be part of many people's image of living a good and considerate life, but it is not criterial or semantically similar or even metaphorically linked to living a good and considerate life. This scale seems to be formed by cultural associations rather than strictly semantic relations.

Thus the *life-ways* as seen in the scales above can best be described as an associative complex or network of schemas linked to each other in different ways. Using the resources of natural language, one can try to create a descriptive phrase for the complex, but since the complex itself is not a schema, it is often difficult to create words for a schema that encompasses all the separate schemas that make up the complex. We have used the term *orientation* as an upper-level term to refer to either the evaluation of a single schema or a complex of schemas. *Orientation* is a positional term whose basic meaning involves the stance of someone in some direction, rather than referring to a collection of objects. In our taxonomy, norms, attitudes, values, and life-ways are all orientations.

The last point to be made about the nature of the scales is that the degree to which the items in a scale need to be treated as a single schema or as a collection of schemas with linking features is affected by the particular rating frame employed. For example, in our research we have found that the rating frame "the time and effort I put into ..."

Table 9.6 Ukrainian individual value scales

alpha	*mean r*			*raw mean rating*
0.55		Finding a good social position		**3.1**
	0.24		Being a leader	**2.7**
	0.20		Feel belonging	**3.1**
	0.19		Being a success	**3.5**
	0.16		Being prosperous	**3.2**
	0.15		Falling in love	**3.0**
0.63		Intelligent, disciplined perseverance		**3.0**
	0.26		Science	**3.3**
	0.22		Pursuing knowledge	**3.5**
	0.20		Being intelligent	**3.5**
	0.19		Being thrifty	**2.8**
	0.18		Being imaginative	**3.3**
	0.17		Being sexually restrained	**2.4**
	0.12		Working hard	**3.3**
	0.09		Having a personally fulfilling life	**3.4**
0.69		Having an outgoing life		**3.0**
	0.33		Being optimistic	**3.3**
	0.33		Being liked	**3.0**
	0.32		Living a life of adventure	**2.7**
	0.31		Making friends	**2.5**
	0.26		Being healthy	**3.4**
0.63		Easy-going		**2.8**
	0.40		Respecting others' privacy	**3.0**
	0.31		Not losing my temper	**3.3**
	0.21		Enjoying life	**1.9**
	0.19		Being tolerant of different ideas and beliefs	**3.0**
	0.15		Having fun	**2.9**

elicits tighter schemas that the "importance" frame, perhaps because the range of things that are similar to each other with respect to "importance" is wider and more heterogeneous than the range of things that are similar with respect to what one puts time and effort into.

The Ukrainian Scales

The same steps were followed for the analysis of the Ukrainian scales – the data was ipsatized, then the 25 items with the highest sum of squared correlations were selected from the intercorrelation matrix and the correlations of these 25 items were subjected to an average link cluster analysis. Four distinct clusters were found, and multi-item scales were constructed for the four sets of items. These results are presented in Table 9.6.

The four Ukrainian scales that emerged from the cluster analysis show both similarities and differences when compared with the University of Connecticut cluster analysis. Two items – "not giving up" and "going against the crowd" – were dropped because of low mean correlations with any of the four scales. The scale with the highest mean rating (3.1) is "finding a good social position." This corresponds to current Ukrainian concerns about employment and one's place in society in the post-1989 world of capitalist and democratic institutions. It is interesting that "being a leader" has the highest mean correlation with this scale, but the lowest mean rating. Being a leader probably receives lower ratings from the Ukrainians because in general Slavs do not stress the ability to lead. Also the inhabitants of post-Soviet territories regard leadership with ambivalence. *Leadership* as a term is reminiscent of Soviet slang and party discourse. There is an anecdote that underscores the perceived inability of leaders to do professional tasks: Someone asks a factory worker: "If you drink a glass of vodka, can you do what you do?" He says, "Yes." "And if two?" "Yes." "And if three?" "I won't be able to do it myself, but will be able to manage/lead [Russian *rukovodit*, Ukrainian *keruvaty*] others, though." Leading has a connotation of manipulativeness rather than competency, and thus while it is important in gaining a good social position, it is not viewed as a means of achieving something of real value.

The inclusion of the item "feel belonging" touches on another aspect of the past, where one's position in the world rested on the legitimacy of one's place in the societal hierarchy. Caroline Humphrey has written about the general Russian strategy of insuring one's own inclusion while excluding certain other people and groups based on criteria of conformist unity, pointing out that in the present world the chance to acquire wealth gives rise to ambivalence and anxiety concerning the legitimacy of inequality (Humphrey 2001). Perhaps these concerns about relatedness account for the inclusion of "falling in love" as an item in this scale.

The scale with the second highest mean rating (3.0), "intelligent, disciplined perseverance," appears to reflect a variety of inner-worldly asceticism, strongly rationalistic and perhaps even anti-hedonistic ("being sexually restrained," "being thrifty"), although "having a personally fulfilling life" is included in the scale. If "finding a good social position" is the goal, "intelligent, disciplined perseverance" appears to be the way to achieve it. A similar group of schemas can be seen in some of the top ratings items listed in Table 9.4 ("being competent and effective," "not giving up," "improving myself"). The linked features that seem to connect the schemas underlying these items seem to be something like "rationality" ... "self-control" ... "good life." Notice that the links between these features are culturally based associations of "what goes with what," not semantic similarity. Nor is there an obvious schema which encompasses all the items of the scale. This scale is an example of an orientation whose cohesion depends on associatively linked features across a variety of schemas.

The third scale, "having an outgoing life," seems to reflect an orientation towards life that is open, upbeat, and interpersonally warm. It also includes the item "being healthy." Ukrainians consider health an important aspect of life. Good health is omnipresent in birthday wishes for every age, and words used to say hello and goodbye literally mean "be healthy." Good heath fits with the other items of this scale in that having an outgoing life requires good health; without health, Ukrainians say, there is nothing. The Georgian quip "If only we get good health, the rest we can buy" is appropriate here. However, Ukrainians are not noted for taking good care of their

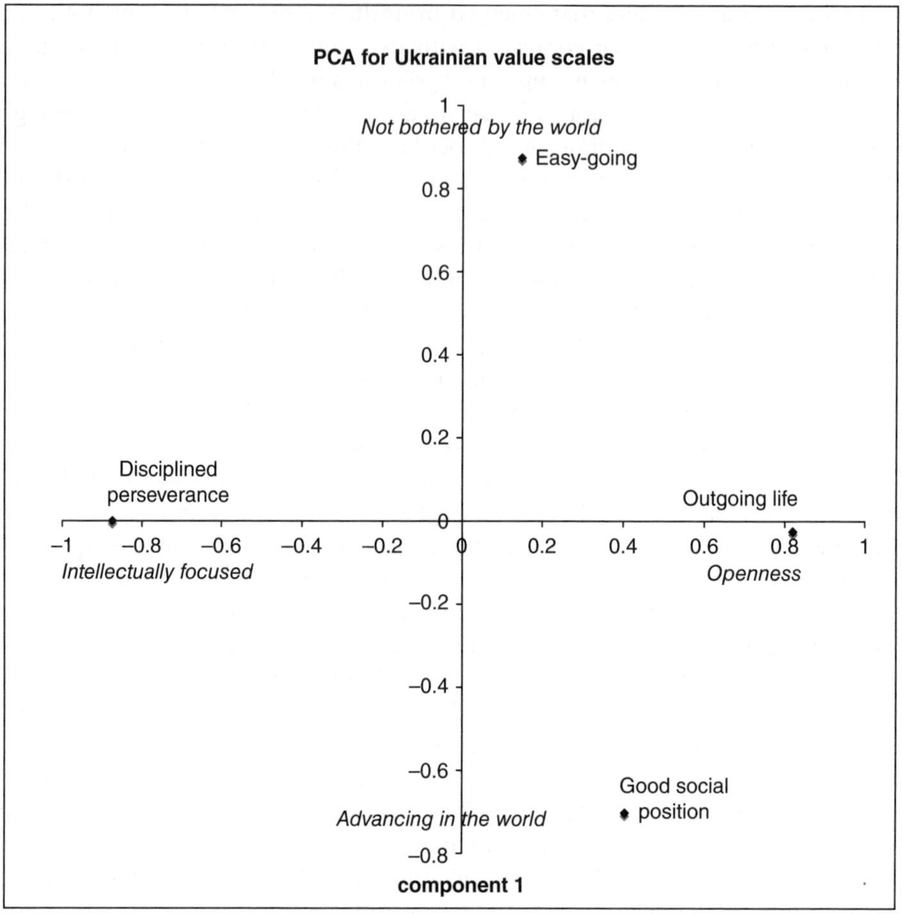

Figure 9.2 Principal components analysis for Ukrainian value scales.

health. Given the decline of the health care system and external events like the Chernobyl disaster, good health is not something Ukrainians expect.

Figure 9.2 presents the principal components analysis of the four Ukrainian scales. "Having an outgoing life" is on the opposite side of the first dimension from "intelligent, disciplined perseverance." Again, it should be noted that the opposite poles of this dimensions, like those of most value dimensions (D'Andrade 2008), is not a contradictory (as would be "stupid, undisciplined giving up"). Rather, opposite poles represent potentially conflictual positions; it appears to the Ukrainian respondents that pursuing an open, optimistic, likable, adventurous, and health-minded orientation conflicts with pursuing a life founded on a knowledge-based, restrained, hard-work orientation. One is seen as what people do at work, the other as what they do over the weekend or on vacation. This is apparently not a salient dimension of conflict for the University of Connecticut undergraduates; their conflicts seem to involve being good to others versus doing good for oneself and basing decisions on what one wants to do oneself versus what is wanted in one's social world.

The Ukrainian low mean importance ratings for "living a life of adventure" (2.7) and "making friends" (2.5) contrast with the University of Connecticut ratings of these items (3.2 and 3.3 respectively). In informal conversations, Ukrainians say that living a life of adventure is hard to imagine in the real world – everyday life is seen as serious, prosaic, and requiring self-control – not as a happy adventure. The "making friends" item shows an interesting contrast to American ideas. Slavs value friendship highly. The typical pattern is that one makes only a few friends in life whom one should hold on to through adversity and physical separation. Making lots of friends is not seen as serving the primary purpose of friendship but instead as indicating that one is not really serious about friendship.

The last scale, "easy-going," has the lowest mean rating of importance (2.8). The focus of this orientation appears to be a kind of personal equanimity with two sides – one involving an internally positive world ("enjoying life," "having fun"), the other involving not being bothered by others ("not losing my temper," "respecting others' privacy," "being tolerant of different ideas and beliefs"). As discussed above, this results in a certain degree of conflict with "finding a good social position" in that "easy-going" focuses on a kind of withdrawal from striving and self-arrogation. It is interesting that "having fun" (2.9) and "enjoying life" (1.9) have such low value ratings. Both are felt to display a lack of maturity and common sense, and even selfishness. Having fun is difficult to translate into Russian or Ukrainian. It is said that relaxing and having fun are Western things that Soviet people lack. Daily life for adults is filled with duties and doing what one has to. There are jokes about enjoying life; it is a common assumption that only a few very fortunate and fabulously rich people will actually enjoy life. The life struggle takes up so much energy in the workplace that one forgets to live. In this context the value of having true friends as an important outlet becomes more apparent.

One caveat is needed: The principal component analyses, because each consists of only four scales, are at best only an approximation to what might be found with ten or 15 scales. This is especially pertinent to the definitions of the dimensions. However, in the case of the University of Connecticut undergraduate data, the two dimensions uncovered are validated by other studies which have found similar dimensions. For example, these same dimensions were found for the USA using 68 multi-item scales (D'Andrade 2008). However, at this time, no other dimensional analysis of variables is available for the Ukraine.

Discussion

Multi-items scales were developed as a way to improve single-item questions. Both reliability and validity are enhanced by the addition of items, as a large literature in statistics and quantitative methodology makes clear (Guilford 1936; Zeller and Carmines 1980; DeVellis 1991). Since multi-items scales can be used for many kinds of measurement, the question that needs to be asked in each case is "Exactly *what* is this scale measuring?" To answer this question both the items that make up the scale and the evaluation frame need to be considered. The upper-level terms used to describe the general class of things that are putatively being measured, such as *attitudes*, *personality traits*, *values*, *behaviors*, and so on, should be regarded with suspicion. For example, the same item can be used in an attitude scale, or a personality scale, or a behavior scale, or a value scale. Personality scales are often found to be systematically correlated with value scales (D'Andrade 2008). Looking at the correlations between value scales and personality scales one suspects that most of the differences are the result of the cognitive set induced by the evaluation frames rather than the result of any substantial difference in what is being referred to.

Perhaps the most outstanding hiatus in multi-item scale research is the absence of theory about the cognitive processes involved in respondent judgments. Obviously, cognition is central in understanding not only *how* respondents make the assessments, but also *what* is being assessed. In this chapter we have argued that people show cognitive and affective orientations to schemas they have developed about the world. We found that while some multi-item scales may assess a single schema, most of the scales involved in our research are not assessments of single schemas, but rather complex connotative associations of linked schemas. For our Connecticut and Ukraine data we have termed the linked schemas that are elicited by our importance frame *life-ways.* As discussed above, life-ways differ from single values in being a complex of associative schemas, rather than a single schema which can be processed as a criterion in making a judgment. Behind these life-ways lie a number of schemas about oneself and the world – how open and rewarding the world is likely to be, what is required by the groups that make up one's social world, what is required to nourish the self, et cetera.

The basic idea of the multi-item scale is that the correlations between the items is a measure of some commonality between the items; some common thing or cognitively established complex of things must be being measured to create these correlations. One question is whether or not the commonality between items is based on a single schema. Another question concerns whether or not the items refer to an institution or norm/policy/law or group of people. In attitude studies the evaluation frame typically has a for or against (pro/con) format, and the investigator assumes the respondent has a well-formed schema about the relevant institution or norm or group. Attitudes are things people are for or against. This, we have argued, is not the case for the scales we have found, which appear to be composed of items with mixed evaluations which refer to schemas grouped into a complex by linked connotative associations.

We would expect values to be related to attitudes; for example, if someone is against the war in Iraq (an attitude), then it should be the case that this person has value criteria by which the war in Iraq has been assessed and found to be immoral, or unnecessary, or badly planned, et cetera. At the next level up we expect values to be organized by affective and cognitive processes into larger life-way complexes such as liberalism, individualism, et cetera. In this account, life-way complexes are not values, but are composed of a connotative associative network of values. Even above life-ways we expect a relatively small number of ontological beliefs which anchor the less abstract orientations into a sense of how the world really is.

The ethnographic project imagined here would attempt an assessment of the norms, attitudes, values (collective and individual), and life-ways for a given group or community. Other kinds of multi-items scales, such as personality scales, happiness and life satisfaction scales, should also be investigated. It would be useful if a reasonably well-tested set of scales could be used for which US baseline results are known. From the initial results, decisions about further work, quantitative and qualitative, could then be used to answer basic ethnographic questions such as how people understand their worlds, both cognitively and affectively.

REFERENCES

Allport, G. W.
1937 Personality. New York: Holt.
D'Andrade, Roy G.
2008 A Study of Personal and Cultural Values. New York: Palgrave Macmillan.
DeVellis, Robert F.
1991 Scale Development: Theory and Applications. Newbury Park, CA: Sage.
Fischer, David H.
1980 Albion's Seed. New York: Oxford University Press.
Guilford, J. P.
1936 Psychometric Methods. New York: McGraw-Hill.
Hofstede, G.
1980 Culture's Consequences: International Differences in Work-Related Values. Beverly Hills, CA: Sage.
Humphrey, Caroline
2001 Inequality and Exclusion: A Russian Case Study of Emotion in Politics. Anthropological Theory 1(3):331–353.
Inglehart, Ronald
1997 Modernization and Postmodernization: Cultural, Economic, and Political Change in 43 Societies. Princeton: Princeton University Press.
Jaeger, Richard M.
1990 Statistics: A Spectator Sport. 2nd edition. Beverly Hills, CA: Sage.
Kenny, David A.
1994 Interpersonal Perception: A Social Relations Analysis. New York: Guilford.
Maltseva, Kateryna
N.d. Individuals, Groups, and Their Values. Unpublished MS, Department of Anthropology, University of Connecticut.
Moffatt, Michael
1989 Coming of Age in New Jersey: College and American Culture. New Brunswick: Rutgers University Press.
Nathan, Rebekah
2005 My Freshman Year: What a Professor Learned by Becoming a Student. Ithaca: Cornell University Press.
Oyserman, Daphna, Heather Coon, and Markus Kemmelmeier
2002 Rethinking Individualism and Collectivism: Evaluation of Theoretical Assumptions and Meta-Analyses. Psychological Bulletin 128:3–72.
Rokeach, Milton
1967 Value Survey. Palo Alto: Consulting Psychologists.
Schwartz, Barry
1993 On the Creation and Destruction of Value. *In* The Origin of Values. Michale Hechter, Lynn Nadel, and Richard E. Michot, eds. Hawthorne, NY: Aldine.
Schwartz, Shalom H., and Anat Bardi
2001 Value Hierarchies across Cultures: Taking a Similarities Perspective. Journal of Cross-Cultural Psychology 32(2):268–290.
Schwartz, Shalom H., Gila Melech, and Arielle Lehmann
2001 Extending the Cross-Cultural Validity of the Theory of Basic Human Values with a Different Method of Measurement. Journal of Cross-Cultural Psychology 32:519–542.

Searle, John R.
1995 The Construction of Social Reality. New York: Free Press.
Strauss, Claudia, and Naomi Quinn
1998 A Cognitive Theory of Cultural Meaning. Cambridge: Cambridge University Press.
Triandis, Harry C.
1994 Culture and Social Behavior. New York: McGraw-Hill.
Zeller, Richard A., and Edward G. Carmines
1980 Measurement in the Social Sciences. New York: Cambridge University Press.

CHAPTER 10 Consensus Analysis

Stephen P. Borgatti and Daniel S. Halgin

Introduction

As developed by Romney et al. (1986), consensus analysis is both a theory and a method. As a theory, it specifies the conditions under which agreement between people can be seen as a sign of knowledge or "getting it right." Many folk epistemological systems rely on the connection between agreement and truth. An obvious example is the court jury system, which does not regard a prosecutor's claims as true unless a jury of 12 independent people agree. Another example is the scientific practice of measuring things multiple times and taking the average as the best estimate. Influential books such as *The Wisdom of Crowds: Why the Many are Smarter than the Few and How Collective Wisdom Shapes Business, Economies, Societies and Nations* (Surowiecki 2004) are based on this argument. Similarly, Adam Smith argued that markets make better decisions about how to allocate goods than any single body could. We also see it in common phrases like "50,000,000 Elvis Fans Can't Be Wrong."[1] And yet, it seems obvious that billions of people *can* be wrong. Agreement does not always imply getting it right. What the theory of consensus analysis does is work out the special circumstances under which agreement really does imply knowledge.

As a method, consensus analysis provides a way of conceptualizing and coping with individual variability. As D'Andrade (1987:194) put it, "For a long time there has been a scandal at the heart of the study of culture. This scandal goes as follows: All human groups have a culture; culture is shared knowledge and belief; but when we study human groups, we find that there is considerable disagreement concerning most items of knowledge and belief." For example, we would like to report that, in Western cultures, the color white connotes purity, but a survey asking respondents to associate colors with qualities will never give a 100 percent association between white and purity. What the

A Companion to Cognitive Anthropology, First Edition. Edited by David B. Kronenfeld, Giovanni Bennardo, Victor C. de Munck, and Michael D. Fischer.

method of consensus analysis does is to provide three things. First, it provides a way to determine whether observed variability in beliefs is cultural, in the sense that our informants are drawn from different cultures with systematically different beliefs, or idiosyncratic, reflecting differences in individual familiarity with elements in their own culture (e.g., some people know the names of more dog breeds than others). Second, within a group that has been determined to constitute a single culture, the method provides a way of measuring how much of the culture each individual knows – "cultural competence." Third, for each culture represented in a data set, the method tries to ascertain the culturally correct answer to every question we have put to our informants.

The method has been found useful in a wide variety of settings across multiple disciplines. For example, consensus analysis has been used to investigate cultural diversity within social movements (Caulkins and Hyatt 1999), Celtic cultures (Caulkins 2001) and Welsh American populations (Caulkins et al. 2005). Scholars have used the method to investigate public health issues such as perceptions of diseases among Guatemalans (Romney et al. 1986), postpartum hemorrhage among Bengalis (Hruschka et al. 2008), pain among Anglo-Americans and Chinese (Moore et al. 1997) and AIDS, diabetes, the common cold, *empacho*, and *mal de ojo* among multiple ethnic groups (Weller and Baer 2001). Others have used consensus analysis to distinguish experts from novices in domains such as fish (Boster and Johnson 1989; Miller et al. 2004), pollution and food safety (Johnson and Griffith 1996), ecological knowledge (Shafto and Coley 2003), medical beliefs (De Munck et al. 1998), and alphabet systems (Jameson and Romney 1990).

Consensus theory, unlike most work in the social sciences, is developed quite formally. It is based on an underlying abstract model, which is then used as a basis for deriving implications which constitute the theory itself. This then makes certain methods possible. We use this structure to organize our discussion.

The Abstract Model

The simplest way to explain the consensus model is to start with a simplified, artificial context. For example, consider a multiple choice exam given in an introductory anthropology class. A possible question might be "The author of the book *Tristes Tropiques* was ...," followed by five choices.

Each student's set of responses consists of a vector of numbers ranging between 1 and L, where L is the number of alternatives in each multiple choice question (5 in our example). If we call a given student's vector z, then her response to question J can be denoted z_j. We can also arrange the whole collection of student response vectors as a response matrix, in which the rows are students and the columns are questions. If we call this matrix Z, then cell z_{ij} gives the response of student I to question J. If N gives the number of students taking the test, and Q gives the number of questions on the test, the matrix Z has N rows and Q columns.

The instructor's answers can also be arranged as a vector t that looks much the same as each student's vector. When we grade the test, we effectively compare each student's row in the response matrix Z with the instructor's vector t. If the two vectors are the same across all questions, the student gets a perfect score. If the vectors are quite different, the student has missed many questions and gets a low score. Thus, a student's exam score or *accuracy* is actually a measure of similarity between the student's and the instructor's

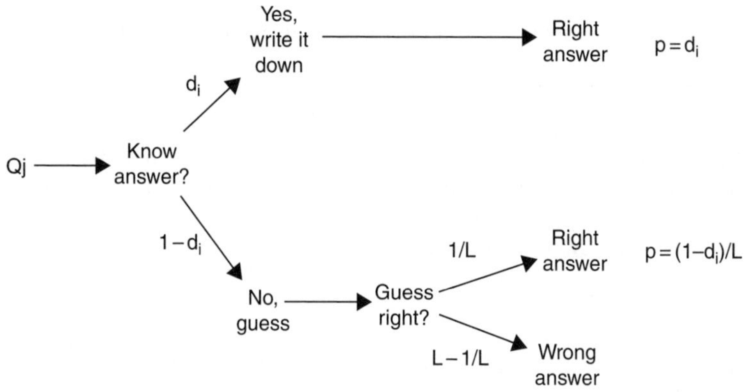

Figure 10.1

vectors. The measure of similarity is the simple match coefficient – the number of times that $z_j = t_j$, where j ranges across all questions, divided by the number of questions q.

Now, to work out the relationship between knowledge, responses on the test, and agreement among students, we build a simple model of how a student goes about responding to a given question on the test. Based on classical test theory, the model is as follows (see Figure 10.1). When a student I confronts a given question, he either knows it or he doesn't. We denote the (unknown) probability of knowing it as d_i and the probability of not knowing it is then $1-d_i$. The quantity d_i is the student's competence in the domain – it is the proportion of all possible questions that could be asked in a given topic that he knows the answer to. In short, d_i is a measure of the amount of knowledge possessed by student I.

Returning to the model, if the student knows the answer, he writes it down and gets it right (this can be made more complicated later to allow for people getting questions wrong that they in fact knew the answer to). If she doesn't know the answer, which occurs with probability $1-d_i$, she guesses. For expository purposes, we will assume she guesses randomly between the L alternatives. However, we can also complicate this model by incorporating certain biases (e.g., adherence to the rule "If you don't know the answer, choose 'c' ") or person-varying talent for knocking out some obviously wrong alternatives.

We can see in the model that the overall probability m_i that a given student I gets a randomly chosen question right is equal to $d_i + (1-d_i)/L$, as shown in Equation 1. In other words, the probability of getting a question right is a function of the probability of knowing the answer plus the probability of not knowing but guessing correctly. By rearranging terms, we can also write the probability of knowing the answer (i.e., competence) in terms of the proportion of correct answers. As shown in Equation 2, a person's competence in a given domain can be modeled as the proportion of correct answers they give, but adjusted for chance guessing. This is a well-known model in classical test theory (Novick 1966).

$$m_i = d_i + (1 - d_i)/L \qquad \text{Equation 1}$$

$$d_i = (Lm_i - 1)/(L - 1) \qquad \text{Equation 2}$$

Table 10.1 Exhaustive enumeration of cases leading to agreement between student I and student J

Case		*Probability*
1	Both I and J know the right answer	$p_1 = d_i d_j$
2	Student I knows the right answer, and student J guesses right	$p_2 = d_i\,(1 - d_j)/L$
3	Student J knows the right answer, and student I guesses right	$p_3 = d_j\,(1 - d_i)/L$
4	Neither knows the answer, both guess the same answer	$p_4 = (1 - d_i)(1 - d_j)/L$

Using this simple model, we can now begin to work out the relationship between agreement and knowledge. We begin by formulating the probability that two students I and J (with knowledge levels d_i and d_j respectively) give the same answer to a given question. As shown in Table 10.1, there are just four ways this can happen. Case 1 is where both students happen to know the answer and therefore provide the same (correct) answer. This happens with probability $d_i d_j$, which is simply the probability that I knows the answer times the probability that J knows the answer. Case 2 occurs when student I knows the answer (with probability d_i) and student J does not know the answer but happens to guess right (which happens with probability $(1-d_j)/L$). The probability of both of these events occurring jointly is their product, $d_i\,(1-d_j)/L$. Case 3 is the mirror image of Case 2. In this case, student J knows the answer and student I does not, but guesses right. This occurs with probability $d_j\,(1-d_i)/L$. Finally Case 4 is where neither student knows the answer and they guess the same thing. Note that it is not necessary that they guess correctly in order to agree. Given that both students are guessing, the probability of agreeing with each other is $L \times 1/L^2$, which is just $1/L$. To see this, consider the probability that both students guess answer "a." Since each is choosing option "a" with probability $1/L$, the probability of both choosing "a" at the same time is $1/L \times 1/L$ or $1/L^2$. Since there are L possible choices, the overall probability of guessing the same thing is $L \times 1/L^2$, which is simply $1/L$. Thus, Case 4 occurs with probability $(1-d_i)(1-d_j)/L$, which is the joint probability that neither student knows the answer and whatever they guess happens to be the same.

Now, since the four cases are independent, to get the overall probability m_{ij} that students I and J give the same answer to any given question, we simply add up the probabilities across all four cases (Equation 3). By rearranging terms, we can simplify this to Equation 4, which says that the agreement m_{ij} between students I and J is a function of the degree to which each is highly knowledgeable plus some agreement due to chance. This shows that, at least in our simplified multiple-choice exam setting, agreement really is an indicator of knowledge.

$$m_{ij} = d_i d_j + d_i(1-d_j)/L + d_j(1-d_i)/L + (1-d_i)(1-d_j)/L \qquad \text{Equation 3}$$

$$m_{ij} = d_i d_j + (1-d_i d_j)\,/L \qquad \text{Equation 4}$$

From a practical point of view, what is particularly interesting about Equation 4 is that we can use it to estimate the amount of knowledge each person has, and we don't need an answer key to do it. To see this, we first rearrange the equation so that joint knowledge ($d_i d_j$) is on the left side of the equation and $(Lm_{ij}-1)/(L-1)$ is on the right. Since L is just a constant, the entire right side is just a linear scaling of m_{ij}, which is the amount of agreement between students I and J. For convenience, we call this adjusted agreement m^*_{ij}.

$$d_i d_j = (Lm_{ij}-1)/(L-1) = m^*_{ij} \qquad \text{Equation 5}$$

The first important thing to realize is that the matrix M* is observable. In our multiple-choice test, we can count up, for each pair of students, how often they agree with each other, and then adjust this for chance agreement to get M*. So it is only the left side that contains unknowns. The second important thing to realize is that the equation $d_i d_j = m^*_{ij}$ is solvable for the values of d. Indeed, standard algorithms for principal factor analysis will take the observed m^*_{ij} values as input and estimate the values of d, which are the factor loadings. In other words, using factor analysis, we can determine each student's amount of knowledge or competence simply by analyzing the pattern of observed agreements among students.

Obviously, there must be a catch. It can't be that we can discover the truth about, say, physical laws, by taking a poll of physicists' opinions. There must be conditions under which this is true. Indeed, there are conditions, and these are entirely contained in the response model shown in Figure 10.1. All that has been shown is that if the response model is true, then we can divine knowledge without the benefit of an answer key. When the model is not true, we really can't draw any conclusions about knowledge.

This may seem very restrictive, and indeed it is, but the good news is that the response model does not have to be exact in every detail. It can be shown (Batchelder and Romney 1988) that Equation 4 holds for any model which embodies the following three assumptions: common truth, conditional independence, and item homogeneity. We discuss each of these in turn.

- *Common truth.* This is the assumption that there is one and only one right answer for every question. It is implicit in the response model which assumes that for each multiple-choice question, one of the answers is correct and the others are wrong. The model shows that there are two branches of the probability that lead to correct answers: knowledge and guessing right.
- *Conditional independence.* This is the assumption that students' responses are independent from each other, both across questions and across other students, conditional on the answer key. In other words, the students do not cheat from each other, and the answers to certain questions do not change the answers to other questions. This assumption is implicit in the second fork of the response model, where, if a student does not know the answer, she guesses randomly from the available choices. The implication of this assumption is that there is nothing attracting students to the same answer other than both knowing the correct answer.
- *Item homogeneity.* This assumption specifies that questions are drawn randomly from a universe of possible questions about a specific topic, so that the probability d_i that student I knows the answer to a question is the same for any randomly chosen question. In other words, all questions are on the same topic, about which a given student has a certain level of knowledge. This is implied in the response

model by the use of a single parameter d_i to characterize a respondent's probability of knowing the answer. Thus, item homogeneity implies that questions about basketball are not mixed with questions about wine, since people can be expected to have different competencies in the two domains.

Together, these three conditions are sufficient to guarantee that we can recover the amount of knowledge possessed by any student, even without the benefit of an answer key. In addition, we can use this method to determine the culturally correct answer key.

Methodology and Empirical Illustration

The consensus method starts with an n-by-m person-by-question response matrix X, in which cell x_{ij} gives the response of person I to question J. We shall assume to start with that the responses are categorical choices obtained from a multiple-choice test (including a true or false test that has just two choices for each question). We presume every question has exactly L possible responses which are numbered 1 through L. The analysis begins by constructing a person-by-person agreement matrix M in which m_{ij} equals the number of questions for which persons I and J give the exact same answers. We then adjust this for chance guessing to obtain the matrix M*, using the formula in Equation 6, where L is the number of choices in the multiple-choice test.

$$m^*_{ij} = (Lm_{ij}-1)/(L-1) \qquad \text{Equation 6}$$

This matrix is then subjected to a principal factor analysis using a method such as Comrey's (1962) method which ignores the diagonals of the input matrix. This results in a set of eigenvectors and associated eigenvalues. We sort the eigenvectors in descending order by the eigenvalues. The principal eigenvector (with the largest eigenvalue) contains the factor loadings which, when all three conditions hold, indicate the amount of knowledge each person has. The eigenvalue can be used to assess the extent to which agreements between persons are explained by a single factor, corresponding to the existence of a single answer key. If the largest eigenvalue is quite a bit larger than the next largest eigenvalue (say, three times as large), we consider this as evidence that the common truth and conditional independence conditions hold, which means we can interpret the factor loadings as competence. In addition, to be consistent with the common truth, all factor loadings should be non-negative or, if negative, negligibly small.

Once each person's competence has been estimated, it is then possible to infer the culturally correct answer to each question by examining the distribution of responses by the competence of each responder. The greater the competence, the more likely their response is the correct one. Effectively, we choose the answer that would maximize the probability of obtaining the pattern of answers we do, assuming the model is perfectly true. The details of this Bayesian inference process are given by Romney et al. (1986).

We now turn to an empirical illustration using an actual multiple-choice exam administered in a Sociology 101 class at the University of South Carolina. The exam consists of 58 multiple-choice questions with 5 possible responses for each question

Table 10.2 Eigenvalues for Sociology 101 exam

Largest eigenvalue	47.903
Second largest eigenvalue	2.839
Ratio of largest to next	16.871

(L = 5). A total of 101 students took the test, yielding a 101 × 58 response matrix X. The analysis procedure in UCINET (Borgatti et al. 2002) was used to analyze the data. After forming the chance-corrected agreement matrix, the program runs Comrey's (1962) minimum residual factor analysis algorithm to obtain the competence estimates d. As shown in Table 10.2, the pattern of eigenvalues is highly consistent with the assumption of a single set of right answers: this is seen in the largest eigenvalue being many times larger than the next largest. This is what we expect in a classroom setting with a single teacher. If the exam had been given to two different classes of Sociology 101 with different professors, we might have seen a result in which the two largest eigenvalues were of similar size, reflecting two different right answer keys in operation and corresponding to the perspectives of different teachers.

Since the first eigenvector turns out to be sufficiently dominant, we can go ahead and interpret the factor loadings (the values of the eigenvector) as estimates of each student's amount of knowledge. Given that in this case we know the correct answers (by definition, they are the teacher's answers) we can compare the model's ranking of students with the instructor's grades for each student. The comparison is shown in Table 10.3. The Pearson correlation between the model's competence scores and the instructor's letter grades is 0.937.[2] Thus, if we regard the instructor's answer key as the gold standard, the model has recovered those scores extremely well, especially considering the letter grade system groups a range of scores together into a single value.

The Model in Anthropological Context

In this section we translate the abstract consensus model into a more general anthropological context. We begin by considering the meaning of the three assumptions.

The first assumption, common truth, is fundamentally a statement about the kinds of informant variability that may exist. From the model's point of view, there are basically two sources of variability in informant responses: culture and competence. Cultural variability refers to variability in responses due to belonging to different cultures, which have systematically different ways of looking at the world – in effect, having different answer keys. Competence variability refers to differences in responses *within* a given culture, which is to say among people for whom the same answer key applies. In any culture, some people simply know more of the cultural truth than others. For example, some people know the names of many different kinds of trees, while others know only a few, even when they belong to the same culture.

The common truth assumption essentially states that, if you want to be able to measure the competence or cultural literacy of informants, they must be drawn from the same culture. Otherwise, the differences in responses you observe could be due to cultural differences.

Table 10.3 Comparison of letter grades and competence scores for 101 students

Letter grade	*Comp.*	*Letter grade*	*Comp.*	*Letter grade*	*Comp.*	*Letter grade*	*Comp.*	*Letter grade*	*Comp.*
A	0.89	B	0.79	C+	0.79	D+	0.70	D	0.59
A	0.89	B	0.79	C+	0.77	D+	0.69	D	0.59
A	0.87	B	0.78	C+	0.77	D+	0.69	D	0.57
A	0.86	B	0.78	C+	0.77	D+	0.68	D	0.56
A	0.85	B	0.77	C+	0.73	D+	0.66	D	0.52
A	0.85	B	0.77	C+	0.73	D+	0.65	D	0.52
B+	0.86	B	0.77	C+	0.73	D+	0.65	D	0.50
B+	0.86	B	0.77	C+	0.73	D+	0.65	D	0.47
B+	0.85	B	0.76	C+	0.72	D+	0.65	D	0.46
B+	0.84	B	0.74	C+	0.72	D+	0.64	D	0.46
B+	0.82	B	0.73	C+	0.70	D+	0.64	F	0.41
B+	0.81	B	0.72	C+	0.64	D+	0.63	F	0.38
B+	0.80	B	0.82	C	0.75	D+	0.63	F	0.38
B+	0.80	B	0.80	C	0.73	D+	0.63	F	0.35
B+	0.79			C	0.71	D+	0.63		
B+	0.77			C	0.70	D+	0.63		
B+	0.77			C	0.68	D+	0.63		
				C	0.68	D+	0.63		
				C	0.68	D+	0.62		
				C	0.66	D+	0.62		
				C	0.64	D+	0.62		
				C	0.62	D+	0.62		
				C	0.60	D+	0.61		
						D+	0.60		
						D+	0.60		
						D+	0.60		
						D+	0.59		
						D+	0.58		
						D+	0.57		
						D+	0.57		
						D+	0.56		
						D+	0.56		
						D+	0.54		

The conditional independence assumption specifies that the only systematic force leading people to give the same answers is the cultural truth. In other words, when people are mistaken about some cultural "fact," their mistakes are not correlated with each other. They might agree on the same wrong answer, but it is just by chance. If this assumption were not true, it would lead to the model overestimating the knowledge of informants, because they would be agreeing at high rates, which would be interpreted as having high levels of knowledge. A key thing to consider here in applying the consensus model is whether the questions are of a factual, recall nature, or whether there are heuristics for figuring out the answer. For example, suppose informants don't actually know whether a given leaf is a maple or not. They may have a rule available to them that says "maple leaves have five lobes," which would lead them to answer "maple" for many different kinds of leaves, sometimes correctly, sometimes not. Heuristics of this type provide an extra degree of association between responses that are not consistent with the conditional independence assumption.

It must be emphasized that the function of the three assumptions is to guarantee that the factor loadings of the agreement matrix can be interpreted as estimates of informant competence in their culture. When the assumptions don't hold, the factor loadings cannot be seen as competence because other factors may be accounting for inter-informant variability. However, estimating competence is not the only important output of the model. In many cases, the key research question is whether or not the informants belong to a single culture, and this can be diagnosed by examining the pattern of eigenvalues. The assumptions of the model do not need to hold in order to make this diagnosis. We now turn to powerful examples of consensus analysis in practice made possible by the loosening of these assumptions.

Consensus Analysis in Practice

Consensus analysis can be used to analyze multiple types of data including true–false, yes–no, multiple-choice, and even open-ended, and to fill in the blank questions (assuming that the assumptions of the model hold). In addition, ways have been proposed to work with ordinal and interval scale data (e.g., Romney et al. 1987; Chavez et al. 1995) and social network analysis data (Kumbasar 1996; Batchelder et al. 1997).

Consider the archival data from NCAA American football shown in Table 10.4.[3] Before the start of each season, sports journalists from competing magazines assess the quality of all football teams and subjectively rank the strongest 25 teams (1 is considered the best). The decisions are made before the teams have played any games and are often influenced by factors such as number of returning players, quality of incoming recruits, strength of schedule, coaching ability, et cetera. To use consensus analysis with these data, we recoded the rankings so that the teams were sorted into six tiers in descending quality. [4] Table 10.4 presents the team quality ratings from ten different judges.

Let's assume that we know very little about NCAA American football and want to learn more about this domain, for example, which teams are considered the best, and which judges are the most informative. From looking at the data, we note that there are clear differences of opinion: *Sporting News* places Auburn in the top tier, but Phil Steele places them in the 3rd tier; ATS places Michigan in the top tier, but *College Football News* has them in the 4th tier; Athlon and *Sporting News* place Southern California in the 2nd tier, but ATS places them in the 6th tier. Without knowing much about the domain, it is difficult to determine the culturally correct ranking of each team, the expertise of each judge, and whether the judges belong to the same culture.

To address the variability in perceived team quality, we might use the modal tier placement of each team as an indicator of quality. For example, all ten judges place Oklahoma and Ohio State in the top tier. We might feel confident that Oklahoma and Ohio State are considered among the best teams in the country. However, there are situations in which there are multiple modal values: four judges place LSU in the 3rd tier, and four place them in the 4th tier. Therefore, the modal approach can fall short because it cannot effectively address these discrepancies.

Table 10.4 NCAA football ratings

	Athlon	*Street & Smith*	*Sporting News*	*Phil Steele*	*College Football News*	*Lindy*	*ATS*	*Game Plan*	*CPA*	*CNN/ SI*
Alabama	5	5	6	6	5	5	6	3	6	6
Arizona State	6	3	6	6	6	5	6	5	6	5
Arkansas	6	6	6	5	6	6	4	6	5	6
Auburn	1	2	1	3	1	2	2	1	3	2
Colorado	6	6	6	6	6	5	5	6	6	6
CSU	6	5	4	6	6	4	6	6	6	6
Florida	4	6	6	6	5	6	4	6	4	6
Florida State	3	4	3	3	5	4	6	2	2	3
Fresno State	6	6	5	6	6	6	6	6	6	6
Georgia	2	3	3	4	3	3	5	2	2	1
Kansas State	1	2	2	3	2	1	3	1	1	2
LSU	4	4	3	3	3	3	5	4	2	4
Maryland	4	3	4	4	2	2	4	4	4	4
Miami-Florida	1	1	1	2	1	1	1	2	1	1
Michigan	2	1	1	1	4	1	1	2	2	3
Minnesota	6	5	6	6	6	6	6	6	6	6
Mississippi	6	6	6	5	6	6	6	6	6	6
Missouri	5	6	6	6	5	6	6	6	6	6
NC State	3	4	5	4	3	4	5	6	4	2
Nebraska	6	6	6	3	6	6	6	3	5	6
Notre Dame	5	5	4	4	4	3	3	4	4	4
Ohio State	1	1	1	1	1	1	1	1	1	1
Oklahoma	1	1	1	1	1	1	1	1	1	1
Oklahoma State	6	5	5	6	6	6	4	4	6	5
Oregon	6	6	6	6	6	6	6	6	6	5
Oregon State	4	6	6	6	4	6	6	6	6	6
Penn State	6	6	6	5	6	6	4	6	5	5
Pittsburgh	2	2	4	1	2	3	2	4	3	3
Purdue	4	6	3	4	5	4	2	3	5	6
Southern Cal	2	3	2	2	2	2	6	3	2	2
Tennessee	5	3	4	2	3	2	2	5	3	4
Texas	2	1	2	1	1	2	1	1	1	1
Texas A&M	6	6	6	6	6	6	6	5	6	5
TCU	6	6	5	5	6	5	6	5	6	6
UCLA	6	6	6	6	4	6	6	6	6	6
Virginia	5	4	2	6	4	5	3	6	4	3
Virginia Tech	3	2	3	2	2	3	2	2	3	2
Washington	3	2	2	2	6	4	3	3	3	3
West Virginia	6	6	6	6	6	6	5	6	6	6
Wisconsin	3	4	5	5	3	6	3	6	5	4

Another approach might be to average each team's tier placement from the ten judges to calculate an aggregate quality score for each team. However, suppose one of the judges knows very little about NCAA football. The averaging method would weight this person's answers equally with all the others, creating an average value that

Table 10.5

Largest eigenvalue	3.82
Second largest eigenvalue	0.36
Ratio of largest to next largest	10.49

Table 10.6

Judge	*Competence*
CPA	0.68
Sporting News	0.67
Athlon	0.67
CNN/SI	0.64
Lindy	0.62
Phil Steele	0.61
Street & Smith	0.61
College Football News	0.60
Game Plan	0.54
ATS	0.53

is quite different from the majority. In addition, the averaging approach cannot distinguish respondents who lack significant knowledge of the domain from those who have significant knowledge but where that knowledge comes from a different culture. In the case of just a few outliers we could turn to more robust measures of central tendency, such as medians and trimmed means. But in the end, all of these methods have no way of discounting the data from judges who really don't know what they are talking about.

A third approach is to use consensus analysis. As discussed earlier, this method can be used to help us identify both the culturally correct quality of each team and the expertise of each judge. This method distinguishes between having low competence in a domain and having a different culture. To analyze these data we transpose the matrix in Table 10.4 to create a judge-by-team matrix in which x_{ij} equals the rating that judge I gave to team J. Table 10.5 gives the output from running consensus analysis on these data using UCINET.

Table 10.5 indicates a good fit with the cultural consensus model in that the ratio of the largest eigenvalue to the second largest is large.[5] As discussed above, the pattern of eigenvalues is highly consistent with the assumption of a single set of right answers and conditional independence. Had there been a group of judges who provided rankings of academic prestige and not football quality, the ratio of the first to second eigenvalue would likely be less than 3 to 1, and the program would notify us that the data do not fit the cultural consensus model.

The high ratio of the first to second eigenvalue allows us to interpret the factor loadings as the competence scores of each judge in the domain of NCAA football. Table 10.6 indicates that CPA has the highest cultural competence, while Game Plan and ATS have the least cultural competence in this domain. If we were interested in learning more about the quality of NCAA football teams, journalists at CPA might be a good source of additional information. If there had been judges that provided

Table 10.7

	Answer key
Oklahoma	1
Ohio State	1
Miami-Florida	1
Texas	1
Auburn	1
Michigan	1
Kansas State	2
Virginia Tech	2
Pittsburgh	2
Southern Cal	2
Georgia	3
Washington	3
Tennessee	3
LSU	3
Florida State	3
NC State	4
Maryland	4
Notre Dame	4
Virginia	4
Purdue	4
Wisconsin	5
Oklahoma State	6
Alabama	6
Florida	6
Arizona State	6
Nebraska	6
Oregon State	6
TCU	6
Arkansas	6
CSU	6
Penn State	6
Colorado	6
Texas A&M	6
Missouri	6
UCLA	6
Fresno State	6
West Virginia	6
Mississippi	6
Oregon	6
Minnesota	6
Southern Miss	6

responses very different from the cultural norm, they would have negative competence scores in this table.

The consensus model also identifies the culturally correct quality of each team, as displayed in Table 10.7. The output provides an "answer" for every team and allows us to easily differentiate the top- and bottom-tiered teams. Note that the answer key

Table 10.8

Judge	*Correlation with actual outcomes*
Consensus analysis answer key	0.64
CPA	0.58
Lindy	0.52
Phil Steele	0.50
Sporting News	0.47
Game Plan	0.46
Athlon	0.44
CNN/SI	0.42
Street & Smith	0.41
College Football News	0.40
ATS	0.23

identifies Southern Cal as a 2nd tier team despite ATS considering them a 6th tier team (we also note that ATS had the lowest competence score).

This data set also allows us to investigate the predictive accuracy of each judge by comparing the pre-season predictions with actual outcomes. At the end of each season the Associated Press ranks teams based on their on-the-field outcomes (i.e., win–loss record, margin of victory, etc.). This outcome measure allows us to compare the accuracy of the perceived quality scores provided by the ten judges and the "culturally true" quality scores derived from consensus analysis. To do this we recoded the final AP rankings using the same method used to recode the pre-season predictions and correlated the results. See Table 10.8.

Findings indicate that the answer key derived from consensus analysis was the most accurate predictor of actual outcomes ($r = 0.64$). In other words, the consensus truth output was a better predictor of actual performance than any of the ten judges individually. In summary, this finding provides additional evidence for the "wisdom of crowds" and highlights the utility of using consensus analysis to get at this "wisdom" and identify competent individuals.

We now turn to an application of consensus analysis to social network analysis. Consider the following example taken from a consulting project in which we studied the relationships between 14 executives forming the top management team of a local organization. Part of this project involved interviewing each executive and identifying how he or she perceived the network connections of each of his or her colleagues. Network ties were evaluated on a 1 to 5 scale, where 5 indicated a stronger tie. One of the driving research questions was whether executives who perceive relationships between others accurately are more effective leaders than those whose perceptions are less accurate. The data collection process involved asking each executive to provide their perception of the relationship between every pair of executives, including themselves. In other words, each executive reported the strength of his or her relationships with other executives as well as his or her perception of the strength of relationship between every possible pair of executives. The resulting data was a collection of fourteen 14-by-14 matrices of perceptions, one for each executive, a type of data known as cognitive social structure data (Krackhardt 1987).

Table 10.9 Eigenvalues

Largest eigenvalue	5.92
Second largest eigenvalue	1.81
Ratio of largest to next	3.27

Table 10.10 Competence scores

Informant	*Competence*
Farhill	0.90
Black	0.78
Mechanic	0.76
Andrews	0.76
Gold	0.76
Godfrey	0.74
Westminister	0.69
King	0.68
Jones	0.67
Long-Rong	0.62
Pyre	0.60
Butler	0.08
Trout	0.06
Agachar	−0.23

We used consensus analysis to identify the consensus view of the network of perceived relationships and determine each individual's competence in perceiving the ties around them.[6] Table 10.9 shows that the largest eigenvalue is more than three times the second largest, suggesting that all of the executives see the network in a fundamentally similar way. Table 10.10 gives the competence scores for each person, showing which individuals have the best understanding of the network around them.[7] We can see that Farhill has the highest score, making him a good choice as a key informant for an ethnographic study (Johnson 1990), and arguably someone who is well positioned to get things done because he understands who is allied with whom. We also note that Butler, Trout, and Agachar have significantly lower competence scores, indicating that they have little idea of who is connected to whom. Interestingly, Trout is the CEO of the organization and Butler is second in command. It is possible that their unique job responsibilities separate them from other executives and might influence their ability to view the network of relationships accurately. Nevertheless, their lack of understanding of the relationships around them is a potential source of serious management problems.[8] Agachar's low score is also interesting because a separate analysis (not presented here) shows that he occupies a highly peripheral position in the informal communication network, which could explain why he knows so little about who is connected to whom. As an aside, if we remove these three individuals with low competence scores and rerun the analysis, we find that the ratio of first to second eigenvalue increases to 10.72, and competence scores for the remaining executives are virtually unaffected (see Tables 10.11 and 10.12).

Table 10.11

Largest eigenvalue	5.85
Second largest eigenvalue	0.55
Ratio of largest to next	10.72

Table 10.12

Informant	*Competence*
Farhill	0.90
Black	0.79
Mechanic	0.77
Andrews	0.76
Gold	0.76
Godfrey	0.74
Westminister	0.69
King	0.69
Jones	0.68
Long-Rong	0.62
Pyre	0.59

Finally, consensus analysis also produces an inferred "true" network of ties based on all respondent points of view. This "true network" is different from simply accepting the majority answer for each dyadic relationship because it takes into account the varying competencies of the judges. It also differs from a network constructed by considering only the responses of the two members of any dyad – an approach Krackhardt (1987) refers to as locally aggregated structures (LAS). Figure 10.2 displays the inferred "true" network of perceived relationships derived from consensus analysis.[9] Figures 10.3 and 10.4 display Farhill's and Agachar's views of the same network. Note that Farhill's view is more similar to the inferred truth than Agachar's, in keeping with their respective competence scores, which is very high for Farhill and very low for Agachar.

In summary, consensus analysis can be used with cognitive network data to reveal very powerful findings not easily obtained from other analytic approaches. These findings can be used to identify potential leaders and to better understand organizational performance and conflict.

Conclusion

The consensus model provides both a powerful theoretical perspective and a very useful analysis methodology. A key theoretical contribution is the distinction made between cultural and competence sources of inter-informant variability. Cultural variability is manifested as systematically different patterns of answers across a survey (or multiple answer keys in the language of the model) that apply to different clusters of informants. Competence variability is the remaining variability between informants

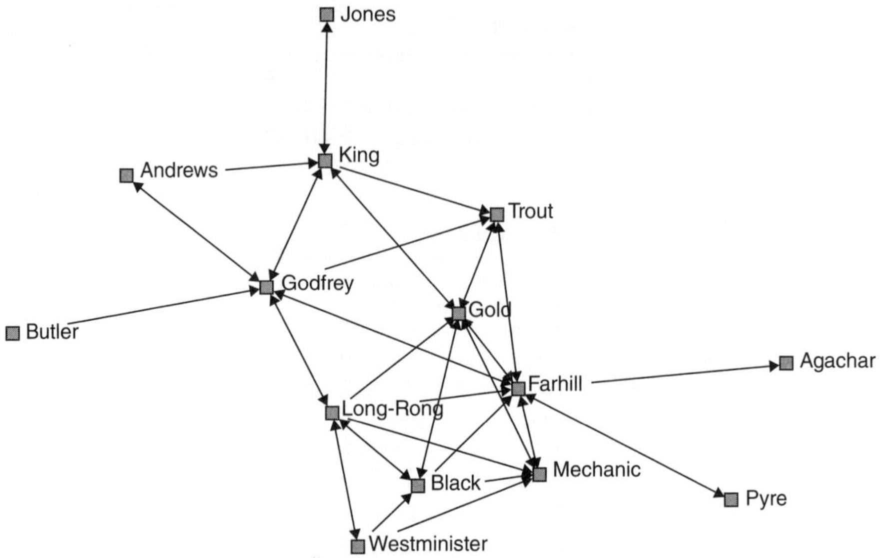

Figure 10.2 "True" network of perceived executive relationships derived from consensus analysis (only displaying ties of strength greater than 4).

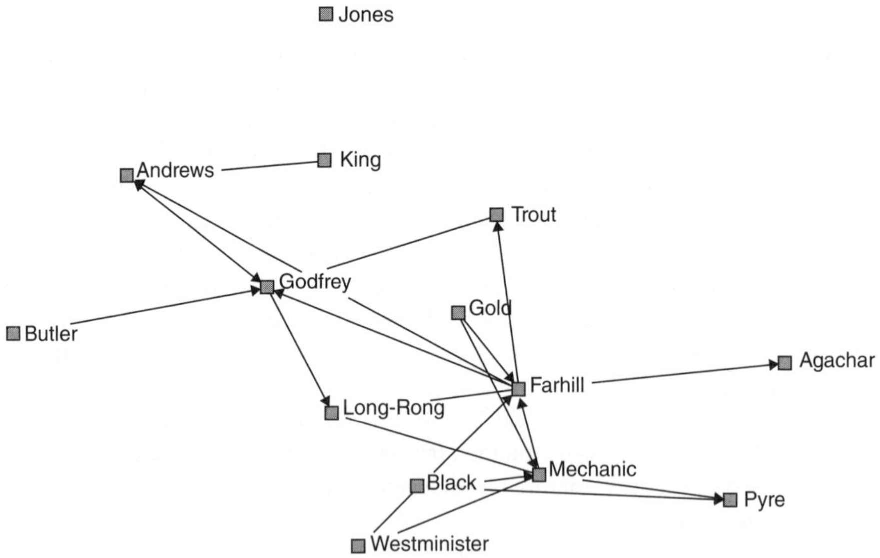

Figure 10.3 Farhill's view of executive relationships (only displaying ties of strength greater than 4).

who are drawn from the same culture, but with perhaps differing access to that culture, leading to some knowing more about some domains than others.

As a methodology, the consensus model can determine whether a given set of informants have consensus, meaning that they share an underlying culture. Given that they do, the model can then provide highly accurate estimates of how much knowledge each person has about the domain. Finally, the model can then use the pattern of who

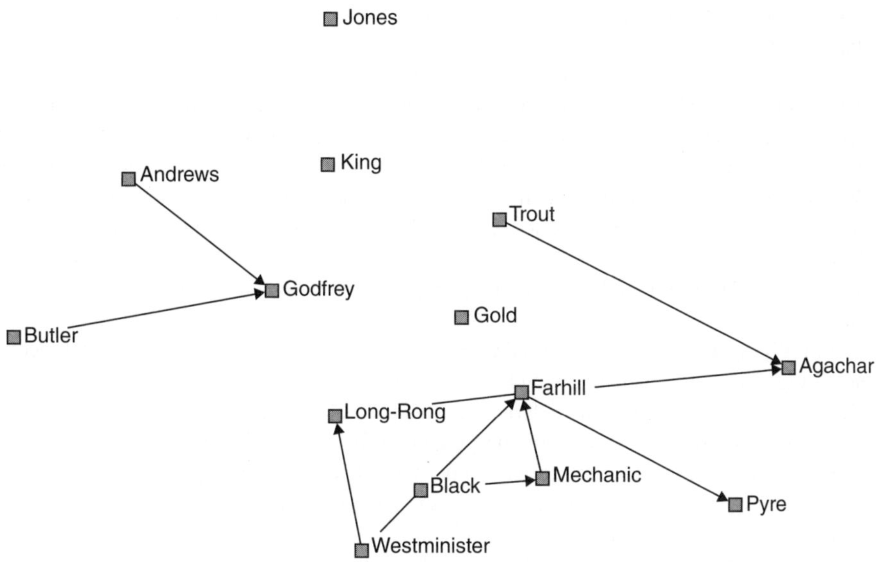

Figure 10.4 Agachar's view of executive relationships (only displaying ties of strength greater than 4).

responded in what way to each question to infer the culturally correct right answers, yielding a more accurate understanding of the culture than that possessed by any one informant.

Of course, the power provided by the consensus procedure does not come without cost (Borgatti and Carboni 2007). The method must be coupled with a qualitative first stage in which the researcher elicits the beliefs of a group in a given domain. The result of this ethnographic work must be a set of discrete propositions or statements of fact that can be used as the basis of a multiple-choice questionnaire. This is a time-consuming process that requires some skill. It also requires a domain that lends itself to being atomized in this way.

Despite these very real limitations, consensus analysis is exceptionally useful. It is also an excellent exemplar of model-based science in which the researcher can capture a social or cognitive process as a simple mathematical model from which he or she can then derive some powerful results, and at the same time specify the conditions under which these results are valid.

As a final note, the consensus model provides a path of reconciliation between scientific and post-scientific epistemologies. The model utilizes a mathematical approach that seems clearly based on a view of knowledge as objective truth, but ends up providing a way to identify and assess culturally relative knowledge.

NOTES

1 The name of an album released by Elvis Presley.

2 The original numeric scores used to assign letter grades are no longer available. The correlation was obtained by converting letter scores to numeric as follows: A = 4.00, B+ = 3.50,

B = 3.00, C+ = 2.5, C = 2.0, D+ = 1.5, D = 1.0, F+ = 0.5, F = 0. Minuses were not used at this university.

3 These data are publicly available at http://football.stassen.com/.

4 We recoded the raw rankings into broader categories to partially address the lack of independence among these data. Our recoding scheme was as follows: Teams ranked 1–5 = 1st tier, 6–10 = 2nd tier, 11–15 = 3rd tier, 16–20 = 4th tier, 21–25 = 5th tier, others = 6th tier. Without the recoding, a judge's choice of a particular rank for one team would (usually) preclude giving that rank to another team, violating the conditional independence assumption of the model.

5 A typical rule of thumb is that the first eigenvalue should be at least three times larger than the second.

6 Technically, data of this type potentially violate the second assumption of the model, because each judge's data is a matrix in which all the cells in a given row correspond to the judge's perceptions of the row person's relationships. If the judge thinks the person is an odd duck, it will influence the perceptions of the person's relations to all others. Maher (1987) has shown via simulation that the model is quite robust to violations of the third assumption, but to date no study has examined violations of the second assumption.

7 All names are pseudonyms.

8 It is presumably no coincidence that the organization was experiencing some problems, which is why consultants were brought in.

9 The networks displayed in Figures 10.2, 10.3, and 10.4 were dichotomized at tie strengths greater than 4.

REFERENCES

Batchelder, W. H., and A. K. Romney
1988 Test Theory without an Answer Key. Psychometrika 53(1):71–92.

Batchelder, W. H., E. Kumbasar, and J. P. Boyd
1997 Consensus Analysis of Three-Way Social Network Data. Journal of Mathematical Sociology 22:29–58.

Borgatti, S. P., and I. Carboni
2007 Measuring Individual Knowledge in Organizations. Organizational Research Methods 10(3):449–462.

Borgatti, S. P., M. G. Everett, and L. C. Freeman
2002 UCINET for Windows: Software for Social Network Analysis. Analytic Technologies, Harvard University.

Boster, J. S., and J. C. Johnson
1989 Form or Function: A Comparison of Expert and Novice Judgments of Similarity among Fish. American Anthropologist 91:866–889.

Caulkins, D. D.
2001 Consensus, Clines, and Edges in Celtic Culture. Cross-Cultural Research 35(2):109–126.

Caulkins, D. D., and S. B. Hyatt
1999 Using Consensus Analysis to Measure Cultural Diversity in Organizations and Social Movements. Field Methods 11(1):5–26.

Caulkins, D. D., M. Offer-Westort, and C. Trosset
2005 Perceiving Ethnic Differences: The Use of Consensus Analysis and Personhood in Welsh-American Populations. Mathematical Anthropology and Cultural Theory: An International Journal 1(4). http://www.mathematicalanthropology.org/pdf/Caulkinsetal1005.pdf, accessed September 16, 2010.

Chavez, L. R., F. A. Hubbel, J. M. McMullin, R. G. Martinez, and S. I. Mishra
1995 Structure and Meaning in Models of Breast and Cervical Cancer Risk Factors: A Comparison of Perceptions among Latinas, Anglo Women, and Physicians. Medical Anthropology Quarterly 9(1):40–74.

Comrey, A. L.
1962 The Minimum Residual Method of Factor Analysis. Psychological Reports 11: 15–18.

D'Andrade, R. G.
1987 A Folk Model of the Mind. *In* Cultural Models in Language and Thought. D. Holland and N. Quinn, eds. Cambridge: Cambridge University Press.

De Munck, V., G. de Alba, V. Guadarrama, and T. Garro
1998 Consensus Analysis: High Blood Pressure in a Mexican Barrio. *In* Using Methods in the Field: A Practical Introduction and Casebook. V. de Munck and E. J. Sobo, eds. Pp. 197–211. Walnut Creek, CA: AltaMira.

Hruschka, D. J., L. M. Sibley, N. Kalim, and J. K. Edmonds
2008 When There is More than One Answer Key: Cultural Theories of Postpartum Hemorrhage in Matlab, Bangladesh. Field Methods 20(4):315–337.

Jameson, K., and A. K. Romney
1990 Consensus on Semiotic Models of Alphabetic Systems. Journal of Quantitative Anthropology 2:289–303.

Johnson, J. C.
1990 Selecting Ethnographic Informants. Newbury Park, CA: Sage.

Johnson, J. C., and D. C. Griffith
1996 Pollution, Food Safety, and the Distribution of Knowledge. Human Ecology 24(1):87–108.

Krackhardt, D.
1987 Cognitive Social Structures. Social Networks 9:109–134.

Kumbasar, E.
1996 Methods for Analyzing Three-Way Cognitive Network Data. Journal of Quantitative Anthropology 6:15–34.

Maher, K. M.
1987 A Multiple Choice Model for Aggregating Group Knowledge and Estimating Individual Competencies. Unpublished doctoral dissertation, University of California, Irvine (AAT 8724745).

Miller, M. L., J. Kaneko, P. Bartram, J. Marks, and D. D. Brewer
2004 Cultural Consensus Analysis and Environmental Anthropology: Yellowfin Tuna Fishery Management in Hawaii. Cross-Cultural Research 38(3):289–314.

Moore, R., I. Brodsgaard, M. Miller, T. Mao, and S. Dworkin
1997 Consensus Analysis: Reliability, Validity, and Informant Accuracy in Use of American and Mandarin Chinese Pain Descriptors. Annals of Behavioral Medicine 19(3):295–300.

Novick, M. R.
1966 The Axioms and Principal Results of Classical Test Theory. Journal of Mathematical Psychology 3(1):1–18.

Romney, A. K., W. G. Batchelder, and S. C. Weller
1987 Recent Applications of Cultural Consensus. American Behavioral Scientist 31(2):163–177.

Romney, A. K., S. Weller, and W. H. Batchelder
1986 Culture As Consensus: A Theory of Culture and Informant Accuracy. American Anthropologist 88(2):313–338.

Shafto, P., and J. D. Coley
2003 Development of Categorization and Reasoning in the Natural World: Novices to Experts, Naïve Similarity to Ecological Knowledge. Journal of Experimental Psychology 29(4):641–649.

Surowiecki, J.
2004 The Wisdom of Crowds: Why the Many Are Smarter than the Few and How Collective Wisdom Shapes Business, Economies, Societies and Nations. New York: Doubleday.
Weller, S. C., and R. D. Baer
2001 Intra- and Intercultural Variation in the Definition of Five Illnesses: AIDS, Diabetes, the Common Cold, Empacho, and Mal de Ojo. Cross-Cultural Research 35(2): 201–226.

CHAPTER 11

Narrative, Mind, and Culture

Benjamin N. Colby

Narrative interchanges between mind and environment, between internal schemas and external patterns, involve interesting and complex cultural processes. As cognitive anthropology absorbs findings in the neurosciences and moves beyond semantic paradigms to narrative and other deeper-level pragmatics it may well fill the embarrassing lacuna in the discipline: the lack of a scientific theory of culture.

The discovery of mirror neurons – a key process involved in cultural transmission – gives us a point of entry for studying the interface between mind and environment. Recent work in biological anthropology (Deacon 1997), behavioral neurology (Damasio 2003), and cognitive linguistics (Halliday and Webster 2007) suggest useful approaches in narrative analysis and from there to broader cultural phenomena.[1]

Even if we have to settle for bridging theories in advance of detailed evidence many advances outside anthropology are directly relevant to narrative and culture theory. What follows are several ways in which discourse generally, and narrative in particular, can yield such bridging theories.

The General Inquirer

My early work with narrative analysis used a computer application, the General Inquirer, which could count themes and show patterns in texts. Although it could handle large numbers of texts, any patterns or relationships found had to be investigated by hand for the kind of insights anthropologists usually seek.

A Companion to Cognitive Anthropology, First Edition. Edited by David B. Kronenfeld, Giovanni Bennardo, Victor C. de Munck, and Michael D. Fischer.

Latent Semantic Analysis

A recent different kind of content analysis, Latent Semantic Analysis (LSA), takes a different approach. Words are analyzed in terms of vectors derived from matrices of words by contexts – a high-dimensional linear associative model (Landauer and Dumais 1997; Landauer 2001). LSA works on a large corpus of texts to provide results that capture the similarity of words and of text passages. Similarity data go beyond contiguous relationships to the larger corpus including texts within that corpus that do not contain a particular word of interest but that nevertheless contribute to a measure of similarity for that word. LSA's ability to bridge the gap between semantic information derived from local text contiguity and the semantic knowledge people extract from their total experience offers an answer, according to Landauer and Dumais (1997), to Plato's paradox – how people seem to learn about an aspect of language in the absence of direct experience with that aspect. That LSA can exhibit this ability comes from indirect inference calculated at an optimal number of dimensions (around 300 arrived at by trial and error) that go beyond relations of direct co-occurrence. LSA is an interesting case where the statistical text analysis procedure came first; only later did results emerge that led to theoretical speculations suggesting that the brain is organized differently than generally thought. However, aside from such suggestive – possibly revolutionary – possibilities, LSA has limited practical use in narrative or discourse study. A variety of LSA programs are available, including one called LIW2007.

Text Ethnography and DRS

While the applications described so far are useful, particularly for handling numerous and large texts, they do not enable the kind of analysis needed for researching pattern–schema connections (patterns = observed culture outside one's head; schemas = postulated neural organizations inside one's head). A useful approach for a more dynamic understanding is one that uses artificial intelligence and interactive analysis.

With the help of Mark James, undergraduate LISP programmer, I designed an interactive Discourse Research System (DRS), coded in Interlisp, a programming environment for LISP (James and Colby 1979). The system provided the analyst with an interactive approach for writing pattern matching rules on the fly as he writes rules and analyzes texts and tests hypotheses.

DRS rules operate on phrases, words, or word parts. Rules for disambiguation are possible. For instance, two meanings for the word *chair* can be assigned features indicated with a plus sign (+) such as [+inanimate +artifact +furniture/+animate +role = manage]. These features can be typed into the dictionary entries but the features can also be used in pattern matching rules that distinguish instances by context (other words and features). Additional features can be assigned for syntactic function such as [+noun] and cohesion features such as [+deictic] or [+non-specific] linking a pronoun to a previously mentioned person. Additional features indicating common contexts and associated objects such as [+table] can be added to the text. Initially the computer reads a text, looks up every word in a feature dictionary and assigns a feature list after each word in the text.

The Emic Quest

While the DRS coding was in process I started to work on ways to segment texts on a basis presumed to underlie the paragraphing of texts. The immediate purpose was to facilitate a division of folktales into smaller chunks for easier analysis with DRS. However, there are other advantages that emerged from the endeavor, as will be seen below.

When we write an essay or anything we expect other people to read, we usually divide what we write into paragraphs. We start new paragraphs when we change the subject or move from one idea to the next. Paragraph indentations alert the reader that there is a change or new idea in the next paragraph. Paragraphing, it turns out, affords an entry port to the underlying pragmatics of a text. To be sure, paragraphing is a poor substitute for the pauses, inflections, gestures, and facial expressions that one experiences with an oral delivery by a good storyteller or simply in any kind of conversation. These are not conveyed in writing except in a very limited fashion: periods, commas, quotation marks, underlining, and paragraphing are an attempt to provide a substitute for the prosodic features of speech events. However limited it is, in comparison with actual speech events, the segmenting of a text into paragraphs directs thinking to the underlying processing of a line of thought. That is our point of entry and it moves us toward a new kind of emic quest.

Only in special cases – as I get to later in eidochronic analysis – does the segmenting or chunking of narrative lend itself to determining stable chunks of thought. These segments involve entire event sequences from what precedes to what follows some particular event. Our brains do this chunking for us at some preconscious level of awareness. This is important, for in recognizing the natural segmentation of events in narrative one is working at a fundamental level of cultural transmission between listeners and hearers.

The bases for paragraphing are variable. But it should be possible to build a model or a set of pattern-matching rules to yield the wide range of information types that can trigger pauses in oral delivery or paragraphs in printed texts. Let's see how it might work for a folktale written with paragraphs.

Segmenting texts and neurological indicators

There are two broad types of indicators for how a text might be chunked to aid comprehension: non-cohesive and cohesive. Non-cohesive juncture indicators suggest natural boundaries in a text. Usually when we start a new paragraph we conclude one mini-theme of thought imagery and move to another. Since this involves a major updating of the narrative situation being modeled in working memory, and since working memory has a limited capacity, part of what has changed is attenuated in working memory to make room for the updated material. What has been replaced thus gets moved to some form of episodic memory – perhaps a "nearby" episodic memory held at the ready for later reference. This is where a narrative grammar would be helpful, on the hypothesis that several higher levels of syntactical categorization would be the route for memory retrieval. The second higher level (above the actual text) would be what I suggest is the emic level.

The converse of junctures is cohesion. The two work in tandem. Linguists measure cohesion through various devices like anaphoric reference or deixis. For example, if a particular character in the story is engaged in some activity, he is first indicated by name or some other term such as the character's role. Then in the sentences that follow, the name or role of the character is simply replaced by the appropriate pronoun. If, however, the paragraph gets overlong, if other characters are referred to in the paragraph, the subject's name or role may be restated before using pronouns for the subject again. If so, this suggests that if no juncture signal appears after a certain amount of additional but not "basic" narrative detail, there has to be a degree of decay in the situational model being maintained in working memory, or if the complexity or "density" (i.e., propositional content, detail, or extensive minutia) of information is very high or not entirely clear, a character's name is reiterated before continuing in further sentences with the appropriate pronoun. If several characters are on the scene in the narrative situation, the clausal or sentence structure may become ambiguous thus increasing the need for reiterating the name. The longer the paragraph the more one has to hold in working memory. If paragraphs are the optimal length, given their propositions or density, then there is an orderly, easy updating of the situation in working memory.

Thus narrative cohesion is concerned with how elements of a narrative form easily digested chunks – that is, chunks that can be easily held in episodic memory, and easily recalled if repeating the narrative on some later occasion – these chunks, I postulate, are the pre-emic units of culture that with time and retellings of a story, or tellings of other stories but with similar chunks, become the emic units of oral narrative.

The following list below gives indicators of junctures in a folktale. My list comes from an analysis of a few fairy tales that might be programmed into a modern-day DRS. Initially, each indicator is intuitively assigned a number representing degree of juncture strength as judged by the analyst. The initial value estimates are iteratively developed depending on the characteristics of whatever corpus is being segmented. If a sentence contains more than one juncture indicator, the values for each indicator are added together for that sentence. Sentences with combined juncture indicators exceeding a certain threshold would thus signal a segment marker. There can be several threshold values, the lower thresholds marking shorter segments, the larger ones marking major segments. These might quite possibly serve to indicate intermediate and high levels of a narrative syntax.

Juncture indicators

A Establishing, specifying, or changing the scene.
B Establishing or changing the time.
C Introducing new characters or making a change in the characters present in a scene, for example, a departure of a character.
D Particularization: a narrowing of focus or time.
E Existentials: existential statements involving participants, conditions, or situations involving *there* or *it* followed by [+be] optional modifiers and [+noun].
F Imperatives.
G Conditions and requirements.

H Interrogative.
I Desiderative.
J Hortatory.
K Valence change: new character appears on the scene with a different valence [+good] or [+bad].
L Potency change (e.g., country girl marries prince or king).

Cohesion indicators Narrative cohesion and hence coherence of narrative is maintained by a more directly linguistic set of indicators, many of which are covered at the clause and sentence level in Halliday and Hasan's *Cohesion in English* (1976).

M Introduction and reiteration of characters versus pronominal reference.
N Additive conjunctions (*and*, *nor*, *or*) counted only in initial positions (otherwise continuity within a sentence is structurally maintained by the conjunction).
O Adversative conjunctions (*but*, *yet*, *though*, *however*).
P Causal conjunctions (*then*, *so*, *because*, *hence*, *therefore*).
Q Temporal conjunctions (*then*, *next*, *after*, *at the same time*, *previously*, *simultaneously*).
R The words *well* and *now* (in initial position).
S There seems to be a continuum according to intonation pattern as to the cohesive, contrastive, or initiating functions of words like *well* and *now* in initial position. In folktales, however, the principal usage signals a new segment, regardless of whether the new segment is by virtue of a contrast with what went immediately before or represents something entirely new.

In work with texts to segment them into natural chunks, the valence assigned to each one of the above indicators is determined by trial and error, simulating various kinds of narrative processing. As in latent semantic analysis, which took a trial and error procedure to discover that 300 dimensions worked best, so also might one attempt a trial and error procedure in assigning valences to different types of juncture indicators in narrative. In such a study the variation found in the chunking valences vary from one genre or cultural system to another or from one storyteller to another, or from one situational context to another. These sources of variation would be a matter for empirical verification but a methodology for discovering criteria that underlie a dynamic system ought to be possible with an updated and much faster DRS-type system. Determining the valences for junctures and the cohesions and how they combine in mental processing (e.g., junctures being assigned positive values, cohesion negative ones, or vice versa) may profitably interface with new approaches using fMRI studies of narrative event boundaries (Speer et al. 2007). That is, the forces of cohesion/juncture are added together for each sentence and given a positive valence as a signal for what stays in situational/working memory and negative for what goes into episodic storage or vice versa depending whether one's focus is on what stays in the narrative situation or whether it is on what gets shunted over into episodic storage.

Determining a threshold value for the decision to set paragraphs opens a window into how the human mind stores and retrieves memories and through that to pragmatic elements that underlie the processing of speech events. Presumably such a threshold varies with people and other factors such as age and situation.

Determining degree of cognitive break is sometimes quite obvious. In the classic phrase "meanwhile, back at the ranch ...," we make a very large cognitive break. We shift our thinking not only in space but also in time. We have to backtrack a little. The mental pause needed during this shifting of mental gears would be larger in magnitude than earlier ones in the text.

While my initial objective was simply to identify major and minor breaks (which would usually correspond with the actual printed paragraphing of a folktale), the later objective focused on a typology of narrative features that add up to trigger a mental pause in a story. These segmenting features are first steps to study the deep-level cognitive mapping that goes on during text comprehension.

This segmentation work was developed in the 1980s in expectation of a faster-running DRS system, which unfortunately did not materialize. Since that time, however, psychologists and psychoneurologists have begun examining segmentation of both texts and perceived behavior – not for purposes of finding emic units in folktales but for studies of memory and reading. It all amounts to the same phenomena and marks the new field of *event perception*. In the next section I restate my earlier approach in terms of recent event perception theory.

Event perception theory Event perception studies look at how people segment experiences into events and sub-events. One keeps track of the current moment in terms of the immediate past and the possible future. With increasing distance from past events, however, those memories attenuate. This memory storage is very different from the storage of physical files in an office where decisions have to be made about how to file something in a linear and hierarchical fashion – the name of the label on the file folder, the name of the drawer the folder is in, and so on. What makes office-filing so vexing – at least when first setting up a system – is that there are multiple ways in which something might be filed and one has to force the choice to a single hierarchical filing system that people in the office must learn to use. For the brain, however, it is a network of thousands of linkages any single neuron might have. As for schemas, one is talking about hundreds of thousands of possible connections in varying degrees of time-traversing strength.

Contemplating this is mindful of how LSA works going way beyond contiguous pairings to how *all* the words relate to each other in 300-dimensional space. No one knows just why 300 dimensions as opposed to 200 or just three or four dimensions work with LSA but that number, 300 dimensions, looks like a new magic number that is far more abstruse than anything George Miller wrote concerning the magic number 7 (plus or minus 2) over 50 years ago (Miller 1956). Event perception research gives segmentation center stage in cognitive functioning and the encoding of memory. Such an endeavor may move us closer eventually to figuring out what in neural integration corresponds with 300 dimensions in LSA.

Though the focus is currently on the brain, attention must also be given to the cultural environment. After all, the brain depends upon cultural patterns and environmental stimulation to organize itself in the first place. When animals are raised in an impoverished environment (cages without toys and other animals) their brains are smaller, especially in the cerebral cortex (Rosenzweig et al. 1964). Since then more studies have confirmed in more detail and specificity that "newly generated granule cells may provide an important cellular substrate by which hormones and experience alter hippocampal function" (Kozorovitskiy and Gould 2008:58).

Segmentation in perception of daily events One way the segmentation process is studied is for subjects to view movies and push a button at their own conscious perception of change in whatever they see happening. There is intersubjective agreement on these points of segmentation. They can occur when actors change their movements, or when there is a change in a goal or a cause. With commercial cinema changes often occur with a change in the camera shot which involves a mixing of segmentation on the part of the viewer and decisions of segmentation on the part of the director, camera man, and film editor. Their expertise would not cut a scene halfway through a movement, but rather at the beginning or end of one as a kind of natural juncture point. People have an intuitive and unconscious sense for natural boundaries which can be articulated in an experimental setting.

Segmentation of narrative Segmentation is so basic to linguistics that, like fish being unaware of water, it is rarely noticed except during conscious analyses of phonemes and other language units. However, that preconscious process is crucial from the lowest level of phonology up to semantics, syntactics, and beyond to narrative structuring and pragmatics.

In language analysis, segmentation is the first thing an anthropologist or linguist has to do when learning the language of the society she studies – a most challenging task when that society is largely illiterate and narrative traditions are primarily by word of mouth. But think about the infant's learning of her mother tongue. The infant too must be able to segment sounds and words. For the child this is all a preconscious speech-orienting process.

In segmenting thoughts, we are creating a frame around those thoughts which link to other frames. This is where the phrase, carving nature at its joints begins to take on meaning through such linkages in the brain; but those "joints" are dynamic and changing. So what are the clues that psychologists and their research participants use for segmenting speech? It turns out that they are essentially the same as those I found during my DRS research for determining paragraphing in discourse. This is a key element in the elusive emic phenomenon that anthropologists wanted to find in the 1960s and 1970s but gave up as cognitive anthropology seemed to be stuck at the semantic level. Perhaps one reason those chunkings were not obvious at the time was that they are so fluid and situationally variable. Another is that the typical anthropological purview rarely extends to that level of analytical delicacy. So far anthropologists have rarely been involved with the neurosciences in spite of Victor Turner's call for an anthropology of the brain in one of his last lectures (Turner 1987) and writings by D'Aquili (D'Aquili et al. 1979; D'Aquili and Newberg 1999). Clearly, discourse and narrative analysis can benefit substantially from interdisciplinary teams that cover a wider range of expertise and interests than a single ethnographer.

Today with narrative study, questions of validity (so intensive in the beginning of cognitive anthropology) are coming back to be addressed in two ways. First is emic validity highlighted by the failed sociobiological ventures into culture theory.

The second way the validity of categories is being re-examined comes from opportunities now available through psychology and fMRI studies.

Biologists explain culture Outside anthropology, biologists were aware of the "emic" objective which was widely advertised by Kenneth Pike, a linguist and missionary who toured the lecture circuit demonstrating how to analyze unknown languages without an intermediate language. He advanced the idea of deriving emic descriptors from native speakers themselves.

Pike's performance must have impressed the biologists. Overnight, it seemed, there was an interest in applying evolutionary theory to culture. The trouble was that evolution in the 1970s was still a highly deterministic gene–culture linkage in the minds of most evolutionary biologists. So when Richard Dawkins and E. O. Wilson started talking about culture, it fit the natural selection ideology of the times. They sought to reduce cultural phenomena to chunks with an emic-like vocabulary but deterministically linked to genes. Richard Dawkins used an eme-like term, *meme*, which he introduced a year after E. O. Wilson's *Sociobiology*. *Meme* resembled an emic unit in name only. Dawkins proposed that memes exist as units that parallel the gene in the sense of being a replicator. A meme was essentially the same sociobiological cultural unit, called "culturgen," proposed by Charles Lumsden and Wilson (Lumsden and Wilson 1981). Curiously their units indiscriminately mixed external or objective phenomena with mental phenomena – or "mentifacts," as Lumsden and Wilson suggested. Further, under mentifacts, Lumsden and Wilson included the widest possible range of phenomena, among them "nearly pure creations of the mind, the reveries, fictions, and myths that have little connection with reality but take on a vigorous life of their own" (316).

Memes don't work Ironically, the meme, proposed by a biologist, simply perpetuates the division between culture and biology that exists in the superorganic view of culture. Perhaps the main reason anthropologists who study culture through ethnography have never taken up *meme* is that *meme* never carried the defining elements of emic solutions so important and enduring in anthropology, namely the distinction captured in the etic–emic contrast which required a *distributional* analysis to carry out an emic solution. Also, emic means "inner view" (the way the natives see their lives) and etic means an "outer view" of culture (the way an outsider might see the lives of the natives through the categories and biases of his own culture). In contrast, Dawkins's memes are not arrived at through analysis or any real data but simply declared by fiat. Cultural anthropologists who have done ethnography rarely if ever use *meme*. Being in the field in the midst of a different cultural reality to be understood and recorded is very different from having an academic armchair conversation about culture.

Psychoneurology As it turns out, only in special cases can we speak of eme-like units of thought that can be detected in narrative. There are at least two reasons for the lack of success in most kinds of discourse that are not part of a long-term interactive tradition (i.e., folktales). First, the higher one goes in general thought processes (as opposed to the very specific imagistic level created by the actual words of a narrative) the more fluid and more interconnected those processes are. Clearly there was some kind of cognition that our prehuman ancestors engaged in before language took off. This prelanguage system today must surely be employed, even if less extensively, along with language. FMRI studies of people reading narrative texts shows that when there is high "imagery" in sound, the primary auditory cortex is activated. When clauses with high motor imagery are read, the somatosensory cortex lights up (Kurby et al. 2008). Before the advent of language, thinking, as a response to sensory input, must have been perceptually processed, primarily organized by sight and remembered as an eidetic process though accompanied by other sensory modalities, for example smell which, being less specific than visual images, evokes generalized mind states or ambience.

Second, thinking, in contrast to simple semantics and taxonomies, has to be more flexible and dynamic because the nature of narrative is so much more complex and because the world itself is continually in process. When people read or listen to narrative, the mind has to fill in the underlying presuppositions that go along with interpreting speech. Unlike the dream process, however, this filling in is constrained by the words a listener hears. Representing that process in any detail by a single ethnographer would indeed be a highly complex and challenging task. Thus what may on first thought be a simple continuum through narrative time are events and experiences that have deep, unconsciously perceived structure. These surely tap into paradigmatic organizations along with the syntagmatic process of the narrative itself. Psychologists are just beginning this task when they focus on event boundaries.

When people go through situations in life, they will occasionally look back over those situations as well as look forward into future possibilities. They look back on what might have been a successful outcome or look back with regret that a better outcome might have resulted if they had acted differently (Marchiori and Warglien 2008). The very process of living involves a time line on which you locate yourself in a present moment, in your past history, or in future possibilities. A frame of the present moment is held in working memory, with everything at the ready for the present and for the immediate future in that situation. Thinking back over some event in your life, you need to call up the memory of that event – bring it back into your working memory.

Now with literacy things have changed. With books events can be recorded and consulted. But whether in the process of reading, writing, listening to, or telling a good story, there is a continual process of information management, of situation modeling, of interpretation, of evaluations, and the rest.

Vladimir Propp

Unnoticed by anthropologists, it turned out that an emic unit had in fact been discovered back in 1928 by the Russian folklorist Vladimir Propp. After Propp was translated into English the French anthropologist Claude Lévi-Strauss mentioned him but without recognizing the true value of what Propp had accomplished: an emic analysis of Russian fairy tales.

It was clear, as Propp saw, that well-told traditional stories begin with a motivating element or some inciting incident that dramatizes a need, a disharmony, a problem, or a villainy that requires corrective action. Out of this motivating element comes a series of actions and finally a resolving event that either supplies whatever was lacking in the beginning of the story or, if the story began with some other motivation like a villainy, defeats any initial villainy that triggered the story. Thus, a typical narrative pattern in oral literature culminates in a resolution that will meet the original need and put the world back into harmony. In between the motivating element and the final goal are the actions required to reach the resolution. These in-between actions carry much of a tale's interest for the audience. Given the repeated presence of the pattern: problem > difficulties > resolution, it seems reasonable to suppose that traditional narratives might have some semblance of organization along the lines of patterns in language proper. Just as speech or written sentences have language grammars, might not stories also have narrative grammars? In other words, narratives seem to consist of a series of building blocks and these blocks may be governed by something like a grammar.

The Russian sequence That is just what Propp found. While he did not develop higher-level categories as would be expected in a narrative grammar, he focused on the general level of actions and events as instanced at a lower level of detail. But what he noticed was that these sequenced events, which he called *functions*, followed the same order if they appeared in a story (with the exception of a single triad of functions which followed one of two different sequences). At the basic level, Propp isolated and described an inventory of 31 of these Russian fairy tale *functions*. For reasons I will give later, these functions are more appropriately characterized as *eidons* (reserving *functions* to apply to higher-level categories and other cultural phenomena). Propp believed that the eidons, though drawn from Russian fairy tales, were universal to all fairy tales. In that he was mistaken, although at higher levels of generality there are levels that might eventually emerge in neurological studies as universal – and at intermediate levels perhaps a convergence toward a universal set of higher-level narrative functions in all societies. Cultural differences appear at the lower levels, including the eidons level.

Eidons in other narrative traditions To replicate Propp's analysis on a different folktale tradition seemed the obvious thing to do. But no one had done so. Ideally one would search collections of folktales from different but relatively homogeneous samples to replicate Propp's analysis on narrative collections from unrelated traditions.

Eskimo traditions a good place

Eskimo folktales seemed ideal for testing Propp's finding. There were numerous publications of collections of Eskimo folktales. The initial analysis could be done on one group, with enough stories from other samples to test the grammar developed from the first sample. The collections were quite sufficient should anyone wish to do a similar study to see if the categories, once determined, followed rules of sequencing. For these reasons, I chose Eskimo narratives as a first replication of Propp's approach.[2]

Turning to Ixil narratives

Later the approach was extended to Ixil Maya folktales with a self-contained collection from a single informant – thus being more tractable, one would think, to distributional analyses. Also facilitating the analysis was ethnographic familiarity with the

Ixil. Since the overall goal reached beyond the study of narrative syntax into the larger study of cultural dynamics and the value core of a society, it was found that core cultural themes in Ixil culture cropped up in different genres and arenas of behaving. When the Ixil work reached a stable set of categories, it was satisfying to find that a distributional analysis of at least two more narrative traditions, Eskimo and Ixil, corroborated Propp's work with the Russian fairy tales. While many categories of a particular narrative sequence occur in narratives native to other societies, their appearance, variants, and sequencing are specific to a particular genre of stories among a specific group of people. The sequence of categories derived from a distributional analysis that Propp proposed supplies the kind of emic units anthropologists were looking for but did not recognize.

What are eidons? Eidons are basic building blocks for representing events and event sequences. While they are generic elements, they have more specific instantiations in a particular story, depending on the characters of the story and the kind of predicament they face. We can represent the units at two levels of generality, for example, "villainy" at the generic level and "X kidnaps Y" at a more specific varietal level. It is not until we get to the higher levels of categorization than those considered by Propp that I think the term *function* might better apply, tied as they are to memory management issues and chunking processes. Since in narrative we are dealing with images (not "image schemas" as currently used in cognitive linguistics) in what I now think must be an eidetic language that predated human language, I prefer to use the term *eidon*, or *eidochronic unit*, for the naturalistic or cultural chunking of narrative units.

Higher-level categories For narrative, you need three major high-level parts: motivation, engagement, and resolution. That's actually rather obvious and is universal in all societies as based in deep neural levels that link up cause and effect reasoning, goal assessment and goal attainment, and more. Less obvious, however, is the linkage of these higher-level units to the intermediate and lower ones.

Cognitive psychology uses top-down In the past when cognitive psychologists talked about story structures, they used this universal structure in a top-down approach. However since they did not use an extensive text corpus they never got to an emic analysis. The superstructure, the higher-level categories of a narrative grammar in some of these studies, was not supported by analysis at the eidochronic level. In true anthropological fashion, a complete narrative analysis must build from the bottom-up, from the eidons and eidon varieties – using top-level categories only tentatively and in terms of their functional role until the actual story events, or eidons, are validated at lower levels.

Narrative grammar within a social network as tradition In short, like a language grammar, we can derive a narrative grammar only from a particular cultural system, from some group of storytellers and listeners – one might say a social network – who share the same culture, including, of course the narratives. Just as a language grammar should account for any utterance in the language, so a narrative grammar should account for any oral narrative (of a given genre) of a particular cultural group. That is, within a properly defined narrative tradition, the narrative grammar should account for all oral productions of a specified traditional type during a particular historical period in a particular social group. The key process in writing a grammar thus becomes the testing of the grammar against new narrative productions in the same genre produced by the same group of people. Once a grammar has been worked out for an extensive corpus one can then attend to what cultural patterns in those stories as cultural models do for people in the network, especially for children and young people.

Common Eskimo concerns The eidochronic patterns found in the Eskimo samples give a rough idea of the kind of concerns common to the Eskimo. Some of these eidons involve magical actions and events. Thus, while the stories may, to some extent, offer models for actual behavior, they also represent wishes or fantasies, religious and magical, which undoubtedly have psychocultural functions. This goes well beyond the characterization of eidons to deep level and more general psychocultural functions of narrative in its capacity for developing neural pathways. As we know through the theory of neural Darwinism advanced by Gerald Edelman and through studies on environmental stimulation of neural growth and genetic expression, narratives have a key role in organizing the idea of progression toward goals over an extended period of time as represented in narrative (Edelman 1987, 2006). Without environmental stimulation brains could not develop. Environmental stimuli also affect genetic expression. Epigenomics, particularly with respect to the development of episodic memory and the processing of goal attainment, is relevant to narrative. They might be usefully analyzed for clues to how narrative models have developmental functions through their transmission. Such transmission is organized at different levels of narrative syntax.

Levels of Narrative Syntax

We can take the following example of an eidon and how it relates to the higher functional level.

Eidon example: magical engagement

Eidon label: *Me*.

Varieties

Me1 (The protagonist engages in a magical contest)

Me2 (The protagonist engages in a unilateral magical action against the adversary)

In either variety, *Me*, if it appears, forms part of the Main Action component, MA. If so the following rule controls the sequential position of *Me*:

MA → (Ak Fh Rv Ps Tr Me Ma El St Ds Dc)

The rule states simply that the Main Action component of Eskimo folktales must contain one or more of the eidons within the parentheses in the order given. For example, if the MA component contains the Magical Engagement (*Me*) eidon, the eidon must precede Elimination of a Character (*El*) if that eidon appears anywhere in the story. If the story has an Attack (*Ak*), *Me* must follow it, not precede it. And so forth.

Each of these eidons has further specification at the varietal level.

Moving to higher levels

We can also move to a higher-level rule, one that determines the appearance of the Main Action component. MA is part of the Engagement Section (*E*) and is positioned by the following rule:

$$E \rightarrow (PA\ MA),$$

where PA is Preliminary Action, which we define by a different set of eidons than those of the Main Action.

As we move up through levels of generality, we come closer to rules common to all oral literature everywhere. Just as in linguistics, where all languages everywhere have noun and verb concepts, so narrative at the higher levels also has rules.

The Engagement Section (*E*) in turn is part of a yet higher-level rule:

$$Resp \rightarrow E\ R,$$

where Resp is Response and R the Resolution component.

At the highest level, of *Move* as a complete episode, we have the following rule:

$$Move \rightarrow M\ Resp,$$

where M is Motivation.

Perception and assumptions about image

At this more specific level of a story, a listener or narrator surely has many ways to bring in his or her own special real life experiences regarding the setting, the situations, the emotional state of the characters, and much more. As the listener hears an eidon, his brain processes this information, mapping it to an integrated emic image. It seems clear that, as the listener hears the narrative and creates the associated images, he also thinks the thoughts associated with the images and events. It isn't clear to what extent thought and image merge, or how that image component is activated. In any case, as one eidon follows another, the listener maps the words of the story onto some understood sense of events creating underlying sequences of images. There thus has to be a generative image system – an eidetic system in the brain. We know such a system operates from our experience with dreaming.

Assumed brain schemas – eidons

In the "stories" that come to us in dreams we often get a weird melange of images that nevertheless come together with a thread – a story of sorts with actions, thoughts, and words. At times we see elements of this process without a thread just before dozing off when we see brief and unconnected hypnagogic images. Both are the result of an eidetic system that ties into what some psychologists and neurologists currently refer to as a preconscious system, or as Epstein calls it, the experiential system (Epstein 1998) or Haidt (2006), more colorfully, the emotional elephant in our neural system ridden by a tiny rational person that the elephant does not always obey. I am convinced that this eidetic system was the main basis for prehominid thought, but with the development of language, the brain, particularly the prefrontal cortex, grew larger and the eidetic system became somewhat more attenuated but nevertheless strongly based emotionally and therefore a powerful motivator often rationalized after the fact in a matter of split seconds via different routings through the brain (LeDoux 1996, 2002).

These emic, functional, or, as I think of them, eidochronic elements strung together in the brain are thus rooted in an eidetic system.[3]

Eidon as a bridging unit

When I use the term *eidon*, I am referring to a postulated (unobserved) neural unit that exists beyond the direct perceptual processing to the meaning-accrual networks of the brain. Even while it is postulated but neurologically unidentified, I also speak of an eidon as psychoculturally real. Just as linguistic units have psychocultural reality, so also do eidons.

Dream language?

In the dream process, where dreams must recombine eidochronic units and associated metaphoric linkages, the consensus is that dreams are involved in memory consolidation. The dream process integrates what is absorbed in previous days' experiences, including narratives heard, to deeper-level neural processes where elements of images from the day are recombined and expressed (usually in some disguised form) to the dreamer. Erich Fromm (1951) called it the "forgotten language."

The emic quest in narrative

In sum, it appears that emic units do, in fact, exist in at least one area of culture beyond the phonemes, morphemes, and syntactic structures of language sentences. As analyzed through distributional analysis they have *cultural reality*. Though conveyed through language, narrative structures and eidons are beyond linguistics proper. Presumably all oral narratives – usually folktales and some kinds of myths – have eidochronic structures. When they are sufficiently regularized through the telling and retelling of stories in more homogeneous societies or social networks characterized by close-knit, widespread, interactive patterns, they are more readily discoverable through distributional analysis.[4]

Natural kinds and emic units

Such an analysis is a primarily bottom-up analysis, an exhaustive distributional analysis of the elements in a collection of narratives of sufficient number to fill out a particular genre (folktales) from a particular society (Eskimo) so as to cover all the eidons or emic units likely to appear in any other, as yet unanalyzed, sample of folktales from the same genre and society. A distributional study looks at all the details of a narrative and classifies those details as sub-units of a particular eidon, as eidons proper and of superordinate units of narrative organization. These would properly come under the heading philosophers sometimes use, "natural kinds," or when they talk about "carving nature at its joints." Events and processes at the lowest levels are directly related to common real-life experiences among a network of people sharing the same narrative tradition. At the higher levels they are less likely to be culture-specific and more likely to be universals of narrative.

The issue of the validity of analyzed cultural units is taken up by Kronenfeld (2008) in his useful discussion of different ways in which *model* is used in anthropology. However, in citing Saussure's distinction between *langue* and *parole* we run into a roadblock to the development of a scientific theory of culture. I do not think it is useful to say that language is different from culture. Saussure's *langue* is the linguistic equivalent of a superorganic view of culture. By ruling out the location of *langue* in the brain (a highly dynamic, ongoing neural process) we run into the same problems that have plagued anthropologists since earliest times. The neurosciences are advancing at an astounding pace. So also are neuroendocrine understandings. We can't ignore their findings. If we are to develop a scientific theory we must recognize that culture and language are located in people's brains. Through mirror neurons, and a host of other devices we humans use to keep on the same page with our families and fellows, we act *as if* culture were out there in the ether somewhere. When we analyze language or narrative we are analyzing cultural patterns. Those patterns are cultural expressions of *schema systems* within the minds of storytellers. For these reasons successful eidochronic analyses of cultural patterns are limited to relatively homogeneous oral traditions, such as Russian fairy tales, Eskimo folktales, and Ixil myths and folktales.

The Ixil sample

The Eskimo work is based on a large sample, as distributional analysis requires. The second analysis – the Ixil Maya stories – was easier to do because of extensive familiarity with the storyteller, the society, and area.

The Ixil results confirm what was found for the Eskimo folktales. Namely, at a higher level of generality, the more general categories of narrative syntax have a more universal character and relate to more general cognitive functions. One can tap into these higher-level units as a functional guide to finding the more culture-specific units at the eidochronic level in the Ixil sample. With those stories, one proceeds through a combination of bottom-up and very tentative top-down processes. However, the end analysis must be validated at the bottom in an exhaustive accounting of every story in a sample. Only through the lowest levels – eidons and eidon varieties – do we have a culture-specific inventory and sequence.

Eidons and motifs: general information

So while motifs and eidons are both eidetic it is anthropologically important to make a distinction between motifs (or mislabeled motifemes) and the units Propp discovered through distributional analysis.

When we recognize motifs as appearing in a number of different traditions in different societies, they are differentially connected in the narrative tradition of any one society. However, if we find a motif to have a particular relationship with other themes in a single oral tradition, and we have identified all the other elements of that tradition as existing in a particular systemic relationship to each other, we can speak of those elements as eidons for that specific tradition.

Tips for doing the analysis

There is a useful distinction between primary eidons and secondary devices that embellish, highlight, or serve as a transition to the next eidon in a story thread. Once these secondary devices are identified they tend to frame the primary eidons (Colby 1973). A program like DRS would assist in doing large studies.

What Next?

Discourse analysis more broadly

LSA does a limited number of tasks exceedingly well (Landauer and Dumais 1997; Landauer 2001). However, for theoretical breakthroughs it is only one of several tools to be used in conjunction with each other. Different levels of generality, the natural junctures or segmentation of texts (for memory encoding), and motives as they are expressed in discourse (McClelland, et al. 1989; McAdams and de St. Aubin 1992; McAdams 1997) are ripe for further development and insights as more pieces of the neurological puzzle fall into place. New, analytical approaches such as a new coding of DRS used in tandem with LSA are much needed. If such a project were undertaken it might well prove valuable for cognitive anthropology. Through collaborative work with cognitive neuroscientists one would expect substantial progress toward a scientific theory of culture.

Folktales

There are compelling reasons for working with oral literature, particularly narrative traditions that have been circulating within a social network over time with a minimum of intrusions from other traditions. Such traditions have taken on a more systemic organization and therefore are more likely to reveal cultural dynamics indigenous to a particular narrative network in a society. In such an endeavor one works with basic models at a level that yields insights both for the folktale genre and also for how motives and values in folktales are echoed in other discourse productions (Colby and Colby 1981).

Cultural dynamics and discourse

We are now on a new time horizon – one where faster computers and programs can enable a number of approaches, such as DRS, which earlier was limited to the analysis of only very short texts (James and Colby 1979). Through discourse analysis of appropriate texts one can approximate native categorizations that go beyond limited, tightly domain-bound and context-independent paradigms to a much broader semantics of actual usage – to sequential data and discovery of cultural dynamics that underlie goal-oriented behavior, collective ideological defenses, and creative thinking. A flexible and interactive computer-assisted text ethnography addresses questions of validity and reliability that have long plagued the ethnographic enterprise.

New findings and understandings are moving apace. Disputes between systemic versus cognitive approaches fade as the recognition of how perceptual and embodied aspects of cultural dynamics drive human beliefs, emotions, attitudes, and behavior (Prinz and Barsalou 2000). The space in between expressed cultural patterns and cognitive schemas – the transmission of culture – can now take center stage for the kind of bridging theories Feldman (2006) calls for.

NOTES

1 Kronenfeld uses the term *pragmatics* to delineate his area of investigation, and though he distinguishes language from culture, I would prefer to speak of language as simply the symbolic realm, one of three realms that constitute culture (the other two being social and material/biological).

2 In retrospect, I have noticed that Eskimo folktales from Greenland appear to be a different tradition and may prove to have a different eidochronic structure.

3 I now wonder whether *listening* to folktales activates a different set of "mirror neurons" from those that mirror actions *observed*.

4 Usually there are not enough myths from the same myth-telling network of people on which one can do a distributional analysis. In the Ixil Maya stories I collected, however, both myths and folktales do appear to fit into the same genre and grammar. Generally, however, I suspect that myths, often being more dreamlike, are a less tightly structured phenomenon than folktales.

REFERENCES

Colby, Benjamin N.
1973 Analytical Procedures in Eidochronic Study. Journal of American Folklore 86(339):14–24.
Colby, Benjamin N., and Lore M. Colby
1981 The Daykeeper: The Life and Thought of an Ixil Diviner. Cambridge, MA: Harvard University Press.
Damasio, Antonio R.
2003 Looking for Spinoza: Joy, Sorrow, and the Feeling Brain. Orlando, FL: Harcourt.
D'Aquili, Eugene G., and Andrew B. Newberg
1999 The Mystical Mind: Probing the Biology of Religious Experience. Minneapolis, MN: Fortress.
D'Aquili, Eugene G., Charles D. Laughlin, and John McManus
1979 The Spectrum of Ritual: A Biogenetic Structural Analysis. New York: Columbia University Press.
Deacon, Terrence W.
1997 The Symbolic Species: The Co-Evolution of Language and the Brain. New York: W. W. Norton.

Edelman, Gerald M.
1987 Neural Darwinism: The Theory of Neuronal Group Selection. New York: Basic Books.
2006 Second Nature; Brain Science and Human Knowledge. New Haven: Yale University Press.
Epstein, Seymour
1998 Constructive Thinking: The Key to Emotional Intelligence. Westport, CT: Praeger.
Feldman, Jerome A.
2006 From Molecule to Metaphor: A Neural Theory of Language. Cambridge, MA: MIT Press.
Fromm, Erich
1951 The Forgotten Language: An Introduction to the Understanding of Dreams, Fairy Tales, and Myths. New York: Rinehart.
Haidt, Jonathan
2006 The Happiness Hypothesis: Finding Modern Truth in Ancient Wisdom. New York: Basic Books.
Halliday, M. A. K., and Ruqaiya Hasan
1976 Cohesion in English. London: Longman.
Halliday, M. A. K., and Jonathan Webster
2007 Language and Society. London: Continuum.
James, Mark, and Benjamin Colby
1979 Discourse Research System: Instructional Manual. *In* Scientiarum Ancillae/School of Social Sciences, UC Irvine. Irvine: University of California.
Kozorovitskiy, Yevgenia, and Elizabeth Gould
2008 Adult Neurogenesis in the Hippocampus. *In* Handbook of Developmental Cognitive Neuroscience. C.A.N.a.M. Luciana, ed. Pp. 51–61. Vol. 1. Cambridge, MA: The MIT Press.
Kronenfeld, David B.
2008 Culture, Society, and Cognition: Collective Goals, Values, Action, and Knowledge, vol. 3. Berlin: Mouton de Gruyter.
Kurby, Christopher, Jeffrey Zacks, and Jonathan Xia
2008 fMRI Evidence for the Activation of Modality-Specific Images during Silent Reading. *In* Annual Conference of the Society for Text and Discourse. Memphis, TN: University of Memphis.
Landauer, Thomas K.
2001 Single Representations of Multiple Meanings in Latent Semantic Analysis. *In* On the Consequences of Meaning Selection: Perspectives on Resolving Lexical Ambiguity. D. S. Gorfein, ed. Pp. 217–232. Washington, DC: American Psychological Association.
Landauer, Thomas K., and Susan T. Dumais
1997 A Solution to Plato's Problem: The Latent Semantic Analysis of Acquisition, Induction, and Representation of Knowledge. Psychological Review 104(2):211–240.
LeDoux, Joseph E.
1996 The Emotional Brain: The Mysterious Underpinnings of Emotional Life. New York: Simon & Schuster.
2002 Synaptic Self: How Our Brains Become Who We Are. New York: Viking.
Lumsden, Charles J., and Edward O. Wilson
1981 Genes, Mind, and Culture: The Coevolutionary Process. Cambridge, MA: Harvard University Press.
Marchiori, Davide, and Massimo Warglien
2008 Predicting Human Interactive Learning by Regret-Driven Neural Networks. Science 319:1111–1113.
McAdams, Dan P.
1997 The Stories We Live By: Personal Myths and the Making of the Self. New York: Guilford.

McAdams, D. P., and E. de St. Aubin
1992 A Theory of Generativity and Its Assessment through Self-Report, Behavioral Acts, and Narrative Themes in Autobiography. Journal of Personality and Social Psychology 62:1003–1015.
McClelland, David C., Richard Koestner, and Joel Weinberger
1989 How Do Self-Attributed and Implicit Motives Differ? Psychological Review 96(4):690–702.
Miller, George A.
1956 The Magical Number Seven, Plus or Minus Two: Some Limits on Our Capacity for Processing Information. Psychological Review 63(2):81–97.
Prinz, Jesse J., and Lawrence W. Barsalou
2000 Steering a Course for Embodied Representation. *In* Cognitive Dynamics: Conceptual Change in Humans and Machines. E. Dietrich and A. Markman, eds. Pp. 51–77. Cambridge, MA: MIT Press.
Rosenzweig, M. R., E. L. Bennett, and D. Krech
1964 Cerebral Effects of Environmental Complexity and Training among Adult Rats. Journal of Comparative Physiological Psychology 57:438–439.
Speer, Nicole K., Jeffrey M. Zacks, and Jeremy R. Reynolds
2007 Human Brain Activity Time-Locked to Narrative Event Boundaries. Psychological Science 18(5):449–455.
Turner, Victor
1987 Body, Brain, and Culture. *In* Waymarks: The Notre Dame Inaugural Lectures in Anthropology. K. Moore, ed. Pp. 71–103. Notre Dame, IN: University of Notre Dame Press.

CHAPTER 12 Simulation (and Modeling)

Michael Fischer and David B. Kronenfeld

Simulation is an alternative to simple speculation, or perhaps a means for evaluating speculation. Instead of simply imagining, arguing, and debating how the different parts of social, cultural, and individual life interact together to form that gestalt, that is the "wholism" anthropologists so value, simulations can be used to examine, explore, and evaluate such interactions within one or more contexts. Simulations are often used to represent "real" events, people, and things, ranging from rituals and objects representing supernatural entities and forces, to calendars, schedules, and essay outlines. Because anthropologists generally use simulations to evaluate judgments and decisions in sociocultural contexts, there is an intrinsically cognitive aspect to most such simulations, where judgments and decisions are often used to mediate people's applications of cultural infrastructure within their physical context.

The fundamental idea underlying simulations is to explore the implication of a set of ideas by their modeling them and their interaction within model processes generated by "well-understood" models (Fischer 1994:182).[1] Simulations are one way of investigating complex interactive aspects of a given research problem in cognitive anthropology. The relevant aspects can be a specific kind of action (e.g., classifying colors), a posited relationship between some actors (e.g., arranging a marriage), changes in a dynamic space (traffic patterns in a city), or an understanding of a process (such as how land use patterns shift as population density grows).

Simulations are useful for many purposes. You explore situations for which it would be difficult or impossible to do research for practical or ethical reasons, such as the impact on group sex composition of male-biased childbirth strategies, or the impact of famine on local political organization. You evaluate the extent to which an anthropologist's account is consistent with the information they provide: do they provide

A Companion to Cognitive Anthropology, First Edition. Edited by David B. Kronenfeld, Giovanni Bennardo, Victor C. de Munck, and Michael D. Fischer.

sufficient information to justify their conclusions? You explore holistic interconnections between relatively simple principles when joined in a common context.

A simulation animates our models to produce data which we can use to evaluate these models. This is of course possible to do without computers, but is a very time-consuming effort. Although most simulations have been applied to theoretical situations where simulation was most useful precisely because it was not possible to observe these directly, in the past few years simulations have been applied back to field research with promising results (see discussion of Bharwani 2005 in this chapter). Simulations put models in context by letting us observe how the model behaves in a complex environment. "Model" literally means to demonstrate or copy. In anthropology "model" more typically means some kind of representation used to account for some ethnographic facts, or to generalize the results of their research.

Simulations can be physical or computational, and computations can be by hand or by machine. Some simulation models are "agent-based" in the sense of actually modeling the actions (including, maybe, thoughts) of individual people and other entities, where the communal or collective patterns of anthropological interest are seen as by-products of some combination of cumulation of individual results and interaction between individuals, while other (i.e., conventional non-agent-based) models deal more directly with communal patterns or with activity rates (under some sets of conditions). Simulations can be mainly quantitative (demographic processes), qualitative (choosing a spouse), or more commonly a hybrid of the two (impact of marriage choices on demographic structure). Simulations become relevant to culture when distinctive cultural patterns are either produced or modeled. Agent-based models become important as a cognitive research tool when the actions of modeled agents are based directly on specific knowledge or cognitive dispositions. Non-agent-based models can be important as tools for cognitive anthropology when the systems modeled are (or can be seen as) based on emergent cognitive operations that characterize members of a cultural group.

In the literature Alan Johnson has defined a computer simulation as

> a computer program that defines the variables of a system, the range of values those variables may take on, and their interrelations in enough detail for the system to be set in motion to generate some output. The main function of a computer simulation is to explore the properties and implications of a system that is too complex for logical or mathematical analysis ... A computer simulation generally has an ad hoc or "home-made" quality that makes it less rigorous than a mathematical model. [Johnson 1978:186–187]

While Bonnie Nardi has offered a slightly different view:

> A computer simulation model ... [provides] the investigator with a simplified analogy ... for the purpose of better analyzing and understanding ... [some] phenomenon. ... it focuses on conducting experiments on a computer in which mathematical or logical operations describing the behavior of a system over time are of primary importance ... Its very purpose, in fact, is the analysis of change over time. ... Computer simulation is a powerful technique, capable of handling large numbers of variables representing complex systems and of simulating the operation of these variables over many cycles. [Nardi 1980:38]

We can see that within anthropology there exists some range of views concerning what simulations (or simulation models) are or do.

In our view, what distinguishes a simulation model from any other model forms is not so much the type of model, but what we do with the model. In the case of simulations we are interested in the behavior of a model and in instances of the application of a model. Simulations do not have solutions in the conventional sense. The most appropriate purpose of a simulation is to generate data, representing the interaction of the models under simulation. The value and purpose of a simulation follows from what is done with this model data (Dyke 1981:204).

Extending this, Fischer proposes a more general structure for computer simulations:

> Abstractly, a simulation model consists of at least one structure, at least one operation which might act on the structure(s), and at least one opportunity to apply operation(s) to structure(s) ... It is the applications of one or more models to create one or more instances. An operation may or may not be based on an analytic model; it can be quite ad hoc. A simulation is at least one instance of an application of operation to structure. This definition does not differentiate between the application of analytic models, such as a discriminant function derived from social data, and less formal models, such as those derived from so-called qualitative analysis of social data. [Fischer 1994:185]

Until recently simulation has been a technique associated with quantitative analysis. As with computing techniques in general, this was due to the historical development of computing and constraints on our knowledge of how to represent models and information of a qualitative and symbolic form. Designing a computer-based simulation involves translating the essential aspects of pre-existing models into a form which can be implemented on a computer so that we can monitor the interaction of the models. Although simulations can be quite abstract and analytic, most anthropologists tend to favor those which are fairly concrete. One reason for this is the emphasis of social anthropology on structural relationships between individuals. If you are investigating the feasibility of literal prescribed matrilateral cross-cousin marriage (see Kundstater et al. 1963), then you must usually simulate a population as a set of people, not as a simple aggregate. Each simulated person must have at least a mother and father, an age, a gender, a marital status, and be subject to birth, marriage, and death, and have, in some cases, a history.

In anthropology the most common (and successful) simulations have been based on the interaction of models of prescriptive or preferential marriage, incest, or other sociocultural phenomena with either demographic models or ecological models (or both) (e.g., Kunstadter et al. 1963; MacCluer and Dyke 1976; Black 1978; Buchler et al. 1986). The fundamental idea underlying these simulations is to investigate the performance of social models in context with "well-understood" models, including the ethnographic model of collection. Most anthropological simulations relate to cognition in the sense that they tend to focus heavily on individual decision-making and its behavioral outcomes rather than on behaviors alone. Whereas in purely quantitative simulations interactions between variables are guided by physical laws and principles, in anthropology they tend to reflect the impact of decision-making within a set of constraints, which themselves (as in the case of ecological models) can be quantitatively represented using known scientific principles. Thus anthropological simulations tend to be hybrid models, integrating qualitative and quantitative components, where the qualitative components are evaluated with respect to their influence on the quantitative components.

In the past anthropologists have argued that there are no practical means for producing directly testable models. We cannot yet produce formally provable models, but there is no reason, though, why at a micro level, we cannot make statements about what we believe we know, and evaluate this with respect to what we think should be the outcome. Analysis should at least be subjectable to a test of the internal consistency of the representation, regardless of how we want to argue about the external reliability or lack thereof. We can then use simulations to examine how well these models succeed in reproducing which aspects of the target phenomena. To the extent that they succeed they represent plausible hypotheses as to what has produced these phenomena in "real life," that is, a successful simulation does not prove that "it" "really happened" that way, but it does prove that it might have – that the modeled concepts and procedures are sufficient explanations, even if not necessarily necessary ones.

For example, Lansing (1991) describes a simulation which resulted from his fieldwork in Bali regarding the role of water temples and the rituals associated with these and the regulation and conservation of irrigation water for rice cultivation, and more controversially, their role in pest control. Although a large part of the simulation related to ecological parameters, the overall significance depended heavily on ethnographic data relating to how the water temples functioned ritually as well, and how information flowed from the water temples to the peasants who used irrigation water for their crops. It appears that among the results of the simulation project was developing a basis for reversing official policy towards the water temple system by the state and development agencies, which are now recognized by the state and "have regained informal control of cropping patterns in most of Bali" (Lansing 1991:125).

Simulations are, as we said, particularly useful to a discipline in which direct experimentation is often immoral – as well as impractical. If and when we get a model of some process that correctly corresponds to known cases, then we can use that model to explore hypothetical cases that deal with novel situations – novel contexts or novel actions – and thereby gain some new perspective on what the relevant parts of existent contexts are and on what is at issue in how people deal with their given situations. Since cognitive anthropology deals with knowledge systems, and "systems" entail productive representations, simulations offer a particularly powerful tool for exploring such systems – especially for systems that are adequately well described.

The following are a few further examples to illustrate the range of simulation possibilities through a set of concrete cases. These examples either directly model shared cultural cognitive processes or indirectly model processes involved in the emergent units produced by such processes.

Philip Wilke, with Leslie Quintero (see, e.g., Wilke and Quintero 1994, 1996, 2009; Quintero et al. 1997; Wilke 2002), has used physical replication as a way of simulating aspects of prehistoric technology. He and fellow flintknappers have carefully replicated the manufacture, use, and maintenance of a variety of stone projectile points, blades, and other tools. This approach has enabled a reconstruction of the life history of a projectile point, including what dulling and breakage occur through use, what changes in shape and size result from resharpening and (as needed) reshaping, and what factors lead to its eventual abandonment. This life history approach, in turn, aids in producing a more fine-grained typology of sites by relating kinds of debitage and abandonment to kinds of activities.

One incidental by-product of this approach has been the realization that some kinds of variation in projectile points that had been taken as markers of different cultures really represented only different life stages of a single point type.

Wilke (1988) used a similar approach in exploring the construction of bow staves by prehistoric people in the inland California desert – where straight wood was very hard to come by. The clue came from notches found in juniper trunks. It turned out that a future bow stave was isolated via side and end notches while still attached to the tree. The notches killed the future stave, while the continuing attachment (over a year or more) allowed the wood to dry and cure, while still being kept straight, before its eventual removal.

This approach is cognitive in the important sense that it gives us a way of exploring the knowledge in action that characterized cultural communities now long dead. The replication represents hypotheses about the goals and actions of those who originally made the target tools. The richness of the replication – that is, the range of observations that were built into the one set of actions – increased the likelihood that the fit with the original data was not accidental or chance, and thus that the goals, understandings, mental templates, and processes (including feedback loops) of the replicative study related directly to cognitive plans of those who made the original tools. Here "richness of the replication" refers not simply to matching the target projectile point shapes, but also the flaking patterns seen on them, the amount and shapes of debitage resulting from their production, the range of shape and size variations found in the population of target points, and the relationship between debitage and the cores from which points were struck. Such replicative studies, thus, are simulations, and ones that directly experiment with hypothesized cognitive processes. As with all simulations, one has no guarantee of how precisely the model captures knowledge (including intent, techniques, ecological knowledge, etc.) that produced the cultural activity being modeled. But the more that unplanned by-products match the observed (here, archaeological) record, the better one feels about the model's accuracy.

David Kronenfeld's (1976) program for simulating an adaptation of Romney's version of a Lounsburian rewrite rule analysis of kin terminologies was a computer variant of Wilke's approach, but where the activity being modeled was the process by which an anthropologist conducted a Romney-type analysis. The initial goal of the analysis was simply to mimic what Romney said an analyst should do (and, ideally, actually did). But, in the course of the simulation, a number of places were found in which analysts subconsciously slid over problems where the dumb and literal-minded computer had to be told explicitly what to do. The mere fact of such raising to consciousness was itself useful, but the raising furthermore revealed both significant presuppositions (that analysts seemed unaware of) and significant ad hoc inconsistencies (doing an operation one way in one place and another way in another place, according to which came out best). The simulation embodies a set of hypotheses about the processes, knowledge, and goals that anthropological analysts bring to the kinterm system analysis task. Additionally, then, the explicitness of the simulation enables experiments with the analytic process aimed at improving it – improvements which can be fed back into the operations of human analysts and into the body of theory from which the analytic process flows. Note – in the context of other approaches to kinterm system analysis included elsewhere in this volume (Introduction, Chapters 13 and 14) – that the simulation does not speak to the preferability of one or another approach or to the empirical cognitive and social goals that each might speak to; it only demonstrates the explicitness and immediate analytic success of this approach.

Romney had envisioned his approach as one that could operate on any imaginable regularities (of the given types) that might appear in the data, while Kronenfeld's implementation required looking for specific known kinds of regularities. For example: (1) Several kinds of unexpected ordering constraints emerged. One had to distinguish unisex terms from explicitly male or female ones initially, or other operations did not get correctly identified. Even though Lounsbury had presented the rewrite rules themselves as an unordered set (any rules that fit a given situation could be applied in any order), the program's process of discovering applicable rules had to consider candidate rules in a particular order. (2) Kinship relations can be seen as a string of relatives connecting some "ego" with some "alter" – going up through ego's ancestors to the point where ego's ancestor is a sibling of alter's ancestor (the "apical sibling pair"), and then down to alter. In analyzing an expression the program had to move along the string in some particular direction. It was found that there was no consistent direction that worked across the whole expression, but that, instead, one had to work from the ends toward the center (i.e., the apical sibling pair). The program reduced the multiple expressions that represented referents of a single kinterm down to a single (or a couple) kernel referent plus a rule; it then used the rule to re-expand from the kernel to the full range of referents of the term.

The program was not a labor-saving device – a competent analyst could analyze a system by hand in the time it took to input the data into the program. The usefulness of the program was, first, to raise to consciousness the operations involved in a successful analysis; second, to detect previously unknown regularities and constraints; and then to demonstrate the successful ability of the amended set of operations to carry out the indicated analysis.

The target of such a simulation is not the cognitive systems of those we study, but a cognitive system of us, the researchers. This is not the leap it might at first seem. Academic communities represent the same kind of subculture of a larger community that local associations or groups represent in the communities we study; the minds being modeled are of the same kind; and the presence of possibly unusual formal strictures on relevant behavior (1) are not necessarily that unusual, and (2) should make the task easier – as was certainly the case for the present kin terminology example.

Christina Gladwin (1975) constructed a flow chart model of the decision process that Fante fishmongers used in their selection of markets in which to sell their fish. Market locations ranged from near the beach (where they bought the fish from the fishermen) to 500 miles or so inland. Transport means varied from physically carrying fish to nearby markets to hiring trucks (or space on trucks) for distant markets, with significant differences in associated costs. Problems of preservation and a short shelf life were involved. The model took account of how the women coded market conditions (numbers of buyers and sellers, demand level, and so forth) and how they related past conditions to present actions (where the markets were often too remote to allow instantaneous information.

The model itself was a simple flow chart built fairly directly from statements the fishmongers themselves made, joined with the ethnographic observations of Gladwin and her husband (Hugh Gladwin). It achieved a better than 90 percent prediction rate (for a corpus of data separate from the corpus used to develop the model) for a whole season's marketing by a community of fishmongers; this rate was considerably better than the best achieved by a variety of micro-economic models (< 60 percent). The difference had to do with how the women processed information. The fishmongers simplified the problem by dichotomizing continuous variables (e.g., price, number of buyers or sellers) at break points, and then by processing their data via a series of simple decisions – as opposed to the instantaneous multivariate combination of continuous variables utilized by the micro-economic models. A lot of the variability in the micro-economic models was ignored by the fishmongers. The difference represented a practical application of insights from Kahneman and Tversky (among others) about how humans process information.

Gladwin constructed a simple descriptive (ethnographic) model of the behavior in question (marketing decisions) that was based directly on what her informants told her and on what she saw them doing. This was as opposed to the theoretically generated micro-economic models with which she compared her flow chart model. At the same time, her exercise was not anti-theoretic or anti-microeconomic. When her successful flow chart model was examined from an economic theory point of view, it was clear that the fishmongers were "satisficing." That is, their marketing consideration started with the closest (best-known and cheapest to reach) markets and worked out from these to more distant ones. They opted for the first (i.e., closest) market that was likely to satisfy their profit needs, and did not look further; they made no attempt to find the best possible market. It was only when the ways in which the market women processed information and structured their decisions were taken into account that the economic picture came into focus.

The Gladwin model was not a perfect replication of all the thought of a Fante fishmonger, but it was shown to successfully capture the structure (with information) of their marketing decisions. As such it represented a notable contribution to cognitive economics, and became the basis for a general approach to culturally structured individual economic decision-making (see Gladwin 1976, 1980; Gladwin and Butler 1984)

Murray Leaf (2000) created a simple but effective simulation of the household economics under varying conditions of Punjabi farmers by eliciting their constraints – how much money or grain et cetera they needed for what purpose; what skills, knowledge, land, and other resources they had available – and their algorithm for combining these – and modeling these in a dynamic spreadsheet (such as Excel). The model was flexible and allowed Leaf to explore how these farmers would be likely to react to a variety of changed conditions, forms of proffered aid, and so forth. This project was part of a large study of the impact of investing in flood control in the Bangladesh delta. The flood control project was intended to have positive outcomes for individual farmers, but Leaf was able to convince them using the empirical data he collected and an earlier version of this model that the impact would likely be not just negative, but devastating. The project was dropped. The published simulation was a direct translation of what he did during the research.

What makes Leaf's approach attractive is its utilization of a simple, readily available calculation device (the spreadsheet) and its direct use of the information and categories of the farmers being studied. In both ways it nicely parallels the Gladwin study as a good example of how ethnographic and other data can be integrated to draw specific, actionable, conclusions.

Kronenfeld and Kaus's (1993) "starling" simulation of Durkheimian emergent properties (see also Kronenfeld and Kronenfeld 2006) was a more abstract agent-based simulation. A set of abstract "critters" were created in a space that contained "food caches," and were given a small set of activities: if see food, head toward it; if on a food cache, consume some food (a little each cycle until the cache was emptied); if no food in sight, move randomly. The size, distribution, and regularity of food caches were experimentally controlled. The "society" constraint was introduced as an experimental variable: don't move further than a given "leash" length from the centroid of the "flock," where the leash length could be varied and its effects examined in relation to the size and distribution of food caches.

Turning the "society" constraint on was sufficient to turn a randomly moving collection of critters into a recognizable mob – a maximally elementary social entity. Individual behavior plus elementary feedback between individuals was shown to be sufficient to produce an emergent social entity.

The payoffs of "society" (thus understood) were then explored – in a context in which there was no predation and no inter-band competition. The society constraint slowed down the net consumption of food but, when food caches were spread out and critter movement slow, the society variable greatly decreased the inter-critter variance in food consumption, and thus contributed to the preservation of what might be interpreted as an adequate breeding population. If the critters could move fast enough and if food was dense enough, then this society variable became superfluous.

A second experimental variable – which allowed critters to recognize which other critters saw food (a kind of "vulture" model, if you will) – was created to further explore the limits of the social variable's usefulness. With it turned on, and with fast critter movement, food was efficiently found and consumed with low inter-critter variance.

This simulation explored the attributes of individual behavior that were needed for collectivities with their own emergent systems to emerge. While not directly cognitive, it explored an important aspect of the basis that was needed for the emergence of any collective cognitive system to emerge. The critters in the simulation do not think per se, but their actions do embody cognitive predilections. And the goal of the simulation project was to develop a feedback model of emergence which could then be applied to the cognitive systems (with their content) that make up language and culture.

Michael Agar (2001; Agar and Wilson 2002) used an epidemiological variant of an agent-based approach to analyze the pattern of heroin use in a community. As heroin was introduced into the community, a few people first use it. Their friends saw them and saw the pleasure that they experienced, and so started using it themselves. This produced a first phase within the community in which use rapidly spread. The bad effects of heroin use took a while longer to develop, but eventually emerged – first in the earliest users. This negative experience spread in a way that tracked the positive one, and led to an increasing pool of people who had not yet started using and who saw the negative effects and then avoided use. In this middle phase use within the community plateaued. Eventually, as the negative experience spread, new use tailed off. In this final phase, the epidemic ended, though with a residual population of hooked users.

This was a very simple and very powerful simulation that led to a new way of thinking about an important social problem. Most of Agar's work since 2000 is derived from and has been directly applied to consultancies, and contributes to policy formation, for example in the Netherlands. It took a bare-bones epidemiological approach in which exposure led to a certain probability of "infection," and in which no other details of the members of the population were considered. The accuracy with which the simulation results matched actual empirical experience provided a telling argument for claiming that the model captured an essential element in the spread of heroin addiction. There is an explicitly cognitive element in the simulation in the sense that it is people's understanding of what they observe in their fellows that drives the epidemiologic process. The accuracy enabled a closer focus on what aspects of the contact situation facilitated or interfered with the spread of the "contagion." At the same time, we want to note that nothing in Agar's model precludes further research into the details that might distinguish those who "caught" the "infection" from those who did not. That is, Agar's simulation was addressed to a specific goal; it did not aim at doing everything! The isolation of different, more or less independent explanatory parameters in a way that allows an independent assessment of the separate effects of each can be another use of simulation models.

Kippen (1988a, 1988b) applied a novel version of simulation to investigate indigenous knowledge systems relating to tabla improvisations (a kind of drum performance prominent in Indian classical music traditions). In 1982 Kippen worked with a group of tabla musicians, and undertook classical training in the instrument. As he began to be able personally to enact some of the requirements of an improvised accompaniment he began working with a computer scientist, Bernard Bel, to develop the Bol Processor (see http://bolprocessor.sourceforge.net/), a program that simulated tabla music based on a set of rules. Kippen worked interactively with tabla performers, eliciting rules, adding these to the Bol Processor, and playing back (by performance) the results to the performers for comment and criticism, and the elicitation of more nuanced rules.

The basic idea was to create a formal set of rules (as used by the Bol Processor) that reflected the knowledge and understanding of the tabla players based on the judgments of tabla players as a part of the overall simulation, creating not a discrete set of recordings, but improvisational "performances" by Kippen's model; literally something new but conforming to a pattern which his expert consultants (tabla musicians) could make judgments about and criticize, and which set up a context for Kippen to elicit new information on which to base modifications to generative rules that could reproduce music consistent with their judgments. Although Kippen was unable to create a model that attained the musical quality of his musician consultants, it did produce "respectable" results that reflected the musical tradition.

In 1982 Fischer (1986) used a similar approach in his research on arranged marriages in a Pakistani community. Using a combination of ethnographic data and survey data he constructed a simulation that used agent-based models to integrate qualitative and quantitative models to simulate indigenous judgments relating to evaluating the suitability of prospective marriages. The model was iteratively refined by asking individuals at different stages (from "sometime in the future" to "the last marriage") for their judgments on its results and eliciting new distinctions and rules based on these judgments for incorporation into the simulation. The quantitative component of the simulation served to describe the "space" within which arranged marriages were considered; the outcomes for a potential union (e.g., arrange, further information needed, flee), key attributes used to assess candidates (e.g., education, social status, intelligence), and the qualitative component described how to navigate this space (e.g., assigning values to key attributes, how to get to an outcome). One of the key insights that emerged from the research was the importance of similarity between the families negotiating a marriage contract and of the bride and groom in particular, in sharp contrast to the principle of hypergamy reported for non-Muslims in northern India (Fischer and Lyon 2000).

In further research over the next two decades Fischer (Fischer and Finkelstein 1991; Fischer 2006) was able to revisit some of these decisions to see how accurate both the model and indigenous judgments were, and to develop a simulation of retrodictive judgments used by people to "explain" the actual outcomes and differences from their earlier judgments.

Schank and Abelson's (1977) simulation of restaurant (and related) conversations offers a different perspective on focusing on individuals in a simulation. They were not looking at any kind of agent-based emergent phenomena or patterns; instead they explored all of the information that was involved in simple restaurant interactions and in conversations about such interactions. What would a computer have to know if it were to be able to successfully mimic a human in this situation? The array of kinds of knowledge that they describe and model is impressive, as is their success in so doing.

One has to know relevant goals: what are the reasons for going into a restaurant? One has to know the canonical trajectory of a restaurant visit (come in, be seated, be given a menu, order, eat with some succession of courses, get the check, leave a tip, pay) along with the additional details that mark subtle subtypes (e.g., fancy restaurant, family restaurant), and the larger divergences that typically mark major variants (e.g., fast food restaurant, cafeteria, etc.). Schank and Abelson distinguish routine scripts that one just follows from plans that need to be created more on the fly. One has to understand what key elements trigger a script or a plan, what elements signal a deviation or an interruption, how an aborted script is to be understood, and so forth.

One also has to know some more general facts about our physical world: what kinds of activities and interactions can take place at a distance, which require proximity and which direct contact. One has to understand about physical conveyance of objects to a place or to a person. One also needs to know what kinds of stuff can be mentally transferred (ideas, wants, etc.) and via what means. One needs similar knowledge for our social world: how close one has to be to talk, and so what the waiter has to do to be able to take one's order; what language is being used, and how the relevant parts work; how one has to mentally process the menu; what the appropriate forms of interaction with the waiter are, with the hostess, with the cashier, et cetera; what one does to show displeasure; and so forth.

Such a simulation represents a major undertaking by a large team. Ultimately its goal is to pass a kind of limited version of a Turing test – that is, to create a record (such as a transcript) of a simulated event that is indistinguishable from a similar record of a real event. The test is to some degree a relative (vs. absolute) one – there always exists room for more detail, for more specificity. Schank and Abelson's success in their limited context was incredibly impressive! They have clearly captured a major part of our understanding of the restaurant event. It is the most complete (broad and accurate) simulation of a collective (i.e., cultural) knowledge with action system that we have yet seen.

But their study also points up some of the dangers of reading such a model as too literal and complete a representation of the modeled reality. For example, for good computational reasons they had to clearly distinguish "scripts" from "plans," while we each know from our own direct experience with different kinds of restaurants that the one grades into the other – that we almost always start with a scriptlike approach, but then commonly have either to recognize more or less standard variants or to adapt to novel variations on the fly (i.e., to produce "plans"). It is this capacity to improvise variations of scripts that characterizes much of our cultural knowledge.

Stuart Plattner (1984) used a fairly straightforward simulation of an institution, St. Louis's Soulard produce market, in novel and useful – and cognitively important – ways. Plattner was interested in how pricing and competition work in a set of competing market stalls. He tried participant observation and interviewing, but important key aspects of pricing decisions remained out of sight, interior to his informants. These aspects were hard to talk about because, in the heat of actual negotiations, informants were too busy to talk, while afterward they could not remember the relevant detail.

So Plattner constructed a computer model of the relevant aspects of the market – in the form of a game in which an informant could operate a virtual stall under realistic conditions. From the players' point of view the computer model itself is a "black box," even though it does embody (presumably standard) hypotheses about market processes. Plattner's simulation discussion did not directly address those processes, since his immediate research goal was the behavior of individual sellers in the market. The game captured the institutional givens and the collective framework within which individual marketer decisions were made. Plattner could freeze the game at any given moment in order to query his informant about an action or decision just made. The simulation game then represented a powerful ethnographic tool – and a powerful device for studying the cognitive processes involved in successful – and unsuccessful – market stall operation.

But the game had two further uses. In the process of constructing the simulation Plattner had continuous recourse to informants who played successive versions and, as they did so, they also told him what worked or did not work in that version. This feedback guided him to a version that felt real to these professional denizens. In that process Plattner gained new insight into the mechanisms of the market itself (where the market is the collective actions of the participating marketers). The second additional use was pedagogical. The game became an excellent hands-on teaching device in his course on economic anthropology.

In this case, what was newsworthy was not so much the market simulation itself (even if it was useful), but the process of its development, the ethnographic interview possibilities it opened up, and the teaching tool that it became. Although all ethnographers will introduce conditionals and hypothetical scenarios in the course of interviews or discussions, as Ellen (1986) notes there is a marked distinction between the kinds of judgments people will make in different contexts; talking about is not the same as doing. These are all uses that are of great potential importance for cognitive anthropology.

A different kind of economically oriented simulation was that of Lawrence Kuznar (see Kuznar and Sedlmeyer 2005; Kuznar 2006), who simulated pastoralist–farmer interactions in Darfur at the community level using an agent-based simulation named

NOMAD. Among the notable outcomes of the simulation was support for the argument that the Darfur crisis was the inevitable result of the breakdown of land use in the face of growing populations, marginal habitats, and an unprecedented ecological crisis. The pastoralists needed products the farmers produced. The question for them was whether to raid for (steal) those products, or to trade for them. The farmers had the problem of encouraging trade if possible, and, if not, deciding whether to resist or to surrender. They also had the option of trying to buy off the raiders or hiring one set of pastoralists to protect them from the others. Kuznar used his simulation to explore the conditions and mechanisms (including knowledge, information, and social relations) that produced one or another of these options.

Bharwani (2005) developed a novel suite of methods to support her research on east Kent farmers and how they reasoned with respect to changing practices such as adapting crop mix or investment in equipment based on their perceptions of climate change. She was especially interested in the impact on farmers' decisions based on what other farmers believed and did, and in particular the extent of consensus and diversity that would emerge. Like Kippen's and Fischer's (above), Bharwani's research was designed from the beginning to collect, model, and analyze data using an agent-based simulation. Her goal was to capture the resolution and breadth of ethnographic methods and integrate these with more formal methods and theory.

She integrated knowledge elicitation using conventional participation, interviewing and observation, rule extraction using algorithms now employed in data-mining, and interactive and iterative testing and modification of these rules with the original ethnographic consultants using what she calls "games," models with which she and the ethnographic consultant interacted and "played" to explore scenarios arising from the ethnographic collection. The game rules could be amended on the spot based on new suggestions by the consultant. From the results of the games, she constructed a knowledge-based model representing the meta-decision capability of the consultant (the range of their capacity to make informed decisions in the relevant domains). These were used in agent-based simulations where there were many agents who could impact each other where each had different knowledge, either representing different ethnographic sources, or with rule variations where the consultant was uncertain. The agents operated within a conventional model of farm economics – with contingent climatic, market, and political conditions – that would determine whether or not they survived (if they made incorrect decisions, they became less viable, and vice versa). Thus computer-based methods are used in conjunction with agent-based methods shaped by ethnographic data collection, providing a more robust and effective method of formalizing and verifying qualitative data while maintaining the involvement of stakeholders and domain experts throughout the process.

Bharwani's project evaluated the capacity and outcomes of adaptive behavior based on a more conventional approach to "adaptive dynamics" developed by J. W. Bennett (1976). His model has features which compliment and fulfill both agent-based methods and ethnographic research. Agent-based methods aim to show how macro-level behavior emerges from various rules programmed at the local, individual level. Bennett's framework also operates on two, similar levels, one which describes low-level, short-term, action–response behavior, resulting in primitive effects, and a further level which describes higher-level, longer-term patterns of behavior, referred to as strategic designs. The ethnographic data collected during the course of Bharwani's research was mapped onto Bennett's framework. The agent-based model is then used to establish which high-level patterns of behavior emerge over time as a result of local behavior, and whether such emergent phenomena are insightful in gaining a clearer understanding of the original ethnographic data.

For Bharwani empirical observation is understood as using a theory – Bennett's adaptive dynamics – that is appropriate to explain the observed behavior (planning and decision-making) of east Kent farmers. Furthermore, both the ethnographic knowledge collection phase of the research and the experiments run within the agent-based simulation allow stakeholders and domain experts to disambiguate their perceptions. In this way, a clearer understanding between observation and theory can emerge.

Bharwani argues that agent-based computer modeling techniques combined with theoretical anthropological approaches promote a better analysis of the behavioral processes with respect to adaptation and transitional behavior. The theoretical anthropological basis helps to identify important properties about the system under study which might not be possible using traditional research methods. The value of using an agent-based model as a tool for analyzing social science theory lies in the potential to reveal new areas of exploration and analysis in further research. Further, there are many advantages in creating a more formalized representation of domain knowledge within anthropology (Fischer and Finkelstein 1991). The benefits of mapping and modeling a complex adaptive system using this framework lie in the ability to identify the characteristics (macro-level strategic patterns or designs) that are important to the functioning of a successful system and its essential underlying components (micro-level strategies with primitive effects which can also be easily identified and analyzed).

Simulation in general, and agent-based simulation in particular, is a promising avenue, since it allows the exploration of the evolution of these models in context and in a more holistic manner. That is, simulations illustrate how systems of different kinds and scales might interact with each other – for example, marriage and population growth, or religion and economics. In many simulations we are interested in the structure and interaction of sub-models more than their content. Agent-based simulations allow us to examine the consequent behaviors of individual strategies on a group. They permit us to better identify incremental complexity and facilitate the identification of critical situations that can lead to prediction outside the simulation, for example, demonstration that some values for the parameters or systems under study are salient enough to drive phenomena, not just be a contributing factor (Fischer 1994:192–196).

Another approach to simulation is seen in cases where the actual simulation itself is made of a heterogeneous collection of ad hoc procedures and mechanisms and used to represent one side in some sort of interaction with, say, humans. What is important about such a simulation is that the output be adequately realistic; there is no particular concern with how it got there.

An early example of such a simulation was "Eliza" (Weizenbaum 1966), which conducted a sort of minimalist psychiatric interview. The program itself was very simple, keying in on a short list of key words, such as "mother," and producing scriptlike messages, such as "Your mother, huh? She must be important to you." What was fun was that it pretty much passed its version of a minimal local Turing test – that is, in any page of a session's transcript there was usually not more than one strange exchange (i.e., not something we'd expect a real psychotherapist to say)!

A larger, more general, and more useful version of this approach is represented by studies of, say, traffic patterns in large cities. The actual simulation is a hodgepodge of different kinds of factual information, different local models, and so forth. So the goal of such a simulation is not to test the capability of some procedure or the working out of some mechanism. Instead, like Plattner's market simulation, it is designed to provide a realistically acting platform on which experiments can be conducted. For example, what happens to your traffic flow if you make Main Street one-way and Church Street one-way in the other direction? Or, what happens when the football game ends and the fans all try to drive home? What happens when you have to close some streets for construction or for a local disaster?

To sum up, there exist a variety of useful kinds of simulation. Sometimes one wants to see how far a given process can be pushed as a potential or plausible explanation of some observed phenomenon. Sometimes one is modeling some mechanism that relates different kinds of systems or communities – again, to see how far the mechanism can be taken as a potential explanation of some target situation. And sometimes the simulation – how it actually works – is not of interest, but instead all that one wants from it is some realistic output which one can then use as a basis for experimentation or reflection.

Simulations never directly explain any actual empirical phenomena; instead they represent a kind of plausibility argument. That is, their strongest claim is that what is modeled in the simulation is logically sufficient to account for the (a?) pattern that one sees in one's observed empirical phenomenon – nothing in the simulation proves necessity. And often, because of the simplifications that the simulator is forced to make, even the plausibility (or sufficiency) argument can be somewhat muddy. But still, simulations provide the most powerful experimental tool available to anthropologists in the normal course of events. And their use can be particularly apropos for those cognitive anthropologists who are aiming to describe, analyze, and understand emergent collective cognitive systems.

Is simulation simply a better form of description, or can it serve as the basis for theory-building? There are, of course, two answers to this question. First, better forms of description are often linked to advances in theory. The main issue is what is "better." Simply representing our subject with a more detailed description, while it might benefit all of us to describe our objects of study in better detail, does not in and of itself lead to better theory. Indeed, if the new description is not amenable to identifying inter-relationships between elements of the data and thus some reduction in the possibilities it may not support the production of theory at all.

We can generally say that a description promotes theory if in conjunction with the theory we can produce a more compact description – that is, a "shorter" description which, in conjunction with the theory, enables the description to apply to a wider range of phenomena, whether more cases, or more aspects of a given case, or both. That is, we evaluate theory by identifying its capacity to reduce the complexity of another description without losing information, or by being able to demonstrate that information lost was of minimal importance with respect to what the theory is attempting to describe or explain. This certainly applies to cognitive phenomena, including collective cognitive systems.

Simulation modeling appears to meet this criterion. While we are describing the constituents of a situation in rather more detail than is normal by avoiding aggregation, we are instead describing how these constituents interact with each other to produce what appears to be a more detailed representation of varied and complex phenomena. If this complexity is reasonably congruent with the observed data (within some level of statistical measurement), then we have produced evidence that the simulation is approximately logically equivalent to whatever processes produced the observed data.

Therefore, while we agree that a simulation is simply a description, it is a description that permits us to evaluate theories far more complex than we can evaluate within the limits of textual narrative, statistical analyses, or rule-based analyses alone (although it is always dependent on the results of one or more of these), and thus it increases our ability to explain the outcomes we identify in a given process and context. Simulation, by opening up the possibilities for testing theory, can be an effective theory-building tool.

NOTE

1 Two different kinds of notions can be contrasted with "well-understood" here. In one sense the contrast concerns whether or not we are able to evaluate the results against some anchor. In the other sense the contrast concerns whether or not the processes themselves (with the operations that represent them) are well understood. Both versions would obtain for a successful simulation.

REFERENCES

Agar, Michael H.

2001 Another Complex Step: A Model of Heroin Experimentation. Field Methods 13(4):353–369.

Agar, Michael H., and Dwight Wilson

2002 Drugmart: Heroin Epidemics As Complex Adaptive Systems. Complexity 7(5):44–52.

Bennett, John

1976 The Ecological Transition: Cultural Anthropology and Human Adaptation. New York: Pergamon.

Bharwani, Sukaina

2005 Adaptive Knowledge Dynamics and Emergent Artificial Societies: Ethnographically Based Multi-Agent Simulations of Behavioural Adaptation in Agro-Climatic Systems. Unpublished doctoral thesis, University of Kent.

Black, S.

1978 Polynesian Outliers: A Study in the Survival of Small Populations. *In* Simulation Studies in Archaeology. I. Hodder, ed. Pp. 63–76. Cambridge: Cambridge University Press.

Buchler, Ira R., Michael Fischer, and Michael McKinlay

1986 Ecological Structure, Economics, and Social Organization: The Kapauku. *In* New Trends in Mathematical Anthropology. G. De Meur, ed. Pp. 57–124. London: Routledge and Kegan Paul.

Dyke, Bennett

1981 Computer Simulation in Anthropology. Annual Review of Anthropology 10: 193–207.

Ellen, Roy F.
1986 Ethnobiology, Cognition and the Structure of Prehension: Some General Theoretical Notes. Journal of Ethnobiology 61:83–98.
Fischer, Michael
1986 Expert Systems and Anthropological Analysis. Bulletin of Information in Computing and Anthropology 4:1–4. http://lucy.ukc.ac.uk/bicaweb/b4_/expert.html, accessed September 20, 2010.
1994 Applications in Computing for Social Anthropologists. London: Routledge.
2006 The Ideation and Instantiation of Arranging Marriage within an Urban Community in Pakistan, 1982–2000. Contemporary South Asia 15(3):325–339.
Fischer, Michael D., and Anthony Finkelstein
1991 Social Knowledge Representation: A Case Study. *In* Using Computers in Qualitative Research. Nigel G. Fielding and Raymond M. Lee, eds. Pp. 119–135. London: Sage.
Fischer, M., and W. Lyon
2000 Model Marriage in Pakistan. *In* Culture, Creation, and Procreation: Concepts of Kinship in South Asian Practice. A. Rao and M. Boeck, eds. Pp. 267–322. New York: Berghahn.
Gladwin, Christina H.
1975 A Model of the Supply of Smoked Fish from Cape Coast to Kumasi. *In* Formal Methods in Economic Anthropology. S. Plattner, ed. Pp. 77–127. Washington, DC: American Anthropological Association.
1976 A View of the Plan Puebla: An Application of Hierarchical Decision Models. American Journal of Agricultural Economics 58:881–887.
1980 A Theory of Real-Life Choices: Applications to Agricultural Decisions. *In* Agricultural Decision Making. P. Barlett, ed. Pp. 45–85. New York: Academic Press.
Gladwin, C. H., and J. Butler
1984 Is Gardening an Adaptive Strategy for Florida Family Farmers? Human Organization 43(3):208–216.
Johnson, Alan
1978 Quantification in Cultural Anthropology. Stanford: Stanford University Press.
Kippen, James
1988a On the Uses of Computers in Anthropological Research. *In* Current Anthropology 29(2): 317–320.
1988b The Tabla of Lucknow: A Cultural Analysis of a Musical Tradition. Cambridge Studies in Ethnomusicology. Cambridge: Cambridge University Press. (Separate cassette tape containing 42 musical items.)
Kronenfeld, David B.
1976 Computer Analysis of Skewed Kinship Terminologies. Language 52(4):891–917.
Kronenfeld, David B., and Andrea Kaus
1993 Starlings and Other Critters: Simulating Society. Journal of Quantitative Anthropology 4:143–174.
Kronenfeld, David B., and Jerrold E. Kronenfeld
2006 CritSim2: A Program for Simulating Society. *In* Cybernetics and Systems 2006, vol. 1. R. Trappl, ed. Pp. 301–303. Vienna: Austrian Society for Cybernetic Studies.
Kunstadter, P., R. Buhler, F. Stephen, and C. F. Westoff
1963 Demographic Variability and Preferential Marriage Patterns. American Journal of Physical Anthropology 21:511–519.
Kuznar, Lawrence
2006 High Fidelity Computational Social Science in Anthropology: Prospects for Developing a Comparative Framework. Social Science Computer Review 24(1): 1–15.
Kuznar, Lawrence, and Robert Sedlmeyer
2005 Collective Violence in Darfur: An Agent-Based Model of Pastoral Nomad/Sedentary Peasant Interaction. Mathematical Anthropology and Cultural Theory: An Interna-

tional Journal 1(4). http://www.mathematicalanthropology.org/pdf/KuznarSedlmeyer 1005.pdf, accessed July 15, 2010.

Lansing, J. Stephen

1991 Priests and Programmers: Technologies of Power in the Engineered Landscape of Bali. Princeton: Princeton University Press.

Leaf, Murray

2000 The Physical Farm Budget: An Indigenous Optimizing Managerial Algorithm. Mathematical Anthropology and Cultural Theory 1(1):1–19.

MacCluer, J. W., and B. Dyke

1976 Minimum Size of Endogamous Populations. Social Biology 23(1):1–12.

Nardi, Bonnie

1980 Use of Computer Simulation for Predicting Sociocultural Change. *In* Predicting Sociocultural Change. S. Abbot and J. van Willigen, eds. Pp. 38–56. Athens: University of Georgia Press.

Plattner, Stuart

1984 Economic Decision Making of Marketplace Merchants: An Ethnographic Model. Human Organization 43:252–264.

Quintero, L. A., P. J. Wilke, and J. G. Waines

1997 Pragmatic Studies of Near Eastern Neolithic Sickle Blades. *In* Prehistory of Jordan II: Perspectives from 1997. H. G. K. Gebel, Z. Kafafi, and G. O. Rollefson, eds. Pp. 263–286. Studies in Early Near Eastern Production, Subsistence, and Environment no. 4. Berlin: Ex Oriente.

Schank, Roger, and R. P. Abelson

1977 Scripts, Plans, Goals and Understanding: An Inquiry into Human Knowledge Structures. Hillsdale, NJ: Lawrence Erlbaum.

Weizenbaum, Joseph

1966 ELIZA – A Computer Program for the Study of Natural Language Communication between Man and Machine. Communications of the Association for Computing Machinery 9:36–45.

Wilke, P. J.

1988 Bow Staves Harvested from Juniper Trees by Indians of Nevada. Journal of California and Great Basin Anthropology 10:3–31.

2002 Bifacial Flake-Core Reduction Strategies and Related Aspects of Early Paleoindian Lithic Technology. *In* Folsom Technology and Lifeways. J. E. Clark and M. B. Collins, eds. Pp. 345–370. Lithic Technology special publication no. 4.

Wilke, P. J., and L. A. Quintero

1994 Naviform Core-and-Blade Technology: Assemblage Character as Determined by Replicative Experiments. *In* Neolithic Chipped Stone Industries of the Fertile Crescent. H. G. Gebel and S. K. Kozlowski, eds. Pp. 33–60. Studies in Near Eastern Production, Subsistence, and Environment no. 1. Berlin: Ex Oriente.

1996 Near Eastern Neolithic Millstone Production: Insights from Research in the Arid Southwestern United States. *In* Neolithic Chipped Stone Industries of the Fertile Crescent and Their Contemporaries in Adjacent Regions. S. K. Kozlowski and H. G. K. Gebel, eds. Pp. 243–260. Studies in Early Near Eastern Production, Subsistence, and Environment no. 3. Berlin: Ex Oriente.

2009 Getting It Straight: Shaft-Straighteners in a Grooved-Stone World. *In* Modesty and Patience: Studies and Memories in Honour of Nabil Qadi Abu Salim. H. G. K. Gebel, Z. Kafafi, and O. Ghul, eds. Pp. 127–134. Yarmouk University, Irbid, Jordan, Monographs of the Faculty of Archaeology and Anthropology 6. Berlin: Ex Oriente.

PART III Cognitive Structures of Cultural Domains

CHAPTER 13 Mathematical Representation of Cultural Constructs

Dwight Read

Introduction

At first glance, mathematical representation of cultural constructs is an oxymoron for those who consider culture to express primarily the humanistic side of what it means to be human and thus to have little to do with the scientific, objective framework associated with mathematics and mathematical modeling. As Clifford Geertz said of ethnographic description more than three decades ago: "it is interpretive; what it is interpretive of is the flow of social discourse" (1973:20). This, he argued makes "the essential task of theory building … not to codify abstract regularities but to make thick description possible, not to generalize across cases but to generalize within them" (26). As a consequence, "cultural theory … is not … predictive" (26) as it is, in the final analysis, not a way to "answer our deepest questions ['the existential dilemmas of life'], but to make available to us answers that others … have given, and thus to include them in the consultable record of what man has said" (30). In this framework, depictions of cultural phenomena that focus on formal order are not only wrong but even pernicious: "Nothing has done more … to discredit cultural analysis than the construction of formal order in whose actual existence nobody can quite believe" (18), for "To set forth symmetrical crystals of significance, purified of the material complexity in which they were located, and then attribute their existence to autogenous principles of order, universal properties of the human mind or vast a priori *Weltanschauungen*, is to pretend a science that does not exist and imagine a reality that cannot be found" (20).

It would be hard to draw a picture more bleak for those who espouse approaching cultural phenomena through the language of mathematical representation, yet Geertz equally recognized that "Our double task is to uncover the conceptual structures that inform our subjects acts, the 'said' of social discourse, and to *construct a system*

A Companion to Cognitive Anthropology, First Edition. Edited by David B. Kronenfeld, Giovanni Bennardo, Victor C. de Munck, and Michael D. Fischer.

of analysis in whose terms what is generic to those structures, what belongs to them because they are what they are, will stand out against the other determinants of human behavior" (1973:27, emphasis added). He went on to assert that "In ethnography, the office of theory is to provide a vocabulary in which what symbolic action has to say about itself – that is, about the role of culture in human life – can be expressed" (27). In a similar vein, G. N. Appell comments: "more explicit attention must be focused on developing … abstract, analytical systems for all cultural domains" (1973:47) and Rodney Needham observes that "comparison stands a better and quite different chance of success if it is conducted in formal terms" (1975:365). For David Schneider the task of anthropology is to "discover how the cultural constructs are generated, the laws governing their change, and in just what ways they are systematically, related to the actual states of affairs of life" (1968:7). Similarly, Pierre Bourdieu recognizes the connection between the "thick description" of social discourse and where the coherence expressed through thick description arises: "Probably the only way to give an account of the practical coherence of practices and works is to construct generative models which reproduce in their own terms *the logic from which that coherence is generated*" (Bourdieu 1990[1980]:92, emphasis added). Each recognizes that culture, however we might define it, is not confined to how we, as culture bearers, act and what meaning our actions may have as actions, but relates more fundamentally to the conceptual systems that underlie our actions and behaviors as social beings.

Without that cultural backdrop – or what Schneider referred to as "the stage, the stage setting, and the cast of characters" (1972:38) – the interpretations of Geertz's thick descriptions of human social interactions would have no more valid reference to "the existential dilemmas of life" than would thick descriptions of social interactions in a species of eusocial insects. Geertz recognizes that ultimately the interpretations made possible by what he calls thick descriptions relate to the deeper questions of how we understand ourselves as humans and not just as another biological species. This cannot be divorced from "the conceptual structures that inform our subject's acts." It is in precisely this sense that mathematical representation of cultural constructs should be viewed, as a way to express and make evident the way in which concepts that make up cultural systems are structured and, through structure, meaning is constructed.

Mathematical representation begins with cultural constructs as they have been elicited through rigorous ethnographic fieldwork (El Guindi 1986; Leaf 2006; Leaf and Read, n.d.) and uses mathematical reasoning to extend anthropological reasoning as a way to elaborate on our understanding of what constitutes cultural knowledge. As Fadwa El Guindi comments regarding algebraic representation of the structure of Zapotec wedding ritual: "We shall first present an ethnographic account of certain events of a ritual and a structural analysis which reveals the basic units and the relations between them; then we shall restate the structural argument in a mathematical form, thereby establishing the inherently mathematical character of the logic which underlies the performance of the ritual" (El Guindi and Read 1979:763). In this manner, mathematical representation becomes a way to carry out the kind of analyses that Geertz and others identify as being at the core of the anthropological enterprise.

Mathematical representations need to delineate the "principles that may be presumed to be at work at their source" (Lounsbury 1964:351) in the form of "generative models which reproduce … the logic" (Bourdieu 1990[1980]:92) that accounts for "how the cultural constructs are generated" (Schneider 1968:7), and thereby enables us to "uncover the conceptual structures that inform our subjects' acts" (Geertz 1973:27). Mathematical representations of cultural constructs can provide the analytical means to achieve these goals for the analysis of cultural phenomena precisely because of what constitutes mathematical reasoning. According to the philosopher Charles Peirce and his mathematician father, Benjamin Peirce, "mathematics is the study of what is true of hypothetical states of things" (C. S. Peirce 1956[1902]:1775) and "is the science which draws necessary conclusions" (B. Peirce 1881:97) from those hypothetical states of things. The "hypothetical states of things" are the cultural constructs and what we want to make evident is what conceptually are the logical underpinnings, and implications, of those cultural constructs. In this way mathematical representation does not become an end in and of itself, but instead "Mathematical models are used ... because there are ethnographic advantages for doing so" (Hage and Harary 1983a:68).

Mathematical Representation of Cultural Constructs versus Mathematical Modeling of Behavior

In his monumental work *Les Structures élémentaires de la parenté* (Elementary Kinship Structures), the French anthropologist Claude Lévi-Strauss (1967[1949]) included an appendix written by the mathematician André Weil. In this appendix, Weil examined the structure entailed by the logic of the marriage rules found in the Murngin Aboriginal society in Australia. For many, this became the canonical example of the benefit to be derived from fusing mathematical formalism with anthropological reasoning and has led to numerous papers that consider marriage rules to be axioms whose logical implications are developed mathematically. The mathematical formalism is not imposed but derived from the ethnographically elicited marriage rules and so what is logically derived through mathematical formalism is, *ipso facto*, what must also be true in the logic of that system of marriage rules, whether or not the mathematical results were ethnographically elicited.

Weil's appendix showed that mathematical formalism could be integrated with ethnographic research with each providing impetus for the other. The mathematical formalism made it possible to derive what structural properties must be part of a system of marriage rules and the ethnographic research can identify structural systems based on axioms different than those considered by mathematicians (see the discussion below on the counting system of the Paiela of New Guinea). In this way, formal representation makes evident the logic of cultural conceptual systems and differs from mathematical modeling of systems of behavior, the more common application of mathematical methods in the social sciences.

A possible downside can occur when the mathematical argument becomes the goal and mathematically derived results are not relinked back to the ethnographic context. There is no reason to assume that all logical implications of a set of cultural concepts have been realized by the society in question and empirically not all implications are realized. As discussed below, the Tiwi on Melville and Bathurst Islands off the north coast of Australia have a kinship terminology that leads to marriages occurring as if the society were divided into two moieties with the requirement that a spouse be obtained from the moiety to which one does not belong. Yet, as Jane Goodale (1994[1971]) makes clear in her ethnography of the Tiwi, they do not have moieties and have no ideology reflecting a moiety structure. Another kind of disjunction can arise when the mathematical analysis depends on mathematical constructs that are not cognitively plausible, as Kronenfeld (2001) has noted with respect to the mathematical analyses made by Franklin Tjon Sie Fat (1998) of Dravidian and Iroquois terminologies.

This line between what may be mathematically elegant, on the one side, and mathematical representation explicitly grounded in, and constrained by, what has been ethnographically elicited, on the other side, has guided Dwight Read's research on making evident the logic of kinship terminology systems (discussed below). Rather than assuming that terminologies either emerge from, or are epiphenomena of, other systems, such as the genealogical grid approach through whose properties kinship semantics are expressed (e.g., Kroeber 1952), the approach in which terminologies are constrained by linguistic properties such as marking rules (e.g., Greenberg 1987), or the polysemic approach reflecting core and extended meanings of terms (e.g., Lounsbury 1964; Scheffler and Lounsbury 1971), Read begins with ethnographic observations that make it evident how culture bearers compute kin relations through the logic of kinterms interconnected in the form of a system of kinship concepts. In this way, the mathematical representation is not imposed but makes explicit an otherwise unseen logic, or as Kroeber (1952:172) has expressed it, "Kin term systems reflect unconscious logic and conceptual patterning."

In contrast, most early examples of mathematical anthropology have focused on behavior, including verbal behavior, as indicated by the content of review articles covering mathematical anthropology (e.g., White 1972; Burton 1973; Kronenfeld 1981) or by the chapters included in edited books such as *Explorations in Mathematical Anthropology* (Kay 1971) and *Genealogical Mathematics* (Ballonoff 1974). Though a few authors engaged early on in the representation of cultural constructs using mathematical or quasi-mathematical representations (e.g., Boyd et al. 1972; Kronenfeld 1980), more exceptional are articles in which the mathematical representation derives explicitly from the ethnographic context, that is, where the mathematical representation is used to make evident the logic entailed by, or underlying, the cultural constructs (e.g., Lehman and Witz 1974; Read 1974, 1984; El Guindi and Read 1979; Hage and Harary 1983b, 1991, 1996). In some cases, mathematical modeling of cultural constructs has brought out the fact that a cultural system, as ethnographically described, is not viable, leading to re-examination of the relevant data sources and subsequent clarification through reinterpretation. Examples include the so-called Natchez paradox derived from Swanton's (1911) account of Natchez social classes and subsequently resolved through reanalysis of the source materials by White et al. (1971) and the use of mathematical graph theory by Hage et al. (1995) to demonstrate that Dumont's (1980) hierarchical opposition model for the structure of Indian caste systems is not a "logical scandal" as he asserted (1980:242).

Mathematical graph theory was used extensively by Per Hage and Frank Harary (1983b, 1991, 1996) to represent and further explore anthropological research and discourse, based on the critical point that graph theoretic constructs provide the mathematical language for so doing. Hage considered anthropological discourse to make use of concepts that lend themselves to mathematical representation and in his books coauthored with mathematician Frank Harary, he showed not only the validity of this claim but, more importantly, the insights and clarifications provided by an appropriate mathematical representation of ethnographic observations. For example, they use the graph theoretic concept of a depth-first search tree to represent the idea of a conical clan as this "gives an exact, general, and intuitively appealing characterization of the conical clan in all of its forms" (Hage and Harary 1996:91). Similarly, they use graph theory to express the underlying structure common to classification systems previously characterized by anthropologists working in different regions as recursive dualism, perpetual dichotomy, recursive complementarity, reciprocal logic, relational contrast, or hierarchical opposition. More in keeping with the theme of this chapter, they argue that the seemingly disparate pollution beliefs in the Mount Hagen area of New Guinea form a culturally structured system with a logic revealed through their mathematical representation and thereby they make evident how the structure in one domain (system of beliefs) can be transformed into a structure in another domain (social organization). It is this use of mathematical concepts for the representation of cultural structures that provides the focus for the remainder of this chapter. To do so we begin with the simplest structure – a structure with a single point – and then systematically expand on the complexity of cultural structures.

Cultural Structures with One Object: Point Structure

A structure with a single object would correspond to a cultural concept whose meaning does not depend on its relation to other cultural concepts. Logically, this means that the negation of the concept is not itself another concept but simply the state of affairs absent from that concept. A simple example is the cultural concept of "human," whereby "human" does not mean simply a member of the species *Homo sapiens* but a concept that distinguishes some members of *Homo sapiens* as being, in some manner, distinct and therefore amenable to categorization as a distinct category. The distinctiveness of being human does not arise from material or biological properties of individuals but from a conceptual distinction that identifies when an individual takes on the property of being human. This distinction can take on many forms, such as the way many hunter-gatherer groups self-identify themselves by an expression that can be translated as "we, the real people"; for example, the expression *ju hoansi* used by the !Kung san, a hunter-gatherer group in the northwestern part of Botswana, for self-identification. In their case, the "real people" are those who are, or can determine, that they are (cultural) kin to each other as determined through their kinship terminology, itself a cultural construct that can be mathematically represented (see below). In the context of the abortion–anti-abortion conflict in US society, humanness is considered to be realized at the time of conception by the anti-abortionists and at the time of birth by the abortionist as the latter signifies (among other things) the ability of the fetus to survive separate from the womb of the woman bearing the fetus. Among the Netsilik Inuit (at least in traditional times), humanness entered in after birth when a woman called out the name of a spirit who helped her during childbirth, with that name becoming the name of the newborn child (Balikci 1970). Humanness is thus a culturally constructed state that can be satisfied by specified criteria, but its negation is simply the absence of that state, not another, specific state.

Not all cultural concepts stand in isolation in this way but instead the meaning of one concept is defined through its relation to another concept such as a pair of concepts conceptualized as being in opposition. Cultural concepts that are seen as in opposition to each other such as man versus woman, parent versus child, good versus evil, white versus black, and so on have the property that conceptually the negation of one concept is the other concept even though logically or empirically this may not be the case. If something is not white we cannot assume it must be black. If someone is not a parent we cannot assume that person must be a child, and so on. The opposition is itself constructed and this construction can be mathematically represented.

Cultural Structures with Two Objects: Binary Opposition

Consider a simple cultural construct defined through the well-known adage attributed to an old Arabic proverb (Al-Amily 2003): "A friend of a friend is a friend, a friend of an enemy is an enemy, an enemy of a friend is an enemy and an enemy of an enemy is a friend." As Cioffi-Revilla (1994:54) notes, the logic of the adage can be traced back to at least 2250 BC in Mesopotamia when Khita of Awan writes to Naram-sin: "The enemy of Naran-sin is my enemy. The friend of Naram-sin is my friend" (Lai 2001:216). The adage has to do with a hypothetical state of things since actual patterns of behavior need not accord with the adage. More precisely, the adage provides a cultural, rather than a behavioral, meaning for the concepts "friend" and "enemy" through the four statements stipulating the meaning of the concepts of "friend" and "enemy" by asserting how "friend" and "enemy" relate to each other as concepts. Through these statements, which express how computations may be made with the concepts, "friend" and "enemy" are culturally constructed as concepts in opposition.

We can mathematically represent the adage by noting that the four phrases define a binary product – denote it by the symbol o – over a set S of concepts: S = {friend, enemy}. Namely, given a pair of elements from S, for example, (friend, friend), the binary product assigns to that pair of elements an element from S; for example, friend o friend = friend by virtue of the first phrase. The logic of the adage may now be mathematically represented using the following symbol substitutions: friend → F, enemy → E, "of a" → o and "is a" → =. The adage, therefore, has a structure determined by a set of elements S = {E, F}, a binary product, o, defined over those symbols that satisfy a set of structural equations, in this case the four structural equations: (1) F o F = F, (2) F o E = E, (3) E o F = E, and (4) E o E = F. The structure so defined can be represented as an ordered triplet, $< S, o, \Sigma >$, where S is a set of elements, o is a binary product defined over the elements in S, and Σ is the set of structural equations satisfied by o for the elements in S. In mathematics, a structure of this kind is known as an *abstract algebra* and the structural properties of abstract algebras (see Box 13.1) may be explored using mathematical reasoning, including the way we may display the structure of the algebra as a graph. In the graph each element in S corresponds to a node and the nodes are connected by arrows, one for each element in a generating set, G, for S, which in this case is just {F, E} when we include the identity element F in G; that is, S is its own generating set.

No structure has been imposed in this mathematical representation of the adage about the "friend" and "enemy" concepts. Instead, the mathematical representation has made explicit the structure expressed in the adage and in so doing enabled that

Box 13.1

Properties important, in general, for the structure of an abstract algebra based on a binary operation, or product, include whether the binary product is *associative*; that is, X o (Y o Z) = (X o Y) o Z for all elements X, Y, and Z (not necessarily distinct) in S and whether the product operation is *commutative*; that is X o Y = Y o X for all elements X and Y in S. Another critical property for characterizing the structure of an abstract algebra with a binary operation is whether the set of symbols contains an identity element, call it I, such that the binary product of any element, X, in S with I yields back the element X; that is, I o X = X o I = X. When an abstract algebra has an identity element, another important structural property is whether each element, X, has an inverse in S, call it X^{-1}, so that X o X^{-1} = X^{-1} o X = I. Finally, we can define a subset, G, of S to be a generating set for S if each element in S is either an element of G or can be written as a binary product of elements in G and there is no proper subset, G*, of G from which the elements of S may be generated. For the friend–enemy algebra, o is associative and commutative, F is an identity element (since F o F = F and E o F = F o E = E) and E is the inverse element for E since E o E = F, the identity element. With these properties, the friend–enemy structure is the smallest non-trivial example of a structure known as an Abelian group, a kind of algebraic structure that plays a central role in the study of algebraic structures. The set G = {E} is a generating set for the algebra since the element F = E o E.

structure to be analytically characterized using mathematical reasoning derived from the study of algebraic structures. The meaning of friend and enemy constructed in the formal structure defined through the adage is that of a binary opposition between the concepts of "friend" and "enemy." Whereas what constitutes friend-like or enemy-like behavior is part of a continuum of behaviors, the formal representation defines "friend" and "enemy" as concepts that form a logically closed system; hence within this construct the negation of "friend" as a concept is "enemy" and the negation of "enemy" as a concept is "friend" even though the negation of friend-like behavior need not be enemy-like behavior. Rather than being derived from behavior, it becomes a prescription for behavior. As Martin Gusinde notes for the Ona of South America, "A person who has quarreled with someone from another group does not hold back his dislike … he wears his innermost feelings clearly drawn on his face as soon as he meets his enemy *or the latter's friends*" (1931:626, emphasis added). In brief, using Geertz's (1973) distinction, the adage is not a model *of* behavior, but a model *for* behavior.

The mathematical representation makes it possible to consider whether other instances of concepts in opposition from other domains use the same structure. Consider some of the structural implications in a moiety system with an exogamous marriage rule. The moiety system can be viewed as forming a social structure characterized by sidedness: *same side* and *opposite side*. "Same side" arises from the lineal rule for the moiety structure and "opposite side" from the exogamous marriage rule. (Sidedness may also arise in some kinship systems even though it is not explicitly identified through a moiety structure, as occurs with the kinship terminology for the Kariera Aborigines of Australia [Leaf and Read, n.d.; see also Houseman 1997; Houseman and White 1998 for a more extended discussion of sidedness].) Sidedness leads to the same algebraic structure as the friend–enemy algebra when we define a binary operation o over S = {same side, opposite side} as follows. If X and Y are elements of the set S, define X o Y to be the side relation – same side or opposite side – that a person A has to person C when A has the side relation X to person B and B has the side relation Y to C. For example, if X = same side and Y = opposite side, A has the same side as B (that is, A and B are in the same moiety) and C is in the opposite side relative to B (that is, C is in the moiety from which persons in the moiety to which A and B belong must obtain spouses), then by virtue of the moiety structure and the marriage rule, A is in the opposite side relative to C and so (same side) o (opposite side) = opposite side. (Note that the binary operation is well defined as it does not depend on which persons are selected as A, B, and C.)

The algebraic structure also underlies culturally constructed analogies such as an analogy between friend and enemy, and same side and opposite side. For this analogy we must logically have friend : same side :: enemy : opposite side since each of friend and same side are identity elements in their respective binary opposition structures. This has the implication that when the analogy is recognized, we would expect one's consanguineal kin (defined as those persons who are in my side) to be conceptualized as friend and one's potential affines (defined as those persons who are in the opposite side with respect to ego) to be categorized as enemy. The analogy may account for ethnographic reports, especially in lowland South America, in which potential affines are both considered, and acted towards, as enemies: "the association of enemy, cannibal and affine is widespread" (Rivière 2004:107). Lowland South American societies are also characterized by a same side–opposite side dichotomy through Dravidian terminologies (Keesing 1975).

The same conceptual structure applies to concepts in other domains. Consider the positive and negative integers and the binary operation of multiplication. For the positive and negative integers, positive × positive = positive, positive × negative = negative = negative × positive and negative × negative = positive. So under the correspondence, friend ↔ positive integer, enemy ↔ negative integer, and o ↔ x, the same structure holds for both friend–enemy and positive integers–negative integers. However, this assumes we already understand what positive and negative numbers are. We cannot merely say that the counting numbers are positive numbers and the negation of a positive number (i.e., a non-positive number) is a negative number, for it is not clear what would be the negation of a positive number absent a prior definition of what constitutes a negative number. In general, what is meant by the negation of a concept is non-trivial. If by a concept is meant a set of attributes that must be satisfied for something to be an instance of the concept, then negation of the concept would include all cases in which that set of attributes does not hold and the latter need not constitute an instance of a concept. For example, if we were to define the concept "friend" by a set of attributes such as "helps without asking for payment" and "can be counted on in adverse circumstances," and so on, then the negation of these attributes, namely, "does not help without asking for payment" or "cannot be counted on in adverse circumstances," and so on, does not define the concept "enemy." Instead, the meaning of "friend" and "enemy" as concepts is structurally defined by constructing "friend" and "enemy" as a pair in opposition (e.g., via the Arabic proverb) without reference to attributes. In the context of the friend–enemy construct, "enemy" becomes the negation of "friend" in the sense that the universe of concepts for this structure consists of exactly two concepts, "friend" and "enemy," and so if the concept in question is not the "friend" concept then it must be the "enemy" concept.

Cultural Structures Based on Three Objects: Mediation Structures

The friend–enemy construct can be viewed as being based on concepts abstracted from persons engaging in behavior that is seen as friend-like, or behavior that is seen as enemy-like. For positive numbers, the counting numbers can play, for numbers, an analogous role to the abstraction from friend-like behavior to the concept "friend," but there are no a priori number quantities that can play an analogous role for the negative numbers that would be comparable to the abstraction from enemy-like behavior to the concept "enemy." Instead, negative numbers must be a constructed concept without reference to prior experience rather than being formed at a higher ontological level (in the sense of more abstract) through experiences one has had at a lower ontological level (as is possible with positive numbers and counting numbers).

Not surprisingly, what is meant by negative numbers has had a long historical development (Knox 2003; Heeffer 2008) and even as late as the mid-eighteenth century, some British mathematicians still asserted that the idea of negative numbers was meaningless (Knox 2003), even though the logic of positive and negative numbers had been worked out in India a millennium earlier by the Indian mathematician Brahmagupta (598–670) using the concepts of debt and fortune. Consider the following summary of Brahmagupta's ideas about numbers included in his text *Brahmasphuta-siddhanta*, written in AD 628:

> A debt [*rina*] minus zero [*sunya*] is a debt.
> A fortune [*dhana*] minus zero is a fortune.
> Zero minus zero is a zero.
> A debt subtracted from zero is a fortune.
> A fortune subtracted from zero is a debt.
> The product of zero multiplied by a debt or fortune is zero.
> The product of zero multiplied by zero is zero.
> The product or quotient of two fortunes is one fortune.
> The product or quotient of two debts is one fortune.
> The product or quotient of a debt and a fortune is a debt.
> The product or quotient of a fortune and a debt is a debt.
> [O'Connor and Robertson 2000]

The last four lines express the same structure for debt and fortune as the Arabic proverb does for friend and enemy and thereby provides the conceptual basis for associating

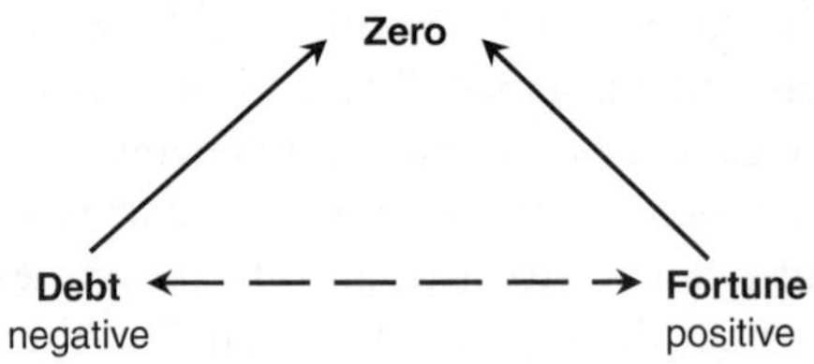

Figure 13.1 Brahmagupta's statements about debt, fortune, positive, negative, and zero are in the form of a mediation structure.

the attribute "negative" with debt and the attribute "positive" with fortune. But fortune and debt differ from friend and enemy by virtue of the fact that these last four lines are not meaningful in isolation. Each of debt or fortune in isolation would just refer to a quantity to which counting numbers would apply since one can count the amount of one's debt just as one can count the amount of one's fortune, hence there is nothing in the concept of debt per se that associates it with "negative" in opposition to fortune associated with "positive." Instead, this required a third concept, that of *zero* (see lines 3 and 7) to connect debt with fortune (see lines 1–2 and 4–6) in a conceptually consistent manner. It is the way each concept is conceptually linked to zero that enables a single structure to be formed that gives rise to debt and fortune as taking on the attributes positive and negative and thus becoming concepts in opposition (see Figure 13.1).

This type of structure, where two concepts are linked to each other in opposition through a third concept and thereby have attributes for one concept that are the opposite of the attributes for the other concept, was identified theoretically and demonstrated ethnographically through research by Fadwa El Guindi (1972, 1973) on the structure of rituals among the Zapotec in the Oaxaca region of Mexico. El Guindi refers to this kind of structure as a *mediation structure* and characterizes it as follows:

> Mediation is … the means by which two [conceptual] categories, otherwise unrelated, are related. The relation is provided by a mediating category and is created in several ways. Among these are defining/differentiating, in which the mediating category plays a semantic/logical role in the definition and maintenance of a structural opposition; transforming, in which it provides the conceptual locus for the change of one category into another; and linking, the linkage of one conceptual domain with another. [El Guindi and Read 1979:764]

Using her terminology, zero in Brahmagupta's set of rules would be a defining/differentiating mediating category for the concept of positive and negative numbers, which is precisely what Brahmagupta's first several rules express.

El Guindi provides examples of mediation structures from Zapotec ritual, myth, and lore such as "cemetery" is a mediating category that links "house" and "field" as conceptual categories in opposition. The latter is indicated by the pairs of "opposite" attributes the Zapotec then associate with "house" and with "field" (see El Guindi and Read 1979:table 1). For the context of a wedding ritual, El Guindi shows how "*compadre*" is a mediating category for constructing an opposition based on

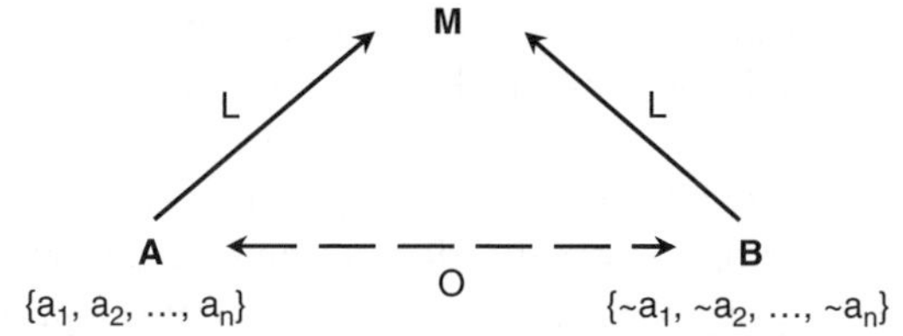

Figure 13.2 Mediation structure. Concepts A and B are in opposition by being linked to a third concept, M, which has the attributes of both A and B.

power–not power between the categories "*caseros*" and "*consuegros*" through the *caseros* (groom's relatives) sending a formal message of invitation enacted by the messengers going from the *caseros* to the *compadres* (marriage godparents) and then to the *consuegros* (bride's relatives): "One cannot move, as it were, from one polar side of the opposition (Caseros) to the other (Consuegros) without first going to a mediating category (Compadres)" (El Guindi and Read 1979:765). Similarly, note that on a number line, one cannot move (conceptually and literally) from positive numbers to negative numbers without going through zero.

Another mediation structure that is part of the wedding ritual consists of "bride" and "groom" in opposition as concepts mediated by the category "marriage godmother." These two mediation structures are formed through categorization of the persons involved in a wedding ritual and "The initial structure, using the conceptual categories Bride, Groom, and Marriage Godmother as elements, is transformed into the final structure, based on the conceptual categories Caseros, Consuegros, and Compadres. That final structure expresses the fundamental, dualistic opposition between bride's side and groom's side which characterizes fandango" (El Guindi and Read 1979:773). The mathematical representation of the mediation structure as an algebra shows "that the logic underlying ritual activity and other aspects of native belief system is inherently structural/mathematical in character" (773). The mathematical (or algebraic) representation of a mediation structure also clarifies, as we will now see, certain of its aspects.

In her theory of mediation structures, El Guindi asserts that the categories in opposition are *closed* "in that they are well-defined, rigidly bounded, and inflexible," whereas the mediating categories are *open* in that they "may combine opposite and contradictory characteristics" (El Guindi and Read 1979:765). Her concept of open and closed as it applies to a mediation structure is made more explicit through the algebraic representation of the mediation structure. Unlike the friend–enemy example, the mediation structure, as it stands, is not the graph of an algebra in that the opposition operation, O, mapping one category in opposition to the other, opposing category (see dashed arrow in Figure 13.2; algebraically speaking, O is a *unary* operation since it acts on a single element), has not been defined for the mediating category M (El Guindi and Read 1979). El Guindi and Read show that the unary operation, O, may be extended to M by defining O(M) = M; that is, M is its own opposition category. For this to be the case, though, the attributes associated with A and their negations associated with B must also be mapped to M by the linking (unary) operation L, so that L not only links the categories A and B to the mediating category M, but the attributes associated with A and B are also mapped to M by L. As shown by El Guindi and Read (1979), at this point we have in the algebraic representation precisely the notion of open and closed categories. The categories A and B are closed by virtue of each having associated with it a (finite) set of attributes that are part of the specification of the category and so each category is well defined. The category M is open as it now combines opposite characteristics since each attribute a_i (associated with A) and its opposite attribute $\sim a_i$ (associated with B) is now associated with M. El Guindi shows that this matches the ethnographic facts for Zapotec rituals. Does it also make sense empirically for the positive and negative integers?

The positive and negative integers are denoted by adding a sign, either + or –, to the symbol used for the natural numbers.[1] Thus the natural number 1 becomes the positive integer +1 or the negative integer –1 through adding the + or the – sign to the natural number 1. In the language of Brahmagupta, +1 would be a fortune of 1 and –1 would be a debt of 1. But what about the number 0? By convention, it neither has the + sign nor the – sign, supposedly as a way to avoid the anomaly of 0 otherwise being both positive and negative. This gives rise to three kinds of numbers: positive numbers, zero, and negative numbers. The convention, though, does not remove the anomaly for if we consider the attributes non-negative and non-positive, then 0 is both non-negative and non-positive, which means it must be both positive and negative despite the convention. Further, a signed 0 with +0 = 0 = –0 is part of the standards for the computer representation of numbers and provides a way to resolve what otherwise would be inconsistencies in computations if one only had an unsigned 0 (Goldberg 1991). The number 0, then, has precisely the property of being an open category as defined by El Guindi since it combines opposite characteristics. The concept of 0, that is to say the absence of something, is in fact conceptually open since we can speak of the absence of something whatever the something may be. The counting numbers, in contrast, apply only to discrete entities but not to substances such as, for example, liquids and gases. We can say that we have 0 water, but we cannot say we have 1 water. Thus, in accordance with El Guindi's argument, 0 as a mediating category is conceptually open whereas the counting numbers correspond to closed categories.

Generative Cultural Constructs: Single Generator

The mediation structure for positive and negative numbers gives rise to another structural property based on the way that the natural numbers are generated from the initial number, one, through recursion via the Peano axioms (see note 1). By recursively operating on the initial symbols, new symbols are constructed with meaning determined through the process by which the new symbols are constructed. Thus from the symbol 1 we form the new symbol 1 + 1 with name 2, from the symbol 2 we form the new symbol 2 + 1 with name 3, and so on. If we instantiate the symbol 1 with a set that contains a single element, then it follows that 2 will be instantiated with a set containing an element and yet another element, and so on. The mediation structure then enables the positive and negative integers to be defined in this manner.

Lest we think that this construction process is limited to constructing the concept of positive and negative integers by reference to the number 0, consider the counting system developed by the Paiela of New Guinea (Biersack 1982). The Paiela count by pairs of numbers, with the pairs determined by positions on the left hand, left arm, left upper torso, and left side of head paired with corresponding positions on the right hand, right arm, right upper torso, and right side of head. The first counting number refers to the left little finger paired with the right little finger, the second counting number refers to the left ring finger paired with the right ring finger, and continues in this paired manner across the fingers, then continues with the wrist, the mid-arm, the elbow, the mid-upper arm, the left shoulder, the side of the neck, and the side of the head. This sequence of paired parts is bounded at one end by the two hands forming a fist associated with an unpaired counting number and by the nose at the other end, also associated with an unpaired counting number.

Counting proceeds by starting with the little finger (beginning either on the left side or the right side of the body), then the ring finger, continuing with the body parts in sequence on one side of the body until the nose is reached, then continuing on the other side of the body in the reverse order for the body parts on the first side until the fist is reached. All told, the counting numbers go from 1 to 28. The names of the counting numbers may be transliterated as "first pair, first pair other side," "second pair, second pair other side," and so on for all the paired body parts. This gives the sequence of counting numbers and counting number names: 1 = first pair (little finger), 2 = second pair (ring finger), ..., 12 = 12th pair (side of face). Then 13 = nose, and the next number begins with the other side so 14 = 12th pair other side (other side of face), 15 = 11th pair other side (other side of neck), ..., 27 = 1st pair other side (other little finger). Finally, 28 = fist. The fist plays the structural role of 0 since the fist links the right side body positions with the left side body positions. The nose plays an analogous role and provides a way to conceptually enable the counting to shift from the one side to the other side of the body through the nose containing both a right nostril and a left nostril. This structure of the integers in the form of pairs of counting numbers based on the left and right sides of the body is literally embedded into the Paiela marriage ritual by erecting two rows of 12 stakes (corresponding to the 12 paired integers) to which the pigs being offered by the groom's lineage to the bride's lineage are tied and ritually counted, then subsequently distributed to the matrilineal and patrilineal relatives of the bride with pigs tied to one row of stakes going to the matrilineal relatives and the pigs tied to the other row of stakes going to the patrilineal relatives (Biersack 1982).

Though they are not usually considered in this manner, the same pattern occurs with the positive and negative integers if we consider +1, −1 to be a pair formed from the counting number 1 with + and − as markers for whether we are considering the number to the right of 0 or the number to the left of 0. Similarly, for the counting number 2 and so on. We can thus relate Paiela counting by pairs to the integers but with the difference that the Paiela use the nose as another position in the structure linking the right side to the left side. For the integers viewed in this manner, counting would begin with +1 immediately to the right of 0, then counting with the positive integers, then shifting over to the negative numbers through a number that connects the positive numbers with the negative numbers, then counting with the negative numbers (in reverse order) until the number 0 is again reached (see Figure 13.3).

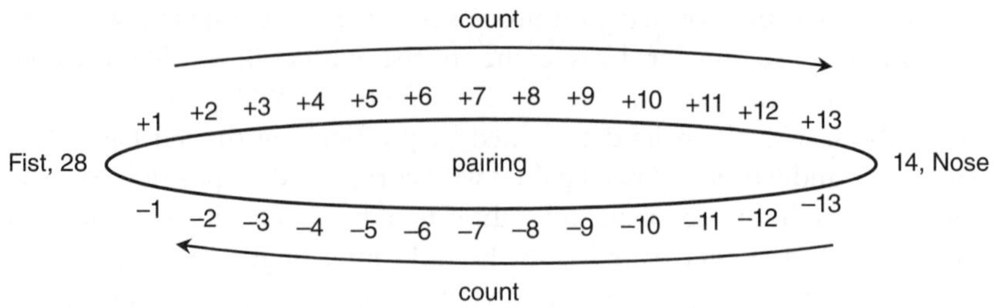

Figure 13.3 Paiela counting by pairs, illustrated with the positive and negative integers.

For both the Paiela counting numbers and the integers, the right side is linked with the left side: with the fist for the Paiela number pairs and 0 for the positive and negative integers. In addition, for the Paiela counting numbers the nose links the left side with the right side through the left nostril and the right nostril. In both cases, what would otherwise be two incompletely defined concepts (e.g., the numbers counted by left and right members of a pair in the Paiela case and the concept of positive numbers and that of negative numbers in the integer case) are linked and thereby form a single structure of well-defined concepts. In addition, the attributes for the linked pairs thereby become conceptual opposites: positive versus negative, debt versus fortune, and left side versus right side.

Generative Cultural Construct: Genealogical Space

The process of generating new concepts from a set of primary concepts not only occurs with examples such as the counting numbers, but is central to the conceptual structures that provide the framework within which kinship relations are activated and played out. Within the domain of kinship, genealogical tracing uses a simple, recursive procedure for generating new relation concepts from a basic pair of relation concepts. The operation of going from a person identified as ego to a female and a male culturally recognized as genealogical mother (m_g for short) and genealogical father (f_g for short) (with culturally specific criterion for making the assignment) can be reapplied, recursively, to the persons so identified and thereby arrive at the new relations m_g's m_g, m_g's f_g, f_g's f_g, and f_g's m_g, and so on.[2] Genealogical tracing of this kind is, of course, the means by which ancestral family trees are constructed.

The genealogical space becomes more complex when we include other aspects of the cultural conceptualization of genealogical spaces. Usually, if not always, descending genealogical pathways using the reciprocal genealogical relations, genealogical son and genealogical daughter, are conceptualized as part of the genealogical space and so we need to allow for descending genealogical pathways to be initiated at any node that is already part of the structure of ascending genealogical pathways. This large genealogical space (discussed in Lehman and Witz 1974) can then be reduced through a series of structural equations (D'Andrade 1970) to arrive at the more familiar idealized genealogical diagram used by anthropologists to express genealogical definitions of kinterms.

Generated Cultural Construct: Kinterm Space

Though genealogy determined through genealogical tracing from a focal individual has been taken as primary for the notion of kinship since the seminal work of Lewis Henry Morgan, the matter is more complex. Kinterms are not simply labels for categories of kin types formed by criteria extrinsic to the kinship terminology, but form a system of concepts expressed in the way users of terminologies compute kin relations. As Levinson observes for Rossel Island:

> Kinship reckoning on Rossel does not rely on knowledge of kin-type strings ... What is essential in order to apply a kin term to an individual X, is to know how someone else, of a determinate kinship type to oneself, refers to X. From that knowledge alone, a correct appellation can be deduced. For example, suppose someone I call *a tîdê* "sister" calls X *a tp:ee* "my child," then I can call X *a chênê* "my nephew," without having the faintest idea of my genealogical connection to X. [Levinson 2002:18]

This quote exemplifies what Read (1984) has called a kinterm product based on the way that kin relations are determined from cultural knowledge about one's kinship terminology without necessary reference to genealogical relations. In general, we can call the product of the kinterms K and L the kinterm that ego would (properly) use for alter 2 when ego (properly) refers to alter 1 by the kinterm L and alter 1 (properly) refers to alter 2 by the kinterm K. We will denote the kinterm product of K and L and the resulting kinterm, M, by the phrase K of L is M. A more formal definition of a kinterm product is given in Read (1984, 2001, 2007), but the details of the formal definition are not needed here. A kinship terminology may be elicited systematically using kinterm products (Leaf 2006: Leaf and Read, n.d.:ch. 4). Unlike the indeterminism that arises for the genealogical definition of kinterms such as "father" or "mother" in classificatory terminologies, a kinship terminology will be logically bounded under kinterm products by virtue of the fact that the elicitation of new kinterms through kinterm products with already elicited kinterms will eventually reach either a response such as (1) the kinterms continue in the same manner (as in parent of grandparent is great grandparent, parent of great grandparent is great-great grandparent, and so on in American and English terminology [AKT]); (2) the product does not yield a kinterm (as in father of father-in-law is not a kinterm in AKT); (3) the product yields the same kinterm (as in *papa* ["father"] of *papaisi shoko* ["great grandfather"] is *papaisi shoko* in the Shipibo terminology [Behrens 1984]); or (4) the product with an ascending kinterm is equated to a descending kinterm, thereby forming a cycle of kinterms (as in *mama* ["father"] of *maeli* ["grandfather"] = *maeli* ["grandson"] is *maiñga* ["son"] in the Kariera terminology [Radcliffe-Brown 1913:154]).

Due to its greater familiarity to most readers, we will use the AKT to exemplify the way in which new concepts (i.e., kinterms) are generated through a structure formed from a set of primary, generating kinterms through repeated use of the kinterm product applied to these terms, along with a set of structural equations satisfied by the kinterm product. A kinterm map for the AKT is shown in Figure 13.4. The kinterm map is based on the generating terms "parent" and "spouse" and the reciprocal generating term, "child." The kinterm map uses a kinterm-specific arrow to show the consequence of taking the product of a kinterm with a generating kinterm;

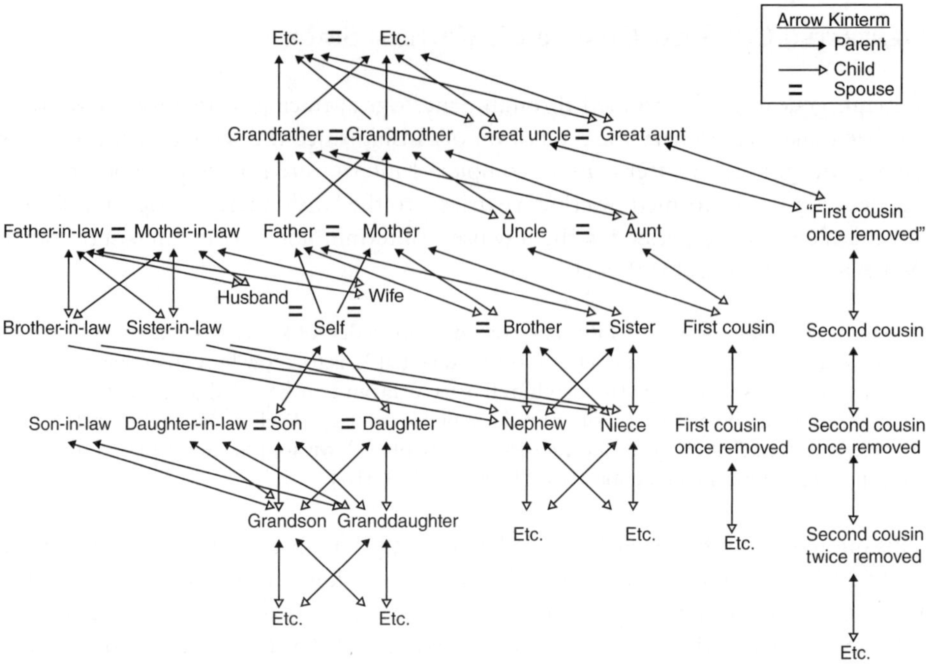

Figure 13.4 Kinterm map for American kinship terminology, based on Parent and Spouse as generating terms and reciprocal generating term Child.

for example, the arrows from "father" to "son" and to "daughter" show that the kinterm product of "father" with "child" is either the kinterm "son" or the kinterm "daughter."

We can model the logic of the kinship terminology structure by formally generating an algebraic structure in which no properties are included except those introduced explicitly through the formalism (see Box 13.2). The assertion that a kinship terminology has the form of an algebraic structure means demonstrating that the formally constructed algebra is isomorphic to the kinterm map structure for the kinship terminology (compare Figures 13.4 and 13.5), which is factually the case for the AKT and all other terminologies considered to date.

The construction of a kinship terminology structure has three components. First, the structure must satisfy properties common to all kinship terminologies. These include the concepts of kinterm reciprocity and of kinterm product closure (i.e., transitivity of kin relations except possibly for products at the boundary of the structure; see Leaf and Read, n.d.:ch. 7). Second, the terminology structure is formed by sequentially introducing the following kinship terminology structures and/or properties: (1) a structure of ascending kinterms, (2) a reciprocal structure of descending kinterms, (3) structurally expressed sex marking of kinterms, (4) an affinal structure introduced either through a "spouse" symbol or through structural transformation of consanguineal kinterms (such as occurs with the Kariera "cross-cousin" marriage rule [see Leaf and Read n.d.:ch. 8]), and (5) local structural rules that do not apply

Box 13.2

Let A = {I, P} be a generating set of algebraic symbols, o the concatenation binary operation defined over A (i.e., if X and Y are algebraic symbol strings, then X o Y is the symbol string XY). Let S be the set of structural equations to be satisfied by o. Define I to be an identity element for o (i.e., the equations I o P = P = P o I are included in S).

1 The algebraic structure A generated by A will be called the ascending structure. A consists of the symbol strings I, P, PP = P^2, PPP = P^3, and so on. Let D = {I, C} be a symbol set isomorphic to A, with P ↔ C under this set isomorphism and include the structural equations, IC = C = CI, defining I as an identity element for products with the element C.
2 The algebraic structure D generated by D will be called the descending structure. D consists of the symbol string I, C, CC = C^2, CCC = C^3, and so on. The union of A and D, call it A ∪ D, consists of the symbol strings ..., C^2, C, I, P, P^2, ...
3 The elements P and C are defined to be reciprocal elements by introducing the structural equation PC = I.
4 Let G = {I, P, C} = A ∪ D be the generating set for an algebra, where I is an identity element, with structural equation S = {PC = I}. The algebra, G, generated by G is isomorphic to the kinterm map of the AKT based on the primary kinterm parent and its reciprocal term child: I ↔ self, P ↔ parent, P2 ↔ grandparent ..., C ↔ child, C^2 ↔ grandchild ..., CP ↔ [brother, sister], C^2P ↔ [nephew, niece], ..., CP^2 ↔ [uncle aunt], ... and so on for all the elements in G and kinterms in the kinterm map based on parent, child, and self.

The remainder of the construction is outlined in Read (2001, 2007).

globally to the entire structure (such as the cousin nomenclature rules for the cousin substructure in the AKT).

The construction proceeds by forming products of the generating elements simplified, where possible, by the structural equations that implement the kinship properties to be satisfied by a particular terminology. Kinship terminology structures vary from one to the other based on differences in the generating elements, in the structural equations relevant to a particular terminology, and through alternative ways to implement the structural components identified above.

In the AKT, the primary terms are "self" and "parent," where "self" – even though it is not usually considered to be a kinterm – is included because of the centrality of the concept of self in any kinship system. The term "self" is an identity element under kinterm products since (self of K) = K = (K of self) for any kinterm K owing to the fact that if ego refers to alter 1 as self, alter 1 refers to alter 2 as K, then ego is alter 1 and so ego refers to alter 2 as K. The complete, formal construction, as outlined in Box 13.2, leads to an algebra structurally isomorphic to the structure of the kinterm map for the AKT (Read and Behrens 1990). One of the key pieces of the construction lies in identifying kinterm reciprocity via a structural equation of the form *ancestral term* of *descendant term* is *self*. The equation is introduced in the construction process prior to the introduction of affinal relations, hence persons linked only through affinal relations are excluded in the instantiation of this equation. For the AKT, the equation *parent of child is self* structurally defines "parent" and "child" to be reciprocal terms. This follows from noting that if ego properly refers to alter 1 as child and alter 1 properly refers to alter 2 as parent, then the equation states that ego properly refers to alter 2 as self, subject to the assumption that the equation is instantiated without reference to affinal relations, hence ego = alter 2 and so alter 1 uses parent reciprocally to refer to the person (ego) who refers to alter 1 as child.

Even more, the procedure for the construction of the descending structure from the ascending structure already motivates this equation. At this stage in the construction, affinal relations are not yet included, hence kin relations based on the terms included in this part of the structure determine non-affinal connections between egos and alters. So suppose ego, alter 1, and alter 2 are not affinally related. If ego refers to alter 1 as child (the AKT kinterm interpretation of the algebraic element, C), alter 1 refers to alter 2 as parent (the AKT kinterm interpretation of the algebraic element P), then alter 2 must be ego and ego refers to alter 2 = ego by self (the kinterm interpretation of the algebraic element I), hence parent of child = self. In other words, the procedure of constructing a descending structure connected to the ascending structure via the common algebraic element I already embodies the concept of kinterm reciprocity. Note that a term and its reciprocal identifies pairs of kinterms such as parent–child, grandparent–grandchild ..., comparable to the way positive and negative identifies pairs of integers, +1/−1, +2/−2, ... and just as the positive and negative integers cannot be defined without the concept of zero (the identity element for addition), kinterms and reciprocal kinterms cannot be defined without the concept of self (the identity element for kinterm products). The algebraic representation has made evident the manner in which the domains of numbers and the domains of kinship find commonality in the construction of concepts in each of these two domains.

The goals for the algebraic representation of kinship terminology structures do not end with discovering isomorphism between the algebraic structure and the kinterm map structure. Rather, this is the beginning point for consideration, in a broader sense, of the ways cultural concept formation will appear and reappear in different domains in the same culture. The most immediate examples relate to demonstrating the way in which the properties of a kinship terminology account for other culturally identified properties of kinship relations such as the "-in-law" suffix for American kinship terms. For English speakers, affinal relations are culturally marked through the "-in-law" suffix, but not consistently since husband of aunt is uncle, not uncle-in-law and wife of uncle is aunt, not aunt-in-law. This anomaly has been attributed to affect (Schneider 1968) or the fact that one (generally) has aunts and uncles prior to one's birth whereas one has in-laws only after one's birth. Neither is satisfactory as both are post hoc rationalizations of a fact, not a principle from which the fact may be derived as an instance. The algebraic argument demonstrates that there is no anomaly as it is logically inconsistent, given the generative structure of the AKT, for there to be in-law suffixes for the aunt and uncle kinterms (Read and Behrens 1990). Instead, the consanguineal kinterms form a two-dimensional structure in which spouse of aunt or

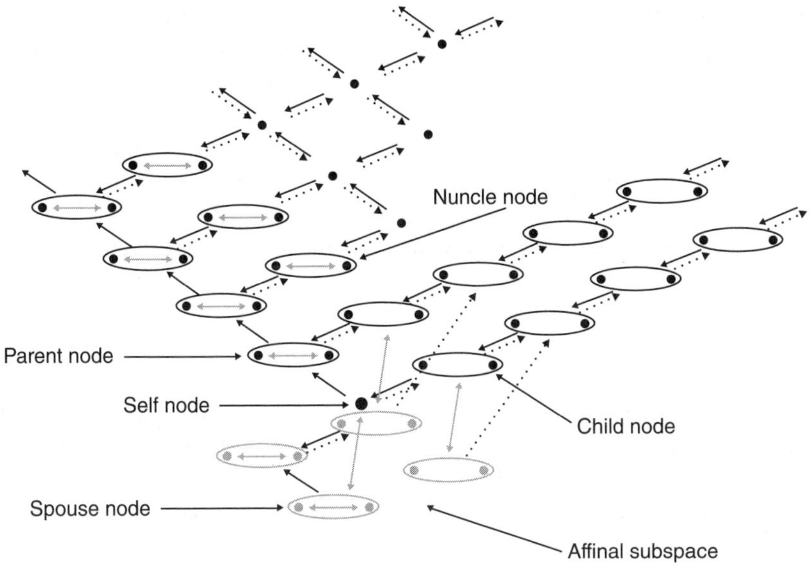

Figure 13.5 Algebraic structure generated as a model for the kinterm map shown in Figure 13.4. The algebraic structure and the kinterm map are structurally isomorphic. "Nuncle" stands for Aunt or Uncle.

uncle is embedded whereas the terms with an in-law suffix (including the affinal terms "husband" and "wife") are in a third dimension orthogonal to that two-dimensional structure (see Figure 13.5). Thus the in-law suffix distinguishes those terms comprising a third dimension for the structure of kinterms in the American kinship terminology as indicated in Figure 13.5.

An even more striking example occurs with the classificatory Polynesian terminologies for which a sibling generator is part of the generative structure. The structural analysis highlights the centrality of the sibling term in these terminologies, a centrality remarked upon as central to social relations by ethnographers of the Oceanic area as discussed in Read (2007). For example, Burridge (1959:130) comments that "the relationship between brother and sister could be said to be the pivot of Tangu social life and culture" (Marshall 1981:7). Further, as noted above, terminologies of this sort typically have a structure of male terms and a structure of female terms with the two structures linked through the sex-marked identity self term of one structure becoming a sibling term for the sex-marked identity self term in the other structure. For a male person identified as ego (that is, the instantiation of the male self term), the structure of the terminology implies that instantiation of the female self term will be his sister and from the perspective of the female structure, she is being identified as the ego for the female structure. This analogy between brother or sister and male ego or female ego is paralleled precisely in the ethnographic description of the Gilbert Islands for whom "brothers and sisters are alter egos" (Lambert 1981:190) and, as Reay (1975–76:80) notes, for Kuma of New Guinea: "Cross-sex siblings together constitute ... a complete human being" (cited in Marshall 1981), which parallels the formation of a whole kinship terminology through the constructed link between male self and female self as cross-sex siblings. That the centrality of sibling is not due to genealogy and descent relations is emphasized by the ethnographers of this area. For example, Schieffelin (1976:56) comments for the Kaluli of New Guinea: "Kaluli ties of sibling relationship are in contradiction to those traced by descent (by genealogical reckoning) and … *the sibling relationship takes precedence over descent* whenever the principles are in conflict" (cited in Marshall 1981:9) and for the Gilbert Islands Lambert notes: "These special responsibilities of a brother [to his sister] … *were not inherent in his genealogical status*" (1981:189, emphasis added).

Conclusion

Despite the negativity expressed by Geertz regarding formal analysis of cultural phenomena, formal analysis derived from ethnographic observations, rather than a priori imposition, will lead to enhanced insight regarding cultural phenomena and uncover commonalities from different cultural contexts. Formal analysis should make commonalities evident and so a good mathematical representation needs to focus on the logic and logical consequences of cultural constructs, thereby enabling their logic to be distilled from specific observations. At first glance, the Arab proverbs about friend and enemy have little in common with the multiplication of +1 and –1, yet the two domains are structured in precisely the same manner owing to both utilizing the structure of two concepts in opposition. At the same time, the representation makes evident a critical manner in which the two constructs differ when we consider the ontogenetic basis for the concepts involved. Though the friend and enemy proverbs may have ontological roots that reflect behavior differences, such as friend-like or enemy-like behavior, and so are plausibly constructs built up from experience, negative numbers do not have empirical referents and instead the concept of a negative number is constructed.

Through this elaboration on the ontogenetic origins of a binary opposition structure for number concepts, we arrive at yet another kind of structure that takes us back to different ethnographic examples through the work of El Guindi on mediation structures that she identified empirically through ritual structures and defined theoretically on the basis of empirical observations. Both the structure for binary oppositions and the mediation structures are algebras since each includes a binary product defined over the elements in the structure. The logic of a binary product opens up yet other avenues for concept formation through binary products of elements that do not map back onto the generating elements. For the numbers it leads to the natural numbers through repeated construction of new numbers by adding the concept of one to an existing number. For genealogical tracing it leads to new genealogical relations through recursive tracing using genealogical mother and genealogical father. In addition, the Paiela counting example demonstrates that structures in one domain – a system of counting through paired body parts – can be exploited for events taking place in another domain – the transfer of pigs from the groom's side to the bride's side as part of wedding ritual. Though recursive genealogical tracing through genealogical mother and genealogical father maintains the structural form of a person linked to a female and a male person that also characterizes the empirical facts of reproduction, with kinship terminologies we find structures with loosened empirical constraint, hence kinship terminology structures can and do vary in accordance with alternative ways that structures can be generated within those constraints. Rather than relegating kinship terminology variation to processes without empirical evidence such as metaphorical extensions, variation can be understood as inherent to the conceptual basis through which kinship becomes a culturally constructed reality and not through reflection of biological or other empirical facts. In so doing, the realities of kinship are constructed through the generation of terminology structure and this leads to concepts that structure not only the domain of kin relations but other aspects of social life such as indicated by the emphasis on brother–sister relations in the Oceanic area. The logic of kinship terminology structures thereby becomes a canonical example of what it means to say that through culture humans live in constructed realities.

NOTES

1 There is a fundamental, conceptual distinction between counting numbers based on the equivalence of sets of objects of the same size and the symbolic system of natural numbers defined via the Peano axioms, which are: (1) there is a number, call it 1, (2) to any number n, the successor number denoted n + 1 is a number, and (3) the induction axiom. Any counting number has a corresponding natural number symbol, but whereas there are an infinite number of natural number symbols, there can be only a finite number of named counting numbers. Arithmetic operations are defined symbolically using the natural numbers, which enables these operations to be carried out without reverting back to manipulating sets of the specified size as is done with the Chinese or Japanese abacus.

2 The expressions "genealogical mother" and "genealogical father" are used here rather than kin type expressions due to both the presumption that the kin types mother and father refer to genitor and genetrix, which makes the concept of a kin type culture-specific, and the polysemy of the terms "mother" and "father" in English as morphemes that can either have a genealogical meaning as in "She is my mother" which, for English speakers, may either have a genetrix connotation ("She is the woman who begat me") or a kinterm connotation ("She is the woman I refer to as mother"). The expressions "genealogical mother" and "genealogical father" make clear that the context is one of genealogical tracing and leaves unstated and variable – hence subject to cultural definition – the criteria by which a female and a male are identified as the persons through whom genealogical tracing takes place.

REFERENCES

Al-Amily, H. M.
2003 The Book of Arabic Wisdom: Proverbs and Anecdotes. Oxford: New Internationalist.
Appell, G. N.
1973 The Distinction between Ethnography and Ethnology and Other Issues in Cognitive Structuralism. Bijdragen tot de Taal-, Land- en Volkenkunde 129:1–56.
Balikci, A.
1970 The Netsilik Eskimo. Garden City, NY: Natural History Press.
Ballonoff, P., ed.
1974 Genealogical Mathematics. Paris: Mouton.
Behrens, C.
1984 Shipibo Ecology and Economy. Unpublished Ph.D. dissertation, University of California, Los Angeles.

Biersack, A.
1982 The Logic of Misplaced Concreteness: Paiela Body Counting and the Nature of the Primitive Mind. American Anthropologist 84:811–829.
Bourdieu, Pierre
1990[1980] The Logic of Practice [Le Sens pratique]. Stanford: Stanford University Press.
Boyd, J. P., J. N. Haehl, and L. D. Sailer
1972 Kinship Systems and Inverse Semigroups. Journal of Mathematical Sociology 2:37–61.
Burridge, K. O. L.
1959 Siblings in Tangu. Oceania 30:128–154.
Burton, M. L.
1973 Mathematical Anthropology. Annual Review of Anthropology 2:189–199.
Cioffi-Revilla, C.
1994 Martial and Political Items in the Mesopotamian Exhibit of the Département des Antiquités Orientales. Louvre Museum: VIth Millennium BC to VIIth Century BC. Working paper, Long-Range Analysis of War Project, University of Colorado.
D'Andrade, R.
1970 Structure and Syntax in the Semantic Analysis of Kinship Terminologies. *In* Cognition: A Multiple View. P. L. Garvin, ed. Pp. 87–143. New York: Spartan.
Dumont, Louis
1980 Homo Hierarchicus: The Caste System and Its Implications. Rev. English edition. Chicago: University of Chicago Press.
El Guindi, F.
1972 The Nature of Belief Systems: A Structural Analysis of Zapotec Ritual. Unpublished Ph.D. dissertation, University of Texas.
1973 The Internal Structure of the Zapotec Conceptual System. Journal of Symbolic Anthropology 1:15–34.
1986 The Myth of Ritual: A Native's Ethnography of Zapotec Life-Crisis Rituals. Tucson: University of Arizona Press.
El Guindi, F., and D. Read
1979 Mathematics in Structural Theory. Current Anthropology 20:761–790.
Geertz, C.
1973 The Interpretation of Cultures. New York: Basic Books.
Goldberg, D.
1991 What Every Computer Scientist Should Know about Floating-Point Arithmetic. ACM Computing Surveys 23:5–48.
Goodale, J.
1994[1971] Tiwi Wives. Prospect Heights, IL: Waveland.
Greenberg, J.
1987 The Present Status of Markedness Theory: A Reply to Scheffler. Journal of Anthropological Research 43:367–374.
Gusinde, M.
1931 The Fireland Indians, vol. 1: The Selk'nam: On the Life and Thought of a Hunting People of the Great Island of Tierra del Fuego. Vienna: Verlag der Internationalen Zeitschrift.
Hage, P., and F. Harary
1983a Arapesh Sexual Symbolism, Primitive Thought and Boolean Groups. L'Homme 23:57–77.
1983b Structural Models in Anthropology. Cambridge: Cambridge University Press.
1991 Exchange in Oceania: A Graph Theoretic Analysis. Oxford: Oxford University Press.
1996 Island Networks: Communication, Kinship, and Classification Structures in Oceania. Cambridge: Cambridge University Press.

Hage, P., F. Harary, and B. Milicic
1995 Hierarchical Opposition. Oceania 65:347–354.
Heeffer, A.
2008 Negative Numbers as an Epistemic Difficult Concept: Some Lessons from History. *In* History and Pedagogy of Mathematics: Satellite Meeting of International Congress on Mathematical Education 11, July 14–18, 2008, Centro Cultural del México Contemporáneo, Mexico City, Mexico. C. Tzanakis, ed. CD-Rom, section 1, 13. Pp. 1–13.
Houseman, M.
1997 Marriage Networks among Australian Aboriginal Populations. Australian Aboriginal Studies 2:2–23.
Houseman, M., and D. R. White
1998 Taking Sides: Marriage Networks and Dravidian Kinship in Lowland South America. *In* Transformations of Kinship. M. Godelier, T. Trautmann, and F. Tjon Sie Fat, eds. Pp. 214–243. Washington, DC: Smithsonian Institution Press.
Kay, P., ed.
1971 Explorations in Mathematical Anthropology. Cambridge: MIT Press.
Keesing, R.
1975 Kin Groups and Social Structure. New York: Holt, Rinehart & Winston.
Knox, K. C.
2003 The Negative Side of Nothing: Edward Waring, Isaac Milner and Newtonian Values. *In* From Newton to Hawking: A History of Cambridge University's Lucasian Professors of Mathematics. K. C. Know and R. Noakes, eds. Pp. 205–240. Cambridge: Cambridge University Press.
Kroeber, A.
1952 The Nature of Culture. Chicago: University of Chicago Press.
Kronenfeld, D.
1980 Particularistic or Universalistic Analyses of Fanti Kin Terminology: The Alternative Goals of Terminological Analysis. Man 15:151–169.
1981 Review: Mathematical Social-Cultural Anthropology. American Anthropologist 83:121–142.
2001 Introduction: The Uses of Formal Analysis re Cognitive and Social Issues. Anthropological Theory 1:147–172.
Lai, D.
2001 Alignment, Structural Balance, and International Conflict in the Middle East, 1948–1978. Conflict Management and Peace Science 18:211–249.
Lambert, B.
1981 Equivalence, Authority and Complementarity in Butaritari-Makin Sibling Relationships (Northern Gilbert Islands). *In* Siblingship in Oceania. M. Marshall, ed. Pp. 149–200. Ann Arbor: University of Michigan.
Leaf, M.
2006 Experimental Analysis of Kinship. Ethnology 45:305–330.
Leaf, Murray, and Dwight Read
N.d. Empirical Formal Analysis in Anthropology: A New Science. Unpublished MS.
Lehman, F. K., and K. Witz
1974 Prolegomena to a Formal Theory of Kinship. *In* Genealogical Mathematics. P. Ballonoff, ed. Pp. 111–134. Paris: Mouton.
Levinson, S. C.
2002 Matrilineal Clans and Kin Terms on Rossel Island. Linguistics 48:1–43.
Lévi-Strauss, Claude
1967[1949] Les Structures élémentaires de la parenté [Elementary Kinship Structures]. 2nd edition. Paris: Mouton. Eng. trans. Boston, MA: Beacon Press, 1971.

Lounsbury, F. G.
1964 A Formal Account of Crow- and Omaha-Type Kinship Terminologies. *In* Explorations in Cultural Anthropology. W. H. Goodenough, ed. Pp. 351–393. New York: McGraw-Hill.

Marshall, M., ed.
1981 Siblingship in Oceania: Studies in the Meaning of Kin Relations. Ann Arbor: University of Michigan Press.

Needham, Rodney
1975 Polythetic Classification: Convergence and Consequences. Man 10(3):349–369.

O'Connor, J. J., and E. F. Robertson
2000 Brahmagupta. http://www-groups.dcs.st-and.ac.uk/~history/Printonly/Brahmagupta.html, accessed September 21, 2010.

Peirce, B.
1881 Linear Associative Algebra. American Journal of Mathematics 4:97–229.

Peirce, C. S.
1956[1902] The Essence of Mathematics. *In* The World of Mathematics, vol. 3. J. R. Newman, ed. Pp. 1773–1783. New York: Simon & Schuster.

Radcliffe-Brown, A.
1913 Three Tribes of Western Australia. Journal of the Royal Anthropological Institute 43:143–194.

Read, D.
1974 Kinship Algebra: A Mathematical Study of Kinship Structure. *In* Genealogical Mathematics. P. Ballonoff, ed. Pp. 135–161. Paris: Mouton.
1984 An Algebraic Account of the American Kinship Terminology. Current Anthropology 25:417–449.
2001 What is Kinship? *In* The Cultural Analysis of Kinship: The Legacy of David Schneider and Its Implications for Anthropological Relativism. R. Feinberg and M. Ottenheimer, eds. Pp. 78–117. Urbana: University of Illinois Press.
2007 Kinship Theory: A Paradigm Shift. Ethnology 46(4):329–365.

Read, D., and C. Behrens.
1990 KAES: An Expert System for the Algebraic Analysis of Kinship Terminologies. Journal of Quantitative Anthropology 2:353–393.

Reay, M.
1975–76 When a Group of Men Takes a Husband. Anthropological Forum 4:77–96.

Rivière, P.
2004 The Amerindinization of Descent and Affinity. *In* Kinship and Family: An Anthropological Reader. R. Parkin and L. Stone, eds. Pp. 104–109. Oxford: Wiley-Blackwell.

Scheffler, H. W., and F. Lounsbury
1971 A Study in Structural Semantics: The Sirionо Kinship System. Englewood Cliffs, NJ: Prentice Hall.

Schieffelin, E. L.
1976 The Sorrow of the Lonely and the Burning of the Dancers. New York: St. Martin's.

Schneider, D. M.
1968 American Kinship: A Cultural Account. Englewood Cliffs, NJ: Prentice Hall.
1972 What is Kinship All About? *In* Kinship Studies in the Morgan Centennial Year. P. Reining, ed. Pp. 32–63. Washington, DC: Anthropological Society of Washington.

Swanton, J. R.
1911 Indian Tribes of the Lower Mississippi Valley. Bulletins of the Bureau of American Ethnology 43:1–387.

Tjon Sie Fat, F. E.
1998 On the Formal Analysis of "Dravidian," "Iroquois," and "Generational" Varieties as Nearly Associative Combinations. *In* Transformations of Kinship. M. Godelier, T. R. Trautmann, and F. E. Tjon Sie Fat, eds. Pp. 59–93. Washington, DC: Smithsonian Institution Press.
White, D.
1972 Mathematical Anthropology. *In* Handbook of Social and Cultural Anthropology. J. J. Honigmann, ed. Chicago: Rand McNally.
White, D., G. P. Murdock, and R. Scaglion
1971 Natchez Class and Rank Reconsidered. Ethnology 10:369–388.

CHAPTER 14

Kinship Theory and Cognitive Theory in Anthropology

F. K. L. Chit Hlaing (F. K. Lehman)

I want, here, to write about the important connection between anthropological work on the domain of kinship and cognitive theory.[1] This is, as I shall demonstrate, a bidirectional connection. On the one hand, one must consider the way in which much work since the 1950s "cognitive revolution," on the analysis of kinship systems and kinship as a domain, has been driven by developments in cognitive anthropology. On the other hand, as I shall try to show in particular, cognitive anthropology itself has been substantially affected by work on the formal, mathematical analysis of social and cultural-conceptual systems This is a somewhat complicated topic, but I have been helped considerably by my recent correspondence with my colleague, the mathematician-anthropologist Dwight Read of UCLA, with whom I am working on a possible monograph on the mathematical analysis of kinship, and who has done so much on kinship and a good deal of work on the relationship between the mathematics of social-cultural systems and cognitive anthropology (see Read and Behrens 1993; Read 2001, 2007, 2010b; and especially now Leaf and Read, in press). So I have decided to try and make only a very few points in this chapter.

First, it is becoming clear that serious work on the cognitive organization of social-cultural systems has to be done in a mathematical framework. That is because what seems essential to the description of any particular social-cultural domain (e.g., kinship) is its conceptual organization as well its particular substantive content (see Lehman 2005). And when one says organization one is necessarily referring to its structure in the sense of *relational* properties, which necessarily entails that "structure" be understood mathematically – as a set of relations closed under a particular algebraic

A Companion to Cognitive Anthropology, First Edition. Edited by David B. Kronenfeld, Giovanni Bennardo, Victor C. de Munck, and Michael D. Fischer.

description; that is, every term in any kinterm system (KTS) has at least one genealogical category mapped in it, and every genealogical category, for example, every well-formed kin type string or word, is mapped uniquely to one kinterm category, a many-to-one mapping. Also, as Read has pointed out in various places, any idea system when applied to the *government* of real time behavior (on human behavior/language above all as *rule-governed*,[2] see the work of Chomsky on generative linguistics, e.g., Chomsky 1957, 1964) is necessarily generative, meaning that one uses it to develop, invent new orderly ways of behaving in real time, new "theorems" if you will, or anyhow output sub-structure for making sense of ways of doing things. Thus, any domain's organizational structure is inherently computational.

So, let us agree to say that what defines any such domain as a distinct culturally defined domain is this computational-generative organization within which the way its substantive content is categorized is, as it were, held together (the relational order of those categories). By way of a useful example in kinship, let me consider now the various, apparently universal facts such as the categories of Mother (M), Father (F), Parent (P), Child (C), Son (S), Daughter (D), and so on. It seems obvious that these elements "make sense" solely with a framework of organization (a structure) involving such dimensions as ascent, descent, generation, lineality, collaterality, and the like (see Lehman and Witz 1974, 1979). Just about all the anthropological kinship literature seems to take this view. But a great deal of it, as I shall argue below, fails to understand it as a formal computational order. And for any given kinship system the same is true (see Read's work again, as cited above). Let us consider, for instance, the English term "uncle." People understand it as B(rother) of P(arent) and then, since B of P can be F of Cousin, as any F of Cousin even if not B of P (so-called Uncle-by-marriage). That is, Cousin = C(hild) of Sib of P, wherewith, by equation, as Read puts it, P of Cousin = Sib of P! In such cases as this one is still involved with the dimensional organization of ascent, descent, generation, and so on, and with collaterality as the dimension defining siblingship, so that cousins are the issue of siblings of lineals! It is clearly not the mere facts of bio-reproduction (the content, so to say) that defines the domain of kinship for human beings, but the conceptual organization and its categories, and this distinguishes human social-cultural kinship from the mammalian or, say, non-human hominid fact of reproduction. There seems to be no evidence from primatology, for instance, that even our nearest anthropoid relatives "recognize" such categories; only that they can somehow relate specially to their own offspring, or fellow offspring of the same mother and so on. Note that "own offspring" is not what we understand by Child, inasmuch as for humans, C implies, by mathematical recursion, the possibility of C being itself a P, and therewith creates the possibility of a grandchild and so on. And similarly, P implies, by the same algebraic generative logic, Grandparent and so on. Likewise "fellow offspring of same M" is not Sibling because, for human cognition, C entails the possibility (the abstract relational category) of what is in English niece or nephew as a relation! And now we note that the recursivity in question (where it is increasingly well understood that it is a special fact of human cognition that our conceptual systems crucially involve recursion) is simply that for any individual (I), if i is categorized in any of the above ways, the possibility necessarily exists of C of i (and, by inversion, P if i) as a relation! So, for instance, the abstract but altogether real category of C of C is relationally defined and, similarly P of P, and so on. And from this we see that kinship as a cultural domain is not about the mere substance of a network of persons linked by reproduction, but about a conceptual structure that can be applied to, indeed imposed upon, networks of persons, assigning *meaning* to those networks. This, as I shall argue below, allows the question to arise as to what kinship, as such networks, is "about" and why it exists, in fact universally for all societies.

Perhaps, now, we can agree that kinship, or indeed any conceptual domain is a system of meaning and knowledge that we use, or rather, construct and learn to relate to our world; construct because it cannot imaginably be acquired by direct information processing, not given the fact of such considerable cultural variation. So, let it be a system of *knowledge*. That is a sufficient premise for what I need to say next.

I must now raise the question of why anthropologists have spent so much effort on the domain of kinship and why so much serious mathematical work has been done on this particular cognitive-conceptual system. I propose that the answer is that in kinship we have a domain of knowledge, or cognition, where we are best able to study its computational properties most readily. Let me explain.

This domain is perhaps uniquely amongst domains of social relations the most *purely relational*. Consider any other social system. To be, say, a student or a teacher one has to know a great deal of the content; one must know how to do all sorts of things. Indeed, all sorts of things are required for any individual to actually be or become either a student or a teacher. To be a student one must know how to study, and so on, and one must be admitted by others to this social identity (SI), using the terminology of the late Roger Keesing (1970). For one to be seen as a student, it is necessary that one be seen or understood to be behaving as such and also that authoritative others be seen to have done something that constitutes one as *admitted*. Now this is true, I claim, in all social domains other than kinship; one has to have learned *how* to be that SI in order to occupy or instantiate it, and it is not sufficient for understanding any such SI to be able just to specify how the different SIs of a domain are related to one another. Teachers are indeed hierarchically above students in terms of *status*, but that is insufficient. Similarly for, say, kings and their subjects, their courtiers, and so on. But to *be* a king it is not enough to be just the son of a previous king; one must be enthroned, installed, and so on. That is, the position can be withheld by others' actions or inactions. What I am pointing out here is that the *role* content of an SI makes all the difference having regard to what I may call individual occupancy of it. And this perhaps explains why Keesing insisted on distinguishing between social identity, role (its enactment, often interactive), and status (what social scientists have usually referred to as the respective rights and duties of SIs to each other in any such system. And so, to know how to *define* an SI in a non-kinship domain requires one to say a lot about role and status. But now consider kinship.

Let us accept to start with the premise that kinship invariably involves, quite centrally, genealogy. Yes, kinship is indeed a social phenomenon. And we can say that it is not simply *about* reproduction (Lehman 1993, 2000).[3] But without question any kinship system is mathematically closed[4] under a map between kinship relations and the space of genealogical categories: for instance, whilst certainly there are adoptive parents and adoptive children and so on, the very meaning of the term *adoption* presupposes non-adoptive, that is, genealogically specified instances of the position. Thus English *uncle* presupposes a male sibling of a parent and so on, as does even the case of the kinship relation of spouse (husband, wife). Although marriage is a cultural matter and involved a jural action on the part of the couple and others as a matter of role and status, one is obliged to define marriage as in some sense legitimizing a connection between a couple such that, at least *inter alia*, where one is a woman she is entitled to bear a child: a relation being established between a man and a woman such that she is a legitimate child-bearer.[5] So even here spouse somehow depends on a presupposed connection between a man and a woman such that it produces a child – whatever the indigenous theory of reproduction may be.[6] So, it is correct to say that spouse is a culturally and jurally sanctioned *form* of being, let us say, "the other parent of one's child." That all sorts of other rights and obligations, legal and otherwise, may attach to marriage, is, for our purposes, beside the point. Thus, for many current societies, it is not problematic if they recognize, for instance, same-sex marriages, granting such couples these culturally or legally particular rights that, *ab origine*, are defined for a mating couple. The argument is not logically different from the one above about adoption.

Proceeding from this, observe something quite unique and important about kinship. Namely, it is a system for which we can most readily study or explore the computational properties because kinship is what one may call *pure relational*. That is to say, what it *means* (taking this term in its cognitive sense) to be an occupant of a kinship category (call it K_{SI}) can at root be defined in purely relational terms. For instance, *child* means immediate lineal descendant (issue, if you will) of a person properly occupying, to oneself, the category of *parent*. So, all one has to be seen to have done in order to be a *child* is exist, that is, to have been born! All anyone else has to do is give birth, which, notice, in English at least (and, for instance, in Burmese and other southeast Asian languages), is not an action verb, but rather a stative verb. By existence, at least in the default, one is the child of one's mother and a woman is the mother of that child. And, inasmuch as it is universally understood that no woman gives birth without in some way or other being paired with a man, that man (whoever he may be) simply *is* father to that child (see above). That he may be, using English common law terms, a person unknown is entirely inconsequential. One has, in virtue of nothing other than one's existence, a F and a M. Furthermore, since each of those is deemed to exist, each also has a F and M (F and M falling into the gender-free category of Parent), and so on recursively. But this gives us only lineal ascent, and, simply by inversion, descent. How about non-lineality?

I start with assuming that parents may have been identified. If at least the M has another child, it is one's sibling (B or Z[sister]), again by virtue of existence alone. The same logic gives siblings, if any of course, to all lineal ascendants, and by inversion, relations of lineal descent from siblings and from parental siblings (say uncles and aunts in English anyhow, that is MB, FB, MZ, FZ, PSib), which gives the genealogical specification for English nieces and nephews and cousins.[7] For, the former are just C of Sibling and C of Sib of P, respectively. And by recursion, C of cousin gives us, in English, cousin, we find that *cousin* is specifiable as any lineal descendant of a parental sibling (for the formal feature specification of such ablineals in Goodenough's (1965) sense, see Lehman and Witz 1974, 1979), whilst for the ablineals from one's own siblings, by a similar logic, "The parent of a niece/nephew is a niece/nephew unless that parent is a sibling (to self)." So there is no way in which one can avoid saying that genealogy "feeds" the meanings of categories in KTS. And (see note 4), whilst indeed there have to be all sorts of encyclopedic meanings for every such category constituting what we know *about* them, there is one remarkable fact about kinship that distinguishes it in its pure relational sense.

That is, a person may be the worst instance of any such category and yet this has no direct bearing upon the relationship in question. True, custody of a child may be legally removed from a bad parent, but they still are, both legally and colloquially (using English examples), "parent and child." If, say, we consider the orthodox Jewish custom of "sitting shiva," where the parents of a child deemed religiously "beyond the pale" declare the child dead and arrange the house in the fashion of mourning, we find that though the parents say "I have no such child," the child, who is obviously not dead, still claims them as parents. Similarly for the less well-understood instances of so-called "disowning" of a wayward child. Note that in such cases whatever relationship is said to be severed, it is not the genealogical connection but rather the jural one involving the KTS, basically, to which is attached all the "rights and duties." Some of these of course are actionable at laws, but none of them defines the relation as non-existent. In other words, adopting some categories from the British social anthropologist M. G. Smith (1974), we may think of the space of genealogical relations as the *commission* underlying the *office* of the jural kin relation.[8] Thus we may say that where a commission is not withholdable, its office's jural rights and duties are not definitive of the relationship inherent in that the office cannot *define* occupancy. And the one social-cultural system that fits this rule is, of course, kinship.

The consequence of this line of reasoning is that uniquely in kinship we can study from a cognitive point of view what a system is all about. That is, the knowledge that people seem to have that makes it possible for them to understand their domain of kinship in the sense of making it definable for them need not work with all the baggage of what I called behavioral "content," which here would be everything about how to be a Son, Daughter, Mother, Father, and so on. What remains, then, means we can do a good job as cognitive scientists by concentrating upon the formal, relational properties of the system! Indeed, as I shall say below, much of the history of anthropological work on kinship for the past 40 or 50 years has been along these lines. To "know" what it takes to "be a …" within kinship is not to know how to enact its role, but rather something more abstractly formal, for example, how to know such things as that if so-and-so is called Cousin (in English), then necessarily, either one of his or her Parents is to be called Uncle or Aunt, or Cousin, such that, eventually one reaches a Cousin whose parent is an Uncle or Aunt. Notice that this is a computational form of knowledge, and this is precisely the focus of all the work of Dwight Read (2001, 2007, 2010b) and his colleagues. To say that people know how to compute such quasi-closed systems of relations is to say that they know its structure. Still, a formal or algebraic description, as in Read's work, *of* that structure can be taken only as a *model* of the cognition; nobody is claiming that ordinary members of society have, as their knowledge of the kinship system, this notational algebra in their heads – certainly not consciously. The same caveat applies *pari passu* to all the work I shall mention below (including my own) on the obviously cognitive question of what it is in our heads that lets us know which of the infinitely many categories in PGS (primary genealogical space) is to be called what in the KTS, in the map under which the latter is closed; where PGS means primary genealogical space of relations, and KTS is the jurally related, culturally specific kinterm space.

I shall say that such specifically cognitive formal work on kinship as a domain started with the beginnings of cognitive anthropology in the 1960s; prior to that time, cognitive issues simply were not raised and the work on kinship was quite generally that of trying to reduce the variety of such systems to some kind of order, to classify them (see Murdock 1949 and references there). This certainly involved working out a language with which to describe systems of kin terminology and thus also to uncover principles of order; and much depended upon a fairly naive and obvious analysis of the space of genealogy. So its organization was considered as having to do with ascent, descent, generation, lineality vs. colaterality and, of course gender, yet no attempt was made to understand these dimensions formally. They were taken as a colloquial heuristic, so that a *typology* of particular systems was to be understood in terms of what happens to these dimensions of genealogical differentiation. So we get the idea of *merging* of collaterality and lineality, the presence or absence of *bifurcation* (tracing through parental links according to parental gender and so on). Such connections were based largely upon categories of descent group organization – agnation/patriliny, uterrinity/matriliny, and the like – but with no attempt to formalize such notions. That is to say, no attempt was made to formalize genealogical space as an algebraic structure.

Why is that important? Because it turns out that the very cognitive problem that cognitive anthropologists began by addressing in kinship could not otherwise be solved. It is the work of Floyd Lounsbury I have in mind (see Lounsbury 1964, 1965; Scheffler and Lounsbury 1971). In effect, he took his cue from Ward Goodenough (1971), who had stated that the goal of cognitive anthropology was to figure out what it is that someone has to *know* in order to act as a member of his or her given society. This assumes that cognitive knowledge generates behavior, whereas we know that the relation between rules and behavior is one of *rule government* in the sense of generative linguistics, where knowledge monitors and allows making sense of behavior and is not itself a performance engine; the evidence is from the common fact of ill-formed behavior. That Goodenough took that view is clear from the fact that he attended to ill-formed behavior by trying to claim that it was generated by "rules for breaking rules," but this leads only to an infinite regress of such rules. Lounsbury's intention was to try to specify what it is that people know in order to be able to say which kin types belong to which kinship terminological categories. Obviously that is a big order because of the at least quasi-infinite size of genealogical space. Memory and knowledge, after all, are in some sense or other "stored" in the brain and therefore, in cases such as this, there must be some finite means for knowing all the mappings from genealogy to kinterm categories.

Lounsbury felt, correctly, that one could hardly memorize it all but had to have in some sense recursive well-formedness rules for that mapping from PGS to KTS as we would now say, following Read and me. However, all he had to work with was the set of kin types, the relative product notation that, I think, we owe originally to Murdock (who was Lounsbury's teacher); and it was this that he used to describe and deal with genealogy. Therefore, he chose to try and formulate rules that took kin type strings into kinterms. For any given kinship system he dealt with (Crow–Omaha, and so on), he had to formulate a very small set of such rules that could apply recursively to any and all kin type strings and these were what are known (borrowing from generative linguistics and its phrase structure-cum-transformation computational algebra) as "rewrite rules." It is easy to show what was involved by taking an example – that of an Omaha system, which places certain kintypes cross-generationally into superior or inferior generations. One of Lounsbury's core rules for such systems was one that lowered kin through one's own out-marrying female agnates: FZ → Z (making an out-marrying father's sister fall together with sister). Then, for any longer kin type string, notated as … FZ …, the rule would apply again and again reducing the string to … Z … This sort of apparatus does capture a degree of *generalization* of the mapping, but clearly it remains to a considerable extent just a point-to-point mapping of categories into categories, because the rules, though themselves a fairly small finite set, must keep applying over infinitely many genealogical kin types to "complete" the map's description of the requisite knowledge. This is again to say that Lounsbury's rewrite system said nothing about the organization of genealogical space itself, and therefore leaves one with the problem of specifying *that* infinite knowledge other than just the relative product string notation or terminology; But one has to question whether that is all there is to the structure of genealogical space. The notation is indeed a finite means for generating infinite output: one starts with a small set of elementary kintypes, F, M, S, D, B, Z, Sp, and one allows them to be composed endlessly by left-to-right concatenation. Thus, for example, FB, FBS, and so on. But somehow what is lacking is anything of the orderly *meaning* of these kin type "words." This problem derives from the essentially positivist and behaviorist assumptions of, for example, Murdock's work and his view that these are just words for positions in actual, observable clusters of actual persons in families. In this view, the core elements of the strings are taken to refer to the elementary (nuclear) family configurations of any speaker – the family of orientation (parents and siblings) and the family of procreation (children, spouses) – and longer strings are taken to refer to positions (or, rather, substantive social relations) in families linked beyond the elementary family; secondary kin are members of families connected through siblings (e.g., one's sibling's family of procreation, one's parents' siblings and their families of procreation, and so on), such that one is taking each primary relative, so to say, and considering his or her family of procreation and so on! The difficulty is that the organization of these families remains unspecified save for the kin type notation, and this is to say that the essential facts about such relations, such as the fact that parents are genealogically ascendant, children descendant (all lineal), that Sp is at least *inter alia* the other P of one's C (real if possible), and so on.

Thus genealogical space can be seen as categories held together along such well-known dimensions as ascent, descent, lineality, collaterality, relative generation, et cetera. The cognitive anthropologist Ward Goodenough (1965) in his work on the kin terminology of American English (a "descriptive" terminology, which does not collapse dimensionally distinct genealogical categories into single kin categories), clarified our understanding of these dimensionalities and pointed out that there is a distinction to be drawn between two sorts of collaterality, or non-lineality, namely, that collaterals who are siblings of lineals have to be seen as what he called colineals, and others as ablineals, as pointed out above. This turned out to be of great importance for the foundations of cognitive anthropology dealing with kinship. In order to make this clear, I must refer to what may amount to the very beginnings of such work, namely, Wallace and Atkins (1960), both of whom had been pupils of Goodenough.

In that seminal paper they built on Goodenough's distinction, and used it to give a meaning account of English kinterms as follows. They proposed, following Goodenough, that the feature composition for uncle/aunt, as against cousin, had to include a specification that amounted to [–lineal, –collateral], which is to say ablineal. For them, uncles/aunts, and also siblings (B, Z) were in some sense nearer to being lineals than other collaterals. Their arguments were disputed by another early paper on the cognitive anthropology of kinship (particularly kinterm) meanings, namely Romney and D'Andrade (1964). Using an experimental technique from psychology, Romney and D'Andrade proceeded to try and test Wallace and Atkins's claim, as stated above. They used the free listing method. They used as subjects undergraduate students at Stanford University and asked them to write down a list of all the English language terms of kin relationship they could think of. They considered the resulting lists and found, not unexpectedly, that there was a statistically significant block ordering of items in the lists; the lists were far from being random. In particular, siblings turned out almost invariably to be in the same early block as M, F, that is, as kinterms for members of one's families of orientation. Arguing from the essentially behaviorist principles underlying free listing experiments, Romney and D'Andrade concluded that such kinterms referred to those relatives that were in some sense closer to the list writers' experience, and that, therefore, siblings were being semantically grouped with immediate ascendants in such a way that there had to be a semantic dimension of "direct" as part of the meaning of such a grouping. This, they argued, disproved Wallace and Atkins's claim that sibling terms had a meaning component (namely, colineality) that separated siblings from parents; that is, the Romney and D'Andrade claim was that "nearness" (to speaker, or ego, or self) in such lists had to correspond with "nearness" in the semantic space defining the terms (along the lines of the then popular componential analysis version of cognitive anthropology). They gave the name of "direct" to a supposed component of that space that they took to replace the lineality dimension of genealogy. That is, for them, siblings were understood as not any less "close" than parents, as opposed to relatives denoted by other kinterms. This is not, I think, the place to argue the merits of this sort of componentialist semantics in the history of cognitive anthropology. Suffice it for now to point out that meaning was being taken as fundamentally referentialist, or Fregean, that is, reducible to behavioral experience. Now, it is altogether likely that for such free listings, subjects will indeed think first of those kin they have had the most or the earliest experience of but it is far from obvious that this gives one unambiguous evidence of the meaning of such words. In particular, other evidence makes it clear that people quite generally do in fact distinguish between lineal ascent–descent (namely, the parent–child relationship) and non-lineal relations and that speakers readily say and understand that siblings are not in the lineal line of descent–ascent – that there is something conceptual that separates siblingship from this. In fact, were this not the case one would be hard put to understand that for English speakers the children of siblings are not "children" of the speaker, just as our Uncles/Aunts are parents not of siblings but of Cousins! But now let us take a closer look at Wallace and Atkins in this connection.

Consider the speaker's own generation (G_0). There is a readily available answer within Wallace and Atkins's analysis of how it comes about that siblings are somehow "thought of" in immediate connection with parents; for, after all, in this generation there is no relationship that is lineal. [+lineal, –ascendant, –descendant] is simply undefined in genealogical space! Hence, one way or the other, siblings/ablineals are just as "near" as are lineals in any other generation. This is to say, essentially with

Wallace and Atkins, that, if indeed lineals are "nearer" than non-lineals – and that is what Romney and D'Andrade are disputing – in G_0 there is, as it were, nothing nearer semantically than ablineals, and, in effect, one's closest kin in one's own generation are not lineal relatives genealogically, semantically, or whatever. In plain language, *ego* is not a term in genealogical space!

Put another way, there is no reason in good cognitive theory about meaning to suppose that experiential "nearness" has to align with conceptual measures of closeness. Let us remember the undergraduate subjects of the Romney and D'Andrade experiment; they were all or nearly all fairly young students; few if any were married. When one uses an older cohort of subjects (and I myself have done this), one finds, significantly, that the lists tend to show Spouse and Child terms in the earliest block or in a very early one, which was not the case with Romney and D'Andrade's lists.[9]

The foregoing ought to make it clear what the beginnings of the cognitive anthropology of kinship were, and it is now necessary to show where it went from there and why. In particular, there is a fundamental difference between (1) accounting for the structure of a kin system (KTS) and (2) accounting for how people know whom to call what! For the structure of a given system of kinterms (a KTS) cannot be understood as a function of the structure of PGS, in spite of the fact that category-theoretic morphisms on the dimensional structure of PGS constitute a proper map to the categories of a KTS (see Lehman and Witz 1979), and despite the fact that such morphisms on PGS essentially constitute a deformation (a sort of folding of dimensions onto dimensions) of PGS that in effect takes PGS as a (quasi-)infinite set of categories into a *much* smaller space – after all, the number of pair-wise distinct terms or categories in any KTS is very small indeed, never more than, say, 30. Indeed, it has always seemed to me that PGS is simply too utterly vast to be useful as a set of categories each of which has associated with it its own behavioral rule or expectations, specifying how one is expected to act as an occupant of such a category, and/or how one is to interact with an occupant of each such category. One could not imaginably keep track of all that for all the categories of PGS; memory, however it is registered in the brain, is in some sense storage, and storage space is necessarily finite. Perhaps, then, this underlies the universal need for such a map.

Nevertheless, there is no evidence to suggest that this compacting of PGS generates the actual structure of any KTS. True, the various different KT systems that have been explored by Read and his colleagues all "inherit" (from *universal* PGS[10]) certain PGS dimensionalities, such as ascent, descent, and generation, but surely that is owing to the fact that what a KTS inherits is fundamentally the fact of parent and child core relations, namely the fact of a person's existence (see above) arising from having been born (to a mother). That and the mathematical operation of recursion create a space of categories linking together "related" sets of such core relations: if C implies M, then, necessarily, for any person_x = M, that person has to have been a C to some other person_y = M, and so forth. Let me quote Dwight Read here:

> how we can begin to relate the general notion of a family and positions in family (not genealogical positions, not kin term positions, but more fundamentally the idea of say motherhood) and how one goes from there to the PGS via recursion and to KTS via

> kin term products, so that products in KTS become a symbolic computational system so that one can go from genealogical tracing to kin term products, calculate the kin term products to arrive at a kin term, and then map back to PGS to construct the genealogical definition of a kin term. [Personal communication, May 2010]

This is relevant to an old issue in the anthropology of kinship from long before the advent of cognitive theory, namely, the possible relationship between kin terminology systems and behavioral social organization. This issue is dealt with to a considerable extent in Murdock (1949). And, of course, all the formal work on systems of marriage, starting with Lévi-Strauss (1949), and all the subsequent applications of group theory in mathematics, starting with André Weil's appendix in Lévi-Strauss's book, is essentially about just this question, as is much of the work – largely in British social anthropology – trying to relate kin terminologies to descent group organization. It is largely the latter lines of work that Murdock argues against successfully. But both the Radcliffe-Brownians and Murdock are positivist behaviorists philosophically and psychologically, and thus both are engaged in trying to reduce abstract conceptual systems to directly observable (objectivist) "facts on the ground" (see Leaf and Read, in press); in Murdock's case, immediate family organization and physical co-residence. Beginning with Lounsbury (cited above) at least, all the cognitive anthropology about kinship term systems has properly rejected accounts of such systems in terms of their supposed reflection of concrete social organization. It is particularly clear that one's knowledge of one's kin terminology system and what genealogical kin belong to what KTS category cannot be accounted for on the basis of similarity of social (e.g., lineage role) position. With regard to Lounsbury's position, there is a wonderful discussion, dated 1974, between him and David Kronenfeld, which I am indebted to Professor Kronenfeld for sharing. Kronenfeld himself (as in his book on kinship theory 2009) makes some use of such behavioral features, and Lounsbury's position is stated clearly in that correspondence:

> I have always felt that the patterns of kinship behavior, and the categorizations of kinsmen effected by such behavior, must have common roots with the kin-labeling behavior and the categorization made by it, but that it would be simplistic and unrealistic to expect that the behavior between persons should generalize along just the same lines laid out in terminological categorization. One would expect rather that for each and every different kind of behavior, considerations at least to some degree different should be relevant. To admit this may restrict somewhat the expected significance of the terminological system as an object of study for the ethnographer, but not to the extent that some of our colleagues – on both sides of the Atlantic – have felt, and certainly not to the extent of removing it from the roster of things meriting the most careful inquiry. [Personal communication from Lounsbury to Kronenfeld, and from Kronenfeld to author]

My position here is this: (1) As stated above, for kinship most particularly, the problem with thoroughgoing appeal to organizational-behavioral facts on the ground to explain kin categorization is that they do not count as anything defining occupancy of a category. In the foregoing quote, something very like this position is adumbrated. (2) In my own work on kin terminologies of a more or less "Omaha" type – based on my ethnographic work with Chin peoples of the India–Burma borderlands, I have had to relate the differential generational skewing (Lehman and Witz 1979) to what amounts to the difference organizationally between wife-giver lineages and wife-taker lineages. However, it turned out that this can easily and appropriately be given in terms of the structure of the genealogical space. That is, wife-givers are readily described as agnates of women married to male agnates (I denoted this with a feature [+maternal agnate]), while wife-takers turn out to be simply the inverse of this specification, namely agnates of issue of sisters and daughters of one's own agnates. And, in general, appeals to social position and so on can always be stated in terms of the structure of genealogical space, often, in fact, in terms of modes of lineation (agnation and so on, but given computationally in terms of direct successions of matri- and patri-filiation). It should be noticed that Read's apparent revival of this issue is stated in such a way as to avoid the aforementioned behaviorist biases of the earlier tradition and is given in terms of the basic relation feeding the recursive computation that lies at the very heart of peculiarly human cognitive capacity.

Now, Read and his colleagues (Read and Behrens 1990, 1993; Read 2001, 2007, 2010a, 2010b; Bennardo and Read 2005, 2007) have shown persuasively that a KTS has a distinct algebraic structure that is not all that much like PGS, and that is altogether unlikely to be generated by the compacting of PGS (see above). For one thing, the equivalent in a KTS, depending upon such things as whether it is a so-called classificatory system (i.e., merging into single categories both PGS lineal and PGS collaterals) or not, or the PGS generating relational element P/C may be something entirely different, such as to include the sibling term; moreover, the structure of a KTS, unsurprisingly, may be sensitive to such things as the sex of "self" (whether "speaker" is male or female). In addition, Read argues that the KTS categories and their relationships may have motivations additional to, or independent of, any PGS dimensionalities PGS → KTS morphisms as dealt with in the immediately preceding paragraph; motivations perhaps not unrelated to the social-organizational considerations dealt with in Read's remarks quoted at length above from his personal communication of May 2010. It seems to me that one of the most significant facts about this work is something that I have never been able to handle effectively from the standpoint of PGS, namely, that Read's algebraic structures are in large measure based upon the kind of knowledge speakers have of the proper way to "navigate" the KTS system. That is, the structure specifies knowledge of the following kind (using examples from English here): "the father of my ortho-cousin is an uncle, the child of a sister/brother is a niece/nephew, the son of a niece is an x-nephew (where x stands for a modifier like "grand," "great," and its iterations such as "great grand," and so on. Or, consider an Omaha-type system such as that of Lai (Haka) Chin from my own field materials. Any speaker simply knows that, for example, C [*fa*] of B [*u-naau*] = C [*fa*], whilst C of Z [*far*] = grandchild [*tu*]. One can more or less indirectly deduce such equations from the logic of the PGS > KTS morphism map, but that is demonstrably not what native speakers do; it is not how they represent or talk about such knowledge. Thus Read is led to argue that the KTS structure is indeed independently motivated and that, as he said in the above quoted communication, one goes "to KTS *via* kin term products, so that products in KTS become a symbolic computational system so that one can go from genealogical tracing to kin term products, calculate the kin term products to arrive at a kin term, then map back to PGS to get or construct the genealogical definition of a kin term." One notes, with Read that the kinterm products, represented by "the x of a y is a z," are algebraically not the same things as the relative products of kin type strings in the conventional genealogical notation; an expression such as FMD directly represents a genealogical category, it is a "string" in the sense of being a wordlike expression of that category. The KTS products are not wordlike in that sense, but rather are ways of proceeding from already existing category to already existing category, representing, as it were, the structural logic of navigating the KTS. Moreover, the navigational algebraic structure closes the KTS! Eventually it takes on back to the "self"-like starting point and does this without, as in PGS, having to calculate inverses. In PGS, one has to know that, for example, C is the inverse of P(arent) and so on, from which one works out that if one calls someone "x," then the person so called must call one "y" (the so-called "ego-alter relation" in traditional work). This is not what is done in navigating a KTS.

Of course to ***know*** a KTS in the cognitive science sense is not in and of itself to know the algebra of the structure. Clearly, ordinary speakers do not, in fact cannot, talk about it in the way they can and do talk about dimensionalities such as ascent, descent, generation, and so on. The algebra does, nonetheless, account for the way one calculates relations between the categories of a KTS.[11]

I have tried here to make as understandable as I can in a brief chapter three things: (1) how the history of anthropological work on kinship has developed in response to the development of cognitive theory in anthropology, (2) how and why so much of the work on kinship has necessarily been formal-mathematical, and (3) what the relation has turned out to be between the so-called kinship-algebra part of anthropology and cognitive theory; what kinship as an especially formal-mathematical domain can teach us about what cognitive anthropology has to be. Obviously, ordinary members of any sociocultural community do not *know*, in the sense of being able to talk about their kinship system or any system of their social-cultural repertoire in the formal language of mathematics. But does this mean that they do not in some genuinely cognitive sense "know" the formal structure? Hardly! After all, we know, for example, our language and its grammar, even though we cannot express that knowledge articulately, and the same goes for our knowledge of the domain of number and so on. Quite generally, people know a great deal they are unable (without the work of technical specialists) to express directly. Our professional work on formalisms is precisely about how to *specify* much of our cognitive knowledge. The domain of kinship turns out to be a lovely case of/for the intimate connection between cognitive and mathematical theory. I have tried to show that here and the matter is spelled out at great length by Leaf and Read (in press), as shown by its very title, *Human Social Organization and the Computational Mind.*

NOTES

1 Let me try to say how I understand the notion of a cognitive domain. Kinship, or any domain, is a system of meanings or knowledge, a way of knowing (assigning interpretation to) parts and aspects of the world.

2 *Rule government* means that formal rules do not act as a performance engine for behavior, but rather as a set of well-formedness conditions that allow an actor or speaker to interpret and evaluate his or her behavior (or that of others); in particular, it is what leads to things like real time self-correction.

3 It is well known that Radcliffe-Brown (1950) set up the distinction between genealogy and jural kin relations. However, it is clear now that reducing genealogy, which is quite an abstract computational order, to bio-reproduction, cannot hold.

4 That is, each and every category in a kinship system has at least one genealogical position in it and this exhausts all genealogical positions, and no other social system is the object of that map.

5 Note that the man may not necessarily be the reproductive father as in the case of the Nayar of southwest India, where, at least in north Kerala, the marriage ceremony is with a chosen *talikettuvar* (in the Malayalam language) and after it a woman may take approved consorts, one of whom may be the birth father of her legitimate offspring, and the *talikettuvar* (literally, the one who ties on the marriage amulet) need not be any of the consorts. And, say, in the case of the Moso of southeast China (Cai 2001; Shih 2001), where a commoner woman need not marry in order to bear legitimate children because for commoners marriage is not required since, politically, they are perpetual minors under the jurisdiction of the chiefs. Here the *talikettuvar* is not a F in any sociocultural sense, only a sort of husband, but in fact it is through him that her children trace what amounts precisely to a genealogical tracing of affinity between their *tarwad* (matrilineage) and the family of the *talikettuvar*. A chosen consort is taken to have legitimately "fathered" the child, and yet he and the *talikettuvar* are not given any jural rights over the woman or the child, nor does he ever reside in her *tarwad*. Nor are they ever given the title or kinterm *appan* (Father) by the child. However, the *talikettuvar* is the object of a period of mourning by the child when he dies, and the connection between his family or lineage and the woman's *tarwad* is kept in the record, constituting what amounts to affinity.

6 If indeed Australian Aborigines and Melanesian Trobrianders used not to understand the male's physical role in conception, it is nonetheless clear that they thought that in some way a man had to have been with a woman physically for her to be impregnated even by some spiritual entity! And parthenogenetic pregnancies, if any, are understood as alternatives to a default kind owing to the ordinary kind.

7 Not a definition, structurally, as Read has cogently argued, but only genealogical specification in the PGS-KTS map (see above). Whilst it remains true that the PGS (primary genealogical space) dimensional features for the default mapping to any KTS category provides a proper lexical meaning for the category (call it *c*), this cannot be taken as *defining c*. The map does not constitute a mechanism that lets PGS *generate* KTS, since it has never been shown that the algebraic structure of KTS is produced by any such map! Similarly, for neither PGS nor KTS does anything like everything a culture supposes (or its bearers *know*) about any category – or what Dan Sperber (1974) calls encyclopedia knowledge about any such category count as defining the category cognitively.

8 As when a military officer is commissioned, which does not give the officer actual rights of command until he or she is posted.

9 This issue is related to another piece of work in the cognitive-formal analysis of kinship, by the early cognitive anthropologist Stephen Tyler (1969), who made it clear once and for all that a genealogical system is a system of algebraic relations amongst categories and therefore has to be freed from the traditional centering on a given person (ego) and his or her kin. "Ego" has (though Tyler failed to make the point) to be an "identity" *on* relations and cannot ever be used as a kinterm, a term for a relation; one's *self* is not a kin relation; more particularly, "Ego" is not any kind of universal reciprocal or inverse of any kin type. Making Ego a sort of central term, as in a usual pedigree chart, hides the inverse relations: the inverse of Parent is not Ego even though I am my own parents' child. The inverse of P is, of course, Child. Furthermore, Tyler criticized the usual analysis of genealogical space in the form of kin type strings (relative product strings), observing that the so-called primitives of the set of kin types are by no means all true primes structurally. Clearly (see above) Spouse

is analyzable at its root, as P of C, whilst, similarly, siblings are C of P (let us say parent's "other" child). The computational organization of genealogical space (PGS) cannot be derived otherwise, that is, in terms of the parent–child core relationship and the associated dimensionalities of ascent, descent, generation, and so on.

10 In fact Atkins (1974) called what we now refer to as PGS (P for "primary") "universal genealogical space," and to say, *pace* Schneider (1972, 1984) and other relativists, that PGS underlies all kinship is only to say that this "inheritance" of dimensional order exists for any KTS. Schneider's position was that ethnographers have used the genealogical method of Rivers (1910) in their fieldwork on kinship, and that this constitutes using a "Western" genealogical "game" with exotic informants or consultants. But even if we were to suppose it is a sort of game, that ordinarily our ethnographic subjects do not talk about kin relations in genealogical terms (a very disputed claim), it remains peculiar that our subjects readily, indeed universally, understand the rules of the game, so that it must, indeed, be a universal of kinship as a conceptual domain.

11 In order to illustrate the foregoing, see Read and Behrens 1990 and Leaf and Read, n.d.:

> The way one elicits the data directly from kinterms without the genealogical method is to get the following kind of data "If I use _____ to refer to X, and X uses _____ to refer to Y, then I should use _____ to refer to Y."
>
> [The] KAES program links an algebraic structure isomorphic to sets of genealogical kin types by first mapping the *generating elements in the algebra* to kin types and then mapping algebraic products to sets of kin types in accordance with the algebraic structure. This yields a mapping of the algebraic structure onto the genealogical space. [Read and Behrens 1993:193, emphasis added]

> I have shown that the structural difference between descriptive and classificatory terminologies may be structurally expressed by whether the kin term structure is generated from a single ascending kin term (such as parent in the case of the AKT [American/English KT]) or is generated by an ascending kin term and a horizontal (sibling) kin term (such as *appa* or *annan* for the Nakarattar [south Indian, Dravidian] terminology). A term used to generate a terminology will be called a *generating term*. The distinction between these two sets of generating terms is whether, as in the AKT, brother and sister are compound terms, namely son of parent = brother and daughter of parent = sister, or whether a sibling term such as *annan* in the Nakarattar terminology, is a primary, hence an irreducible, kin term. [Leaf and Read, n.d.]

REFERENCES

Atkins, John R.

1974 GRAFIK: A Multipurpose Kinship Metalanguage. *In* Genealogical Mathematics. Paul A. Ballonoff, ed. Pp. 27–52. The Hague: Mouton.

Bennardo, G., and D. Read

2005 The Tongan Kinship Terminology: Insights from an Algebraic Analysis. Mathematical Anthropology and Cultural Theory 2. http://www.mathematicalanthropology.org/pdf/Bennardo&Read1205.pdf, accessed September 22, 2010.

2007 Cognition, Algebra, and Culture in the Tongan Kinship. Journal of Cognition and Culture 7:49–88.

Cai, Hua

2001 A Society without Fathers or Husbands: The Na of China. New York: Zone.

Chomsky, N. A.

1957 Syntactic Structures. The Hague: Mouton.

1964 Current Issues in Linguistic Theory. The Hague: Mouton.

Goodenough, Ward H.

1965 Yankee Kinship Terminology: A Problem in Componential Analysis. American Anthropologist 67(5.2):259–287.

1971 Culture, Language and Society. Addison-Wesley Modules in Anthropology. Reading, MA: Addison-Wesley.

Keesing, Roger M.

1970 Toward a Model of Role Analysis. *In* A Handbook of Method in Cultural Anthropology. R. Cohen and R. Narroll, eds. Pp. 423–453. New York: Natural History Press.

Kronenfeld, David B.

2009 Fanti Kinship and the Analysis of Kinship Terminologies. Urbana: University of Illinois Press.

Leaf, Murray, and Dwight W. Read

In press Human Social Organization and the Computational Mind: Ethnology as a Formal Science.

Lehman, F. K.

1985 Cognition and Computation. *In* Directions in Cognitive Anthropology. Janet W. D. Dougherty, ed. Pp. 19–48 Urbana: University of Illinois Press.

1993 The Relationship between Genealogical and Terminological Structure in Kinship. Journal of Quantitative Anthropology 4(1):90–122.

2000 Aspects of a Formal Theory of Kinship: The Functional Basis of Its Genealogical Roots, and Some Extensions in Generalized Alliance Theory. Anthropological Theory 1(2):212–239.

2005 On the "Globality Hypothesis" about Social/Cultural Structure: An Algebraic Solution. Special issue, "Cultural Systems," Cybernetics and Systems 36(8):803–816.

Lehman, F. K., and Klaus G. Witz

1974 Prolegomena to a Formal Theory of Kinship. *In* Genealogical Mathematics. Paul A. Ballonoff, ed. Pp. 11–134. The Hague: Mouton.

1979 A Formal Theory of Kinship: The Transformational Component Committee on Culture and Cognition, University of Illinois at Urbana–Champaign, Report no. 11.

Lévi-Strauss, Claude

1949[1969] Les Structures élémenaires de la parenté. Paris: Presses Universitaires de France. *English translation*: The Elementary Structures of Kinship. Boston, MA: Beacon.

Lounsbury, Floyd G.

1964 A Formal Account of the Crow- and Omaha-Type Kinship Terminologies. *In* Explorations in Cultural Anthropology. Ward Goodenough, ed. Pp. 251–293. New York: McGraw-Hill.

1965 Another View of Trobriand Kinship Categories. American Anthropologist 67(5.2):142–185.

Murdock, George Peter

1949 Social Structure. New York: Macmillan.

Radcliffe-Brown, A. R.

1950 Introduction. *In* African Systems of Kinship and Marriage. A. R. Radcliffe-Brown and C. D. Forde, eds. Oxford: Oxford University Press.

Read, Dwight W.

2001 What is Kinship? *In* The Cultural Analysis of Kinship: The Legacy of David Schneider and Its Implications for Anthropological Relativism. R. Feinberg and A. Ottenheimer, eds. Pp. 78–117. Urbana: University of Illinois Press.

2007 Kinship Theory: A Paradigm Shift. Ethnology 46:329–364.

2010a The Generative Logic of Dravidian Language Terminologies. Mathematical Anthropology and Cultural Theory 3(7). http://www.mathematicalanthropology.org/pdf/Read.0810.pdf, accessed September 24, 2010.

2010b The Logic and Structure of Kinship Terminologies: Implications for Theory and Historical Reconstructions. *In* Per Hage and the Renaissance in Kinship Studies. D. Jones and B. Milkic, eds. Salt Lake City: University of Utah Press.

Read, Dwight W., and C. Behrens

1990 KAES: An Expert System for the Algebraic Analysis of Kinship Terminologies. Journal of Quantitative Anthropology 2:353–393.

1993 KAES: An Expert System for the Algebraic Analysis of Kinship Systems. Journal of Quantitative Anthropology 4(1): 353–393. http://kaes.anthrosciences.net, accessed September 22, 2010.

Rivers, W. H. R.

1910 The Genealogical Method of Anthropological Enquiry. Sociological Review. 2:1–12.

Romney, A. Kimball, and Roy G. D'Andrade

1964 Cognitive Aspects of English Kin Terms. American Anthropologist 66(1):146–170.

Scheffler, Harold W., and Floyd G. Lounsbury

1971 A Study in Structural Semantics: The Siriono Kinship System. Englewood Cliffs, NJ: Prentice Hall.

Schneider, David

1972 What is Kinship All About? *In* Kinship in the Morgan Centennial Year. Priscilla Reining, ed. Washington, DC: Anthropological Society of Washington.

1984 A Critique of the Study of Kinship. Ann Arbor: University of Michigan Press.

Shih, Chuan-Kang

2001 Genesis of Marriage among the Moso and Empire Building in Late Imperial China. Journal of Asian Studies 60(2):381–412.

Smith, M. G.

1974 Corporations and Society. Chicago: Aldine.

Sperber, Dan

1974 Rethinking Symbolism. Cambridge: Cambridge University Press.

Tyler, Stephen A.

1969 The Myth of P: Epistemology and Formal Analysis. American Anthropologist 71(1):71–78.

Wallace, Anthony F. C., and John R. Atkins

1960 The Meaning of Kinship Terms. American Anthropologist 62(1):58–60.

CHAPTER 15 Numerical Cognition and Ethnomathematics

Andrea Bender and Sieghard Beller

In 2004, *Science* published an article on numerical cognition that created a stir. Its author claimed that the language spoken by the Amazonian Pirahã contains numerals for one and two only, and that it is this restricted numeration system that prevented them from accomplishing a range of apparently simple numerical tasks (Gordon 2004). While Gordon himself took these findings as evidence for the assumption that numerical cognition depends on language, others disputed this strong conclusion (Frank et al. 2008; and see comments in Everett 2005).

One of the unresolved questions concerns the direction of causality: Have the Pirahã no concept of exact numerosity because they lack the respective words, or did they never develop such words because they were simply not interested in numbers? Related to this, but addressed less explicitly, is a second question: How and when do specific components of numerical cognition evolve? A particularly strong position is held by Premack and Premack (2005), who suppose that a genuine number representation did not start before the transition from hunting-gathering to agriculture, pastoralism, and trade. While the first question on the direction of causality cannot be resolved in retrospect, the latter, more general, question can be tackled by a comparative approach.

This chapter discusses how people represent numbers and perform numerical operations depending on the specific tools provided by their languages and cultures. The controversy regarding Pirahã numeration system, together with its cognitive implications, helps to illustrate some of the prime questions addressed here:

1 What do we know about the cognitive architecture for numerical cognition?
2 Which tools, both mental and material, are required for number representation and numerical operations?

A Companion to Cognitive Anthropology, First Edition. Edited by David B. Kronenfeld, Giovanni Bennardo, Victor C. de Munck, and Michael D. Fischer.

3 Which implications do the tools' properties have for cognitive processes?

As mathematics is not confined to numerosity, the last section of this paper will go beyond numbers in highlighting some other, more implicit, mathematical fields, thereby also addressing the final question:

4 Do patterns have to be *intentionally* mathematical to be considered as mathematical?

In order to answer these questions, we draw on findings and insights not only from anthropology, but also from other disciplines such as mathematics, linguistics, psychology, and cognitive sciences. We also draw on various instances from both ancient and contemporary cultures, and will present a wide range of notions, from the most obvious part of numerical cognition – counting – to the more complex and intriguing aspects of ethnomathematics.

The Cognitive Architecture of Numerical Cognition

One of the simplest mathematical facts is that objects occur in diverging numbers. A tree can bear five apples or a basketful of apples or so many that nobody would wish to count them. While it may be a question of definition, whether the shriveled fruit dangling from the upmost branch should be considered an apple, the number itself is not. If it counts as an apple, it has to be counted. Although number is an abstract property, it is one that matters: with a basketful of apples, the tree will feed many more people than with only a handful.

In a limited manner, number can be perceived directly. If you try to assess the number of items in each group of Figure 15.1, you may realize a difference: Most likely, you will have an instant impression of the number of dots in (a), but not of the diamonds in (b). Of course, counting 16 items requires more time than counting four, but the difference reaches deeper.

The relatively small number of dots is open to immediate perception called "subitizing." This process is accurate for samples of one and two items, but then continually decreases in accuracy. Usually, *four* is deemed the limit for subitizing (Mandler and Shebo 1982). This is sufficient for the dots, but not the diamonds; obtaining their exact number requires counting. The ordered presentation of squares in (c) contains the same number of items as (b), but can be assessed more quickly and easily owing to its structure of four groups of four squares. In this case, however, the apparently immediate "perception" differs crucially from that in (a): in addition to subitizing four squares as well as four groups of squares, we also need to retrieve from memory the information that four times four equals 16.

Findings like these indicate that numerical cognition is based on two distinct systems (Feigenson et al. 2004): an ability to roughly estimate an amount (*analog numeracy*) and an ability to exactly assess a certain number (*digital numeracy*). On the basis of neuropsychological studies, researchers like Dehaene (1992; and see Campbell 1994) further differentiate digital number representations into those for spoken words and those for written symbols (Figure 15.2).

Quantities, whether distinct or fuzzy, may be assessed by subitizing or estimation. They are then represented in an analog *magnitude code* that allows for the comparison of quantities and approximate calculations and thus constitutes the core preverbal

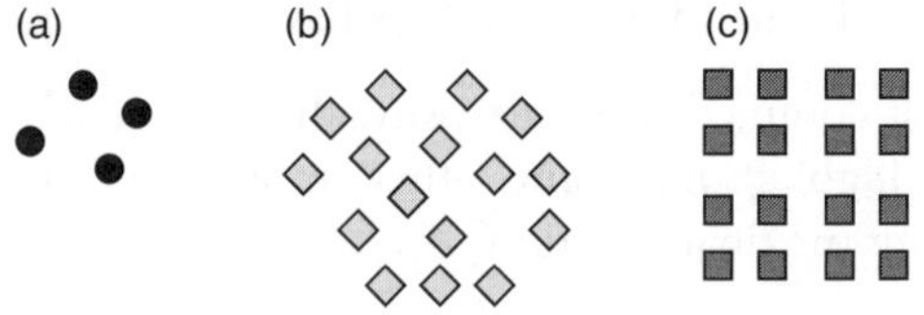

Figure 15.1 How many items are there in each group?

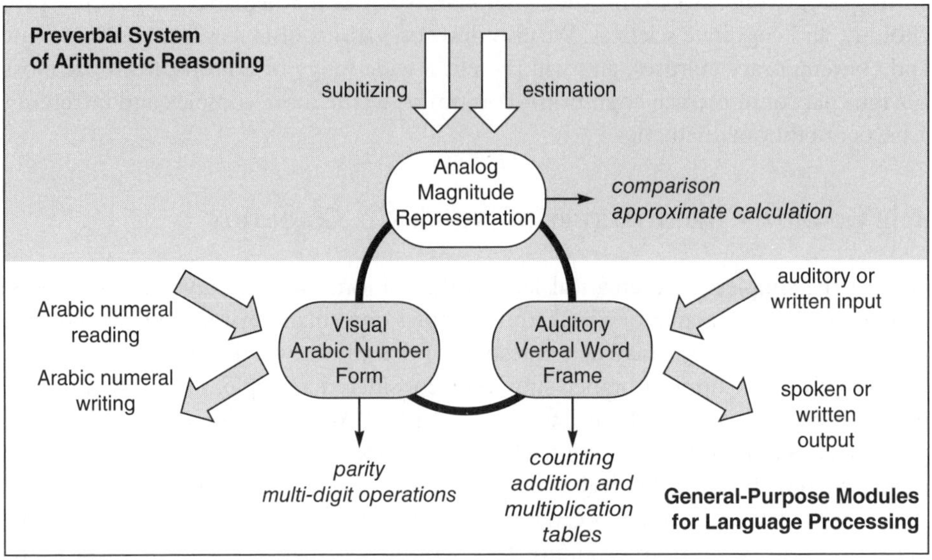

Figure 15.2 The triple-code model for numerical cognition (adapted from Dehaene 1992:31). The three core representations are circled. The large arrows indicate input–output processes; the thin arrows indicate operations specific to each representation. The black circle indicates translation processes between the representations.

system of arithmetic reasoning. In order to achieve an exact assessment of numbers beyond four and to perform exact calculations, items have to be counted. This requires a counting sequence that can be represented as number words only or as external representations, for instance with Arabic numerals. If perceived as words, numbers are represented in an auditory *verbal word code*. This representation not only allows for counting but also provides the addition and multiplication tables necessary for calculations. If numbers are perceived as written symbols (e.g., as Arabic numerals), they are represented in a visual *Arabic number code* that allows for assessment of parity and for more complex calculations. These three codes can be translated into each other to a certain extent, but each representation depends on distinct input processes and enables similarly distinct output processes and operations.

Please note that the model depicted in Figure 15.2 describes the assumed cognitive architecture for people who are fluent in the Arabic numeration system. The model may have to be modified for people not familiar with a notational system and the Arabic system in particular, but attempts to address this concern have been rare. A notable exception is found in the studies on the Pirahã and the Mundurukú in the Amazonian Basin (Gordon 2004; Pica et al. 2004).

Other than the system for analog numeracy that we share with non-human species, the one for digital numeracy is restricted to symbolic representations like language, and thus to humans. Number words and counting sequences form the basis of this digital numeracy (Hurford 1987; Dehaene 1997; Wiese 2003), and as these are to a large extent culture-specific, they offer a great opportunity to study interactions between culture and cognition.

Properties of Numeration Systems

All counting sequences refer to the same entities, namely to a certain section of integers. How this is done, however, is open to a large degree of freedom. The number words, of which these counting sequences consist, therefore constitute specific numeration systems with distinct properties. Among the most relevant properties are extent, dimensionality, base and structure, regularity of composition, degree of abstraction, and availability of a notational system.

Extent

In theory, counting sequences could be infinite; in practice, however, they are not. The finite set of lexemes that constitute natural languages also restrict the system of regularly composed number words. Greenberg (1978:253) defines the *limiting number L* as the next number beyond the highest possible composition. In a regular decimal system with a lexeme for "hundred" as the highest numeral, for instance, the limiting number is 999 + 1 = 1,000.

Languages differ largely with regard to the extent of their numeration system. The Pirahã language, for instance, encompasses words for one and two only (Gordon 2004). Polynesian numeration systems, on the other hand, reach as far as 10^{10} (Bender and Beller 2006b). Whereas the highest number in a numeration system is a matter of great variation, the lowest is not. As natural languages do not need a symbol for zero, the smallest number with which counting starts is typically one (Greenberg 1978).

This does not imply that counting has to proceed in counting units of one. Most languages in Polynesia and some in Micronesia, for instance, adopted and preferred other counting units (such as 2, 4, 5, or 20), at least for some objects of prime cultural significance (Bender and Beller 2006a, 2007).

Dimensionality

Zhang and Norman (1995) distinguish three types of dimensionality. A one-dimensional (1D) system consists of a distinct lexeme for each number, as for instance in the body-part systems abounding in Papua New Guinea (e.g., Saxe 1981; Wassmann and Dasen 1994; and see Figure 15.3).

Two-dimensional (1 × 1D) systems employ a recursive principle for composing number words out of a finite set of numerals, for instance by combining *base* and *power* as in English.

Three-dimensional ((1×1) × 1D) systems are an extension of 1 × 1D systems as they combine main power with sub-base and sub-power. The Roman numeral system

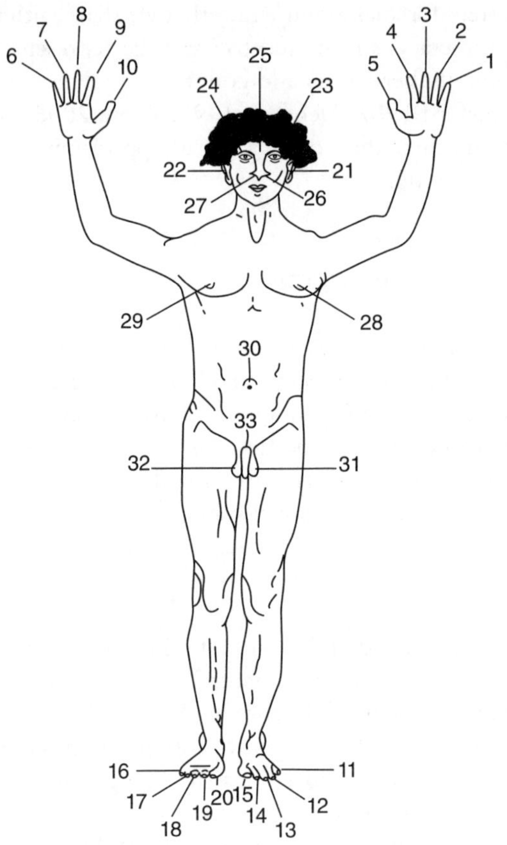

Figure 15.3 Yupno counting sequence (Wassmann and Dasen 1994:84). Due to the symmetry of the human body, most number words occur twice.

is an illustrative case: In addition to a decimal base, it also employed specific symbols for 5, 50, and 500 that served as sub-bases.

Base and structure

Two-dimensional (1 × 1D) systems that operate with base and power require only a small set of basic numerals, the last of which constitutes the endpoint of the prime counting cycle (in the decimal English system, this is "ten"). From this point onwards, a new counting cycle starts, consisting of the base and the same basic numerals as before (exceptions to this general rule in English are discussed below).

Base 10 is rather widespread among the languages of the world, but by far not the only one. The Yuki of California adopted base 8, classic Mayan and Nahuatl base 20, and the Babylonians base 60 (for further base systems, see Menninger 1969; Ifrah 1985).

Two-dimensional systems may also differ with regard to how they compose number words. The decimal English system encompasses basic numerals for the numbers from 1 through 9 and for the base itself; two further numerals denote the next powers of the base, 100 and 1,000. Number words beyond the basic numerals are generated by listing the multiples of the base raised to various powers, for instance: "two hundred" ($2 \cdot 10^2$), "thirty" ($3 \cdot 10^1$), and "eight" ($8 \cdot 10^0$). The composition of the power terms follows the multiplication principle, while the complete number word is composed by joining all power terms according to the addition principle. Other principles (e.g., subtraction) can also be found in natural languages, but rather rarely (Greenberg 1978).

Regularity of composition

The composition of number words in English contains several irregularities. Whereas hundreds and thousands are counted by simply placing a basic numeral in front of the power term (as in "three thousand"), multiples of ten are composed differently (e.g., as "thirty" instead of "three ten"). Furthermore, the order of the power terms switches between 12 and 20: While 103 is glossed as "hundred and three," 13 is not glossed as "ten and three" but as "thirteen." This implies three slightly different forms to denote the base 10: "ten," "-teen," and "-ty" (in addition to alternative forms for 3 and 5). Finally, certain numbers are denoted with specific numerals not composed of the basic numerals at all, namely "eleven" and "twelve."

There are further instances for irregularities in other languages, in particular among the Indo-European relatives of English. The number words for 80 and 90 in French, for instance, are composed as *quatre-vingts* ($4 \cdot 20$) and *quatre-vingt-dix* ($4 \cdot 20 + 10$).

Although such irregularities often occur as side effects of language evolution, they are not inevitable. Chinese provides an instance for a regular system, in which the number words reflect the polynomial structure without distortions (Fuson and Kwon 1991).

Degree of abstraction

Number is not confined to homogeneous groups of objects. For instance, the number of objects depicted in Figure 15.1 can easily be assessed as 36, despite their different shapes and colors. Many numeration systems reflect this abstractness of number by providing a single counting sequence for any type of object. In some cases, however, particular objects are counted specifically: a pair of pheasants as "brace," a pair of husband and wife as "couple," and a pair of siblings born on the same day as "twins." Even the term *pair* itself differs from the abstract number word *two*.

A more systematic manner of counting different things differently is adopted in numeral classifier languages. In these languages, classifiers are obligatory components of counting constructions (Lehman 1979, 1990; Aikhenvald 2003). The closest counterpart in English are words like *sheet* in "two sheets of paper." Although classifiers typically do not add any lexical content, they group the associated nouns into classes and are therefore treated as a sub-domain of taxonomy (Berlin and Romney 1964; Craig 1986; for a discussion of their numerical dimension, see Silverman 1962; Bender and Beller 2006b).

In Micronesia, a region where numeral classifier systems abound, such systems range from a binary distinction in Kosraean to more than 100 classifiers in Chuukese (Benton 1968; Harrison and Jackson 1984). Still, for the majority of their diverging counting sequences, Micronesian languages adopt counting units of one. In Polynesia, differentiation went one step further: Here, the distinct sequences for specific

Table 15.1 Different notational systems: the base in each system is shaded (adapted from Zhang and Norman 1995)

Arabic	*Egyptian*	*Greek*	*Roman*	*Aztec*	*Mayan*
1	|	α	I	•	•
2	||	β	II	••	••
3	|||	γ	III	•••	•••
4	||||	δ	IIII	••••	••••
5	|||||	ε	V	•••••	
6	||||||	ς	VI	••••• •	• ——
7	|||||||	ζ	VII	••••• ••	•• ——
8	||||||||	η	VIII	••••• •••	••• ——
9	|||||||||	θ	VIIII	••••• ••••	•••• ——
10	∩	ι	X	••••• •••••	
20	∩∩	κ	XX	P	• ——
100	𓍢	ρ	C	PPPPP	
200	𓍢𓍢	σ	CC	PPPPP PPPPP	

objects were also based on counting units different from one (Bender and Beller 2006a, 2006b, 2007).

Notational system

Although a sequence of number words suffices for counting, most numerical operations heavily rely on external representations (Figure 15.2). The currently most proliferate system is that of Indo-Arabic origin (for a description of its development, see Ifrah 1985). It is a 1 × 1D system with base 10 and figures for the numbers one through nine. According to the *place-value principle*, powers are indicated by a figure's place within a complex number, with 0 indicating an empty place:

$$3{,}208 = 3 \cdot 10^3 + 2 \cdot 10^2 + 0 \cdot 10^1 + 8 \cdot 10^0$$

The value of a figure depends on the figure itself and on its position in the array. For instance, the value 200, signified by the figure 2, is derived from its position as the third figure from the right.

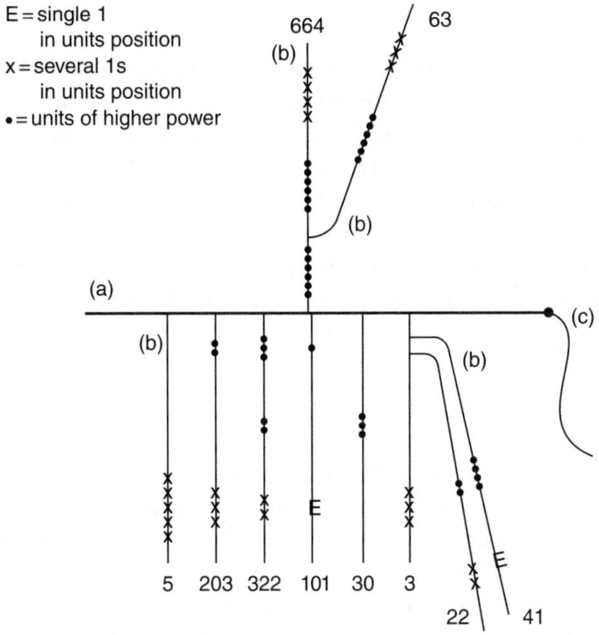

Figure 15.4 Schematic presentation of a *quipu* (adapted from Ascher 1998[1991]:24).

Notational systems differ largely, both with regard to the symbols they employ and their specific properties (see Table 15.1). For instance, the Egyptian and Aztec systems did not employ distinct symbols for each basic number as the Arabic system does, but used one symbol perpetually for each power level. Therefore, • in the Aztec system represented single items, with ••• indicating three of these, while P indicated scores of items, with PPPP indicating four of these. The Roman and Mayan systems were similarly structured, but with a sub-base each. And Mayan differed further with regard to the power dimension, where the same symbols recurred according to the place-value principle. As most of the properties of notational systems are analogous to those of verbal numeration systems, they will not be elaborated on here (for detailed analyses, see Nickerson 1988; Zhang and Norman 1995; Chrisomalis 2004, 2010; Schlimm and Neth 2008).

Not all notational systems are based on script, though, and one that differs considerably from the written symbols of the Indo-Arabic tradition is the Inca *quipu* system (Ascher and Ascher 1981; Urton 1997; Quilter and Urton 2002; and see Figure 15.4). A *quipu* consists of a main cord (a), to which different types of counting cords (b) and the dangle end cord (c) are tied. Color, length, and number of cords depend on the kind and number of objects to be counted.

Three types of knots denote the number: the figure-eight knot represents a single 1 in the unit position; the long knot represents several 1s in the unit position, with one turn for each item; and single knots represent units of higher powers. The reading direction is from inside out, that is, the highest power term is closest to the main cord. As the *quipu* system adopts the place-value principle, single knots (•) could be used to represent different numbers, depending on their relative position.

Conclusion

Counting sequences provide the most important tool for numerical cognition, without which specific operations are difficult or impossible to accomplish. This cannot be surprising, though. The same applies for any task that requires tools (just try to imagine the sculptor Rodin carving his *Thinker* with bare hands). What we consider more interesting and more important is the following question: Does the way in which these tools are shaped affect the way in which they are used? In other words: Do the culture-specific numeration systems – by way of their distinct properties – interact with cognitive processes in general and with numerical operations in particular?

Cognitive Implications

Essential for most cognitive processes, particularly when operating with numeration systems that lack notation, are the various parts of our memory: the long-term memory in which our knowledge is stored, and the short-term memory in which operations are performed (Baddeley 2006[1999]). Numeration systems consisting of short number words should therefore generally facilitate mental arithmetic. Obviously, notational systems further relieve the memory capacity, but these properties are not the only dimensions, on which numeration systems differ with regard to their implications for cognitive processing.

Extent

Apparently the limiting number L confines regular counting and thus exact assessment of number to amounts below L. Pirahã with an assumed L = 3 is a case in point: When asked to reproduce the amount of a set of objects, Gordon's participants responded less than perfectly for numbers beyond 3 (Figure 15.5, task 1). This performance even declined when they had to rely entirely on their memory for the original amount (Figure 15.5, task 2). Importantly, the same results are obtained with English speakers who are prevented from verbally counting the presented objects (Frank et al. 2008), which again emphasizes the crucial role of linguistic tools for these kinds of tasks.

However, extent is one of those properties that can be most easily adapted if people gain interest in higher numbers. Even without changing a system per se, a numeration system can be extended beyond its limiting number, either by saying "and one more" or by multiplying powers of the base as in English "ten thousand" and "hundred thousand." The Yupno, whose one-dimensional system terminates when a body is completely counted (see Figure 15.3), could restart with a second body if the counting had to go further (Wassmann and Dasen 1994).

A particularly intriguing strategy for extending the range of counting was adopted in Polynesia. Numeration systems like that in Tongan or Mangarevan were not extended by shifting L, but by enlarging the counting unit. Particular objects such as coconuts or fish were counted not as single items but as pairs or quadruples or scores of items. The same number words as in ordinary counting could thus be used to reach larger numbers (Bender and Beller 2006a; Beller and Bender 2008).

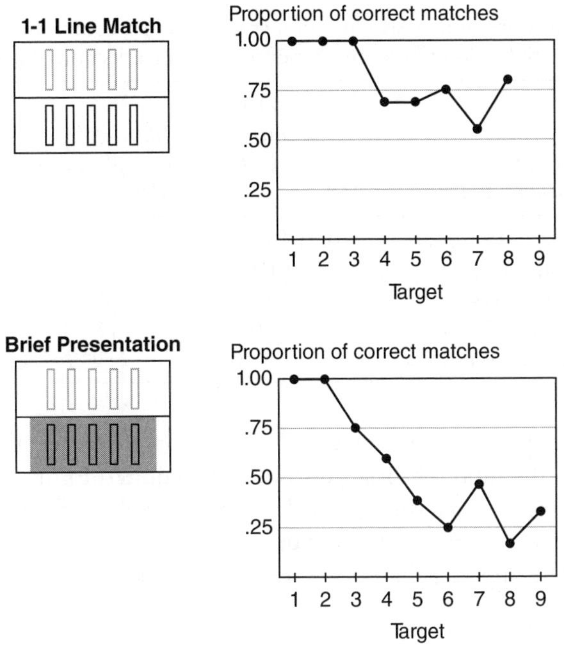

Figure 15.5 Results of two number tasks with Pirahã villagers (n = 7) (adapted from Gordon 2004:497). Participants were asked to reproduce the number of objects presented in the lower array. The original sample remained visible in the 1–1 line match task (task 1), but was hidden after 1 second in the brief presentation task (task 2).

Dimensionality

One-dimensional systems are conceptually simple as they denote each number with a distinct numeral. Its users do not have to learn a generative principle or particular rules for composition, and they need not adapt to potentially occurring irregularities. As long as they are only concerned with small numbers, one-dimensional systems are therefore perfectly adequate.

However, when large counting sequences are required, two-dimensional systems are more comfortable. Their recursive pattern for number word composition helps to keep the number words compact while dramatically reducing the amount of lexemes needed. A small set of basic number words suffices, even though most natural languages also use specific lexemes for the powers of their base (Table 15.2). And two-dimensional systems yield a second advantage: specific calculations are facilitated, depending on the base used, as will be discussed below.

Base and structure

In two-dimensional systems, the base is the prime structuring component. Its size determines the number of different numerals contained in the system and the compactness of the representation (Table 15.2): the larger the base is, the shorter and more compact are words for high numbers. Systems with larger bases are therefore more efficient for encoding and memorizing big numbers. But the base entails a cognitive

Table 15.2 Implications of base size for number of numerals, compactness of representation, size of addition/multiplication tables, and basic factors, for a selection of bases

Base	*Number of numerals (for counting up to 10^6)*		*Compactness of representation (illustrated for 148_{10})*	*Addition/ multiplication tables*	*Basic factors*
2	20	1 basic + 19 powers	10,010,100	3	2
5	12	4 basic + 8 powers	1,043	15	5
10	15	9 basic + 6 powers	148	55	2, 5, and 10
12	16	11 basic + 5 powers	104	78	2, 3, 4, 6, and 12
20	23	19 basic + 4 powers	78	210	2, 4, 5, 10, and 20

trade-off, as it also determines the extent of addition and multiplication tables, and the larger the base is, the more of these equations are required for numerical operations. And finally, the base also determines which operations will be particularly simple. In a base 10 system, multiplication with (and division by) 10 is trivial, while multiplication with 3 is tricky. The opposite holds for a base 12 system.

Regularity of composition

The prime factor influencing the ease with which number words are learnt and operated is regularity. As we have seen above, completely regular systems are rather the exception than the rule. Most European languages contain numeration systems with a range of irregularities: they include special number words, they switch the order of constituents, or they use sub-bases to construct power terms.

East Asian numeration systems, on the other hand, are constructed regularly according to the place-value principle, and this implies crucial advantages: Comparative studies with children showed that irregularities slow down the acquisition of the numeration system (Figure 15.6) and the comprehension of its base, and even influence calculating strategies (Fuson and Kwon 1991; Miura et al. 1993; Miller et al. 1995; Geary et al. 1996). Even in adults, they still occasionally cause mistakes. It is like using a knife with a jagged blade: usually, it will work well, but under pressure the results may be impaired.

Degree of abstraction

Languages employing specific number words such as "brace" have long been regarded as disadvantaged in a general manner (e.g., Menninger 1969; Ifrah 1985), for at least two reasons. First, such terms unnecessarily duplicate the amount of number words to be learnt. And second, they appear to prevent abstract operations like adding all objects on a table irrespective of their shape or size: two braces of pheasants and four pairs of oranges cannot be accounted for as "six braces of food."

However, such an assessment of specific counting terms neglects the practical context for their employment. If people wish to figure out the number of food items on the table, they can easily come up with "six pairs" or "twelve items." What terms like "brace" and "six-pack" in English or the numeral classifiers in Micronesian languages

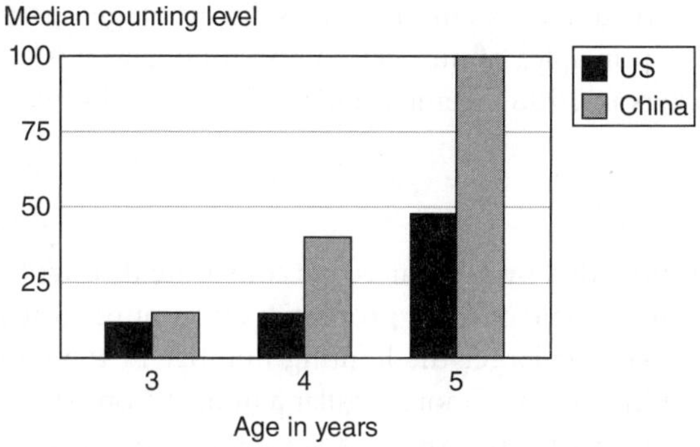

Figure 15.6 Median level of number up to which 3- to 5-year-olds counted correctly in the USA and China (adapted from Miller et al. 1995:57).

do is establish counting units in which things are measured. For each group of objects, these units define a comfortable scale for the objects to be counted. Adding entities of different measures, on the other hand, is normally neither reasonable nor required. Polynesian and Micronesian languages had consistently used this principle to enlarge their counting systems – as well as facilitate mental arithmetic with larger numbers – for their most important and most frequently used objects (Bender and Beller 2006a, 2006b, 2007).

Notational systems

As external representations relieve working memory, they tremendously facilitate all types of cognitive operations. Being accompanied by a notational system is therefore a particularly influential property of numeration systems per se. Due to their specific properties, different notational systems further affect numerical cognitive processes in different ways.

One of the most crucial properties of notational systems is which parts of the numerical information they represent explicitly and which they leave implicit. Those aspects left implicit have to be known and retrieved from memory while operating with number symbols and thus add to the cognitive load (Zhang and Norman 1995). In the Egyptian notation system, for instance, numerosity is explicitly represented: The number of figures on each power level reflects the number of items (Table 15.1). The power level itself, however, remains implicit; the meaning of the respective figure has to be retrieved from memory. The order of the single items in a complex figure, finally, is irrelevant.

In systems adopting the place-value principle like the Indo-Arabic or the Mayan system, the order of single items in a complex figure is crucial. Here, the power level is represented by the position of a figure. Whether such figures are to be read from left to right or vice versa, for instance, and which number is the base for the system, has to be already known to interpret the figure correctly.

However, there is not a single "perfect" system. People who frequently use their notational system internalize both its form and its structure and then find it hard to change to other notational systems. Despite the cognitive advantages propelling its proliferation, the Indo-Arabic system also entails disadvantages, particularly an intransparency of some key principles of number composition, and it is harder to learn than other systems (Nickerson 1988). Similar trade-offs can be observed for most systems.

Conclusion

The number words provided by each language constitute distinct numeration systems with specific properties. Some of these properties affect numerical cognition straightforwardly. For instance, the larger the limiting number L, the more extensive is the range for exact counting, and the more regular a numeration system, the easier it is to learn and handle. Base size, however, is associated with a cognitive trade-off as it affects the compactness of representation and the size of addition and multiplication tables in diverging ways.

Consequently, numeration systems differ with regard to how efficient they are as tools for cognitive arithmetic. Efficiency is not an abstract feature, though, but depends both on the nature of the task and on the context of usage. If counting large clusters of objects is required, then two-dimensional systems with medium base size may be most efficient. If, however, exact numbers are of no interest, learning such a complex system is futile. Yet, cultures differ not only with regard to their interest in numerosity, but also in mathematical domains in general.

Implicit Mathematics

Mathematics contains more than just counting and calculating, and even in cultures that make no consequent use of numeration systems, other concepts (e.g., from topology and geometry) may be well established (Dehaene et al. 2006). While some anthropologists have taken great pains to document such alternative and implicit "ethnomathematical" patterns (e.g., Deacon 1934), it probably required fully trained mathematicians like Marcia Ascher to discover and illuminate the richness of such notions across the world. For a wide range of pastimes, rituals, and institutions, Ascher uncovered and analyzed the mathematical principles on which they are based: chance and strategy in games and puzzles, principles of stochastic in the methods for divination, calculations for time-keeping and navigation, or relational and group theoretic principles structuring kinship algebra (Ascher 1988a, 1988b, 1998[1991], 2002; see also Crump 1990; for navigation, see Gladwin 1970; Hutchins 1983; and for kinship, see Lehman, Chapter 14 in this volume). Due to restrictions of space, only one domain will be addressed in more detail here: graphs.

Graphs are arrays of points (or *vertices*), connected to each other by lines (*edges*). Two-dimensional graphs, whose vertices are all part of the same network, are called "connected planar graphs" (for a popular instance, see Figure 15.7). Two figures are considered equivalent (*isomorphic*) if they have the same structure in terms of vertices and edges, whereas shape is irrelevant.

One of the core questions of graph theory is whether each vertex can be connected by a single continuous path that covers each edge once and only once (*Eulerian path*). The answer depends on the degree of vertices, defined by the number of edges emanating from a vertex: an Eulerian path can be found if a graph has not more than one

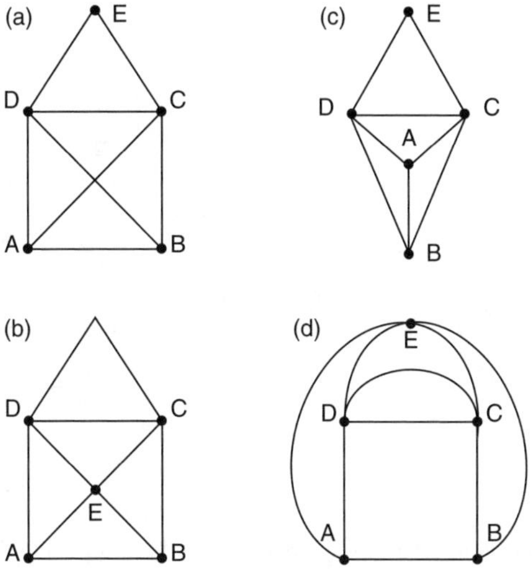

Figure 15.7 "This is the house of Santa Claus." The figure has to be drawn without interruption, each edge accompanied by one syllable of the rhyme. The original folklore version is depicted in (a), a differently defined graph with identical shape in (b). Figures (c) and (d) are isomorphic versions of (a) and (b), respectively.

pair of odd vertices. If it has only even vertices, the path will end in the same vertex where it began, thus constituting an *Eulerian cycle.* For the "House of Santa Claus," a continuous Eulerian path can be found, but not an Eulerian cycle.

Respective graphs are documented for a wide range of different cultures: as *kolam* in Tamil Nadu, India (Ascher 2002), as sand figures among the Bushong in Zaire (Torday 1925; Ascher 1988b), as *sona* among the Tshokwe in Angola and Zaire (Ascher 1988b; Gerdes 1997), or as *nitus* on Malekula in Vanuatu (Deacon 1934).

At first glance, these graphs appear widely different, with some entirely consisting of straight lines and corners, others comprising curves and loops. In some cultures dots are used as vertices, while in others the lines are carefully drawn around the dots. Yet, these graphs also share important features: They are all used to separate at least two regions of the plane, and they reveal a genuine concern with Eulerian paths and often with cycles. The drawing procedures can be translated into a set of instructions, some of which consist of systematic sequences of procedures. The story associated with a graph is connected to how the path is taken. Typically, each figure has its own name, but isomorphic graphs are treated similarly.

A particularly well-documented case are the *nitus* from Malekula. A proper *nitus* requires at least an Eulerian path; if it even allows for an Eulerian cycle, it is called *suon.* In addition, most *nitus* entail rotational and/or axis symmetry. For the more complex *nitus* (like the one in Figure 15.8), a few basic motions are linked recursively into larger procedures, sometimes combined with systematic size modification or with rotation, thus creating visual complexity from structural simplicity. The mathematical distinction between graphs consisting of even-degreed vertices only and those consisting of odd-degreed vertices is reflected in different tracing procedures and visual appearance in the *nitus* (Ascher 1988a).

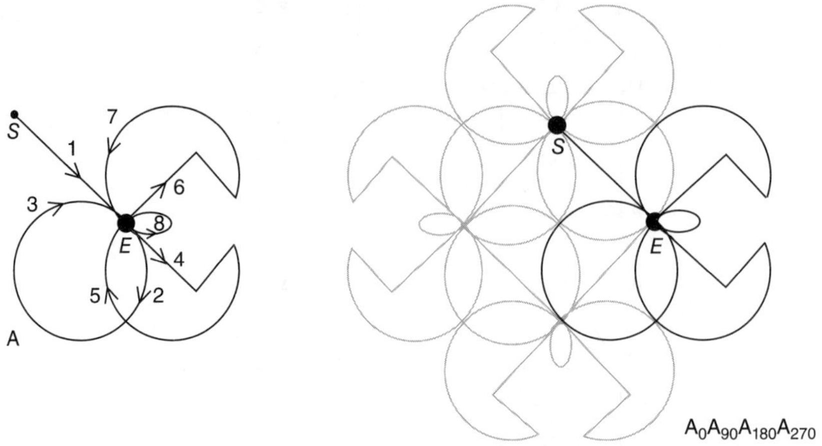

Figure 15.8 The *nitus* "yam" from Malekula (adapted from Ascher 1998[1991]:53). The basic tracing unit (A) is depicted on the left, with *S* indicating the starting point and *E* the end point. For completing the *nitus* (right), A is supplemented by three more units, rotated by 90, 180, and 270 degrees, respectively.

On Malekula, passage to the land of the dead depends on competence in drawing one's figures properly, without hesitation or backtracking. But as the shapes and tracing patterns of graphs differ widely across cultures, so do their functions. In the West, they are predominantly used for studying flows through networks and solving technical problems such as traffic regulation. The *kolam* figures in Tamil culture are placed on thresholds each morning after a purification ritual, to mark the boundary between interior and exterior, offer protection for the house, and welcome guests. For Bushong children, graphs appear to have been used only in games, while the Tshokwe *sona* were exclusively men's business, connected to mythological stories and rites of passage.

In conclusion, graphs may not be treated explicitly as mathematical representations in any of these cultures. Yet they are based on mathematical principles: they are produced in a systematic and structured manner, drawing on concepts of number, logic, and spatial configurations. These principles are not only noticed, but even emphasized by their practitioners. In addition, the procedures follow strict algorithms and are transformed to create more complex graphs. This formal transformation constitutes a "process algebra," in which variables are operated upon according to specific rules, and in this sense, graphs are genuinely mathematical in any of the instances described above. Recent studies even suggest that the geometrical and topological concepts required for such expressions of ethnomathematics are most likely universally shared (Dehaene et al. 2006).

General Conclusion

Although several scholars dispute that mathematics exists "outside people's heads" (e.g., Davis and Hersh 1981; Lakoff and Núñez 2000), its patterns are ubiquitous. Laws of physics follow mathematical equations, biological evolution can be assessed with stochastic algorithms, and some basic facts of life are so evidently numerical that even non-human species perceive and consider them. Still, the way in which we represent these patterns and the emphasis we place on them differs across languages and cultures. Numerosity as the most obvious part is captured by counting sequences distinct for each language. Other aspects such as stochastic or graph theoretic notions are molded into cultural patterns even more strongly (see Wilder 1981).

The intricate relationship of mathematical notions, cognitive processing, linguistic phrasing, and cultural shaping is best captured and disentangled by a joint endeavour of various disciplines. Such an endeavour, however, is still in its infancy. With a few exceptions only some of which could be acknowledged in this chapter (for others see Gay and Cole 1967; Lancy 1983; Closs 1986; Lave 1988; Washburn 2004), most mathematicians focus on "pure" mathematics, cognitive scientists and psychologists on numerical cognition in Western countries, and anthropologists more on the cultural context of ethnomathematical notions than on the notions themselves. Each approach is important in its own right and yields essential insights – but how much more could be achieved by joining forces!

Mathematicians, for instance, while contributing to the identification and adequate assessment of mathematical patterns, could profit by discovering novel approaches to old problems. Cognitive scientists and psychologists, exploring the foundations of numerical cognition, could gain insights for adapting their models to non-literate populations and to alternative conceptual systems. And anthropologists, whose expertise is required for accounts of how mathematical concepts are culturally embedded, socially distributed, and passed on, are well advised to take insights from other disciplines seriously in interpreting cultural patterns.

For the re-evaluation of Polynesian numeration systems (Bender and Beller 2007; Beller and Bender 2008), for instance, considering such diverse knowledge was indispensable. Mathematical understanding was required to assess Polynesian numeration systems not as vigesimal, but as genuinely decimal, and their apparently mixed bases as enlarged counting units. The strategies behind these modified counting sequences became fully comprehensible only when further combining anthropological insights in the importance of redistribution for status in Polynesian societies with cognitive insights in how properties of numeration systems affect numerical operations.

Joining efforts in such a manner would eventually also allow us to formulate more convincing answers to the general questions posed in the introduction. Why, for instance, do some people not count at all (like the Pirahã) or not very far (like the Yupno)? Does a lack of extensive counting sequences reflect a lack of number concepts as has been assumed by Gordon (2004)? And if so, is this conceptual lack merely a consequence of not having learnt counting sequences (Gelman and Gallistel 1978; Dehaene 1997; Wiese 2003), or is it a consequence of not having taken the evolutionary leap from hunter-gatherer to agricultural subsistence (Premack and Premack 2005)?

There is good reason to doubt this latter assumption. First, such a link between numeration systems and subsistence does not hold. In some Aboriginal hunter-gatherer societies in Australia, numeration systems extend beyond numerals for one and two only (Harris 1987). And vice versa, the Amazonian Mundurukú, claimed as employing no exact number words (Pica et al. 2004), base their subsistence on agriculture.

Even languages that appear to have only a few number words nowadays may have had more in the past (Beller and Bender 2008). Adzera, for instance, a language spoken in the Morobe Province of Papua New Guinea, contains a numeration system whose basic numerals do not exceed two and appear to have not been used in an exact manner (Holzknecht 1986). However, as a member of the Oceanic branch of the Austronesian language family it belongs to a linguistic cluster whose proto-language already contained a numeration system with base 10 and numerals for powers up to 10^3 (Lynch et al. 2002). The Iqwaye, on the other hand, neighbors of the Adzera in Morobe Province, yet of Papuan origin like the Yupno, have developed an extended vigesimal system linked in a complex and fascinating manner to kinship and cosmology (Mimica 1988).

Many more instances could be mustered to demonstrate that numeration systems do not always evolve from simple to more complex systems and not necessarily along with patterns of subsistence. Due to their specific properties, each numeration system sets limits for its users. How tight these limits are varies across languages, and how content its users are with these limits varies across cultures. Only if a simple evolutionary approach is given up in favor of the assumption that numerical concepts and numerical tools like number words *co-evolve* (Wiese 2007) – and may do so in various directions (e.g., Donohue 2008) – can findings on both cognitive universals and cultural variety be integrated. For such an endeavor, cognitive anthropology is in dire need. Each culture has developed its own idiosyncratic representation of mathematical concepts. How people express these concepts, what they achieve thereby, and how this feeds back to other domains of culture still belong to the most fascinating – and least explored – domains for cognitive anthropology.

REFERENCES

Aikhenvald, Alexandra Y.
2003 Classifiers. Oxford: Oxford University Press.
Ascher, Marcia
1988a Graphs in Cultures: A Study in Ethnomathematics. Historia Mathematica 15:201–227.
1988b Graphs in Cultures (II): A Study in Ethnomathematics. Archive for the History of Exact Sciences 39:75–95.
1998[1991] Ethnomathematics. Pacific Grove: Brooks/Cole.
2002 Mathematics Elsewhere. Princeton: Princeton University Press.
Ascher, Marcia, and Robert Ascher
1981 Code of the Quipu. Ann Arbor: University of Michigan Press.
Baddeley, Alan D.
2006[1999] Essentials of Human Memory. Hove: Psychology Press.
Beller, Sieghard, and Andrea Bender
2008 The Limits of Counting: Numerical Cognition Between Evolution and Culture. Science 319:213–215.
Bender, Andrea, and Sieghard Beller
2006a "Fanciful" or Genuine? Bases and High Numerals in Polynesian Number Systems. Journal of the Polynesian Society 115:7–46.
2006b Numeral Classifiers and Counting Systems in Polynesian and Micronesian Languages: Common Roots and Cultural Adaptations. Oceanic Linguistics 45:380–403.

2007 Counting in Tongan: The Traditional Number Systems and Their Cognitive Implications. Journal of Cognition and Culture 7(3–4):213–239.
Benton, Richard A.
1968 Numeral and Attributive Classifiers in Trukese. Oceanic Linguistics 7(2):104–146.
Berlin, Brent, and A. Kimball Romney
1964 Descriptive Semantics of Tzeltal Numeral Classifiers. American Anthropologist 66(3):79–98.
Campbell, Jamie I. D.
1994 Architectures for Numerical Cognition. Cognition 53:1–44.
Chrisomalis, Stephen
2004 A Cognitive Typology for Numerical Notation. Cambridge Archaeological Journal 14:37–52.
2010 Numerical Notation: A Comparative History. New York: Cambridge University Press.
Closs, Michael P., ed.
1986 Native American Mathematics. Austin: University of Texas Press.
Craig, Colette., ed.
1986 Noun Classes and Categorization. Amsterdam: John Benjamins.
Crump, Thomas
1990 The Anthropology of Numbers. Cambridge: Cambridge University Press.
Davis, Philip J., and Reuben Hersh
1981 The Mathematical Experience. Brighton: Harvester.
Deacon, Arthur Bernard
1934 Geometrical Drawings from Malekula and Other Islands of the New Hebrides. Journal of the Royal Anthropological Institute 64:129–175.
Dehaene, Stanislas
1992 Varieties of Numerical Abilities. Cognition 44:1–42.
1997 The Number Sense. Oxford: Oxford University Press.
Dehaene, Stanislas, Véronique Izard, Pierre Pica, and Elizabeth Spelke
2006 Core Knowledge of Geometry in an Amazonian Indigene Group. Science 311: 381–384.
Donohue, Mark
2008 Complexities with Restricted Numeral Systems. Linguistic Typology 12:423–429.
Everett, Daniel L.
2005 Cultural Constraints on Grammar and Cognition in Pirahã. Current Anthropology 46(4):621–646.
Feigenson, Lisa, Stanislas Dehaene, and Elizabeth Spelke
2004 Core Systems of Number. Trends in Cognitive Sciences 8:307–314.
Frank, Michael C., Daniel L. Everett, Evelina Fedorenko, and Edward Gibson
2008 Number as a Cognitive Technology: Evidence from Pirahã Language and Cognition. Cognition 108:819–824.
Fuson, Karen C., and Youngshim Kwon
1991 Chinese-Based Regular and European Irregular Systems of Number Words: The Disadvantages for English-Speaking Children. *In* Language in Mathematical Education. K. Durkin and B. Shire, eds. Pp. 211–226. Milton Keynes: Open University Press.
Gay, John, and Michael Cole
1967 The New Mathematics and an Old Culture: A Study of Learning among the Kpelle of Liberia. New York: Holt, Rinehart, & Winston.
Geary, David C., C. Christine Bow-Thomas, Fan Liu, and Robert S. Siegler
1996 Development of Arithmetical Competencies in Chinese and American Children: Influence of Age, Language, and Schooling. Child Development 67:2022–2044.
Gelman, Rochel, and C. R. Gallistel
1978 The Child's Understanding of Number. Cambridge, MA: Harvard University Press.

Gerdes, Paulus
1997 Ethnomathematik, dargestellt am Beispiel der Sona-Geometrie. Heidelberg: Spektrum Akademischer.
Gladwin, Thomas
1970 East Is a Big Bird: Navigation and Logic on Puluwat Atoll. Cambridge, MA: Harvard University Press.
Gordon, Peter
2004 Numerical Cognition without Words: Evidence from Amazonia. Science 306: 496–499.
Greenberg, Joseph H.
1978 Generalizations about Numeral Systems. *In* Universals of Human Language, vol. 3: Word Structure. J. H. Greenberg, ed. Pp. 249–295. Stanford: Stanford University Press.
Harris, John
1987 Australian Aboriginal and Islander Mathematics. Australian Aboriginal Studies 2:29–37.
Harrison, Sheldon, and Frederick H. Jackson
1984 Higher Numerals in Several Micronesian Languages. *In* Studies in Micronesian Linguistics. B. W. Bender, ed. Pp. 59–78. Canberra: Australian National University.
Holzknecht, Susanne
1986 A Morphology and Grammar of Adzera (Amari Dialect), Morobe Province, Papua New Guinea. Pacific Linguistics, series A, 70:77–166.
Hurford, James R.
1987 Language and Number: The Emergence of a Cognitive System. Oxford: Blackwell.
Hutchins, Edwin
1983 Understanding Micronesian Navigation. *In* Mental Models. D. Gentner and A. L. Stevens, eds. Pp. 191–225. Hillsdale, NJ: Lawrence Erlbaum.
Ifrah, Georges
1985 From One to Zero: A Universal History of Numbers. New York: Viking.
Lakoff, George, and Rafael E. Núñez
2000 Where Mathematics Comes from: How the Embodied Mind Brings Mathematics into Being. New York: Basic Books.
Lancy, David F.
1983 Cross-Cultural Studies in Cognition and Mathematics. New York: Academic Press.
Lave, Jean
1988 Cognition in Practice: Mind, Mathematics and Culture in Everyday Life. Cambridge: Cambridge University Press.
Lehman, F. K. L. (Chit Hlaing)
1979 Aspects of a Formal Theory of Noun Classifiers. Studies in Language 3(2):153–180.
1990 Outline of a Formal Syntax of Numerical Expressions, with Especial Reference to the Phenomenon of Numeral Classifiers. Linguistics of the Tibeto-Burman Area 13: 89–120.
Lynch, John, Malcolm Ross, and Terry Crowley
2002 The Oceanic Languages. Richmond: Curzon.
Mandler, G., and B. J. Shebo
1982 Subitizing: An Analysis of Its Component Processes. Journal of Experimental Psychology: General 111:1–21.
Menninger, Karl
1969 Number Words and Number Symbols. Cambridge, MA: MIT Press.
Miller, Kevin, Catherine M. Smith, Jianjun Zhu, and Houcan Zhang
1995 Preschool Origins of Cross-National Differences in Mathematical Competence: The Role of Number-Naming Systems. Psychological Science 6:56–60.

Mimica, Jadran
1988 Intimations of Infinity: The Mythopoeia of the Iqwaye Counting System and Number. Oxford: Berg.
Miura, Irene T., Yukari Okamoto, Chungsoon C. Kim, Marcia Steere, and Michel Fayol
1993 First Graders' Cognitive Representation of Number and Understanding of Place Value: Cross-National Comparisons – France, Japan, Korea, Sweden, and the United States. Journal of Educational Psychology 85:24–30.
Nickerson, Raymond S.
1988 Counting, Computing, and the Representation of Numbers. Human Factors 30:181–199.
Pica, Pierre, Cathy Lemer, Véronique Izard, and Stanislas Dehaene
2004 Exact and Approximate Arithmetic in an Amazonian Indigene Group. Science 306:499–503.
Premack, David, and Ann Premack
2005 Evolution versus Invention. Science 307:673.
Quilter, Jeffrey, and Gary Urton, eds.
2002 Narrative Threads: Accounting and Recounting in Andean Khipu. Austin: University of Texas Press.
Saxe, Geoffrey B.
1981 Body Parts as Numerals: A Developmental Analysis of Numeration among the Oksapmin in Papua New Guinea. Child Development 52:306–316.
Schlimm, Dirk, and Hansjörg Neth
2008 Modeling Ancient and Modern Arithmetic Practices: Addition and Multiplication with Arabic and Roman Numerals. *In* Proceedings of the 30th Annual Conference of the Cognitive Science Society. B. C. Love, K. McRae, and V. M. Sloutsky, eds. Pp. 2097–2102. Austin, TX: Cognitive Science Society.
Silverman, Martin G.
1962 Numeral-Classifiers in the Gilbertese Language. Anthropology Tomorrow 7:41–56.
Torday, Emil
1925 On the Trail of the Bushongo. Philadelphia: Lippin.
Urton, Gary
1997 The Social Life of Numbers: A Quechua Ontology of Numbers and Philosophy of Arithmetic. Austin: University of Texas Press.
Washburn, Dorothy K., ed.
2004 Embedded Symmetries, Natural and Cultural. Albuquerque: University of New Mexico Press.
Wassmann, Jürg, and Pierre R. Dasen
1994 Yupno Number System and Counting. Journal of Cross-Cultural Psychology 25:78–94.
Wiese, Heike
2003 Numbers, Language, and the Human Mind. Cambridge: Cambridge University Press.
2007 The Co-Evolution of Number Concepts and Counting Words. Lingua 117: 758–772.
Wilder, Raymond L.
1981 Mathematics as a Cultural System. Oxford: Pergamon.
Zhang, Jiajie, and Donald A. Norman
1995 A Representational Analysis of Numeration Systems. Cognition 57:271–295.

CHAPTER 16

"Indigenous Knowledge" and the Understanding of Cultural Cognition: The Contribution of Studies of Environmental Knowledge Systems

Roy Ellen

Defining Our Terms of Reference

The term "indigenous knowledge" arose largely in its modern setting as a designation for the technical or empirical knowledge of mainly non-Western peoples, of the kind also described as ethnoscience. As a category it is problematic, and has become ideological through its entanglement in political debates about indigeneity. Applying the adjective "indigenous" to the substantive "knowledge" raises the same complications that we find with the category "indigenous peoples." Indigeneity is an often contested status, and it has been suggested that terms such as "traditional" or "local" might be preferable. But these too have their limitations, as what is traditional is not necessarily indigenous or local, and what is local is not always indigenous or traditional. The designations "folk" or "ethno-" (as in, say, ethnobiological or ethnomedical knowledge) are current in academic work, but have less currency outside the academy.

A Companion to Cognitive Anthropology, First Edition. Edited by David B. Kronenfeld, Giovanni Bennardo, Victor C. de Munck, and Michael D. Fischer.

Many ethnoscience domains have been the subject of systematic documentation and theorization, both in terms of the encyclopedic information they encode (especially their classificatory apparatus) and also in terms of their underlying explanatory and organizational logics. My main focus here will be on studies of environmental knowledge systems, but because we are not referring to scientific knowledge in the accepted narrow sense (only as a comparator and means of evaluating other bodies of knowledge), we inevitably imply the existence of a dualistic "other." Indeed, there is a danger in seeming to essentialize the features of non-scientific environmental knowledge systems by contrasting them with scientific knowledge; or to conflate the dualism as a whole with the distinction between Western and non-Western. It is difficult to generalize about these features, as in the widest sense they must apply to all those diverse knowledges that lie outside of science as it emerged as an ideal and institutionalized body of global practice. As a category, "indigenous knowledge" also sustains an ambiguity in relation to how we should regard the great literate scholarly traditions of knowledge (such as Ayurveda or early modern European herbalism), which in turn are often distinguished from local oral traditions, but with which they have continuously interacted historically. However, it has become conventional (see, for example, Ellen and Harris 2000) to characterize folk knowledge in particular as rooted in the experience of living in a particular place, and as orally or performatively transmitted. Despite often being seen as static, folk knowledge is actually remarkably fluid, a consequence of a practical and experimental engagement with everyday life. Folk knowledge is more culturally distributed and shared than scientific knowledge, not existing in its totality in any one person or group. However, particular kinds of knowledge may be the domain of specialists or particular sub-groups. Though characteristically embedded in other aspects of culture, and often described as holistic and integrative, it is precisely the difficulty of separating the technical from the social, and the rational from perceived non-rational elements, that has made it easy to ridicule as a kind of pseudo-science. The same interconnections have, by contrast, encouraged activist and spiritual representations of indigenous knowledge as intrinsically mystical, and through this have perpetuated mythologized notions of tribal environmental wisdom (Ellen 1986).

Most accounts of indigenous knowledge are summations of what people know, or qualitative descriptions that are not really relevant to the objectives of this chapter. Those who seek to apply indigenous knowledge to practical problems of development often tend to be more inclusive in their use of the term (e.g., Warren et al. 1995; Sillitoe et al. 2002), applying it to, say, philosophical or medical knowledge. However, it is mainly knowledge of the natural world (ethnobiological knowledge, ethnoecological knowledge, landscape classification, and conceptions of nature in a more general sense, together with some applications of such knowledge) that have made the most obvious contribution to our understanding of cognition, especially concerning the interplay between linguistic, cultural, environmental, social, and evolved factors. It is upon these that I focus here. I will also look at aspects of cultural cognition involved in technology and material culture, spatial orientation and way-finding, insofar as these connect with the preceding themes. It is partly because the greatest impact of indigenous knowledge studies on cognitive anthropology has been through ethnobiology and studies of material technologies, and because a line has to be drawn somewhere, that I shall confine myself to these areas. Cognitively speaking, "indigenous knowledge" is not one single homogeneously identifiable thing, or indeed something that is easily divisible. It might, for example, be seen as a series of overlapping domains, some of which share organizational features, some of which may acquire a certain "systematicity," but often the domain boundaries and systemic features are more heuristic than empirical.

The Beginnings of Anthropological Approaches to the Study of Environmental Cognition

The history of the study of indigenous environmental knowledge systems has revealed a twin-track approach, directed in part by the search for fundamental truths about how people organize sense data about the natural world, and in part by a more pragmatic concern for the empirical content of that knowledge and how it might assist in development contexts. Our concern here, as I have indicated, is with the former.

Anthropologists studying the classification of plants and animals and the distribution of ethnobiological knowledge have made a particular contribution to the development of field methods, and from the earliest days, studies of knowledge systems have been closely associated with the emerging paradigm of cognitive anthropology, largely through the work on ethnoscience in the late 1950s and early 1960s, and its strong association with the American school of ethnosemantics (Sturtevant 1964), the guiding methodology of which entailed the use of formal protocols to yield sufficient data for an ethnographer to successfully replicate native language behavior in a designated context (e.g., Frake 1980). Although the approach failed as a way of reporting ethnographic data more generally, it proved to be a productive paradigm in terms of the studies of ethnobiological knowledge they inspired, and provided elicitation techniques and an analytical language that persists (for example, the received concept of "cognitive domain"). In particular, they enabled a clearer understanding of the relationship between category and word, and demonstrated that the correspondence between the two in category formation, classification, knowledge distribution and transmission, was seldom straightforward. These developments were made possible by mapping folk categories onto their phylogenetic denotata. Such a linguistic approach to folk classification is perhaps best exemplified in the work of Harold Conklin (1954, 1962) and Brent Berlin (Berlin et al. 1974). In other words, biological kinds provided a "natural metric" for cultural comparisons, and a way of linking work in cognitive anthropology and cognitive psychology.

The early influence of linguistics was reflected also in the prominence of the distinctive feature model, emphasizing category boundaries and reflected in the semantic structuralism of Edmund Leach (e.g., 1964) and Mary Douglas (e.g., 1975). The immediate stimulus of this work was Lévi-Strauss (1962:1–33), though ultimately it was inspired by Émile Durkheim and Marcel Mauss (1963[1901–02]) who had prefigured a sociological theory of classification. Since then, debates around the role of metaphor, totemism, animism, and the construction of "nature," have supported the view that the interrelationships between symbolic and mundane classification are often far from clear (e.g., Rosaldo 1972; Ellen 1993; Healey 1993). However, initial approaches in this tradition were generally untested in either field or laboratory settings, and new evidence soon showed that categories are much more fuzzy, and more realistically modeled using notions of polythesis, or in terms of semantic cores and peripheries, which assume the pre-eminence of particular cognitive prototypes.

The more recent work of Berlin (1992), Atran (1990, 1998), Hunn (1977), and Boster (1996) all bear testimony to the fertile synergy between research on ethnobiological knowledge and cognitive studies more generally. With a shift away from the dominance of distinctive features, and an emphasis on core–periphery models and cognitive prototypes, and with a growth in the use of psychological at the expense of linguistic approaches, greater recognition has been given to how we might engage with differences in the world without using language as an intermediary. In recent decades more work has been undertaken on intracultural variation, on degrees of consensus, on knowledge transmission, and on the interactive relationship between cognitive process and learned bodily routines. I shall develop these themes later in this chapter.

Language and Cognition

It has long been known that language gives us our most accessible clues as to how categories and knowledge are organized. Plant binomials, for example, usually indicate the existence of a *kind of* relationship. A shared name is generally the outcome of a process whereby a percept is registered through repeated perceptual events, reinforced over the longer term and transmitted between individuals. As we have seen, it was first assumed that this was through a process of contrasting distinctive features, a model derived from lexicography and logic (Conklin 1962). Thus, birds have wings, feathers, beaks and fly, in contrast to fish, which swim and have fins. However, it was soon noted that the systematic patterns of contrast necessary for this model to work were not always present. For example, category A might be linked to category B through common attribute *a*, but category B linked to category C through common attribute *b*. This connected categories A and C even where they had nothing in common. This process, which we now know more generally as "polythetic classification," has been documented for folk classifications of plants and animals, where it has been described as "chaining" (e.g., Hays 1976; also Ellen 1993:121). As research on ethnobiological classification developed it became apparent that the digital distinctive feature model explained only certain kinds of fairly self-conscious classifying behaviors, and that an analog approach based on the notion of cognitive prototype presented a better way of modeling the cognition of basic and more inclusive categories. In this model, incoming perceptual images from the environment are matched by the brain with pre-existing cultural images of, say, "birdness" or "treeness," where the presence or absence of specific characteristics is not an overriding consideration, only closeness or marginality of overall match (Rosch 1977). Thus in British English classification of birds a robin would configure closely the core prototype, but an ostrich would be marginal, whereas in the famous Kalam example described by Bulmer (1967), the perceptual marginality of the cassowary is reinforced culturally so that it ceases to be a "bird" altogether. In everyday cognitive practice, therefore, we use the notions of both contrasting features and cognitive prototypes, and move freely between the two.

As the Kalam example shows, the difficulties we face in assigning things to categories are simplified by imposing culturally agreed boundaries, or indeed by instituting these by the ways we manipulate the natural world, for example, breeding varieties of plants or animals that emphasize phenotypic difference for aesthetic reasons, marvelously illustrated in Darwin's famous account of the Spitalfields pigeon-fanciers (Feely-Harnik 2007) or in Fukui's (1996) account of Bodi cattle patterns and colors, or Shigeta's (1996) study of Ari ensete selection. Thus, because parts of our experience of the world are complexly continuous it is occasionally necessary to impose boundaries to produce categories at all, and sometimes these are remarkably arbitrary. Consider, for example, what we conceive of as the technically precise area of engineering design, where as Lemonnier (1992) has demonstrated, the scope for cultural arbitrariness over technical necessity is as great, if not greater, than in the making of Anga fiber capes in the New Guinea highlands.

We may conclude that language is a good first guide to thought. Thus, the very sounds we use may identify certain species or groups of animal, as in onomatopeia (e.g., Nuaulu *kukue* [*Cuculus saturates*] and English "cuckoo"), or in the kind of verbal mimesis reported by Berlin (2006) in which there is a plausible correlation between bird morphology and the openness or closure of vowels in cross-language data. We can also infer cognitive process to some extent from the morpho-syntactic structure of names and their meanings. But all this is rather imperfect, and often language evidence may obscure cognitive process, for example, that related to artisanal performance (Dougherty and Keller 1982). Lexicalization and other forms of linguistic encoding are often prompted by the social need to exchange information, and where this necessity does not arise we need not expect language to predict cognition. Rather different is the delay in the erosion of category labels once these have been absorbed into language as morpho-syntactic classifiers (e.g., numerical classifiers), and where apparent linguistic indicators may sometimes be at variance with otherwise cognized groupings (e.g., Grinevald 2000).

Nested Classifications and the Problem of "Taxonomy"

It is now well attested that cognitive domains of environmental phenomena are established at varying degrees of classificatory inclusiveness. Thus, depending on a locally defined situation or the focus of analysis, we might isolate "all living things," "plants," "trees," and "oak," where each appears to be related through a "kind of" relationship. In such cases domain boundaries reflect distinctions that are empirically important for the population who share them. Thus if a population has no concept of "fish" then "fish" cannot be a cognitive domain. However, categories can exist without labels, even at the domain level. Thus, the lexical field, for say plants, may not correspond with the cognitive domain because of the existence of covert categories at various levels of inclusiveness, including the "unique beginner" for the domain (e.g., Taylor 1984).

The internal subdivisions of cognitive domains have often been represented as taxonomies, in the sense of a hierarchical model of contrast and class inclusion, partly because these are so prevalent in literate Euro-American literary scientific culture, most obviously reflected in the tradition emanating from Linnaeus. In the context of cognitive anthropology, Brent Berlin (1972, 1992; and Berlin et al. 1974) has put forward a strong claim for logical taxonomy as the general way in which ethnobiological classification operates universally, hypothesizing a series of levels broadly reflecting the Linnaean rank: unique beginner, life form, intermediate, generic, specific, and varietal. This is a persuasive argument, and provides a powerful inductive framework for generating data and for making systematic inferences about the properties of organisms. However, nestedness need not imply taxonomy in the formal or domain-specific sense. These features of classification are particularly striking in plants and animals because of the discreteness and concreteness of individual organisms, and because the patterns of physical and behavioral similarity between taxa strongly reflect evolutionary process and phylogenetic distance. So, in the domain of living kinds classificatory tendencies converge in a special way because of regularities in the objective world which is classified, and to which the mind responds, not obviously because of the character of the mind which does the classifying.

We know that taxonomic thinking as a way of representing relationships between things is more important in some cultural populations than in others (see, for example, Lancy and Strathern 1981), and some domains more than other domains, such as natural history and some groups of cultural objects, but even within natural history domains some work better than others taxonomically, such as plants more than fungi (Ellen 2008), and other domains (such as color) are surprisingly resistant to taxonomic thinking, while some subcultural learning and teaching contexts encourage it more than others. Moreover, because of the propensity of most anthropological researchers to rely heavily on an approach embedded in Western science, it is easy to yield taxonomies in patterns of data collected from non-literate informants. In asserting a universal "abstract taxonomic structure" the methodology all too often seems to be one in which inconvenient features of peoples' classifying behavior which do not fit the expected pattern are systematically ignored or explained away as exceptions, until a suitably "taxonomic" pattern is obtained. But if we accept instead the centrality of prototypical thinking and polythesis in classifying activity, it is not at all surprising that it is often difficult to establish systematic and consistent hierarchical relationships between superordinate and subordinate categories (Edelman 1992:236; see also Hunn 1977; Friedberg 1990; Ellen 1993; Sillitoe 2003).

Berlin's model also works best if we claim a universal distinction between general purpose and special purpose classifications (a distinction, for example, that the findings of Atran [1998:563] no longer uphold), between those that are "natural" from those that meet particular specialized cultural requirements, such as cooking. Any demonstration of the empirical primacy of taxonomy depends on the extent to which categories can be shown to be linked in a particular way, despite the existence of other ways of classifying that undermine implicit levels and contrasts, and upon the ease with which transitivity statements can be elicited in fieldwork situations. Atran now accepts that taxonomic organization of the world is much more situationally generated, and does not necessarily define the inferential character of folk biology as suggested in his *Cognitive Foundations of Natural History*. This is consistent with other data (e.g., Ellen 1993:123–124). Like Itza' Maya, Nuaulu do not "essentialise ranks," which would violate their prioritization of "ecological and morpho-behavioural relationships" over abstract principles. Scientific systematics, by contrast, has until recently rejected such cross-cutting classificatory relationships (Atran 1998:561–562). Indeed, a central problem of folk biological methodology has been that much of data are acquired not knowing quite how independent the system of ranks discovered is from the analytic concepts with which we start. A more plausible working model is that we assume for any one population a flexible system of relationships between categories, which allows for the generation of particular "classifications" depending on context, although the aggregation of contexts may well favor particular kinds of "natural" classifications. A good example of the pre-eminence of local ecological and cultural considerations, and also of some general fundamental ambiguities, is found in the position occupied by "palms" in different ethnobotanical schemes and the nebulousness of their position as a "life form," intermediate or "unaffiliated generic." On balance, it must be the case (as Atran asserts), that the denser our knowledge the more we deviate from any general model, and that taxonomies might better be accommodated by treating them as simplifications of experiential complexity in ways which make knowledge less useful. Thus, when we find plant and animal domesticates as salient components in elicited schemes of folk classification we cannot just reject them as "special cases," or cross-cutting utilitarian artifacts, that evolved after the arrival of agriculture, simply because they seem to violate some evolved predisposition.

Modularity and Ethnobiological Knowledge Organization as an Evolved Capacity

We have long known that the brain has a propensity to store information in ways that make best use of the perceptual and cultural resources available, what Rosch (1977) calls "cognitive economy." I have discussed above the role the study of systems of classificatory knowledge have played in exemplifying how the mind models "fuzzy" concepts and "core" prototypes, some of which in turn provide a repertoire of artifacts through the physiology of perception which in turn can be used to organize perceptual and symbolic data.

The concept of cognitive domain as a methodological tool reflecting the tendency to cognize "areas of conceptualization" (D'Andrade 1995:34) has long been advocated, but in addition has given rise to the notion of domain specificity, that is, the idea that the attributes of one domain might be different from another (as between language, mathematical ability, intuitive physics, and so on). Moreover, since their popularization by Fodor (1983), our understanding of the evolution of the hominid brain has been much influenced by modular theories in cognitive psychology, which stress the differential development of categorizing abilities in different functionally discrete domains, which are claimed in some cases to be rooted in evolved neurobiological proclivities. Thus, there are special features relating to essence, rank, and basic category that are more likely to reflect evolved features in the domain of biological knowledge, than in, say, the domain of cultural artifacts (Atran and Medin 2008:65; also Brown et al. 1976 versus Atran 1987).

The difficulty for anthropologists and psychologists alike here has been in identifying cultural and cognitive traits of sufficient discreteness to be accepted as unitary modules in the first place, and the ways in which the human mind unhelpfully interferes with the conventional forces of selection by reforming such units, linking them together in novel ways and attributing to them new (and sometimes contradictory) linkages and meanings (Aunger 2000). If cross-cultural similarities in ethnobiological classification are a legacy of a universal "evolved predisposition" in *Homo sapiens* (Mithen 1996), or if natural history knowledge – say – is a "meme," and if Bruner

(1996:101) is correct in his claim that the intersubjective, the actional, and the normative probably all have biological roots in the genome, then science and folk, or indigenous, knowledge are cognitively closer than we might think. In the light of the new neurobiology, however, this view of the brain, with its computational and algorithmic representation, is increasingly incompatible with what we now know of brains and bodies and how they interact with the world.

Thus, categorization and classification are embodied and experienced, not just imposed or constructed (Edelman 1992:236): they proceed as synesthetic processes, combining all our senses (Varela et al. 1993:172–177). Symbols arising from complex cultural traditions mold the prefrontal cortex through neural plasticity to transform our conscious minds. We see a nice illustration of this in Berlin's (2006) work on verbal mimesis, with its strong echo of the relevance of the co-evolutionary.

Ethnobiological Universals

One source of evidence for domain specificity and evolved tendencies has been claims for the existence of lexical and classificatory universals in the natural history domain. Historically, this has been an important area for the investigation of cognitive universals, and although the recognition of universals does not in itself imply non-cultural "evolved" origins, it has often been assumed to represent strong evidence in its favor. Some of the conclusions of this research are still contested, but there is a small but growing body of secure knowledge. Many aspects of rule-governed category formation and classification work in the same way irrespective of cognitive or semantic domain, but there are also significant differences between domains, some of which have major theoretical and methodological implications.

Since folk classifications of biological species must co-evolve with the plants and animals that are their subject, we can agree with Boster (1996), in the most general sense, and at the level of clearly discriminated prototypes of natural kinds, that humans "carve nature at the joints." In other words, there are certain discontinuities that are so protean, so much part of the lives of so many human populations, that they might be said to be universal. To begin with, this appears to be true for natural kinds as a phenomenal type and is evident in the universal recognition of "animacy." Additionally, few would now deny that all classifications display some concept of logically "basic" category or "level" applied to biota (or things in nature, or natural kinds), the segregates of which are then either aggregated or disaggregated to create complex classifications. For Haudricourt (1973:268) and for Berlin (1992) it is the genus that gives us the basic level for plants in many languages, while species obtain priority only with Linnaeus, though doubt has been expressed as to the level at which basic categories of natural kinds might be found (Bulmer 1970; Ellen 1993:67–71).

Universals have also been claimed to exist at the level of "unique beginner," such as plant or animal. The argument here is supported by both linguistic and experimental sorting data, but also by negative inference, in that it is difficult to see how cultural and developmental factors in themselves could generate such salient if sometimes lexically covert categories (Boyer 2001). Ethnobiological universals are also argued for in respect to life forms (e.g., Berlin et al. 1973), some of which appear to be more obvious than others. These latter vary cross-culturally, but do not always partition "the living world into broadly equivalent divisions" (Atran 1998:n. 5). Thus, though the "tree" concept may have existed for millions of years, it has been suggested that the life-form category and term are linguistically recent (Witkowski et al. 1981), while its earliest naming appears to have involved functional considerations reflected in tree–wood polysemy (Ellen 1998:71). The work of Brown (1984) demonstrates the universality of a few life forms and the order in which they are added to language, but also confirms the diversity of the many. Moreover, while some (e.g., Brown 1984; Boster 1996) have emphasized the origins of natural kind classification in evolutionary psychology, we might equally demonstrate non-cultural recognition abilities and the evolutionary antiquity of cross-cutting functional classifications, such as "edible–non-edible" and "predator–non-predator" (Johns 1990).

Only "natural kinds" match directly real and discrete objects in an objective world. But even with biodiversity, some gaps between purportedly discrete kinds and objects are bigger and more salient than others, in most environments, and therefore serve as more widespread (even perhaps universal) markers in classifying behavior. Human experience, in many diverse environments, does not mean, for example, that we automatically recognize a "tree" as a bounded kind of thing, as we can see in any photograph of a stretch of forest. Trees often merge imperceptibly into bushes. The definition is therefore polythetic, single features being neither essential nor sufficient to allocate a percept to a category. In an important sense, then, the objective "thinginess" of the biota sets it apart from many other semantic domains (social as social relations, color, taste, or smell), and what separates it from other domains that classify objects (say, cultural objects) is the degree to which we can organize it according to its plausibly conjectured evolution. Thus, grouping natural objects *a* and *b* is more likely to indicate historical affinities (common origin) than, say, a classification of furniture. To refer to the thinginess of the natural world is simply to acknowledge the universal human imperative to turn the natural world into things and to think of the things so prehended in terms of their essential qualities. This is not to say that such a capacity is innate in the sense of springing into action from the first moment of post-partum development: it is simply to recognize the existence of a process that takes place over time, a consequence of interaction between normal developmental processes and environmental stimuli.

We cannot keep semantic domains separate, and no one domain can be represented in its own terms. It is always necessary to translate into a second domain in order to be understood. This is why the metaphorical and the symbolic are so central to cognition. The way in which we use the domain of social experience to make sense of the natural world has long been argued, by such as Mauss and Lévi-Strauss, but this now begins to make much more sense given what we know about the role and dominance of the social intellect in primate evolution (e.g., Dunbar 2003). But it is precisely this mutual explanation of the material in terms of the social and the social in terms of the material (however arbitrary these ideas might be in empirical terms) that entrenches in cognition the methodology we call Cartesian dualism. Though ultimately a distortion of experience, this notion works sufficiently well most of the time for most of us to place confidence in it for practical purposes. But not only do we use distinctions derived from one domain to organize another; we repress certain characteristics and exaggerate and foreground others to better organize the world. Any one species, entity, or percept is far too complex an aggregation of traits to be stored and retrieved as information in any one-dimensional form. The processes of simplification required sometimes gives us more naturalistic classifications, and sometimes more symbolic ones.

Inferential Knowledge of Living Organisms

By ethnobiological knowledge I have in mind local knowledge of the living environment, including plants, animals, and the human body: ethnobotany, ethnozoology, and ethnoanatomy, including the applied knowledges that arise from these, such as ethnomedicine. Hitherto, most studies of such knowledge undertaken by anthropologists have focused on individual folk species and their classification into more inclusive schemes. But when it comes to understanding how knowledge about the environment is more generally organized, we need to note that identification of types is only the start. Thus, individual natural kinds provide a conceptual focus for the aggregation, storage, and understanding of species-specific knowledge (autoecological knowledge), while the classification of organisms in a particular way provides a basis for inferring features of common biology that may not be specifically remembered. In addition, from systems of partonyms for particular organisms, and groups of organisms, we can further infer aspects of people's biological understanding, and from indirect features, for example leaf variegation in manioc, we might infer important information about the toxicity of otherwise edible tubers. In this way apparently inconsequential features of identification can be seriously adaptive. In this way also we can see how the mind can make sense of ecological knowledge, and transmit it, without necessarily converting it into language (Ellen 2003a:47–48; 2003b:62–63). It is just one of many possible examples that show us that while knowledge of plants and animals may often be lexicalized, we need to differentiate between lexical and non-lexicalized substantive knowledge, and that this non-lexicalized knowledge in non-literate populations heavily outweighs that committed systematically to language.

Taxa-specific knowledge of the above kind needs to be distinguished cognitively from knowledge of general principles of biology that may be more important than simply the aggregation of knowledges of individual species or groups of species. In this kind of knowledge, what is crucial is the ability to transfer (or infer) lessons learned from one organism in one context to a second or more organisms in different contexts. One of the most obvious areas in which we can see this happening is in the transfer of lessons learned in using the properties of medicinal plants for humans to veterinary care, or of inferences about bitterness and toxicity in food to medicinal or poisoning applications, or from observations of the internal organs and functioning of the bodies of hunted animals to understanding the workings of the human body (Ellen 2003b:57–64). While such knowledge is subject to widespread diffusion, sometimes in the hyper-organized form of traditional medical practices, universal human knowledge of generic biological principles has led to the repeated independent discovery of ecological properties using common patterns of causality in different cultural settings (see the work of Sinclair and his group as reported in, for example, Walker et al. 1999). Something similar may be apparent in the demonstration of cross-cultural convergence in adult concepts of biological inheritance found by Astuti et al. (2004), even though patterns of development may vary culturally. Such evidence supports the claim by Johnson-Laird (1982) that storing knowledge as causal hypotheses (or models) is more efficient than "databank" models because humans have insufficient memory to make the right responses by induction alone (and we might add, relying on oral culture and low levels of division of labor).

Ethnoecology, Landscape, and Nature

Not all knowledge of the natural world is perceived, logged, ordered, or activated through models based on individual organisms, nested folk classifications of "natural kinds," or inferences based on observations of general organismic principles. Ethnoecological knowledge of places, or systemically and functionally organized spaces, rather than typologically related organisms, plays an important role in the way we model and understand the natural world. Such folk synecological knowledge involves overlapping understandings of the non-living environment, such as water, soil, rocks, climate, topography, intuitive physics, and computation, and the patterns and movements of astronomical bodies.

People perceive, group, and understand individual organisms in terms of second order categories based on physical and ecological proximity, through what we call habitats, landscape types, or ethnoecological categories. There are a growing number of analyses of how people organize knowledge at this level (e.g., Conklin 1976; Meilleur 1986). For example, some studies on the ethnoecological classifications of tropical forest peoples (e.g., Shepard et al. 2001:31–32) have suggested the existence of common themes and patterns, factors such as topography, flooding, other disturbance regimes and soils generating a small number of general categories, distinctions between primary and secondary forest, including various stages of swidden fallow regeneration. Indeed disturbance history is probably the single most important dimension in classifying forest for people engaged in swidden cultivation. In other words, we find a widespread conceptual model based on a limited number of dimensions of perceived experience. However, these same data also raise issues regarding overall category differentiation, degree of lexicalization and, most specifically, in relation to the claim of the extent to which biotic features – mostly indicator plant species – are used to define more specific habitat types. Other data (e.g., Ellen 2007; Widlok 2008) emphasize the difficulties of eliciting ethnoecological classifications independent of distinctions based on use strategies, land tenure, and other contingent contextual information. These suggest that it is often inappropriate to treat complex multidimensional landscape categories in the same way that many have analyzed folk classifications of species. We should not expect the degree of shared systematic categorization implied in the Matsigenka data of Shepard et al., for example, to be necessarily repeated elsewhere, and would expect people to lexicalize their environment more flexibly and with more limited shared encoding.

The issues raised by ethnoecological classifications lead us directly to the literature on the construction of "nature" as a more abstract category. The category of nature has been extensively critiqued from a perspective of social constructivism (e.g., Descola and Pálsson 1996; Ellen and Fukui 1996), and it is now very clear that not only do many languages have no word for nature, but that the contrast between "nature" and "culture" is far too simplistic to explain how most people perceive, interact with, and represent the world; that the way we define nature alters over time, and that particular human populations use the concept of nature in numerous and often contradictory ways. However, the data elicited by anthropologists on the classification of natural kinds, on symbolic classifications, orientation, and social deixis, provide powerful evidence in support of some kind of cognitive architecture yielding categories at this level of generality, based on (1) the propensity to perceive entities in the real world that represent so many concrete kinds which can then be grouped into increasingly larger groups based on family resemblance (e.g., sparrow–bird–animal, oak–tree–plant), (2) the tendency to distinguish self from other (village:forest, land:sea, here:there), and (3) a notion of internal essence that captures the "nature" of some entity, as when we talk of certain behaviors being "natural." Depending on the social context this can be an affirmative announcement, or it can be negative, requiring control. What is interesting about notions of this kind is that they bring together ideas originating in work on biocognition with ideas generated through work on social cognition (Ellen 1996), reinforcing the argument of the previous section regarding the consubstantiality and essential interdependence of different semantic domains.

As Atran and Medin (2008) have recently noted, there is often considerable variability in the systematic folk ecology of groups living in the same area, as well as qualitative differences in folk biological understanding. Indeed, their data show greater similarities between experts in modern cultures and people from small-scale societies, and greater levels of abstraction and induction in societies where knowledge of, and "cultural support" for, learning about the natural world is eroded as a result of diminishing contact with living kinds in urban societies and in majority culture. There is, therefore, a disjunction between empirical knowledge of biological diversity, objective biological diversity, and linguistic encoding, the consequences of which can sometimes be dramatic. A particular concern is how cognitive and cultural change results in some people protecting their environment and others destroying it. Itza' Maya, for example, with few cooperative institutions but with mutually reinforcing spirit beliefs and rich ethnoecological knowledge, promote forest replenishment and show awareness of ecological complexity and an aptitude for sustainability. By comparison, Q'eqchi (with highly cooperative institutions and dense internally connected social networks) acknowledge few ecological dependencies and foster rapid depletion. Ladinos are in between, closer to the behavior of native Maya than immigrant Maya, it is claimed, because they have more open social networks with close links with Itza'.

The Contribution of Studies of Technological Skills to Cognitive Anthropology

What we conveniently describe as "indigenous knowledge" is inevitably a combination of what Lévi-Strauss recognized as a purely intellectual compulsion on the part of collective human minds to make sense of the world, and useful bits of knowledge to better act upon it. For this reason it is difficult to separate domains of technological knowledge (domains of application) from domains of understanding. Technology draws on both natural history and intuitive physics in order to achieve selected material objectives: organizing time, making artifacts, getting and producing food, managing natural resources, processing food, navigation … and many more. In cognitive anthropology, the contribution of studies of way-finding has had a particularly privileged position, given the extensive literature on, for example, traditional oceanic navigation (e.g., Gladwin 1970; Frake 1985; Gell 1985; Akimichi 1996). This has raised many issues of cognitive significance, including whether we navigate using map-like structures – abstract networks and spaces viewed from above – or by employing a succession of linear signposts, whether visual, auditory, tactile, or olfactory (Gell 1985). The ethnography suggests that how we combine these strategies depends on the kinds of environments we are traversing (for example, whether dense tropical forest, open desert, or a highly culturally modified urban neighborhood), and on our access to forms of symbolic storage, such as maps *sensu stricto*.

When we look at a particular technological activity we can see that it is composed of cultural elements that we might hypothesize as cognitive "archaeotypes," each having been discovered many times by humans, and for this reason presumably drawing on an evolutionary predisposition to identify and solve problems in similar ways, what Mithen (1996) and others have described as "technical intelligence." What is more difficult to explain are local combinations of these archaeotypes, how people learn to link them together in a process of qualitative innovation (Barnett 1953:7). If we look at the example of Nuaulu sago starch processing in eastern Indonesia (Ellen 2004a), the most complex operation is that linking separation of starch granules through pounding, the addition of water to create a suspension, the combination of pressing of wet pulp and filtering, and the retrieving of flour following sedimentation. There is much to be said for seeing the entire process, from cutting to heating, as a single integrated body of knowledge and material actions, but if we concentrate on starch separation, the key conceptual breakthrough in the innovation of palm starch technology is the discovery that by leaching inedible pith edible flour can be extracted. This required recognition that starch granules could be separated from fibrous pith and that this could be achieved by mixing the unprocessed pith with water, using a semi-permeable membrane to separate starch in suspension from fiber, and then separating the starch through sedimentation. Regardless of the particular constellation of equipment and material actions employed to realize this objective, such a combination of understanding, once embedded in a population's collective knowledge base through repeated sharing, may be said to represent a *cultural schema* in the sense used by D'Andrade (1995) and others (e.g., Gopnick and Wellman 1994; Keller and Keller 1996:22): meaning an empirical generalization representing particular plans, procedures, tools, and artifacts, typically organized through multinodal structures which can potentially incorporate visual, kinesthetic, oral, and propositional information. However, in the case of sago-processing the inscription required *third order* problem-solving. Where palms are domesticated or used for their fruit, cabbage, leaves, leaf stalks, the process by which opportunities might have been prehistorically translated into regular resource use is relatively straightforward and easy for us to appreciate. These innovations required the solving of what we might characterize, cognitively, as *first order* food-processing problems. Where palms are tapped for their juice and subsequently fermented we might speak of *second order* food-processing problems, since the solution requires analogical reasoning, perhaps drawing on existing uses of more readily accessible and useful stem sugars (maple syrup, cane sugar). However, in the case of palms utilized for their solid starch, the cognitive problem might be said to be a *third order* one, since there are few obvious parallels on which to draw. We can observe similar kinds of cognitive activity in the recognition of toxicity in plants, and in the techniques devised for its reduction (as in processing yams containing dioscorine), and the selective use of low levels of toxicity for therapeutic purposes (Johns 1990).

Intracultural Variation, Change, and Transmission

Early studies of indigenous knowledge tended to consist of connected normative statements, of the kind "The X believe that ..." The methodological challenge to the "omniscient speaker–hearer" model was particularly articulated from within the ethnoscience community. Increasingly, ethnographic practitioners began to actually measure the variable distribution of knowledge within a population (e.g., Gardner 1976), or variation in the significance of particular species (Turner 1988; Stoffle et al. 1990). Studies of variability are now numerous (Berlin 1992:199–231), but once it became empirically evident that fundamental knowledge might vary within a population, the data raised important issues concerning the extent of "cultural consensus" (Romney et al. 1986; Ellen 2003b; Sillitoe 2003:109–116), constraints on transmission of knowledge networks deriving from structured bias and stochasticity (Casagrande 2002), knowledge exchange and flow, the information upon which subsistence decision-making might be based, and strong evidence of the role of social and situational factors. Here again ethnobiological knowledge provided convenient data with which to explore new methods (Boster 1984, 1986), including free-listing and pile-sorting (as in Werner and Schoepfle 1987). Such studies reinforced a distributional view of knowledge, never existing in its totality in any one place or individual, despite the widespread anecdotal reports of the knowledgeability of particular individuals, and the well-documented accounts of key indigenous research participants such as Méndez Ton Alonso (Berlin 2003) or Ian Saem Majnep (Marcus 1991). Indeed, to a considerable extent classificatory knowledge has become increasingly devolved not in individuals at all, but in cultural artifacts, and in the practices and interactions in which people themselves engage. But as knowledge remains orally articulated, or even devolved in non-linguistically coded tacit experience, it often poses obstacles to effective reproduction through the literate mode, inviting serious over-simplification, straining the limits of ordinary language as a medium of transmission, and giving rise to specialized forms of language (such as mathematical notation) or devolved in practical interactive demonstrations of which language may be the lesser part. Consider, for example, how you would explain to a child how to tie a shoelace – over the telephone.

As individuals vary in their classificatory, substantive, and applied knowledge, we can infer that these things are constantly changing. The data concerning how classifications change in the short term through category extension (as reflected in, for example, lexical marking behavior), category obsolescence, are now well attested, though inferences concerning the way ranks grow over the longer term, and how new life forms are added to natural history knowledge, are less secure (Berlin 1972; Brown 1984). Much more attention has been paid in recent years to interindividual knowledge transmission, a focus that has been accompanied by acquisition of data on the distribution of knowledge by age and generation (e.g., Stross 1973). Models for analyzing transmission have been influenced by the work of Luigi Cavalli-Sforza (Hewlett and Cavalli-Sforza 1986; Ohmagari and Berkes 1997), emphasizing simple contrasting types of transmission (vertical versus horizontal) and assuming knowledge to be a kind of stuff to be transmitted meme-like between individuals, rather than the outcome of an interactive process between individuals, or between individuals, knowledge, and the properties of the materials on which the technology depends. There has been particular emphasis on studies of ethnobotanical knowledge erosion, and a body of evidence (e.g., Atran and Medin 2008:47) suggesting that substantive knowledge declines faster that lexical knowledge. However, studies of knowledge acquisition and erosion have tended to focus on acquired or eroded elements of a single domain, as, for example, the transmission of plant knowledge, ethnomedical knowledge, food knowledge, and so on. What such an approach ignores is the relevance to transmission of simultaneous membership of several domains. Thus, erosion of knowledge in one domain may accelerate erosion in another of which that plant is a member; or alternatively, maintenance of knowledge of the plant in the context of one domain will enable retention of knowledge in another. The more complex the domain, the more this kind of overlap is likely to be significant (Ellen 2009).

Atran and Medin suggest that an appreciation of values and meanings in environmental decision-making and management helps to explain why Menominee children reveal progressively poorer subject scores for science as they move through the school system. This is attributed to differences in specific goals, and to media coverage. Expertise cannot be separated from cultural context, even when people engage in the same activities. Moreover, despite common processes for cognizing nature, cultural variation in its understanding is related to critical differences in their respective "framework theories," in decision-making and management, as well as to group conflict and stereotyping arising from these differences. It demonstrates effectively how erosion of knowledge amongst ordinary people is linked to diminishing contact with nature, and the cognitive consequences of how we humans act upon the world in different cultural contexts.

The Impact of Literacy, Scholarly Knowledge, and Science

Folk knowledge of the environment is typically orally transmitted, through imitation, demonstration, and interactive rediscovery. For as long as technical knowledge was oral and shared it was constantly being reinforced by the elasticity of the brain and the distribution of knowledge across individuals, but it was ultimately subject to the cognitive limitations of both brain and body, and in particular "cognitive economy." However, through specialist divisions of technical labor (professional remembrancers, and technical occupational specialization) these limits could be exceeded, a process accentuated through the use of visual images and material culture. This process in turn made it possible for particular domains and classifications to acquire semi-autonomous histories, displaying "emergent" properties and characteristics determined by a cultural framework unfettered by ecological experience and ordinary cognitive constraints. However, writing has been the technology that has had most impact on environmental cognition, permitting long-term storage, unconstrained by (even distributed) memory, and permitting new ways of manipulating data (e.g., Goody 1977; Ong 1982). Writing knowledge makes it more portable and permanent, increases the quantities that can be stored in one form, allows for new kinds of representation and connections, and reinforces the dislocation that arises when knowledge rooted in a particular place and set of experiences (i.e., local or indigenous) and generated by people living in those places is transferred to other places. Thus, the same Tibetan herbal text might integrate environmental knowledge of medicinally important plants from very different habitats over the wider Himalayan area and as far north as Mongolia. Similarly, people can agree on categories even where there is apparent disagreement over descriptions of what is to be put in them. Such artifacts as manuscripts are every bit as much part of what indigenous knowledge systems can tell us about cultural cognition as data obtained from knowledge transmitted orally.

It is, therefore, perhaps unsurprising that early anthropological models of category formation too were not only heavily constrained by adherence to linguistically defined approaches but also to a writing-based interpretation of how knowledge is everywhere organized, what Bloch (1991) has called the "linear-sentential" model of culture. Moreover, we now understand that the distinctions sometimes made between what we call science and other knowledge-making processes are less than clear. Intuitive or local knowledge exists at the interface of most sophisticated technologies, and in many populations the products of formal science routinely hybridize with established local knowledge to produce new indigenous knowledges. Historically, much European science emerged and built upon what we would now describe as European folk or expert local knowledge (as in the work of Linneaus and Galileo), and during the seventeenth and eighteenth centuries scholars became conscious of this interplay through contact with new knowledge from the rest of the world. Today, things have come full circle, and we can find virtue in looking at cognitive organization of scientific knowledge much as we would look at folk knowledge.

From Cognitive Anthropology to Cultural Cognition

Studies of "indigenous" systems of environmental knowledge have been at the center of cognitive anthropology as it emerged as a distinct intellectual practice during the second half of the 20th century. They have provided a laboratory in which some of the key concepts and methodologies have been fashioned and tested, partly because the physical sense data that are their referents had a greater fixity than, say, social relationships or other indirectly apprehended phenomena. Work on these forms of knowledge has provided data drawn from ethnographic settings on the capacity of the human mind, and of distributed minds, to store, evaluate, and utilize knowledge of the natural world and the broader environment, aided by language; and has been at the forefront of major theoretical advances, in particular in relation to: (1) the universal shared properties of thought in relation to evolved features, (2) the distributed character of knowledge, (3) the role of situated bodily practice, and (4) the social context of knowledge. It has also been important in (5) redrawing methodologically the boundary between psychology and anthropology. Overall, we might characterize this shift (especially in the context of the emerging enculturation of the mind model of contemporary neuroscience) as one from cognitive anthropology to cultural cognition. In conclusion, it is useful to expand upon each of these themes.

Universals and evolved features

Historically, work on natural kinds has been a major forcing ground for identifying the issues and testing propositions. If the work on cognitive universals has sometimes seemed problematic, the capacity of culture and the mind to continually rediscover the same basic ecological processes, through patterns of causality repeatedly in different cultural settings, seems to demonstrate a place for underlying evolved structures in achieving this, but equally demonstrates that at every stage it relies on and is constrained by local cultural and ecological particularities. Similarly, while drawing on social cognition and models, technological knowledge builds upon a knowledge of the properties of natural species, combined with a knowledge of intuitive physics encoded in other ways: knowledge as a musical score as extemporization; the universality of the experimental method.

Distributed knowledge

There is now recognition that culture has allowed for degrees of complexity in the arrangement of categories that individual brains cannot accommodate. The boundary between shared and individual representations is increasingly difficult to maintain (Sperber 1985), such that personal cognitive organization as well as what is shared culturally becomes a proper focus of anthropological scrutiny (Strauss 1992). Thus, following Sperber (e.g., Sperber and Hirschfeld 2006), Atran and Medin (2008) argue that environmental knowledge comprises causally distributed networks of mental representations and external linguistic, social, and material expressions, about complex distributions of causally connected representations across minds. Their point of departure is the modeling of micro-processes of individual cognition and practice, and from this macro-structural norms and other regularities emerge from decentralized local interactions, in which content is unstable and seldom reliably replicated.

Bodily and situational practice

Cognitive engagement with the physical world involves not only interlection but sensation. Much knowledge relating to the functioning of organisms, or systems of organisms, is unlexicalized and unspoken in traditional populations, part of habitual taken for granted practice. Whereas cognition and perception suggest purely cerebral processes, we now recognize them as complexly "embedded," with the character of what I have elsewhere described as *prehension* (Ellen 2005:27–29), and emphasizing the difficulties of distinguishing mind from matter, thinking from doing or speaking, individual from group, cerebral from social, and natural from cultural. Cognition in this sense is context-dependent, involving the whole person as he or she moves around the world in space and time (e.g., Dougherty and Keller 1982). While it can be accepted that the notion of "embeddedness" is often prone to insufficient specification (Vayda et al. 2004:37–38), we cannot empirically understand cognition without going beyond it to show how mental processes relate to habitual somatic behavior. Increasingly our understanding of cognition is therefore "experientialist" and "embodied" (Lakoff and Johnson 1980:178), relying on a definition of culture that is intrinsically interactive and intersubjective, colonizing the different brains it encounters. All of this echoes Varela et al. (1993:173), who emphasize too how sensory and motor processes, perception and action, are fundamentally inseparable in lived cognition. They argue that "mind and the world together arise in *enaction*, [though] their manner of arising in any particular situation is not arbitrary" (177, emphasis added); while knowledge, located at "the interface between mind, society, and culture, rather than in one or even in all of them ... does not preexist in any one place or form but is enacted in particular situations" (179).

Social context

Since so much of what we sense and experience is mediated by social consciousness, and since the boundary between the mundane (technical) and symbolic is often unclear, it has sometimes been difficult, in practice, to know how to divide these two axes: symbolic things are in an important sense practical, and practical classifications of the non-social world often rely on metaphors which are ultimately social, as in the use of the terms *genus* and *family* to organize plants and animals. We therefore anthropomorphize nature through cognitive fluidity, merging and transposing different kinds of thought process. And we all know that many cognitive domains overlap not simply in the way they are used to describe each another, but in their empirical content. One striking example of this is the essential unity and continuity of natural and supernatural, of visible and invisible, forms (see, for example, Boyer 1993).

Most practical technologies, including those involving sophisticated insights about the working of the world, are often embedded in folk-cosmological frameworks. This has often led scientists and other experts to assume that the embedded technical knowledge was valueless. Justifying the importance of such knowledge in the context of development projects is sometimes embarrassing and difficult for anthropologists, since it suggests that effective decisions about, say, choice of an appropriate medication, or where to find game, are influenced by irrational claims. But such frameworks need not necessarily reduce the effectiveness of technical knowledge, and may indeed enhance its utility. Notions of myth and sacredness provide what Atran and Medin (2008) have called "cultural support." Thus, describing a group of trees as sacred provides a powerful positive sanction over behavior related to the extraction of its resources. Even the most abstract and sophisticated scientific knowledge will be situated in some symbolic matrix and associated with ideas that are not in themselves "scientific." My favorite example here (Ellen 2004b:429–430) is of the Micronesian *etak* reported by numerous ethnographers (but see particularly Akimichi 1996), in which various kinds of observations and inferences concerning tides, currents, winds, animal behavior, weather systems, and astronomical movements are integrated and understood with reference to mythical and invisible entities and rationalizations to effect an accurate technology of navigation. Similarly, it has shown how more arcane aspects of biocognition actually relate to practical problems of resource allocation and development, and that Marvin Harris's criticism of ethnoscience as mentalist trivia has not been sustained. It is these kinds of interconnections that have finally undermined the classic notion of "primitive thought" and shown it to be chimerical. Studies of local environmental knowledge among traditional peoples have shown us the ways in which different kinds of knowledge might be constituted in different cognitive practices, and how successive versions of "the great cognitive divide" (as – say – between literacy and non-literacy) need to be much more carefully nuanced before resorting to simple dualist typologies. Indigenous knowledge systems are no different from any other kind of knowledge system in most cognitive respects.

The boundary between psychology and anthropology

Perhaps most importantly, and as empirical knowledge systems have been associated with methodological innovations, Atran and Medin (2008) show how cognitive psychology is severely limited by the dominance of laboratory studies using "standard" populations of unknowledgeable college students, which inevitably fail to capture the significance of cultural variation, and therefore have little to say about "real universals," while ignoring altogether certain basic human processes of categorization and reasoning applied to the conception of biological kinds. Here the authors argue for strong universal evolutionary limits on the organization of biological knowledge as a "learning landscape" shaping the way inferences are generalized from empirical instances or experiences.

REFERENCES

Akimichi, Tomoya
1996 Image and Reality at Sea: Fish and Cognitive Mapping in Carolinean Navigational Knowledge. *In* Redefining Nature: Ecology, Culture and Domestication. Roy Ellen and Katsuyoshi Fukui, eds. Pp. 493–514. Oxford: Berg.
Astuti, R., G. E. A. Solomon, and S. Carey
2004 Constraints on Conceptual Development: A Case Study of the Acquisition of Folkbiological and Folksociological Knowledge in Madagascar. Monographs of the Society for Research in Child Development. Oxford: Blackwell.
Atran, S.
1987 Ordinary Constraints on the Semantics of Living Kinds. Mind and Language 2:27–63.
1990 Cognitive Foundations of Natural History: Toward an Anthropology of Science. Cambridge: Cambridge University Press.
1998 Folk Biology and the Anthropology of Science: Cognitive Universals and Cultural Particulars. Behavioural and Brain Sciences 21:547–609.
Atran, Scott, and Douglas Medin
2008 The Native Mind and the Cultural Construction of Nature. Cambridge, MA: MIT Press.
Aunger, R., ed.
2000 Darwinizing Culture: The Status of Memetics as a Science. Oxford: Oxford University Press.
Barnett, Homer Garner
1953 Innovation: The Basis of Cultural Change. New York: McGraw-Hill.
Berlin, Brent
1972 Speculations on the Growth of Ethnobotanical Nomenclature. Language in Society 1:151–186.
1992 Ethnobiological Classification: Principles of Categorization of Plants and Animals in Traditional Societies. Princeton: Princeton University Press.
2003 How a Folk Botanical System Can Be Both Natural and Comprehensive: One Maya Indian's View of the Plant World. *In* Nature Knowledge: Ethnoscience, Cognition, and Utility. G. Sanga and G. Ortalli, eds. Pp. 38–46. New York: Berg.
2006 The First Congress of Ethnozoological Nomenclature. *In* Ethnobiology and the Science of Humankind. Roy Ellen, ed. Pp. 29–54. Oxford: Blackwell.

Berlin, B., D. E. Breedlove, and P. H. Raven

1973 General Principles of Classification and Nomenclature in Folk Biology. American Anthropologist 75:214–242.

1974 Principles of Tzeltal Plant Classification: An Introduction to the Botanical Ethnography of a Mayan Speaking People of the Highland Chiapas. New York: Academic Press.

Bloch, M.

1991 Language, Anthropology and Cognitive Science. Man 26:183–198.

Boster, J.

1984 Inferring Decision Making from Behaviour: An Analysis of Aguaruna Jivaro Manioc Selection. Human Ecology 12:347–358.

1986 Exchange of Varieties and Information between Aguaruna Manioc Cultivators. American Anthropologist 88:428–436.

1996 Human Cognition as a Product and Agent of Evolution. *In* Redefining Nature: Ecology, Culture and Domestication. R. Ellen and K. Fukui, eds. Pp. 269–289. Oxford: Berg.

Boyer, P.

1993 Cognitive Aspects of Religious Symbolism. Cambridge: Cambridge University Press.

2001 Cultural Inheritance Tracks and Cognitive Predispositions: The Example of Religious Concepts. *In* The Debated Mind: Evolutionary Psychology versus Ethnography. H. Whitehouse, ed. Pp. 57–90. Oxford: Berg.

Brown, C. H.

1984 Language and Living Things: Uniformities in Folk Classification and Naming. New Brunswick, NJ: Rutgers University Press.

Brown, C. H., J. Kolar, B. J. Torrey, T. Trung-Quang, and P. Volkman

1976 Some General Principles of Biological and Non-Biological Folk Classification. American Ethnologist 3:73–85.

Bruner, J.

1996 Frames for Thinking: Ways of Making Meaning. *In* Modes of Thought: Explorations in Culture and Cognition. D. R. Olson and N. Torrance, eds. Pp. 93–105. Cambridge: Cambridge University Press.

Bulmer, R.

1967 Why is the Cassowary Not a Bird? A Problem of Zoological Taxonomy among the Karam of the New Guinea Highlands. Man 2:5–25.

1970 Which Came First, the Chicken or the Egg-Head? *In* Échanges et communications: Mélanges offerts à Claude Lévi-Strauss. J. Pouillon and P. Maranda, eds. Pp. 1069–1091. The Hague: Mouton.

Casagrande, D. G.

2002 Ecology, Cognition, and Cultural Transmission of Tzeltal Maya Medicinal Plant Knowledge. Unpublished Ph.D. dissertation, University of Georgia.

Conklin, H. C.

1954 The Relation of Hanunóo Culture to the Plant World. Unpublished Ph.D. dissertation, Yale University.

1962 Lexicographical Treatment of Folk Taxonomies. *In* Problems in Lexicography. F. W. Householder and S. Saporta, eds. Pp. 119–441. Bloomington: Indiana University Research Center in Anthropology, Folklore, and Linguistics.

1976 Ethnographic Semantic Analysis of Ifugao Land-Form Categories. *In* Environmental Knowing: Theories, Research and Methods. G. T. Moore and R. G. Golledge, eds. Pp. 33–59. Stroudsburg, PA: Dowden, Hutchinson and Ross.

D'Andrade, Roy

1995 The Development of Cognitive Anthropology. Cambridge: Cambridge University Press.

Descola, P., and G. Pálsson, eds.

1996 Nature and Society: Anthropological Perspectives. London: Routledge.

Dougherty, J., and C. M. Keller

1982 Taskonomy: A Practical Approach to Knowledge Structures. American Ethnologist 9:763–774.

Douglas, M.

1975 Implicit Meanings: Essays in Anthropology. London: Routledge and Kegan Paul.

Dunbar, R. I. M.

2003 The Social Brain: Mind, Language, and Society in Evolutionary Perspective. Annual Review of Anthropology 32:163–181.

Durkheim, É., and M. Mauss

1963[1901–02] Primitive Classification. London: Cohen and West.

Edelman, G. M.

1992 Bright Air, Brilliant Fire: On the Matter of the Mind. London: Penguin.

Ellen, R. F.

1986 What Black Elk Left Unsaid: On the Illusory Images of Green Primitivism. Anthropology Today 2(6):8–12.

1993 The Cultural Relations of Classification: An Analysis of Nuaulu Animal Categories from Central Seram. Cambridge: Cambridge University Press.

1996 The Cognitive Geometry of Nature: A Contextual Approach. *In* Nature and Society: Anthropological Perspectives. P. Descola and G. Palsson, eds. Pp. 103–123. London: Routledge.

1998 Palms and the Prototypicality of Trees: Some Questions Concerning Assumptions in the Comparative Study of Categories and Labels. *In* The Social Life of Trees: Anthropological Perspectives on Tree Symbolism. L. Rival, ed. Pp. 57–79. Oxford: Berg.

2003a Arbitrariness and Necessity in Ethnobiological Classification: Notes on Some Persisting Issues. *In* Nature Knowledge: Ethnoscience, Cognition and Utility. G. Sanga and G. Ortalli, eds. Pp. 47–56. Oxford: Berghahn.

2003b Variation and Uniformity in the Construction of Biological Knowledge across Cultures. *In* Nature across Cultures: Views of Nature and the Environment in Non-Western Cultures. H. Selin, ed. Pp. 47–74. Dordrecht: Kluwer.

2004a The Distribution of Metroxylon Sagu and the Historical Diffusion of a Complex Traditional Technology. *In* Smallholders and Stockbreeders: Histories of Foodcrop and Livestock Farming in Southeast Asia. P. Boomgaard and D. Henley, eds. Pp. 69–105. Verhandelingen van het Koninklijk Instituut voor Taal-, Land- en Volkenkunde 218. Leiden: KITLV.

2004b From Ethno-Science to Science, or "What the Indigenous Knowledge Debate Tells Us about how Scientists Define Their Project." Journal of Cognition and Culture 4:409–450.

2005 The Categorical Impulse: Essays in the Anthropology of Classifying Behaviour. Oxford: Berghahn.

2007 Plots, Typologies and Ethnoecology: Local and Scientific Understandings of Forest Diversity on Seram. *In* Local vs Global Science: Approaches to Indigenous Knowledge in International Development. P. Sillitoe, ed. Pp. 41–74. Oxford: Berghahn.

2008 Ethnomycology among the Nuaulu of the Moluccas: Putting Berlin's "General Principles" to the Test. Economic Botany 62:483–496.

2009 A Modular Approach to Understanding the Transmission of Technical Knowledge: Nuaulu Basket-Making from Seram, Eastern Indonesia. Journal of Material Culture 14(2):243–277.

Ellen, R., and K. Fukui, eds.

1996 Redefining Nature: Ecology, Culture and Domestication. Oxford: Berg.

Ellen, R. F., and H. Harris

2000 Introduction. *In* Indigenous Environmental Knowledge and Its Transformations: Critical Anthropological Perspectives. R. Ellen, P. Parkes, and A. Bicker, eds. Pp. 1–33. Amsterdam: Harwood.

Feeley-Harnik, G.

2007 "An Experiment on a Gigantic Scale": Darwin and the Domestication of Pigeons. *In* Where the Wild Things Are Now: Domestication Reconsidered. R. Cassidy and M. Mullin, eds. Pp. 147–182. Oxford: Berg.

Fodor, J. A.
1983 The Modularity of the Mind. Cambridge, MA: MIT Press.
Frake, C. O.
1980 Language and Cultural Description: Essays by Charles O. Frake. Anwar S. Dil, ed. Stanford: Stanford University Press.
1985 Cognitive Maps of Time and Tide among Medieval Seafarers. Man 20:254–270.
Friedberg, C.
1990 Le Savoir botanique des Bunaq: Percevoir et classer dans le Haut Lamaknen (Timor, Indonésie). Mémoires du Muséum National d'Histoire Naturelle, Botanique 32. Paris: Muséum National d'Histoire Naturelle.
Fukui, K.
1996 Co-Evolution between Humans and Domesticates: The Cultural Selection of Animal Coat Colour Diversity amongst the Bodi. *In* Redefining Nature: Ecology, Culture and Domestication. R. Ellen and K. Fukui, eds. Pp. 319–385. Oxford: Berg.
Gardner, P.
1976 Birds, Words and a Requiem for the Omniscient Informant. American Ethnologist 8:446–468.
Gell, A.
1985 How to Read a Map: Remarks on the Practical Logic of Navigation. Man 20:271–286.
Gladwin, T.
1970 East Is a Big Bird: Navigation and Logic on Pulawat Atoll. Cambridge, MA: Harvard University Press.
Goody, J.
1977 The Domestication of the Savage Mind. Cambridge: Cambridge University Press.
Gopnick, A., and H. M. Wellman
1994 The Theory Theory. *In* Mapping the Mind: Domain Specificity in Cognition and Culture. L. A. Hirschfeld and S. A. Gelman, eds. Pp. 294–316. Cambridge: Cambridge University Press.
Grinevald, C.
2000. A Morpho-Syntactic Typology of Classifiers. *In* Systems of Nominal Classification. G. Senft, ed. Pp. 50–92. Cambridge: Cambridge University Press.
Haudricourt, A.
1973 Botanical Nomenclature and Its Translation. *In* Changing Perspectives in the History of Science: Essays in Honour of Joseph Needham. M. Teich and R. Young, eds. Pp. 265–273. London: Heinemann.
Hays, T. E.
1976 An Empirical Method for the Identification of Covert Categories in Ethnobiology. American Ethnologist 8:489–507.
Healey, C.
1993 Folk Taxonomy and Mythology of Birds of Paradise in the New Guinea Highlands. Ethnology 32:19–34.
Hewlett, B. S., and L. L. Cavalli-Sforza
1986 Cultural Transmission among Aka Pygmies. American Anthropologist 88:922–934.
Hunn, E.
1977 Tzeltal Folk Zoology: The Classification of Discontinuities in Nature. New York: Academic Press.
Johns, T.
1990 With Bitter Herbs They Shall Eat. Tucson: Arizona University Press.
Johnson-Laird, P.
1982 Mental Models. Cambridge: Cambridge University Press.
Keller, C. M., and J. D. Keller
1996 Cognition and Tool Use: The Blacksmith at Work. Cambridge: Cambridge University Press.
Lakoff, G., and M. Johnson
1980 Metaphors We Live By. Chicago: Chicago University Press.

Lancy, D. F., and A. J. Strathern
1981 Making Twos: Pairing as an Alternative to the Taxonomic Mode of Representation. American Anthropologist 83:773–795.
Leach, E.
1964 Anthropological Aspects of Language: Animal Categories and Verbal Abuses. *In* New Directions in the Study of Language. E. H. Lenneberg, ed. Pp. 23–63. Cambridge, MA: MIT Press.
Lemonnier, P.
1992 Elements for an Anthropology of Technology. Anthropological Papers Museum of Anthropology University of Michigan no. 88. Ann Arbor: Museum of Anthropology, University of Michigan.
Lévi-Strauss, C.
1962 The Savage Mind. London: Weidenfeld and Nicolson.
Marcus, George E.
1991 Notes and Quotes Concerning the Further Collaboration of Ian Saem Majnep and Ralph Bulmer: Saem Becomes a Writer. *In* Man and a Half: Essays in Pacific Anthropology and Ethnobiology in Honour of Ralph Bulmer. Andrew Pawley, ed. Pp. 37–45. Auckland: Polynesian Society.
Medin, D., and S. Atran, eds.
1999 Folkbiology. Cambridge, MA: MIT Press.
Meilleur, Brien A.
1986 Alluetain Ethnoecology and Traditional Ecology: The Procurement and Production of Plant Resources in the Northern French Alps. Unpublished Ph.D. dissertation, University of Washington, Seattle.
Mithen, S.
1996 The Prehistory of the Mind: A Search for the Origins of Art, Religion and Science. London: Thames and Hudson.
Ohmagari, K., and F. Berkes
1997 Transmission of Indigenous Knowledge and Bush Skills among the Western James Bay Cree Women of Subarctic Canada. Human Ecology 25:197–222.
Ong, W. J.
1982 Orality and Literacy: The Technologizing of the Word. London: Methuen.
Romney, K., S. Weller, and W. Batchelder
1986 Culture as Consensus: A Theory of Culture and Informant Accuracy. American Anthropologist 88:313–338.
Rosaldo, M. Z.
1972 Metaphors and Folk Classification. Southwestern Journal of Anthropology 28:83–99.
Rosch, E.
1977 Human Categorisation. *In* Studies in Cross-Cultural Psychology, vol. 1. N. Warren, ed. Pp. 1–49. London: Academic Press.
Shepard, Glenn H., Douglas W. Yu, Manuel Lizarralde, and Mateo Italiano
2001 Rainforest Habitat Classification among the Matsigenka of the Peruvian Amazon. Journal of Ethnobiology 21:1–38.
Shigeta, M.
1996 Creating Landrace Diversity: The Case of the Ari People and Ensete (Ensete ventricosum) in Ethiopia. *In* Redefining Nature: Ecology, Culture and Domestication. R. F. Ellen and K. Fukui, eds. Pp. 233–268. Oxford: Berg.
Sillitoe, Paul
2003 Managing Animals in New Guinea: Preying the Game in the Highlands. Studies in Environmental Anthropology 7. London: Routledge.
Sillitoe, P., A. Bicker, and J. Pottier, eds.
2002 Participating in Development: Approaches to Indigenous Knowledge. ASA Monograph 39. London: Routledge.

Sperber, D.
1985 Anthropology and Psychology: Towards an Epidemiology of Representations. Man 20:73–89.
Sperber, D., and L. Hirschfield
2006 Culture and Modularity. *In* The Innate Mind, vol. 2: Culture and Cognition. P. Carruthers, S. Laurence, and S. Stich, eds. Pp. 149–164. Oxford: Oxford University Press.
Stoffle, Richard W., Michael J. Evans, and John E. Olmsted
1990 Calculating the Cultural Significance of American Indian Plants: Paiute and Shoshone Ethnobotany at Yucca Mountain, Nevada. American Anthropologist 92:416–432.
Strauss, C.
1992 Models and Motives. *In* Human Motives and Cultural Models. R. D'Andrade and C. Strauss, eds. Pp. 1–20. Cambridge: Cambridge University Press.
Stross, B.
1973 Acquisition of Botanical Terminology by Tzeltal Children. *In* Meaning in Mayan Languages. M. S. Edmonson, ed. Pp. 107–141. The Hague: Mouton.
Sturtevant, W. C.
1964 Studies in Ethnoscience. American Anthropologist 66:99–131.
Taylor, P. M.
1984 "Covert Categories" Reconsidered: Identifying Unlabelled Classes in Tobelo Biological Classification. Journal of Ethnobiology 4:105–122.
Turner, N. J.
1988 "The Importance of a Rose": Evaluating the Cultural Significance of Plants in Thompson and Lillooet Interior Salish. American Anthropologist 90:272–290.
Varela, F. J., E. T. Thompson, and E. Rosch
1993 The Embodied Mind: Cognitive Science and Human Experience. Boston, MA: MIT Press.
Vayda, A. P., B. B. Walters, and I. Setyawati
2004 Doing and Knowing: Questions about Studies of Local Knowledge. *In* Investigating Local Knowledge: New Directions, New Approaches. A. Bicker, P. Sillitoe, and J. Pottier, eds. Pp. 35–58. Aldershot: Ashgate.
Walker, D. H., P. J. Thorne, F. L. Sinclair, B. Thapa, C. D. Wolod, and D. B. Subba
1999 A Systems Approach to Comparing Indigenous and Scientific Knowledge: Consistency and Discriminatory Power of Indigenous and Laboratory Assessment of the Nutritive Value of Tree Fodder. Agricultural Systems 62:87–103.
Warren, D. M., L. J. Slikkerveer, and D. Brokensha, eds.
1995 The Cultural Dimension of Development: Indigenous Knowledge Systems. London: Intermediate Technology.
Werner, O., and G. M. Schoepfle
1987 Systematic Fieldwork, vol. 1: Foundations of Ethnography and Interviewing. Newbury Park, CA: Sage.
Widlok, T.
2007 Conducting Cognitive Tasks and Interpreting the Results: The Case of Spatial Inference Tasks. *In* Experiencing New Worlds. J. Wassmann and K. Stockhaus, eds. Pp. 258–280. Oxford: Berghahn.
2008 Landscape Unbounded: Space, Place, and Orientation in ≠Akhoe Hai//om and Beyond. Language Sciences 30:362–380.
Witkowski, S. R., C. H. Brown, and P. K. Chase
1981 Where Do Tree Terms Come From? Man 16:1–14.

CHAPTER 17

Emotions, Motivation, and Behavior in Cognitive Anthropology

E. N. Anderson

Introduction

Cognition and emotion are now known to be inseparable in normal human thought, but these two types of mental action have long been separated, and remain separate for many analytic purposes. Recent work has tended to break down the distinction.

Early Work

Early work in cognitive anthropology and related fields tended to ignore emotion. Since Descartes, cognition had been separated, in philosophy and in psychological theories, from emotion (affect, sentiment). Cognitive theorists worked with knowledge and the supposedly rational aspects of thought, while Freudians and other specialists worked with affect. There was little meeting across the divide. The "cognitive revolution" in psychology took place largely at Harvard and Yale in the 1950s (Gardner 1985), and firmly placed itself in this tradition. Much of the early work in cognitive anthropology took place at the same two schools, among anthropology students interested in psychology or in traditional knowledge. They naturally followed this classic separation (see, for example, such early collections as Romney and D'Andrade 1964).

Moreover, structuralism, a field closely related academically to cognitive anthropology, tended to dismiss "sentiment" out of hand. Rodney Needham, in an influential and widely read book, *Structure and Sentiment* (1962), lashed out in a full-scale

A Companion to Cognitive Anthropology, First Edition. Edited by David B. Kronenfeld, Giovanni Bennardo, Victor C. de Munck, and Michael D. Fischer.

diatribe against injecting sentiment into studies of family and kinship systems (as had been advocated by David Schneider and others). For Needham, and most kinship students of his time, kinship systems were pure structural abstractions, and the family sentiments that might flow along kin lines were an irrelevant distraction. Anthropology's leading structuralist, Claude Lévi-Strauss, was noted for his "cool" interpretations of culture. Culture, for him, was a beautiful, logical array, free from the messy world of emotion and day-to-day interaction (see, for example, Lévi-Strauss 1962). Structural linguistics, especially the influential Chomskian form, focused on grammar, a cool, unemotional realm. Investigation of emotional communication was limited. Farther afield, economics had become a highly mathematicized and militantly rationalist discipline; it had enormous influence on cognitive anthropology as well as on political science, sociology, and philosophy. "Rational individual self-interest" became paradigmatic; the best source on this in anthropology is Marshall Sahlins's merciless dissection of it (Sahlins 1976).

Furthermore, when cognitive anthropology began in the 1950s and 1960s, anthropology was recovering from certain perceived excesses of the "culture and personality" movement. Many of the early cognitivists sought consciously to distance themselves from that sub-field, which had become identified with studies of sentiment and feeling and with a narrow neo-Freudian perspective and a very low confirmation rate.

However, others took a different view. From the culture and personality side, John and Beatrice Whiting, who were senior scholars at Harvard during the "cognitive revolution" and who therefore taught many of the early cognitive anthropologists, had incorporated cognitive themes in their work (see Whiting 1994). The Whitings were influenced by the sole significant collaboration of a psychological anthropologist and a cognitive psychologist, John Dollard's work with Neal Miller (1950). Dollard and Miller integrated cognition and emotion, laying a groundwork for further research in that area.

Anthony Wallace's *Culture and Personality* (1st edition 1961) attempted to integrate that field with cognitive studies. B. N. Colby and Roy D'Andrade began studies of personhood and affect that would lead to further work in later years. Somewhat related was a concern for heuristics and biases in thought, which followed from Herbert Simon's influential work in the 1950s (Simon 1957). Concerns were purely cognitive at first ("cool cognition"), but quickly expanded to look at "hot cognition" – emotional distorters of thought (see Nisbett and Ross 1980). Recent work has centered on showing how these "irrational" heuristics help us rather than hinder us in coming to decisions; Gerd Gigerenzer, the leader in this field, has provided a delightful popular account (2007; see also D'Andrade 2001).

The real reversal of cognitive psychology's position began in 1980 with Robert Zajonc's paper "Feeling and Thinking: Preferences Need No Inferences" (1980). Zajonc reviewed a large body of research (including Osgood et al. 1957, whose findings on human dichotomous evaluative reactions had already had some influence on cognitive anthropology). Zajonc showed that people invariably evaluate every perception as good or bad, dangerous or safe, positive or negative, before they consciously notice it or identify it. One gets a strong feeling of threat before one has even recognized the lion in the grass. The survival value of this for humans and other animals is obvious, and this rapid assessment mechanism is presumably far older and deeper in the brain than rational thought. Zajonc showed that humans simply do not consciously perceive or notice genuinely neutral stimuli. All conscious perception, and indeed all conscious mentation, involves some affect. Admittedly, Zajonc was talking about something much more basic and elementary than "emotions" in the full sense of the term (Lazarus 1984), but he forced psychologists to recognize that pure rational cognition did not really exist. (The question of how to define "emotion," and how it relates to terms like "feeling," "sentiment," "affect," and "mood," remains highly contentious; see, for example, Elster 1999; Nussbaum 2001; Stets and Turner 2006. The present review will simply use the terms as they are used by the cited authors, thus leaving definitional issues unresolved.)

Zajonc's paper was little noted in anthropology, but was closely paralleled by a major shift in ethnography. Emotions began attracting ethnographic attention, often from people closely associated with the cognitive anthropological universe. The link was, once again, often through the close institutional ties of cognitive anthropology and psychological anthropology, including culture and personality. One influential early example was Edward Schieffelin's *The Sorrow of the Lonely and the Burning of the Dancers* (1975, new edition 2005), which focused on emotions of grief and loss among the Kaluli of Papua New Guinea. Studying and working with Edward and Bambi Schieffelin was Steven Feld, who made the leap of combining their psychological approach with the techniques of cognitive anthropology in the major work *Sound and Sentiment* (1982, with important accompanying sound recording, n.d.[c.1982]). Feld used ethnoscientific and cognitive methodology to sort out types of music and song, cues and features thereof, and underlying thoughts and attitudes. Lila Abu-Lughod (1985) studied a rather similar situation in Egypt, where Bedouin women used song to express emotions and feelings impossible to discuss openly in words. Indeed, since responses to arts and performances inevitably include emotion, all of the enormous anthropological literature on those subjects should be consulted. However, it is outside the bounds of this review.

Emotions as Cultural Constructs

Slightly later, Renato Rosaldo, who had been educated at Harvard at the height of the cognitive revolution, reasserted the importance of emotions in thought (Rosaldo n.d.[c.1985], 1989) on the basis of both research and personal tragedy in Luzon. Keith Basso, another product of Harvard's cognitive days, also integrated cognitive techniques with broader psychological concerns (e.g., Basso 1996). He collaborated with Steven Feld in editing a major collection of studies of landscape that fused the examination of traditional ecological knowledge with analysis of attitudes and emotions toward the land (Feld and Basso 1996). A large number of books following this have dealt with environment and emotional responses or total experience in the Kantian sense (integrating sensation, emotion, and cognition; see, for example, Rose 2000). Clayton and Carole Robarchek studied the relationships of fear and anger in an extremely non-violent society and an extremely violent one (Robarchek 1989a, 1989b; Robarchek and Robarchek 1998).

Slightly after this time, there arose a brief flourishing of attempts to show that emotions were culturally constructed, with little or no innate component. In psychology, Richard Lazarus and Beatrice Lazarus (1994; R. Lazarus 1984, 1991) maintained that the term "emotion" should be restricted to the subtle, complex, learning-influenced feelings of humans, postulating that these have little or no resemblance to animal passions. (Possibly they never owned a dog or cat.) In linguistics, Anna Wierzbicka (1992, 1999) developed a detailed theory (outside the purview of this article) of semantic primes underlying emotional words. She also wrote of cultural emotions that lack equivalents elsewhere. For instance, her Polish background included a uniquely Polish form of nostalgia, apparently deeper and sadder than others' nostalgia – though her description of it does not appear to most readers to be beyond comparison with, say, Marcel Proust's or Thomas Hardy's accounts of similar emotions. Wierzbicka's theory was critiqued in detail by D'Andrade (1995), who remains skeptical of the uniqueness of Polish nostalgia.

In sociology, Rom Harré (1986) took perhaps the most extreme position, not only maintaining stoutly that some emotions had no equivalent in other cultures, but going further to say that emotions are essentially cultural constructs with little or no biological ground. He therefore expected them to vary enormously across cultures. One adduced bit of evidence is the alleged Spanish emotion *vergüenza ajena*, "shame for the stranger," in which one is acutely embarrassed by the behavior of a stranger (or other person irrelevant to oneself; see Harré 1986 and essays therein). Unfortunately, this term is otherwise unreported, and my repeated questioning of Spanish speakers in Spain and Latin America has failed to find it. Moreover, the feeling itself is well known worldwide, perhaps especially among teenagers. It fails both the test of cultural construction (it is not a widespread part of Hispanic culture) and of cultural uniqueness.

The trend in sociology is to see emotions as universal and biological (Stets and Turner 2006, but see Peterson 2006). However, a very important book by Arlie Hochschild, *The Managed Heart* (1983), recounted in exquisite ethnographic detail how airline flight attendents – "stewardesses" in those sexist days – were trained not only to *act* caring and help-oriented toward passengers, but actually to *be* so. Stewardesses who failed to be caring and empathetic did not last long. Hochschild's important work has had major effects on sociology. The knowledge that emotions may be innate but can certainly be trained and culturally managed has led to much research.

In anthropology, extreme views of the cultural nature of emotions have been associated with a group that crystallized around Richard Shweder (yet another product of Harvard's cognitive revolution days) and his "cultural psychology," developed from culture and personality traditions (Shweder and LeVine 1984; Stigler et al. 1990; Shweder 1991, 2003). Shweder had worked in Orissa, and along with Orissan colleagues he explored in detail the differences in Orissan and "American" (i.e., northeastern North American middle-class white) construction of self. Orissans reportedly have a much more social conception of self. The Orissan self is more involved in social transactions, and more protean according to social settings. A self may be very different in different social contexts. (Indianists often use the word "dividual," as opposed to "individual.") This is apparently related to the wide and deep social gulfs between castes, language groups, occupational categories, and other social worlds in India. Shweder avoids blanket generalizations about Indians or Americans, but the implication is that India in general has more broadly social and group-oriented selves than America; Hazel Rose Markus (2008) provides a valuable recent review situating his work with other cross-cultural research from the psychological side. American individualism is, of course, well documented (e.g., Bellah et al. 1996).

A similar case for a "more social" vs. "more individual" self has long been made for China as opposed to "America" or "the West." Early work, focusing on America, was conveniently reviewed in Hsu (1953). The view has gained much support from rigorous experiments, surveys, ethnographic work, and other sources (again, conveniently reviewed: Bond 1986, looking at "the West" in general; the latest major item as of this writing is Oyserman and Lee 2008; see also D'Andrade 2008; for Japan, see Nisbett 2003). This view has been qualified (Anderson 2007), since Chinese are often highly individualistic and independent, and can wall themselves off from others, but the general phenomenon is hard to deny. Self-concepts appear more collectivist than actual emotions, but the obvious implications of such a self-concept for emotional life have been well documented.

Catherine Lutz (1988), also associated with the cultural psychology group, reported an emotion called *fago* (pronounced "fango") from Micronesia. This emotion she considered culturally unique. It implies a deep, caring, tender concern for others – possibly a cultural construction of parent–child love. It appears similar to the Tahitian *arofa*, reported *inter alia* in a similar important study of Oceanian emotion management, *Tahitians* by Robert Levy (1973). (Levy was a slightly earlier member of the same intellectual world, and his book can be seen as a transitional work from culture and personality to cultural psychology.) In any case, in spite of its alleged cultural uniqueness, Lutz does a particularly brilliant job of explaining it in a way that makes it not only comprehensible, but palpable, to the non-Micronesian reader.

All this brought anthropologists back to the age-old questions of how well words *represent* thought, and how much words *influence* thought. The former is as old as philosophy, having been raised by Socrates in Greece, Zhuang Zi in China, and Nagasena in India. (Significantly, all three of them appear to have concluded that words do a sorry job – not only of influencing thought, but even of communicating it.) The latter is known in anthropology as the "Sapir–Whorf hypothesis," but it has a longer lineage, going back at least to the speculation of the early linguist Wilhelm von Humboldt in the early 19th century. Wierzbicka provides a solid, rather favorable case. D'Andrade, in his important review of cognitive anthropology (1995), deals with this question in the context of Lutz's and Wierzbicka's work, as well as his own major projects of research on emotion and personality terms in English. As implied above, he viewed cultural psychology with skepticism, concluding that emotions were not shown to differ greatly – certainly not as greatly as the different words used to define them. The fact that the Greeks distinguished *eros* from *caritas*, and had a verb *philein* with still different connotations, does not necessarily mean that their experiences of love were phenomenologically different from those of us in less verbally subtle cultures. English surely needs new words to separate erotic love, parental love, love for Bach's suites, and love for macaroni and cheese. Yet, D'Andrade's own work disclosed that emotion words in English are incredibly complex and subtle, and are not easily reduced to the simple tables and multidimensional scales usable for fish names, illness terms, or kinship categories.

More generally, researchers from Roger Brown (1958) to Bruno Latour (2005) have concluded that humans work hard and interact complexly with reality to make their words reliable enough to allow communication. A linguistic community finds words that represent adequately what its members want to tell each other. This conclusion implies considerable cultural construction, but enough interaction with external realities to permit actual communication about tasks and needs. This obviously allows plenty of leeway. One does not expect a one-to-one correspondence between words and things; one does not find cultural construction in a vacuum, with concepts unrelated to any reality at all (Latour 2005). Somewhere between, there is space for easy translation of most emotion words, if perhaps not for *fago*.

Philosophers who have recently written major works on emotion (Elster 1999; Nussbaum 2001) were also prone to credit the subtle, learned, and culturally constructed nature of emotions. They also tend to follow the classic philosophical tradition (which goes back to ancient Greece) of seeing emotions as mere disarrangers of the important matters, the purely cognitive and rational side of human mentation. At best (Frank 1988; Gibbard 1990; Nussbaum 2001), emotions are simple things that can become useful workers for cognitive tasks. In general, these philosophers seem to find emotions to be very minor, easily ignored, and easily controlled parts of mental life – a conclusion in sharp contrast with the observations of the novelists cited by Nussbaum, and with the findings of recent psychological work.

Emotions as Universal

In spite of the later date of some of these books, work implying that emotions were overwhelmingly cultural constructs (rather than biologically innate) dates primarily from the 1980s and very early 1990s. The principal reason was that the tide turned rather dramatically in the early 1990s. Paul Ekman, for instance, showed that emotional expressions and the emotions themselves are basically the same among all humans. (Good, accessible summaries of his diverse and widely scattered work are found in Ekman 1992, 2007.) This left open the question of how "basic" was "basic"; Ekman's very broad categories – fear, anger, happiness, surprise, disgust, sadness, and contempt – left a great deal of room for cultural fine-tuning. He himself pointed out the cultural nature of such things as *Schadenfreude* (the German delight in the misfortunes of others) and wonder (whatever that may be cross-culturally; Ekman 2007). Kemper (1987) pointed out that emotions are an open set. Not only are there guilt, shame, interest, excitement, enthusiasm, and many other mood states, but one can always split off some new feeling and give it a name. Many others are also critical of such cut and dried lists (see also Neisser 1976; D'Andrade 1995; Milton 2005).

Darwinian theorists pointed out that the mind has evolved; human minds have certainly evolved from higher primate minds. Basic similarities, driven by adaptive needs to respond to comparable real-world problems such as threat and mating, are to be expected. This point was widely recognized by anthropologists after 1990 (e.g., Barkow et al. 1992) and sociologists (Turner 2000; Hammond 2006; Stets and Turner 2006). This is not to say that dogs experience the subtle nuances that Proust experienced while nibbling his famous *madeleine* – Richard and Beatrice Lazarus certainly have a case here – but the dog and the human are linked by broad contours of natural selection for rapid reaction to universal needs. If a dog or a human had to wait to assess a lion's taxonomy and biology before fleeing, the lion would have a good meal. (This example is used in almost all works on the generality of immediate emotional reaction.)

On the universality and powerful, life-transforming effects of emotion, one may also consider novels and similar literature. Western readers have had little problem – once they learn alien cultural manners – in relating emotionally to the characters in Lady Murasaki's *Tale of Genji*, Cao Xueqin's *Story of the Stone* (an 18th-century Chinese novel), or the works of Dostoevsky, Tolstoy, and Chekhov. Nor have Chinese and Japanese readers been slow to appreciate Shakespeare, Poe, or Hemingway. Translations of poetry from or into every major language sell widely, and literary critics have difficulty with symbols and interpretations but do not seem to find alien and incomprehensible emotions. On the other hand, the ways that emotions are fine-tuned and expressed can vary enormously, not only from culture to culture but even from writer to writer within the same culture (consider Dostoevsky and Tolstoy, or Hemingway and Faulkner).

Meanwhile, psychologists belatedly undercut the assumptions of the culture and personality school by showing that personality traits, like basic emotions, were universal, cross-cutting cultural lines (McCrae and Costa 1997). As with emotion, however, a vast space is left for cultural fine-tuning. Also, devastating attacks on Freudian theory (many summarized in Grünbaum 1984; Dawes 1994) have shown that it has serious limits as a source of useful concepts for anthropology, though some anthropologists, notably Melford Spiro (1987), continue to find valuable inspiration and ideas within the Freudian corpus. (For a superb and witty case study of Freudianism gone wrong in cultural interpretation, see Amborn 2008.)

New Work on Emotions in the Brain

More important has been the discovery of the basic neurology of emotion. This work did not affect anthropology for some years, but it had immediate and dramatic effects on psychology and cognitive studies.

The most widely visible bodies of work were those of Joseph LeDoux (1996) and Antonio and Hannah Damasio (Damasio 1994, 1999). LeDoux's work showed that the amygdala, a small structure deep in the brain, was critical to feelings of fear. It was closely connected to the hippocampus (associated with memory and emotion in general) and with other structures that mediated mood and arousal. LeDoux later expanded his work to cover other emotions, as well as self-concept (LeDoux 2002). Important here was the realization that emotional primes are localized in particular deep-brain structures, and that the physiological basis of affect is the same for all mammals – however much the peripheral guidance and expression of particular feelings may be modified by species-specific developments. Electrical and chemical stimulation of the brain was known to evoke strong feelings in some cases, but this was different: actual localization of a true emotion in a particular neural circuit.

The Damasios' work was specifically on humans, and was more revolutionary in impact. They demonstrated that normal humans always automatically integrate emotion and cognition in social life, decision-making, and indeed simply living. Hence the title of Antonio Damasio's book *Descartes' Error* (1994). Almost 400 years of philosophical and psychological separation was ended overnight. The Damasios found that individuals with traumatic damage to the orbito-frontal cortex (low in the front brain) cannot integrate cognition and emotion adequately, and thus lead most abnormal lives, being incapable of social self-regulation. They cannot figure out how to act appropriately or respond to others' feelings. Humans need to integrate emotions and feelings with cognition in order to have any sort of functional social life.

Further work by a number of neuropsychologists has shown that social behavior, including fine-tuning of social sensitivity, empathy, and "appropriate" social behavior, is centered in the anterior cingulate cortex (in monkeys as well as humans). Here also, emotion and cognition are inseparably united.

The fact that emotion and cognition are inseparable, and indeed necessary parts of a *single* process, began to influence anthropology after the late 1990s. Kay Milton in *Loving Nature* (2002) provided a phenomenological account of environmentalists and their actions in England and the Continent, and showed how the Damasios' findings could make sense of otherwise incomprehensible, "irrational" conflicts between different environmentalist camps over such things as whether to save or exterminate an introduced duck species that was genetically swamping a local south European one. What appeared to be an exceedingly narrow technical point, of interest only to a few waterfowl geneticists, blew up into a huge conflict that led to street demonstrations, violent emotions, and even physical threats.

Milton (2005) has gone on to provide an excellent overview of emotion in social science, emphasizing that it needs to be examined ecologically – in a very broad sense of that word: individuals relating to their environments. She calls for "methodological individualism," in contrast to others (many cited above) who have emphasized the strongly social and cultural nature of emotions. She continues to stress the embodied nature of emotions and the wrongness of Descartes, though her recursion to the old William James (or James–Lange) theory that emotions are actually *caused* by body reactions is unfortunate. (She maintains that crying *causes* sadness; this goes against the experience of American males, who are socialized not to cry but who have no problems feeling sad at appropriate times.)

Ethnography based on cognitive anthropology has yet to incorporate these insights fully. Indeed, ethnography throughout the whole field of cultural anthropology has remained surprisingly resistant to continuing the work of Feld or Rosaldo. An important exception is Kimberly Hedrick's study of cattle-ranching (2007), which is cognitive-based but draws on Milton as well as Feld and Basso (among others). She followed the decision-making methodology of Gladwin, Randall, and others (see Kronenfeld 2009:ch. 2) but, unlike previous workers, took full account of emotion. The ranchers' complex and highly emotional feelings about the land were basic to their decision-making. So was their profound factual and rational knowledge of cattle, grass, trails, forest, economics, bureaucracy, and much more. Their embodied procedural knowledge of riding, herding, and maintenance was also relevant. Thus their decisions were not economically "rational," but were heavily conditioned by emotions, including the emotionally given goal of maintaining their beloved way of life.

Naomi Quinn (2006) has drawn on neuropsychology, notably including LeDoux, to address anthropological ideas of the self. Much further work using the Damasios' findings has taken place in psychology and sociology (Stets and Turner 2006) and in political science (Marcus 2002; Westen 2007). Today, thus, we may follow Hyde et al. (2008:291) in speaking of "the ABCs" of thinking: "affective, biological and cognitive" models or influences.

Motivation

This recent work provides a bridge to the topic of motivation. Anthropologists, cognitive and otherwise, have been remarkably silent on the topic of motivation, largely because it is an article of faith throughout anthropology that people do what their "culture" tells them to do. However, the idea of people as virtually mindless followers of "culture," identified with Leslie White (1949), has been substantially abandoned in contemporary anthropology, in favor of views more associated with agency. The late Pierre Bourdieu takes much credit for this (see Bourdieu 1977, 1990; see also Latour 2005). Motivation theories have been slow to catch up. Bourdieu himself emphasized negotiation for individual self-interest within hierarchic social settings. Recent anthropology has more often focused on individual desire or structural pressure for power over people; in this case the immediate stimulus is Michel Foucault, though the concerns go back to Marx and Weber. (This is a drastic oversimplification of Bourdieu and especially of Foucault, but serious consideration of their theories is unfortunately impossible in this short review.)

Most of this speculation is outside of cognitive anthropology per se, but within cognitive anthropology a substantial literature has recently developed. A volume of exploratory essays, edited by D'Andrade and Claudia Strauss, appeared in 1992. General reviews of the field since then (notably including Kronenfeld 1996, 2008; Strauss and Quinn 1997; Shore 1998; Quinn and Strauss 2006) have at least touched on issues of feeling and motive, including issues of classifying people, perniciously or otherwise (Kronenfeld 1996), and managing social situations sensitively (Shore 1998). Particularly important is an article by Claudia Strauss (2007), with appended discussion and debate, on American emotional and cognitive reactions and explanations after the deadly shootings at Columbine High School in Colorado. In all these sources, cognitive anthropology merges into the huge literature on agency, motive, and person that has emerged in cultural anthropology in the last 30 years (a literature unfortunately outside our purview here; for cognitive anthropological reviews of relevant concepts, see Quinn and Strauss 2006).

Many decision-making studies have been concerned with goals. The vast majority of decision-making studies (largely outside anthropology) have concerned economic behavior, and assume maximization of a material or monetary return as the goal, but anthropological research has led to major modifications of this general assumption. Robert Randall found that Samal fishermen were largely concerned with "making a living" (maximizing overall utility) as opposed to simply maximizing fish catches. Quinn and Holland found desire to marry was influenced not only by biology but also by local culture, which put tremendous pressure on girls to find a partner (see Strauss and Quinn 1997, and esp. Holland and Eisenhardt 1990). Hedrick's findings on lifestyle have been noted above. All anthropological studies show that decisions are made within cultural norms – people attend to the side goal of doing what is "right" or "appropriate" or "praiseworthy."

Recent concern for the environment has inspired a rapidly growing number of studies by cognitive anthropologists of traditional, local, or national values and levels of motivation to save or manage environmental resources. Willett Kempton studied decision-making for saving energy in American homes, and, with James Boster and

Jennifer Hartley, explored the wider question of how motivated Americans are to save their environment (Kempton et al. 1996). A group including the cognitive anthropologists Scott Atran and Norbert Ross and the cognitive psychologist Douglas Medin has recently produced a number of studies of Native American environmental values in Mexico and the United States (see, for example, Atran et al. 1999; Ross 2003; Medin et al. 2006).

Studies of folk taxonomy have shown that people develop classification systems for use (Hunn 1982, 2008), but also because humans simply want to classify things – they have a drive to classify (a *vis classificatrix* in the phrase of Berlin 1992). This is presumably derived from the universal animal property once called "stimulus generalization." As early as 1798, Immanuel Kant, in the first significant book about "anthropology," observed that people aggregate stimuli that evoke similar responses, differentiate those that require different ones (Kant 1978[1798]). So classification is shaped by use, but classifying in order to develop an efficient general purpose classification system is itself a use, since such a system is so widely useful, and since to pick out "useful" plants one needs a more general system for looking at plants – unknown ones could prove useful (Hunn 1982). In any case, traditional ecological knowledge always goes well beyond mere utility (Berlin 1992). It may include astonishingly accurate knowledge of extremely arcane details of local biology, such as Maya farmers' awareness of the rare and obscure Piratic Flycatcher's practice of taking over nests from other birds (Anderson and Medina Tzuc 2005) – a bit of knowledge of no conceivable use to the Maya, but intrinsically interesting to them.

Anderson (1996) drew on Abraham Maslow (1970) to develop a more comprehensive theory of motivation. Briefly, Maslow (and Anderson) propose basic survival needs as most immediate but least important for long-term well-being, and social and life management needs as the reverse. The progression runs from air and water through temperature regulation (clothing, fire, shelter) to health, reproduction, control over one's life (autonomy and security), and social existence (sociability, love, care, conflict management). Maslow additionally hypothesized a need for "self-actualization" – never defined, but probably close to the better-defined and better-studied "ultimate meaning" of Frankl (1959, 1978). Emotions were discussed as part of thought, rather than as part of the basic motivational system. This now requires amendment. Emotions are involved in every stage of goal-setting and motivation. Sometimes they serve as direct motivators – most clearly when raw fear makes us run from a lion or an advancing car, but also when love makes us blind, grief makes us drink, or loneliness makes us seek company.

A vast black hole in all social science literature concerns *interest* – being interested in something, even to the point of devoting one's life to studying it. Interest is not really an "emotion," not even quite a "feeling," yet it is clearly emotional and motivational rather than rational-cognitive. Perhaps academics are so deeply involved in being interested in things that they are like the proverbial fish who "does not know water." Though briefly mentioned in very comprehensive works (Kemper 1987; Elster 1999), interest has apparently escaped serious study by any scholar in any field. Yet it is a powerful motivator – surely by far the most powerful one for academics, but also for inventors and other transformers of the world.

Robin Dunbar (1996) showed that gossip makes up about two-thirds of all conversation, a figure that holds up cross-culturally. Clearly, people are most interested in each other, especially within intimate circles. Primates, dogs, and other highly social animals show every evidence of comparable interest in social familiars. Of course, every animal must also be interested in making a living – in finding resources for survival. For social animals, one's fellows are vital in that endeavor.

Beyond that, in humans, interest is clearly heavily shaped by culture. In the United States, for instance, one is expected to be interested in sports and in the lives of movie stars, but only to a certain degree; the reciter of endless sports statistics is "boring." Other cultures direct more attention to wild plants, or ritual, or poetry, or fish, or almost anything else imaginable. People from a given culture often find the interests of "others" strange, if not downright decadent or contemptible. More broadly, culture shapes the landscape and lifestyle choices recorded in the phenomenological research noted above (Feld and Basso 1996; Milton 2002; Hedrick 2007; etc.).

More sinister aspects of culturally conditioned wants have been widely explored, especially by Michel Foucault, who devoted his career to dissecting ways that power is used to manipulate belief (e.g., 1965[1961], 1970[1966], 1978[1976], 1980), and earlier by Karl Marx ("false consciousness"). These thinkers have inspired a long-standing critical tradition in anthropology. Power is most effective when it convinces people that they actually *want* to do what the powerful want them to do. This is done crudely in advertising, more subtly through all manner of media manipulation. The success of oil and automobile companies at making the world not only use internal combustion vehicles, but also idealize them as lifestyle and even cult objects, is a dramatic but far from unique case in point (see also Stets and Turner 2006). Within cognitive anthropology, the negative aspects of cultural direction for young women to "want romance" instead of a career or personal success are explored by Holland and Eisenhardt (1990). Political scientists have now discovered Damasio, emotion, and the emotional nature of political motivation, producing some work that is important for cognitive studies (e.g., Taylor 2006; Westen 2007).

The end result of motivation and knowledge is behavior: people decide to seek resources, marry, raise children, and live their lives; for all this, they must make informed choices. Emotions and basic biological drives serve as the ultimate motivators. Cognition is involved as people bring knowledge to bear to inform their decisions. The more accurate, organized, and efficiently retrieved this knowledge is, the more useful it will be. The large literature on heuristics and biases shows us that accuracy is commonly sacrificed to efficiency, and that this is often a good thing (Gigerenzer 2007). Emotions can help or harm the process (Vohs et al. 2008), serving as valuable guides or as distorters. A major frontier for cognitive anthropology is to explore the ways this happens, the ways cultures construct emotions, and the ways that people (necessarily within cultures) think about emotions and motivation.

Conclusion

Emotion, selfhood, and personhood are all to some degree culturally constructed, as are systems of knowledge (cognition). On the other hand, emotions clearly draw on innate responses and states, which have some degree of Darwinian explanation. Recent work in social theory has begun to take account of the fundamentally emotional nature of much that was once thought "rational" (e.g., Marcus 2002; Milton 2002; Westen 2007). Anthropological research integrating studies of cognition, emotion, and motivation is expected to increase.

ACKNOWLEDGMENTS

I am grateful to Julie Brugger, Eugene Hunn, and David Kronenfeld for help with this chapter.

REFERENCES

Abu-Lughod, Lila
1985 Veiled Sentiments: Honor and Poetry in a Bedouin Society. Berkeley: University of California Press.
Amborn, Hermann
2008 Dr. Freud Was Not a Kafa: A Classical Case of Anthropological Overinterpretation from Ethiopia. Anthropos 103:15–32.
Anderson, E. N.
1996 Ecologies of the Heart. New York: Oxford University Press.
2007 Floating World Lost. New Orleans: University Press of the South.
Anderson, E. N., and Felix Medina Tzuc
2005 Animals and the Maya in Southeast Mexico. Tucson: University of Arizona Press.
Atran, Scott, Douglas Medin, Norbert Ross, Elizabeth Lynch, John Coley, Edilberto Ucan Ek, and Valentina Vapnarsky
1999 Folkecology and Commons Management in the Maya Lowlands. Proceedings of the National Academy of Sciences 96:7598–7603.
Barkow, Jerome, Leda Cosmides, and John Tooby
1992 The Adapted Mind: Evolutionary Psychology and the Generation of Culture. New York: Oxford University Press.
Basso, Keith
1996 Wisdom Sits in Places: Landscape and Language among the Western Apache. Albuquerque: University of New Mexico Press.
Bellah, Robert, Richard Madsen, William M. Sullivan, Ann Swidler, and Steven M. Tipton
1996 Habits of the Heart: Individualism and Commitment in American Life. Berkeley: University of California Press.
Berlin, O. Brent
1992 Ethnobiological Classification. Princeton: Princeton University Press.
Bond, Michael, ed.
1986 The Psychology of the Chinese People. Hong Kong: Oxford University Press.
Bourdieu, Pierre
1977 Outline of a Theory of Practice. Richard Nice, trans. New York: Cambridge University Press.
1990 The Logic of Practice. Richard Nice, trans. Stanford: Stanford University Press.
Brown, Roger
1958 Words and Things: An Introduction to Language. Glencoe, IL: Free Press.
Damasio, Antonio
1994 Descartes' Error: Emotion, Reason, and the Human Brain. New York: G. P. Putnam's.
1999 The Feeling of What Happens: Body and Emotion in the Making of Consciousness. London: Heinemann.

D'Andrade, Roy
1995 The Development of Cognitive Anthropology. New York: Cambridge University Press.
2001 Everyday Irrationality: How Pseudo-Scientists, Lunatics, and the Rest of Us Systematically Fail to Think Rationally. Boulder, CO: Westview.
2008 A Study of Personal and Cultural Values: American, Japanese, and Vietnamese. New York: Palgrave Macmillan.
D'Andrade, Roy, and Claudia Strauss, eds.
1992 Human Motives and Cultural Models. New York: Cambridge University Press.
Dawes, Robyn
1994 House of Cards: Psychology and Psychotherapy Built on Myth. New York: Free Press.
Dollard, John, and Neal Miller
1950 Personality and Psychotherapy: An Analysis in Terms of Learning, Thinking and Culture. New York: McGraw-Hill.
Dunbar, Robin
1996 Grooming, Gossip, and the Evolution of Language. Cambridge, MA: Harvard University Press.
Ekman, Paul
1992 Are There Basic Emotions? Psychological Review 99:550–553.
2007 Emotions Revealed: Recognizing Faces and Feelings to Improve Communication and Emotional Life. 2nd edition. New York: Holt.
Elster, Jon
1999 Alchemies of the Mind: Rationality and the Emotions. Cambridge: Cambridge University Press.
Feld, Steven
1982 Sound and Sentiment: Birds, Weeping, Poetics and Song in Kaluli Expression. Philadelphia: University of Pennsylvania Press.
N.d.[c.1982] Music of Oceania: The Kaluli of Papua Niugini, Weeping and Song. Vinyl recording. Kassel, Germany: Musicaphon.
Feld, Steven, and Keith Basso
1996 Senses of Place. Santa Fe, NM: School of American Research.
Foucault, Michel
1965[1961] Madness and Civilization: A History of Insanity in the Age of Reason. Richard Howard, trans. New York: Random House.
1970[1966] The Order of Things: An Archaeology of the Human Sciences [Les Mots et les choses]. New York: Random House.
1978[1976] The History of Sexuality, vol. 1: An Introduction. Robert Hurley, trans. New York: Random House.
1980 Power/Knowledge: Selected Interviews and Other Writings, 1972–1977. Colin Gordon, ed. New York: Pantheon.
Frank, Robert H.
1988 Passions within Reason: The Strategic Role of the Emotions. New York: W. W. Norton.
Frankl, Viktor
1959 Man's Search for Meaning: An Introduction to Logotherapy. Boston, MA: Beacon.
1978 The Unheard Cry for Meaning: Psychotherapy and Humanism. New York: Simon and Schuster.
Gardner, Howard
1985 The Mind's New Science: A History of the Cognitive Revolution. New York: Basic Books.
Gibbard, Allan
1990 Wise Choices, Apt Feelings: A Theory of Normative Judgment. Cambridge, MA: Harvard University Press.

Gigerenzer, Gerd
2007 Gut Feelings: The Intelligence of the Unconscious. New York: Viking.
Grünbaum, Adolf
1984 The Foundations of Psychoanalysis: A Philosophical Critique. Berkeley: University of California Press.
Hammond, Michael
2006 Evolutionary Theory and Emotions. *In* Handbook of the Sociology of Emotions. Jan E. Stets and Jonathan H. Turner, eds. Pp. 368–385. New York: Springer.
Harré, Rom, ed.
1986 The Social Construction of Emotion. Oxford: Blackwell.
Hedrick, Kimberly
2007 Our Way of Life: Identity, Landscape, and Conflict. Unpublished Ph.D. thesis, Department of Anthropology, University of California, Riverside.
Hochschild, Arlie
1983 The Managed Heart: The Commercialization of Feeling. Berkeley: University of California Press.
Holland, Dorothy, and Margaret Eisenhardt
1990 Educated in Romance: Women, Achievement, and College Culture. Chicago: University of Chicago Press.
Holland, Dorothy, and Naomi Quinn, eds.
1987 Cultural Models in Language and Thought. New York: Cambridge University Press.
Hsu, Francis L. K.
1953 Americans and Chinese: Two Ways of Life. New York: H. Schuman.
Hunn, Eugene S.
1982 The Utilitarian Factor in Folk Biological Classification. American Anthropologist 84:830–847.
2008 A Zapotec Natural History. Tucson: University of Arizona Press.
Hyde, Janet Shibley, Amy H. Menzulis, and Lyn Y. Abramson
2008 The ABC's of Depression: Integrating Affective, Biological and Cognitive Models to Explain the Emergence of the Gender Difference in Depression. Psychological Review 115:291–313.
Kant, Immanuel
1978[1798] Anthropology from a Pragmatic Point of View. Victor Lyle Dowdell, trans. Carbondale: Southern Illinois University Press.
Kemper, Theodore D.
1987 How Many Emotions Are There? Wedding the Social and Autonomous Components. American Journal of Sociology 93:263–289.
Kempton, Willett, James Boster, and Jennifer Hartley
1996 Environmental Values in American Culture. Cambridge, MA: MIT Press.
Kronenfeld, David
1996 Plastic Glasses and Church Fathers. New York: Oxford University Press.
2008 Cultural Models. Intercultural Pragmatics 5:67–74.
2009 Culture, Society, and Cognition. Berlin: Mouton de Gruyter.
Latour, Bruno
2005 Reassembling the Social. Oxford: Oxford University Press.
Lazarus, Richard S.
1984 On the Primacy of Cognition. American Psychologist 39:124–129.
1991 Emotions and Adaptation. New York: Oxford University Press.
Lazarus, Richard S., and Bernice N. Lazarus
1994 Passion and Reason: Making Sense of Our Emotions. New York: Oxford University Press.
LeDoux, Joseph
1996 The Emotional Brain: The Mysterious Underpinnings of Emotional Life. New York: Simon and Schuster.

2002 Synaptic Self: How Our Brains Become Who We Are. New York: Viking.
Lévi-Strauss, Claude
1962 La Pensée sauvage. Paris: Plon.
Levy, Robert
1973 Tahitians: Mind and Experience in the Society Islands. Chicago: University of Chicago Press.
Lutz, Catherine
1988 Unnatural Emotions: Everyday Sentiments on a Micronesian Atoll and Their Challenge to Western Thought. Chicago: University of Chicago Press.
Marcus, George E.
2002 The Sentimental Citizen: Emotion in Democratic Politics. University Park, PA: Pennsylvania State University Press.
Markus, Hazel Rose
2008 Pride, Prejudice, and Ambivalence: Toward a Unified Theory of Race and Ethnicity. American Psychologist 63:651–671.
Maslow, Abraham
1970 Motivation and Personality. 2nd edition. New York: Harper and Row.
McCrae, Robert R., and Paul T. Costa Jr.
1997 Personality Trait Structure as a Human Universal. American Psychologist 52:509–516.
Medin, Douglas, Norbert O. Ross, and Douglas G. Cox
2006 Culture and Resource Conflict: Why Meanings Matter. New York: Russell Sage Foundation.
Milton, Kay
2002 Loving Nature. London: Routledge.
2005 Emotion (or Life, the Universe and Everything). Australian Journal of Anthropology 16:198–211.
Needham, Rodney
1962 Structure and Sentiment: A Test Case in Social Anthropology. Chicago: University of Chicago Press.
Neisser, Ulric
1976 Cognition and Reality: Principles and Implications of Cognitive Psychology. San Francisco: W. H. Freeman.
Nisbett, Richard
2003 The Geography of Thought: How Asians and Westerners Think Differently … and Why. New York: Free Press.
Nisbett, Richard, and Lee Ross
1980 Human Inference. Englewood Cliffs, NJ: Prentice Hall.
Nussbaum, Martha
2001 Upheavals of Thought: The Intelligence of Emotions. New York: Cambridge University Press.
Osgood, Charles E., George J. Suci, and Percy H. Tannenbaum
1957 The Measurement of Meaning. Urbana: University of Illinois Press.
Oyserman, Daphna, and Spike W. S. Lee
2008 Does Culture Influence What and How We Think? Effects of Priming on Individualism and Collectivism. Psychological Bulletin 134:311–342.
Peterson, Gretchen
2006 Cultural Theory and Emotions. In *Handbook of the Sociology of Emotions.* Jan E. Stets and Jonathan Turner, eds. Pp. 114–134. New York: Springer.
Quinn, Naomi
2006 The Self. Anthropological Theory 6:362–384.
Quinn, Naomi, and Claudia Strauss, eds.
2006 The Missing Psychology in Cultural Anthropology's Key Words. Special issue, Anthropological Theory 6(3).

Robarchek, Clayton A.

1989a Hobbesian and Rousseauan Images of Man: Autonomy and Individualism in a Peaceful Society. *In* Societies at Peace. Signe Howell and Roy Willis, eds. Pp. 31–44. New York: Routledge.

1989b Primitive Warfare and the Ratomorphic Image of Mankind. American Anthropologist 91:903–920.

Robarchek, Clayton A., and Carole Robarchek

1998 Waorani: The Contexts of Violence and War. New York: Harcourt Brace.

Romney, A. Kimball, and Roy D'Andrade, eds.

1964 Transcultural Studies in Cognition. Washington, DC: American Anthropological Association.

Rosaldo, Renato

N.d.[c.1985] Grief and a Headhunter's Rage: On the Cultural Force of the Emotions. Southwestern Anthropological Association, Newsletter 22(4)–23(1):3–8.

1989 Culture and Truth: The Remaking of Social Analysis. Boston, MA: Beacon.

Rose, Deborah

2000 Dingo Makes Us Human: Life and Land in an Australian Aboriginal Culture. New York: Cambridge University Press.

Ross, Norbert A.

2003 Culture and Cognition: Implications for Theory and Method. Newbury Park, CA: Sage.

Sahlins, Marshall

1976 Culture and Practical Reason. Chicago: University of Chicago Press.

Schieffelin, Edward

1975 The Sorrow of the Lonely and the Burning of the Dancers. New York: St. Martin's.

Shore, Bradd

1998 Culture in Mind: Cognition, Culture and the Problem of Meaning. New York: Oxford University Press.

Shweder, Richard

1991 Thinking through Cultures: Explorations in Cultural Psychology. Cambridge, MA: Harvard University Press.

2003 Why Do Men Barbecue? Recipes for Cultural Psychology. Cambridge, MA: Harvard University Press.

Shweder, Richard, and Robert LeVine, eds.

1984 Culture Theory: Essays on Mind, Self and Emotion. New York: Cambridge University Press.

Simon, Herbert

1957 Models of Man. New York: John Wiley.

Spiro, Melford E.

1987 Culture and Human Nature: Theoretical Papers of Melford E. Spiro. Chicago: University of Chicago Press.

Stets, Jan E., and Jonathan H. Turner, eds.

2006 Handbook of the Sociology of Emotions. New York: Springer.

Stigler, James, Richard Shweder, and Gilbert Herdt

1990 Cultural Psychology: Essays on Comparative Human Development. New York: Cambridge University Press.

Strauss, Claudia

2007 Blaming for Columbine: Conceptions of Agency in the Contemporary United States. Current Anthropology 48:807–832.

Strauss, Claudia, and Naomi Quinn

1997 A Cognitive Theory of Cultural Meaning. New York: Cambridge University Press.

Taylor, Michael

2006 Rationality and the Ideology of Disconnection. New York: Cambridge University Press.

Turner, Jonathan
2000 On the Origins of Human Emotions: A Sociological Inquiry into the Evolution of Human Affect. Stanford: Stanford University Press.
Turner, Jonathan H., and Jan Stets
2005 The Sociology of Emotions. Cambridge: Cambridge University Press.
Vohs, Kathleen D., Roy Baumeister, and George Loewenstein, eds.
2008 Do Emotions Help or Hurt Decision-Making? A Hedgefoxian Perspective. New York: Russell Sage Foundation.
Wallace, Anthony F. C.
1961 Culture and Personality. New York: Random House.
Westen, Drew
2007 The Political Brain: The Role of Emotion in Deciding the Fate of the Nation. New York: Public Affairs.
White, Leslie A.
1949 The Science of Culture. New York: Grove.
Whiting, John
1994 Culture and Human Development: The Selected Papers of John Whiting. Eleanor Hollenberg Chasdi and Roy D'Andrade, eds. New York: Cambridge University Press.
Wierzbicka, Anna
1992 Semantics, Culture and Cognition. Oxford: Oxford University Press.
1999 Emotions across Languages and Cultures. Cambridge: Cambridge University Press.
Zajonc, R. B.
1980 Feeling and Thinking: Preferences Need No Inferences. American Psychologist 35:151–175.

CHAPTER 18

Social Networks, Cognition, and Culture

Douglas R. White

Networks

Network studies are an important adjunct to further development of cognitive anthropology and theory. When reliable means of identifying relational properties of behavior, cognition, and cultural structures or systems are available they help overcome limitations of other types of descriptive studies, descriptive statistics, or ad hoc inferences about how mind, culture, and social behavior interact.

Roles

Roles form into key network and institutional structures which can be understood in relation to social processes. Network ethnography can also operate in this way to further understanding (White and Johansen 2006:ch. 1). Network studies enhance our understandings of cause and effects of emergent roles and their dynamical patterns of shifting stability, including hierarchy. Finding hierarchy and its network embeddings, for example, often depends on global as well as local information on how local patterns fit within global ones. Both the understanding of global network structure and analysis of micro–macro linkages are additional advantages. If we wanted to find the leaders in a large urban community (see Freeman et al. 1960), for example, we could start from a sample of potential leaders, ask *them* who the leaders are, and iteratively construct a snowball sample of higher order leaders until finally a leader sub-network or evidence of a single leader emerges.

Cohesive groups

Cohesive groups have patterned interactions that are self-reinforcing and self-stabilizing in certain spatio-temporal frames. Study of these interactions can also account for individual choices, the emergence of cohesive units as socially and cognitively recognizable

A Companion to Cognitive Anthropology, First Edition. Edited by David B. Kronenfeld, Giovanni Bennardo, Victor C. de Munck, and Michael D. Fischer.

entities and the consequences of these units and their changes through time for coordinated group behaviors. This kind of information may differ significantly from interview or observational accounts of individuals acting independently. The network concept of ***structurally cohesive*** sub-networks of varying intensity, as defined by ***the least number of disjoint redundant links*** between each pair of their nodes, provides ways to study to what extent social groups, affected by their patterns of cohesion, come to be self-reinforcing and consequential in their effects.

Cognition

Formally defined core concepts from network science help capture how cultural consensus forms and changes around emergent roles and cohesive groups, given that humans are cognizant of role and group structure. Such concepts provide the bases needed for explanatory theory about sharing and differentiation in societies and cultures. Both cognitive and brain networks include various types of hierarchical organization. The human eye and visual perception per se do not allow us to truly "see" reality but rather to extract patterns of perception at successively higher levels.[1] There are no inherently "true objects" or "natural attributes" of objects corresponding to our perceptual world(s), but rather complex patterns of relations that identify objects cognitively with varying coherence and descriptive categories involving variable salience. As with other species, our views of the world have evolved adaptively as per our Gibsonian affordances – that is, the means by which we relate to our environment. The organism–environment system is a relevant network for study.

Deeper Problems: Mind, Logics, and World

The frequent disconnect between social behavior and cognition is a useful problem for study in the context of social networks, cognition, and culture. D'Andrade's (1974) "behaviorscope" experiment showed that the categories subjects list in conveying their immediate judgments of others' behaviors differ greatly from those they later report from long-term memory of the same events. The experiment also showed that the similarity structure of categories used in memory-based judgments is closer to those of the linguistic categories involved in expressing recovered memory and uncorrelated with those used in immediate judgments of these events. No wonder, then, that the studies of Bernard, Killworth, and Sailer (Bernard and Killworth 1977; Bernard et al. 1980, 1982; and with Kronenfeld in Bernard et al. 1984) showed that there is roughly only 50 percent agreement between the network links that people form and their mental recall of these links. Freeman et al. (1987) showed that the "best" informants on behaviors in groups, according to consensus, "can be used to reveal long-range stable patterns of events," while average non-consensual judgments of the worst informants can be more useful "to reveal the details of a particular event of special interest" (the accident bystander phenomenon, for averaging perceptions of completely independent observers). These findings connect with the theories proposed by Gibsonian psychological studies reviewed herein: namely, that experience and memory are stored in continuous perceptions, feelings, and "narrative-like" constructions about ongoing interactions, that is, in episodes, rather than in bits of time or cognitive categorization.

Network science is not simply a "method" of data collection and analysis but theory-driven in ways that begin from decisions about coding or structuring data so as to focus the analysis on theoretical questions. Results are heavily dependent on mathematical theorems about graphs, networks, and relational algebra that capture "necessary connections" (see White 1974; White and Reitz 1983; White and Harary 2001) for results that are not prima facie visible to the observer, as either ethnographer, preceptor of a network graphic, or network participant. Local choices and subsequent behavior in networks, for example, have necessary implications for global features of networks, and vice versa. Some of these properties are best examined through formal definitions and theorems. Through proper tuning and validation of how to code networks (e.g., "experientially"), network modeling can contribute to ethnography and to cognitive anthropology, and vice versa.[2]

The three-world problem

Popper and Eccles (1977) debated aspects of what they call the three-world problem, which also confronts cognitive anthropology:

World 1: The physical world (and human brain and behavior in that world).
World 2: Mental activity and human consciousness.
World 3: Objective culture, "which is the creation of World 2 but takes on its own distinct and permanent existence."[3]

The topics of the present essay, and those of Read (2008) and Leaf (2007, 2008) on formal empirical models, confront the question of how these three worlds are related. How is it possible for "objective" culture to take on a distinct and durable existence? Figure 18.1 brackets the three-world problem at two levels: that of the sciences (networks, cognition, and culture) and how these play out at the individual level of brain, mind, and behavior or organism–environment linkage. Arguments between scientists such as neurophysiologist Damasio (2007) and philosophers like Gluck (2007), seemingly irreconcilable, fail to resolve these problems. Anthropology currently wrestles with apparently incommensurate dualities in the interfaces between brain as a physical organ and the mind as a non-material dynamical organized response pattern mediating the organism–environment, ego–alter, and other interfaces.

The sciences today are undergoing major transformations, rethinking, and resynthesis. They in turn are affected by transformations in physics, biology, and ecological psychology in dealing with complex systems and, in particular, the dynamics of complex systems. I address here how these new syntheses affect anthropology and those social sciences concerned with human cognition, culture, and networks. Cognitive anthropology is caught in a position of having to reconcile individual cognition in the human brain with the existence of cultural patterns in terms of shared and meaningful symbols.

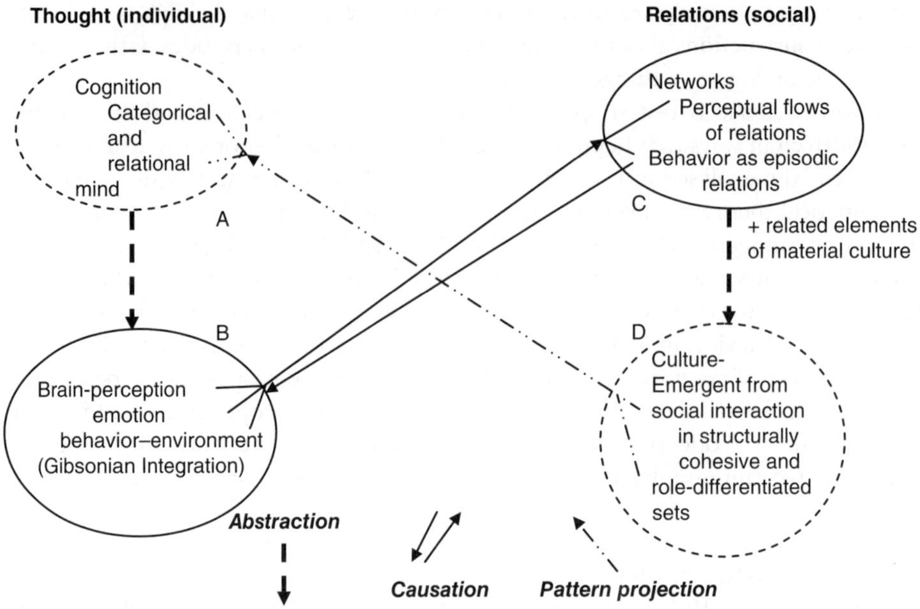

Figure 18.1 The three-world problem at two levels: individual and social, thought and relations. Arrows suggest directed cycles. Placement of Cognition and Culture avoids the implication that culture is superorganic or reified as "distributed cognition." Rather, from a not always consistent distillation of practices, culture emerges in roles and cohesively organized groups that can be cognized, and a reflexive cognitive D–A link for thinking about culture but no directed A–D link because "culture" does not "think." There are network and environmental physical B–C brain–behavior loops and an A–B–C–D cycle with non-material elements including mind and culture. The network oval C evokes the idea that episodic behaviors are internally (experientially) and externally perceptual and can be represented as network flows with an episodically temporal ordering in behavior that draws on restructured and weakly encoded memory of episodic experience. Solid and dashed ovals encircle material and immaterial elements, with causality between material items, pattern projections between thought and culture, and abstractions between material and immaterial counterparts: "mind studies brain, behavior models culture."

Figure 18.1 expresses a view which helps us to understand the relations between networks of behavior and cognition, mind and culture.[4] The upper ovals involve what individuals "do" in terms of thinking (internally) and behaving (externally). The lower ovals involve brain and the Gibsonian organism–environment interaction (left oval) and the non-material elements of culture (right). The left downward arrow (abstraction) refers to our cognitive ability to think about and study our brain, while the right abstraction arrow refers to our ability, through behavior, to project or reinvent culture. Culture, in turn, expresses our ability through learning to project culture into thought, including relational thinking. Rather than a positivist reduction to causal relations between acts → perceptions → thoughts (with incommensurate physical actions and immaterial thoughts), Figure 18.1 expresses how the three worlds may be related by material, abstract, and projective connections. It is also able to incorporate an A–C link that would support a network-based A–C–D cognitive modeling of cultural phenomena.

Relational thought

For humans, the assumption that mind operates largely through categories fails to be convincing because humans also think relationally, as has been demonstrated experimentally (Hummel and Holyoak 2005; Penn et al. 2008). One problem with 1960s cognitive anthropology was that meaning was seen as defined by categories, an element in the upper left oval of Figure 18.1, without the element of relational cognition.

An experimentally supported solution to the mind–body conundrum is that organism and environment constitute a single system (Turvey and Shaw 1979, 1995; Gibson 1966, 1979; West and King 1987; Swenson and Turvey 1991; Turvey 1991, 2009; Oyama 2000; Wagman and Miller 2003). Events are bounded in perception by changes in action that have networks of connected parts within events and recurrence across events. These views accord with those of Hutchins (1991, 1994) on the human–cognitive environment connection and the use of environmental material anchors in studies of human cognition, where part of cognition is "outside" but does not constitute "distributed cognition," which connotes direct immaterial mind–mind connection.

Time series of episodic events as experiences thus lend themselves *perceptually* to network coding and analysis. Such studies may be done at many different time scales. In our studies of kinship networks, for example (see White and Johansen 2006 for an ethnographic example) there are intergenerational events such as marriage, childbirth, death, migration, and proximal interactions within the culturally recognized and individually perceived event boundaries and time scales of event sequences. The network links between events and actors exhibit structural and dynamical patterns, including recurrences for which tools exist for studying complex dynamics (see Carollo and Moreno 2005 for methods), fractalities (White and Johansen 2006:136–137), and *structural cohesion* as a predictive network variable relating to shared-culture formation.

Cohesive groups in networks

Cohesive blocks (*maximum sub-networks in which each pair of nodes are connected by a certain minimum number k of disjoint paths*) are found operationally in a manner that fits the basic conceptual form for the idea of the cohesion of groups, the way cohesion is perceived for groups, and the way that cohesion ties a group together both internally and by resistance to being dismembered. It also shows the way that networks provide a particular set of the degrees of freedom in how cohesive groups may relate to one another through overlap (e.g., membership in multiple communities) and through core–periphery sub-group hierarchies for levels of cohesion. This opens the way to the following hypothesis.

The Cohesion and Consensus Hypothesis

Levels and variations of cohesion within social networks for society as a whole and within its varying segments, measured within networks for cohesive blocks (sub-networks) with a minimum level *k* of disjoint paths between every pair of their nodes, tend to predict levels and variations in cultural consensus, provided that the connections that define the network have some positive perceptual relation to the subject or contents of cultural consensus.[5]

This hypothesis was suggested by Schweizer (1996:116) but without an analytic measure of cohesion. It was reiterated by Ross (2004:124), who took density as a measure of cohesion, which it is not. White and Harary (2001) were the first to both formulate a formal measure of network cohesion that drew from the theory of graphs, and to test the predictiveness of the concept with a simple empirical example. They predicted how a karate club studied for two years by Zachary (1977) divided its membership between the club owner and the instructor, and the order of secession of members as the teacher formed a new club. This has a cognitive dimension because to decide with whom to disconnect individuals had to assess (1) their relation to others relative to the themselves, and owner and instructor, and (2) who their closer or more distant friends in the network were and how those allies stood in relation to the two leaders. Defectors moved to the teacher's side by breaking with those on the owner's side but did not follow a simple individual-level decision rule; rather, their behavior entailed a perception of group cohesion by breaking ties that were less cohesive with the owner's side than the ties they kept, and, for ties of the same level of cohesion, breaking the more distant tie from the owner. Attributes of the leaders with respect to those of students were not predictive.

Atran et al. (2002) tested friendship and social interaction as predictors of cultural agreement for environmental cognitions for populations but found no correlation (Ross 2004:122). Boster (1986) found kinship as a source of agreement among Peruvian manioc cultivators but, again, had no measure of cohesion and no findings for a cohesion consensus hypothesis. Interaction alone and network density alone, in these studies, were not predictive of cultural consensus. Atran et al.'s (2002) expertise networks, however, did predict cultural agreements, and might have been more cohesive.

Moody and White (2003) tested the predictiveness of White and Harary's structural cohesion measure, and showed that: (1) students' level of structural cohesion in friendship group "blocks" strongly predicted their reports of attachment to high school; and (2) cohesive strengths of co-memberships in the cohesive blocks of business alliances predicted similarities in the choices of firms in their political party alliances. In both cases, none of the other network or attribute variables – including density, centralities, and dyadic tie measures as well as student attributes – outperformed the predictiveness of the cohesion measure.

Powell et al. (2005), using the Moody–White measurement of structural (block) cohesion, analyzed time-lagged effects from year to year of multiple variables in the choice of partners for strategic collaborations in the biotech industry. They found that diversity of level of cohesion in the cohesive blocks to which potential partners belonged the year before were strong predictors of partner choice. Here, none of the other network or attribute variables outperformed the predictions of cohesion and diversity measures.

Multi-connectivity for networks of organizations, especially those with structurally cohesive block circuitry, is like a series of stacking blocks as shown in Figure 18.2: a child's stacking blocks game. Each successively smaller block may be stacked on a peg, here representing successively more *k*-cohesive groups, each with (by definition) a

Figure 18.2 Stacking blocks, analogous to three cohesive hierarchies with overlaps of nodes in common.

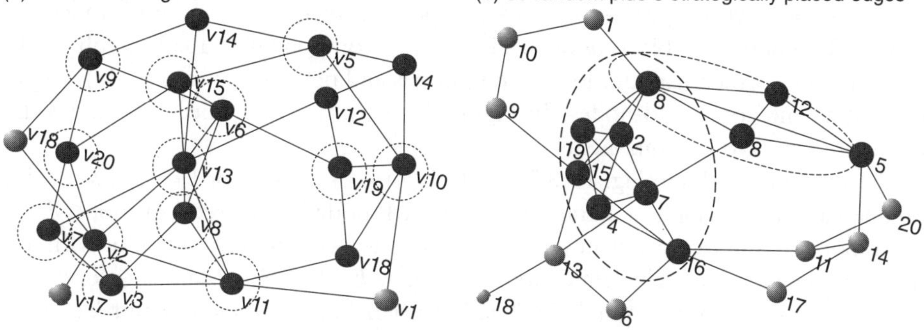

Figure 18.3 Cohesive blocking in graphs with 20 nodes and differing numbers of nodes and random edges, with additional edges added in (b). Shades of *k*-cores are *k* = 3 in black, *k* = 2 in gray, and *k* = 1 in white. This differs from sorting by *degree* (number of links per node), as shown by circled nodes in (a) for nodes with degree ≥ 4. (a) has a single cohesive hierarchy. (b) has two *k*-components that are not differentiated by the *k*-core concept but belong to the same 3-core. If the two 3-blocks in (b) were social groups, the cohesion and consensus hypothesis would predict greater consensus in each of the two 3-components than in their combined *k*-core (black nodes). For social interaction networks, greater consensus might be expected by the cohesion consensus hypothesis the greater the cohesion of a *k*-component.

non-increasing number of group members. The top block in each stack represents its most cohesive sub-graph for that stack of nodes in a network. What differs from the children's game is that blocks on different stacks may be part of a shared platform for their upper blocks, a platform representing overlap for their lower blocks.

The complexity of this example is difficult to envision because each *k*-component contains all blocks above a certain level and overlaps apply downwards to the blocks below. It is best stated abstractly as a mathematical definition for precisely bounded maximal sub-graphs of a larger graph whose sub-groups for levels *k* are found by blocking algorithm. The resultant blocks are most easily perceived by humans when the stacks and blocks are few and when viewed in a suitable format such as the spring embeddings of Pajek (Batagelj and Mrvar 1998).[6]

Figure 18.3 shows, with two different network structures, how cohesive blocks are defined and stacked by internal level of network-tie cohesiveness. The differences between (a) and (b) illustrate two slightly different model networks: (a) an "integrated" single stack of cohesive blocks and (b) a network with multiple cohesive blocks that are segregated but overlapping. In (a) the ties are fully randomized. Random edges always tend to create embedded levels of "socially integrated" *k*-cohesion, like a nest of Russian dolls, that is, forming a single hierarchy of cohesion. The biotech networks studied by Powell et al. (2005), for example, have single stack cohesion with maximum cohesiveness varying from 4 to 6 from year to year.

Each of the two graphs in Figure 18.3 has 20 nodes, but while (a) has 38 all-random edges, (b) has 33 random edges plus three strategic ties placed to create the greater complexity of two cohesive but overlapping sub-groups. The random graph in Figure 18.3(a), with its 20 nodes and 40 links (each link adding one degree to each of the two nodes linked) has an average degree per node of 4 edges (some with more and some with less). Those that have degree four or more are circled but no set of the 14 nodes with degree 4 forms a 4-component. Instead, there are 17 nodes that form a 3-component (black nodes). Here the 3-component is a sub-graph of the 2-component, which has additional (gray) nodes and nests in the largest (1-)component of all the connected nodes. In Figure 18.3(b), however, the black nodes differentiate into two 3-components.

The shades of nodes in Fig. 18.3 illustrate *k*-cores. A *k*-core (for $k = 1, 2, 3, \ldots$) is a unique largest sub-graph of a graph in which each node has degree *k* or more. Every *k*-component is a *k*-core but not every *k*-core is a *k*-component or *k*-block. In any network these are uniquely defined for the integers $k = 1, 2, 3, \ldots$, allowing for higher *k*-cores that are empty. In graph 18.3(a) but not 18.3(b) the *k*-cores and *k*-components are identical for each *k*. The *k*-cores of a graph are easily computed, for example, by Pajek (Batagelj and Mrvar 1998: menu/net/partitions/core), which deletes all nodes with less than the highest degree *k* and then recomputes degree, retaining those with *k* or more links, iteratively. Like the measure of sub-graph density, the use of *k*-cores (defined by Seidman and Foster 1978; Foster and Seidman 1989) is often taken in network analysis as a measure of group cohesion, even though this usage is invalid. A *k*-core for any value of *k* with more than $2k$ nodes may be completely disconnected. Even a sub-graph of two cliques (each completely connected) may have 50 percent density and yet be disconnected. Densities, like *k*-cores, are not measures of cohesion. For small graphs, the combination of spring embedding and *k*-core coloring usually allows visual identification of *k*-components, just as people with mature skills in relational cognition can often identify the unique *k*-components in their friendship groups. For a more sophisticated use of *k*-cores as fingerprints of network structure, recognizing that cores may be disconnected, see Alvarez-Hamelin et al. (2006).

Figure 18.4 shows the results of cohesive blocking applied to Figure 18.3(b) using the algorithm of Moody and White (2003, in a version implemented by McMahan 2007). Nodes in both 3-components (3-connected) are black but, as also shown in the splitting diagram to the right, there are two overlapping 3-connected components. The output vector computed by the McMahan (2007) algorithm tells exactly which nodes are in each of the 3-components, as shown by dotted ovals in (b):

> [[3]] [1] "v2" "v3" "v4" "v7" "v15" "v16" "v19"
> [[4]] [1] "v3" "v5" "v8" "v12" (NB node "v3" is shared with 3-cohesive block [[3]].)

Note that "v3" occurs in both 3-components in the separate but overlapping dashed ovals.

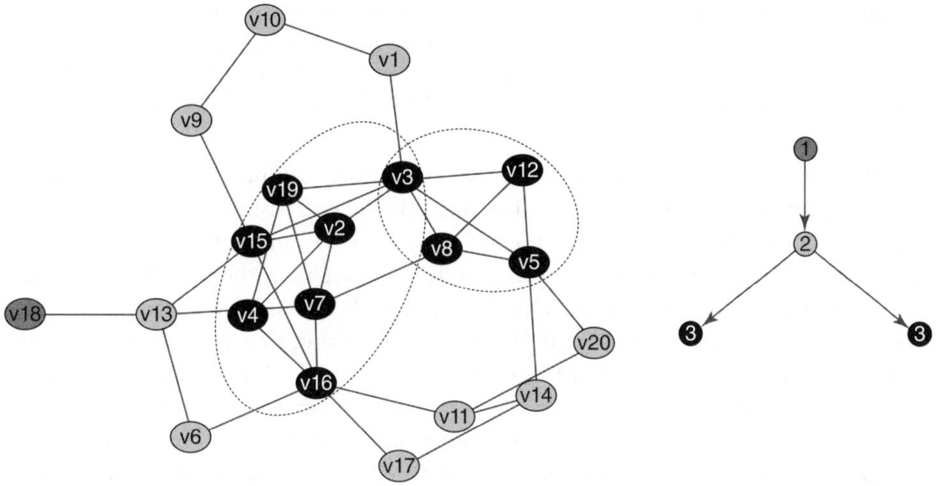

Figure 18.4 Cohesive blocking of the graph in Figure 18.3(b). The graph to the left is the network in Figure 18.3(b), also spring-embedded, but now with *k*-connectivity calculated by the cohesive blocks algorithm programmed in R freeware by Peter McMahan from the Moody and White (2003) algorithm. An appendix (White 2010a) gives cut-and-paste execution instructions in R.

Armed with this way of measuring the *distribution of cohesive groups at different levels of cohesion*, it is easy to see how a cohesion and consensus hypothesis could be tested by direct correlation with a pair-wise cultural consensus matrix (Romney et al. 1986). A single-consensus model would perfect match a network of type (a) – integrated cohesive groups, but a divergent-consensus model might match one of type (b) – separate even if overlapping cohesive groups, or one with more, or more discrete, components of cohesion. Areas in the graph of higher and lower correlation between consensus and cohesion could be mapped and compared.

Test of Structural Cohesion and Cultural Consensus

San Juan Sur (SJS) is a peasant community in the Turialba Canton of Costa Rica studied by Loomis and Powell (1949) in contrast to a nearby hacienda community (Atirro). Their network study is one of the few with data available to directly address issues of networks, cognition, and culture, for which the hypothesis linking structural cohesion to cultural consensus can be tested.

Costa Rica was then seen as the most democratic country in Latin America, "the land of peasant proprietors," where many of the rising hacendado class arose from peasant communities. The focus of their study was the transition to more stratified society, as

> peasant holdings are being gradually throttled by the large *fincas* and corporations thus reducing the status of the people from that of peasantry to peonage. Increasingly larger numbers of people are becoming *journaleros* and working for a subsistence wage as peons

> of the large land owners. What, then, might be expected if the country continues in the present trend toward a peon–patron type of system? For example, is there really a larger lower class on the hacienda than in the peasant community? How do the classes in these two situations compare with those in society at large? [Loomis and Powell 1949:448]

One focus of this study was on the impact of formal and informal social systems – social networks – on social change. Loomis investigated visiting relations between peasant proprietor families living in the SJS neighborhood and in the nearby hacienda of Atirro. The visiting network data they collected were published as simple directed graphs, without giving the number of visits but with arcs showing "frequent" visits from one family to another. For SJS 92 percent of visiting ties were within the community, and kinship ties were most often to the wife and/or husband's parents.[7] Line values classified the visiting relations: value one for ordinary visits, two for visits to kin, and three for those of ritual kin: god-parents, god-children and *compadres*. Judges and members of each community were asked to rate one another on a scale of social class from 1 to 10 (1–100 for the sum of ten judges). These data allow comparison of structural cohesion with consensual social class ratings in the two communities.

SJS and Atirro differ organizationally. The 60 Atirro residents interviewed were *finca* employees who worked for a small daily wage, lived in a tightly nucleated cluster, were much more mobile than the SJS residents (16 had lived there for less than a year) but enjoyed a rent-free *casa* during their employment. An administrator directed the work of the *finca* and a *mandador* directed the workers and was answerable to the *finca* owner. Here, structural cohesion would be expected to be fragmented but with some fragments indicating organizational specialization, as for example, in the *finca* hierarchy. The results of testing the cohesion–consensus hypothesis are positive for SJS but not for Atirro, where social cohesion in visiting is disrupted by turnover and *finca* organization.

SJS judges agreed on four classes for Atirro and SJS: upper and lower middle (18 percent of SLS) and upper and lower in a lower class (59 percent and 24 percent). The SJS peasant community is described ethnographically as egalitarian with no upper middle class. Nine of the ten judges in SJS rated themselves identically to how others rated them (Loomis and Powell 1949:149), and an SJS leader rated himself one rank lower than others rated him. Seven of the ten rated each other mutually as middle class. Figure 18.5, showing the SJS network, contains three types of directed ties: kinship visits were the most frequent, visits to ritual kin less frequent, and ordinary visiting infrequent. Reciprocal arcs are symmetric ties, as opposed to asymmetric directed arcs.[8]

For the cohesion–consensus hypothesis, SJS cohesive blocking shows black nodes for the large structurally integrated 3-component of the network, gray nodes that add to the 2-component, and a single white node that adds to the 1-component. SJS has the community integration structure associated with a single cohesive hierarchy, as in Figure 18.3(a). The correlation between upper middle-class families and levels of structural *k*-cohesion in ties for visiting kin in SJS is highly significant ($p < 0.003$) and somewhat less so ($p < 0.04$) are the ratings by judges of middle and upper low class (76 percent of the network) vs. lower low class (24 percent) with cohesive 3-component vs. lower cohesion correlation.[9] The correlation between *k*-cohesion and leadership status is equally significant.

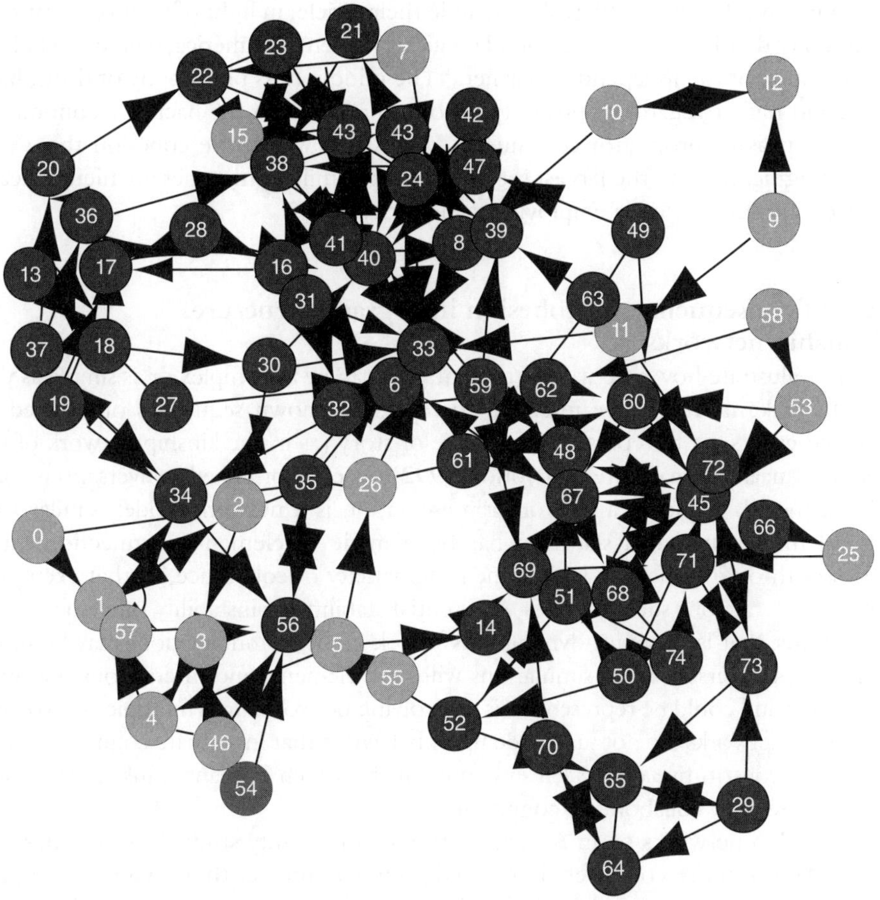

Figure 18.5 SJS network, with major contrasts between the structurally cohesive 3-component (dark nodes) of the network and the larger 2-component which also contains the lightest nodes. The one gray node adds to the 1-component, which includes the entire network. Kinship links are common within the 3-component, supplemented by a clustering of fewer non-kinship ties in the dense upper part of the graph, and very few scattered ritual kinship ties. These contrasts show up better at http://intersci.ss.uci.edu/wiki/pdf/Social_Nets_Cog-May2010_29pp_a.pdf. Edges without arrows are symmetric, arcs with arrows asymmetric.

In the Atirro *finca* there are no correlates of cohesion with class rank or leadership. "In Atirro the two upper classes have associations directed largely outside the community and little interaction orientated to other people in the village" (Loomis and Powell 1949:157). "The top prestige leaders … were not chosen from these two upper groups and there exists a barrier of significant proportion between the two lower groups and the two upper groups" (low and upper middle class). "The lack of informal communication between leaders [of the two lower classes] and the *finca* and commissary directors in the classes above is noteworthy." Mutual agreement on class levels does occurs for eight of ten judges but the community was split equally in their ratings of one resident and, for a leader, three judges agreed with his rating while six judged him higher.

Loomis and Powell (1949:157) conclude their article, in light of their concern with community disaffection in the hacienda regions of Central America, where Costa Rica was a bastion of the independent farmer. "The middle class philosophy of thrift, hard work, and higher regard for property is not as prevalent in the hacienda community as in the peasant proprietor community." In Atirro what little cohesion there is is highly fragmented and the largest set of extended family visiting ties are hierarchically connected to the hacienda employment hierarchy.

Tests of consequences of cohesion in P-graph structure of kinship networks

P-graphs illustrate how a network representation can be as complex or as simple as you want to make it. It may be intended to represent known sequences of selected or observed events, or to represent a narrative or story (as in the kinship network of the biblical Canaanites in White and Jorion 1992), a series of linked conversations, or a cultural model. Typically a network representation is a network model, similar to a cultural model in that a selection has been made of elements, connections, and processes through time that have some systematicity or coherence, or that exemplify complex interactions such as cycles, differential stability, or instability of elements and interactions, that is, complex dynamics. Network models of interactions may be simulated, and, conversely, most simulations will have elements and interactions that map out in time and could be represented as an evolving network, or as multiple co-evolving networks. Networks are not just made up of behaviors that instantiate cognition (Read 2008) but constitutive of the felt environment by which humans think, individually, and socialize their collaborative cognition.

For kinship networks of an Austrian farming community studied by Brudner and White (1997), more cohesively integrated members predict those who inherit productive property as opposed to those who do not and who tend to leave their natal community. For a Turkish nomad clan, more cohesively integrated members tended to predict those who would stay with the clan rather than emigrating to cities, inheriting in this case the productive property of pastoralism. Predictions of this sort are reviewed in White (2010b). To better study the structure of kinship networks the network units were converted from individuals to couples (P-graphs, as defined by White and Jorion 1992) so that cycles of marriage as well as marriage between consanguineal kin could be detected. These cycles are a special case of structure cohesion or k-connective where $k = 2$ (bi-components) are the maximal level of cohesion (two is the maximum number of parents in a P-graph and standard genealogy). This type of biconnectivity excludes cohesion within families and captures kinship units of *structural endogamy* (White 1997) within communities.

Perception and action based on cohesive structure

Case study findings such as those of Moody and White (2003) on school friendship networks and of business alliances in relation to political affiliation, and of Powell et al. (2005) on human biotech collaborations, each imply an ability to *act upon perceptions of* cohesive network structure even without any linguistic labeling of the cohesive groups or levels of cohesion, and that these perceptions proved to be largely correct.

The first is an example of friendships in relatively small networks within single organizations (high schools), while the second and third are medium- and large-sized networks of firms *and* other alliances of the firms (in the first, political parties, in the second, other organizations that serve functions for the biotech firms). A cognitive ability that would allow individuals or firms to act in such a way that their choice behavior for network ties is predicted by structural cohesion presumes recognition of cohesive structure even when names for *k*-components are lacking in ordinary discourse.[10]

The fallacy that thought depends on language

We know from experimental comparisons between human and other animals that relational reasoning (Hummel and Holyoak 2005) is critical to humans' ability to negotiate their extensive skills in social networks. The special relationship between human cognition and the complexity of human social networks includes those of "non-perceptual relational similarity based on logical, functional, and/or structural similarities between relations and systematic correspondences between the abstract roles that elements play in those relations" (Penn et al. 2008:111).[11]

Dominant anthropological views of the early 1960s, however, assumed that cognition and culture were largely constructed through language and linguistic categories, which in an extreme case can be problematized in a quote from Helen Keller: "Before I had words I had only sensations." Keller, however, was deafblind. It has been shown experimentally that with sight alone humans have enormous complexity in their understanding of social relations. Orang-utans and other higher primates also have understanding of complex relations acquired by watching and listening. This hints at where words and language fit in Figure 18.1 as opposed to non-linguistic, for example relational, cognition.

We can narrativize culture as a phenomenon taking on "its own distinct and [durable] existence," and as such stories are supported experientially by the duration of network groupings with a high degree of structural cohesion (Moody and White 2003) and where social networks form detectable communities (Estrada and Hatano 2008). The algorithmic science of finding unique "strong boundaries" of cohesive network sub-groups, as proven mathematically for cohesive blocking (overlap detection for hybrid communities) is barely in its infancy. Yet White and Harary's (2001) time-series predictions of karate club member decisions are replicated in Estrada and Hatano's model, and serve as an example of precisely matching predictive models for how ties dissolve as a club splits in two during a conflict between leaders. For every population in which there are data on the kinds of elements that constitute a culture or subculture, tests can now be constructed using cohesive blocking models and also Estrada's community detection algorithm to predict consensus or other patterns of behavior.

Co-descendant sidedness: South Asia

Humans can cognize complex role and structural patterns in social networks, only some of which are encoded in language. An illustration of complexity in pattern recognition is explicit in South Asian kinship cognition, expressed in discourse that is explicitly computational. When two people in a Dravidian language region are uncertain how they are related, for example, it is a computational discussion of whether they have a common close ancestor that allows them to decide whether they are "parallel kin" or marriageable "cross" relatives. This calculation expresses the existence of positions in the kinship network connecting same or opposite sides of two sets of intermarrying male lines (*viri*-sides) so if there is an *even number* of their female links – mothers of male or agnatic ascendants linking them to an ancestor – then they are cross and marriageable (Kris Lehman, personal communication), as with ♂ZD, ♂FZD, ♂MBD, or more remote cross-sided kin (♂MZS of course is not marriageable either). Otherwise they are same-sided, as with Z, FZ, MB. This shows cognizance of a balance principle of signed graphs that is proven as a theorem by Cartwright and Harary (1956): If we regard the male links as (+) same-side ties and female links as (–) opposite-side in a marriage network, the balance theorem partitions all and only the (+) links into one of two sides, assures that (–) links connect opposite sides, and that all cycles contain only even numbers of (–) links (but any number of (+) links). Descendants with overlapping ancestors need only marry properly sided consanguines (e.g., ZD, FZD, MBD) to form *viri*-sides (opposing sets of agnatic lines) that intermarry. The *viri*-sided balance principles implicit in Dravidian egocentric kinship terminology organize coherent sidedness for networks of consanguineal marriages. Caveats for consistency are that sidedness can incorporate totally foreign spouses but cannot apply to distant families related through marriage, for the practical reason that (1) there are too many paths to follow, unlike tracing near ancestors, and (2) these may not be among "your" kin who share a common network structure of sidedness. Thus, a network of consanguineal marriages will be sided if everyone follows the local co-descendant *viri*-sidedness rule (or, in a matrilineal society, a *uxori*-sided rule wherein an even number of *fathers* of *uterine* ascendants will create same-sidedness in a *uxori*-sided consanguineal marriage network).

The structure of kinship networks is often valuable in understanding how kinship works, even at the terminological level. Leach's (1961) *Pul Eliya* contains a complete genealogy of a Sri Lankan community with agnatic compounds and cross and parallel kinship terms with Dravidian sidedness rules. Named matrimonial moieties are absent. The restudy of these data, analyzed by Houseman and White (1998a) and White (1999), shows that among those kin linked by common ancestors, 100 percent of the male links in the kinship network can be divided into *viri*-sides such that women from one side marry men on the other (Houseman and White 1998b). We show that the Dravidian "practice" of sided marriage in a kinship network of this sort is sufficient to result in a sided "structure" of a network of consanguineal marriages, without recourse to sides as named social groups, or as defined by unilineal descent. Pul Eliyans lack a rule for membership in corporate male descent groups that is consistent with network male-based (*viri*-)sidedness. Thus, language categories themselves, such as Dravidian kinterms, do not inevitably tell us what we might wish to know about kinship reasoning.

Although Pul Eliyans have a concept for network sidedness that is rooted in kinship terminology, there is a minority of wrong-sided marriages between non-consanguines. The name for them is *dos*, "improper," marriages. They also have a reason *not* to practice *viri*-sidedness village-wide or with outsiders because irrigation rights and extended family residences in compounds are normally inherited by sons and allocated to a daughter when she lacks brothers. To inherit *and* avoid *dos* marriage, the heiress will marry a man from a distant village whose sidedness can be ignored (some brothers from distant villages are able to marry women on opposite sides). Thus, community members have an elaborate understanding of network sidedness expressed in their kinterms and they retain consistent sidedness among the majority of the village that are connected through common ancestors, while a minority of non-sided marriages occur for those who do not marry consanguines within the core community. Strategic marriages preserve cognatic inheritance relations without violating the integrity of a cognized but not fully articulated linguistic inscription of network sidedness. Sidedness and its strategic alterations are difficult to perceive in Leach's (1961: flyleaf) genealogy but rather easy to interpret in the *viri*-sided P-graph diagrams of Houseman and White (1998b:figs. 4.3, 4.4, 4.5).

Residential inheritance dependence: The Chuukese puzzle

Another example important for understanding kinship is how behavior choices are made as part of "shared culture" but in ways that are ascribed by fixed categories such as descent or residential groupings. Relational thinking about where to reside after marriage, for example, is analyzed in a network study by Skyhorse (1998) of the Romanum Chuukese (aka Trukese) genealogies. This is a question that spawned the Fischer–Goodenough residential rules controversy (Goodenough 1956; Fischer 1958): should residential choice be broken down into categories based on the lineage of the wife or husband, with the wife's father's maternal uncle, or husband's father, and so forth, and should the categories be "emic" (how people think about these choices) or "etic" (describing choices in the observer's language). Skyhorse, however, shifted the question to show cultural uniformity in terms of how the context of networks relationships predicted choice. Nearly 100 percent of the couples she studied with the aid of complete Romanum genealogies went to live with the holder of lineage land who was "closest" to the husband or the wife in terms of the rules for inheriting land. This is the kind of decision analysis (Fjellman, Geoghegan) reviewed in White (1974), but now contextualized by how people were embedded by meaningful links within the global kinship network of genealogical links.

Sub-group versus individual centrality

In the two examples discussed above, and in my karate club example, network-based cognitions and decisions play out in the mutualities of how two people regard each other with respect to others: in the "sidedness" of mutual ancestral descent, the mutual considerations of alternative inheritances by spouses play a leading part in residential choice, and dyadic considerations about dropping friendships in factional disputes. In sociology these are known as Simmelian effects of the network embedding of dyads within triads, or how network structure and groups influence behavior. While the centrality of individuals has been shown to be an important influence on their behavior (Freeman 1979 distinguishes effects of betweenness versus closeness or simply number of connections, for example), Estrada and Hatano (2008) test a more Simmelian measure of *sub-group* centrality that characterizes the relative participation of each individual node in all sub-graphs in a network. This measure, over a large sample of empirical networks, is almost totally uncorrelated with betweenness centrality for individual nodes. Estrada and Rodriguez (2005) go a step further to exploit their group-oriented method to define uniquely determined network communities based on patterns of shared sub-group centrality and the clustering of "communicability" in networks. Measures based on group effects such as these (and structural cohesion) should predict degree of cultural sharing between members of a network, no matter how extended, and effects on individual agency and on the potential agency of groups.

Diversity and sharing

The integration of network approaches into cognitive anthropology reopens significant new problems of sharing and diversity; continuity and discontinuity in culture; and stability, metastability, and instability in complex systems (including culture). New approaches can help in new syntheses at the ethnographic level and theoretical level, including comparison and explanation. The concepts of structural cohesion are ones around which communication, social reinforcement, and agreement may shape cultural consensus. These group-oriented network measures also identify social boundaries that may overlap and that may change rapidly. Members of a cohesive group may also affiliate elsewhere to create complex network formations.

Continuity

Many anthropologists have felt obliged to explain how continuity in culture occurs. Sir Herbert Spencer coined the term "superorganic," as if society were an organism whose existence required shared culture. This pseudo-explanatory word game was continued by Durkheim who referred to collective consciousness. Alfred Kroeber and Leslie White continued the use of the superorganism concept as if it were an explanation, and we see the term "distributed cognition" in use today in cognitive anthropology. J. W. Powell in 1880 coined the term "enculturalation" to describe what we see today in evolutionary syntheses of developmental (ontogenetic) processes. For Oyama (2000:71) and many contemporary researchers, "What passes from one generation to the next is an entire developmental system" that is inheritance-dependent but, as the outcome of a dynamical process; this is a view that can benefit from further empirical research testing the modern synthesis in developmental and cognitive psychology supported by new experimental evidence of *direct perception* (Michaels and Carollo 1981:11–13), with network and organism–environment embeddings as part of unexpected solutions to the mind–body two-world problem.

Discontinuity

Dynamical processes, like episodic direct perception, have discontinuities, often cycling between different states. Leach's (1961) study of the Pul Eliya emphasizes that there is no corporate charter of norms linked to the permanency of descent groups that continue indefinitely, and all is not harmony: most of the many conflicts he described involved failures of delayed reciprocation in discretional transfers of property between matrimonial sides. Statistical changes as well as institutional ones (like policies introduced by British colonial authorities) may change frequencies of behavior that change the context in which new expectations and norms are formed around changed network formations of structurally cohesive groups.

Metastability and instability in complex systems, including culture

Re-examining the problems of continuity and discontinuity in culture, sharing and diversity, and stability, metastability, and instability in complex systems (including culture) can help in a new synthesis of cognitive and social anthropology. These include problems of theory and method and issues of dualist versus monist social theories as described by Leaf (1979).

White and Johansen (2006) provide a longitudinal network study that exemplifies metastability by documenting the ethnogenesis, growth, and decline of ten lineages linked through structurally endogamous marriages in a nomad clan and the formation of new groups as clan members emigrate or resettle in urban areas. It focuses on how the initial formation of a structurally endogamous group through strategic intermarriage provides the cohesion for a leader of a long-range migration to form a new clan and move to occupy new territory. It then focuses on how equalitarian rotating leadership creates a period of reciprocal interlineage alliances that holds the growing population together for many generations. Intense competition for resources favor large sibling sets with many siblings-in-law while population pressure shunts less competitive smaller families off to resettle in towns and cities. The growing numbers of interlinked nomads and ex-nomads eventually support the movement of wealthier lineage leaders and their families to the city, and ties between the lineages gradually thin out to the point where the clan ceases to be cohesive, as new occupational forms are taken up.

Conclusion

I have provided here the first true tests, using data from the San Juan Sur and Atirro studies in Costa Rica, of various hypotheses about how aspects of cultural consensus are predicted by measures of sub-group cohesion in social networks based on formal graph-theoretic concepts, aka structural cohesion or multiple (*k*-)connectivity.[12] These kinds of hypotheses provide explanations for how multiply reinforcing social interactions can serve as key mechanisms for the emergence of cultural sharing. This extends as well to sharing in social roles where the role occupants interact cohesively with the overlapping role alters. The latter hypothesis has been extensively tested in sociology using the formal measure of structural equivalence and by Reichardt and White 2007 in their overlapping role equivalence models of complex networks.[13] Cohesion in overlapping role equivalence and the cohesiveness of groups provide theoretical bases for the emergence of cohesion-based institutional structures as an aspect of cultural organization.[14] Models of cohesive groups and role overlap structures, as formal measurement concepts, also predict that cohesion-based aspects of culture will be cognized in patterned ways that are likely to be shared between individuals (i.e., because of the common group or role overlap in environmental perceptions). Studies that integrate networks, cognition, and cultural frameworks ought to be far more effective than studies that divorce these topics from one another in the study of culture.

This paper advanced the propositions that: (1) cognition is not exclusively based on language; (2) human cognition is well capacitated to perceive complex relational structures in networks of behavior without a necessary dependence on named concepts or categories; (3) behaviors can be organized on the basis of these perceptions; and (4) reliance on categories and typologies as the exclusive basis of individual or culturally shared cognition is ill advised. There is weighty scientific evidence for these propositions. This brings weight to the idea that network structure and dynamics are key components for understanding human behavior, adding to but semi-independent of symbols, language, narratives, and other needed components.

Another proposition is that the most useful codings of social networks are those that emerge from a narrative structure, regardless of whether these narratives are explicit in speech or text. This is supported by the Gibsonian propositions that (1) a relevant network for study beyond just individual organisms and their ties is the organism–environment behavioral system, including what is afforded in this interaction that become sources of adaptation; and (2) types of human experience as cognitively encoded in Gibsonian psychological formats (as in the studies reviewed here) can fit into the conceptualization of social networks. That is, if experience and memory are stored in continuous perceptions, feelings, and "narrative-like" constructions about ongoing interactions, that is, in episodes, rather than in bits and pieces of categories, modeling these interactions as networks may be more useful. These ideas may suggest useful ways for social networks data to be encoded. Multiple types of directed links may represent different modes of interaction between two or more individuals in episodes of joint experience.

Ways of coding networks may also be tied in with newer models and measures of cohesive groups wherein interactions are likely to develop that help to coordinate behavior, cognition, mutually understood use of language and communications, and where the development of cultural models is within bounded social units. Extension of cohesion-based models of roles can help to understand how role interactions in organizational settings can become institutional. Contemporary network studies (Powell et al. 2005; Vedres and Stark 2008) are uncovering the benefits of research on such topics as internal group cohesion versus extra-group structural holes in networks role structure (Burt 2001) that reflect a congruence between anthropological ideas about benefits to groups in shared culture and roles in broader organizational structure. An anthropological approach to networks and culture, then, through proper tuning and validation of how networks are coded in terms of these experiential encodings, provides network modeling that can contribute to cognitive anthropology, and vice versa.

Because groups and roles are given to instabilities or meta-stabilities in complex interactive structures it may be useful to succinctly code and analyze network interactions through time to understand interaction system dynamics. The synthesis of cognition and network embedding in joint study offers an enrichment of the fields of cognitive studies, network studies, and cultural studies.

General problems of culture and cognition are also complemented by the "memes" approach, for example, of Sperber and Wilson (1986). Cultural units of meaning or "memes" can be studied "epidemiologically" through diffusive percolation, through convective network routes or role transmissions, or through propagation by omnidirectional radiation, for example popular media. Memes do not simply diffuse, but are also carried by interactions that can be shaped in cohesive groups and spread in cohesion-based networks of roles. And, at the cognitive level, networks of relevance give interpersonal focus to attention and thus to shared understandings that are spread by various mechanisms.

Two of the most basic concepts relevant to social sciences have been those of group and role. In this paper I have tried to move the status of these concepts up from the descriptive level (or middle-range theoretical constructs) to a level of measurement in networks of interactions where more formal and thus measurable theoretical concepts can be tested at a causal level, exemplified by how cultural emergence can be explained and predicted as consensus at the level of cohesive group emergent out of interaction, and predictive consequences of levels of structural cohesion in groups and role structures.

My model of process, shown in Figure 18.1, is that perceptions of material and behavioral entities and relations (C) flow into behavior–environment systems with organism–brain sentience and emotion (B). These networks are abstractly parsed in mind–cognition (A) which can recognize abstracted patterns in other (B, C) networks, the compounds in these cases constituting joint entities. This parsing flows back recursively within the mentally constructed network of episodic memory (A), coupled to perception–emotion responses (B), to produce networks of self-generated and both self- and other-perceived behavior structured into network-codable episodes (C), the compounds in these cases constituting joint entities. The shared cohesive patterns of these networks (D) can be recognized in mind (A), abstracted by mind–cognition back from emergent patterns of shared culture (D). This model has room for network analyses at multiple levels. It is not as simple as a positivist reduction to causal relations between acts → perceptions → thoughts, which mixes levels of the material and the immaterial. In separating the elements and relations of actions, thoughts, and culture, and analyzing their network components and effects, we may come to better understand human behavior, cognition, and culture.

NOTES

1 Because these patterns are constructed in the mind by interactions of neural networks, our mind has a perception of durability and continuity in our experiences, chunks of which will persist in various aspects of memory and mental schemata even as our attention is intermittently shifting from one experience to another.

2 Biotech organizations (Powell et al. 2005), for example, self-report their new collaborative contracts annually in their trade journal *because* collaborations contribute value to reputation; Aydını nomads proudly report their marriages and ancestors to ethnographers (White and Johansen 2006); network surveys may constrain and limit responses but also ask respondents to report on personal experience as well as experiential observations. The dyadic self–other reporting may provide estimates of the reliability of such reports.

3 See, further, http://intersci.ss.uci.edu/wiki/index.php/Culture%2C_science_and_the_world - _note-1, accessed October 4, 2010.

4 See the concepts of schema, prototype, and instantiation summarized by D'Andrade (1995:122–124). The positivist "model of the mind," however, in contrast to Figure 18.1, attributes causality to relations between material and non-material ("reified") entities, conflates constructs of mind (thought, wish, intention) with materially causal agents, mediates feelings through thought, and conflates them with "mindless" action.

5 There are, of course, other network predictors of cultural consensus, such as parentage or ancestry, common history, common educational experience, or exposure to the same media sources such as specific TV and radio sources. These are "vertical" rather than "horizontal" influences as in structurally cohesive groups. There are also "oblique transmission" influences such as effects of common types of prestigious figures that inspire learned agreement.

6 The spring embedding or FDP (force-directed placement) visualization algorithm pulls nodes together if they are connected and pushes them apart according to the length of the singular chains that connect them but which are not embedded in cohesive blocks.

7 These ties show an extended family structure in SJS with a common – consensual role – pattern in the visiting behaviors for kin. Removing symmetric ties for visiting between kin gives 46 remaining asymmetric visiting ties that form a connected but partially ordered visiting hierarchy differing significantly from random rearrangements of ties ($p = 0.00000000000003$). This is evidence of the salience of a P-graph structure (see following section) for the kinship network (individual members of couples and their siblings linked to parental couples).

8 These contrasts can be seen in color at http://intersci.ss.uci.edu/wiki/pdf/Social_Nets_Cog-May2010_29pp_a.pdf, accessed September 24, 2010.

9 Figure 18.4 has 54 red nodes and 20 green–blue nodes (one node is obscured), and nine green–blue nodes with social class ratings below 46 on the scale 0–66 in figure 2 of Loomis and McKinney (1956:407).

10 The cohesive blocks in the biotech industry were unnamed, and it is doubtful that the friendship groups were named because they cut across grade levels and they partitioned groups within grade levels.

11 Cohen (1969; Cohen et al. 1968) had shown evidence of modes of reasoning using relational reasoning rather than analytical categories of non-verbal tests but such evidence has been largely ignored.

12 For SJS the direction of this radix prediction (one predictor, many dependent variables) for multiple aspects of consensus (among judges of middle-class position, for upper- to middle- vs. lower-middle and lower-class ranking of individuals, and for leadership roles, etc. is more likely prima facie than the multiple regression prediction (many predictors, one dependent variable). Atirro lacks all but very fragmented social cohesion or cultural consensus.

13 The concept of role models with overlaps of alters is that every occupant of a role X which interacts with role Y has some overlap with common alters and thus a partially shared perceptual environment. A dynamical model of overlapping roles computes this algorithm in successive time periods. Reichardt and White (2007) give an example of a role overlap model for the 2000 global economy.

14 It may make more sense for the study of culture to ground the notion of systemic cohesion not by "institutions" but by substituting a term for more concretely cohesive entities such as "organizations." This specifies more concrete linkages, objectives, and adaptive redesign (Leaf 2008). Then in the domain of adaptive cognition (Posner 1989) and language there are two concrete adaptive levels for conceptual networks with concrete linkages that are either tighter through logical construction or looser through Ashby's principle of adaptive variability, where collaborative cognition occurs through the natural and constructed environment, artifacts, and observables (Hutchins 1991).

REFERENCES

Alvarez-Hamelin, José Ingacio, Luca Dall' Asla, Alain Barat, and Alessandro Vespignani
2006 Large Scale Networks Fingerprinting and Visualization Using the K-Core Decomposition. *In* Advances in Neural Information Processing Systems 18. Y. Weiss, B. Schölkopf, and J. Platt, eds. Pp. 41–50. Cambridge MA: MIT Press.

Atran, Scott, D. Medin, N. Ross, E. Lynch, V. Vapnarsky, E. Ek' Ucan, J. Coley, C. Timura, and M. Baran
2002 Folkecology, Cultural Epidemiology, and the Spirit of the Commons. Current Anthropology 43:421–450.
Batagelj, Vlado, and Andre Mrvar
1998 Pajek – Program for Large Network Analysis. Connections 21(2):47–57.
Bernard, H. R., and P. D. Killworth
1977 Informant Accuracy in Social Network Data II. Human Communication Research 4(1):3–18.
Bernard, H. R., P. D. Killworth, and L. Sailer
1980 Informant Accuracy in Social Network Data IV. A Comparison of Clique-Level Structure in Behavioural and Cognitive Data. Social Networks 2(3): 191–218.
1982 Informant Accuracy in Social Network Data V: An Experimental Attempt to Predict Actual Communication from Recall Data. Social Science Research 11:30–66.
Bernard, H. R., P. D. Killworth, D. Kronenfeld, and L. Sailer
1984 The Problem of Informant Accuracy: The Validity of Retrospective Data. Annual Review of Anthropology 13:495–517.
Boster, James
1986 Requiem for the Omniscience Informant: There's Life in the Old Girl Yet. *In* Directions in Cognitive Anthropology. J. Dougherty, ed. Urbana: University of Illinois Press.
Brudner, L. A., and D. R. White
1997 Class, Property and Structural Endogamy: Visualizing Networked Histories. Theory and Society 25(2):161–208.
Burt, Ronald
2001 Structural Holes versus Network Closure as Social Capital. *In* Social Capital: Theory and Research. N. Lin, K. Cook, and R. S. Burt, eds. Pp. 31–56. New York: Aldine de Gruyter.
Carollo, C., and M. Moreno
2005 Why Nonlinear Methods? *In* Tutorials in Contemporary Nonlinear Methods for the Behavioral Sciences. M. A. Riley and G. Van Orden, eds. Pp. 1–25. http://www.nsf.gov/sbe/bcs/pac/nmbs/nmbs.jsp, retrieved March 1, 2005.
Cartwright, D., and F. Harary
1956 Structural Balance: A Generalization of Heider's Theory. Psychological Review 63:277–293.
Cohen, Rosalie A.
1969 Conceptual Styles, Culture Conflict, and Nonverbal Tests of Intelligence. American Anthropologist 71(5):828–856.
Cohen, Rosalie, Gerd Fraenkel, and John Brewer
1968 The Language of the Hard Core Poor: Implications for Culture Conflict. Sociology of Education 41:201–220.
Damasio, Antonio
2007 Descartes' Error: Emotion, Reason and the Human Brain. London: Penguin.
D'Andrade, Roy G.
1974 Memory and the Assessment of Behavior. *In* Social Measurement. T. Blalock, ed. Pp. 139–186. New York: Aldine de Gruyter.
1995 The Development of Cognitive Anthropology. Cambridge: Cambridge University Press.
Denham, Woodrow W., and Douglas R. White
2005 Multiple Measures of Alyawarra Kinship. Field Methods 17:70–101.
Estrada Ernesto, and Naomichi Hatano
2008 Communicability in Complex Networks. Physical Review E 77(036111):1–12.
Estrada, Ernesto, and Juan A. Rodriguez
2005 Subgraph Centrality in Complex Networks. Physical Review E 71(056103):1–9.

Fischer, J. L.
1958 The Classification of Residence. American Anthropologist 60:508–517.
Foster, Brian L., and Stephen B. Seidman
1989 A Formal Unification of Anthropological Kinship and Social Network Methods. *In* Research Methods in Social Networks Analysis. L. C. Freeman, D. R. White, and A. K. Romney, eds. Pp. 41–59. Fairfax, VA: George Mason University.
Freeman, L. C.
1979 Centrality in Social Networks: I. Conceptual Clarification. Social Networks 1: 215–239.
Freeman, L. C., W. Bloomberg Jr., S. P. Koff, M. H. Sunshine, and T. J. Fararo
1960 Local Community Leadership. Syracuse, NY: University College.
Freeman, L. C., A. K. Romney, and S. Freeman
1987 Cognitive Structure and Informant Accuracy. American Anthropologist 89:310–325.
Gibson, James J.
1966 The Senses Considered as Perceptual Systems. Boston, MA: Houghton Mifflin.
1979 The Ecological Approach to Visual Perception. Hillsdale, NJ: Lawrence Erlbaum.
Gluck, Andre
2007 Damasio's Error and Descartes' Truth: An Inquiry into Epistemology, Metaphysics, and Consciousness. Scranton, PA: University of Scranton Press.
Goodenough, Ward H.
1956 Residence Rules. Southwestern Journal of Anthropology 12:22–37.
Houseman, Michael, and Douglas R. White
1998a Network Mediation of Exchange Structures: Ambilateral Sidedness and Property Flows in Pul Eliya (Sri Lanka). *In* Kinship, Networks and Exchange. T. Schweizer and D. R. White, eds. Pp. 59–89. Cambridge: Cambridge University Press. http://eclectic.ss.uci.edu/~drwhite/pub/PUL-CAMB1a.pdf, accessed September 24, 2010.
1998b "Taking Sides": Marriage Networks and Dravidian Kinship in Lowland South America. *In* Transformations of Kinship. M. Godelier and T. Trautmann, eds. Washington, DC: Smithsonian Press.
Hummel, J. E., and K. J. Holyoak
2005 Relational Reasoning in a Neurally Plausible Cognitive Architecture. Current Directions in Psychological Science 14(3):153–157.
Hutchins, Edwin
1991 Organizing Work by Adaptation. Organization Science 2(1):14–39.
1994 Cognition in the Wild. Cambridge, MA: MIT Press.
Leach, Edmund R.
1961 Pul Eliya. Cambridge: Cambridge University Press.
Leaf, Murray
1979 Man, Mind, and Science: A History of Anthropology. New York: Columbia University Press.
2007 Empirical Formalism. Structure and Dynamics: eJournal of Anthropological and Related Sciences 2(1):7–27. http://repositories.cdlib.org/imbs/socdyn/sdeas/vol2/iss1/art2, accessed September 24, 2010.
2008 Indigenous Algorithms, Organizations, and Rationality. Structure and Dynamics: eJournal of Anthropological and Related Sciences 3(2), article 3. http://repositories.cdlib.org/imbs/socdyn/sdeas/vol3/iss2/art3, accessed September 24, 2010.
Loomis, C. P., and J. C. McKinney
1956 Systemic Differences between Latin-American Communities of Family Farms and Large Estates. American Journal of Sociology 61(5):404–412.
Loomis, C. P., and R. M. Powell
1949 Sociometric Analysis of Class Status in Rural Costa Rica – A Peasant Community Compared with an Hacienda Community. Sociometry 12(1–3):144–157.

McMahan, Peter
2007 Cohesive Blocks: R Program for Use with Digraph. Documented for usage in R at http://intersci.ss.uci.edu/wiki/index.php/Peter_McMahan, accessed September 24, 2010.
Michaels, Claire F., and Claudia Carollo
1981 Direct Perception. Englewood Cliffs, NJ: Prentice Hall.
Moody, James, and Douglas R. White
2003 Structural Cohesion and Embeddedness: A Hierarchical Conception of Social Groups. American Sociological Review 68(1):1–25.
Oyama, S.
2000 Evolution's Eye: A System's View of the Biology–Culture Divide. Durham, NC: Duke University Press.
Penn, D. C., K. J. Holyoak, and D. J. Povinelli
2008 Darwin's Mistake: Explaining the Discontinuity between Human and Nonhuman Minds. Behavioral and Brain Sciences 31:109–178 (with 24 commentaries and authors' responses). http://reasoninglab.psych.ucla.edu/KH%20pdfs/Penn,%20Holyoak,%20Povinelli.2008.pdf, accessed October 4, 2010.
Popper, Karl, and John Eccles
1977 The Self and Its Brain: An Argument for Interactionism. London: Springer.
Posner, Michael I., ed.
2000 Foundations of Cognitive Science. Cambridge, MA: MIT Press.
Powell, Walter W., Douglas R. White, Kenneth W. Koput, and Jason Owen-Smith
2005 Network Dynamics and Field Evolution: The Growth of Interorganizational Collaboration in the Life Sciences. American Journal of Sociology 110(4):901–975.
Read, Dwight
2008 A Formal Explanation of Formal Explanation. Structure and Dynamics 3(2): 123–140. http://repositories.cdlib.org/imbs/socdyn/sdeas/vol3/iss2/art4, accessed September 24, 2010
Reichardt, Jörg, and Douglas R. White
2007 Role Models for Complex Networks. European Physical Journal B60:217–224.
Romney, A. K., S. C. Weller, and W. H. Batchelder
1986 Culture as Consensus: A Theory of Cultural and Informant Accuracy. American Anthropologist 88:313–338.
Ross, Norbert
2004 Culture and Cognition: Implications for Theory and Method. Thousand Oaks, CA: Sage.
Schweizer, Thomas
1996 Muster Soziale Ordnung: Netzworkanalyze als Fundament der Sozialeethnologie. Berlin: Reimner.
Seidman, Stephen B., and Brian L. Foster
1978 Graph-Theoretic Generalization of Clique Concept. Journal of Mathematical Sociology 6(1):139–154.
Skyhorse, P.
1998 Adoption as a Strategy on a Chuukese Atoll. History of the Family 3(4):429–439.
Sperber, Daniel, and Deirdre Wilson
1986 Relevance: Communication and Cognition. Cambridge, MA: MIT Press.
Swenson, R., and M. T. Turvey
1991 Thermodynamic Reasons for Perception-Action Cycles. Ecological Psychology 3: 317–348.
Turvey, Michael T.
1991 Thermodynamic Reasons for Perception–Action Cycles. Ecological Psychology 3: 317–348.

2009 On the Notion and Implications of Organism-Environment System. Ecological Psychology 21(2): 97–111.

Turvey, Michael T., and Robert E. Shaw

1979 The Primacy of Perceiving: An Ecological Reformulation of Perception for Understanding Memory. *In* Studies of Memory: In Honor of Uppsala University's 500th Anniversary. L.-G. Nilssen, ed. Pp. 167–222. Hillsdale, NJ: Lawrence Erlbaum.

1995 Toward an Ecological Physics and a Physical Psychology. *In* The Science of the Mind. Robert L. Solso and Dominic W. Massaro, eds. Pp. 144–172. Oxford: Oxford University Press.

Vedres, Balazs, and David Stark

2008 Opening Closure: Intercohesion and Entrepreneurial Dynamics in Business Groups. MPIfG Discussion Paper 09/3. Max-Planck-Institut für Gesellschaftsforschung. http://www.mpifg.de/pu/mpifg_dp/dp09-3.pdf, accessed October 4, 2010.

Wagman, J. B., and D. B. Miller

2003 Nested Reciprocities: The Organism-Environment System in Perception-Action and Development. Developmental Psychobiology 42:317–334.

West, M. J., and A. P. King

1987 Settling Nature and Nurture into an Ontogenetic Niche. Developmental Psychobiology 20:549–562.

White, Douglas R.

1974 Mathematical Anthropology. *In* Handbook of Social and Cultural Anthropology. J. J. Honigmann, ed. Pp. 369–446. Chicago: Rand McNally.

1997 Structural Endogamy and the Graphe de Parenté. Mathématiques, Informatique, et Sciences Humaines 137:107–125. http://eclectic.ss.uci.edu/~drwhite/pw/str-endo.pdf, accessed September 24, 2010.

1999 Controlled Simulation of Marriage Systems. Journal of Artificial Societies and Social Simulation 2(3). http://jasss.soc.surrey.ac.uk/2/3/5.html, accessed September 24, 2010.

2010a Appendix to Social Networks, Cognition and Culture: Activating the Cohesive. Blocks Algorithm to Produce Fig. 2. http://intersci.ss.uci.edu/wiki/index.php/Appendix_to_Social_Networks,_Cognition_and_Culture, accessed September 24, 2010.

2010b Kinship, Class, and Community. Sage Handbook of Social Networks. Peter Carrington and John Scott, eds. Cambridge: Cambridge University Press.

White, Douglas R., and Frank Harary

2001 The Cohesiveness of Blocks in Social Networks: Node Connectivity and Conditional Density. Sociological Methodology 31:305–359.

White, Douglas R., and Michael Houseman

2002 The Navigability of Strong Ties: Small Worlds, Tie Strength and Network Topology. Complexity 8(1):72–81.

White, Douglas R., and Ulla Johansen

2006 Network Analysis and Ethnographic Problems: Process Models of a Turkish Nomad Clan. Boston, MA: Lexington.

White, Douglas R., and Paul Jorion

1992 Representing and Computing Kinship: A New Approach. Current Anthropology 33(4):454–463.

White, Douglas R., and Karl Reitz

1983 Graph and Semigroup Homomorphisms. Social Networks 5:193–234. http://eclectic.ss.uci.edu/~drwhite/pub/whitereitz.pdf, accessed September 24, 2010.

Zachary, Wayne W.

1977 An Information Flow Model for Conflict and Fission in Small Groups. Journal of Anthropological Research 33:452–473.

PART IV

Cognitive Anthropology and Other Disciplines

CHAPTER 19

Culture and Cognition: The Role of Cognitive Anthropology in Anthropology and the Cognitive Sciences

Norbert Ross and Douglas L. Medin

INTRODUCTION

Human beings are thinking, talking organisms. It seems obvious that cultural anthropology and, specifically, cognitive anthropology would be a central player in studies on the relationship between cognition and culture. This is not the case. Cultural anthropology largely operates at a qualitative level without sensing the need to examine individual cognition. In turn, cognitive psychology has placed its bet that it can understand the human mind without taking into account the social processes within which the human mind operates. Although theories and quantitative methods of cognitive psychology are elaborate they derive almost exclusively from undergraduates performing 50-minute tasks on computers. No surprise then that cognitive anthropology – far from being a central player – is something of an orphan within the cognitive sciences.

On a more optimistic note, in the cognitive sciences there has been an increase in focus on the role of both language and culture in cognition. This upsurge ranges from a powerful revival of linguistic relativity theory (e.g., Gentner and Goldin-Meadow 2003) to the idea that culture not only affects what people think but also how people

A Companion to Cognitive Anthropology, First Edition. Edited by David B. Kronenfeld, Giovanni Bennardo, Victor C. de Munck, and Michael D. Fischer.

think (e.g., Nisbett 2003). Cognitive anthropologists have taken tentative steps to reconnect with the other cognitive sciences as well as with evolutionary models of cultural dynamics. They also show signs of questioning the Lone Ranger model of research, supplementing it with the idea that research collaborations drawing on a diversity of skills and perspectives may be more effective.

But even this limited optimism must be tempered with caution. Though "cultural psychology" has broadened the cultural base for psychological studies, the heavy focus on college students continues. Only now student participants are selected by their non-European ethnic background (within or outside the USA). Cognitive anthropologists, on the other hand, by ignoring laboratory studies of cognition in principle, find that their knowledge of theories and related data is outdated. In brief we are short of the conditions that would foster the mutual respect and interest to make cognitive anthropology a key player in both anthropology and in cognitive science.

This chapter is intended to help bridge the gap and for that purpose we proceed as follows. First, we elaborate a bit on the history of cognitive science and its relation to cognitive anthropology in order to provide one perspective on the relation between cognition and cognitive anthropology. Next, we argue that this perspective is outdated and ineffective. Then we turn to the relation between cognitive anthropology and other approaches to the study of culture and cultural processes. This will lead us to our central thesis – that cognitive anthropology must be central both to studies of culture and to studies of cognition. To do so, however, it must stretch and bind itself to its neighbors. With these arguments as background, we illustrate these themes with some facets of our ongoing research.

Cognitive psychology was a reaction to and grew out of behaviorism, and has always emphasized tight experimental control of variables and other forms of methodological rigor. By the time the Cognitive Science Society was founded in the late 1970s, however, cognitive psychologists were at home studying meaningful materials such as text. Under the influence of cognitive scientists such as Robert Abelson and Roger Schank (e.g., Schank and Abelson 1977), theoretical constructs like schemas and scripts came into use.

This richer set of theoretical tools and perspectives was broadly attractive to cognitive scientists. Philosophers of language, linguists, artificial intelligence (AI) researchers, and cognitive anthropologists each seemed to have something to offer. Perhaps buoyed by these developments, in one of the early issues of the society's new journal *Cognitive Science* cognitive anthropologist Roy D'Andrade (1981:182) suggested a convenient division of labor between psychology and anthropology: psychologists would study *how* people think and anthropologists would study *what* people think, using the conceptual tools growing out of cognitive science research.

We believe that the distinction between process and content was meant to be a division of labor under the common goal of understanding the human mind in its social context. In practice, however, it became a rationale for mutual disinterest between cognitive anthropology and the rest of cognitive science. In addition, more recent developments in the cognitive sciences indicate that *what* people think is inseparably linked to *how* people think and vice versa.

Cognitive psychology has methodological commitments that get in the way of a broad cognitive science. We do not think it is an exaggeration to say that cognitive psychology suffers from rigor mortis. For each novelty in research materials or procedures a cottage industry tends to develop. Phenomena are studied in such minute detail that there is the danger that researchers are learning about properties of the paradigm rather than properties of the mind. Researchers quickly hone in on materials that produce effects of interest, but, as a consequence, it is difficult to assess the robustness and generality of the phenomena in question (Medin et al., in press). Add to this the convenience sample of undergraduates and there's not much to excite cognitive anthropologists.

Anthropologists conceptualize people as social beings, adapting to real-world environments where history and context are central. Cognitive anthropologists obtain their data by collecting data in real-world contexts, not by sitting participants down in front of a computer and keeping social interaction to a minimum.

Round one goes to cognitive anthropology, if you're willing to tolerate the sort of stereotyping we've adopted. But by the same rules cultural anthropology doesn't fare so well in round two. Historically speaking, cultural anthropology has wavered between two untenable positions. One is the view that "participant observation" allows access to the "omniscient informant," leading to claims like "the people of culture x believe y" without any apparent need to report actual data. The second and contrasting view comes from what is often considered as one offshoot of postmodern criticism on anthropological research. Contributors to this line of thought argue that hopes of understanding another culture are illusory. In its extreme form this critique suggests that the observer and the observed are so intertwined that one cannot tell which is which, irretrievably undermining much of what social science strives for. The best anthropology can hope for, on this view, is for researchers to describe their experiences and encounters with other people. We agree that the problem of the observer has to be taken seriously, yet disagree with the impossibility of conducting comparative research.

A further complication is that it's not always clear what the proper unit of analysis should be in cultural anthropology. Most researchers who study cognition, and presumably nearly all cognitive psychologists, locate cognition in individual minds. But some anthropologists treat culture as a "super-organism" with emergent (cognitive) properties (see Atran et al. 2005 for a review) and researchers who take a "situated cognition" perspective locate cognition to activities in particular contexts, explicitly denying that cognition is a property of individuals (e.g., Lave 1988; Hutchins 1995). Even if this difference in perspective is just a matter of definitions, it is an impediment to bridging the gap between cognitive anthropology and the rest of cognition.

In summary, from the perspective of cognitive psychology, cultural anthropology involves exotic people, unclear methods, and very little actual data. From the perspective of cultural anthropology in general, and cognitive anthropology in particular, the data from cognitive psychology are so artificial as to be useless and largely irrelevant to any of anthropology's concerns. As a consequence these two disciplines have had very little to do with each other.

Even worse, we see cognitive anthropology as having distanced itself from debates in cultural anthropology. We identify with cognitive anthropologists' worries about explicit and formal field methods, but sometimes these worries have come at the expense of an involvement with important questions of wider anthropological theory. Hence cognitive anthropology may have lost relevance for the wider field of anthropology.

We do not pretend to have provided an overview of the history of cognitive anthropology and we plead guilty to trafficking in stereotypes. But we don't think we are far off in our conclusion that cognitive anthropology has been widely isolated from both of its parent disciplines: cultural anthropology and the cognitive sciences. This isolation comes at a time when cognitive anthropology may be instrumental for significant advances in both disciplines. It is to this possibility that we will now turn our attention.

Cognitive anthropologists view the rising interest in cross-cultural studies in the cognitive sciences as a mixed blessing. The idea that a cognitive psychologist can call up a colleague in Tokyo, persuade him or her to run some task with Tokyo undergraduates, and thereby become a cultural researcher just may not sit well. Aiming to understand culture in terms of values on two dimensions (e.g., Eastern collectivism versus Western individualism) may be useful for some purposes, but it is not the sort of take on culture that anthropologists live and labor for. A more conceptual criticism is that most of these studies treat language and/or culture as independent variables; we will return to this point.

There has also been a recent upsurge of interest in modeling cultures as dynamic systems using evolutionary models (for an account of social cooperation in general and altruism in particular see Hamilton 1964; Trivers 1971; see also Axelrod 1997). This focus has been broadened to include attempts to understand the epidemiology of ideas (Blackmore 1999; for alternative frameworks see Aunger 2000; Sperber 2000; Richerson and Boyd 2004).

However, usually such evolutionary models have not been (well) informed by research in either cognitive anthropology or cognitive science more broadly. For example, the main mechanism for cultural transmission in these models is *imitation* and although theories assume that successful and powerful others are more likely to be imitated (e.g., Henrich and Gil-White 2001), there are deep conceptual issues associated with the very notion of imitation that have tended to be ignored (see Henrich and Henrich 2007 for a notable exception). Also, imitation is only one of a set of possible learning and reasoning mechanisms (Atran et al. 2005). For example, children do not acquire adult beliefs simply by being exposed to them (Quinn 1997; Hirschfeld 2002). Cultural anthropologists generally have not weighed in on these issues, despite the fact that their research seems highly relevant.

The preceding material is one view of the current state of the art. The gist of things is that there are grounds for optimism with respect to the relation between cognitive anthropology and cognition on the one hand and anthropology proper on the other. But translating this opportunity into meaningful engagement and interdisciplinary collaboration and cooperation remains a serious challenge.

We offer four main suggestions. First, an understanding of how the mind works (cognition) is needed to better understand the mechanics of cultural processes, arguably the goal of anthropological research. Second, an understanding of social processes and the specific environment (social and physical) within which the mind develops and operates is essential to better understanding cognition, arguably the goal of the cognitive sciences. As both cognitive and social factors are heavily interconnected, they must be explored in conjunction with one another. Cognitive anthropology is ideally positioned to pursue these sorts of interactions. Third, given that cognitive anthropology is not currently pursuing this goal, we offer suggestions with respect to theory and methods for doing so. Fourth, we'll argue that "culture" should be studied as the *outcome of social and cognitive processes*, as an emerging product rather than a set of rules, grammars to be detected, or as an independent variable.

Overview on Human Cognition

Much of the development of the human brain takes place after birth. Hence, experience with the environment provides important input for brain development (Linden 2007). On the other hand, infant learning is guided by a series of innate and quickly acquired skeletal principles that are specific to particular domains such as language, (naive) physics, (naive) biology, (naive) psychology, and number (e.g., Carey and Spelke 1996; Bloom 2002; Baillargeon 2004). It is between these two interacting poles that cognitive anthropology needs to locate its research, incorporating and providing a theoretical understanding that accounts for both aspects: innate principles and malleability of neural structures. As a result, cultural knowledge is not simply copied from one brain to the next, nor is it irrelevant for the developing mind.

This perspective suggests a balance of attention between "universal or at least bounded cognitive mechanisms" and an embedded cognition where cognitive and social factors interact. Before proceeding, we first sketch a definition of culture that we consider useful in our attempts to understand the interaction of culture and cognition.

Culture: The outcome of cognitive and social factors

In our view, culture comprises both mental and public representations such as material productions, speech, and other aspects of behavior in particular ecological contexts (see Sperber 1996; Ross 2004). What we refer to as culture or cultural concepts are those representations that are relatively stable and systematically distributed within a population (Atran et al. 2005). Much of our view concurs with ideas often summarized as "distributed cognition" (Vygotsky 1978; Hutchins 1995; Cole 1996). We see cultural processes as the outcome of the complex interaction of individual cognitive processes interacting with each other and their social environment. This view of culture has several consequences.

First, adopting this perspective forces us to perceive cognitive processes as *situated or embodied manifestations*; that is, as mental activities relevant to an individual's life, which take place within a specific context. Consequently, it reinforces a research strategy of examining cognition in relevant contexts.

Second, this view of culture enables us to better illuminate the interaction of cognitive and social processes. When we talk about cultural change, we are talking about conceptual change (within and across individuals) as well as about changes in the distribution of specific concepts within populations. To the extent that the formation and transmission of concepts depends on the flux of information, it is important to widen our analysis of *information* to any kind of information input or cultural practice, and not focus solely on explicit propositional content. "Culture" and "cultural differences" cease to be the endpoints or even the focal points of our research. Instead, we focus on the distribution of representations within and between populations with the goal of explaining patterns of agreement and disagreement. Both cultural processes as well as the resulting distribution of agreement patterns form part of a dynamic system we describe as culture. In this approach it is as important to explain both *cultural stability and resiliency* as well as *cultural change* as the outcome of complex processes (Ross et al. n.d.).

Third, viewing culture as a distribution of ideas and practices avoids essentializing culture or defining it only in terms of consensus or agreement. Instead of treating disagreement as failure to form or maintain a consensus, it becomes central to our distributional approach. Both agreement and disagreement need to be explained as structures emerging from the interplay of social and cognitive factors.

Note that regarding culture as an independent variable is inherently circular unless the notion is unpacked into a series of dimensions or values that could in principle be manipulated. In this case, however, the concept of culture becomes empty and can be discarded. Simply naming differences "cultural" does not add anything to our understanding of either "culture" or "cultural processes" or their interaction with cognition.

We will revisit our definition of culture toward the end of this chapter. For now we turn to some research findings that illustrate the main points of our argument. Much of our data come from the domain of folk biology, a domain we are most familiar with.

Categories, Reasoning, and Expertise

Below we discuss four questions that direct ways we can think about "cultural and experiential differences" in categorization, conceptual organization, and the use of categories in reasoning.

Do experts and non-experts agree on concepts and categories?

This was a question Linda Garro tackled in her study of curers and non-curers in Pichataro, Mexico. In her study Garro was able to show that both groups agreed on a common model of disease (and health) with curers agreeing more with one another than non-curers. This higher agreement implies *more knowledge* with respect to the culturally appropriate beliefs (Garro 1986, 2000).

Ross et al. (n.d.) revisited the study after 30 years, including biomedical personnel that arrived in the community shortly after Garro's initial study. Despite a plethora of changes that occurred in the community, we found that experts and non-experts still agree with one another (and with the models from 30 years ago), but disagree systematically with the biomedical staff working in the community clinic and pharmacies (Ross et al., n.d.). This study showed not only the persistence of cultural knowledge, but also agreement across levels (but not kind) of expertise.

Does expertise affect category organization?

Boster and Johnson (1989) conducted research with respect to the effects of different levels of expertise in categorization. Specifically, they examined knowledge and sorting pattern (categorization) among expert fishermen and novices (college students).

These researchers noted that, while morphological information about fish (provided as drawings) is available to novices and experts alike, access to more specific information related to functional and utilitarian aspects requires expertise. (See Chi and Koeske 1983; Gobbo and Chi 1986; Johnson and Mervis 1998 for converging evidence from cognitive developmental research.)

Boster and Johnson found that novices relied more on morphology when sorting fish than did experts, whereas experts relied more on functional information based on commercial fishing goals. They argue that shifts associated with the development of expertise do not resemble a change from an incoherent to a coherent model, but represent a change from a readily available default model to a newly acquired model, based on different goals and information. (See Medin et al. 1997 for data with tree experts showing that different types of expertise lead to different categorization schemes.)

These data are interesting on two accounts. First, they pose the existence of a default system of folk-biological categorization (Boster et al. 1986; Boster 1987; Berlin 1992) and, second, they point toward the acquisition of expertise as a process of modifying conceptual structures based on different kinds of information and goals.

Barsalou's (1991) analysis of goal-driven categorization (different goals lead to different categorization schemes) presents at least in part a good basis for understanding these types of results. Changes in categorization schemes based on new information can also be observed in the history of sciences. For example, Dupre (1999) has shown that historically the categorization of whales shifted, not in response to more knowledge about whales, but rather because of changing concepts of what it means to be a fish.

Does culture affect categorization?

There are clear effects of culture on sorting behaviors (e.g., Lopez et al. 1997). These cultural differences remain even when overall expertise is controlled for. Medin et al. (2002, 2006) examined the sorting of local freshwater fish among both experts and non-experts of two adjacent populations in Wisconsin: Menominee Native American and European Americans. European American fishermen tended to organize categories in terms of goals and in terms of taxonomic relationships. Menominee fishermen also used these strategies but, in addition, showed a strong tendency to sort in terms of ecological relationships (e.g., habitat). (Ross et al. [2003] report similar differences for children, initiating an exploration into the emergence of cultural models.)

In the initial sorting task participants were asked to pile-sort 44 local fish (written on cards) into groups based on similarity (see Chapters 7, 10, and 27, this volume). Individual fish–fish distance matrices were created and compared across participants. Resulting patterns of agreement and disagreement were explored across lines of expertise and culture.

Using the cultural consensus model (Romney et al. 1986) we established that both groups shared an overall agreement. We aggregated the data for each group into a combined model, which was analyzed using multidimensional scaling. In order to represent the model of the European American experts two dimensions were needed, correlating with desirability and size. For the Menominee data three dimensions were needed to achieve a fit for their sorting data. Two dimensions correlated with size and desirability and the third dimension – not found among European Americans – correlated with what we termed an ecological dimension (e.g., sorting by habitat).

This task was followed, months later, by several different tasks. First, we asked participants to describe fish–fish interactions for all possible pairs of 21 fish species (e.g., "Does the largemouth bass affect the river shiner or the river shiner affect the largemouth bass?"). As before we found cross-group consensus, but Menominee experts held a clear sub-model not shared by European American experts. Menominee experts reported more relations overall and more reciprocal relations. We also noted that European American fishermen mainly reported interactions involving adult fish of the kind "a musky will eat a northern." Menominee reported these relations too, but also added relations between fish during the whole life cycle (e.g., "a musky will eat a northern, and northern fry hatch out two weeks earlier in the spring so northern fry will eat musky fry") as well as non-food-chain relations (destroying the nesting place of X). In contrast, the small set of relations reported exclusively by European Americans appear to be overgeneralizations. They typically involved food-chain relations between predator and prey fish that are rarely found in the same waters. Had the studies stopped here one would conclude that we were observing cultural difference in knowledge and we might have been able to weave a story about why European American fishermen mainly learn about adult fish. Readers in anthropology might have liked our conclusion with respect to the intricate knowledge of indigenous people. However, here is where ethnography and spending plenty of time with fishermen outside of a formal interviewing situation came into play. What made our results puzzling was that we had heard more than one European American expert mention that northern hatch out in the spring a few weeks before muskies do. It also seemed implausible that European American fish experts would have so little ecological knowledge.

Hence, we followed up with a second experiment exploring the knowledge individuals hold about fish habitats. In this task participants sorted the fish according to different habitats. Two findings are important here. First, members of both groups did *not* differ in their responses and, second, European American experts correctly described fish as not sharing a habitat, even for pairs for which in the previous task they had described a "big eats small" relationship. These data reinforced the notion that the differences did not represent a simple cultural difference with respect to ecological knowledge.

Instead of representing differences in knowledge per se, perhaps the cultural differences encountered were more about *knowledge organization* and related *accessibility*. The sorting task suggests that Menominee fishermen make use of an ecological organization, which might facilitate answering questions about fish–fish interactions. On the other hand, if the European American experts focus more on taxonomic relations it may take more time and effort to retrieve information about ecological relations. Several months later we repeated the fish–fish interaction task but this time reduced the number of probes from 441 to 35, while still allowing an hour for the task. If our analysis was correct we should have found that: (1) the cultural differences would disappear, (2) European American experts should start to answer in terms of the full life cycle of fish, and (3) Menominee experts would be relatively less affected by the pace of the task. All three predictions received strong support.

We take these data to indicate two things. Experts of the two groups share a good amount of base knowledge with respect to ecological relations and fish habitats. This ecological knowledge is not equally accessible. We find systematic group differences (that one might be tempted to call cultural), yet these differences are not in knowledge per se but in access to this knowledge.

These findings have important implications for our theories of culture and cognition. For starters they illustrate the importance of a combination of formal quantitative tasks and ethnographic methods. With respect to the formal approach, our findings show that it is important to pay attention to the nature of the interview and the probes applied. Instead of attempting to find some "gold standard" task that will reveal what people think or know, it is only by coordinated and converging measures across a range of tasks that one begins to understand cultural differences.

Many of the studies we reviewed have been dealing with categorization in relation to expertise and culture. Two questions emerge immediately. Are the categories elicited in our research meaningful? Or asked differently, do the elicited categories more or less reflect the knowledge organization of our participants? The second question is: If categories are affected by culture and expertise, do we find the same influence with respect to reasoning strategies?

Do expertise and culture affect reasoning?

Clearly if categorization provides the building blocks of thought (reasoning) and if categorization is influenced by expertise and culture, reasoning necessarily differs along these lines as well. However, the more interesting question at this point would be whether the use of categories in reasoning differs across expertise and culture.

Reasoning strategies can be described as heuristics for inference-making (or decision-making) when relevant information is incomplete. In these situations humans make use of heuristics or strategies to fill in the blanks and make inferences. We will focus on two kinds of reasoning. The first is inductive reasoning about categories and their properties (what is often called category-based induction), especially in the biological domain. Cultural research has shown the importance of framework theories and the organization of knowledge to this kind of reasoning. The second, related form of reasoning is causal reasoning, a domain in which interesting cross-cultural research is also being done (Burnett and Medin 2008).

Research on the use of categories in reasoning has been guided by theories of induction that suggest principles of induction that may be universal. Probably the best-known theory is the Osherson et al.'s (1990) similarity coverage model. Three phenomena associated with the theory have received the most attention: *similarity*, *typicality*, and *diversity*.

The *similarity* principle of induction describes the fact that two kinds seen as similar (more closely related in terms of their taxonomic distance) are more likely to share a previously unknown (and invisible) property or characteristic than two kinds that are taxonomically more distant. For example, informants usually judge mice and rats as more likely to share some unknown property than mice and penguins.

The *typicality* principle describes the fact that more typical members of a category are more likely to have features common to all the category members than less typical ones. For example, if informants are told that sparrows have some protein x inside them and that penguins have some protein y inside them, they judge that it is more likely that all birds have protein x rather than protein y.

Finally, the *diversity* principle describes the fact that individuals are usually more likely to ascribe a property to the whole category when told that two taxonomically different category members share that property, than when told that two taxonomically similar category members share a property. A projection from mice and cows to all mammals is stronger than a projection from mice and rats to all mammals.

These three phenomena are very robust when tested with undergraduate populations in the USA. However, cross-cultural and cross-expertise studies reveal quite a different picture. Lopez et al. (1997), for example, compared the categorization and category-based induction of University of Michigan students with Itza' Maya of the tropical rainforest of Guatemala with respect to local mammals (for each group a slightly different set of mammals was used). They found that Itza' Maya and Michigan undergraduates tended to sort mammals in more or less similar ways, yet only the Itza' included ecological factors in their considerations. Both groups showed similarity and typicality effects in reasoning. However, only undergraduates relied on the diversity principles.

While the study has obvious limitations (for one, it confounds cultural differences with differences in age, education, et cetera and most notably expertise), the results do challenge the universality of at least one of the reasoning principles, *diversity*. The challenge is to understand why the two groups reasoned so differently when it came to taxonomic diversity.

Subsequent studies pinpoint domain knowledge and expertise as being the critical factor (see, for example, Proffitt et al. 2000; Bailenson et al. 2002; Shafto and Coley 2003; Shafto et al. 2007) and it appears that ecological and causal reasoning can override category-based reasoning when sufficient knowledge (deemed relevant) is available.

Summary

Let's recap our findings. In general, both experts and novices make use of category structure in their reasoning strategies. Reasoning strategies often are linked to *causal understandings*. Experts, however, having more and different kinds of knowledge available, are more flexible in their causal reasoning. Causal stories, however, are not uni-dimensional, but are often influenced by the foregrounding or backgrounding of specific kinds of information, as in Barsalou's (1991) goal-derived categorization that makes certain kinds of knowledge more or less accessible. On this account, cultural differences may often be saliency effects driven by framework theories or epistemological orientations that lead to differences with respect to some domain such as folk biology or the relation of human beings to the rest of nature (Bang et al. 2007).

Implications for Conceptions of Cultural Change and Cultural Learning

Anthropological lore has it that knowledge is passed down from elders (experts) to younger generations (novices) and therefore culture is carried through time and space. But we need to examine whether and how this is actually accomplished. The idea that the passing down is no more complicated than handing down an heirloom substantially underestimates the complexity of cultural transmission and begs one of the central questions in cultural anthropology and cognitive science. It assumes an unproblematic, faithful reproduction of models and knowledge through time (stability of culture), where change is seen as rupture that needs to be explained. It also assumes that all knowledge is somehow *passed on*, relegating learning to the passive act of receiving information. Furthermore, it fails to account for the fact that faithful transmission or copying of information is almost impossible (Sperber 1996). Finally, and perhaps most important for the anthropological context, it ignores the fact that much (if not most) of cultural knowledge is not explicit. In this section we take up questions about what is transmitted in cultural transmission, how it might be transmitted, and whether it leads to cultural stability.

Stability and instability

Earlier we mentioned the study conducted by Ross and collaborators in Pichataro (Mexico). The research consisted of a restudy of work conducted by Linda Garro some 30 years ago (1986, 2000). Exploring whether curers and non-curers shared a common folk-medical belief system, Garro found that, overall, members of the two groups agreed with respect to their folk-medical understandings, with the experts having the highest level agreement with one another.

Soon after this initial research a clinic emerged in Pichataro, introducing free biomedical services as well as health education. Furthermore, a large flow of transnational migration to the USA led to an influx of money and medical knowledge. Finally, improved infrastructure opened Pichataro up to information from the nearby towns and, through phone and internet services, to the world at large. In short, one might expect significant changes in folk-medical models over the last 30 years.

In our restudy we used the same question–answer frame applied by Garro. Adding biomedical staff, we matched our participants as closely as possible with the individuals interviewed by Garro. Rather than asking whether the same individuals changed their models over the last 30 years, we asked whether the knowledge available to adult women in the community had substantially changed over the last 30 years – both with respect to curers and non-curers.

Introducing biomedical experts allowed us to link potential changes to the emergence of the clinic. Several findings are important for our current purposes. Thirty years after the initial study curers and non-curers still share a common folk-medical model. The model held by curers and non-curers is significantly different from the model held by biomedical staff. Curers and non-curers agree with one another as much as they agree with the general folk-medical model held in Pichataro some 30 years ago (Ross et al. n.d.).[1]

Taking into account that we did not interview the same participants as Garro did 30 years ago, these findings are striking. The folk-medical model learned by a new generation of curer and non-curer adult women in Pichataro has not significantly changed over the last 30 years. The presence of a medical clinic did not affect the acquisition or production of folk-medical models over the last 30 years. We say *production of folk-medical models* as these models are not talked about much and, as a result, each individual needs to generate a good part of the answers rather than copying the model from experts. It is important to note that, from its inception onward, the clinic was well attended, making it even more surprising that the models of the biomedical staff seem not to have affected the folk-medical models entertained in the community.

Although these data are encouraging with respect to the maintenance of cultural knowledge, data from other parts of Meso-America are less positive. Previously, we documented cultural differences between Itza' Maya and Ladino farmers in mental models of the forest, the nature of the forest spirits, and the sustainability of agroforestry practices (Atran et al. 2002, 2005). Since that time substantial changes have come to this part of Guatemala, including a blacktop road linking Flores to Guatemala City, the development of ecotourism and Spanish-language schools, as well as continuing Ladino immigration. LeGuen et al. (n.d.) have recently assessed the intergenerational stability of mental models of the forest and conceptions of forest spirits. Both Itza' and Ladinos show substantial loss of ecological knowledge and a shift in value orientation towards economic concerns. Although we had earlier reported that Ladino farmers showed deference to Itza' Maya farmers and sought out their expertise, there is no evidence of intergenerational change in the direction of the Maya model. Instead, LeGuen et al. found that the Itza' notion of the forest guardians, the Arux, had become assimilated towards the Ladino understanding of the Duende.

These two case studies raise a central problem for cognitive and cultural anthropology. Why, in the first case, is there little change over three decades despite the introduction of Western medicine but, in the second case, there is dramatic change over a single generation? In the latter case we are also challenged to explain why the change has taken the particular form that it has. *One can always speculate after the fact but post hoc theorizing underlines just how incomplete our understanding of cultural learning is.*

How then should we envision cultural learning?

First a disclaimer. Much more research is needed to better understand the processes, channels, and units by which knowledge is transmitted. While some copying might go on, it is very rarely flawless and most of the time it is simply impossible as the main process of learning. If not copying, what kind of processes would produce the results described above? How – in the absence of copying – is cultural stability or systematic cultural change achieved across time and individuals?

One productive line of research lies in the area of reasoning strategies. Category-based and causal reasoning strategies allow individual learners to use existing frameworks to make their own inferences, generating knowledge on their own by filling in the blanks when needed. In this account, framework theories in the form of categorization schemes and abstract relational expectations might provide the groundwork upon which individuals reflect when in need of an answer (e.g., when asked by the occasional anthropologist).

Two kinds of frameworks have been argued for in the literature: *innate biases* as well as *cultural frameworks*, like the one described for the Menominee above. *Innate biases* are domain-specific biases. For example, Waxman et al. (2007) found that Menominee, as well as rural and urban European American children, ascribe an essence to species of living kinds. In this view, species are what they are because of their essence. On top of this general framework (see also Astuti et al. 2004) Menominee children – drawing on salient discourse about ethnic or racial identity in terms of blood quantum – may tend to identify blood as a carrier of essence.

Employing the often used "adoption paradigm" we asked children whether an animal adopted at birth by an animal from another species (pig and cow) would grow up to be a member of the species of the birth parents or of the adoptive parents. In a series of tasks several conditions were described (such as "always snuggling up with the adoptive mother," "eating the same food as adoptive mother," "drinking the milk of the adoptive mother," etc.). Only in the case of a total blood transfusion (the target animal was described as being sick and in need of a compete blood exchange) with the blood from the adoptive mother were some Menominee children willing to change their predictions concerning the kindhood of the adopted animal when grown up.

Even the cryptic description of the task makes it clear that children could not possibly have copied their parents (or other experts) when responding to our research questions. Does this make the questions useless? We don't think so. Most cultural knowledge is implicit. Responses to our questions are systematic across individuals, indicating that children used similar strategies and extracted similar background information when producing new knowledge. The result is agreement on a topic, which they probably had never thought about before, using innate structures as well as publicly available knowledge as the basis.

We noted earlier that both Menominee fishermen and Menominee children show greater attention to ecological relations than their rural European American counterparts. How does this ecological orientation get passed on? One possibility is explicit teaching, but that is only one. Bang et al. (2007) asked Menominee and European American children and adults about the nature and frequency of their outdoor practices. They found that European Americans were much more likely to engage in practices that background nature (e.g., playing baseball) compared to practices that foreground nature (e.g., berry-picking). There is independent evidence that what we might call "psychological distance" affects cognitive processing in a variety of ways, including inferences and attributions (see Trope and Liberman 2003; Liberman and Trope 2008).

A related set of observations come from Unsworth (2008). She asked European American and Menominee adults to describe the last encounter they had had with a deer. The author recorded the content of the stories as well as the gestures used. The two groups did not differ in the overall likelihood of using gesture, but they showed a very large effect of perspective when gesturing about deer. European American adults would "place" the deer in some location (using their hands) but a significant proportion of Menominee adults "became" the deer in gesture. That is, they were more likely to reliably take the deer's perspective in gesture than European American adults. We are currently conducting studies to examine whether this difference in gesturing affects children's learning, reasoning, and discourse concerning nature.

This leads us to one final study. We just argued that perspective-taking is related to the differences of how Menominee and European American hunters see the world. "Becoming the deer" takes into account the surrounding world from a perspective other than direct, human, egocentric interaction with the environment. Rather than being the center of the universe, where nature becomes a backdrop for hunting and fishing, Menominee seem to explore nature at least in part through multiple lenses and perspectives.

We have evidence for similar multiperspective-taking from Tzotzil Maya of Chiapas, Mexico, in the form of spatial encoding. The specific studies were designed to test the relation of language and spatial cognition – one of the strongest arguments for linguistic relativity theory (Brown and Levinson 1992; Levinson 2001, 2003; Levinson et al. 2002). Findings suggested that speakers of languages that do not encode right and left encode spatial arrangement in different ways (maintaining, for example, absolute directions, such as north and south). The most forceful data come from the "recall under rotation" paradigm. Here participants are asked to reconstruct an observed spatial arrangement after being rotated by 180 degrees. English speakers usually arrange the items on the recall table by maintaining the right–left order violating absolute directions (north–south). However, Maya speakers do the opposite – arranging items according to an absolute system of spatial references that violates the relative frame of reference. Important criticisms of the research methods have appeared but do not provide an alternative account of the data (Li and Gleitman 2002).

Using the rotation paradigm, we conducted studies with Tzotzil Maya as well as Spanish speakers jointly living in a community in the Highlands of Chiapas, Mexico (Ross et al. n.d.). Much to our surprise both Maya as well as Spanish speakers seemed to employ an absolute orientation (Spanish makes heavy use of relative spatial references). Clearly then language did not predict the outcome of the rotation task. What then could account for the data? In several of our trials the stimuli *faced* participants rather than being lined up in front of them from left to right. In these cases many participants arranged the items on the recall table *facing away* from themselves while also maintaining the absolute direction of the arrangements. This suggests that the participants might not have used an absolute system of spatial encoding, as suggested by the original researchers, but instead combined *perspective-taking* with a relative frame of reference – from the viewpoint of the stimuli items. Ethnographic interviews support this idea, as several participants explained that their parents had always told them about the importance of taking into account what other elements – such as animals – might think or feel. In this account, the participants take themselves out of the scenario, rather than seeing themselves as the center of attention. Not surprisingly, what has been described as the use of an absolute reference frame has only been reported for small-scale indigenous groups, with a focus on older, culturally more expert participants. The relative frame of reference with the participant at the center of attention might well be the product of Western urban thought. We need more data to pursue this issue.

From an anthropological perspective these data are important as they undermine the notion of language as an independent variable and instead put epistemological framework theories (Ross et al. 2007) at the center of potential explanations.

Culture: The Precipitate of Cognition and Communication

It should be clear that category structure is only one anchor for human reasoning and that category structures themselves need to be explored in terms of their specific properties. Other anchors are provided by causal theories, general habits, biases, et cetera. We further argued that knowledge organization influences the accessibility of certain types of knowledge. Differences in accessibility affect the kind of knowledge that is generated and becomes salient within a population.

Where and what is culture in this account?

"Culture" is an elusive concept that cannot serve as an explanatory tool to understand specific processes of human behavior, as the very same behavior is part of that culture informing further processes of inference-making. As a result, "culture" becomes an emergent property of agreement patterns within and across populations. Studying culture becomes the exploration of patterns of agreement and disagreement, linking them to specific constellations of cognitive and social factors. Looking at culture and cultural processes from this perspective, it is clear that they are intertwined with individual cognitive processes explored by the cognitive sciences.

Despite their serious limitations, experimental studies conducted in the psychological laboratory can be useful in providing methodologies and theoretical tools for further field research. But lab studies continue to suffer from the lack of attention paid to the social and physical environment within which cognitive processes are produced, transmitted, acquired, and shaped. To attend to these issues will require supplementing the control provided by the laboratory and artificial stimuli with in-depth studies conducted in the real world, combining ethnographic work with experimental research.

Cognitive anthropology can provide the ideal bridge between the two fields of which it forms a part. It deals with just the kind of populations cognitive science needs, in order to make arguments about cognitive mechanisms and could provide the ethnographic insights needed to understand experimental data. It can contribute concise field experiments, providing at the same time the necessary ethnographic context to design, run, and interpret such studies. In sum, cognitive anthropology has the potential to provide the conceptual bridge for an interdisciplinary focus on the central question of how human cognition and social life interact to create human culture. Clearly this issue is of equal importance to both cognitive science and cultural anthropology, bringing us back to the point we made previously. Cognitive anthropology should claim a central role in both fields, bridging two related, yet separate disciplines. In order to do so, the field of cognitive anthropology, like any bridge, needs to be firmly grounded in the theories and methods of both disciplines. We hope this chapter will provide some starting points for this endeavor.

ACKNOWLEDGMENTS

The writing of this chapter was supported by NSF grants 0726107 to Norbert Ross and 0527707 to Norbert Ross and Tom Palmeri. Support was also provided by AFOSR grant 5710001864 to Douglas Medin and NSF grants DRL 0815020 and BCS 0745594 to Douglas Medin and Sandra Waxman.

NOTE

1 Unfortunately we were not granted access to the original data and hence could not make direct comparison across time and expertise.

REFERENCES

Astuti, R., G. Solomon, and S. Carey
2004 Constraints on Conceptual Development. Monographs of the Society for Research in Child Development 69(3):vii–135.
Atran, S., D. Medin, and N. Ross
2005 The Cultural Mind: Environmental Decision Making and Cultural Modeling Within and Across Populations. Psychological Review 112(4):744–776.
Atran, S., D. Medin, N. Ross, E. Lynch, V. Vapnarsky, E. U. Ek', et al.
2002 Folkecology, Cultural Epidemiology, and the Spirit of the Commons: A Garden Experiment in the Maya Lowlands, 1991–2001. Current Anthropology 43(3):421–450.
Aunger, R., ed.
2000 Darwinizing Culture: The Status of Memetics as a Science. Oxford: Oxford University Press.
Axelrod, R. M.
1997 The Complexity of Cooperation: Agent-Based Models of Competition and Collaboration. Princeton: Princeton University Press.
Bailenson, J. M., M. S. Shum, S. Atran, D. L. Medin, and J. D. Coley
2002 A Bird's Eye View: Triangulating Biological Categorization and Reasoning Within and Across Cultures and Expertise Levels. Cognition 84(1):1–53.
Baillargeon, R.
2004 Infants' Physical World. Current Directions in Psychological Science 13:89–94.
Bang, M., D. L. Medin, and S. Atran
2007 Cultural Mosaics and Mental Models of Nature. Proceedings of the National Academy of Sciences 104:13868–13874.
Barsalou, L. W.
1991 Deriving Categories to Achieve Goals. *In* The Psychology of Learning and Motivation. G. H. Bower, ed. Pp. 1–64. New York: Academic Press.
Berlin, B.
1992 Ethnobiological Classification: Principles of Categorization of Plants and Animals in Traditional Societies. Princeton: Princeton University Press.
Blackmore, S.
1999 The Meme Machine. Oxford: Oxford University Press.
Bloom, P.
2002 Mindreading, Communication, and the Learning of the Names for Things. Mind and Language 17:37–54.
Boster, J. S.
1987 Agreement between Biological Classification Systems Is Not Dependent on Cultural Transmission. American Anthropologist 89:914–920.
Boster, J. S., and J. C. Johnson
1989 Form or Function: A Comparison of Expert and Novice Judgments of Similarity among Fish. American Anthropologist 91(4):866–889.
Boster, J. S., B. Berlin, and J. O'Neill
1986 The Correspondence of Jivaroan to Scientific Ornithology. American Anthropologist 88(3):569–583.
Brown, P., and S. Levinson
1992 "Left" and "Right" in Tenejapa: Investigating a Linguistic Conceptual Gap. Zeitschrift für Phonetik, Sprachwissenschaft und Kommunikationsforschung 45(6):590–611.
Burnett, R., and D. L. Medin
2008 Reasoning across Cultures. *In* Reasoning: Studies of Human Inference and Its Foundations. L. Rips. and J. Adler, eds. Cambridge: Cambridge University Press.

Carey, S., and E. Spelke
1996 Science and Core Knowledge. Philosophy of Science 63(4):515–533.
Chi, M. T. H., and R. D. Koeske
1983 Network Representation of a Child's Dinosaur Knowledge. Developmental Psychology 19:29–39.
Cole, M.
1996 Cultural Psychology: A Once and Future Discipline. Cambridge, MA: Harvard University Press.
D'Andrade, R. G.
1981 The Cultural Part of Cognition. Cognitive Science 5:179–195.
Dupre, J.
1999 Are Whales Fish? *In* Folkbiology. D. Medin and S. Atran, eds. Pp. 461–476. Cambridge, MA: MIT Press.
Garro, L.
1986 Intracultural Variation in Folk Medical Knowledge: A Comparison Between Curers and Non-Curers. American Anthropologist 88(2):351–370.
2000 Remembering What One Knows and the Construction of the Past: A Comparison of Cultural Consensus Theory and Cultural Schema Theory. Ethos 28(3):275–319.
Gentner, D., and S. Goldin-Meadow
2003 Language in Mind: Advances in the Study of Language and Mind. Cambridge, MA: MIT Press.
Gobbo, C., and M. Chi
1986 How Knowledge Is Structured and Used by Experts and Novice Children. Cognitive Development 1(3):221–237.
Hamilton, W. D.
1964 The Genetical Evolution of Social Behavior. Journal of Theoretical Biology 7(1):1–52.
Henrich, J. P., and F. J. Gil-White
2001 The Evolution of Prestige: Freely Conferred Deference as a Mechanism for Enhancing the Benefits of Cultural Transmission. Evolution and Human Behavior 22: 165–196.
Henrich, N., and J. P. Henrich
2007 Why Humans Cooperate: A Cultural and Evolutionary Explanation. Oxford: Oxford University Press.
Hirschfeld, L. A.
2002 Why Don't Anthropologists Like Children? American Anthropologist 104: 611–627.
Hutchins, E.
1995 Cognition in the Wild. Cambridge, MA: MIT Press.
Johnson, K. E., and C. B. Mervis
1998 Impact of Intuitive Theories on Feature Recruitment throughout the Continuum of Expertise. Memory and Cognition 26:382–401.
Lave, J.
1988 Cognition in Practice. New York: Cambridge University Press.
LeGuen, O., R. Iliev, S. Atran, X. Lois, and D. L. Medin
N.d. A Garden Experiment Revisited: Inter-Generational Changes in the Sacred and the Profane in Petén, Guatemala. Unpublished MS.
Levinson, S.
2001 Covariation between Spatial Language and Cognition. *In* Language Acquisition and Conceptual Development. M. Bowerman and S. C. Levinson, eds. Pp. 566–588. Cambridge: Cambridge University Press.
2003 Space in Language and Cognition. Cambridge: Cambridge University Press.

Levinson, S., S. Kota, B. M. Haun, and B. Rasch
2002 Returning the Tables: Language Affects Spatial Reasoning. Cognition 84: 155–188.
Li, P., and L. Gleitman
2002 Turning the Tables: Language and Spatial Reasoning. Cognition 83:265–294.
Liberman, N., and Y. Trope
2008 The Psychology of Transcending the Here and Now. Science 322:1201–1205.
Linden, D.
2007 The Accidental Mind. Cambridge, MA: Harvard University Press.
Lopez, A., S. Atran, J. D. Coley, D. L. Medin, and E. Smith
1997 The Tree of Life: Universals of Folkbiological Taxonomies and Inductions. Cognitive Psychology 32:251–295.
Medin, D., W. Bennis, and M. Chandler
In press The Home Field Disadvantage. Perspectives in Psychological Science.
Medin, D., D. Lynch, J. D. Coley, and S. Atran
1997 Categorization and Reasoning among Tree Experts: Do All Roads Lead to Rome? Cognitive Psychology 32:49–96.
Medin, D., N. Ross, S. Atran, R. C. Burnett, and S. V. Blok
2002 Categorization and Reasoning in Relation to Culture and Expertise. Psychology of Learning and Motivation 41:1–41.
Medin, D., N. Ross, S. Atran, D. Cox, J. D. Coley, J. B. Proffitt, et al.
2006 Folkbiology of Freshwater Fish. Cognition 99(3):237–273.
Nisbett, R.
2003 The Geography of Thought. New York: Free Press.
Osherson, D., E. Smith, O. Wilkie, A. Lopez, and E. Shafir
1990 Category-Based Induction. Psychological Review 97:85–200.
Proffitt, J. B., J. D. Coley, and D. L. Medin
2000 Expertise and Category-Based Induction. Journal of Experimental Psychology: Learning, Memory, and Cognition 26(4):811–828.
Quinn, H.
1997 Convergent Evidence for a Cultural Model of American Marriage. *In* Cultural Models in Language and Thought. D. Holland and N. Quinn, eds. New York: Cambridge University Press.
Richerson, P. J., and R. Boyd
2004 Not by Genes Alone: How Culture Transformed Human Evolution. Chicago: University of Chicago Press.
Romney, A. K., S. C. Weller, and W. H. Batchelder
1986 Culture as Consensus: A Theory of Culture and Informant Accuracy. American Anthropologist 88(2):313–338.
Ross, N.
2004 Culture and Cognition: Implications for Theory and Method. Thousand Oaks, CA: Sage.
Ross, N., and J. Shenton
N.d. Language, Cultural Models and Spatial Cognition. Unpublished MS.
Ross, N., D. L. Medin, J. D. Coley, and S. Atran
2003 Cultural and Experiential Differences in the Development of Folkbiological Induction. Cognitive Development 18:25–47.
Ross, N., D. L. Medin, and D. Cox
2007 Epistemological Models and Culture Conflict: Menominee and Euro-American Hunters in Wisconsin. Ethos 35(4):478–515.
Ross, N., C. Timura, and J. Maupin
N.d. Stability in Emergent Cultural Systems: Globalization and Cultural Resiliency in Folk Medical Beliefs. Unpublished MS.

Schank, R., and R. Abelson
1977 Scripts, Plans, Goals and Understanding: An Inquiry into Human Knowledge Structures. Hillsdale, NJ: Lawrence Erlbaum.
Shafto, P., and J. D. Coley
2003 Development of Categorization and Reasoning in the Natural World: Novices to Experts, Naïve Similarity to Ecological Knowledge. Journal of Experimental Psychology: Learning, Memory and Cognition 29:641–649.
Shafto, P., J. D. Coley, and D. Baldwin
2007 Effects of Time Pressure on Context-Sensitive Property Induction. Psychonomic Bulletin and Review 14:890–894.
Sperber, D.
1996 Explaining Culture: A Naturalistic Approach. Cambridge: Blackwell.
2000 An Objection to the Mimetic Approach to Culture. *In* Darwinizing Culture: The Status of Memetics as a Science. R. Aunger, ed. Oxford: Oxford University Press.
Trivers, R.
1971 The Evolution of Reciprocal Altruism. Quarterly Review of Biology 46(1):35–57.
Trope, Y., and N. Liberman
2003 Temporal Construal. Psychological Review 110(3):403–421.
Unsworth, S. J.
2008 The Influence of Culturally Varying Discourse Practices on Cognitive Orientations Toward Nature. Unpublished doctoral dissertation, Northwestern University, Evanston, IL.
Vygotsky, L.
1978 Mind in Society. Cambridge, MA: Harvard University Press.
Waxman, S. R., D. L. Medin, and N. Ross
2007 Folkbiological Reasoning from a Cross-Cultural Developmental Perspective: Early Essentialist Notions Are Shaped by Cultural Beliefs. Developmental Psychology 43(2):294–308.

CHAPTER 20

Cultural Models, Power, and Hegemony

Halvard Vike

Introduction: The Problem of Power and Ideology

To what extent do theories of ideology and hegemony contribute to our understanding of power? The modest version of my own view is that they leave several fundamental questions quite open. The strong version is that they in fact explain surprisingly little. Such a view may seem somewhat odd from the vantage point of cognitive anthropology, which has not been very concerned with power. Cognitive anthropology is generally seen as a set of approaches mainly developed and put to work in attempts to understand the mechanisms of the mind, and the analytical range of these approaches are largely seen as much more limited than that of anthropological perspectives on political systems and power. This is in part due to cognitive anthropology's tendency to focus on the individual, systems of classification, on small-scale social contexts, and on ideal test cases, which all contribute to create severe limitations when it comes to understanding larger contexts in which human behavior and knowledge are shaped. However, I would like to argue that cognitive anthropology has much to offer, and that it may profit greatly from focusing systematically on power and politics. Indeed, I believe that the questions asked by cognitive anthropologists may make us better equipped when it comes to trying to understand issues of domination. I moor my optimism in two generalizations concerning the anthropology of power in general. First, it seems to me that the idea that power, for example class-based power, is legitimated through hegemonic ideas, is not well enough founded. Far too often anthropologists and other critical social scientists apply such reasoning as a type of explanatory default, inferring from observations of social differences, domination, and meanings in use and concluding that the dominated have internalized a version of the world that serves those in power. As a consequence – and this is my second

A Companion to Cognitive Anthropology, First Edition. Edited by David B. Kronenfeld, Giovanni Bennardo, Victor C. de Munck, and Michael D. Fischer.

point – anthropologists seeking to understand systems of domination too often fail to understand individual subjectivity and practice relating to such systems. Put bluntly, it seems that we have a tendency to reify both ideology (as "hegemonic") and individual consciousness (as "agency" or "subjectivity").

If domination does not necessarily rest on ideological systems that take on hegemonic functions, it must be fruitful to look for other explanations as to how domination occurs and is reproduced. The empirical record clearly indicates that domination in most forms is not at all incompatible with lack of consent, the existence of criticism, resistance, and the like. Indeed, many forms of hierarchy may be more fruitfully understood as systems of distributed sanctions (and anticipated sanctions) than as systems of shared meanings which serve to legitimize power. The fact that the oppressed and dominated to some extent embrace, or seem to embrace, the values which legitimate their subordination cannot be taken as evidence of the existence of hegemony. Conforming to official norms is often a highly pragmatic affair, and does not exclude knowledge of alternative possibilities and strategies, or the will to pursue them. Systems of distributed sanctions may not have much to do with hegemony, in the sense that such systems install in people's minds and bodies beliefs and representations which can be demonstrated to serve the dominant classes. If we understand hegemony as false consciousness, forms of dominance in the most general sense (as "the hegemony of late capitalism"), or somewhat more fruitfully either as contradictions between official norms and lived experience or even as ideas inherited from the past – or all the above (see Roseberry 1989) – we should be very careful not to rule out the fact that, in all societies, most people will to some extent have a pragmatic interest in trying to control the actions of their relevant others and thus take part in dominance. In this sense, culture as such may be seen as having a "conservative" effect. Even though this may serve the status quo and benefit some interests at the cost of others, so as to inspire the observing anthropologist to explain how power works, hegemony may not be very relevant. Workers may be well aware of the fact that some of the value they produce is reified and fetishized as surplus value and capital, masquerading as the origin of growth and prosperity, private property and commodities. In most such cases, there are a large number of reasons why workers fail to change or destroy this logic other than some kind of twisted consciousness. And even if they don't know about the actual paths the value that they produce actually follows, these reasons – most of which may reasonably be conceptualized as pragmatic – seem likely to be highly relevant. What power does is, among other things, define the limits of what is pragmatically possible. If that is indeed the case, the analytical task of explaining domination does not necessarily become less challenging, but the role of ideology and hegemony certainly becomes a somewhat trivial issue, and the question turns out to be different than what the Marxist inspiration in the social sciences has made us think. Turning to the issue of individual consciousness, it is striking that the anthropology of power has paid so little attention to knowledge, that is, to the careful exploration of how it is organized and put to use for various purposes – most of which are deeply engrained in processes of power. Even when arguing that people we study take part in the production of meaning of a kind which serves to undermine their own interests, anthropologists must of course know that when their opportunity to break out is very limited, they are not necessarily interested in talking much about these opportunities or acting upon them. When the people we study "fail" to oppose power, or do not explicitly reflect upon its nature and how to relate to it, we as anthropologists have very little reason to assume that power works through forming people's preferences (Lukes 2005). In other words, it is not reasonable to assume that "hidden agendas" and "hidden transcripts" that are not necessarily officially sanctioned are out of reach and/or beyond conscious reflection. Indeed, to the extent that anthropologists get access to information which speaks to such matters, this information may concern primarily how people talk about how they deal with sour grapes (Elster 1983). These are some of the kinds of problems that cognitive anthropology and the study of cultural models is well equipped to ask. A sound anthropology of knowledge is vital to the study of power.

Cognitive Anthropology and Practice

In 1984, Ortner made the important observation that since the sixties, anthropological theories seemed to have moved toward theories of practice. Somewhat disillusioned by systems theories of various kinds, ethnoscience's seemingly naive focus on systems of classifications, and narrow, "economic man"-based versions of transactionalism, many realized that the time had come for approaches that enabled anthropologists to grasp the links between systems and individual agency. One major influence was Bourdieu, especially his Kabyle work (Bourdieu 1977). Interestingly, Bourdieu retained an idea of "objective structures" and dealt with it as an ordered system of symbolic and social difference which was assumed to become reproduced through social practices that are generated by internalized dispositions specific to each social category (such as those of gender and class). As Ortner pointed out, Bourdieu became a leading figure in the practice school because he actually provided an alternative to structural theories without ignoring the structuralist ambition to understand large-scale systems. In practice, as it were, he criticized them for their tendency to reify systems and apply mechanical explanatory models. His own alternative – which became extremely influential in anthropology – was a theory of internalized dispositions; the habitus. Although this attempt is generally viewed as successful, it seems to me that his conceptualization of the habitus, although extremely fruitful in the sense that it re-emphasizes and reintroduces the explanatory power of social practice, motivation, and knowledge, has very serious shortcomings. It is simply extremely hard to grasp what the habitus is, especially since Bourdieu's own emphasis is so strongly biased toward routine behavior – "what goes beyond saying." Differences between forms of knowledge, and thus between forms of motivation and forms of action, are more or less totally ignored. I will come back to this issue later on, and now make two claims which are important to my argument. One unfortunate consequence of Bourdieu's influence is that we are left with a strong tendency to reify both systems (as "objective structures") and consciousness. The latter, implied by the focus on internalization, seems to have been generally accepted and has contributed to strengthening the belief that most forms of power *must* be legitimated in order to exist – by forms of knowledge that are either not fully conscious and/or not possible to articulate.

In this light, I want to argue that what is needed in order to develop a sound theory of practice that may enable us to understand power is a better grasp on knowledge and motivation as part of a single, but yet differentiated, cognitive system – one which needs to be much less mystifying than is the case with the concept of the habitus.

Simultaneously, what is needed is also a less mystifying understanding of social systems. Although both anthropologists and the people we study talk about such systems, or aspects of such systems, as things, we need to acknowledge that such talk makes use of conventional metaphors, that is, practical reifications. It is reasonable to assume that it is precisely such reifications, especially as they are put to work in anthropological analyses, which inspire us to think that the legitimation of power must rest on some form of internalized knowledge. But the relative stability of any hierarchy of power is more likely to result from complex forms of aggregation and non-planned patterning of pragmatic and/or institutionalized action than from hegemonic beliefs and values. In any society, very few actors – whether the dominated or those in power – have any precise knowledge of what their actions actually do on a large scale, and people may have many reasons to act in relative accordance with what they think is expected of them, and with what seems sensible in the short run. That the cumulative effects of processes of aggregation serve power interests differently is to a large degree a different matter – an observation which critics of functionalist thinking made long ago.

Anthropologists have long known that in order to understand social complexity, we need to realize that the question of what knowledge is cannot be separated from what it does. Here is one of the paradoxes of culture: although it provides us with procedures for simplification, and thus helps us to interpret social situations without spending a great deal of time and energy, it leaves us with no other option than to actually reflect and test alternative, potentially applicable models. Thus culture cannot be habitual in the sense that social practice is made automatic. As a consequence, the significance of culture is not how it makes us follow rules and prescriptions, and provide automatic, ant-like responses, but rather how it makes us able to adapt knowledge in ways that are relevant but not too costly. Culture represents a stock of knowledge which is organized so as to make this possible. The way we model our world and apply our models in social situations is a matter of picking between alternatives and constructing more encompassing plans and scripts, even though most often we may not do this very self-reflexively. Looking at how cultural knowledge is organized requires that knowledge is seen as situated and practical, but at the same time organized so as to enable us to select from alternative behavioral options and interpretations in ways that make these – in the eyes of the observer – appear more or less automatic, that is, not too demanding. One of the main functions of culture is to enable us as humans to make contextual shifts. The ability to shift between, adapt to, and transform contexts cannot be fully accounted for by changed external factors, coincidence, or unconscious adjustment; they may more fruitfully be seen as results of cognitively effective ways of dealing with options, anticipating scenarios and possible sanctions, more or less on the spot, that is, ways of monitoring several models simultaneously. The idea that culture is internalized and becomes deeply embedded dispositions which generate behavior in the Bourdieuan "what goes without saying" sense underestimates the complexity of culture and the way it is used as a reservoir rather than as prescriptions.

When we analyze meaning and power, our focus on knowledge has the advantage over culture in that it makes it much clearer that social practice is a product of what people think, understand, and feel, that is, of what's in their heads and bodies. As the critique of the Geertzian idea of culture made clear (see below), culture seems too often to be conceptualized as a phenomenon somehow separated from people, constituting some kind of public style or pattern to which individuals conform. Humans actively model the world they live in, and it is these models that are the basis of culture. Humans learn about the world by incorporating what they observe and are taught not primarily through remembering explicit messages, but by passively learning from them and then transforming this experience into models that enable them to act meaningfully and purposefully in a variety of contexts – even contexts they have never before encountered, constantly adjusting and attuning their knowledge and its organization so as to be able to cope. "Culture" is both what individual models share – the overlapping content, as well as what may not be directly shared but which is nevertheless acknowledged and treated as a property of communities of interaction. In other words, culture consists of the mechanisms that link different and differentially distributed models to each other.

> Cultural models, by this view, then, are not in any sense simply mechanically or automatically followed or instantiated by members of a culture; they are, instead, utilized in the construction of an understanding of a situation that enables a person to interpret what is going on and respond both appropriately and effectively. This abductive use would seem to preclude cultural models from being deeply "internalized" into individuals' construction of self, but, rather, suggests that they are used more externally (as the grammar of a language) to construct and interpret social situations; as is the case with language, any individual may participate in a variety of cultural systems (with, perhaps, varying degrees of expertise) and may "code switch" among them. [Kronenfeld 2009:6]

The starting point is: how do we, as humans, know? And how should we, as anthropologists, go about the task of accounting for the forms of knowledge which people we study most probably use but rarely provide us with? The question is relevant to the anthropology of power in much the same way as was the critique against ethnoscience. Analyses of power generally have little to say about how ideology, hegemony, and legitimation relate to "psychological reality," that is, to how and what people know when interacting within systems of power, and what this leads to in terms of social aggregation.

Cultural knowledge takes on many forms, many of which function as models *of* the world. There are many reasons to assume, however, that models *for* action are much more salient. The cultural models we use to organize our experience and sort out – among massive loads of information – what is relevant from what's not, are action models, models which are not necessarily mediated by language. They are, as Kronenfeld puts it, "prototypical formulations of cultural content" (2009:5), and

> [do] not provide us with a set of instructions or "thou shalt"s, but instead [provide] us with a tool kit or vocabulary of goal instantiations, categories of objects and actions, means toward ends, ways of conveying or reading motives, attitudes, desires, and the like, schematic "pictures" or story lines that link these, and so forth. [2009:97]

Such prototypical formulations are organized by criteria of relevance which make it possible for humans in most situations to act meaningfully without necessarily paying much attention to all potentially relevant alternatives. For any observer, it may be hard to realize that any given path of action or some post factum rendering of it is more or less habitual, and not necessarily a product of some prior dialogue with other possibilities. But in analytical terms there is simply no good reason to assume that people do not continuously consider alternative paths of action, despite the fact that such considerations must be made on the basis of some evaluation of their cost, in terms of both the time and the energy it takes to process them, but also in terms of the possible sanctions they may generate if opted for. Such a perspective on cultural knowledge provides additional support for the assumption that power does not necessarily work through some form of direct influence on how people's existence is (wrongly) represented in their consciousness. Cultural knowledge is deeply social, but "culture" as such must be seen as fundamentally epiphenomenal. Anthropologists' idea of culture, perhaps especially in the Geetzian, Bourdieuan, and Marxist versions, is heavily influenced by natives' (including the anthroplogists themselves as natives) inclination to talk about the patterns they relate to as things in themselves, and to act accordingly. We all seem to live by our reifications, and our reifications serve many important purposes. They make it possible to communicate effectively about phenomena of a general nature, and they enable us to make sense of variation, complexity, patterns, and aggregate phenomena through meaningful simplification, for example by attributing agency and motives to such phenomena. Models of the world seem to be made up of such reifications, many of which are not at all understood as things in the literal sense but rather as conventional ways of speaking about them and grasping some of their relevant properties. It comes naturally to us as humans to deal with culture and society as things. As a consequence, much of our behavior must be understood as an "as if" type of behavior. When we say that "society," "God," "the economy," "culture," "globalization," et cetera have done this or that, we reify our environment but the degree to which we do it may actually derive from our immediate, pragmatic purposes. We reify in many ways and for various purposes. In Kronenfeld's words:

> if culture itself only exists in our separate representations of it, and if these representations depend on our experience and are changing, then culture becomes only a kind of epiphenomenon. Its reality – and its force – lies not in any kind of independent, objective existence but instead in, and only in, our acting as if it had such existence. [Kronenfeld 2009:87–88]

There are both epistemological and methodological reasons to believe that cultural knowledge is a more complex phenomenon than influential theories of culture have been able to fully acknowledge. Culture is profoundly social, public only in a secondary sense, epiphenomenal and organized as more or less tight systems of action schemas. Our reifications, which constitute an inherent aspect of linguistic categorization, allow for communicative efficiency and serve as "as if" approaches, which provide us with practical hypotheses and attempts at pragmatic generalizations. An essential part of knowledge and social practice, and indeed culture, is the assumption we make about the knowledge and actions of others. One interesting aspect of this is our tendency to attribute agency to statistical distributions of individual actions that appear as patterned, systematic, and thus intentional. Adapting to such patterns, whether driven by the belief that the patterns are really motivated, or just by pragmatically adjusting to what's considered normal and perhaps expected, contribute heavily to social regularity and conformity. Such a perspective on cultural knowledge

> highlights the apparent paradox of the Durkheimian conception: our thought and behavior are constrained and shaped by collectivities to which we do not intrinsically belong – regarding each of which we each see our own selves as standing outside and looking in. [Kronenfeld 2009:43]

The argument that power and dominance is most often made more or less legitimate by means of ideology, which in some way or other misrepresents reality and or the experience of those suffering from it, is based on the presupposition that power is realized through lack of knowledge, or "false" or inappropriate knowledge. One element in this is the idea that dominance "needs" ideological legitimation, in other words, that power rests on some kind of consensus across great divides of power differences. This understanding is clearly very different from the idea that power is realized through the control over social contexts and people's choices. The latter may be much more important than ideological power, and may have very little indeed to do with hegemony as some form of misrepresentation.

Political Economy, Power, and Ideology

In the 1980s and 1990s, key figures in the political economy school such as Wolf and Roseberry took issue with culture in new ways, trying to break loose from mechanical materialism, postivist structuralism, and functionalist perspectives on culture as ideology. Their aim was to stick to the Boasian heritage, and retain the concept of culture, combine it with a historical perspective, and incorporate this into a class analysis framework. In this pursuit, they had to take issue with the Geertzian influence, which in their eyes had done much to push the situatedness of culture into the background. "Geertz *seems* to be working with a concept of culture as socially constituted and socially constituting" (Roseberry 1989:21). For example, Geertz states that the Balinese cockfight is a "status bloodbath," which enables the Balinese to tell themselves about their "texts," that is, their culture. We learn about caste and status differences, but only as a general background for the reading of the texts, not how they have in fact been shaped and significantly changed by colonialism and state formation (Roseberry 1989:23). Roseberry points out that Geertz shares a common conceptual ground with some of the American materialists, such as Harris, in that they all conceive of culture as a form of "superstructure," "simply as ideas" (26). According to Roseberry, we need to ask "who is talking, who is being talked to, what is being talked about, and what form of action is called for" (28). The same kinds of questions are relevant to Sahlins too, despite his attempts to transcend the limitations of the Geertzian perspective and to look for culture in practice and historical transformation. From the viewpoint of cognitive anthropology, it is of course interesting to note that Sahlins made a serious attempt to understand culture as a set of interpretative schemes. Yet Sahlins's focus is on how "events" are incorporated in "structure," and although he shows that the transformations that occur in this way involves the changing of the relationships between cultural categories, the idea of transformation itself as well as the "practice" that makes it come about is quite mechanical (Roseberry 1989:9). In both Geertz's and Sahlins's writings, then, culture "is enacted rather than acted" (10). The way out of this impasse, in Roseberry's vision, is through the connecting of political economy and symbolic anthropology, as is done in works such as Anderson's *Imagined Communities*, which deal not with nationalism in the abstract but in particular settings, and develop historical scenarios where people act on meanings in moments of great political and economic turbulence and in the process change them. Echoing earlier Marxists, particularly Godelier and Bloch, Roseberry claims that Marx himself conceived of the material not as matter but as social practice – an active materialism that focuses on how people "enter into definite relations with others and with nature" (38). This is the source of Roseberry's notion of hegemony. Hegemony, in his view, is a product of the way social reality tends to be misrepresented as a result of the hierarchically differentiated experience that the materialist perspective allows us to account for.

Wolf, in his latest works, attempts to bring political economy in contact with more recent developments in cognitive anthropology through the concept of ideology. For this purpose he draws on, and tries to systematize, the idea that "minds interpose a selective sieve or screen between the organism and the environment through which it moves" (Wolf 1999:3). Ideology, then, understood as "unified schemes or configurations developed to underwrite or manifest power" (4) is a representational device which is mapped onto the world rather than mirroring it. Moreover, ideology is about something and does something for people, and thus is related to people's concrete concerns in particular contexts. Wolf distinguishes between four modalities of power: (1) the Nietzschean (about how people are drawn into a play of power); (2) the Weberian (the imposition of ego's will upon others); (3) a modality in which power represents some people's control over interactional contexts; and (4) "structural power" which refers to ways in which power provides someone with the ability to organize and orchestrate "the settings themselves" (5), and to specify "the direction and distribution of energy flows" (5). A focus on power, Wolf insists, links the analysis of communication and the codes which organize them to the exploration of what it really is about, "what it asserts or denies about the world beyond the vehicle of discourse or performance itself" (8). When involving ourselves in such explorations we should direct attention to the division of labor in society, and try to grasp how collective representations tend to arise from a variety of socially positioned and diverse sets of imaginings. The concept of ideology is attractive to Wolf because it mirrors so well anthropology's own history, torn as it has been between Enlightenment ideas as well as the reactions to it. Culture, in the American tradition especially, draws originally on (among others) Herder's vision of the *Volksgeist*, while the concept of ideology in its pre-Marxist version came from the idea that humans are perfectible, by means of science and "true ideas," education, and enlightened leadership – rule by reason. In Marx and Engels, the concept of ideology was first given an almost formal definition and understood as a form of misrepresentation on the part of both the dominant and the dominated, but was anchored in the idea that capitalism tends to generate a particular form of cognitive deception: commodity fetishism, understood as a form of "escalated animism" (35).

As for the relationship between class and culture, Wolf insists that both terms claim too much and too little, and the two concepts need to be wed because each one has really never served us well in grasping the totality in its own right. "The pragmatic turn" in anthropology enables us to understand communication not as an application of a Saussurian *langue*, but as the contextual formulation and function of signs within a network of practices and communications (culture). Power enters this in deciding "who can talk, in what order, through which discursive procedures, and about what topics" (Wolf 1999:55), and is a part of a social system organized around the marshalling of social labor (class). In his exploration of three cases of historical transformation in which crises arising from the organization of social labor occurred and provided new possibilities for elites – the Kwaikutl, the Aztecs, and National Socialist Germany – Wolf attempts to demonstrate that ideology is indeed powerful and an active force. In all three cases ideology drew on pre-existing cultural materials, yet addressed the experiences of people as they felt the consequences of new forms of differentiation, and at the same time rooted power in the cosmos (274). His third case is particularly telling in this regard. National Socialist Germany clearly demonstrates how the particular mix of Enlightenment ideas and archaic understandings (related to *das Volk*, premodern social order, rights, and statuses) were put to work as a means to provide meaning to people's frustrated and confusing experiences in a rapidly changing and threatening new order.

Although, of course, not wholly representative of the neo-Marxist inspiration in anthropology, Roseberry and Wolf formulate some key concepts in the attempt within the anthropological political economy school to come to terms with the concept of culture. They seek to reintegrate it with social practice, to take systems of ideas seriously as mental models, to retain the "functionalist" idea of power as related to the control of labor, and the equally "functionalist" idea that some cultural models are primarily about the legitimation of such control. In this regard Wolf's reformulation of the relationship between culture and class must be considered highly successful; it is far more sophisticated than the perspectives of Geertz, Sahlins, and Bourdieu in that it conceptualizes power as socially generated, dynamic, and at the same time as contingent. However, apart from this, Roseberry and Wolf have very little specific to say about ideology and hegemony as mental models, that is, how they constitute a part of people's knowledge and motivation for action. What they do is discuss a few, although basic, insights from linguistics and cognitive anthropology, and establish that ideology is not a mere reflection of some kind of societal infrastructure, but they say almost nothing about how people actually use them, what kind of system they constitute, and what the relationships between their constituent parts may be. Roseberry's conclusion that our understanding of materialism needs to be revised, and Wolf's important insights in the relationship between class and ideology (based on the idea of commodity fetishism laid out in *Das Kapital*) both seem essential, but do not take us *very* far beyond the anthropological influences they criticize.

Internalization

Strauss and Quinn's seminal essay "Anthropological Resistance" (1997) has contributed a great deal to clarify what various influential theorists have had to say about knowledge. They begin by taking issue with the Geertzian conceptualization of culture as exclusively "public," with the looseness of the idea of culture as "a web of meaning," and with the almost complete lack of any consideration of agency. To some extent their perspective echoes Wikan's (1987) and Barth's (1993) interesting critiques of Geertz's Bali work. They all point to his failure to link public webs of meaning to the real concerns of individuals, and of projecting public cultural models into their minds, thus blending motives and concerns, agency, and cultural forms. Strauss and Quinn argue that Geertz and his followers established a false dichotomy "between meaning as public (in several senses) and meaning as a cognitive-emotional state" (1997:13), and gave analytical priority to "models of" at the cost of "models for." Although he clearly acknowledged that culture somehow leads to action, they argue that it is very unclear how that happens. Strauss and Quinn thus stress that "meaning can only be evoked in a person" (20), and they quote Spiro (1987[1982]):

> In sum, symbolic analysis needs to be supplemented by research that takes note of which symbols people attend to and which they ignore: varying ways a given set of symbols is interpreted by different social subgroups and over time (Roseberry 1989); and the socializing situations that lead some symbols to be motivating while others make no difference in what people do. [Strauss and Quinn 1997:23]

> we should ask questions such as: what are the diverse experiences from which people gain their interpretative frameworks? Do some experiences create schemas that challenge the schemas gained from other experiences? On which schemas do people act in a given situation and why? [Strauss and Quinn 1997:38]

Strauss and Quinn understand culture as positioned, somehow more or less shared, and generated by motives that are in part formed by the culture they generate. We will return to this point later, but emphasize here that this is the typical Berger and Luckman (1966) position, which sees the social construction of reality as a dynamic process involving externalization, objectification, and internalization. Their critiques of Geertz and many other key figures and traditions seem adequate in precisely such terms: Geertz has no good grasp on the relationship between practice and cultural systems, and poststructuralists either let the subject be absorbed by discourses (see Butler 1990, 1997; Mahmood 2001) or the opposite: model the subject as a relatively free agent without specifying what subjectivity is, how practice is motivated, or what cultural systems are. As for neo-Marxism, Strauss and Quinn argue that, although both Roseberry's and Wolf's versions represent a search for ways to understand culture as an aspect of systems of power which is constituted by the interplay between the socially positioned versions of culture that each actor has, they seem to lack a good grasp of why people act the way they do. Are they motivated by ideology? In the case of Comaroff and Comaroff (1991), Strauss and Quinn point out, the relationship between culture and power comes in two forms: as ideology and as hegemony. Only the latter constitutes a field of negotiation, debate, and explicit struggle. It would appear that most of the time people are subject to dominance, and most of the time they have internalized it and don't question it. Strauss and Quinn's critique and position is, however, best illuminated through their discussion of the Bourdieuan theory of practice. Bourdieu argues in *Outline of a Theory of Practice* (1977) that much of what we know and do is embodied in and in some way due to some non-reflexive habit, which is internalized relatively passively by socially positioned individuals. The popularity of Bourdieu's perspective is interesting in light of the fact that he does not distinguish at all between various ways of knowing, for instance between what we don't talk about because it's improper and what remains silent because it is hard to articulate. Nor has he presented any theoretically informed idea of what kind of system culture is, what people share and don't share, what motivation is and how it works, et cetera.

Cognitive anthropology has never been much concerned with power or, for that matter, complex social domains. That may be one reason for the divide that seems to have existed between social/cultural approaches and cognitive anthropology. Strauss and Quinn are a very good case in point. They do indeed cross the divide, but their critique of Bourdieu, for instance, has not influenced anthropologists working with politics. And they themselves have not to any considerable degree brought their own cognitive approach into complex social domains. One key insight from their and other related work is that culture is organized as a hierarchical system of models, and people learn to relate situations and contexts to models for interpretation and action. Such models are systematically related, for instance taxonomically, and entail – or are driven by – motives and goals. The use of one general model as a general entry into a complex situation may imply a number of others at lower levels, and these models are more like concrete scenarios. The use of such models is not necessarily purely instrumental or habitual, or mental. For example, a person may be motivated by a scenario – or action scheme – and learn to identify it with an attractive emotional state. The instantiation of the scheme may be emotionally and non-reflexively driven. It is this phenomenon that Strauss and Quinn talk about as "internalization." Part of this idea seems inspired by Bourdieu, but clearly it is in accordance with common sense in the social sciences. By internalization they seem to mean that our minds – our motives and practices – are to some extent formed and directed by culture. Cultural models become a part of us in the sense that they motivate action. In this way they substantiate Bourdieu's general perspective. Although humans are more flexible than he thinks, they have more ways of dealing with alternative models and situations than Bourdieu allows for. However, since culture in Strauss and Quinn's perspective is what motivates them, the difference is not substantial, apart from the fact that the latter are able to account for much more of social behavior than is Bourdieu.

Resistance and Knowledge

Political anthropology has two poles, and the integration between them seems always to have represented a challenge. This challenge is what "practice" became a much celebrated answer to. On the one hand, the anthropology of dynamic political systems – think of *African Political Systems* (Fortes and Evans-Pritchard 1940), *Political Systems of Highland Burma* (Leach 1954), *Political Leadership among Swat Pathans* (Barth 1959), *Strategems and Spoils* (Bailey 1969), et cetera – and the strategies that created such systems had little to say about power. On the other hand, while the anthropology of power achieved much in terms of understanding culture as ideology, and the ways in which power is made legitimate, it rarely looked at the relationship between individual choice, aggregation, and functional integration in social systems. The concept of ideology strongly implies the absence of choice, a divide between knowledge and appropriate action of the kind that may shake a social system. Ideology and hegemony are very often seen as positive legitimating devices; they consist of ideas that serve somebody's class interests and that are taken over by the rest, so that people more or less wrongly believe in the order that they have before their eyes. Roseberry's and Wolf's versions only carefully modify this assumption in that they acknowledge that ideology may not appear as misrepresentations for the oppressed.

Both these poles, which are here somewhat caricatured, contain serious shortcomings. It is striking that political anthropology has largely failed to contribute more to our understanding of what people actually know, what they do with their knowledge, and how what they do generates systems of power. One of the best commentaries to these shortcomings is, in my view, Scott's work on resistance. In *Weapons of the Weak* (1985) he introduces the argument that the idea of hegemony is largely misconceived. The marginalized and poor peasants of Malaysia whom he studied were not at all subject to someone else's worldview. Instead they played according to the public transcript as long as it seemed too costly not to. In this context "costly" would mean provoking the owners of the means of production, who made decisions concerning who was getting access to work. Conforming to the public transcript often has very little to do with some sort of hegemonically imposed moral conviction to do so, Scott insists. To the contrary, the marginalized have a "hidden transcript" that provides them with alternatives, alternatives that may be acted upon more consistently and more publicly if power weakens. Scott argues that the normative order in the village of Sedaka is not in any sense "outside and above" (1985:305) the poor villagers, but an "environment of conflict and divergent interpretations" "through which self-interested action must pass" (306). Consequently, what is at stake for anthropological theory is not to understand normative consensus, but to critically re-evaluate how the people we study often distinguish between "what is inevitable" and "what is just" much more effectively than anthropologists themselves (317). As I pointed out earlier, options that seem out of reach may nevertheless constitute an essential part of people's stock of knowledge, but anthropologists rarely seek the information necessary to understand this (325). The point may be generalized. The empirical record does not seem to support the view that, although dominant ideologies may well exist, partly due to the need for elites to understand and try to legitimate their own position, such ideologies are normally not successful in the sense of being internalized by the subordinate classes (320). One of many illustrations of this is Willis's (1977) study of how English working-class kids, through their intense resistance to middle-class standards, authority, and rules, socialize themselves into a position as uneducated, powerless, manual laborers, just like their fathers.

Scott's generalization has far-reaching consequences. The following, apparently very naive question comes to mind: why have the concepts of hegemony and ideology been so tightly tied to the idea of cultural dominance, that is, the diffusion of the worldviews of the dominant? If dominance is, indeed, possible without such a mechanism, what then is legitimacy?

> theories of hegemony frequently confound what is inevitable with what is just, an error that subordinate classes rarely, if ever, make. [Scott 1985:317]

If hegemony is supposed to mean something different and more than simply any set of ideas that somehow seem especially important and thus serve power, we need to reformulate the question of how someone's control over the social contexts within which people's thought and action take place, is realized and reproduced.

> From a much more modest view of what hegemony is all about, it might be said that the main function of a system of domination is to accomplish precisely this: to define what is realistic and what is not realistic and to drive certain goals and aspirations into the realm of the impossible, the realm of idle dreams, of wishful thinking. [Scott 1985:326]

Theories of hegemony seem to have contributed to the same type of reification that the Geertzian concept of culture did, or that the Bourdieuan idea of habitus did and still does. Power and dominance are much more about control over social contexts than about the concepts through which people think. Cognitive anthropology may make us able to see this more clearly and to follow its implications more thoroughly, because its insights strongly suggest that cultural models are structured by relevance, are quite easily accessible and adaptable by individuals, and are thus flexible – although they are not always possible to articulate or worth talking about even when the anthropologist is observant enough to ask about them. If most people know much more about their own worlds than we as anthropologists tend to think, and actively make choices but still, perhaps more often than not, tend to conform to expectations in their relevant environment that they feel exposed to, then their social contexts should not be analytically depicted as defined by cultural concepts that inappropriately represent their real experience, but rather as a very complex aggregate outcome of pragmatically motivated interactions.

> ... no symbol represents a meaning in itself but only evokes one in its interaction with an actor's particular knowledge, agenda, and positioning. It follows that we cannot usefully inspect an abstracted tradition for its entailments; we must observe the uses to which real people put its concepts, in their practices of a range of actors in a range of circumstances. [Barth 1993:349–350]

In Barth's perspective, people's daily concerns are clearly informed by culture, but not in the sense of being internalized as values that play a key part in guiding action. Cultural categories are more transparent than that, and people are able to use them for their various purposes. In this pursuit, they are of course strongly constrained, and there is often no other way to go about one's daily life than to act and communicate in terms that are meaningful and acceptable to one's relevant others. Although Barth's theory of culture, which is really a perspective on knowledge, does not contain elaborate discussions of the self, he clearly supposes that that there is an active self "behind" the collective representations we make use of.

> Above all, we need to recognize the continual flux in which these actions occur. I take it that every performed and interpreted act will change, slightly, the meanings that are ascribed to any following choice, act, or expression within the circle of persons in which it was visible. The result is a low degree of order and a high degree of flux – a flux that comes about through small and humble steps yet may cumulatively challenge, invade, and transform the relevance of whole constructed worlds. [Barth 1993:323]

It is interesting to note, then, that his inclination to avoid the question of internalization altogether seems closely related to his reputation as a "transactionalist" who carries with him a reductionist perspective on motivation and agency. I suggest that, however, precisely because he does not support the idea that knowledge is internalized in any deep sense, his perspective on knowledge is in fact able to transcend what we may call the mystical view of power. By *mystical* I mean the tendency to try to explain power with reference to the internalization of (aspects of) cultural forms in a way that influences people's understanding of the world and thus makes the order of things more or less acceptable – *instead* of studying power as an emergent property of complex processes of aggregation. By the latter I mean processes involving the ways in which social contexts are shaped, mainly unintentionally and as cumulative effects of intentional practices. The main theoretical problems with the hegemony hypothesis, as I see it, are the following. First, it translates from forms to subjectivity far too easily. Second, it is based on the assumption that because people, through their daily practices, largely fail to change the overall order of things (for instance, the cultural form of late capitalism) and thus take part in their own subordination, this is caused by lack of some "appropriate" (presumably more critical) consciousness. Third, the critical interest in power, especially when wed to the Marxist idea of class, assumes largely uncritically that because people's perspectives of the world and of themselves are hierarchically positioned, the order of things becomes legitimated through their internalizations of the structural limitations to which they are exposed. I will argue, too, that all these problems may be related to the moral predicament inherent in the Marxist perspective on power, which, I hasten to add, has contributed so much to anthropology. Since power has so much to do with class, and since the worldviews of the dominant classes are so dominant in the public discourse, it seems morally problematic to insist that power is, like culture, primarily epiphenomenal, and that the relative absence of visible forms of resistance does not necessarily have much to do with ideology and hegemony. There is of course no doubt that many forms of power are products of intentions, or that these intentions may represent the interests of, say, a dominant class, and are structurally embedded in institutions. But in order for any system of power to be reproduced, the cumulative effects of the myriad of actions and projects that make up any such system can only very rarely be directly regulated or controlled. That these effects may nevertheless be regulated in ways that serve collective interest should not inspire us to assume that there are certain values and beliefs that cause this connection. Because of this, ideology and hegemony should be regarded as effects, that is, as aggregate social and cultural forms – and thus mainly epiphenomenal. Returning to Wolf, we should emphasize again that power of the kind he describes is primarily about the control over contexts in which people act. Such control is only rarely direct, and to the extent that it is seemingly exercised ideologically, this is normally not because ideology shapes consciousness but because certain systems of symbols are used by people in order to act meaningfully, but more basically to pursue ends that may be more or less independent of them. Anthropologists often seem to miss this essential distinction between selves and motives, on the one hand, and the symbols through which people's actions are communicated, on the other. As I have argued, this may be due to the anthropologists' tendency to reify culture, ideology, and power in much the same way as people we study do. Depending on their social position, the people we study make generalizations about the complex patterns that they see, and in that very process, reify them for the purpose of understanding them and act upon them. As consciousness, such generalizations are probably rarely "correct." But I want to argue that it is hardly fruitful to assume that that is the reason why power works. The questions we are disposed to ask when we believe that ideology is internalized may prevent us from realizing that the symbols which people think with, and think through, have far less explanatory power than, for instance, penetrating analyses of how social contexts are shaped, how people deal with them, and what happens as a result of the paths of action people do not choose to follow. The mystery of power is perhaps more than anything else about why, in most situations, coordinated action is so hard to realize.

Cultural Models and Power Reconsidered

I have argued that because knowledge is a concept which lends itself more easily to understanding how people operate in their world, it is for many purposes more fruitful than the concept of culture. The concept of culture – in much the same way as ideology and hegemony, which the concept of culture has inspired – easily leads us to impose a misplaced concreteness on the patterns and forms which we tend to think about as "society." Among the anthropologists who have formulated this point most clearly, Barth – especially in his work on Bali – is perhaps paramount. His generative perspective on "society" provides us with an analytical framework which makes it possible to think about culture not as ideology, but as a cumulative set of effects that people need to relate to and make use of. Contrary to what many seem to believe, this is not a perspective that ignores power, nor one that reduces motives to instrumental self-interest. It simply turns the mystery of power around and avoids the question of how it is made legitimate though some form of incomplete consciousness. As Scott and others have shown, the empirical record does not indicate that subordinate people necessarily lack the ambition to improve their situation and hence do not develop practical strategies to realize it. That they may not succeed may have nothing to do with hegemony. If by hegemony we refer simply to the distribution of power being unequal and more or less stabilized, then hegemony becomes a purely descriptive device, simply a way of labeling a certain pattern. We may add to this that although patterns may be controlled, used, and always entail real effects, ideological dominance may be only a marginal aspect of this.

Recent contributions in cognitive anthropology point in the same direction as Barth's and Scott's perspectives. That is my main reason for arguing that cognitive anthropology, although traditionally not very concerned with power, has a lot to offer. Strauss and Quinn's seminal essay "Anthropological Resistance" seems to me to represent the most pertinent critique of practice theories to date (see chapter 2 in Strauss and Quinn 1997). They argue convincingly that most of the time most people know a lot more, and different things, than the rendering of their knowledge by anthropologists would have us believe. But one modification of this view is strongly needed. When criticizing Bourdieu for applying a very undifferentiated and functionalist view of knowledge, coined in the concept of the habitus, Strauss and Quinn fail to let go of the idea of internalization, which is an essential part of that concept. Thus they are bound to explain power with reference to what people don't know or take for granted. This, it may be reasonably assumed, is one important reason why so much time and effort is spent on trying to establish analytically to what extent people actually "have agency" and are "at least partially 'knowing,' and thus able to act on and sometimes against the structures that made them" (Ortner 2006:110, with reference to Giddens 1992). In his recent book on cognitive models, Kronenfeld argues convincingly that the significance of cultural knowledge, organized primarily for us as models for action, is fundamentally flexible. It provides the "overhead" that enables complex, distributed systems of knowledge to work. According to this perspective, as anthropologists we should be more concerned with how this system works. Understanding power then, becomes, at least in one very important sense, a question of studying how knowledge is systematically organized and put to use by social actors. Both reproduction and change, both consensus and resistance, depend on people acting. And if their actions are not based on internalized knowledge primarily, but on more or less continual reflection on how to act and why, their knowledge becomes an important key to understanding how their social environment is perceived, presumably through some kind of combination between the understanding of patterns, norms, and pragmatic consideration. The cumulative effects are of course always related to power and dominance, but the relationship is perhaps not mediated by shared norms and ideological beliefs. The kind of system we should pay attention to, according to this reasoning, is the knowledge people have and how individual versions of distributed systems of cognition are interrelated – as well as how actions and the patterns they generate are interpreted and changed. As a consequence, such a call is simultaneously a call for a genuinely generative social anthropology which incorporates insights from cognitive anthropology. Culture is not primarily about worldviews, but about the toolkit people use when dealing with social encounters. Such encounters generate complex patterns, which feed back into the encounters, and the knowledge needed to come to grips with this complexity demands different, and both more differentiated and more flexible forms of knowledge than concepts such as culture, ideology, and the habitus inspire us to believe.

REFERENCES

Bailey, F. G.
1969 Strategems and Spoils: A Social Anthropology of Politics. Oxford: Blackwell.
Barth, F.
1959 Political Leadership among Swat Pathans. Oxford: Berg.
1993 Balinese Worlds. Chicago: University of Chicago Press.
Berger, P., and T. Luckmann
1966 The Social Construction of Reality: A Treatise in the Sociology of Knowledge. New York: Penguin.
Bourdieu, P.
1977 Outline of a Theory of Practice. Cambridge: Cambridge University Press.
Butler, J.
1990 Gender Trouble: Feminism and the Subversion of Identity. New York: Routledge.
1997 The Psychic Life of Power: Theories in Subjection. Stanford: Stanford University Press.
Comaroff, J., and J. Comaroff
1991 Of Revelation and Revolution: Christianity, Colonialism, and Consciousness in South Africa, vol. 1. Chicago: University of Chicago Press.
Elster, J.
1983 Sour Grapes: Studies in the Subversion of Rationality. Cambridge: Cambridge University Press.

Fortes, M., and E. E. Evans-Pritchard
1940 African Political Systems. London: Oxford University Press.
Giddens, A.
1992 The Transformation of Intimacy: Sexuality, Love and Eroticism in Modern Societies. Cambridge: Polity.
1940 African Political Systems. London: Oxford University Press.
Kronenfeld, D. B.
2009 Culture, Society, and Cognition: Collective Goals, Values, and Knowledge. Berlin: Mouton de Gruyter.
Leach, E.
1954 Political Systems of Highland Burma: A Study of Kachin Social Structure. London: Continuum.
Lukes, S.
2005 Power: A Radical View. Basingstoke: Palgrave Macmillan.
Mahmood, S.
2001 Feminist Theory, Embodiment, and the Docile Agent: Some Reflections on the Egyptian Islamic Revival. Cultural Anthropology 16(2):202–236.
Ortner, S. B.
1984 Theory in Anthropology Since the Sixties. Comparative Studies in Society and History 26(1):126–166.
2006 Anthropology and Social Theory: Culture, Power, and the Acting Subject. Durham, NC: Duke University Press.
Roseberry, W.
1989 Anthropologies and Histories: Essays in Culture, History, and Political Economy. New Brunswick, NJ: Rutgers University Press.
Scott, J.
1985 Weapons of the Weak: Everyday Forms of Peasant Resistance. New Haven: Yale University Press.
Spiro, Melford E.
1987[1982] Collective Representations and Mental Representations in Religious Symbol Systems. *In* Culture and Human Natures: Theoretical Papers of Melford E. Spiro. B. Kilborne and L. L. Langness, eds. Pp. 161–184. Chicago: University of Chicago Press.
Strauss, C., and N. Quinn
1997 A Cognitive Theory of Cultural Meaning. Cambridge: Cambridge University Press.
Wikan, U.
1987 Public Grace and Private Fears: Gaiety, Offense, and Sorcery in Northern Bali. Ethos 15(4):337–365.
Willis, P.
1977 Learning to Labour: How Working Class Kids Get Working Class Jobs. Aldershot: Gower.
Wolf, E. R.
1999 Envisioning Power: Ideologies of Dominance and Crisis. Berkeley: University of California Press.

CHAPTER 21

Cognitive Anthropology through a Gendered Lens

Carol C. Mukhopadhyay

Feminist and Cognitive Anthropology: Two Separate Worlds?

Cognitive and feminist anthropology seem to inhabit two separate worlds, despite the pioneering work on gender by cognitive anthropologists, the significance of gender in human culture and, therefore, in the culture–cognition interface, and the potential relevance of cognitive anthropology to a feminist anthropology project. Historical overviews of both sub-fields yield a Mars–Venus scenario, at least judging from "origin" stories, descriptions of major founders and lineages, dominant methodologies and theoretical paradigms, questions posed, and influential thinkers. Significant publications exhibit virtually no overlap in references or contributors. Core community members do not draw upon each other for theoretical or methodological insights, at least in recent years. Cognitive anthropology seems unaware of or at least uninvolved in and unaffected by current theoretical conversations in feminist theory. And feminist anthropology seems largely oblivious to the existence of cognitive anthropology.

This same situation may characterize the relationship between feminist scholarship and psychological anthropology. Susan Seymour's introduction to the *Ethos* special issue on "Feminist Psychological Anthropology" (2004) reviews the history of their interaction and argues that, despite much overlapping research on gender, psychological anthropology has been surprisingly untouched by feminism. At the same time, she finds numerous examples of how feminist scholarship outside psychological anthropology has appropriated psychological concepts (or at least psychological terminology) and psychological-type explanatory paradigms without drawing upon psychological anthropology resources.

A Companion to Cognitive Anthropology, First Edition. Edited by David B. Kronenfeld, Giovanni Bennardo, Victor C. de Munck, and Michael D. Fischer.

Should We Care?

One could argue that feminist and cognitive anthropology have little in common. Cognitive anthropology investigates abstract philosophical questions, of mind, language, thought; how humans process and utilize ideas, emotions; the relationship between the individual and culture. Feminist anthropology, on the other hand, grew out of a broader societal movement, feminism, fundamentally concerned with gender inequality. As such, some would argue, feminist anthropology is inherently both political and pragmatic, driven by real-world concerns and potential applications to gender justice issues.

Early feminist anthropological research focused on women's status, exploring links between aspects of social-economic organization and gender inequality. Many of these domains, such as kinship, figure in the work of cognitive anthropologists. Even here, feminist and cognitive anthropologists seem interested in different questions and theoretical goals, and rarely cite each other's work.

Why should this apparent mutual disinterest concern us? Anthropology is a diverse discipline that attempts to understand not only the entirety of human cultural productions and processes (including language) but human biology. Even among cultural anthropologists, there are hundreds of specialties, interest groups, regional concentrations. It's impossible to keep up with what's going on in the field. And for what purpose?

Yet, the history and contemporary trajectories of feminist and cognitive anthropology have more in common than is at first apparent. The history of feminist anthropology, fully written, would locate some early advocates in cognitive anthropology.[1] There are feminist anthropologists today, myself included, who either have academic roots in cognitive anthropology or were mentored by cognitive anthropologists. Some mentors played a significant role in feminist anthropology. Others, while not engaged in feminist research or gender theory, might describe themselves as feminists.

Key, some might say foundational, writings in feminist anthropology have come from people trained in cognitive anthropology, including two seminal *Annual Review* articles on the status of women (Quinn 1977; Mukhopadhyay and Higgins 1988). The direction much feminist anthropology has taken in the past two decades is arguably either implicit in or has actually been pioneered by cognitive anthropologists.

On the other hand, cognitive anthropology has benefited, theoretically and methodologically, from gender-related and other research by feminist cognitive anthropologists (see Kronenfeld 2008). Key cognitive anthropology figures, such as Naomi Quinn and Dorothy Holland, contributed to the development of feminist anthropology through their research on gender, through the Association for Feminist Anthropology and through efforts to integrate feminist perspectives into psychological anthropology. Cognitive anthropologists organized the first conference on feminist psychological anthropology in Sweden (2000), and produced the first issue of *Ethos* devoted to feminist psychological anthropology (2004). I believe the two fields overlap, have much to gain from each other and may, indeed, need each other if they are to individually and collectively survive and thrive.

Caveats

This account, like any, reflects my experiences and perceptions of cognitive and feminist anthropology. These have been influenced by when and where I discovered anthropology and feminism. I have seen many changes in approaches, goals, personnel, and descriptive labels for what I am calling "cognitive" and "feminist" anthropology.

At the time of my first encounter with anthropology, in 1969, as a civil rights activist seeking intellectual escape from junior high school teaching, there was no feminist anthropology, no women's studies, and only a faint recognition that gender (labeled "sex") was worth studying and that the ethnographic record could benefit if women were not virtually invisible. Since then, there has been an explosion of research on gender and an accompanying adjustment of language and labels.

One label that emerged is "feminist anthropology" along with an organization, the Association for Feminist Anthropology. I do not wish to get mired in debates about the meaning of "feminist," "feminism," "post-feminism" or what constitutes or should constitute feminist anthropology. Indeed, I do not know how the Association for Feminist Anthropology got its name. I recall thinking that the Anthropology of Gender better reflected my own scholarly orientation and goals, albeit goals partially motivated by feminism. Until recently, most major volumes and literature reviews used *gender* or some version of the anthropology of gender in their titles (see di Leonardo 1991; Mascia-Lees and Black 2000; Brettell and Sargent 2005[1993]). Were it not so bulky, I would use "gender/feminist anthropology" to best describe the body of work to which I am referring. Nevertheless, for readability, I will use "feminist anthropology" as a convenient shorthand, partly reflecting current usage (see Geller and Stockett 2006), partly in recognition of a shared set of perspectives articulated by feminist anthropologists, including, for many of us, a commitment to politically engaged scholarship (see Morgen 1989; Mascia-Lees and Sharpe 2000; Lewin 2006).

The field of cognitive anthropology has also evolved over time. My first exposure to cognitive anthropology was in a graduate seminar for which I was totally unprepared, having taken no anthropology courses prior to entering an MA program at a local university. I recall being confused and intimidated by something called "componential analysis," a part of ethnoscience, somehow related to linguistics. In another course, I tried to stay engaged while an ABD instructor diagrammed relationships between categories of "witches," using data "elicited" from his Liberian "informants."

It was not until I entered the University of California, Riverside Ph.D. program in anthropology that I acquired a fuller understanding of ethnoscience, its roots, goals, methodologies, links to linguistics and other philosophical traditions striving to understand language, mind, and thought. Kronenfeld recently described cognitive anthropology as going through three stages of "successively wider, cumulative developments ... classification, decision models, and cultural models" (2008:38). The classification stage, with its immersion in native systems of classifications, and in theoretical and methodological foundational literature for identifying and analyzing such systems, certainly characterized my initial graduate school experiences.

I soon was caught up in the second stage, exploring with Kronenfeld and other UCR students the exciting developments in language, thought, and cognition coming out of computer science and psychology, including artificial intelligence and expert systems. Instead of reading about how non-Western groups categorize things, we turned to how real people make decisions, whether house-buying, selecting marriage partners, or fish-catching/selling.

My graduate training and dissertation research was most heavily influenced by this decision model stage of cognitive anthropology. "Cultural models" research and the more elaborate cultural knowledge structures that some of us were finding, if not consciously pursuing, were on the horizon but not yet articulated.

I thought of myself primarily as a cognitive anthropologist. Gender-related research was exploding, new data were being collected, old data reanalyzed, long-cherished explanatory models challenged. I identified strongly with the new wave of activity and was hoping my research, as a cognitive anthropologist, would be part of this movement. Yet ... I felt a certain discomfort with the "cognitive anthropology" identity and approach.

At this point, however, I am simply clarifying what I mean by cognitive anthropology here. Cognitive anthropology has moved far beyond my graduate school days. There is a more sophisticated understanding of language and semantics, and its relationship to conceptual systems, as articulated in Kronenfeld's work on extensionist semantics (1996). New research in cognitive science and cognitive psychology has given us mental models, schema theory, and distributed parallel-processing models. Cognitive anthropologists have applied these insights to culture and the relationship between culture and the individual (Kronenfeld 2008).

Most important, new research on language, cognition, and culture coalesced in third-stage cultural models research in the 1980s and 1990s (see Holland and Quinn 1987; Strauss and Quinn 1997). I have found this new work methodologically and theoretically both useful and liberating, addressing some of the troubling issues that came up during my own fieldwork and dissertation (see Mukhopadhyay 1980, especially introduction and literature review).

So, why the perception – and perhaps reality – of a disconnect between feminist and cognitive anthropology? This chapter is, in part, an effort to understand that perception and my attempts to balance feminist and cognitive anthropology selves in a changing anthropological world. The following sections provide a rather personalized historical overview of the two sub-fields. I suggest some areas of divergence and factors underlying the perception of incompatibility. Finally, I describe areas of potential convergence.

Potential Synergies: Cognitive Anthropology and Gender in the 1970s

The 1960s and 1970s were exciting times for a graduate student. Both cognitive and feminist anthropology had just come onto the scene and offered fresh, new directions and opportunities. Both promised, rather ambitiously, to revolutionize anthropological thinking about and to produce a new theory of culture!

Cognitive anthropology arose as ethnoscience. Through linguistically oriented analyses and methodological rigor, anthropologists would uncover cultural knowledge, construct a cultural grammar of each culture and, perhaps, even discover universal cultural principles.

This emphasis on culture as a mental phenomenon and on emic perspectives held promise for a deeper understanding of gender. Ethnoscience implicitly rejected what are now called "essentialist" views, arguing against the imposition of Western categories on other cultures. Instead, it sought to discover native categories, conceptual structures, systems of classification, cultural meanings. From my perspective, cognitive anthropology offered a way to document and extend Margaret Mead's pioneering observations about gender – that concepts of gender are not fixed but culturally variable and culturally constructed. A thorough exploration of gender concepts and ideologies, cross-culturally and in the United States, could finally commence!

There were other appealing aspects of cognitive anthropology. It offered a scientific approach to an emotional, intensely political and politicized, intensely personal and personalized topic. Everyone experiences gender and has opinions and beliefs on the subject. Everyone is to some extent an expert. And ... there are powerful vested interests in maintaining gender inequality, whether at home or in the public realm. It is precisely, I thought, this type of topic which demands scientific rigor, empirical data, an explicit methodology, formal models subject to hypothesis testing, conclusions clearly linked to evidence. From a pragmatic and activist standpoint, also, change requires substantive, accurate knowledge of how gender systems operate.

Finally, the decision models phase of cognitive anthropology critiqued 19th-century arguments about "primitive" vs. "modern" minds, the latter associated with "rational" decision-making, the former with the "blind follower of culture" model. These discussions seemed applicable to gender, to the operation of systems of gender inequality, the question of what is now called "agency" and to social change processes.

My sense of a potential synergy between cognitive and feminist anthropology was reinforced by graduate school readings. As mentioned earlier, gender research was virtually non-existent in the early 1970s. Yet Maccoby's seminal 1966 volume included a cross-cultural overview by cognitive anthropologist Roy D'Andrade. Another 1966 D'Andrade article (in Maccoby 1966) challenged the empirical basis for gendered personalities by showing that "observed" personality trait clusters could be predicted by semantic relations between English terms.

As I ploughed through Tyler's *Cognitive Anthropology* (1969), I saw potential applications to gender, despite gender-biased language and the apparent irrelevance and invisibility of gender and women, including in the popular topic of kinship. Greenberg's (1966) marking theory helped me understand, if not accept, male-biased language in English while revealing it was not universal. Language offered numerous entry points into understanding how gender operates. Of course gender as category and classifying principle is ubiquitous. Beyond that, there was everyday discourse as well as academic and other dominant discourses, saturated with gender. What a rich minefield to explore!

I also encountered cognitive anthropologists who addressed gender-relevant domains of social structure. Some, like Peggy Sanday, subsequently concentrated on gender. Others, like Naomi Quinn, Hugh Gladwin, Christina Gladwin, Stuart Plattner, and Mike Burton spanned both sub-fields.

By this time I was focusing on gender-differentiated activities, naively called *the* sexual division of labor. Prevailing anthropological theories and US folk explanations linked women's inequality to their economic dependence or to male dominance through aggression. Biological differences, such as "strength", were central in such arguments and in explanations of the sexual division of labor cross-culturally (see Mukhopadhyay and Higgins 1988).

Virtually no ethnographic research had studied, from an emic perspective, the actual processes producing the sexual division of labor in families or communities.[2] Theoretical discussions explored origins or employed statistical analyses of cross-cultural precoded gender data on technological activities in pre-industrial societies.

Early challenges to these essentially biological-reproductive determinism arguments came from cognitive anthropologists. Burton et al. (1977) used "entailment analysis" to dispute the role of strength in the sexual division of labor. Nerlove (1974) went further, arguing that childcare responsibilities were *adapted to* economic activities, rather than the opposite.

Ironically, neither presented systematic evidence (objective or informant-based) that activities possessed the features attributed to them. Words like "heavy," "dangerous," "distant" were not yet perceived as culturally embedded, complex, and part of larger semantic domains, as my own subsequent research showed (Mukhopadhyay 1980). A Durkheimian–Parsonian functionalist model of gender roles dominated, reflecting a longer-standing and pervasive American meritocracy folk model of society for both race (Mukhopadhyay et al. 2007) and gendered academic career paths (Mukhopadhyay 2004). Yet despite their limitations, I was inspired by these early works and determined to apply cognitive anthropological approaches to *my* study of the sexual division of labor!

At the same time, I recall struggling to integrate my immersion in cognitive anthropology with gender.[3] There was no resistance by faculty, just an inability to provide much substantive guidance, given the state of anthropology at the time.[4] I and fellow students searched out gender-relevant classics (H. L. Morgan, Engels, McLennan) and topics (e.g., dowry, bride wealth, kinship) for our graduate seminars. We taught the first anthropology class on gender at UCR, "Women in Cross-Cultural Perspective," using the just published Rosaldo and Lamphere collection, *Women, Culture and Society* (1974).

Struggling to Fit the Body into the Shoe

Applying 1970s cognitive anthropology methods and theories to my dissertation research proved easier in the abstract than in reality. My goal was to understand the decision processes underlying the sexual division of labor in households. My fieldwork was in Los Angeles, California, with 18 families of 19 hospital nurses (18 females, 1 male). I used standard ethnoscience and other verbally oriented methods to identify task categories, alternative performers, task performance occasions, and salient task and performer attributes that I (naively) assumed were decision criteria for allocating household tasks.[5]

I soon discovered that identifying or applying classification rules for matching tasks and performers would not be easy. Familiar concepts like "housework," "child care," or "cleaning the stove" turned out to be complex, entailing hundreds of lower-level items, with fuzzy boundaries and attributes, and (at the time) unconventional structural relationships and classification principles. But I was not dealing with conventional domains, or even nouns, but verbs, activities ("cooking") and complex activity traits ("heavy," "dirty"). As a native, I was aware of deeper shared assumptions (and conceptual structures) behind words, subtleties of meaning conveyed by tone, facial expression, and body movement, and creative applications of words. I found infinitely more ways of matching tasks and performers than I had imagined – how were alternatives reduced to a manageable set? And I encountered what Holland (1992) later called "messy" situations, tasks not covered by existing rules or schemas, requiring novel solutions and more active and creative thinking.

With many activities, performed frequently, not always routinely, by many potential performers, how could one formally model or predict anything? An impossibly complex mental process was required. Clearly, existing approaches to ethnographic decision-making, decision models, and tests of such models, and what they represented were naive and oversimplified. I developed the term "cultural precedents" for the normal reliance on what are today "cultural schemas," a semi-automatic process without active thought or comparison of alternatives, decision criteria, or task attributes (Mukhopadhyay 1980; see also Kronenfeld 2008 on my work). But even "cultural precedents" were not uniformly shared.

Most surprising, my informants were not particularly interested in "truth," that is, in logically or objectively applying categorization rules to a given situation. They were not simply trying to figure out the most efficient fit between task and performers. I witnessed creative applications of words, driven by a search for a culturally plausible rationale for a desired outcome. In short, I found that my informants had motives, emotions, likes and dislikes, egos, images to preserve, and goals embedded in larger social and conceptual structures. I could not formally model the decision to barbecue without understanding broader concepts ("a man's job") which referenced and were embedded in broader US cultural models of gender, family, and "work."

Finally, I was not dealing with the conventional one-person decision process model. Most household activity decisions implicate at least two people, each with some right to consent … or not comply. So … I was dealing with collective decisions with multiple decision-makers, each with activity concepts, goals, cultural models, strategies, and potential resources (not always equal). Fascinatingly rich data for understanding processes; virtually impossible to model.

It was not until long after my dissertation (1980) that I realized my problems reflected the state of cognitive anthropology at the time. We had not yet discovered more complex knowledge systems that underlie single words, such as "commitment" or "bachelor," or recognized the role of narratives, experience, embodiment in human thought and reasoning.

The 1980s and 1990s

My feminist cognitive anthropology orientations continued beyond graduate school as I attempted to remain an active scholar while teaching eight courses per year at a predominantly undergraduate state university. I recall struggling with which academic conversation to join or, rather, how to identify scholars and journals speaking my language. Clearly, my work was relevant to ethnographic decision-modeling (Mukhopadhyay 1984; Kronenfeld 1996, 2008). And new cognitive structures, ways of coding cultural knowledge, foreshadowed the cultural models and other boundary-expanding developments that emerged in the late 1980s and 1990s (see Holland and Quinn 1987). By 1992, pragmatics entered cognitive anthropology discussions, complicating simplified conceptions of schema and introducing the situated nature of action, power, emotions, motivation, and other complexities in real-world settings (D'Andrade and Strauss 1992).

Cognitive anthropologists were also exploring gender-related substantive areas. Quinn, as early as 1982, published work on US cultural models of marriage and Holland and Quinn's (1987) volume included several articles on marriage. D'Andrade and Strauss's (1992) volume dealt primarily with gender-related topics of romance, marriage, and parenting. Contributors were predominantly women I would consider feminist anthropologists.

This potential synthesis of feminist and cognitive anthropology approaches was clearest in Holland and Eisenhart's exploration of US cultural models of school-going and romance (1990). I became aware of their research in the mid-1980s when I was extending my own work on gender-differentiated activities into academic and occupational choices. Engineering and the emerging field of computer science represented prototypic US male fields and lucrative careers, and were of theoretical interest. But they were also becoming hot topics.

Americans were increasingly worried about women's under-representation in science and engineering. Chancellor of the California State University system, Ann Reynolds, organized an intercampus task force to review existing research and make campus-wide policy recommendations. Before my appointment, the task force did not include a single social scientist or even educational researcher. Instead, it consisted of women scientists, engineers, and mathematicians![6]

This was typical of early research on gendered science. The dominant paradigm came from educational psychology before it discovered qualitative methods. US survey or aggregated educational or labor statistics were described (less often analyzed) using standard statistical techniques.

From my perspective (and apparently Holland and Eisenhart's, independently), such approaches gave little insight into the role of culture in individual science-related decisions. Why not use a cognitive anthropology approach to understand the processes underlying gendered academic choices, including the broader cultural and social context in which such processes occur.[7] With a bit of local funding, I initiated an exploratory project, using ethnosemantic methods and participation observation, on the culture and academic choice processes of US computer science majors (Mukhopadhyay 1984). Subsequently, given the paucity of research on gendered science in non-Western cultures, I undertook a larger, comparative research project in India (Mukhopadhyay 2001).

The Growing Disconnect between Feminist and Cognitive Anthropology

Despite exciting developments in cognitive anthropology, my heart was in feminist anthropology. Or rather, I was more attracted to this work. I found it more path-breaking, compelling, and theoretically stimulating. Equally important, I found the research more relevant to ordinary human lives and to issues of social justice. Indeed, it is feminist anthropology's explicit commitment to politically relevant research that, I believe, significantly differentiates it from cognitive anthropology and that has shaped the trajectories of the two sub-disciplines.

As cognitive anthropology's attention turned to cognitive science developments, and to exploring the neuroscience of the brain, after a short flirtation with this literature, my own interest waned. To me, gender-related substantive work in cognitive anthropology was being applied to advance cognitive theory and not gender theory.

Cognitive anthropology also emphasizes understanding the individual mind, albeit as shaped by extra-individual forces, including culture and society. Yet I was as interested in the operation of those external forces (social, economic, political, educational) as in their manifestation at the individual level. True, most anthropologists, whether cognitive or feminist, explore the individual–culture nexus. But cognitive anthropology begins with, focuses on, and does not go much beyond the individual in this culture–individual equation. This is reflected in Strauss and Quinn's book title *A Cognitive Theory of Cultural Meaning* (1997), a theory that does not "encompass public culture or explain the shape it takes" (1997:253) but only how cultural meaning manifests itself in the individual mind, how individuals internalize and utilize culture in thinking, reasoning, and acting.

But cross-cultural variation in cultural knowledge, cultural meanings, and gender systems makes it clear that extra-individual, collective, external processes are involved and must also be studied. Cognitive anthropologists do not deny this but this is not their focus. The original goals were "a descriptive theory of specific folk knowledge" (Kronenfeld 2008:55) rather than understanding the culturally rooted shape of that knowledge. Strauss and Quinn recognize that neither their theory "of how cultural meaning is internalized in individuals" (1997:9) nor a theory of "public culture" can stand alone. And they call for an integration of these perspectives. But for them, origins are secondary: "however such solutions are invented, once in existence as cultural schemas they are spread" (128–129).

Other cognitive anthropologists reiterate the individual psychological-cognitive focus (see Schwartz et al. 1992). More recent attempts to theorize "public culture" (see Kronenfeld 2008) still move from the individual outward and have not yet reached major cultural institutions. An exception is Holland's work on schooling and cultural reproduction (see Levinson et al. 1996).

Nor is power easily theorized within a cognitive anthropology perspective, although it cannot be ignored, as Holland pointed out in 1992. A theory of cultural meaning has to take into account the power, individual impacts, and processes generating popular culture, whether music videos, television, movies, video games, or advertising. Organized religion, too, wields enormous power, through its multiple verbal and non-verbal manifestations. Public culture is powerful, regardless of how fragmented or diffused it is, and some individual voices are significantly louder than others.

Finally, cognitive anthropology, with its structural linguistic roots and commitment to a scientific study of culture, emphasizes, indeed prides itself, on producing formal models. Such models require simplified worlds, indeed elegance is equated with simplicity. Yet real life, especially in politically charged domains such as gender, does not lend itself well to such simplifications, methodologies, or formal representations; and complexities are difficult to model and even more difficult to test. For some of us, our subject matter requires that we complexify rather than simplify, forgoing, at least temporarily, the elegance of formal models in favor of the messy reality and everyday politics of life (see Quinn 2005).

Feminist Anthropology in the 1980s and 1990s

Ironically, feminist anthropology in the 1980s and 1990s took the lead pursuing the messier complexities of gender, including how it operates ideologically, linguistically, conceptually. This was partly a logical outcome of the critique of grand theories of gender inequality that initially preoccupied feminists.

The early 1980s witnessed an outpouring of research and writing on gender, both within anthropology and in other disciplines. There were, as now, multiple feminist languages and academic communities and I recall not being sure where I, as a scientifically trained and oriented cognitive feminist social anthropologist fit!

Women's studies programs and journals were getting underway and drew from multiple disciplinary perspectives in the social sciences and humanities. I was invited in 1981 to a Duke University seminar on women and politics. Naomi Quinn was a participant, if not co-organizer, along with Jean Barr, a political scientist. Despite the US focus of my dissertation, I was asked to contribute a paper on India, perhaps due to my earlier research (with political scientist Suresht Bald) on Indian women's political participation. The result was my first comparison of US and Indian gender concepts, "Sati or Shakti: Women, Culture, and Politics in India" (Mukhopadhyay 1982).

The cognitive anthropology influence was my exploration of cultural models of gender, this time as related to legitimate female power and authority. On the other hand, my paper didn't employ typical methodology. I used secondary sources of data to study what Strauss and Quinn (1997) would later call "public culture," images of women found in Hindu ideology, myths, stories, and popular culture. And women's political participation data came from published government statistics.

By the mid- to late 1980s, the gender literature just within anthropology was overwhelming. There was so much to discover and think about once woman/women entered the anthropological mix. The early naive treatments of the status issue, first critiqued by Quinn in 1977, were under increasing attack, supported by new research. It was time to update Quinn's article. A colleague and I undertook the task of summarizing trends and literature in the previous decade. Published in 1988, the article, "Anthropological Studies of the Status of Women Revisited: 1977–1987" (Mukhopadhyay and Higgins 1988), critically examined theoretical, methodological, and cultural barriers to objectively evaluating women's status cross-culturally. We described the florescence of ethnographically based writings covering diverse aspects of women's lives in a multitude of cultures around the world. This rich, grounded literature stimulated and provided empirical grounds for rejecting existing paradigms, hypotheses, and conceptual frameworks, including the universalizing theories used to analyze gender inequality. It also challenged the reliability and objectivity of traditional ethnographic data and methods, the positivist-empiricist orientation, the focus on cause–effect relations rather than the interpretation of processes.

These trends, thicker ethnographic description, reflexive critique of prevailing theories and concepts, narrowing scope, attention to context, variability, and agency; recognition of multiple social roles (vs. only "wives"), going beyond economics, exploring cultural symbols and meaning, continued into the 1990s and signaled a broader directional change within cultural anthropology. The rise of symbolic anthropology and postmodernism, the shift from more scientific to more literary orientation, and the perception, by some, of cognitive anthropology as anti-symbolism, overly formalistic, and oblivious to public culture (di Leonardo 1991),[8] widened the gap between cognitive and feminist anthropology.

The Shift from the Status of Women to Cultural Meaning

Perhaps the most dramatic change within feminist anthropology was the shift to cultural meaning. As early as the 1970s, some feminist anthropologists began to explore language–gender links. Ortner, in an oft-cited 1974 essay, applied Lévi-Strauss's proposed universal culture–nature dichotomy to the area of gender. By the early 1980s, however, Ortner's nature:culture::female:male analogy, and other prevailing binary conceptual frameworks (public vs. private/domestic spheres) were criticized as rooted in Western cultural models. Contributors to *Nature, Culture and Gender* (MacCormack and Strathern 1980) used cross-cultural ethnographic data to refute the universality of the categories, their meanings, their gender associations (i.e., male–culture, female–nature), and/or their link to gender rather than other social categories, like age. MacCormack, though not a linguist, pointed out that concepts like nature and culture are polysemic and metaphoric and can be applied inconsistently and selectively (Mukhopadhyay and Higgins 1988:480).

"Cultural constructionist" approaches produced accompanying critiques of universalizing Western categories, and explorations of local gender concepts and ideologies. Feminist anthropologists scrutinized cultural meanings of all aspects of gender, from menstruation, motherhood, paternity, the body, to clothing and other commodities. Ortner (and Whitehead) led the way with *Sexual Meanings: The Cultural Construction of Gender and Sexuality* (1981). Eventually Marxists and materialist-oriented scholars jumped on the bandwagon of cultural meaning, recognizing that culture and power reside not just in material goods but in the meanings they embody. By the end of the 1980s, gender scholarship, according to Ortner, exhibited a rapprochement between symbolic, structuralist, Marxist, and political-economic approaches and a merging of theoretical streams in a unified search for a "theory of action" and an emphasis on how cultural meanings inform and generate such action (Mukhopadhyay and Higgins 1988:486). Cognitive anthropology, interestingly, was not mentioned.

Nevertheless, from my perspective, feminist anthropological analyses, especially of the systematic aspects of gender concepts, were consistent with, if not derived from, cognitive anthropological understandings, including extensionist semantics (Kronenfeld 1996). Feminist anthropological analyses recognized that gender systems are embedded in and generated by local contexts. This applied to conceptual systems as well as other dimensions of inequality. Hence, attention shifted to intercultural and intracultural variability, to local descriptive theories, including of the biological facts of life.

Second, gender conceptions were viewed as a system of concepts, embedded in a larger conceptual and ideological system. Delaney, for example, located a Euro-American concept of paternity within the larger ideological edifice of Christianity, including a monotheistic, male-created, empowered universe. These ideas have always guided my own work (see Mukhopadhyay 2004).

Interestingly, in one of the few reviews of feminist anthropology that mentions cognitive anthropology, di Leonardo (1991) approvingly described recent work as moving from "a less scientistic and universalizing tack" to softer and more emotion-laden topics like marriage. She cites Lutz's (1988) critique of universalizing notions of emotion and gender and Holland and Quinn's 1987 volume, the latter described as "explicitly feminist work looking at the gendered character of cognition" (di Leonardo 1991:19), although I'm not sure I would characterize it that way.

Exploration of cultural meaning, gender-related linguistic and conceptual frameworks, gender and sexual categories, in more localized contexts, without universalizing assumptions, has continued (see Geller and Stockett 2006). However, it has primarily been feminist anthropologists not trained in cognitive anthropology who have undertaken the most thorough, sustained, gender-focused critical analyses and cross-cultural descriptions of gender-related cultural knowledge, cultural models, and cultural meanings. These feminist anthropologists, often with little background in formal linguistics, have appropriated linguistic approaches and terminology to unravel the language and conceptual structures of the domain of gender. They have undertaken the cognitive anthropologists' project of exploring key terms and other recurring phrases, metaphors, and implicit assumptions embedded in natural discourse (Strauss and Quinn 1997) … the natural discourse of gender.

Feminist symbolic anthropologists have subjected kinship and other anthropology theories to the kind of comparative critical analysis that one would have expected from cognitive anthropology (but see Ethos 2004). Collier and Yanagisako (1987) argued that an American folk model of kinship, in which the central element is the biological facts of sexual reproduction, has permeated and biased the entire field of kinship theory. They called for interrogating all gender–family–kinship folk theories, including the assumption that "motherhood" is the central defining concept of womanhood or, even, that "male" and "female" are universal, "natural" categories (see also Seymour 1999). Questioning the universality of male and female as either biological or social categories has intensified, influenced by Butler (1990), performance theory, and critiques of "heteronormativity" (see Moore 1994). Archaeologists question whether sexuality as a determinant of social identity is a universal phenomenon or a modern, Western phenomenon (see Voss 2008).[9]

Feminist anthropology also addressed issues of power, drawing on sources outside of cognitive anthropology to explore the power of language, especially discourse and narratives.[10] Feminist anthropologists began scrutinizing and unraveling expert discourses in Western social science, such as human origins narratives (see review in Mukhopadhyay and Higgins 1988; more recently in Geller and Stockett 2006). Emily Martin, citing the need to "wake up" "sleeping metaphors" in science, took on the medical profession, looking at female reproduction-related discourses, such as fertilization and menstruation. Others analyzed colonialist, nationalist, and development discourses as related to gender.

Critical analyses increasingly come from archaeologists and physical anthropologists (see Conkey and Gero 1997). Recently, Walrath (2006) applied both a critical literary perspective and genetic research data (on tri-nucleotide CAG repeat sequences in primates) to challenge the human birth narrative in paleoanthropology. She argues that this discourse problematizes the female body, posing an "inevitable obstetric difficulty" from bipedalism and a big-brained human baby, thus requiring cultural intervention (monogamy). Her own empirical research suggests an alternative interpretation.

Initial challenges to dominant discourses in academia produced a sometimes controversial critique of science, especially of its objectivity. I think such critiques are largely thoughtful and warranted and do not, contrary to some stereotypes (by some cognitive anthropologists and feminists), reject empirical data, hypothesis-testing, or the scientific enterprise. They essentially argue that science, like other cultural domains, and scientists, like other humans, are culturally located and have internalized cultural models which guide, often subconsciously, their theorizing, perceptions, and interpretations. In short, it is basic cognitive anthropology applied to science! Anyone familiar with old Western scientific arguments on gender (or race) can supply plenty of examples of culture shaping science.

Feminist anthropology, through its emphasis on agency and subjectivity has tried to understand both public culture and individuals, rejecting the fax model of culture that Strauss and Quinn (1997) rightly bemoan. Feminist research describes how individuals resist and reinterpret public culture, whether in religious, educational, or family contexts.[11]

Feminist anthropologists have gone beyond dominant discourses; they've analyzed how ordinary folks talk about politically charged topics like abortion, new reproductive technologies, female circumcision, and sexual preference (see Visweswaran 1997). Instead of homogenizing women, careful attention is given to ethnic, class, regional, sexual, and other areas of variability. Recent work addresses violence, analyzing individual discourses, interrogating categories and assumptions, such as the unmarked treatment of gendered (predominantly male) violence, linking it to larger discourses of militarism and the state (Das 2008).

Feminist anthropologists have explored the individual–culture nexus but, unlike cognitive anthropology, emphasize external social, economic, and political institutions, forces, and processes that generate public meanings and public culture. They try to elucidate gender symbolism by reference to broader structures of inequality in the society. Research explores the impact of global institutions on individuals, through gendered commodities like clothing or food, shop-floor (factory) experiences, and immigration. Feminist anthropologists have also probed popular culture, analyzing the stories told, learned, and drawn upon to interpret and act in the world (see Lewin 2006).

A Feminist Cognitive Anthropology: Does This Marriage Have a Future?

In retrospect, the appeal of feminist anthropology over the past decades has come primarily from its pursuit of the type of analysis I originally sought from cognitive anthropology. In short, feminist anthropologists, mainly without the aid of cognitive anthropology, have taken on the task of describing the cultural knowledge or, more broadly, the culture associated with the domain (semantic, conceptual, social) of gender. Feminist anthropology has probed native or emic cultural meanings of the big semantic and conceptual categories (male, female), the language of gender at the discourse level, and the larger conceptual and ideological frameworks (cultural models) in which they are embedded. Feminist anthropology has tried to link cultural meaning and action and to explore the relationship between the individual and culture, although with more emphasis on public culture and institutions.

Not surprisingly, then, I see the two sub-disciplines, especially given recent developments in cognitive anthropology, as compatible and having many common goals. Both are fundamentally interested in cultural meaning, in the relationship between culture and the individual, in how humans individually and collectively construct, internalize, and use culture. Both seek culture in part through studying language, in analyzing categories, narrative, discourse, for clues to cultural models, to conceptual frameworks that shape thought, emotion, motives, and action. Both have developed insights and approaches that, I think, can be fruitfully shared and mutually beneficial.

What Cognitive Anthropology Offers

Perhaps more than anything, cognitive anthropology offers a more sophisticated conceptual framework and methodology for eliciting, analyzing, and understanding culture, especially through language, and for constructing "a descriptive theory of specific folk knowledge" (Kronenfeld 2008). Cognitive anthropology pioneered systematic methods for analyzing language–culture connections. Recent advances, especially dealing with larger constructions and discourse in natural settings, offer a more empirically based, sophisticated approach to gender-related language than is currently employed (see Quinn 2005). Such methods would enable feminist anthropology to go beyond the current, almost metaphorical, application of linguistic theory to the analysis of cultural meanings and cultural categories.[12] My own recent work on gender utilized these methods, along with other techniques (see also Strauss 2004).

Cognitive anthropology also offers a sophisticated conceptualization of both language and cognition, including how cultural knowledge is structured, encoded, stored, retrieved, processed, distributed. The "cultural models" concept and approach is spreading beyond cognitive anthropology. Such understandings, if nothing else, allow us to evaluate the validity of our descriptions and analyses (Kronenfeld 2008). I also think the decision models approach, if modified and combined with other research strategies, can be useful to feminist anthropologists, as my gendered science research in India demonstrates.

Feminist anthropology can draw on cognitive anthropology's traditional commitment to science to improve its own standards of data collection and analysis and to recommit itself to theory-building, albeit of limited scope. Social justice and equity are furthered, not retarded, by applying critical standards to data and theory. Many feminist anthropologists recognize this and feel it is time to return to (if indeed they ever left) an enlightened science of gender (see Mascia-Lees and Sharpe 2000; Quinn 2000). This includes accepting some simplification in theory-building, a renewed commitment to more systematic cross-cultural comparison, and acknowledgment that infinite, obsessive concern with difference is unproductive (see Moore 2006).

Feminist anthropology can benefit from cognitive anthropology's probing the actual processes through which individuals internalize culture, construct or perform selves, interpret and apply cultural schema. Psychological and cognitive anthropologists, such as Strauss and Quinn (1997), Seymour (2004), and Mattingly et al. (2008) note, correctly, that despite a commitment to agency and subjectivity, feminist anthropology has not drawn sufficiently upon psychological anthropology understandings. But feminist anthropologists from other traditions, such as Moore (2006), also argue that individual processes of agency have not been adequately studied or theorized. Indeed, Moore argues that in the name of agency, we have instead simply produced more essentialist models.

What Feminist Anthropology Can Offer

Feminist anthropology pioneered critiques of academic and other expert theories of gender, exposing hidden assumptions, culturally rooted categories and binary oppositions, and false universals. This critical stance towards received wisdom should be extended to cognitive and psychological anthropology. Prevailing theory about the formation of gender identity, sexual preference, transgendered identities, et cetera is ripe for study by cognitive anthropologists.

Useful also are thoughtful critiques of science, especially on the limits of objectivity, and a greater emphasis on reflexivity, especially the impact of one's position (and definitely, one's gender) on how one selects, approaches, prioritizes, and theorizes problems. Positionality issues also affect our informants. I am still surprised that some cognitive anthropologists are surprised that gender might be a significant variable to consider in studies of values (D'Andrade 2008), empathy (Strauss 2004), or other cultural conceptualizations. Gender is a powerful defining principle in our own and in many other societies; and women constitute approximately half of the population. How can we describe a culture or put forth cultural models without asking about gendered versions of those models? How can we talk about cultural construction of selves without theorizing gendered selves?

Feminist anthropology's critique of universalizing theories, of over-homogenizing culture, its emphasis on variability, on difference, on gender, ethnicity, class nationality, on intersectionality, has value. Cognitive anthropological analyses have tended to downplay or even ignore difference, blithely describing "American" (or "Indian") culture on the basis of small, narrowly constituted, selective samples of informants. The question of multiple (not just distributed) cultural schema, cultural models, semantic meanings, versions of culture is a thorny one, but one that cannot be ignored, especially as our research increasingly takes place in large-scale, complex societies.

Cognitive anthropology, like feminist anthropology, can focus more on research domains that have contemporary significance for real people. Given limited resources, why not select research problems with social justice or policy implications? More pragmatically, contemporary students seem attracted to fields which (and professors who) address current social problems, justice issues, including gender inequality in its various manifestations. Images matter ... and images of sub-disciplines attract (or don't attract) graduate students, sustain graduate departments, and produce academic lineages.

Cognitive anthropology must deal more effectively with the issue of power. This requires greater consideration of the world outside the individual, whether the intimate social contexts of everyday interactions or the broader public culture, regardless of how distributed, and the powerful external forces which shape individual lives, perceptions, and choices. Clearly, individual schema do not develop in a power vacuum.

"Popular culture" exemplifies how some cultural forms, produced by small segments of society, have enormous impact on the public culture individuals experience and, to varying degrees, internalize. US children experience approximately 40 hours per week of mainly commercial media, including music videos, video games, and television. Researchers have documented the powerful impact of these visual images, the kinds of stories children (and adults) are learning about gender, sexuality, entitlement, and violence. Without the benefit of cognitive anthropology training, apparently, scholars have contributed insightful (and frightening) analyses of how cultural models of gender are transmitted and acquired, and how they mediate interpretations and behavior, including sexual coercion (see Media Education Foundation videos and narration in Dreamworlds, Tough Guise).

Cognitive feminist anthropologists can apply our theoretical and methodological insights to exploring in greater depth how and to what extent and under what conditions powerful popular culture images are internalized, utilized, resisted, manifested. This is particularly important cross-culturally as popular culture becomes more global. And it is what Strauss and Quinn (1997) call for: looking more systematically and intensively at how real individuals experience public culture.[13]

The Future

I end this paper more enthusiastic about future synergy between feminist and cognitive anthropology than when I began. In some ways, both sub-disciplines are marginal to the centers of power, have not been able to claim center stage and define the prestige topics for the past several decades. Both feminists and cognitive anthropologists have seen the center stage taken over by other folks (males, symbolic-poststructuralists-interpretivists) and have been under pressure to follow their lead or be confined to obscurity. Dominant groups *lead* ... or rather, are *read* and *cited*. Marginal groups ... well, the opposite follows.

Perhaps, as Quinn (2000) suggests in an extremely thoughtful and disturbing paper, this is why powerful male anthropologists have generally neither been interested in nor felt compelled to read feminist anthropology. But the power dynamics may be even greater for marginalized groups. This may partly explain the cognitive–feminist anthropology divide I described at the beginning of this paper. Maybe this also explains why the special edition of *Ethos* on feminist psychological anthropology (2004) seems to have gone unnoticed or at least uncited by some major figures in cognitive anthropology, despite the inclusion of at least two articles by feminist cognitive anthropologists (Strauss and Quinn), and one article whose title specifically refers to a "feminist cognitive anthropology" (Mukhopadhyay 2004). It might shed light on why some former "cognitive" or "feminist" anthropologists are dropping these labels from their self-descriptions (Ethos 2004; Quinn 2005). And perhaps this accounts for the gender of cognitive anthropology (virtually all male) and Association for Feminist Anthropology (virtually all female) sessions and volumes. But, on a hopeful note for the future, my 2008 Association for Feminist Anthropology-sponsored "Gender and Politics" session had both male and female feminist cognitive anthropologist panelists and audience participants.

NOTES

1 Feminist anthropology has created its own "origin stories" which emphasize certain lineages while excluding others. Several prominent reviews ignored the seminal *Annual Review* articles by Quinn (1977) and Mukhopadhyay and Higgins (1988). Cognitive anthropologists are rarely mentioned, although see di Leonardo (1991).

2 I realize now that by "actual" processes I meant not ultimately the immediate ones but the larger extra-individual processes through which individuals came to utilize cultural precedents in most situations.

3 UCR graduate school in the 1970s, and my dissertation adviser, Martin Orans, was committed to scientific approaches of all types.

4 Academics were still arguing over whether women were intrinsically better at typing than males, part of the prevailing general model of biological determinism.

5 My methods were influenced by sociology, home of family research, but also by cross-cultural "time allocation" studies.

6 I worked on the Chancellor's Office's final report and subsequently developed a detailed plan for implementing the report recommendations at the San Francisco State University campus.

7 Holland and Eisenhart's work took more of a "cultural models" than "decision models" approach but included questionnaires and surveys developed for the project, thus providing a larger database for statistical analysis. Creating culturally meaningful questionnaires from ethnosemantically elicited data came from early cognitive anthropologists. My India research utilized these approaches and produced a "database" of over 5,000 questionnaires of various types (Mukhopadhyay 2001).

8 Strauss and Quinn (1997:ch. 9) describe Geertz's damning critique of cognitive anthropology's definition of culture as "cultural knowledge." But I recall stereotypes of cognitive anthropology as not interested in "cultural meanings"!

9 Voss's (2008) recent review of feminist archaeology is an excellent introduction to the volume and quality of work over the past three decades. It also belies the stereotype of feminist anthropology as solely humanist-literary, anti-empirical, anti-science.

10 Common references are to Foucault, Kristeva, feminist psychologist Judith Butler, semiotics (Peirce, Fernandez), occasionally Lakoff and Johnson.

11 Cognitive anthropologists have always, at least implicitly, recognized agency. In fact, decision models seemed to explicitly start with this assumption! But "agency" and "subjectivity" were viewed by many feminists, in the mid-1980s, as new "discoveries."

12 Feminist anthropologists, for example, study the meanings attached to consumption objects, and how their meanings shift over time and context. They often employ linguistic concepts, especially from Saussure.

13 Psychologists have studied the impact of violent and "seductive" pornography on male arousal. But I believe they measured "arousal" through physical sensors rather than doing detailed interviewing and analysis of talk. Anthropologists working in the USA are often not fully aware of the research of sibling disciplines who focus on the USA. There is too much to read. Yet we risk reinventing the wheel (and a crude one at that) when we turn our eye on American culture.

REFERENCES

Brettell, Caroline B., and Carolyn F. Sargent, eds.
2005[1993] Gender in Cross-Cultural Perspective. 4th edition. Upper Saddle, NJ: Pearson Prentice Hall.
Burton, Mike, L. Brudner, and Doug White
1977 A Model of the Sexual Division of Labor. American Ethnologist 4:227–251.
Butler, Judith
1990 Gender Trouble: Feminism and the Subversion of Identity. New York: Routledge.
Collier, Jane, and Sylvia Yanagisako, eds.
1987 Gender and Kinship. Stanford: Stanford University Press.
Conkey, Margaret, and Joan M. Gero
1997 Programme to Practice: Gender and Feminism in Archeology. Annual Review of Anthropology 26:411–437.
D'Andrade, Roy
1966 Sex Differences and Cultural Institutions. *In* The Development of Sex Differences. Eleanor Maccoby, ed. Pp. 174–204. Stanford: Stanford University Press.
2008 A Study of Personal and Cultural Values. Basingstoke: Palgrave Macmillan.
D'Andrade, Roy, and Claudia Strauss, eds.
1992 Human Motives and Cultural Models. Cambridge: Cambridge University Press.
Das, Veena
2008 Violence, Gender and Subjectivity. Annual Review of Anthropology 37:283–299.
di Leonardo, Micaela, ed.
1991 Gender at the Crossroads of Knowledge. Berkeley: University of California Press.
Dreamsworlds
2007 Dreamsworlds 3: Desire, Sex and Power in Music Video. Sut Jhally, writer, narrator, and editor. Media Education Foundation.
Ethos
2004 Feminist Psychological Anthropology. Special issue, Ethos 32(4).
Geller, Pamela L., and Miranda K. Stockett, eds.
2006 Feminist Anthropology: Past, Present, and Future. Philadelphia: University of Pennsylvania Press.
Greenberg, Joseph H.
1966 Language Universals with Special Reference to Feature Hierarchies. The Hague: Mouton.
Holland, Dorothy
1992 The Woman Who Climbed Up the House: Some Limitations of Schema Theory. *In* New Directions in Psychological Anthropology. Theodore Schwartz, Geoffrey M. White, and Catherine A. Lutz, eds. Pp. 68–79. Cambridge: Cambridge University Press.
Holland, Dorothy, and Margaret Eisenhart
1990 Educated in Romance. Chicago: University of Chicago Press.
Holland, Dorothy, and Naomi Quinn, eds.
1987 Cultural Models in Language and Thought. Cambridge: Cambridge University Press.
Kronenfeld, David
1996 Plastic Glasses and Church Fathers. New York: Oxford University Press.
2008 Culture, Society, and Cognition. Berlin: Mouton de Gruyter.
Levinson, Bradley A., Douglous E. Foley, and Dorothy C. Holland, eds.
1996 The Cultural Production of the Educated Person: Critical Ethnographies of Schooling and Local Practice. Albany: SUNY Press.
Lewin, Ellen, ed.
2006 Feminist Anthropology. Malden, MA: Blackwell.

Lutz, Catherine
1988 Unnatural Emotions: Everyday Sentiments in a Micronesian Atoll and Their Challenge to Western Theory. Chicago: University of Chicago Press.
Maccoby Eleanor, ed.
1966 The Development of Sex Differences. With contributions by Roy D'Andrade and others. Stanford: Stanford University Press.
MacCormack, Carol, and Marilyn Strathern, eds.
1980 Nature, Culture and Gender. Cambridge: Cambridge University Press.
Mascia-Lees, Frances, and Nancy Johnson Black
2000 Gender and Anthropology. Prospect Heights, IL: Waveland.
Mascia-Lees, Frances E., and Patricia Sharpe
2000 Taking a Stand in a Postfeminist World: Toward an Engaged Cultural Criticism. Albany: SUNY Press.
Mattingly, Cheryl, Nancy C. Lutkehaus, and C. Jason Throop
2008 Bruner's Search for Meaning. Ethos 36(1):1–28.
Moore, Henrietta L.
1994 A Passion for Difference. Bloomington: Indiana University Press.
2006 The Future of Gender or the End of a Brilliant Career? *In* Feminist Anthropology: Past, Present, and Future. Pamela L. Geller and Miranda K. Stockett, eds. Pp. 23–42. Philadelphia: University of Pennsylvania Press.
Morgen, Sandra, ed.
1989 Gender and Anthropology. Washington, DC: American Anthropological Association.
Mukhopadhyay, Carol C.
1980 The Sexual Division of Labor in the Family: A Decision-Making Approach. Ph.D. dissertation, University of California, Riverside. Ann Arbor, MI: University Microfilms.
1982 Sati or Shakti: Women, Culture, and Politics in India. *In* Perspectives on Power. Jean O'Barr, ed. Pp.11–26. Durham, NC: Center for International Studies, Duke University.
1984 Testing a Decision Model of the Sexual Division of Labor. Human Organization 43(3):227–242.
1994 Family Structure and Indian Women's Participation in Science and Engineering. *In* Women, Education and Family Structure in India. C. C. Mukhopadhyay and S. Seymour, eds. Pp. 103–133. Boulder, CO: Westview.
2001 The Cultural Context of Gendered Science: The Case of India. http://www.sjsu.edu/people/carol.mukhopadhyay.
2004 A Feminist Cognitive Anthropology: The Case of Women and Mathematics. Ethos 32(4):458–492.
Mukhopadhyay, Carol, and Patricia J. Higgins
1988 Anthropological Studies of the Status of Women Revisited: 1977–1987. Annual Review of Anthropology 17:461–495.
Mukhopadhyay, Carol C., Rosemary Henze, and Yolanda T. Moses
2007 How Real is Race? Lanham, MD: Rowman and Littlefield.
Nerlove, Sara
1974 Women's Workload and Infant Feeding Practices. Ethnology 13(2):207–214.
Ortner, Sherry, and Harriet Whitehead, eds.
1981 Sexual Meanings: The Cultural Construction of Gender and Sexuality. Cambridge: Cambridge University Press.
Quinn, Naomi
1977 Anthropological Studies of Women's Status. Annual Review of Anthropology 6:181–225.
2000 The Divergent Case of Cultural Anthropology. *In* Primate Encounters: Models of Science, Gender, and Society. Shirley C. Strum and Linda M. Fedigan, eds. Pp. 223–242. Chicago: University of Chicago Press.

Quinn, Naomi, ed.
2005 Finding Culture in Talk. New York: Palgrave Macmillan.
Rosaldo, Michelle, and Louise Lamphere, eds.
1974 Woman, Culture and Society. Stanford: Stanford University Press.
Schwartz, Theodore, Geoffrey M. White, and Catherine A. Lutz, eds.
1992 New Directions in Psychological Anthropology. Cambridge: Cambridge University Press.
Seymour, Susan C.
1999 Women, Family, and Child Care in India. Cambridge: Cambridge University Press.
2004 Introduction. Special issue, "Psychological Anthropology," Ethos 32(4):416–431.
Strauss, Claudia
2004 Is Empathy Gendered and If So, Why? Special issue, "Psychological Anthropology," Ethos 32(4):432–457.
Strauss, Claudia, and Naomi Quinn
1997 A Cognitive Theory of Cultural Meaning. Cambridge: Cambridge University Press.
Tough Guise
2002 Tough Guise: Violence, Media, and the Crisis in Masculinity. Sut Jhally, dir. Susan Ericsson and Sanjay Talreja, producers. Jackson Katz and Jeremy Earp, writers. Media Education Foundation.
Tyler, Steven, ed.
1969 Cognitive Anthropology. New York: Holt, Rinehart and Winston.
Visweswaran, Kamala
1997 Histories of Feminist Ethnography. Annual Review of Anthropology 26:591–621.
Voss, Barbara L.
2008 Sexuality Studies in Archeology. Annual Review of Anthropology 37:317–336.
Walrath, Dana
2006 Gender, Genes, and the Evolution of Human Birth. *In* Feminist Anthropology: Past, Present, and Future. Pamela L. Geller and Miranda K. Stockett, eds. Pp. 55–70. Philadelphia: University of Pennsylvania Press.

CHAPTER 22

Sociality in Cognitive and Sociocultural Anthropologies: The Relationships Aren't Just Additive

Lynn Thomas

INTRODUCTION

This chapter examines the various kinds of potential relationships between cognitive anthropology and sociocultural anthropology that have remained neglected to this date.[1] Its object is to suggest in some respects what a cognitively oriented social anthropology might be like. It presumes a shared goal of both cognitive and social anthropology to produce theoretically informed, and informing, ethnographic work. Sociocultural anthropological work of course gives serious attention to social aspects of the human life-ways it examines. Cognitive organization – and even social cognitive organization – is often submerged and made subservient to other issues (see the example from Philippe Bourgois below).

Little work in sociocultural anthropology is informed by the central concerns of standard American-style cognitive anthropology (see D'Andrade 1995; Brown 2006; Colby, Chapter 11, this volume). In addition to American cognitive anthropology, there is also the work of Sperber (see below for a glimpse of one aspect of that important work), and some of Bloch's work (see in particular Bloch 2005; and Bloch and Sperber 2002 on the reconstruction of a classical social anthropological problem). This important work is quite relevant to sociocultural anthropology and is underappreciated. It might seem that cognitive anthropological work is just too

A Companion to Cognitive Anthropology, First Edition. Edited by David B. Kronenfeld, Giovanni Bennardo, Victor C. de Munck, and Michael D. Fischer.

peripheral to the central goals of understanding and, where possible, also explaining the patterning of people's lives and life-ways. But the appearance is misleading. And we can find ways to yet improve cognitive anthropological work so that it might better help with sociocultural anthropological analysis. Much that is valuable – and too often also underappreciated – consists of much work in cognitive anthropology conducted matter-of-factly as a part of the common endeavor with its parent, or supervening, discipline.[2]

The Role of Cognitive Anthropology in American Cultural Anthropology

There are important antecedents (see Boas, Sapir) to the cognitive anthropology that developed in the 1960s, mainly in the United States. But the aim here is to stick closely to the present day and to suggest lines of thinking that might better integrate at least one variety of social anthropology and some threads of current cognitive anthropology. Persons interested in cognitive anthropology have suggested that it has fallen on hard times; in one version it is "vanishing" from the cognitive sciences and in another its practice in social and cultural anthropology is quite weak (Brown 2006). There is little doubt that there is some truth to such claims, although strong caveats also need to be registered. The first is that one needn't look far to find full-bodied and vibrant cognitive anthropological work, as is attested by the papers in this volume, and the work to which these papers refer.

Any diagnosis of the condition of cognitive anthropology needs to attend to sources of its condition. Cognitive anthropology began as a small part of the small discipline of anthropology. Cognitive anthropology never took over, nor was it in a position to threaten to take over, the discipline and unify it. Cultural anthropology has had an intellectual influence on its sister disciplines in the social sciences disproportionate to its size. One prominent example is the spread of distinctively anthropological culture concepts to other social sciences, however fatuously deployed in some contexts, as when culture plays the role of leftover residual, after politics and economics have been "factored out." Another important example is the practice of ethnography – however thinly practiced in the other disciplines. Cognitive anthropology seemed for a time poised to garner recognition for significant influence in social and cultural anthropology in reforming how fieldwork is understood. Giving concepts carefully detailed analysis and setting higher standards for ethnographic description and explanation are among the important practices by which cognitive anthropology has and could still serve the whole discipline and other social scientists as well.

However, even as cognitive anthropology was being consolidated, American cultural anthropologists were beginning in large numbers to more firmly disavow "scientific" research practices, such as those espoused by virtually all of the important cognitive anthropologists. The anti-science mindset in anthropology led to one or two department split-ups and, eventually, the massive disavowal of training in statistics or other formal methods of research (see many of the selections in Moore and Sanders 2006). Consistent with these developments is the expression of concern by senior anthropologists that anthropologists decreasingly do serious fieldwork. Thus, just at the time when cognitive anthropologists were striving to practice a scientific approach to ethnographic data collection and analysis, a majority of anthropologists came to understand scientific approaches to be unsuited to the discipline.[3]

Additionally, by the 1970s many scholars in the disciplines of the history and the philosophy of science, were rethinking the purportedly dominant views of how science works: there was a shift from positivist prescriptions to Kuhnian "paradigms" (see Kuhn 1996[1962]; Weinberg 1998; Chalmers 1999) and, less so, Feyerabendian anti-method notions of "anything goes" (Feyerabend 1987; Chalmers 1999). Significant numbers of social scientists were also pushing hard in the direction of interpretive or hermeneutic approaches. In what seems a somewhat retrograde movement, the interpretive approaches were often conceived to be opposite to what these practitioners understood to be scientific.[4] Some interpretivist and hermeneutic postmodernist scholars seemed to define their work (in significant part) in the very terms of the "enemy" camp of scientifically oriented workers as the privileged approach to the study of culture or society. Culture concepts were caught up in some postmodern(ist) discussions in anthropology, just as they were important in some varieties of the "culture wars" debates. In one respect cognitive anthropology was well ahead of the postmodern game: cognitive anthropologists were increasingly dissatisfied with conceptions of culture as homogeneous bounded wholes, favoring a more shreds-and-patches, contingent, and dynamic understanding of culture. Anthropologists were in general working to come to terms with the multivocality and fluid assemblages of materials associated with culture at least a decade prior to that multiplicity becoming a cause célèbre of American postmodernists. Despite the evident agreement that the concept of culture needed to be reconsidered in fundamental ways and a consensual rejection of the homogeneous holistic approach between cognitive, postmodern, and (for lack of a better word) "mainstream" cultural anthropologists, there could be no comfortable integration or "live and let live" accommodation of a science and anti-science approach under the banner of cultural anthropology. As anthropology turned in important respects more and more anti-science, and since cognitive anthropology cast its lot with science (but see Tyler 1978, 1984), the field simply presumed the demise of cognitive anthropology and lost its relevance to most practicing cultural anthropologists. Though there has been a revival of cognitive anthropology, it is mostly connected, and marginally so, to sub-disciplines in psychology and to the interdisciplinary field of "cognitive sciences." To date there has been little attempt to discover or find a niche for cognitive anthropology within mainstream social and cultural anthropology.

In what follows I would like to characterize what a socially oriented cognitive anthropology might look like. This hypothetical discipline – "cognitive social anthropology" – would be an interpretive discipline that has well-developed sociological concepts which do not reduce human life-ways to descriptions of cultures (for some of the issues involved in this claim, see below and see Moerman 1988; Carrithers 1992, 2001). Such a cross-fertilization would focus on viewing local epistemologies in terms of social-cum-cognitive concepts and processes. The aim would be to interpret the mechanisms by which cognitive processes are tied to cultural and sociological processes and context. That is, how what we can say about cognition interrelates with what we can say about social life, human actions, and people's actual understandings or interpretations of both. Cognitive social anthropologists would need to be attentive to moral concepts and moral cognition, remembering that the emerging social sciences were once "moral sciences." Further it would need to attend, where appropriate, to hot as well as cold cognition (Elster 1983).

The Lie of the Land

In the following sections of this chapter, then, I will work out some of the aspects of this cognitive social anthropology program. I will illustrate four instances of social-cognitive work that helps to explain certain localized (in space and time) patterns of social-cultural life worlds. In the first instance, I will first present two versions of interpretive approaches, one by Weber, the other by Wittgenstein. These two approaches illustrate a range of possibilities for a cognitive social anthropology along an individual–social dimension, with Weber representing the former end and Wittgenstein the latter. The second example presents one small example of Dan Sperber's work, which is the only attempt I am aware of to bridge in a strong way the divide between social-cultural anthropology and cognitive science and to integrate them. The third example is that of a once influential epistemology, crafted by the philosopher Quine (and Ullian) for educational purposes. This example is meant to stress the potential gains from in-depth examination of epistemologies (and ontologies) by anthropologists. The example raises the question of how this most cognitive of cognitive matters, a version of meta-cognition, has been omitted from the agenda of cognitive anthropology. Of course different parts of epistemological formations can be emphasized by different practitioners, and Quine and Ullian's effort illustrated here may have been understood as a unified composite. The fourth and last example is an effort to bring a number of elements of the paper together. It also brings political economy, and with it power asymmetries, into the picture. So two of our instances of topics are methodological, the interpretive example and the snippet of Sperber's work. The example of an epistemology can be understood as baseline cognition. The example from Bourgois is a particularly rich putting together of many elements relevant to the concerns of the chapter. Bourgois attends to a broadened notion of political economy and political economic history. Cognitive social anthropology could be more aware of history (not just cultural or language history) and more cognizant of the importance of political economy in people's lives and life-ways than cognitive anthropology has been and is at present. As understood here, political economy has to do with power and resources in human social life, their interrelationships, and their relationships with other facets of life.

With all the considerations dealt with in this chapter, it will serve the reader well to understand that the author of this paper doesn't presume that some kind of (misplaced) holism means that all the concerns treated here are items to be checked off on a to-do list. The instinct many cognitive anthropologists have to take small problems and work them in detail has been productive of some of the best work in the subdiscipline and should continue to be honored in its reformulation, whatever directions that takes.

A special word about Sperber and Carrithers (the latter is as yet unintroduced, but see below). Both recognize how variation and change are central aspects of how sociocultural patterns operate. Sperber has framed his epidemiology in terms of a number of interacting factors that go part of the way toward formulating and accounting

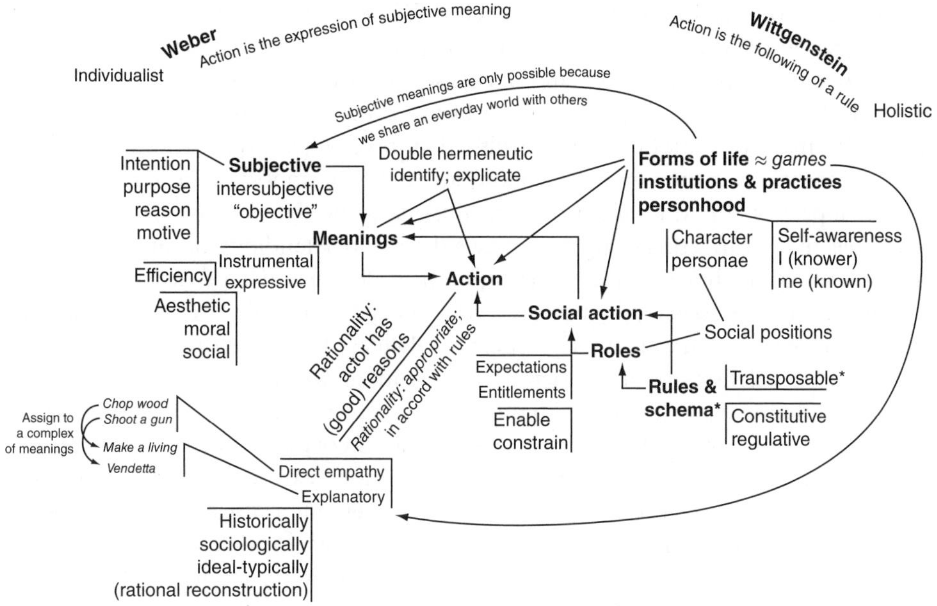

Figure 22.1 Interpretive social science: Hollis's compromise (based on Hollis 2002 and Sewell 1992).
* See note 6.

for such facts: one part of his formulation suggests how the epidemiology works in terms of flows of information internally (in the human mind) and publicly (here understood as the world outside the mind, including that of another person or of other people in the environment). Information flows from the mind-internal component to the mind-external one and vice versa. The flows in these two directions alternate indefinitely for the lifetime of the sociocultural pattern examined. Revisions in the information and the nature and causation of its flow can be expected, variably, to occur along the way (hence Sperber's rejection of Richard Dawkins's memetic approach). I will address Carrithers later, all too briefly, but be forewarned that Sperber and Carrithers might find issues that separate them. Let us, then, proceed to work through the examples and illustrations.[5]

Interpretive Social Science

Martin Hollis (2002) gives an unusually complete rendering of two important varieties of interpretive social science, Weberian and Wittgensteinian. Figure 22.1 is meant to capture and integrate the main elements and relations of Hollis's discussion.[6] On the diagonal from the upper left to lower right are items in bold face. These are central common elements of the two programs. Elements above and to the right of the diagonal represent specifically Wittgensteinian elements or emphases. To the lower left are Weberian elements. The arrows represent major substantive flows of elements of meaning and their characterizations as to type and function. While it might not be a mistake to understand the diagram as suggesting that Wittgenstein provides theoretically some of the social considerations that are implicit in Weber's work, it does, however, seem that Weber and Wittgenstein are not entirely compatible in this respect. Some have chosen one more than the other, and of course Weber has been the vastly more influential of the two. But perhaps something like a composite of the two is a (part of a) default for many practitioners of sociocultural anthropology: explication of meanings, their interrelations, their coherence conditions, and their import in life-ways.[7]

One appeal of the interpretive program seems to be the promise that it is more adaptable than competing programs to yielding understandings of alternative, layered, meanings as they occur in differing human life-ways. Even that basic appeal is somewhat blunted however by the ease with which a seemingly "deep" and close or "experience near" rendering of, say, aspects of Balinese life, turns out upon reflection to suggest a celebration of exoticized American notions. For example, Geertz's famous rendering of Balinese cockfights might seem to an observer to depend on what looks a lot like an American-style hydraulic theory of emotions at work. Do Balinese share that theory? Though they may it is not clear from Geertz's work that they do. Or consider Geertz's book on Balinese statescraft as theater. While suggesting to some a profoundly different, commensurable pattern to statescraft compared with European patterns, it might also suggest to a student of American politics something not so similar to how things work here. Thus, once more, we do not know if Geertz's interpretations, and their appeal to (some) North Atlantic readers are based on readers' prior, given, cognitive schemes and theories of emotions, social relations, and statecraft or are actually derived from his observations, independent of his putative ethnocentricism. This could be akin to the surmise of Charles Taylor to the effect that Western observers may export to their studies of "others," a mentality that sharply distinguishes the instrumental (us) from the expressive (them). Under this reading, Geertz might be foisting on others a dualism that stems from his own society.

The sometimes stolid cognitive anthropological emphasis on working out objective analyses (see D'Andrade 1995) is an already well-established antidote to interpretive flights of fancy. But it is not clear that either cognitive anthropologists or interpretivists have created a high road to prevent ethnocentric readings of concepts (see the comments above on Geertz, and Wierzbicka's occasional criticisms of cognitive anthropological work (e.g., Wierzbicka 1989:n. 1)), nor presumably has anyone else, though perhaps Wierzbicka comes as close as anybody.

Cognitive anthropology seems to need an interpretive component, if for no other reason than to help remind practitioners that meanings (or individual instances of same) live in the contexts not only of sets of meanings but also of practices and perhaps more importantly in the latter. With these considerations in mind, something like a synthesis of Weberian and Wittgensteinian approaches such as attempted in Figure 22.1 might make sense, if steered clear of excessive holistic integration. In virtue of its strong emphasis on sociocultural meaning, interpretive anthropology needs cognitive anthropology for its attention to the close analysis of concepts and conceptual relations. And cognitive anthropology needs concerted prior attention to sociality. This brings us, then, directly, so to speak, face to face with cultural forms.

The culture concepts in cognitive anthropology presented some distinct advantages over traditional culture concepts: investigations of "intracultural" variation, as in Romney and D'Andrade's (1964) and Kronenfeld's (1980) work on kinship categories; its pioneering work on the internal structure of concepts (Kronenfeld 1975,

1996). Culture is already pluralized internally in these works, ahead of the game. The internal heterogeneity suggests, moreover, an external one by de-essentializing conceptualizations. But this work also carried disadvantages as well, most notably perhaps its somewhat sometimes narrowed, and decontextualized, construals of cognition and culture and its equation of the two.

Cultural anthropologists sometimes work with a conceptualization of culture that fits well with cognitive anthropology's strengths while not suffering its defects. Some greater explicitness on this culture concept might be helpful (see for broader considerations Eagleton 2000, 2007[1991]; Shweder 2001). What follows is a brief attempt to construct a culture concept that allows pluralization while maintaining some element of what I take to be an appropriate general conceptualization of the contexts of cultures. In brief, the culture concept I have in mind holds culture to be *the social and mental life of meanings, especially in and of practices.* That's it. Somewhat elaborated, cultures consist of socially produced, reproduced, and distributed sets of meaningful practices. The "meaningfulness" is internally organized as conceptual sets, and as "practices" externally organized in divisions of labor and other social divisions. Further, this conceptualization includes the meanings and valences (i.e., good and bad in moral senses and emotional import) integral with practices.

Although it is not treated here, it is important to recognize that sociocultural patterning in the formulation suggested by this chapter, is understood to be spatially and temporally localized in communicationally contiguous units,[8] in human bodies, families, and communities, for example, and their reproductive cycles (Goody 1958); and maximally in longer-term eras and regions of varying scales (see, for example, Goody 2010, and the very different work of Friedman and Friedman 2008a, 2008b).

One of the original emphases in American anthropology was on the sharedness of the culture, but the sharedness was always problematic. It sometimes masked a tacit claim that a culture is homogeneous tradition, passively so. Sperber's thinking about cultural distributions helps here (1996; see Figure 22.2). In developing his epidemiology of representations (aka, in this chapter, "meanings"), he holds a methodological individualist's construal of meaning, though with ample room for socialization. Consider how much room there is for social play in the intermediate parts of the diagram, and especially in the lower left part. The figure illustrates his sense that cultural representations are those that last longer among more people, without a set boundary where "individual" leaves off and "culture" begins. For representations to last longer among more people they need to be externally expressed. And for their communication, of course, they must be present in interpersonal contexts in formats such that their meanings (or something similar to them) are appropriated, actually inferred, and reproduced in forms that have purchase in the frameworks of meanings and purposes of the persons in these social settings. But here the discussion must take a turn. The next three elements of the definition given above of culture as the social life of meanings need to be brought in, and of them, practices matter most. Configurations and reconfigurations of meanings don't just happen. They are involved in the doings of life typically in public contexts (in the sense of Sperber). And some of the more important doings of life are sets of actions, and of activities systematized as full-fledged practices, deployable from available or extemporaneously built meanings and resources. These activity sets and practices have direction and import in people's concrete daily lives and are sometimes configured as singular institutions in their own right. Meanings

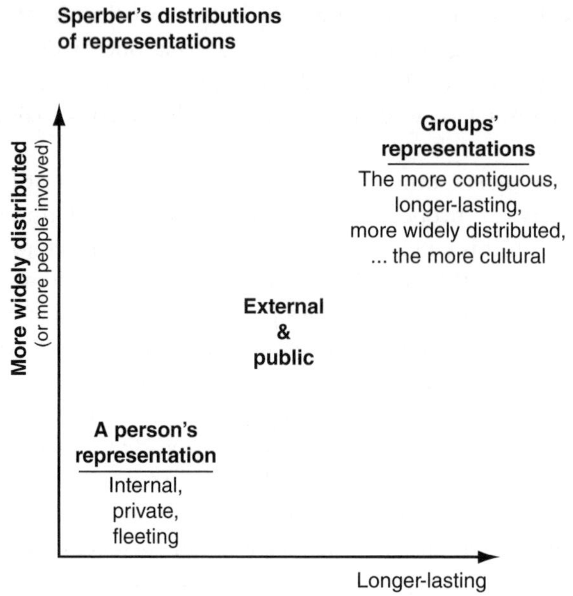

Figure 22.2 Sperber's distributions of representations (based on Sperber 1996).

of course are also much involved in the nuts and bolts of practices, and practices are materially involved in the world as well, and entail material configurations of resources. See Figure 22.3 illustrating Bourgois's work for concrete instances interpretable in terms of these rather abstracted – decontextualized – understandings.

Noticing that cultural patterns are localized in space and time in contiguous units and may have wider and larger-scale temporal and spatial distributions is part of this picture. It may also be the case that spatial and temporal sociocultural forces and movements developed elsewhere may be separately brought forward so as to impinge upon and affect redeployments of other resources–meanings–practices sets. There are also the possibilities that Jonathan Friedman has drawn attention to – replications of sociocultural patterns in societies located in very different historical settings but with similar reactions to similar trajectories of their respective world systems.

There is more, though, to the prospects for keeping nuts and bolts in mind, something that one can begin to do by maintaining strong connections with Sperber's epidemiology of representations. A certain kind of bridging of the sort that might be especially helpful here is strikingly well illustrated by Bloch and Sperber (2002). They take as a deceptively simple case in point a classical problem in social anthropology addressed by Junod, Radcliffe-Brown, Fortes, and Goody. The problem involves a sister's son's rights to his mother's brother's properties in societies with patrilineal descent groups.

Interesting though they are, this is not the place to rehearse the various arguments that have been attempted as explanations of the pattern of privileging the sister's son. Whether the pattern is unitary is a problem that Bloch and Sperber discuss but cannot fully address without more ethnographic information. But Bloch and Sperber's suggestion of an approach to explanation – which is multifactorial – frames the representations and categories, and proceeds from there. They can only gesture in the essay under consideration in the direction of the cognitive elements but it is clear that they

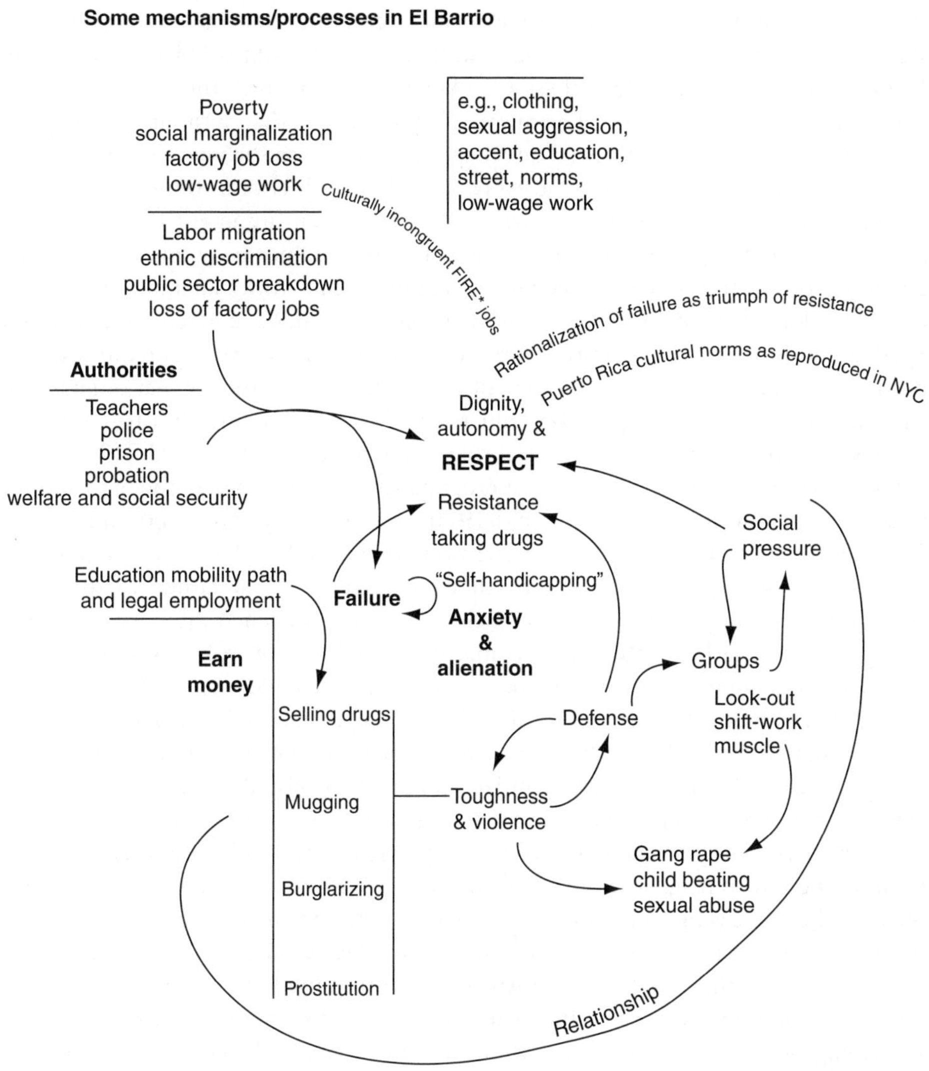

**FIRE = finance, insurance, real estate.*

Figure 22.3 El Barrio crack dealers (based on Bourgois 2002[1995]).

are important in their explanatory work. They turn to biology which mediates between cognition and social cultural patterning. They don't take the turn to a memetic approach, for reasons each of them in separate essays have rejected while nevertheless expressing approval of the effort to bring biology significantly into social anthropological work. Their biologizing is more nuanced than many of the sociobiological and evolutionary approaches with which anthropologists will be familiar.

So Sperber's epidemiology of representations is applied in sorting out issues and in framing the representations and categories involved. The epidemiology of representations involves attention to multiple forces that are causally implicated in the explanation of whatever pattern of sociocultural facts the analyst is working on, in this case the privileging of the sister's son. Here, they base something akin to Radcliffe-Brown's, Fortes's, and Goody's notion of a universality of bilateral kinship in Hamilton's classic sociobiological essay on kin altruism in which the sharing of genes with siblings extends the role of altruism. They point out that, although Hamilton's theory is biologically universalist, a direct application of it to such patterns as involved in sister's privilege won't work: "the expression of genes is always contingent on environmental factors" (Bloch and Sperber 2002:730). Their argument holds that biological facts and the generalized importance of them need not be cognized as such by people (a consideration that has been important in Bloch's work), an important indication of the limitation of purely cognitive approaches in general research programs. But Sperber and Bloch place cognition centrally in their program: "We wanted to explain, defend, and illustrate an 'epidemiology of representations,' a theory that differs from classical anthropological approaches and recent biological approaches to culture in various ways, in particular in the central role it assigns cognition" (2002:742).

One more point on the Bloch and Sperber paper: Minangkabau in the highlands of west Sumatra, Indonesia, as of the mid-1970s, was a society with important, operative, matrilineal descent groups. The question arises whether they had an equivalent of privileging sister's son? The answer: they did ... sort of. The father's, father's sister's, and their matrilineal relatives are included in the broadened category of "matrilineage of one's father" (the father is matrilinealized as it were). A saying "*bak di rumah bako*" suggests that *anak pisang* (matrilineal male children) are "treated like a king." *Anak pisang* are the reciprocal of *bako*, except that while *bako* are a lineage, *anak pisang* are individuals, children of males of a matrilineage – *anak pisang* can expect good food, service, sleeping in late, joking relations; also, the duty of *bako* is always to aid *anak pisang*, to provide a seat of honor for *anak pisang* at feasts, to show special respect to *anak pisang*, to give *anak pisang* presents, and under certain special circumstances to put up with insults from *anak pisang* to *bako*. There is, though it seems to be decreasing in importance, a property transfer of sorts called *pambaon* – involving usufruct rights to land from *bako* to *anak pisang* (Benda-Beckmann 1979). The similarity to the sister's son's privileging is intriguing. The exact social circumstances are different from those Bloch and Sperber discuss, but it is intriguing to find something not dissimilar so far away, not at all cognate with the African materials. One important difference is that there is something of a matrilineal constitution of *anak pisang*, in that their reproduction is that of a male of the matrilineage. The honoring and giving of allowances to *anak pisang*, then, involve Fortes's bilaterality, internally integrated to the *bako–anak pisang* relationship.

The point of this section is twofold: that culture (or replacement concepts for it) still need(s) rethinking and can bear it, and that distributions of representations matter. In both respects might cognitive anthropology be contributing more to the discussions, or have more to offer?

Epistemology and Ontology

Why haven't cognitive anthropologists paid more attention to local epistemologies (and ontologies), as part of an effort to understand out how cognition works in different sociocultural systems? A notable (but relatively unknown) exception is the exceptionally rich body of work by a social anthropologist, Overing (1985a, 1985b, 1988, 1989, 1993, 2003, 2007), who deals with the connection between epistemology and ontology. As a readily accessible gesture in a very different context to some of the general considerations in this work, see Figure 22.3, which shows an elementary version of an epistemology from Quine and Ullian (1978). This particular epistemology was authored by a professional philosopher (Quine) and an English professor. Their purpose was instruction of undergraduates, and the book's directive was concerned with "right thinking," and the acquisition of "right beliefs."[9] Should it appear that, by attending to professional philosophers' epistemological pedagogical issues, I am departing too much from an anthropological frame of reference, let me add that I am interested in their exposition for two reasons. First, it is an instanced specimen. Second, I will not here try to situate Quine and Ullian in their larger pedagogical environment or in philosophical discourses and communities, although it is worthwhile pointing out that "right thinking" became an American pedagogical movement in higher education in the 1970s or so, and continued to be practiced, though perhaps not so saliently as it once was (see, for example Ruggiero 1991; Moore 1993). My present point is to highlight, by means of the figure, the respects in which social relations of meanings – "beliefs" – are involved in the various tenets of the formulation. At the same time, I've taken care not to depart too much from the safety of methodological individualism (see Sperber and Kronenfeld). The diagram stresses the role of personal cognition, and understandably since, as noted, Quine and Ullian's purpose was to prescribe "best cognitive practices" in their formulation. They are trying to teach undergraduates how to think. Their purpose is far from mine, at the moment, and what I take to be cognitive anthropology's, in that I wish to better understand how cognition – in this case people's folk theories of knowledge – work rather than tell people how to think.

A final illustration: El Barrio crack dealers

In his monograph *In Search of Respect: Selling Crack in El Barrio* (2002[1995]), Philippe Bourgois uses "social reproduction" theory along with delineations of social history, context-setting, and narrative to convey a richly textured ethnography of the lives of drug dealers. In my teaching (in an introductory social anthropology course), two things sometimes stood in the way of students' fully grasping the role of "respect" in the account: (1) students sometimes got lost in detail and didn't connect key concepts; (2) additionally, they sometimes missed contrasts of their own lives with the everyday lives of non-drug dealers in the community in contextualizing the drug dealers' lives. On the latter, Bourgois isn't quite silent, but seems to depend somewhat on readers being able imaginatively to fill in missing, or de-emphasized material. Some students, in a recurring pattern in different uses of the book in the same course over a period of a few years, ended up taking Bourgois's emphasis on agency much further than Bourgois himself takes it in the book, such as to lose sight of the context of agency and the directions and force of agency in sharply constrained social settings. They mentally transformed unsatisfactory social adaptations to unsatisfactory conditions back into their own life-way's terms, and then couldn't understand why these people acted as they did (self-defeating as it was). These are students who in principle quite readily, sometimes glibly, acknowledge the role of ethnocentrism in misunderstandings of the ways of "others." It was just that they found it too much to bring that lesson home in the case of Bourgois's account. And in a few instances, students were unaware that anything was at issue until confronted by the professor in comments on their writings about the book.

Arguably the gap between what the book does richly convey and what some students got out of it is not a simple failure to grasp concepts. Perhaps it is more a failure to engage an appropriate "depth psychology" with a contextualization that make clear the moral-emotional import of circumstances, given social-cultural background and the pressing need to hitch oneself to endeavors that allow one to get on with life, and even make a success of oneself such that the respect is truly garnered and owned. By a depth psychology I have in mind such considerations as sour grapes and wishful thinking (see Elster 1983, 2007).

More on Sociality

All three of the figures in this chapter have been drawn so as to highlight the social aspects of each of the respective realms, as if they are seen through one social anthropologist's initial examination. The elements of the figures should carry that idea far enough for the present purpose.

It is worthwhile reiterating a point made by Carrithers (mentioned above; see, for example, 1990, 1992, 2001), which leads to the conclusion that we might need more of a cognitive anthropology supplementing social anthropology than we are in need of a merely socially qualified cognitive anthropology. Perhaps social cognition, including notions of distributed cognition, need rethinking, recontextualing, or replacing. The misgivings about social cognition have to do with how limited, even anemic, the social side of things is in these formulations. Rather than get into a fight with anyone concerning this issue, let me reiterate Carrithers's point and leave it at that, hoping that his point will be picked up and developed. His point is that there is a (qualified, to be sure) primacy of the social over and above the cultural, and in the present context that also, in part, means the cognitive, since the cognitive is so often conceived of as reduced to the cultural and then again the cultural to the cognitive. Neither reduction is convincing, nor is the interpretive one either, for the reason Carrithers gives for the primacy of the social, and in this case over the cultural, but not, perhaps, contrary to his intentions, over the cognitive. In close, but abbreviated paraphrase: (1) People live by means of relationships as well as cognition (which might be understood here to include morality and emotionality; see the papers by Overing). (2) Human cultural patterning depends on, and so makes sense in, the perspective of people's concrete relationships with others, so culture makes sense only given those relations with others. (3) Culture as mentation is intelligible only by virtue of social relationships. No comparable or as strong a case can be made for the opposite, that is the ways social relations depend on culture, and so this isn't a case of the chicken and the egg. Of course the social and the cultural are not all there are: human minds "live" in brains, which "live" in bodies, which live in material worlds, which is where social lives occur. But if the social has a qualified primacy, that should be reflected in our theories and empirical work. Carrithers would prefer a stronger formulation. He puts the point this way: "Alongside an ontology of schemas, narratives, etc., we had [better] assume an already existing ontology of people in [social] relations" (personal communication,

March 27, 2010). It is well to take seriously the idea that, as sociality theory suggests, "people do things in relation to, with and in respect to each other" (Carrithers 1992:34), things that we would be too hasty to reduce to culture or to a cognition that isn't a thoroughly socialized cognition (see also 1990, 2001).

Conclusion

This chapter argues for a more ambitious cognitive anthropology. Ambition along the lines of Dan Sperber's epidemiology of representations makes good sense. So do elements of the other approaches, to varying degrees. Another thread of unity running through the illustrations is sociality. This thread is extravagantly developed in Bourgois's work. In Sperber's epidemiology of representations, seemingly the least socialized of the examples (or sharing that place with Quine and Ullian's), sociality is built in via communication and cognition (see also Sperber and Wilson 1995[1986]); the thread then runs to sociality as part of an epistemology (which happens to be a version of a classical North Atlantic one). The thread culminates, as it were, in Bourgois's Barrio – as mentioned. This instance is strongly social; and one notices in this situation of poverty that human and personal resources are central, vindicating Sewell's (1992) classic paper joining the conceptual (if not the cognitive yet) with the social.

Power relations are a part of most modes of sociality and are actually present, though silent, in most of the illustrations, least so in the interpretive, epistemological, and epidemiological approaches. Sperber's epidemiology, for example, incorporates power quietly, but perhaps potentially powerfully for its methodological individualism: communication and epidemiology both give allowances to stronger and differential rhetorics. Power is yet differentially incorporated into Quine and Ullian's epistemology; some argue that such epistemologies are inherently attempts at hegemony and represent means of control. Finally the instance of the barrio is deeply constituted of power differentials, both externally (involving, for example, the authorities) and internally (involving, for example, differential respect and sanctioning). Another example needs to be mentioned here as well; though unfortunately not discussed, it shows strong connections between power, sociality more generally speaking, and cognitive issues in an instance of city-planning in Denmark. Flyvbjerg's account (1998) shows the stylizations of sociality in magnificent detail, but in a chapter already grown too long Flvyberg's account has to be omitted here.

NOTES

1 For present purposes take sociocultural anthropology to be the generalized melding of social and cultural anthropologies. The focus here, however, will be on social anthropology, understood broadly as the tradition of British anthropology that was developed early in the 20th century and influenced by Durkheim and others centered around L'Année Sociologique, whose focus of interest is not structural functionalism but rather its emphasis is on social life, social relations, and institutions, that is, it emphasizes the social more strongly than present American cultural anthropology. On both sides of the Atlantic there are partisans of social and cultural and, even more, of the melded sociocultural anthropology. I am not so much concerned with the partisanship and its institutionalism as with the need

for present purposes for a relatively clear delimitation between anthropologies emphasizing culture (not 'cultural'?) concepts and those emphasizing social concepts.

2 It does not seem to me controversial to point out that cultural anthropology is the most proximate supervening discipline for cognitive anthropology. Cognitive anthropology also grew up as part of the "cognitive revolution," and often in close affiliation with linguistic anthropology and linguistics, cognitive science, and cognitive psychology.

3 All the while conflating, in a great many cases, positivism with "scientific approach."

4 Hesse (1976, 1980a, 1980b, 1980c, 1982) recognized that just as some social science practitioners were disavowing scientific methodologies in favor of interpretive ones, some work in the philosophy of science was suggesting that, in many respects, science works more in the fashion interpretive work suggests than in a "positivist" style (narrowly understood).

5 How to understand the diagrams: First, they originated in a desire to help students see both "the big picture" and some of the patterns of relationships among systemically connected entities in their readings and class discussions. Their purpose is to informally and metaphorically "model" sociocultural mechanisms and processes at work. It is unfortunate that my drawing abilities and other constraints prevent any attempt at conveying a sense of dynamics in particular, concrete circumstances. The conventions used in the diagram are these: Simple lines mean a substantive connection, often inclusion, or representation of a set of related items; arrowed lines suggest asymmetry, often a causal connection. Sometimes, instead of a causal connection, arrows mean something like "involves" or "includes" in chains of connections. The diagrams are not meant to supplant fuller discussion or as formalizations. The literature cited for each diagram offers a fuller discussion of what the diagram is intended to represent.

6 I have added in a notion of transposable rules and schemas from a paper on practice theory by Sewell (1992).

7 Practice theory, variously understood and centered on some of Bourdieu's work might come about as close as any formulation these days to a "default generalized sociocultural theory," but nevertheless it has often been wedded more or less closely to interpretive approaches.

8 The phrasing is meant to allow for such things as the electronically contiguous communicative forms of internet "communities."

9 Notions of belief and believe have become problematical. See Needham 1972; Ruel 1982; Smith 1998[1979]; Pouillon 2008[1982].

REFERENCES

Benda-Beckmann, F. von

1979 Property in Social Continuity: Social Continuity and Change in the Maintenance of Property Relationships through Time in Minangkabau, West Sumatra. Verhandelingen van het Koninklijk Instituut voor Taal-, Land-, en Volkenkunde nr. 86. The Hague: Martinus Nijhoff.

Bloch, Maurice

2005 Essays on Cultural Transmission. Oxford: Berg.

Bloch, Maurice, and Dan Sperber

2002 Kinship and Evolved Psychological Dispositions. Current Anthropology 43(5): 723–748.

Bourgois, Philippe

2002[1995] In Search of Respect: Selling Crack in El Barrio. Cambridge: Cambridge University Press.

Brown, Penelope
2006 Cognitive Anthropology. *In* Language, Culture, and Society. C. Jourdan and K. Tuite, eds. Pp. 96–114. Studies in the Social and Cultural Foundations of Language. Cambridge: Cambridge University Press.
Carrithers, Michael
1990 Why Humans Have Cultures. Man 25(2):189–207.
1992 Why Humans Have Cultures: Explaining Anthropology and Social Diversity. New York: Oxford University Press.
2001 Sociality: Anthropological Aspects. *In* International Encyclopedia of the Social and Behavioral Sciences. N. J. Smelser and P. B. Baltes, eds. Pp. 14500–14504. Miamiasburg, OH: Elsevier. Access available via ScienceDirect.
Chalmers, A. F.
1999 What Is This Thing Called Science? Indianapolis, IN: Hackett.
D'Andrade, Roy
1995 The Development of Cognitive Anthropology. Cambridge: Cambridge University Press.
Eagleton, Terry
2000 The Idea of Culture. Malden, MA: Blackwell.
2007[1991] Ideology: An Introduction. New York: Verso.
Elster, Jon
1983 Sour Grapes: Studies in the Subversion of Rationality. Cambridge: Cambridge University Press.
2007 Explaining Social Behavior: More Nuts and Bolts for the Social Sciences. Cambridge: Cambridge University Press.
Evans-Pritchard, E. E.
1956 Nuer Religion. Oxford: Clarendon.
Feyerabend, Paul
1987 Farewell to Reason. London: Verso.
Flyvbjerg, Bent
1998 Rationality and Power: Democracy in Practice. S. Sampson, trans. Chicago: University of Chicago Press.
Friedman, Kajsa Ekholm, and Jonathan Friedman
2008a The Anthropology of Global Systems: Historical Transformations. Blue Ridge Summit, PA: AltaMira.
2008b Modernities, Class, and the Contradictions of Globalization: The Anthropology of Global Systems. Lanham, MD: AltaMira.
Goody, Jack
2010 The Eurasian Miracle. Cambridge: Polity.
Goody, Jack, ed.
1958 The Developmental Cycle in Domestic Groups. Cambridge: Cambridge University Press.
Hesse, M.
1976 Models versus Paradigms in the Natural Sciences. *In* The Use of Models in the Social Sciences. L. Collins, ed. Boulder, CO: Westview.
1980a In Defense of Objectivity. *In* Revolutions and Reconstructions in the Philosophy of Science. Bloomington: Indiana University Press.
1980b Revolutions and Reconstructions in the Philosophy of Science. Bloomington: Indiana University Press.
1980c Theory and Value in the Social Sciences. *In* Revolutions and Reconstructions in the Philosophy of Science. Bloomington: Indiana University Press.
1982 Science and Objectivity. *In* Habermas: Critical Debates. J. B. Thompson and D. Held, eds. Cambridge, MA: MIT Press.

Hollis, Martin

2002 Philosophy of Social Science. *In* A Blackwell Companion to Philosophy. N. Bunnin and E. Lsui-James, eds. Pp. 375–402. Malden, MA: Blackwell.

Kronenfeld, David

1975 Kroeber vs. Radcliffe-Brown on Kinship Behavior: The Fanti Test Case. Man 10:257–284.

1980 Particularistic or Universalistic Analyses of Fanti Kin-Terminology: The Alternative Goals of Terminological Analysis. Man 15(1):151–169.

1996 Plastic Glasses and Church Fathers: Semantic Extension from the Ethnoscience Tradition. New York: Oxford University Press.

Kuhn, Thomas

1996[1962] The Structure of Scientific Revolutions. Chicago: University of Chicago Press.

Moerman, Michael

1988 Talking Culture: Ethnography and Conversational Analysis. Philadelphia: University of Pennsylvania Press.

Moore, Henrietta L., and Todd Sanders, eds.

2006 Anthropology in Theory: Issues in Epistemology. Malden, MA: Blackwell.

Moore, Kathleen Dean

1993 Reasoning and Writing. New York: Macmillan.

Needham, Rodney

1972 Belief, Language, and Experience. Chicago: University of Chicago Press.

Overing, Joanna, ed.

1985a Reason and Morality. London: Tavistock.

1985b There is No End of Evil: The Guilty Innocents and Their Fallible God. *In* The Anthropology of Evil. D. Parkin, ed. Pp. 244–278. Oxford: Blackwell.

1988 Personal Autonomy and the Domestication of the Self in Piaroa Society. *In* Acquiring Culture: Cross Cultural Studies in Child Development. I. M. Lewis and G. Jahoda, eds. Pp. 169–192. London: Croom Helm.

1989 The Aesthetics of Production: The Sense of Community among the Cubeo and Piaroa. Dialectical Anthropology 14(3):159–175.

1993 The Anarchy and Collectivism of the "Primitive Other": Marx and Sahlins in the Amazon. *In* Socialism: Ideals, Ideologies, and Local Practice. Pp. 43–58. ASA Monographs 31. New York: Routledge.

2003 In Praise of the Everyday: Trust and the Art of Social Living in an Amazonian Community. Ethnos 63(3):293–316.

2007 The Stench of Death and the Aromas of Life: Poetics of Ways of Knowing and Sensory Process among Piaroa of the Orinoco Basin. "In the World and about the World: Amerindian Modes of Knowledge," special issue in honor of Prof. Joanna Overing. Tipití: Journal of the Society for the Anthropology of Lowland South America and Sao Paulo: Revista de Antropologia.

Pouillon, Jean

2008[1982] From Remarks on the Verb "To Believe." *In* A Reader in the Anthropology of Religion. Michael Lambek, ed. Pp. 1–8. Malden, MA: Blackwell. *Repr. from* Between Belief and Transgression: Structural Essays in Religion, History, and Myth. M. Izard and P. Smith, eds. Pp. 1–8. Chicago: University of Chicago Press.

Quine, Willard van Orman, and J. S. Ullian

1978 The Web of Belief. New York: Random House.

Romney, A. K., and R. G. D'Andrade

1964 Cognitive Aspects of English Kinterms. American Anthropologist 66(3.2):146–170.

Ruel, M. J.

1982 Christians as Believers. *In* Religious Organization and Religious Experience. J. Davis, ed. Pp. 9–31. New York: Academic Press.

Ruggiero, Vincent Ryan
1991 The Art of Thinking: A Guide to Critical and Creative Thought. New York: HarperCollins.
Sewell, William H., Jr.
1992 A Theory of Structure: Duality, Agency and Transformation. American Journal of Sociology 98(1):1–29.
Shweder, R. A.
2001 Culture: Contemporary Views. *In* International Encyclopedia of the Social and Behavioral Sciences. N. J. Smelser and P. B. Baltes, eds. Pp. 3151–3158. Amsterdam: Elsevier. Available online via ScienceDirect.
Smith, Wilfred Cantwell
1998[1979] Faith and Belief: The Difference between Them. Oxford: Oneworld.
Sperber, Dan
1996 Explaining Culture: A Naturalistic Approach. Cambridge, MA: Blackwell.
Sperber, Dan, and Deirdre Wilson
1995[1986] Relevance: Communication and Cognition. Oxford: Blackwell.
Tyler, Stephen A.
1978 The Said and the Unsaid: Mind, Meaning, and Culture. New York: Academic Press.
1984 The Vision Quest in the West, or What the Mind's Eye Sees. Journal of Anthropological Research 40(1):23–40.
Weinberg, Steven
1998 The Revolution That Didn't Happen. New York Review of Books 45:48–52.
Wierzbicka, Anna
1989 Soul and Mind: Linguistic Evidence for Ethnopsychology and Cultural History. American Anthropologist 91(1):41–58.

CHAPTER 23

Cognitive Anthropology and Education: Foundational Models of Self and Cultural Models of Teaching and Learning in Japan and the United States

Hidetada Shimizu

Recently, I made some short video documentaries for research about the lives of high school students in a Japanese and an American high school (Shimizu 2006a, 2006b). The videos show students presenting digital photographs they took of their daily lives, typical high school events (homecoming and school festival), as well as students answering short questions about their sense of self and morality, such as "Describe yourself" and "What is the right way to live?" When one Japanese student (senior, female) watched the footage from both schools and was asked for her reaction, her first comment was, "What stood out for me was for American students, their sense of self originates from within and from there, they try to influence their outside world." In contrast, she characterized the Japanese students' sense of self as being "outside in." She elaborated her point by saying that for the Japanese, the individual sense of

A Companion to Cognitive Anthropology, First Edition. Edited by David B. Kronenfeld, Giovanni Bennardo, Victor C. de Munck, and Michael D. Fischer.

self originates from without, or from the nexus of human relations and social context in which one is embedded, and it is from that nexus that they would consider the influence on their *own* thoughts, feelings, and behavior.

Interestingly, this way of looking at oneself in relation to others (people, things, and situations) corresponds to what Bennardo calls "radiality," a global cognitive schema whereby

> What happens to an individual's ego is not the focus of that same individual's attention. One focuses on other-than-ego individual (or more than one individual, or a group) and the consequences of one's behavior on that other-than-ego person/s. In other words, a point, that is, a place, a person, or event, is chosen in the field of ego, that is, the spatial field, the social field, or the event field, and other points are put in relationship to the previously chosen one, either centripetally, that is, toward it or centrifugally, that is, away from it. [Bennardo 2009:1–2]

Quoting D'Andrade (1989:809), Bennardo explains that radiality is a class of cultural model – that is, a cognitive schema or a blueprint of reality that are "intersubjectively shared by a social group" – which "consists of bits of knowledge organized in such a way as to facilitate storage and/or retrieval/use of that same knowledge" (Bennardo 2009:11). However, radiality is not simply one among many cultural models in that it is a *foundational* cultural model: it functions as a general purpose "assemblage of knowledge that can generate other more complex models when used to merge a larger number of units of knowledge" (Bennardo 2009:12). For example, among Tongans, the cognitive schema of locating oneself spatially from the viewpoint of other-than-ego (radiality) is globally and repeatedly found at the core of the Tongan ways of conceptualizing space, time, possessions, and kinship terminology.

In this chapter, I extend Bennardo's notion of radiality and non-radiality (i.e., egocentricity) to equally "foundational," and hence ideologically dominant, cultural models in Japan and the United States – interactional relativism and unilateral determinism (Lebra 1976) – to shed light on how they serve as basic templates for both formal and informal educational processes in Japan and the United Sates. Subsequently, I examine possible psychological and behavioral outcome of earlier educational experiences in an older age group, adolescents, in the two countries by using data I collected through "multivocal videography" of adolescents in Japanese and American high schools (Shimizu 2007).

Unilateral Determinism and Interactional Relativism as Foundational Cultural Models

Many psychologists and anthropologists, including Bennardo, have used the notion of the sociocentric–relational self as a dominant model of selfhood among non-Westerners, including East Asians, and the egocentric–individualistic self, of Westerners and Americans (see Strauss 2000 for more detail). In the case of selfhood among the Japanese, however, there has been consistent evidence from the "classics" ethnography of Ruth Benedict to more recent ethnography of the psychosocial development of Japanese adolescents and adults that the lived experience of an individual Japanese is often characterized by the coexistence of sociocentric–relational and egocentric–individualistic selves (see Shimizu 2000a, 2000b; D'Andrade 2008). As David Reynolds noted:

> The Japanese are not merely group oriented. They are among the most self-centered, self-seeking people I have ever encountered. They are also among the most self-sacrificing, unselfish, other-directed peoples of the world. I am not talking here about variations among different Japanese individuals, although tremendous variations do exist; I am talking about variations in one individual over time and situation and even in one individual at one moment. [Reynolds 1980:1]

Rather than starting from the sociocentric–relational vs. egocentric–individualistic models of selves as a point of departure, I adopt Lebra's notion of the presence vs. absence of a "prime mover" – that is, an object or being is perceived as a non-relative, self-derived, and self-sustaining "cause, origin, purpose, initiator, or controller of the behavior of elements of the universe" (e.g., omnipotent God or sovereign nation) (1976:7) – as the basis for two contrasting cultural models ("ethos," to use her term): "unilateral determinism" and "interactional relativism," respectively. Her explanatory system cuts through the distinction between sociocentric–relational and egocentric–individualistic selves and delineates instead the coexistence of the two orientations in the cultural models and experience of self in both Japan and the United States (and elsewhere). Lebra notes, for example, that a prime mover "may be located on the side of either the actor [i.e., ego] or the object [i.e., other-than-ego]" (1976:7). On the one hand, the prime mover exists on the ego side "to the extent the actor feels that physical or symbolic objects are to be created, manipulated, exploited, or controlled, the prime mover exists within the actor and may be identified as his wish, goal or power." On the other, "if these objects are taken as the ultimate reality or irresistible force [such as a 'god'] that demands reverence and submission, the prime mover exists on the side of object world [i.e., other-than-ego]." In either case, "the prime mover may be identified variously as the cause, origin, purpose, initiator, or controller of the behavior of elements of the universe," and when the "influence flows unilaterally from center to periphery," this orientation is called "unilateral determinism" (7).

With the prior assumption of a prime mover – or by using the cultural model of unilateral determinism – one grants an individually transcendent power to a being or spirit (e.g., a monotheistic god with absolute power), an idea (e.g., Platonic realism), a principle (a "natural law" of "science" or "history" in a Hegelian sense), or even to "an ordinary citizen … as in sanctified individualism" over and beyond other such beings. With interactional relativism, however, one cannot pinpoint the prime mover, nor is it relevant to do so. Rather, the focus is on understanding and acting in accordance with *relative positions* of the ego and the other-than-ego – or "Alter" in Lebra's terms. Specifically, the "Ego acts upon or toward Alter with the awareness or anticipation of Alter's response, and Alter in turn, by responding according to or against Ego's expectation influences Ego's further action" (1976:7). In a given social interaction, *who* is being the cause, origin, or the mover of the social transaction

> cannot be attributed to either Ego or Alter exclusively but to both or to the relationship between the two. The actor is unable to locate the prime mover and is likely to be indifferent to its existence. Instead, he is more aware of influence *flowing both ways*

> *between himself and his object* ... In interactional relativism, an actor acts in a certain way not because he is forced to do so by an external prime mover such as an environmental force, nor because he is driven by an internal prime mover such as an irresistible passion or desire; his behavior is, rather, *a result of interaction and mutual influence between himself and his object.* [Lebra 1976:7, emphasis added]

While Bennardo sees a foundational cultural model as a fundamental cognitive structure underlying a more specific and varied cognitive scheme from which they are derived, I see unilateral determinism and interactional relativism as pervasive *forces* – both cognitive and psychodynamic – that *motivate* educational activities and processes in the United States and Japan at various developmental stages and in various educational settings (see D'Andrade and Strauss 1992 for this position).

Divergent Patterns of Teaching and Learning in Japan and the United States

I now examine comparative educational research done in Japan and the United States, both in the informal education setting that takes place in the context of mother–child interactions and relationships, and in the formal education setting that takes place at school and in the classroom. Throughout, I argue that the two forces of interactional relativism and unilateral determinism shape differentiated patterns of teaching and learning in Japan and the United States, respectively. The former predisposes the educating agent (mother/teacher) and the learner (child/student) to orient their attention to the *mutually influencing processes* that take place *between* them, and relatively less emphasis is placed on each as a prime mover. The latter predisposes the educating agent and the learner to focus their attention on *themselves* as "prime movers" (autonomous, self-constituting, and self-governing entities), whose intention, interests, motives, and goals reside within himself or herself, and relatively less emphasis is placed on the mutually influencing processes that take place between the teacher and learner.

Informal Education Setting: Mother–Child Interactions

Infancy

The mother–child interactions during infancy (0–2 years of age) provide a primary context in which the child's preverbal, yet ontologically basic, sense of self is developed: that is, through daily and routine interactions with its mother, the child comes to understand its most prototypical sense of being-in-the-world.

A study, which laid the foundation for understanding the cultural nature of mother–child interactions during infancy in Japan and the United States, is the longitudinal, comparative study of mother–infant interactions by William Caudill (1973) (but see also Caudill and Weinstein 1969). Caudill and Weinstein (1969) conducted home observations of naturally occurring interactions between 30 mother-and-infant pairs, with firstborn infants, three to four months of age, divided equally by gender, from urban middle-class families in Japan and the United States. They found a basic similarity in the amount of time mothers spent to meet biological needs of the infants in the two countries (e.g., feeding, dressing the baby). However, the mothers in the two cultures engaged in different *styles* of caretaking. For example, American mothers engaged in a greater amount of *vocal* communication with infants; they talked to the child and stimulated them more to engage in physical activities and exploration. In contrast, Japanese mothers spend more time being in *direct bodily contact* with their infants and soothed them toward quiescence and passivity.

They also found correlations between the patterns of caretaking and infants' behavior. American infants' *happy vocalization* was correlated with mothers' chatting to and looking at the baby. In contrast, Japanese infants' happy vocalization did not show any relationship to maternal behavior; instead, the happy vocalization of Japanese infants was correlated with the mothers' *soothing and quieting behaviors.*

Caudill notes that these findings are consistent with general cultural expectations of the two cultures. In America, the emphasis is placed on verbal communication, and in Japan, the non-verbal, bodily contact is used as a means of communication. As for the possible impacts of these two distinct communicative styles on the child's emerging sense of self, Caudill notes:

> In Japan, in contrast to the situations in America, the mother views her baby much more as an extension of herself and *psychologically the boundaries between the two of them are blurred.* Because of the great emphasis on the close attachment between mother and child in Japan, the mother is likely to feel that *she knows what is best for the baby*, and *there is no particular need for him to tell her what he wants, because after all they are virtually one.* Given this orientation, the Japanese mother puts *less emphasis on vocal communication and more on physical contact* ... In America, the mother views her baby, at least potentially, as a *separate and autonomous being* who should learn to do and think for himself. For [the mother], the baby is from birth a *distinct personality with his own needs and desires*, which she must learn to recognize and care for. She helps him learn to express these needs and desires through her emphasis on vocal communication so that he can "tell" her what he wants and she can respond appropriately. [Caudill 1973:72]

From Caudill's empirical data and interpretations, one may infer that the Japanese pattern of caretaking supports the worldview that minimizes the presence of a prime mover. What is emphasized here is the oneness (*ittaikan*) of the mother and the child, which is so close that the pair do not even have to communicate verbally with one another. The motives, feelings, and behaviors are intimately *shared* between the two. The American pattern, on the other hand, seems to affirm the worldview with two separate prime movers: the mother and the child. What is emphasized here is that each has a psychological and motivational universe of his or her own, and the content of this universe has to be communicated (rather than co-possessed as in the Japanese case) to others in terms of vocal (rather than bodily and intuitive) communication.

Language socialization

Ordinarily, language acquisition signifies becoming a competent user of a given language. Equally important, however, is internalizing cultural beliefs and norms encoded in a language through everyday use of it. Schieffelin and Ochs (1986) call the latter processes of acculturation *through* language, language socialization. Seen from this perspective, mothers in Japan and the USA seem to talk (or not to talk) to their children in such ways as to affirm the cross-culturally divergent ontological assumptions about the nature of self in its psychosocial environments, as just described above.

For example, Clancy (1986), a sociolinguist who studies the language acquisition of young Japanese children, gives the following overview of basic characteristics of Japanese language and communicative styles. First and foremost, quoting Azuma et al. (1980), it is "context dependent, indirect, and rich in connotation and evasive in denotation" (Clancy 1986:213). Japanese talk less than Americans (Barnlund 1975). Explicit verbal communication is actually looked down upon as too superficial, such that, according to Barnlund (1975:133), "to give in so many articulate words one's innermost thoughts and feelings is taken as an unmistakable sign that they are neither profound nor very sincere" (cited in Clancy 1986:214).

Given the importance of such intuitive communication style, it is not surprising that a significant portion of Clancy's (1986) data collected from daily interactions between middle-class Japanese mothers and their roughly two-year-old children (between one year and 11 months and two years and two months) contained explicit teaching of empathy (*omoiyari*) on the part of the Japanese mothers. For example, although she urged the mother–child pairs to act as naturally as they would without her presence, the Japanese mothers "seemed to seize upon [the researchers'] visits as occasions for socializing their children into appropriate patterns of polite interactions with people outside of the family circle" (1986:219). While Japanese mothers gave a wide range of directive commands to the child – from very direct (e.g., *nasai*, meaning "do" this and that) to very indirect ones (e.g., if you do this it will hurt a person or an inanimate object [so don't do it]) – close to half of all the utterances (45 percent) emphasized the child's need for "sensitivity to the needs, wishes and feelings of others" (232). When one child was eating a tangerine, for example, the mother suddenly suggested to the child, "The girls [researchers] also say, 'We want to eat,'" although they had not indicated such desire themselves (233). When a child was misbehaving, the mother, taking advantage of the presence of the researcher, indicated her disapproval to the child by saying, "Older sister [the researcher] is saying, 'I am surprised. I'm surprised at Mayo'" (234).

In Ochs and Schieffelin's (1984) dichotomous typology, while the Japanese mothers expect the *child* to adapt to the needs of others (other-centered, or radiality in Bennardo's term), the American mothers adapt *themselves* to accommodate to the needs of the child. One way that the latter accomplish this goal is by treating the child as a communicative partner worthy of receiving their full attention. Starting in infancy, for example, the American mothers engage in face-to-face interactions with the child using eye contact. They not only talk directly to them, but also expect them to play the role of "communicative partner" in "dyadic, turn taking" communicative style (Ochs and Schieffelin 1984:286).

Often, the child's language is too limited for them to act as a communicative partner. One way the mother deals with this limitation is to lower the complexity of her speech directed at the child (called "child-raising" strategies by the authors) so that the child is treated *as if* it were a "competent" speaker. For example, in eliciting a story from her child, a mother often asks her child questions such as "Where did you go?" "What did you see?" – questions she knew in advance that the child would be able to answer. As a result, "the child is seen as telling the story even thought she or he is simply supplying the information the adult has preselected and organized" (Ochs and Schieffelin 1984:287). Another strategy for "child-raising" is where "a caregiver construct[s] a tower or other play object [by] allowing the young child to place the last block" or lets the child win a game, "acting as if the child can match or more than match the competence of the adult" (287). Mothers also make much effort to interpret unintelligible or partially intelligible utterances of young children by paraphrasing them or using question intonations (Cazden 1965, cited in Ochs and Schieffelin 1984:288).

Maternal socialization goals and strategies for regulating children's behavior

The sociolinguistic studies just introduced show that the ways in which Japanese and American mothers communicate with one another transmit powerful messages about how one is expected to relate to the outside world: the Japanese child must learn to identify with the needs and motives of others and to accommodate itself to them (interactional relativism), and the American child is required to identify and verbalize its own needs and feelings verbally to others (unilateral determinism).

These contrasting models of relating to one's world were given further support when mothers in both countries were asked about the age at which they expected their children to master certain skills as well as what strategies they would use to regulate children's behavior in hypothetical situations (Hess et al. 1980). For example, when asked about the age at which they expect their children to master varied skills, Japanese mothers desired early mastery of "emotional maturity," such as getting over anger by themselves; coping with disappointment without crying; "compliance with adult authority," such as coming or answering others when called, not doing things forbidden by parents; and "politeness," such as greeting family members courteously. American mothers, on the other hand, desired early mastery of "social skills," such as taking initiative in playing with others, getting their way by persuading friends, and "verbal assertiveness," such as stating their own preference when asked, and standing up for their own rights in relation to others. In short, "the Japanese mothers tended to be concerned about skills that show self-control, compliance with adult authority, and social courtesy in interaction with adults. The American mothers appeared to be more concerned with individual action, standing up for rights and other forms of self-assertion" (Hess et al. 1980:265).

Moreover, when the Japanese and American mothers were asked how they would respond to their misbehaving child, more Japanese mothers preferred strategies which would evoke the child's voluntary desire to comply with their request than their American counterparts; more American mothers preferred the use of direct commands than Japanese mothers (Conroy et al. 1980). Specifically, mothers were asked to imagine six hypothetical situations in which they would want to alter their child's behavior, such as bothering customers in a supermarket, drawing on the wall, or refusing to eat vegetables at dinner. Then, they were asked what they would say to the child in each situation. Maternal responses were classified into four major categories: appeals to the mother's authority (e.g., "I told you not to do that"), appeals to rules (e.g., "Walls are not for drawing"), appeals to feelings (e.g., "How do you think I will feel if you don't eat the vegetables I cooked for you?"), and appeals to consequences (e.g., "If you eat your vegetables, you'll be strong and healthy") (see Hess et al. 1986:155–156).

The results showed that significant numbers of Japanese mothers (22 percent) relied more on appeals to feelings compared to their American counterparts (7 percent), and more American mothers (50 percent) appealed to their authority than Japanese mothers (18 percent). Aside from the large statistical differences between the two groups, the qualitative differences in the content of mothers' responses were equally compelling. The Japanese mothers appeared to behave as if refusing to play the role of an authoritative teaching agent (i.e., a prime mover) for fear that doing so would injure the relationship she is trying to build toward a spirit of mutual collaboration (interactional relativism). As Hess and Azuma (1991) note:

> Japanese mothers tended to avoid explicit confrontation lest it damage the closeness with the child. In encounters where the child persisted in resisting the mother's efforts (e.g., eat vegetables), about 20% of the Japanese mothers who started with a firm demand for compliance gradually moderated their demands, often yielding altogether. Except in situations that presented danger, few mothers attempted to gain compliance by using their authority as a rationale. More often they used a strategy of *damashi* – a kind of deception in which the child's attention was diverted so that he or she would make the compliant response without being aware of the underlying dispute with the mothers. [Hess and Azuma 1991:5]

The Japanese mother's use of relationships and empathy as a primary medium of teaching, and the American mother's use of her own intention and authority in regulating children's behavior, were also found when mothers were asked to engage in teaching tasks in an experimentally controlled setting. In Dickson et al. (1979), Japanese and American mothers were asked to engage in tasks which required one person (mother) to describe to another (child) an object that the latter could not see. For example, they were given a notebook with pages presenting four figures – of which only one was the target. The mother was asked to describe this figure to the child, so that the child can push the button under the correct pattern on the page. The analysis of the transcripts of the maternal speech revealed nuanced but critical differences between the two groups of mothers.

The Japanese mothers seemed to rely on the child's willingness and ability to empathize with the mother's problem-solving strategies, so that they could solve the problem collaboratively. The American mothers, on the other hand, seemed to rely on the child's ability to solve the problem on their own. For example, in her effort to help her child find the correct answer, an "American mother might say to her child, '*Can* you push the red button under the picture that looks like a triangle?' A Japanese mother might say, 'I see a shape that looks like a crooked triangle. *Do* you see something that looks a little bit like a triangle?' " (Dickson et al. 1979:5, emphases added). As Miyake (1977) who oversaw the Japanese segment of the study observed, the "can you" question (American pattern) is concerned with the child's *intra*-cognitive capability, whereas the "do you" question (Japanese pattern), with their *inter*-cognitive capability. Hess and Azuma (1991) corroborate this point by saying that the keys for the Japanese model of socializing are "*attention to and close identification with others.* The keys for the [American model] are to *set one's own goals, be clear about what one wants, and view socializing persons as 'others' in a position of authority, able to offer punishments or rewards contingent on one's behavior*" (Hess and Azuma 1991: 5–6, emphases added).

Formal Education Setting: Culturally Guided Teaching and Learning in School

In this section, two separate examples of teaching and learning in formal educational settings in Japan and the United Sates are discussed: preschooling and eighth-grade mathematics education. In both cases, I argue that as in the mother–child interactions described above, the Japanese instructions are guided by the principles of interactional relativism, de-emphasizing the role of the teacher and student as a prime mover, and their American counterparts by unilateral determinism, accentuating their roles as prime movers.

Preschool education

Do the goals and practices of educating very young children differ between Japan and the United States? Tobin and his colleagues (1989a, 1989b) developed an innovative method to answer this question. In his "multivocal visual ethnography," he videotaped a "typical day" in a preschool in each county. First, he showed the video footage to the teachers and administrators in which the filming took place to gain their insiders' explanations about their educational beliefs and practices. He also showed the video to preschool teachers and child development specialists (e.g., college professors) in different regions of the countries to get a sense of the diversity of opinions. Finally, he showed the clips to similar audiences in the paired foreign country. The study was replicated in 2001–02 (Tobin 2009) with additions of different types of schools (more "progressive" vs. "typical") in each country.

Tobin and his colleagues' findings from both the "old" and "new" studies show that one central goal of preschool education in Japan is to instill in children two separate (i.e., *interactionally relative*) senses of self cultivated at home in the close, dyadic relationships with their mothers (called *honne*, or "real self") and that which is cultivated at school in the milieu of group-based life with peers (called *tatemae*, or "formal self"). Tobin (1989a, 1992) explains that the post-World War II erosion of the extended family and the proliferation of the nuclear family increased the time and resources mothers invest in their children at home (see Vogel 1971). However, this trend also decreased the child's opportunity to develop a more outward-looking sense of self (*tatemae*), geared specifically towards life as a member of a group, or *shudan seikatsu* (group life). This became a source of concerns for both parents and teachers.

Specifically, in the traditional model (*shitsuke*), child-rearing operated on the values placed on the complementarity (i.e., relativity) between the dimensions of selfhood called *omote* (outside) and that of *ura* (inside, or backside) (see Doi 1986 for detail). The outside (*soto*) is where the formal and outbound sense of self conforming to the norms of social behavior called *tatemae* (i.e., correct appearance or "form") are required and practiced. An example would be where a young child is nudged by his mother to intuit and respond to the (unstated) needs of the guest (Clancy 1986). The inside (*uchi*), on the other hand, is where the intimate and inwardly spontaneous sense of self and norms of behaviors, called *honne* (i.e., real feelings underlying or concealed behind *tatemae*), are expected and expressed. An example would be where the child who needed to attend to the needs of a guest can unwind and be allowed to play as it wishes after the guest leaves.

Relevantly, Tobin found that one essential goal of preschool curriculums in present-day Japanese preschool is to instill in children the ability to discern between the formal (*soto*) and informal worlds (*uchi*); and once this distinction (*kejime*) is realized, to cultivate dimensions of selfhood which affirms *both* the formality of group life and the "joy" of realizing one's authentic self in it. It is to learn about the complementarity, rather than opposition, between the formal and informal selves, knowledge that is difficult to obtain at home.

To American observers, the Japanese preschool looks "rowdy" and "chaotic." There are as many as 30 children in a classroom with only one teacher. The teacher seems "unable" to pay individual attention to students, nor do students appear to be given enough "choice" to choose from a variety of activities tailored to meet the differential needs and interests of them as individuals. On the contrary, the Japanese teachers and administrators who saw the footage of the Japanese preschool day generally approved of the pedagogical practices it represented.

For example, they felt that the high student–teacher ratio was something necessary to develop students' outward-oriented sense of self appropriate for *shudan seikatsu*, or group life. At the same time, a Japanese teacher who saw the American classroom with a much lower student–teacher ratio commented: "I cannot help feeling that there is something sad about a class that size. Don't American teachers worry that children may become too independent and individualistic? I wonder how you teach a child to be a member of a group in a class that small" (Tobin 1989b:184).

Another poignant example of a cross-cultural difference became evident when the behavior of one boy, Hiroki, who misbehaved all day long, speaking up haphazardly in classroom, and hitting and kicking his classmates, was shown to both American and Japanese viewers. In none of these instances did the teacher say or do anything to stop Hiroki misbehaving. While these scenes generated sharp criticism among American viewers regarding the teacher's "inability" to "control" the situation, the staff from the Japanese preschool approved of the teacher's practice. They felt that children could not be so one-dimensional as to know only how to behave correctly (*tatemae*). Children also needed to act spontaneously and in a "childlike" way (*kodomo rashii*) as children of this age. The principal of the school explained:

> I worry more about some of the other children who never misbehave than I worry about Hiroki. He'll be okay. It's easier to teach a mischievous child to behave than to teach a too good child to dare to be naughty. In the old days, children had more chances to play freely, without adults always peering over their shoulders. These days, children don't know how to really play, to play like children, which includes being mischievous … fighting's not a problem. Fighting at this age is natural. If there were no fights, that would be a problem. Children need to learn how to fight when they're young so they won't have to fight when they get to junior high school and could really hurt someone. [Tobin 1992:30]

In contrast with the Japanese preschool educators who insisted that children behave appropriately *both* as members of a group *and* as unique individuals (i.e., interactional relativism), American educators projected much more dualistic views of how children should behave. They insisted that there should be clear and inviolable boundaries between people – between the teacher and the child, the parent and the teacher, and between children themselves. Not only should the children respect the individuality of other people, but they should also develop their own independent talent and potentials as unique and creative individuals (i.e., unilateral determinism).

In both his old and his new studies, Tobin contends that the core goals and practices of the American preschool can be summarized in terms of values and principles stated in the US Constitution: "free choice, self-expression, individual rights and pursuit of happiness" (Tobin 2009:193). In the American preschools, for instance, the idea of "freedom" entails freedom to *choose*, not freedom to play (*jiyuu asobi*): "the teachers in Japan gave greater emphasis to the children *being* free, the US teachers put the greater emphasis on choice" (194, emphasis added). American children are given not only a clear set of options to choose from – for example, what activity to do, what to play with, what area of the room to play in, who to play with – but are also expected to "develop a meta-awareness and a meta-discourse of the techniques and language of choosing" (195). One such belief is that "children should not only have opinions about what they want to do, but they should verbalize them" (197). Children are routinely reminded, " 'Tell me,' 'Use your words' ... throughout the day ... not only to encourage children to verbalize their choices of activities, but also for mediating disputes, narrating and recapitulating play, and dictating stories" (197–198).

Another set of values and practices which pertain to freedom of choice is the notion of "individualized education." Tobin found that almost all American teachers he interviewed had negative views of teacher-led whole-group instruction with high teacher–student ratios (as in the Japanese classroom), yet enthusiastically endorsed the moral and pedagogical superiority of "individualized," "child-centered" teaching. For example, according to American teachers' folk theory of teaching, choice is tied up with the idea of "an inalienable right to the pursuit of happiness and fun" such that "activities that are individually chosen are assumed to be inherently more pleasurable than those that are collectively chosen or assigned" (Tobin 2009:195). Choice is also tied up with the democratic sense of fairness whereby "letting children choose between building with Legos [*sic*] and playing at the water table is seen as providing practices in exercising the right of democratic citizenships and more generally, of 'independent decision making' " (195).

It is noteworthy that the value placed on individualized education is often elevated to the level of social policy. Individualized education plans (IEPs) and other programs targeted at the "special needs" of a single student or a group (e.g., bilingual education, Head Start) are good examples. In Japan (and other countries such as France), for example, the main goal of preschool is to provide equal (uniform and universally available) education for all children. American education, on the other hand, "emphasized equality of *opportunity*, which means not the same education for all, but education tailored to the needs of individual and communities" (i.e., prime movers) (Tobin 2009:204, emphasis added).

Cultural scripts for teaching mathematics and science

The educators' assumptions about students' sense of self – as contributing members of a class in Japan, and as autonomous beings with their own needs and talents in the United States – are also reflected in ways in which mathematics is taught in the two countries. In the Video Study portion of the Third International Mathematics and Science Study (TIMSS), for example, Stiger and Hiebert (1999) found that eighth-grade math teachers in Japan and the United States had different teaching goals and procedures for teaching mathematics. When randomly selected Japanese and American eighth-grade math teachers were asked what they tried to accomplish through their teaching, the Japanese teachers emphasized helping students *understand* mathematical concepts through structured *interactions* between themselves and the teacher, while the American teachers emphasized *skills* that enable them to solve mathematic problems *individually*.

Specifically, when a group of mathematics education experts analyzed the contents of videotaped eighth-grade mathematics lessons, they found that the lessons in the two countries followed different scripts. In a typical Japanese lesson, for example, the teacher starts the lesson by reviewing the concept from the previous class. He then presents a challenging conceptual problem, the problem for the day, which students try to solve individually first and then in a group. After about 20 minutes, the teacher selects one or more solution methods (not the answer) of students and discusses them with the class in detail. At the end of the class, and sometimes during the lesson, the teacher summarizes the main principle involved in the lesson.

In a typical American lesson, on the other hand, the teacher starts the lesson by reviewing the previous material by checking homework or engaging students in a warm-up activity. Here, rather than asking the whole class to think about a conceptually challenging question, each student called on by the teacher answers a simple fill-in question taken from a workbook. This is followed by the teacher's demonstration of how to solve the problem for the day, whereby the teacher often "engages students in a step-by-step demonstration by asking short-answer questions along the way" (Stiger and Hiebert 1999:80). The next step is practice, where individual "seatwork is assigned and students are asked to complete problems [alone] similar to those for which the solutions methods was demonstrated" (80–81). Finally, the teacher corrects some of the student solutions by showing the correct method and answer, and ends the class by assigning homework.

Although there were some minor variations, the core aspects of the two scripts for teaching mathematics remained constant in elementary-grade mathematics (Stiger et al. 1996) and science (Azuma and Walberg 1985, cited in Hess and Azuma 1991) classes. Hess and Azuma (1991) characterized the general patterns of these two contrasting models of teaching as "sticky-probing" (for the Japanese pattern) and "quick and snappy" (for the American pattern). In "sticky-probing," the teacher typically "select[s] a seemingly small problem that most of the children would not otherwise notice, probe into it through deliberative group discussion and teacher–pupil exchange, and thus spend[s] considerable time on reflecting, explaining, and digesting the problem." In contrast, in the "quick and snappy" approach, the lessons are divided into "small steps or concepts, each of which is quickly mastered, promptly rewarded, and identified as a correct term, concept, or procedure" (Hess and Azuma 1991:6).

As with the divergent patterns of the mother–child interactions in Japan and the United States, these two dominant pedagogical scripts in the classroom give support for the principles of interactional relativism and unilateral determinism respectively. The sticky-probing approach, for example, "demands patience and compliance because … [while students] must resist feelings of satiation and boredom … they are [also] expected to probe, to stay with a topic, and to examine an issue from several perspectives, rather than to push quickly for a solution or 'correct' answer" (Hess and

Azuma 1991:6). Fundamentally, a lesson with "sticky-probing" lacks a fixed prime mover in that neither the teacher nor the students are unilaterally in control of the classroom discourse at any given time. Rather, much of the emphasis is placed on the teacher guiding students to *work together as participants of a mutually collaborative problem-solving process.* In one sense, the Japanese teacher's refusal to give away the correct answer and let students come up with their own solution parallels the Japanese mother's and preschool teachers' refusal to step in and solve children's disputes. In both cases, the main goal is to help children understand (*wakaru*) how to conduct themselves appropriately even without adult guidance. According to Lewis (1988:164), one elementary school teacher noted: "I don't want to create children who obey [just] because I am here. I want children who know what to do themselves and who learn to judge things themselves" (Hess and Azuma 1991:7).

In contrast with "sticky-probing," which is built on the assumption of each student's willingness to *identify* with the goal of collaborative problem-solving, the "quick and snappy" approach is built on the assumption of the separateness, individuality, and autonomy of each student (i.e., prime mover), particularly in terms of his or her *own motivation* to learn. Accordingly, the quick and snappy approach uses the principle of contingency management (behaviorism) whereby the teacher entices (rather than assumes) the interests of individual students with appropriate stimuli (e.g., motivating lessons) or rewards and punishment (e.g., praise given to a student response or lack thereof). In a typical American math class, for example, the teacher asks students questions easy enough so that the lesson can move along at a brisk pace as well as give the students a chance to receive immediate and positive feedback for their answer, both of which help to maintain students' interests and motivation. This teaching method is consistent with the common assumption of American educators that "the teacher and curriculum must learn the student's attention ... [such that the] success and quality of schools are judged by [teachers'] ability to arouse interests in the students" (Hess and Azuma 1991:7).

Cultural Scripts for Self-Descriptions among Adolescents

Having examined how children are educated at home and in school, I now ask: What are the psychological and behavioral consequences of early socialization and the education practices of Japanese and American children when they reach adolescence? While it would be difficult to make direct links between the educational processes described above and their psychological and behavioral impacts on children in later years, one may at least get a glimpse of their consequences by looking at how adolescents talk about themselves in a *public* discourse.

Specifically, in a part of a large-scale study, I asked 11 Japanese and 10 American high school students, roughly divided by gender, to "describe themselves" in a videotaped interview (Shimizu 2007). Since they were told that the video would be shown to their peers and parents and teachers in their own school, as well as those in the paired foreign country, it was expected that students would present culturally appropriate, if not personally revealing, answers. Taken as culturally appropriate scripts for describing themselves, their responses yielded intriguing cross-cultural differences: (1) Japanese students' narratives were often spoken from the perspective of someone other than themselves, or elaborated in a context of interpersonal and social relationships, whereas their American counterparts simply defined themselves on their own terms (i.e., self-referred and determined); and (2) a good majority of Japanese students' self-description contained self-criticism, whereas their American counterparts contained no criticism but, instead, positive personal attributes such as individual ability, interests, and activities. All the following excerpts from my (unpublished) interviews were responses which immediately followed the question ("describe yourself") and were not purposely selected from other segments.

For example, a 17-year-old Hiroko (pseudonym), described herself as follows:

> HIROKO: My friends tell me that I'm *akarui* [amiable] and interesting.
> INTERVIEWER: What do you mean by *akarui*?
> KEIKO: This is what my parents told me. *They said that my teacher told them that I was a pipeline between the boys and the girls in the classroom and helped to improve the overall atmosphere of the class. The teacher said it was a very commendable thing to do. I guess that's me.* [emphasis added]

While many of her Japanese peers engaged in such a reflective mode of self-description, none of their American counterparts did so. Instead, their self-descriptions were "self-referred," that is, not attached to any reference to other-than-ego perspectives as the following examples show:

> I'm like artistic … can draw, athletic like play basketball and soccer. I like to get to like know people … just asking, like talk to people and I like Martial Arts … like Kung Fu type of stuff like Bruce Lee and stuff like that, very fun. (Mark, 17)

> I have a lot of friends. I think I'm pretty outgoing. I like to get involved in stuff and that's pretty much it. I'm kind of loud. I like to smile a lot. (Kristy, 17)

In some cases, the Japanese students' self-descriptions were also self-critical as the following examples show:

> I'm a negative thinker. I'm also self-centered. I have a tendency to try to read into other people's thoughts. You could say I don't trust people easily but I also have fun with people. (Seiko, 15, female)

> I'm indecisive and self-centered. *For example?* Here's a little thing. I can't make decisions right away. People criticize me for that … I tell my friends what I want to do and force them do that with me. When I want to do something I let other people know about it. But when I'm down, I don't listen to other people. (Yumiko, 15, female)

While more female than male students appear to see themselves critically, Hiato, a 17-year-old boy, also described himself as follows:

> HIATO: I tend to think of myself first. Even when I'm taking other people into consideration, I still tend to think of myself first.
> INTERVIEWER: Are other people like that, too?
> HIATO: I'd say I'm the only one.
> INTERVIEWER: So you feel you're different from others?
> HIATO: Yes, I think I'm egotistical.

None of the American students' self-descriptions were self-critical; instead, they conveyed a sense of self-contentment and self-confidence:

> I would describe myself as a leader in the school, someone who is always busy. I love being busy so ... And I don't know just somebody who's pretty much never really sits down, somebody that stays pretty involved and yeah. Yeah. (Michelle, 17)
>
> I would describe myself as someone who has a lot to give. I really like helping people and friends are important to me. I like making people laugh. It's just something that I can't really get through the day without. (Eric, 16)
>
> Describe myself? I would say I'm outgoing and it's hard to describe myself. I love to have fun. I like to do things that I will have a memory of. When I look back on my life, I want to have a story. So when I do something, I like to say when I think back on this, is it going to be a good experience? Am I going to laugh? When I tell a story, are people going to enjoy it? (Sarah, 17)

In sum, in the Japanese students' self-descriptions, the role of self as a prime mover – "the cause, origin, purpose, initiator, or controller of the behavior of elements of the universe" (Lebra 1976:7) – is intentionally de-emphasized by referencing ego from the perspective of other-than-self, or downplaying its positive attributes. As such, instead of its "influence flow[ing] unilaterally from center to periphery" (unilateral determinism), the self is presented to others as a projection of its awareness of other people's perceptions of it (interactional relativism).

Comments about the Japanese students' self-descriptions by cultural insiders and outsiders provided support for the pervasive and taken-for-granted nature of this self-presentation. First, while Japanese students' circuitous self-descriptions struck nearly all American viewers as being "modest," and their self-criticism as (too) "honest," none of the Japanese viewers even noticed such features, and described them as being "fairly typical" (*goku futsuu*). When they were told how surprised the American viewers were about teenagers criticizing themselves in public, however, one Japanese mother suggested that the self-criticism did not indicate self-negation, but rather, a conventional discourse in which a person anticipates a gracious treatment of themselves by others in light of their self-effacing gesture: "When you criticize yourself like that, you don't really mean it, I don't think. You do so because you are expecting/counting on others to deny it by saying, 'No, you aren't like that'" (interactional relativism).

American students and teachers who saw the American students' self-description did not see anything special about them, either. However, unlike Japanese parents and teachers who criticized their children or students for being too timid compared to their American peers – who "look as if they received special training to speak well/highly of themselves" – many American teachers praised their students off-handedly. One teacher said she had great "respect and admiration" for her students because they take initiatives in helping other people (e.g., "grouping around" to help a peer with family illness). Furthermore, when American students were shown the clip of Japanese students' self-effacing self-descriptions, most students commented that they would focus on the positive, instead of the negative, qualities about themselves. As one student noted: "most people here, if you ask them what they were like, would only state the positive things about themselves ... because for the most part, most kids in America are like that." A teacher also corroborated this point by saying:

> I thought it was very interesting how honest [Japanese students] were, you know, I mean the one girl just flat out comes out and says, "I'm self centered." You know, they're just very honest about who they are and I think that's definitely a non-American trait. That seems to be something that's solely a Japanese trait from what I have seen. Because here in America, we're very conscientious about, you know, what we're like and I think sometimes we're not totally honest about who we are. For high school students to be able to say that, I thought that was pretty mature of them to be able to do that, to be forward about some of their shortcomings.

These comments made by Japanese and American viewers reveal how each group sees their way of talking about themselves – presenting themselves critically as seen from the perspective of others (interactional relativism) and highlighting positive aspects of themselves and their life as viewed solely from their own perspective (unilateral determinism) – as perfectly "normal" as judged by their "cultural common sense" (Geertz 1983:73–93). This evidence is consistent with the general observation of experienced ethnographers that the values and norms that exert the most fundamental and pervasive power over people's thinking and behavior are, for the most part, out of their awareness (see D'Andrade 2005:89–98, for methods to tap into such assumptions). Nonetheless, as the evidence above shows, what is most ordinary and unremarkable to one group is often a profound source of "astonishment" to the other (see Shweder 1991:1–23). As I will discuss next, in this very gap between the unexamined, taken-for-granted perspective of the cultural insiders and that of the cultural outsider lies a significant yet unexplored potential for future research at the intersection of education and cognitive anthropology.

Implications for Cognitive Anthropology and Education

In this chapter, I have argued that interactional relativism and unilateral determinism are two *foundational* cultural models guiding the educational process of children in Japan and the United States. The normative and generative influences of these models are so penetrating and pervasive, albeit tacit and unnoticed by cultural insiders, that they span various developmental periods – that is, infancy, early and middle childhood, and adolescence – as well as educational processes and settings – that is, infant care, language socialization, maternal education at home, preschool curriculums, and mathematics education.

What does this evidence mean for cognitive anthropology's present and future roles in the interdisciplinary field of education? Presently, the vast majority of mainstream (i.e., domestic, non-cultural, and non-anthropological) educational and developmental research (as represented in such flagship journals as *American Educational Research Journal* or *Developmental Psychology*, respectively) pays relatively little attention to the notion of culture, except as it relates to racial, ethnic, and sociocultural "diversities" (pluralism) within the United States (e.g., Greenfield and Cocking 1994). There has been only a handful (relatively speaking) of culturally and anthropologically informed research on a more global scale. Of these projects some trace their roots to anthropology of education (e.g., Spindler 1974), and others to cultural and psychological anthropology (e.g., LeVine and New 2008).

Still, very few of these studies make a deliberate and systematic link between collectively shared *mental* representations of individuals (e.g., cultural models), on the one hand, and the cultural institutions (e.g., school) and practices (e.g., home and community socialization) that make the acquisition of such cognitive structures possible, on the other. In fact, it was the "culture and personality" study during the period 1930–1955 which attempted to systematically link and correlate the triad of variations in (1) shared mental and behavioral characteristics of individuals (or culturally constituted "personality") across human populations, (2) educational practices (e.g., parental and communal socializations) and institutions (e.g., schools) that produce these mental and behavioral characteristics, and (3) the effects that the mental and behavioral variations have on the functioning of sociocultural institutions (e.g., parenting, informal and formal teaching, and schooling) (see LeVine 1982:3–14).

For various historical reasons, this ambitious attempt to link the mental lives of individuals, educational process, and institutional contexts was abandoned with the "fall" of the culture and personality school. Cognitive anthropology can be a vital force in a renewed effort to bring back culturally shaped and shared *mental* processes – via cognitive schemas, models, maze ways, et cetera – to the forefront of psychosocial research on how individuals become acculturated and educated members of the social institutions in, for, and by which they function.

REFERENCES

Azuma, H.
1986 Why Study Child Development in Japan. *In* Child Development and Education in Japan. H. Stevenson, H. Azuma, and K. Hakuta, eds. Pp. 3–12. New York: Freeman.

Azuma, H., and H. Walberg
1985 Kagakuteki gainen no shutoku, teichaku, ten-i ni oyobosu kyojuhoho no eikyo [The influence of teaching method on acquisition, retention, and transfer of scientific concepts]. *In* Department of Curriculum and Instruction Research Report. T. Inagaki, ed. Pp. 208–277. Tokyo: Faculty of Education, University of Tokyo.

Azuma, H., R. D. Hess, K. Kashiwagi, and M. Conroy
1980 Maternal Control Strategies and the Child's Cognitive Development: A Cross-Cultural Paradox and Its Interpretation. Paper presented at the International Congress of Psychology, Leipzig.

Barnlund, D. C.
1975 Public and Private Self in Japan and the United States: Communicative Styles of Two Cultures. Tokyo: Simul.

Bennardo, G.
2009 Language, Space, and Social Relationships: A Foundational Cultural Model in Polynesia. Cambridge: Cambridge University Press.

Bjork, C.
2009 Moderated Discussion: Preschool in Three Cultures Revisited. Comparative Education Review 53(2):259–283.

Caudill, W.

1973 Psychiatry and Anthropology: The Individual and His Nexus. *In* Cultural Illness and Health: Essays in Human Adaptation. L. Nader and T. Maretski, eds. Pp. 67–77. Anthropological Studies 9. Washington, DC: American Anthropological Association.

Caudill, W., and H. Weinstein

1969 Maternal Care and Infant Behavior in Japan and America. Psychiatry 32:12–43.

Cazden, C.

1965 Environmental Assistance to the Child's Acquisition of Grammar. Unpublished doctoral dissertation, Harvard University.

Clancy, P.

1986 The Acquisition of Communicative Style in Japanese. *In* Language Socialization across Cultures. B. Schieffelin and E. Oches, eds. Pp. 213–250. New York: Cambridge University Press.

Conroy, M., R. D. Hess, H. Azuma, and K. Kashiwagi

1980 Maternal Strategies for Regulating Children's Behavior: Japanese and American Families. Journal of Cross-Cultural Psychology 11(2):153–172.

D'Andrade, R. G.

1989 Cultural Cognition. *In* Foundations of Cognitive Science. M. I. Posner, ed. Pp. 795–830. Cambridge, MA: MIT Press.

2005 Some Methods for Studying Cultural Cognitive Structure. *In* Finding Culture in Talk: A Collection of Methods. N. Quinn, ed. Pp. 83–104. New York: Palgrave Macmillan.

2008 A Study of Personal and Cultural Values: American, Japanese and Vietnamese. New York: Palgrave Macmillan.

D'Andrade, R. G., and C. Strauss

1992 Human Motives and Cultural Models. New York: Cambridge University Press.

Dickson, W. P., R. D. Hess, K. Miyake, and H. Azuma

1979 Referential Communication Accuracy between Mother and Child as a Predictor and Cognitive Development in the United States and Japan. Child Development 50:53–59.

Doi, T.

1973 The Anatomy of Dependence. Tokyo: Kodansha International.

1986 The Anatomy of Self. Tokyo: Kodansha International.

Geertz, C.

1983 Local Knowledge: Further Essays in Interpretive Anthropology. New York: Basic Books.

Greenfield, P. M., and R. R. Cocking

1994 Cross-Cultural Roots of Minority Child Development. Hillsdale, NJ: Lawrence Erlbaum.

Hess, R. D., and H. Azuma

1991 Cultural Support for Schooling: Contrasts between Japan and the United States. Educational Researcher 20(9):2–8, 12.

Hess, R. D., K. Kashiwagi, H. Azuma, G. G. Price, and W. P. Dickson

1980 Maternal Expectations for Mastery of Developmental Tasks in Japan and the United States. International Journal of Psychology 15:259–271.

Hess, R. D., H. Azuma, K. Kashiwagai, W. P. Dickson, S. Nagano, S. Holloway, K. Miyake, G. Price, G. Hatano, and T. McDevitt

1986 Family Influences on School Readiness and Achievement in Japan and the United States: An Overview of a Longitudinal Study. *In* Child Development and Education in Japan. H. Stevenso, H. Azuma, and K. Hakuta, eds. New York: Freeman.

Lebra, T. S.

1976 Japanese Patterns of Behavior. Honolulu: University of Hawaii Press.

Lewis, C.

1988 Japanese First Grade Classrooms: Implications for U.S. Theory and Research. Comparative Education Review 32(2):159–172.

LeVine, R. A.
1982 Culture Behavior and Personality: An Introduction to the Comparative Study of Psychosocial Adaptation. New York: Aldine.
LeVine, R. A., and R. S. New
2008 Anthropology and Child Development: A Cross-Cultural Reader. Malden, MA: Wiley-Blackwell
Miyake, K.
1977 Out-of-Code Impressions on American Mother–Child Interactions. Unpublished paper, Chukyo University, Toyota, Japan.
Ochs, E., and B. B. Schieffelin
1984 Language Acquisition and Socialization: Three Developmental Stories and Their Implications. *In* Culture Theory: Essays on Mind, Self, and Emotions. R. A. Shweder and R. A. LeVine, eds. New York: Cambridge University Press.
Reynolds, D. K.
1980 The Quiet Therapies: Japanese Pathways to Personal Growth. Honolulu: University of Hawaii Press.
Schieffelin, B. B., and E. Ochs
1986 Language Socialization across Cultures. New York: Cambridge University Press.
Shimizu, H.
2000a Beyond Individualism and Sociocentrism: An Ontological Analysis of the Opposing Elements in Personal Experiences of Japanese Adolescents. Human Development 43(4– 5):195–211.
2000b Japanese Cultural Psychology and Empathic Understanding: Implications for Academic and Cultural Psychology. Ethos 28(2):224–247.
2006a A Video Accompaniment to Adolescence in Three Culture Studies: Joseph High School of Japan.
2006b A Video Accompaniment to Adolescence in Three Culture Studies: Lutheran High School of the United States.
2007 Cultural Models of Self-Presentations in Japan and the United States: A Multivocal Videography Study. Presentation at the annual meeting of the Society for Anthropological Sciences, San Antonio, Texas.
Shweder, R. A.
1991 The Astonishment of Anthropology. *In* Thinking through Cultures: Expeditions in Cultural Psychology. Cambridge, MA: Harvard University Press.
Spindler, G. D.
1974 Education and Cultural Process: Toward an Anthropology of Education. New York: Holt, Rinehart and Winston.
Stiger, J. W., and H. Hiebert
1999 The Teaching Gap: Best Ideas from the World's Teachers for Improving Education in the Classroom. New York: Free Press.
Stiger, J. W., C. Fernandez, and M. Yoshida
1996 Cultures of Mathematics Education in Japanese and American Classrooms. *In* Teaching and Learning in Japan. T. P. Rohlen and G. K. Letendre, eds. New York: Cambridge University Press.
Strauss, C.
2000 The Culture Concept and the Individualism–Collectivism Debate: Dominant and Alternative Attributions for Class in the Unites States. *In* Culture, Thought, and Development. L. P. Nucci, G. B. Saxe, and E. Turiel, eds. Pp. 85–114. Mahwah, NJ: Lawrence Erlbaum.
Tobin, J. J.
1989a Preschool in Three Cultures: Japan, China, and the United States. New Haven: Yale University Press.

1989b Visual Anthropology and Multivocal Ethnography: A Dialogical Approach to Japanese Preschool Class Size. Dialectical Anthropology 13:173–187.

1992 Japanese Preschools and the Pedagogy of Selfhood. *In* Japanese Sense of Self. N. R. Rosenberger, ed. New York: Cambridge University Press.

2009 Preschool in Three Cultures Revisited: Japan, China, and the United States. Chicago: University of Chicago Press.

Vogel, E.

1971 Japan's New Middle Class: The Salaryman and His Family in a Tokyo Suburb. Berkeley: University of California Press.

CHAPTER 24

Archaeological Approaches to Cognitive Evolution

Miriam Noël Haidle

The evolution of the human mind is an old question in Paleolithic archaeology (e.g., Verworn 1915).[1] The flourishing of cognitive science, beginning in the 1950s, did not touch the discipline's potential, however: for a long time archaeology and cognitive science widely ignored each other. While Leroi-Gourhan (1964) sketched a singular developmental picture of the paleontology of human thought, most other archaeological inquiries into cognition were raised predominantly to redefine human uniqueness, after widely recognized studies of animal tool behavior, documenting several animal species' use of stones as tools, demonstrated that tool use could no longer be considered an exclusively human marker. Today, regarding typically human cognitive performance and its origin, the focus in archaeology has narrowed to so-called non-functional, symbolic artifacts related to "modern" human behavior as art, religious actions, and indirectly language, combined with planning and foresight (e.g., Mellars 1996; 2005; Noble and Davidson 1996; Klein 2000; McBrearty and Brooks 2000; Coolidge and Wynn 2001; Klein and Edgar 2002; d'Errico 2003, 2007; d'Errico et al. 2003; Henshilwood and Marean 2003; Mithen 2006). Yet, cognitive archaeology covers more than that. This chapter tries to sketch the theoretical basis of a very heterogeneous field of the archaeological discipline and to outline some attempts to track down and explain the singularity and origin of the human mind.

Cognitive Space and the Potential of Paleoanthropological and Archaeological Remains

Access to original data on the cognitive evolution of *Homo* can be gained only on intricate trails. The basis of cognitive behavior is the individual cognitive space (or mind) (Haidle 2008), which can expand along three dimensions (Figure 24.1): the

A Companion to Cognitive Anthropology, First Edition. Edited by David B. Kronenfeld, Giovanni Bennardo, Victor C. de Munck, and Michael D. Fischer.

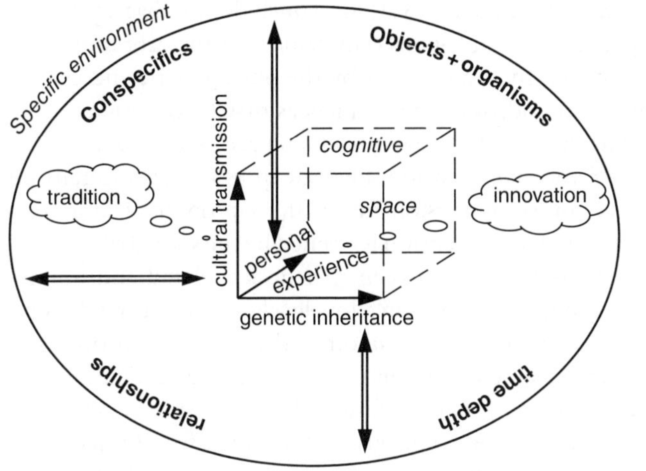

Figure 24.1 A model of cognitive space.

phylogenetic, the ontogenetic, and the historical-cultural. The phylogenetic dimension of an individual's or a species' mind expresses the genetic potential derived from evolutionary processes. The exploitation of the phylogenetic potential cannot ever be assumed to reach completion, because it depends on the two other factors, the ontogenetic-individual and cultural-historical dimensions; therefore, even if two individuals or populations have the same phylogenetic cognitive potential, their cognitive performance as seen, for example, in artifacts may be completely different according to their cultural background and individual experiences.

Phylogenetic development in human cognitive evolution can be assumed, since great apes demonstrate marked differences in cognitive behavior, regardless of whether they grew up in an intact natural group of their own species or received individual cognitive support in a modern cultural-historical environment. The cause of this development in humans may be related to physical features like the increase of relative brain size (McHenry and Coffing 2000) and possible changes in brain anatomy (Falk 1987; Bruner 2007). The genetic basis of brain size regulation and the specific human development of the brain cortex has at least partially been identified in recent years (Evans et al. 2005, 2006; Mekel-Bobrov et al. 2005; Pollard et al. 2006). A dating of developmental details (e.g., Tobias 1995), however, is problematic, as brains are not preserved in the fossil record. Only natural and artificial endocasts of fossil skulls give a rough sketch of the brain's outer form and hints on the anatomical development of some brain areas, but not on their function (Wilkins and Wakefield 1995). Genetic studies suggest other or additional possible agents which cannot be traced morphologically, like increased gene activity in the brain (Enard et al. 2002a), or the mutation of *FOXP2*, a gene involved in linguistic articulation (Enard et al. 2002b; Krause et al. 2007); their specific roles, however, remain unclear.

The ontogenetic-individual dimension incorporates the cognitive elements originating in individual actions and experiences, be they accidental or intentional. This dimension is limited by the biological potential to think and act, given by genetic characters derived from phylogeny, and is influenced by opportunities to interact with the environment. Behavioral innovations, which do not directly descend from genetic mutation, originate in this individual dimension. For the expression of the ontogenetic-individual dimension, the frame is set by the phylogenetic and the cultural-historical dimension, although individual performances may lie outside the population's mean range which is normally extrapolated from archaeological data.

The cultural-historical dimension, finally, expresses the culturally fostered factor of the mind, the cognitive dimension that is most prominent in and, in its full range, exclusive to humans. This dimension is opened by the spread of innovation in behavior, not by genetic transmission, between genetically related and unrelated individuals, within and between generations. On a low level of this cultural dimension, individuals adopt a certain behavior, whose outcomes they observe in others, by emulating it until they are personally content with the result. In a real cultural setting, however, with teaching and learning between individuals and shared attention on a problem, children do not have to find solutions on their own for problems that arise, but can rely on culturally stored solutions invented by individuals in past decades, centuries, or millennia. This historically grown solution set makes up a part of the individual's environment that can be acted on and used as a basis for further innovation – the so-called ratchet effect (Tomasello 1999). The cultural-historical dimension of the mind does not expand constantly; instead this dimension, and with it the spread of innovations, are strongly influenced by interdependent social parameters like intra- and intergroup communication, population density, social structures, the position of innovators in their groups, and general group-specific attitudes about learning, innovation, and progress (Rogers 1995). Factors such as communication that may hamper or foster the increase of the cultural dimension, have their origins partially in the phylogenetic dimension, probably with the language faculty or the capability to understand others as intentional actors (Tomasello 1999).

Cognition is the main basis of what prehistoric groups did, and this is partially expressed in the artifacts that have been preserved to our times. Thus artifacts are a means for detecting the cognitive background behind their creation. This is not easy. Indications of prehistoric people's cognitive potential – what they could think and do – have to be separated out from behavior compelled by the restrictions of the natural and social environment. Archaeology can help to delineate the cognitive space of prehistoric groups and to trace the development of the cognitive dimensions, especially the cultural-historical factor. Prehistoric archaeological research uses artifacts – objects and features created by humans – as its primary source. Their interpretation is based on the fundamental assumption that they were produced intentionally: conscious and unconscious mental decisions dictated their manufacture in this specific way and not another. On this basis, prehistoric research pursues typological approaches to the differentiation of groups and the establishment of relative chronologies, and technological approaches that illuminate the history of how the technical knowledge of early populations was applied to the manufacture of objects. Research focusing on functional aspects deals with the probable and actual use of artifacts, while spatial approaches try to discover spatial and stratigraphical structures and relations. Those four methodological approaches, which are closely connected to the material aspects of prehistoric remains, form the core of prehistoric archaeology. Social and cognitive aspects, on which the artifacts can also inform, can typically not be extrapolated from the immediate find context or the description of a complete object or its significant details, but have to be deduced through a more interpretative approach. Yet loss of evidence within the archaeological record must also be factored in; it must be kept in mind that absence of evidence cannot be equated with evidence of absence, and in not only material, but also cognitive, terms (Speth 2004). What we can detect in the archaeological record is only a group's minimum cognitive potential, which has been manifested in artifacts. Cognitive faculties that are apparently unexpressed in material remains because a group did not manifest these faculties in a material way, or because an archaeological analyst failed to recognize them, might have been present; yet researchers can only then state the lack of indication (Haidle 2007).

Theoretical Approaches to Cognitive Archaeology

Despite sometimes vivid discussions during the last decades, the rather peripheral areas of cognitive archaeology are only slowly gaining importance. The introduction to an early discussion panel entitled "What Is Cognitive Archaeology?" in the *Cambridge Archaeological Journal* (1993 3[2]), subsumes the cognitive approach to archaeology as follows: "Cognitive archaeology ... should be that part of archaeology which deals with concepts and perception. In an archaeological context this may be taken to cover the whole spectrum of human behavior, with especial reference to religion and belief, symbolism and iconography, and the development and expression of human consciousness" (p. 247) The main topics of cognitive archaeology have surfaced repeatedly ever since archaeology emerged as a field of scientific study, but were rarely the goal of deliberate research. The first systematic studies on the cognitive foundations of archaeological phenomena stem from the 1960s and 1970s. "Cognitive archaeology," a term in use since the 1980s, first emerged as a line of research in the 1990s, mainly in the United Kingdom and the United States. However, its focal points of interest and its methodological approaches to the extraction of cognitive information from artifacts remain inconsistent, owing to its widely differing theoretical foundations.

Anglo-American Cognitive Archaeology

"Cognitive archaeology" itself formed as a response to new archaeology, a process-oriented and functionalist approach with behavioristic tendencies focusing on environmental influences, settlement and subsistence patterns. Cognitive archaeology, instead, is mainly culture-oriented. It focuses on the cognitive processes that lie behind the material remains and searches the human mind for explanations of behavioral strategies and their material expression in artifacts (Whitley 1998). This line of research is not based on a unified theory and its development was undefined and unsystematic (Flannery and Marcus 1993:260). Five contributions to "Viewpoint: What is Cognitive Archaeology?" published in the *Cambridge Archaeological Journal* (1993 3[2]:247–270) mirror this diverse understanding of cognitive archaeology. Colin Renfrew (1993) defines it as a cognitive extension of the processual approach. In his opinion, the main question in cognitive-processual archaeology is not *what* earlier populations were thinking, since the ancient significance of objects and symbols is difficult to establish, but *how* – how were cultural expressions used in their specific individual context? Additionally, Renfrew detects two key aspects of cognitive archaeology. One is concerned with the connection between cognition and tool production as well as language evolution during the course of human evolution; the other is focused on the study of cultural changes among modern humans, such as sedentarization, the formation of cities and states, the emergence of agriculture, writing, metallurgy, and organized religion and ideologies. In Renfrew's approach, aspects of economic and settlement history are not rejected but incorporated and elaborated upon through the study of their cognitive foundations.

In his definition of cognitive archaeology, Christopher Peebles (1993) stresses the importance of mental capacities and the knowledge that was applied to mastering the respective natural and social environments of prehistoric societies. The study of these aspects is based on the cultural remains that mirror the use of this knowledge. Following Ian Hodder (1993), cognitive archaeology works with the symbolic and structural content of material remains, incorporates their social and historical context, proceeds hermeneutically in the search for the significance of artifacts within this context, and interprets. Hodder suggests studying cognition only in connection with the respective society and the social significance of its artifacts. Barbara Bender (1993) does not recognize cognitive archaeology as an independent line of research but sees it merely as a form of cultural materialism. Bender focuses mainly on the question of power – in prehistoric societies as well as in modern academia. Cognitive archaeology helps to identify power structures in prehistoric societies; physical structures like hill forts, enclosures, and ditch systems can express power by the way they include or exclude, signify permission or prohibition, limit, or exert pressure. As extreme representatives of a processual cognitive approach, Kent Flannery and Joyce Marcus (1993) view cognitive archaeology as a complement to basic subsistence and settlement archaeology. Its key points of research are, in their opinion, all those aspects that stem from the human mind, such as cosmology, religion, ideology (expressed in concepts, philosophy, ethics, and values), iconography, and all other forms of intellectual and symbolic behavior. Flannery and Marcus stress that these topics are not peripheral phenomena, but often form the basis of an understanding of subsistence and settlement behavior and changes therein. They reject the notion of "cognitive archaeology" as a separate line of research and argue for a generally more holistic approach, since studying the cognitive foundations of material phenomena, where applicable, is part of every archaeologist's task. Taken together, the five positions do not offer a clear definition of the theoretical and methodological lines along which cognitive archaeology is structured. Rather, it resembles a patchwork of different directions taken in the assessment of its key topic: the mental foundations of archaeological remains.

From Theory to Practice in Cognitive Archaeology

When considering publications with cognitive archaeological content (e.g., Gibson and Ingold 1993; Renfrew and Zubrow 1994; Lock and Peters 1996; Mellars and Gibson 1996; Mithen 1996; Renfrew and Scarre 1998; de Beaune et al. 2009), rather than the associated theoretical discussion, it becomes increasingly clear that cognitive archaeology incorporates processual as well as post-processual elements and does not view itself as an extension of an archaeology primarily concerned with settlement and subsistence questions. Rather, it constitutes its own line of research, the key interest of which lies in studying the development of human thinking – an original approach not covered by other lines of research. When dealing with the evolution of human thinking, models derived from developmental psychology are often used as a basis, and archaeological remains are sifted for their equivalents. Examples of this practice include Jean Piaget's theories on logical and spatial intelligence (see Piaget 1985), used in the works of Thomas Wynn (1979, 1981, 1985); Howard Gardner's model of multiple intelligences (1993) in the studies of Kate Robson Brown on early Paleolithic artifacts (1993); and the studies by John Tooby and Leda Cosmides (1989, 1992) and Annette Karmiloff-Smith (1992) on the transition from specific intelligences for certain areas of knowledge to a generalized intelligence, which influenced the writings of Steven Mithen (1994, 1996).

In an epistemological assessment of studies on Paleolithic cognition, Isabelle Saillot et al. (2002) detect three core themes:

1 The search for indicators of modern cognitive capacities, where the evaluation of the same indicators varies according to the initial view taken ("capability x is recent"; "capability x is old").
2 The reconstruction of the development of cognitive capacities, which is either approached as a theoretical question or as a matter of tool development, or is summarily rejected.
3 The development of models of cognitive capacities during the Paleolithic. While some researchers deem this development basically impossible, others insist on new, specific approaches, since they consider models developed for modern humans as non-transferable to animals or premodern humans. A third group considers the deduction of Paleolithic cognition models from modern ones as feasible.

After Saillot, it is not possible to compare the different studies on Paleolithic cognition directly, since the terminology they employ is derived in part from different fundamental concepts that are often not clearly defined. For example, the term "planning," as used in the context of tool manufacture, describes a mental concept of sequential actions and thus differs from "planning" in terms of subsistence, or the spatial planning of settlements or temple compounds. The approaches also differ in their fundamental theoretical views of the development of the human mind – genetic, cognitivistic, looking for increasing complexity, focused on primatology or zoology in general – and their assumption of what constitutes typical human behavior (e.g., language, symbolism, complex behavior, or no special characteristics). The choice of the method of research and the archaeological material considered as relevant is completely dependent on the choice of approach (Saillot et al. 2002:9).

The French Way: The Technological Concept of *Chaînes Opératoires* and the *Schéma Conceptuel*

Parallel to the Anglo-American discussions of cognitive archaeology, another cognitive-archaeological line of research, this one based on ethnological approaches (Lemonnier 1983; Karlin et al. 1991), emerged in France during the 1980s (Pélégrin et al. 1988; Nelson 1991; Pélégrin 1993; Sellet 1993). Based on technological processes that are interpreted as action chains – *chaînes opératoires* – it attempts to approach the thinking processes these chains are based upon – the *schéma conceptuel*; its main employ is in the study of Paleolithic groups. Ideally, all technical and decision processes that occur during the "lifetime" of an artifact – from the selection of the raw material through the manufacture of its basic form, its modification by shaping or remodeling, to its final discarding – can be recorded as a *chaînes opératoires*, that is, organized chains of individual actions. Within archaeology, stone tools constitute an ideal data set, since they occur frequently and are mostly resistant to erosion, so that even the debitage from their manufacturing process can be recorded, and reconstitution allows an almost unbroken reconstruction of subsequent actions.

This rather technologically oriented French line of research has so far gained little access into Anglo-American dominated cognitive archaeology (e.g., Schlanger 1994, 1996), even though it constitutes one of the stipulated methods in the research of prehistoric concepts. Similarly, the theoretical approach to cognitive archaeology has met with only minimal notice in France and central Europe. One result of this non-ideological approach to specifically human behavior and the method of process description is that the concept of *chaînes opératoires* could be transferred to animal tool production (Beyries and Joulian 1990; Joulian 1996); thus, human cognition derived from artifacts can be considered on a directly comparable level.

Models of Cognitive Evolution

The different theoretical foundations and methodological approaches to the extraction of cognitive components in archaeological inventories show a very heterogeneous picture. Their lowest common denominator is the certainty that artifacts constitute the realization of ideas in objects. The answers to whether these cognitive elements are, in fact, accessible and how this access can be realized, are as diverse as those to the questions about the physical and psychical basis of human cognition. Outside the mainstreams of latter 20th-century archaeological theory, there have been different attempts to consider cognitive evolution archaeologically. The following examples give an overview on the diversity of approaches; the list does not aim at being comprehensive.

The Paleontology of Human Thought

One archaeological attempt to illuminate the evolution of cognition appears in "Le Geste et la parole," a pioneering work by French paleontologist and prehistorian André Leroi-Gourhan (1964), who saw the development of the modern human mind paleontologically as a process in which the physical evolution of the brain released new capacities for thinking. The early development of bipedal locomotion, for instance, not only freed the hands for technical actions but, with the shift of the *foramen magnum*, also enabled an increase in size of the occipital lobes. Subsequent simple technical solutions like primitive stone tools allowed the reduction of the masticatory apparatus, which made further change in skull architecture possible;

specifically, the parietal and especially the frontal lobes could gain their modern anatomical forms and structures, and the mouth, with decreased nutritional functions, could be used for vocal communication. Brain volume is of secondary significance to Leroi-Gourhan; besides the anatomical features of an upright posture, a short face and hands not engaged in locomotion, the main marker of humankind has been the manufacture and use of tools.

Leroi-Gourhan posits that human cognitive evolution was dominated by increases in technical intelligence and vocal capabilities, capacities that developed slowly until *Homo erectus*, and then became more sophisticated, though still mainly technical, in Neanderthals. Only with the unfolding of the prefrontal cortex, bringing capacities for foresight, consciousness, the control of affect, and the ability to discern and thus to reflect on behavior, could late Neanderthals and, later, anatomically modern humans develop non-functional actions, symbolic capabilities, and creative consciousness. Thus, development was not bound solely to biological evolution, with memory encoded predominantly in the genes and with individuals inventing technical operations on their own. Rather, the new cognitive capacities fostered the ethnic group as a social memory pool with true language as a cultural storage facility, allowing the development of operational sequences in super-individual processes: in teaching and in sharing problems and solution attempts with other members of the groups. The result was the explosion of artifact varieties and symbols in the Upper Paleolithic. In sum, Leroi-Gourhan's focus lies on the physical basis of cognitive evolution with secondary support by archaeological evidence. His model concentrates on the expansion of the phylogenetic dimension of cognitive space, with the cultural-historical factor becoming important only at the end of the Middle Paleolithic.

Early *Homo* Capabilities in the Light of Piaget's Theory

A second and completely different perspective on human cognitive evolution has been taken by Thomas Wynn (1979, 1981, 1985), who applied Jean Piaget's model of ontogenetic developmental stages in children's object behavior to Lower Paleolithic artifacts, and thereby to human phylogeny. The first developmental stage, young infants' sensorimotor intelligence, characterized by pure activity-based intelligence without inner representations of the actions, can also be observed in primate tool behavior; in this stage, activity cannot be reasoned out in advance. The second stage, pre-operational intelligence, is marked by inner representations of single consecutive tasks, so that anticipation of the results of an action is limited to the change in only one variable at time; planning of an action is therefore restricted to trial and error. Wynn (1981) has identified this stage in chimpanzee tool manufacture, as well as in the simple technology of Oldowan core tool assemblages.

The next stage, the concrete-operational phase, allows coordination of changes in several variables. It is now possible to anticipate the result of an operational sequence or to construct the operational sequence for reaching a desired result, so complex planning can proceed, and errors can be envisioned and corrected before they are executed. This concrete-operational stage, which, according to Piaget, should be fully developed by age 11 to 13, is identified by Wynn (1979) in the bifacial technology of Acheulian handaxes. Diverging from Piaget (1972, 1985), who differentiated between concrete-operational intelligence in children and the formal-operational intelligence that succeeds it in modern adults, Wynn merges these two stages and concludes that human phylogenetic development of cognition – as it can be seen from technological perspective – reached modern competence around 300,000 years ago, at the latest. Although Wynn's interpretation needs re-evaluation in light of challenges to Piaget's theory by modern psychology, his attempt to adapt an object-directed psychological theory to archaeological analysis of artifact traits is an interesting example of a cross-disciplinary approach. A summary of Wynn's model of the development of spatial cognition and the significance of symmetry can be found in Wynn (2002) together with several comments.

From Domain-Specific Intelligence to a Fluent Mind

A third approach has been developed by Steven Mithen (1994, 1996), who created a hypothetical model of the phylogenetic development of human cognition, based on psychological models of different cognitive domains in modern humans. Mithen identifies four distinct domains of intuitive intelligence in modern children that, he believes, reach back to Pleistocene times: linguistic, social, technical, and natural history. Only when these types of intelligence are combined can the knowledge specific to one domain be generalized to the other domains and made usable beyond the circumstances in which it arose, enabling creativity to develop. Analyzing the technical and environmental behavior of modern chimpanzees, as well as the assumed behavior of the common ancestors of humans and chimpanzees, and assessing that both originate in a basic general intelligence domain, Mithen detects in these species only one specialized domain, social intelligence, which, he believes, became fully developed in early *Homo* at around 2 million years. In his opinion, the technical and natural history domains arose sometime up to 1.8 million years and allowed the *Homo* genus' expansion out of Africa and spread to large parts of the Old World. For the following one million years, mental organization did not show major changes, paralleling a trend of stagnation in relative brain growth. Mithen expects that linguistic intelligence came into being between 0.5 and 0.1 million years, but was initially bound to social intelligence; he assumes that technical and environmental issues could not be talked about at that time because these issues were still encapsulated in their own domains. A cultural explosion took place between 60,000 and 30,000 years before present, when, according to Mithen, the knowledge stored in specific intelligence domains became accessible to the other domains. This cognitive fluidity is evidenced in archaeological artifacts like bone and antler tools, blade technology, grave goods, the expansion of occupation to Australia, personal ornaments, and art – all of which require a combination of knowledge from social, linguistic, technical, and natural history domains. This model, while provocative, consists of open generalizations that fail to account, for example, for how the Late Acheulean wooden spears from Clacton or Schöningen could be manufactured before the development of a cognitive synthesis. Thus, Mithen's model of distinct intelligence domains becoming fluent on the eve of modern behavior can be summed up as adapting hypotheses from evolutionary psychology to human cognitive evolution by matching them in a rather speculative way to selected parts of the archaeological record.

Language and Symbolic Behavior as Milestones of Cognition

In a fourth prospective on the cognitive basis of early human tool behavior, the psychologist William Noble and the archaeologist Iain Davidson erect a phylogenetic model of human cognitive development on the premise that, unlike chimpanzees, modern humans can share their awareness of objects and events, to which they can give socially constructed meaning with the help of language (Noble and Davidson 1996). Their research starts with observations of aimed throwing as the hypothetical germ of pointing, a primeval mode of sharing awareness intentionally. Aiming or pointing, they posit, could have developed into iconic, representational gestures that, in their repetition, could have left chance traces on some material. Once recognized and imitated as representatives of the gesture, these signs might have become symbols; and once the principle of representing symbols was understood, the faculty of language might have arisen as a result of the shared meanings. Language, then, allowed ways of thinking which had been impossible without it: it permitted the description of perceptions, reflections, memories, plans for the future, and awareness of oneself as part of the world and as a perceptive individual. To support their model of the development of shared assignment of meaning through language, Noble and Davidson look for evidence of symbolic behavior and planning in archaeological remains. Up to and including the Middle Paleolithic, they find that no specific artifact forms were produced in a goal-directed process, and that the observed progress is only technological, not conceptual. For the authors, however, Upper Paleolithic art and the colonization of Australia by boat are the most prominent among the first markers of modern cognitive aspects which derive from language, constituting true manifestations of symbols and planning. This model, again, constitutes an attempt to parallelize ideas derived from psychology with some selected artifacts and events in prehistory.

The Frontal Lobe – Home of Modernity

In a fifth approach, Frederick Coolidge and Thomas Wynn (2001, 2004, 2005) pick up the model of the phylogenetically evolved frontal lobe of the brain as the seat of executive functions and the working memory, which is the ability to hold a variety of information in active attention. The development of the cortical frontal lobe was already viewed by Leroi-Gourhan (1964; see above) as a factor in the evolution of modern human cognition. From the observation of behavioral problems in people with damage to the frontal area of the brain, either caused by accidents or congenital, several executive functions of this part of the brain could be deduced: decision-making, formulation of objectives, planning and organization as well as the development of strategies to achieve a goal, and the exertion of control in case of the disruption of planned actions, their obstruction, and their mental integration through space and time or sequential memory. In their search for the key factor of modern human behavior, which they locate around the beginning of the Late Paleolithic, Frederick Coolidge and Thomas Wynn (2001, 2005) revisit the hereditary executive functions of the frontal lobe and the working memory as the crucial characteristic. In their opinion, the transition to modern cognitive capacities is not linked to an anatomical change visible in the skeleton – such as Leroi-Gourhan's (1964) "unlocking of the forehead"– but can be viewed as neuronal reconnections caused by simple changes on the genetic level.

To corroborate their hypothesis, Coolidge and Wynn (2001) search for indicators of some of these executive functions within the archaeological material. The function of sequential memory is the basis of complex action sequences. It is only for between 100,000 and 50,000 years before present that they accept evidence of a truly multistage technology. A second executive function, the suspension of an immediate reward for an action or the action itself, can be detected in the archaeological context at the earliest during the Late Paleolithic, finding its expression in storage, the cultivation of plants, animal husbandry, or indirect means of capture such as traps. Organization or planning as a third executive function of the frontal lobe coordinates different actions; the transport of raw materials over several kilometers does not meet these conditions, according to the authors, and has to be omitted from the evidence for the thus defined form of planning. Like Noble and Davidson (1996), they cite the colonization of the Sahul region (Australia, New Guinea, and Tasmania) by *Homo sapiens* around 60,000–50,000 years before present as the earliest unambiguous product of the planning function of the frontal lobe. Neanderthal cognition, in contrast, shows modern aspects in expert performance in problem-solving via the long-term working memory. Neanderthals' working memory capacity, however, may not have been as large as that of modern humans (Coolidge and Wynn 2004; Wynn and Coolidge 2004).

In their studies, Coolidge and Wynn do not follow the evolution of cognition as visible in archaeological artifacts but search for the possible cause of a jump in evolution that would explain the changes in artifact inventories at the transition from the Middle to the Late Paleolithic. Older aspects of the human mind, such as spatial cognition (see Wynn 1979, 1981, 1985), are assumed; thus, the evolution of human thinking took place in several independent steps, the latest of which – the expansion of the executive function of the frontal lobe and the working memory – led to modern human behavior. A broader multidisciplinary discussion of the "working memory" approach is given in Wynn and Coolidge (2010).

Increasing Distances between Problems and Solutions

A sixth approach to human cognitive evolution on the basis of tool behavior focuses on a particular attribute of artifacts: the dissociation of problems and solutions. In his famous experiments, especially with chimpanzees, in the early 20th century, Köhler (1963) recognized tool behavior as an extension of the process of loop way thinking. If tool use is considered to solve a problem, then the immediate desire, to get a fruit, for example, has to be set aside for one or several intermediate objectives, such as finding or producing an appropriate tool. Thus, at least in the short term, thinking and resulting physical actions must depart from the immediate problem. Separated from each other, the different elements of mental or physical operations may not seem to be useful; if one is unable to conceptualize a tool for termite-fishing, it does not make sense to look for a thin and flexible twig in the bushes five meters away from the termite mound. However, only in the combination of these different operational elements can the final aim be reached. In essence, thinking shifts from the immediate givens of a problem to abstract conceptualizations of possible solutions and sequences of means, necessitating appropriate tools, for achieving these solutions in the future. The more tools and their manufacture can be dissociated from immediate subsistence aims, the more soluble problems become (Haidle 2008, 2010).

When a herbivore feels the need to feed, and looks for some grass and eats it, there is the minimum distance between problem (hunger) and solution (eating grass). Any tool use extends the problem–solution distance (see above). An increasing distance between problems and solutions in human evolution can in fact be observed by coding different human artifact behavior in cognigrams and comparing it with animal tool behavior, respectively, on a chronological scale. Examples of major extensions of the problem–solution distance and thus the range of soluble problems are the use of secondary tools (tools to produce tools to solve a problem; see Kitahara-Frisch 1993) first manifested in stone tools flaked with the help of a stone hammer 2.5 million years ago (Semaw et al. 1997). The increasing extensions of distances for raw material acquisition up to several kilometers from circa 2 million years on reveal the perception of a sub-acute need, followed by long-term actions that may have been interrupted (but not stopped) by other problems. The special form concept of hand axes, a distinct stone artifact type from circa 1.5 million years on (Asfaw et al. 1992) with simple to very sophisticated realizations, then requires the adjustment of the manufacture process to a mental template. Evaluating several variables at a time, the knapper had to regularly control intermediate results with the final aim and to match the following actions in recursive loops (Haidle 2006). The duration of the manufacturing process of wooden spears as those from the 300,000–400,000-year-old site of Schöningen (Thieme 1997), finally, can be estimated on the basis of experiments to a minimum length of several days (Haidle 2009). The operational sequence is extremely extended in both duration and complexity. This high level of complexity in tool behavior is possible only by decoupling satisfaction and basic need, such that the manufacture and curation of tools can become an aim and a satisfaction in and of itself, independent of current basic needs. The resulting small operational units, each autonomous with its own intermediate aim, can be assembled in a modular way within different operational sequences: several operational units can be combined side by side, or in an effective chain. Thus, the modular way of handling tools allows a level of behavioral flexibility and complexity – for example, in composite tools such as spears with hafted projectile points – barely conceivable without the modular simplification. Decoupling of need and satisfaction and the consequent modular tool behavior are the basis for the increasing acceleration and diversification in the development of material culture with prominent stages like the emergence of figurative art at around 40,000 years before present, of sedentarism and food production at around 10,000 years before present, and of the industrial and the digital revolution in the last two centuries.

Conclusions

The evolution of cognition is a process as multifaceted as cognition itself. The prehistoric evidence of its manifestation is plentiful but extremely selected. Only some of the facets can eventually be tracked down in the archaeological record. Thus it is obvious that none of the attempts to study human cognitive evolution can be explaining the complete spectrum. Cognitive archaeology relies on different psychological models, uses neuro-anatomical hints and seeks evidence of increasingly complex thoughts and higher mental states in artifacts. Theories and methods vary tremendously. The approaches can be judged on their theoretical basis – often borrowed from other disciplines – or on the methods or archaeological data used to match to the theories. A world formula that is able to delineate the whole process of cognitive evolution by retracing the development of one super-trait is an illusion. A multitude of approaches is needed. Yet, Colin Renfrew's (1996) fundamental critique, namely, that the presented indicators of changes accompanied by a cognitive revolution around 40,000 years before present are sparse and often include circular arguments, still applies. His ensuing demand for the development of more effective methods for the study of cognitive processes should be taken as an incentive to further methodological and theoretical developments within cognitive archaeology.

NOTE

1 Paleolithic: Stone Age before the Neolithic development of agriculture and sedentary way of life, from first evidence of human material culture around 2.5 million years ago to around 10,000 BC.

REFERENCES

Asfaw, B., Y. Beyene, G. Suwa, R. C. Walter, T. D. White, G. WoldeGabriel, and T. Yemane
1992 The Earliest Acheulean from Konso-Gardula. Nature 360:732–735.
Bender, Barbara
1993 Cognitive Archaeology and Cultural Materialism. Contribution to "Viewpoint: What Is Cognitive Archaeology?" Cambridge Archaeological Journal 3(2):257–260.
Beyries, S., and Frédéric Joulian
1990 L'Utilisation d'outils chez les animaux: Chaînes opératoires et complexité technique. Paléo 2:17–26.
Bruner, Emiliano
2007 Cranial Shape and Size Variation in Human Evolution: Structural and Functional Perspectives. Child's Nervous System 23:1357–1365.
Coolidge, Frederick L., and Thomas Wynn
2001 Executive Functions of the Frontal Lobes and the Evolutionary Ascendancy of *Homo Sapiens*. Cambridge Archaeological Journal 11(2): 255–260.
2004 A Cognitive and Neuropsychological Perspective on the Chatelperronian. Journal of Anthropological Research 60(1):55–73.
2005 Working Memory, Its Executive Functions, and the Emergence of Modern Thinking. Cambridge Archaeological Journal 15(1): 5–26.
de Beaune, A. Sophie, Frederick L. Coolidge, and Thomas Wynn, eds.
2009 Cognitive Archaeology and Human Evolution. New York: Cambridge University Press.
d'Errico, Francesco
2003 The Invisible Frontier: A Multiple Species Model for the Origin of Behavioral Modernity. Evolutionary Anthropology 12:188–202.
2007 The Origin of Humanity and Modern Cultures: Archaeology's View. Diogenes 54(2):122–133.

d'Errico, Francesco, Christopher Henshilwood, Graeme Lawson, Marian Vanhaeren, Anne-Marie Tillier, Marie Soressi, Frédérique Bresson, Bruno Maureille, April Nowell, Joseba Lakarra, Lucinda Backwell, and Michèle Julien

2003 Archaeological Evidence for the Emergence of Language, Symbolism, and Music: An Alternative Multidisciplinary Perspective. Journal of World Prehistory 17(1):1–70.

Enard, Wolfgang, Philipp Khaitovich, Joachim Klose, Sebastian Zöllner, Florian Heissig, Patrick Giavalisco, Kay Nieselt-Struwe, Elaine Muchmore, Ajit Varki, Rivka Ravid, Gaby M. Doxiadis, Ronald E. Bontrop, and Svante Pääbo

2002a Intra- and Interspecific Variation in Primate Gene Expression Patterns. Science 296:340–343.

Enard, Wolfgang, Molly Przeworski, Simon E. Fisher, Cecilia S. L. Lai, Victor Wiebe, Takashi Kitano, Anthony P. Monaco, and Svante Pääbo

2002b Molecular Evolution of *FOXP2*, a Gene Involved in Speech and Language. Nature 418:869–872.

Evans, Patrick D., Eric J. Vallender, and Bruce T. Lahn

2005 Molecular Evolution of the Brain Size Regulator Genes CDK5RAP2 and CENPJ. Gene 375:75–79.

Evans, Patrick D., Sandra L. Gilbert, Nitzan Mekel-Bobrov, Eric J. Vallender, Jeffrey R. Anderson, Leila M. Vaez-Azizi, Sarah A. Tishkoff, Richard R. Hudson, and Bruce T. Lahn

2006 Microcephalin, a Gene Regulating Brain Size, Continues to Evolve Adaptively in Humans. Science 309:1717–1720.

Falk, Dean

1987 Hominid Paleoneurology. Annual Review of Anthropology 16:13–30.

Flannery, Kent V., and Joyce Marcus

1993 Cognitive Archaeology. Contribution to "Viewpoint: What is Cognitive Archaeology?" Cambridge Archaeological Journal 3(2):260–270.

Gardner, Howard

1993 Frames of Mind: The Theory of Multiple Intelligences. New York: Basic Books.

Gibson, Kathleen R., and Tim Ingold, eds.

1993 Tools, Language and Cognition in Human Evolution. Cambridge: Cambridge University Press.

Haidle, Miriam Noël

2006 Menschen – Denken – Objekte: Zur Problem-Lösung-Distanz als Kognitionsaspekt im Werkzeugverhalten von Tieren und im Laufe der menschlichen Evolution. Habilitation thesis, Faculty of Geosciences, Eberhard Karls University of Tübingen.

2007 Archaeology. *In* Handbook of Palaeoanthropology, vol.1: Principles, Methods, and Approaches. W. Henke and I. Tattersall, eds. Pp. 261–287. Heidelberg: Springer.

2008 Kognitive und Kulturelle Evolution, with critiques of Bernd Baldus, Thomas Bargatzky, Andrea Bender, Olaf Breidbach, Ditmar Brock, Lutz Fiedler, Ulrich Frey, Matthias Herrgen and Winfried Henke, Maria Kronfeldner, Ulrich Krull, Rolf Löther, Heinz-Jürgen Niedenzu, Rolf Oerter, Heidi Peter-Röcher, Helmut Prior, Peter Schauer, Thomas Schauer, Thomas Sukopp, Natalie Thaïs Uomini, Jörg Wettlaufer. Erwägen–Wissen–Ethik 19(2):149–209.

2009 How to Think a Simple Spear? *In* Cognitive Archaeology and Human Evolution. Sophie A. de Beaune, Frederick L. Coolidge, and Thomas Wynn, eds. Pp. 57–73. New York: Cambridge University Press.

2010 Working Memory Capacity and the Evolution of Modern Cognitive Capacities: Implications from Animal and Early Human Tool Use. Current Anthropology 51(suppl. 1): S149–S166.

Henshilwood, Christopher S., and Curtis W. Marean

2003 The Origin of Modern Behavior: Critique of the Models and Their Test Implications. Current Anthropology 44(5):627–651.

Hodder, Ian
1993 Social Cognition. Contribution to "Viewpoint: What is Cognitive Archaeology?" Cambridge Archaeological Journal 3(2):253–257.
Joulian, Frédéric
1996 Comparing Chimpanzee and Early Hominid Techniques: Some Contributions to Cultural and Cognitive Questions. *In* Modelling the Early Human Mind. Paul Mellars and Kathleen Gibson, eds. Pp. 173–189. Cambridge: McDonald Institute for Archaeological Research.
Karlin C., P. Bodu, and J. Pélégrin
1991 Processus techniques et chaînes opératoires: Comment les préhistoriens s'approprient un concept élaboré par les ethnologues. *In* Observer l'action technique des chaînes opératoires, pour quoi faire? H. Balfet, ed. Pp. 101–117. Paris: CNRS.
Karmiloff-Smith, Annette
1992 Beyond Modularity: A Developmental Perspective on Cognitive Science. Cambridge, MA: MIT Press.
Kitahara-Frisch, Jean
1993 The Origin of Secondary Tools. *In* The Use of Tools by Human and Non-Human Primates. A. Berthelet and J. Chavaillon, eds. Pp. 239–246. Oxford: Clarendon.
Klein, Richard G.
2000 Archaeology and the Evolution of Human Behavior. Evolutionary Anthropology 9:17–36.
Klein, Richard, and Blake Edgar
2002 The Dawn of Human Culture. New York: John Wiley.
Köhler, Wolfgang
1963 Intelligenzprüfungen an Menschenaffen. Facsimile of 2nd rev. edition of "Intelligenzprüfungen an Anthropoiden I." Abhandlungen der Preussischen Akademie der Wissenschaften Jahrgang 1917, Physikal.-Mathem. Klasse 1, 1921. Berlin: Springer.
Krause, Johannes, Carles Lalueza-Fox, Ludovic Orlando, Wolfgang Enard, Richard E. Green, Hernán A. Burbano, Jean-Jacques Hublin, Catherine Hänni, Javier Fortea, Marco de la Rasilla, Jaume Bertranpetit, Antonio Rosas, and Svante Pääbo
2007 The Derived FOXP2 Variant of Modern Humans was Shared with Neandertals. Current Biology 17:1–5.
Lemonnier, Pierre
1983 La Description des systèmes techniques: Une urgence en technologie culturelle. Techniques et Culture 1:11–26.
Leroi-Gourhan, André
1964 Le Geste et la parole. Paris: Albin Michel.
Lock, Andrew, and Charles R. Peters, eds.
1996 Handbook of Human Symbolic Evolution. Oxford: Oxford University Press.
McBrearty, Sally, and Allison S. Brooks
2000 The Revolution That Wasn't: A New Interpretation of the Origin of Modern Human Behavior. Journal of Human Evolution 39:453–563.
McHenry, Henry M., and Katherine Coffing
2000 *Australopithecus* to *Homo*: Transformations in Body and Mind. Annual Review of Anthropology 29:125–146.
Mekel-Bobrov, Nitzan, Sandra L. Gilbert, Patrick D. Evans, Eric J. Vallender, Jeffrey R. Anderson, Richard R. Hudson, Sarah A. Tishkoff, and Bruce T. Lahn
2005 Ongoing Adaptive Evolution of ASPM, a Brain Size Determinant in Homo Sapiens. Science 309:1720–1722.
Mellars, Paul
1996 Symbolism, Language, and the Neanderthal Mind. *In* Modelling the Early Human Mind. P. Mellars and K. R. Gibson, eds. Pp. 15–32. Cambridge: McDonald Institute for Archaeological Research.

2005 The Impossible Coincidence: A Single-Species Model for the Origins of Modern Human Behavior in Europe. Evolutionary Anthropology 14:12–27.
Mellars, Paul, and Kathleen R. Gibson, eds.
1996 Modelling the Early Human Mind. Cambridge: McDonald Institute for Archaeological Research.
Mithen, Steven S.
1994 From Domain Specific to Generalized Intelligence: A Cognitive Interpretation of the Middle/Upper Palaeolithic Transition. *In* The Ancient Mind: Elements of Cognitive Archaeology. Colin Renfrew and Ezra B.W. Zubrow, eds. Pp. 29–39. Cambridge: Cambridge University Press.
1996 The Prehistory of the Mind: A Search for the Origins of Art, Religion and Science. London: Thames and Hudson.
2006 The Singing Neanderthals: The Origins of Music, Language, Mind, and Body. Cambridge, MA: Harvard University Press.
Nelson, M.
1991 The Study of Technological Organization. *In* Archaeological Method and Theory, vol. 3. M. B. Schiffer, ed. Pp. 57–100. Tucson: University of Arizona Press.
Noble, William, and Iain Davidson
1996 Human Evolution, Language and Mind: A Psychological and Archaeological Inquiry. Cambridge: Cambridge University Press.
Peebles, Christopher S.
1993 Aspects of a Cognitive Archaeology. Contribution to "Viewpoint: What is Cognitive Archaeology?" Cambridge Archaeological Journal 3(2):250–253.
Pélégrin, Jacques
1993 A Framework for Analysing Prehistoric Stone Tool Manufacture and a Tentative Application to Some Early Stone Industries. *In* The Use of Tools by Human and Non Human Primates. A. Berthelet and J. Chavaillon, eds. Pp. 302–317. Oxford: Clarendon.
Pélégrin, J., C. Karlin, and P. Bodu
1988 "Chaînes opératoires": Un outil pour le préhistorien. *In* Technologie lithique. J. Tixier, ed. Pp. 55–62. Notes et Monographies Techniques no. 25. Paris: CNRS.
Piaget, Jean
1972 The Theory of Stages in Cognitive Development. *In* Critical Features of Piaget's Theory of the Development of Thought. F. Murray, ed. Pp. 116–126. New York: MSS Information.
1985 Meine Theorie der geistigen Entwicklung. Frankfurt am Main: Fischer.
Pollard, Katherine S., Sofie R. Salama, Nelle Lambert, Marie-Alexandra Lambot, Sandra Coppens, Jakob S. Pedersen, Sol Katzman, Bryan King, Courtney Onodera, Adam Siepel, Andrew D. Kern, Colette Dehay, Haller Igel, Manuel Ares Jr., Pierre Vanderhaeghen, and David Haussler
2006 An RNA Gene Expressed During Cortical Development Evolved Rapidly in Humans. Nature 443:167–172.
Renfrew, Colin
1993 Cognitive Archaeology: Some Thoughts on the Archaeology of Thoughts. Contribution to "Viewpoint: What is Cognitive Archaeology?" Cambridge Archaeological Journal 3(2):248–250.
1996 The Sapient Behaviour Paradox: How to Test for Potential? *In* Modelling the Early Human Mind. Paul Mellars and Kathleen R. Gibson, eds. Pp. 11–14. Cambridge: McDonald Institute for Archaeological Research.
Renfrew, Colin, and Chris Scarre, eds.
1998 Cognition and Material Culture: The Archaeology of Symbolic Storage. Cambridge: McDonald Institute for Archaeological Research.
Renfrew, Colin, and Ezra B. W. Zubrow, eds.
1994 The Ancient Mind: Elements of Cognitive Archaeology. Cambridge: Cambridge University Press.

Robson Brown, Kate
1993 An Alternative Approach to Cognition in the Lower Palaeolithic: The Modular View. Cambridge Archaeological Journal 3(2):231–245.

Rogers, Everett M.
1995 Diffusion of Innovations. 4th edition. New York: Free Press.

Saillot, Isabelle, Marylène Patou-Mathis, and Marcel Otte
2002 Une critique épistémologique des analyses de paléocognition. Préhistoire Européenne 16–17(2000–2001):9–15.

Schlanger, Nathan
1994 Mindful Technology: Unleashing the *Chaîne Opératoire* for an Archaeology of Mind. *In* The Ancient Mind: Elements of Cognitive Archaeology. Colin Renfrew and Ezra B. W. Zubrow, eds. Pp. 143–151. Cambridge: Cambridge University Press.
1996 Understanding Levallois: Lithic Technology and Cognitive Archaeology. Cambridge Archaeological Journal 6(2):231–254.

Sellet, F.
1993 Chaîne Opératoire: The Concept and Its Applications. Lithic Technology 18(1–2):106–112.

Semaw, S., P. Renne, W. K. Harris, C. S. Feibel, R. L. Bernor, N. Fesseha, and K. Mowbray
1997 2.5-Million-Year-Old Stone Tools from Gona, Ethiopia. Nature 385:333–336.

Speth, J. D.
2004 News Flash: Negative Evidence Convicts Neanderthals of Gross Mental Incompetence. World Archaeology 36(4):519–526.

Thieme, H.
1997 Lower Paleolithic Hunting Spears from Germany. Nature 385:807–810.

Tobias, Philipp V.
1995 The Communication of the Dead: Earliest Vestiges of the Origin of Articulate Language. Kroon-Vordracht 17.3. Amsterdam: Stichting Nederlands Museum voor Anthropologie en Praehistorie.

Tomasello, Michael
1999 The Cultural Origins of Human Cognition. Cambridge, MA: Harvard University Press.

Tooby, John, and Leda Cosmides
1989 Evolutionary Psychology and the Generation of Culture. Part I: Theoretical Considerations. Ethology and Sociobiology 10:29–49.
1992 The Psychological Foundations of Culture. *In* The Adapted Mind: Evolutionary Psychology and the Generation of Culture. Jerome H. Barkow, Leda Cosmides, and John Tooby, eds. Pp. 19–136. New York: Oxford University Press.

Verworn, Max
1915 Die Entwicklung des menschlichen Geistes. 3rd edition. Jena: Gustav Fischer.

Whitley, David S.
1998 New Approaches to Old Problems: Archaeology in Search of an Ever Elusive Past. *In* Reader in Archaeological Theory: Postprocessual and Cognitive Archaeology. David S. Whitley, ed. Pp. 1–28. London: Routledge.

Wilkins, Wendy K., and Jennie Wakefield
1995 Brain Evolution and Neurolinguistic Preconditions. Behavioral and Brain Sciences 18:161–226.

Wynn, Thomas
1979 The Intelligence of Later Acheulean Hominids. Man 14:371–391.
1981 The Intelligence of Oldowan Hominids. Journal of Human Evolution 10:529–541.
1985 Piaget, Stone Tools and the Evolution of Human Intelligence. World Archaeology 17:32–43.
2002 Archaeology and Cognitive Evolution. Behavioral and Brain Sciences 25:389–438.

Wynn, Thomas, and Frederick L. Coolidge
2004 The Expert Neanderthal Mind. Journal of Human Evolution 46:467–487.
2007 Did a Small but Significant Enhancement in Working Memory Capacity Power the Evolution of Modern Thinking? *In* Rethinking the Human Revolution. P. Mellars, K. Boyle, O. Bar-Yosef, and C. B. Stringer, eds. Pp. 79–90. Cambridge: McDonald Institute for Archaeological Research.
Wynn, Thomas, and Frederick L. Coolidge, eds.
2010 Beyond Symbolism and Language: An Introduction to Supplement 1, Working Memory. Current Anthropology 51(suppl. 1): S5–S16.

PART V

Some Examples of Contemporary Research

CHAPTER 25 The Distributed Cognition Model of Mind

Brian Hazlehurst

The cognitive revolution of the 1950s forged a particular division of intellectual labor between psychologists and anthropologists which persists in the modern study of mind. Cognition, for psychologists, is typically defined by the properties of processing over internal knowledge states. Culture, for anthropologists, is generally defined by properties of human living stemming from a people's shared history. For many anthropologists studying living peoples, culture is defined to be what members of such groups know, which directs or informs the way people act, and make sense of, their world. The cognitive revolution, in other words, provided a common framework for these disciplines in which the mechanism of knowing – processing over internal knowledge states – could be integrated with the content of what is known – the mental products of histories of social living (e.g., Hutchins 1980; Quinn and Holland 1987; D'Andrade 1989a).

While the fields of anthropology and psychology have always defined their subject matter in relation to the boundary provided by individual persons, the cognitive revolution consecrated this boundary with the development of a specific architecture for human cognition. This architecture was created in the image of the digital computer or Turing machine, as the general formulation is known. In the late 1950s, this architecture (we will call it the Turing machine mind, or TMM) provided the foundation for an emerging sub-discipline in computer science – artificial intelligence – whose charter mission was to investigate the possibility that computational processes embodied by the Turing machine constitute human cognition and intelligence generally (e.g., Turing 1950; Feigenbaum 1963; Newell and Simon 1963).

Below I argue that the conception of mind forged in this era – which continues today in the cognitive sciences – has led to some theoretical impasses in the study of culture and cognition. An alternative model of mind is then advanced based upon a reconstruction of the natures of, and relationships between, culture and cognition.

A Companion to Cognitive Anthropology, First Edition. Edited by David B. Kronenfeld, Giovanni Bennardo, Victor C. de Munck, and Michael D. Fischer.

This reconstruction, a model of mind employing the perspective of "distributed cognition," is founded upon the notions that (1) cognition is built out of interactions among structures providing the building blocks for information-processing that supports organized behavior; (2) these interactions (instances of processes which employ and create structures) are not limited to events internal to agents, but distribute across diverse media, social space, and time; and (3) culture is itself such a process, generating many of the structures and processes constituting human cognition. The paper addresses how the model resolves the theoretical impasses brought on by a commitment to the TMM as cognitive architecture. It is argued that the model implicates a renewed role for anthropology in the interdisciplinary study of cognition. It is also argued that the distributed cognition model of mind holds promise for advancing a theory of culture that is useful to anthropology.

The Turing Machine Mind (TMM) as Cognitive Architecture

A Turing machine is an abstract device consisting of a *tape* which can store an infinite number of *symbols* (instances of members of a finite set of *basic symbols*), and a *head* which can read and write symbols at a single location (i.e., where the head is positioned) on the tape. The head, in turn, is under control of a finite set of rules (the *program*) which can interpret the symbols read off the tape, deterministically change the internal state of the machine, generate symbols to be written to the tape, and move the head across the tape (Hopcroft and Ullman 1979). This device describes the logical essence of all modern digital computers. The machine's program defines a set of conditions under which – beginning with some start state – possible final states can be achieved. For present purposes, let us focus upon two key aspects of this formulation.

1 There is a fundamental division between program and data. Data are instances of elements from the finite set of basic symbols. Data reside on the tape – whether put there by an external agency or by the internal program. The program directs processing – the deterministic, serial organization of input from and output to the tape, together with control of transition of the machine through an internal state space which defines the functions performed.
2 The symbols which inform processing are inherently representational in the sense that their existence and meanings are assumed by the program. The symbols encountered on the tape are always of some type or class which is (syntactically) well defined over the set of rules making up the program and (semantically) well defined over the world in which the machine operates.

The concept of mind built in the image of digital computers (TMM) can now be stated in terms of the following correspondence between the functional physiology of humans and the computational properties of a Turing machine:

3 Cognition can be explained as the manipulation of mental representations according to the functional constraints of physiology. Computation is the manipulation of data according to constraints provided by the rules of a program.

The TMM has been consecrated in a set of methodologies which treat it as fundamental to research programs for the study of mind. Cognitive psychologists have held that evidence for physiological constraints (the program) can be generated by controlled laboratory study of instances of cognition in which the nature of mental representations (data) and their manipulation (effects of the program) can be specified (e.g., Miller et al. 1960; Pylyshyn 1990[1980]). Complementing this, practitioners in artificial intelligence (e.g., Newell and Simon 1963, 1990[1976]) have held that by building simulations of cognitive behavior, manipulations of data (taken to be mental representations) will yield valid models of human physiology (the program). Finally, cognitive anthropologists have pursued a cross-cultural search for relations between mental representations (data) which, as shared knowledge, inform local competence (effects of the program) and universal properties (the program) of the human mind (e.g., Wallace 1961; D'Andrade 1981; Boyer 1994).[1]

Three Theoretical Impasses Introduced by the TMM

Clearly, the central point of contact between cognitive science and anthropology has been the notion of ***knowledge*** which emerges from the TMM. In particular, knowledge is the data in a cognitive system which is bounded by the skull of an individual. As such, knowledge is composed of symbols (tokens stored on the tape of a symbol processing machine) which have certain properties. For instance, symbols are members of classes and can be combined to form larger symbol structures under the operations of the program (Fodor and Pylyshyn 1988). This notion of ***compositionality*** is essential to the TMM, for it must be the case – having closed out the external world from playing any active processing role – that meaningful complex constructions can be generated from basic symbols by the application of rules from the program.[2]

However, by subordinating a theory of knowledge to the requirements of compositionality the TMM generates a theoretical impasse, the Ungrounded Symbols Impasse:

> How can knowledge (instances of symbol structures, physically realized internal to individuals) simultaneously be connected to the world and be elements of the private machinations of brains?

In order to ensure compositionality in the TMM, symbols must be predominantly syntactic objects. The operations performed by the rules of the program, if they are to generate intelligence, cannot be held hostage to complexity in the relationships between symbols and the world (Fetzer 1992). The notion of compositionality requires that symbols' essential contributions to cognitive functions be derived from their syntactic structure – that is, their membership in class hierarchies which define the ways they are to be treated by rules of the program (e.g., Haglund 1985; Fodor and Pylyshyn 1988; Newell and Simon 1990[1976]). And yet, there is significant empirical evidence for the argument that cognitive actions are essentially tied to the world and construal of experience in the world. This has been documented in domains as diverse as planning and action (Suchman 1987; Kirsh and Maglio 1994), problem-solving (Goodwin and Goodwin 1996; Ochs et al. 1996; Hutchins and Palen 1997), reasoning (Johnson-Laird and Wason 1977; D'Andrade 1989b), and language (Langacker 1986; Lakoff 1987; Levinson and Brown 1992). The Ungrounded Symbols Impasse is a symptom of the fact that *symbols are unproblematically representational in the TMM. Once imported into the system, they fill certain formal or syntactic roles which enable idealized cognitive functions without further recourse to the world.*

The second theoretical impasse, the *Homogeneous Agents Impasse*, arises from what the TMM implies about a group of individuals who share experience or a cultural history, namely:

> How can knowledge (internal structures built from a single, finite set of basic symbols) do the work necessary to accomplish coordinated behavior among all of the members of a group who are said to share a culture?

The most obvious solution is to assume – as anthropologists typically have – that knowledge is shared by members of a culture. For both implicit and explicit subscribers to the TMM, culture is or is derived from shared knowledge responsible for behavior. The implication is that the same symbol structures must be resident within each individual. The empirical facts are, however, that intracultural variation in knowledge is pervasive (Boster 1987; Gatewood 2001; Atran et al. 2005) – that is, individuals' knowledge structures are *often distinct and perhaps never equivalent.* But if individuals are using the same program with significantly different data structures, then how are complex acts of coordination such as effective communication possible, let alone commonplace accomplishments? The TMM offers no alternative to shared knowledge as explanation for the preponderance of coordinated behaviors among individuals which is routinely exhibited in human activities. The Homogeneous Agents Impasse is a symptom of the TMM's commitment to bounding the cognitive system at the skin of the individual. *The operation of rules upon symbols bounded in this way addresses the processing of an idealized subject, but fails to account for the empirical facts about variability in knowledge and thus has no explanation (because it ignores) the phenomena of coordinated action.*

The third, and final, impasse discussed here arises from the ontological status of the TMM as a system that entails knowledge or knowing. The *Teleological Symbols Impasse* can be stated as:

> How can basic knowledge (the finite set of basic symbols) ever have come into existence in the first place?

Since all symbols are composed of discrete tokens imagined to instantiate well-defined epistemic contents (knowledge, propositions, or concepts), the creation of *basic* knowledge is a mystery in the TMM (Bickhard 1987; Hutchins and Hazlehurst 1995). Where do basic symbols come from in the first place? Perhaps – it is popular to speculate – evolution engineered basic knowledge over phylogenetic history. However, since the TMM does not afford the possibility of a "partial symbol," or a "partial rule," it is hard to imagine how evolution could be the engine for producing complete symbols and complete rules. The Teleological Symbols Impasse is a symptom of the fact that the TMM is inherently epistemic rather than providing a mechanism for the emergence of knowledge processes from non-epistemic properties of the system. With the Turing machine model of mind *there is, paradoxically, no mechanism for the creation of basic symbols on which the model depends.*

In sum, the three theoretical impasses discussed above create a bind for much orthodox thinking about the nature of mind and the relationship of mind to human physiology and social living. One way out of the bind is to reject the TMM as cognitive architecture and replace it with a reconstructed model of mind. The reconstruction proposed here, employs the perspective known as "distributed cognition" (Hutchins and Hazlehurst 1991, 1995; Hazlehurst 1994; Hutchins 1995a) – and is discussed below as the distributed cognition mind, or DCM.

The Distributed Cognition Mind (DCM)

The DCM draws upon the insight that *higher-level conceptual and symbolic abilities are emergent products of lower-level perceptual, motor, and memory processes which are tightly coupled to the task worlds of situated actors* (McClelland et al. 1986; Rumelhart et al. 1986). In brief, research demonstrates that humans effortlessly excel in those areas of cognition traditionally labeled "primitive" (e.g., pattern-matching, motor skills, and the employment of implicit procedural knowledge) and labor in those areas of cognition traditionally labeled to be "higher level" (e.g., deductive reasoning, and the manipulation of propositional knowledge). This implies – on both empirical and logical grounds – that the TMM's attempt to directly incorporate these properties of "higher intelligence" (e.g., symbol structures and rule mechanisms for operating on them) into the basic architecture of the individual mind/brain, is a mistake. For cognitive anthropology, the implication is that taking language-like propositional structure as basic elements of individual minds – and their unproblematic sharing as the basic feature of culture – may be a mistake.[3] The challenge and opportunity provided by these insights is development of a theory of how human activities turn basic pattern-matching capacities and sociohistorical circumstance into complex cognitive systems.[4]

The central tenet of the DCM is that individuals routinely build internal structure through interacting in a world which is populated with naturally and sociohistorically generated structures. These interactions create functional dependencies among structures realized in diverse information-processing mechanisms, which both enable and result from organized, goal-directed behavior. The ontology of the DCM consists of three classes of structures – *internal*, *artifactual*, and *natural* – as well as processes which employ and create those structures. *Natural structure* is created by processes of nature which are not of human manufacture; for example, the cycle of tidal activity along a coastline caused by gravitation associated with the lunar orbit. *Artifactual structure*, on the other hand, is created by processes which do entail human design and manufacturing activities; for example, a tide chart which records the learned relationship between astronomical events and tidal activity. Finally, *internal structure* is built in the process of individuals acting in the world; for example, neural organization which results from employing structures found on a tide chart for predicting the extent of land and water at the beach.

In addition, the ontology of the DCM includes *processes* which bring structures into interaction with each other. These processes implement information-processing mechanisms by tying structures together into functional arrangements – possibly for exploitation by other processes and often generating structure at the same time. This nesting of process and structure, involving diverse media, can create quite complicated cognitive systems. Take, for example, an individual's recognition of a constellation among a collection of visible stars. This is a process which (via electrical activity in the individual's brain) brings into coordination a distribution of light impinging upon the individual's retinas and a cultural prescription for how to "see" particular regions of the sky. This coupling of structures, when coordinated with additional structure (e.g., a label or a map) can be employed in yet other processes – for instance, the term or chart may be used in a navigational procedure. Cognition, in other words, is constituted in the interactions among structures that achieve organized, goal-directed behavior in specific task environments. It is instantiated by processes that coordinate structures, enabling efficient processing of information, to meet functional demands posed by accomplishing objectives in the world. These structures and processes are not strictly confined by the boundaries of individuals, and typically distribute across individuals, time, and space.

In this model, *knowledge* resides in arrangements among structures on the insides and structures on the outsides of agents. Such arrangements are inherently "grounded" in the world of cognitive and social action (Impasse 1) because they imply the world through mediating action in it. Knowledge in this model is inherently derived from the world because it mediates the accomplishment of objectives in the world, affording resolutions to the problems of where knowledge comes from (Impasse 3) and how it can vary across individuals yet still provide the basis for coordinated interactions (Impasse 2). For example, an individual's "knowing" about astronomical events may evolve from recognition of pictures of these events, to facility with terms describing the events, to an ability to manipulate the laws of physics in order to postulate something theretofore unknown about the heavens! Knowledge, in other words, is constructed out of particular experiences, within the contexts provided by particular cultural histories. The model posits variation in knowledge as a product of situated learning while promoting functional interdependence through negotiation of shared experience.

The model also clearly posits a central role for culture in the constitution of mind. The laws of physics are an achievement for which no individual can claim complete responsibility, and yet the formulation of these laws is most certainly a human accomplishment. The laws of physics are an outcome of many interactions among individuals and between individuals and the world, organized by institutions, tools, language, presuppositions, and so on. Culture, in other words, is the process which organizes the traffic in structures that are endemic to human activity. Figure 25.1 depicts the cultural process. It represents the distributed cognition model of mind seen from the vantage point of a history of structures and processes which propagate structures through time.

A fundamental implication of the change in perspective offered by the DCM is that symbols no longer exist as constituents of closed formal systems of computation serving as an unproblematically shared language of thought within the skulls of individuals. Rather – as philosophers such as Wittgenstein and Peirce told us long ago – the ontology of symbols is located in a network of relationships among three kinds of structures: (1) residues of the embodied experiences of social agents (internal

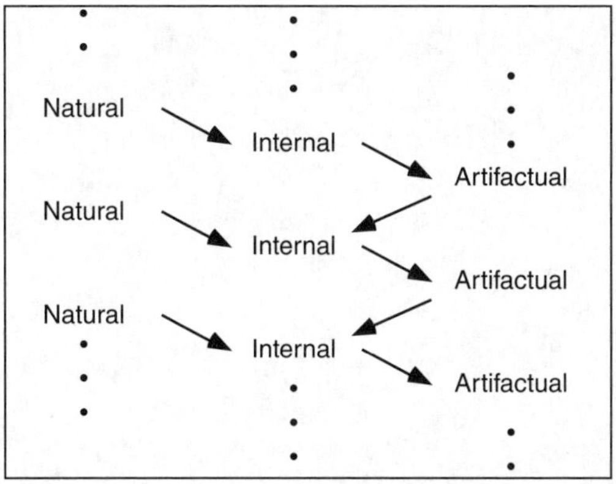

Figure 25.1 A schematic of the cultural process showing the relations of natural, internal, and artifactual structure through time. The arrows represent propagation of constraints upon interactions involving these different kinds of structure.

structures), (2) material forms created for the purpose of mediating goal-directed behavior (artifactual structures), and (3) referents in the world (natural and artifactual structures) and in the mind (internal structures) whose access facilitates that goal-directed behavior. The challenge for modern cognitive science lies in understanding how this characterization can provide methodological and theoretical insight. The empirical route seems clear: cognition in the world requires ethnographic description of cultural processes to explicate the network of relationships among structures that enable organized, goal-directed behavior. In these descriptions, the trafficking in structures entailed by situated human activity is made explicit, as in the example below from an ethnography of herring fishing on the west coast of Sweden. Clearly, anthropology has a major role to play in this undertaking. Furthermore, the DCM holds an opportunity for advancing theory in anthropology – development of a process model of culture which reunites the material and social with the cognitive.

As part of an ethnography of fishing practices on an island village off the west coast of Sweden, the author conducted an investigation of communications about sonar displays of underwater schools of herring which make "seeing" fish and the conduct of successful fishing possible (Hazlehurst 1994:ch 5; see Figure 25.2). Fishermen's reports of fish seen often entail descriptions which are grounded in the properties of sonar display devices. Thus common descriptors such as *strö* (sprinkle), *fläckar* (flecks), *prickar* (dots or marks), *punkter* (points), *klungar* (clusters or groups), *rand* (stripe), *skuga* (shadow), *tunn* (thin), *tätt* (tight), *spritt* (dispersed), *röd/gul/blå* (red/yellow/blue), or holding one's thumb up to indicate size or shape, are all ways of communicating the nature of the representation generated by the sonar device as a means to convey the fish seen. Other methods of constructing descriptions entail using positional or scale properties of the representation to depict the size and location of the fish in the water. Descriptions that entertain aspects of the state (or future state) of the fish themselves might also be employed, such as an estimate of the catch size of a school (e.g., "600 boxes") or the behavior of the school (e.g., "tight to the bottom"). In addition, the prospects for using one's particular equipment to capture the fish

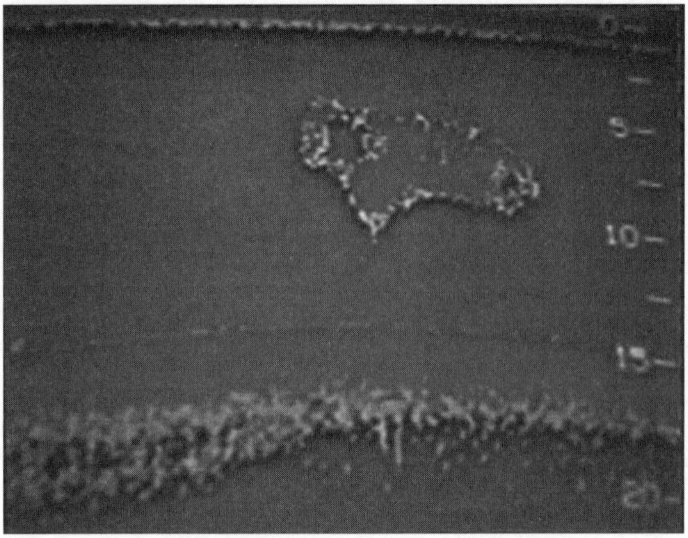

Figure 25.2 A sonar display image. One of the 50 images used in a simulation experiment to assess communications of sonar representations of herring among Swedish fishermen from a west coast island village.

might enter into the description (e.g., "they stand well for catching" or just "it looks productive"). These descriptions have evolved as the technology both for displaying sonar and for catching fish have taken on different forms through time.

Sonar displays are communicated between captains of teams of cooperating ships by radio during prolonged periods of search for herring in some fishing practices (e.g., purse seining) and for monitoring and adjustments to catching equipment during extended periods when capturing herring "on the run" in other fishing practices (e.g., mid-water pair-trawling). Each of these types of practices, and the roles of individuals within those practices (e.g., captains vs. regular crew members) shape the nature of fishermen's engagement of sonar displays and are thus relevant variables regulating the "trafficking in structures" related to sonar displays. Such traffic includes the regular interpretation and communication of sonar displays as representations of schools of herring and as calls to action required for successful outcomes in each type of fishing practice.

Support for the DCM in this case comes from a demonstration that fishermen's symbols for understanding and communicating about herring are products of constraints brought to bear by the material and social world in which the activity of fishing is situated. Cultural practices organize the distributed cognitive resources that accomplish the tasks required by fishing, and the symbols invented, used, and communicated by radio channel are among those resources. Analysis of ethnographic data supports the argument that the symbols employed for communicating and understanding sonar displays are constructed and grounded in the course of their use in mediating work routines.

Quantitative evidence that symbols, knowledge, technology, and cultural practices mutually determine each other in a cognitive ecology is provided by measuring the strength of relationships among (1) fisherman experience with different types of fishing practice, (2) fishermen's roles (as either captains who perform most of the decision-making using sonar or regular crew members who are primarily deckhands and less actively in the communication loop about what is being "seen" for fish), and (3) the distribution of agreement among fishermen when using symbols in simulated communication tasks involving sonar images (Hazlehurst 1994:ch. 5; see Figure 25.2). It was hypothesized that participation in different fishing practices, which entail distinct constraints on technology-mediated task performance in the real world, would determine fishermen agreement in the simulated communication tasks. Similarly, fisherman level of experience using the symbols required for communicating about sonar was hypothesized to predict competence in the simulated communication tasks as measured by who agrees with whom the most about the forms and meanings of the symbols used. Results from the simulation experiments were consistent with theory-driven expectations that captains would be more reliably understood in their communications and that communications would be more "accurate" (i.e., shared meanings more often established between interlocutors) when interlocutors engage in the same type of practice than when they engage in different fishing practices.

The cognitive ecology here that enables successful communications about fish taps into generic and fundamental human capacities which, when organized by valued cultural practices, creates a powerful cognitive system that (in this case) enables search and capture of huge quantities of herring. Qualitative analysis of task-relevant communications showed, for example, that symbols used to communicate what fishermen are "seeing" for fish can simultaneously and productively mix properties of the representing device (the sonar display), the represented object (the school of fish), and the shared task and goal of interlocutors (catching the mother lode with the equipment and method at one's disposal). Thus, for instance, although "red," "yellow," "blue," and "white" literally refer to properties seen on the sonar display screen these colors are simultaneously and effortlessly used and understood to refer to the properties of the fish themselves. Common examples included "red groups which lie on the bottom," and "productive sprinkle with a little red up there near the surface." In both of these examples, red is a property used to modify nouns ("groups" and "sprinkles," respectively) which are somehow simultaneously on the display (that is where the representations emanate from) and located in the water ("on the bottom" and "near the surface," respectively).

Such capacities to project shared experience onto perceptual regularities created through socially mediated interactions with structure in the world is possibly a basic feature of the human mind. Whether projecting constellations onto patterns of light seen in the night sky (Gladwin 1970) or projecting human activity onto stains apparent in the dirt of archaeological digs (Goodwin 1994), the human capacity to project complex and socially constituted meanings onto perceptual regularities provides the raw materials for powerful distributed cognitive systems. Such systems are organized by specific cultural practices. In the case of describing sonar displays for purposes of communicating about underwater schools of fish, this generic capacity is orchestrated by specific fishing practices, as evidenced in the patterns of agreement in the simulated communication task.

Symbols, consensual codes of shared experience, make possible the accomplishment of sophisticated collective activity. In general, once symbols exist they enable employment of collective experience, driving the accumulation of knowledge across time and space. The boundary of this symbol system is defined not by any individual, but by a cultural process which guides the evolution of an ecology of structures mediating the organization of goal-directed behavior. Individuals, while they actively employ elements from the ecology of structures in order to accomplish tasks, do not in themselves constitute symbol processing systems as the TMM would have it. Rather, individuals learn to coordinate internal structure with structures available and emerging in the public task environments, affording the exploitation of a historically and socially distributed body of understandings.

Unraveling the TMM

The model of mind proposed here challenges the historical implicit agreement between anthropology and psychology regarding how to understand the relationship between cognitive and cultural phenomena. That agreement, which persists in the orthodoxy of modern cognitive science and cognitive anthropology, emerged under the influence of a particular conception of mind – what I have called the Turing machine mind or TMM. However, the TMM suffers from a number of problems related to positing that individual brains constitute formal symbol-processing machines. Three problems were identified at the beginning of this chapter as theoretical impasses to the study of culture and cognition created by the TMM. These were labeled the Ungrounded Symbols Impasse, the Homogeneous Agents Impasse, and the Teleological Symbols Impasse, respectively.

The perspective advanced here explicitly rejects the TMM and replaces it with a model of mind – the distributed cognition mind, or DCM – founded upon the notions that (1) cognition is built out of interactions among structures providing the building blocks for information-processing that supports organized behavior, (2) these interactions (instances of processes which employ and create structures) are not limited to events internal to agents, but distribute across diverse media, social space, and time, and (3) culture is itself such a process, generating many of the structures and processes constituting human cognition – effectively embedding human activities in sociohistorically constructed ecologies of structures.

The Ungrounded Symbols Impasse of the TMM results from the fact that symbols in the TMM are inherently – that is, ontologically granted as – representational objects of cognitive systems. Symbols represent by fiat established by a priori relations to rules of the program and understandings of the programmer/analyst, rather than as a consequence of the system interacting with (and as one part of) the task world. This is so because symbols in the TMM are required to fill formal computational roles inside the cognitive system (as well-defined data for the program) without significant recourse to the world.

The nature of symbols in the DCM is quite different. Symbols have material forms in the world – for example, verbal descriptions of sonar displays – which individuals create, try out, and modify in order to accomplish objectives in that world. The activities in which these acts are embedded are organized by constraints imposed by sociohistorical practices – for instance the methods used to capture fish, the radio channels through which talk about sonar propagates, and the social and economic constraints which define who is listening to whom. Fishermen, in order to communicate with others in the collective activity that ensures successful fishing outcomes, must employ terms for describing sonar displays which classify what they are seeing in ways which enable the sharing of meanings between interlocutors and allow achievement of shared goals. There is no singular way to accomplish this. There is no set of constraints automatically available to individuals that determines how this is done. Instead, fishermen construct the physical forms, and mappings from forms to meanings, in the course of their shared experiences on the water. The fishermen who interacted with each other most in the collective activity of making sense of sonar displays to catch fish also shared more of the language – the forms and meanings – used for communicating about sonar displays (Hazlehurst 1994:ch 5).

Of course, once created, terms of the language are susceptible to stability – even apparent fixation – if the task environment promotes or accommodates it. It may be that mistaking stability in such structures for a fixed nature has led researchers to overlook processes involving joint activity and negotiation of a shared world as foundational mechanisms of mind (Freyd 1983, 1990; Hazlehurst and Hutchins 1998).

The Homogeneous Agents Impasse of the TMM results from the fact that the TMM treats an idealized individual as the unit of cognitive analysis. The implication for members who are said to "share a culture" is that the individuals' knowledge structures must be carbon copies of each other. While empirical research has made clear the artificiality of this notion, there has been little reflection upon what this implies for the TMM, which is generally assumed by the same research. In particular, if knowledge varies substantially between individuals, how can coordinated activity even be possible? Having bound the processing system at the (idealized) skull of an (idealized) individual, the TMM cannot address processes which are distributed across individuals entailing variability in cognitive resources.

The DCM treats the interactions between individual persons, and those between individuals and the task environment, to be as "cognitive" as interactions which take place within an individual's brain. The structures are different, the processes which bring the structures into interaction are different, but all of these interactions are part of the cognitive system and all participate in determining how the activity is organized. Having reconstituted the boundary of the cognitive system to include the task world involving (typically) several or many actors, the Homogeneous Agents Impasse dissolves. Coordinated activities among individuals are accomplished via the employment of mediating structure in the world. There is no need to posit equivalent structures internal to each agent in order to accomplish this coordination because functional equivalence is built in the course of sharing public mediators of goal-directed activity.

Finally, the Teleological Symbols Impasse of the TMM results from the fact that symbols in the TMM are granted their epistemic contents by fiat, leaving the origins of those contents a mystery. This follows directly from the division of the system into data and program (and a corresponding exclusion of the task world), in which the data must be of a particular ontology in order for it to be intelligible to the program – basic symbols in the TMM must be given, a priori, to the cognitive system. Insofar as those given symbols carry semantic contents, the TMM fails to give any account of where the basic symbols of the system could come from. Pushing the burden of explanation for the origins of basic symbols/knowledge onto an unspecified process of biological evolution is unsatisfactory. The evolutionary solution creates an incoherence for the

TMM because it is not clear how "partial symbols" or "partial rules" could be a possibility in this framework – and yet such partial products would certainly be entailed by any evolutionary process.

The DCM treats symbols as constructed, pliable, and negotiated mediators of action in the world. Symbols gain their epistemic properties via individuals grounding their private experiences in the appropriation of public structures which do certain kinds of work in the world. There is no mystery about how symbols come into existence in the DCM: symbols are, first, simple material entities in the world whose meanings are built from the ways they enter into human activity. Typically, this entails individuals coming into coordination with symbolic structures via the production of internal structures which support use of the symbols to accomplish tasks, typically joint tasks requiring coordinated, coarticulated action. Furthermore, there is no mystery about how complex knowledge comes into existence in the DCM: knowledge is a result of processes in which individuals build internal structures in support of manipulations of the task world. The same mechanism can account for the origins of both *basic* and *complex* knowledge, therefore the resort to a genetic mechanism for basic knowledge becomes unwarranted.

Moving on from the TMM

The past decade in theorizing about mind has brought about a shift in emphasis from computation (logical symbol manipulation) to biology (embodiment), partly in reaction to inadequacies of the TMM (see Clark 1997; Gibbs 2006). This shift is evidenced in neuroscience (Damasio 1994; Chiel and Beer 1997; Thompson and Varela 2001) and cognitive linguistics (Lakoff 1987; Fauconnier and Turner 2002; Johnson 2007), in robotics (Brooks 1991; Beer 2003) and in a resurgence of interest in the link between biological evolution and cognition (Lakoff and Johnson 1999; Pinker 2000). The brain, the body, and biological ancestry are now central theoretical foci for investigating mind. Cognition as "disembodied" computation is now replaced by research addressing "embodiment" or the interaction of mind, brain, and world. As Gibbs (2006:9) puts it:

> People's subjective, felt experiences of their bodies in action provide part of the fundamental grounding for language and thought. Cognition is what occurs when the body engages the physical, cultural world and must be studied in terms of the dynamical interactions between people and the environment. Human language and thought emerge from recurring patterns of embodied activity that constrain ongoing intelligent behavior. We must not assume cognition to be purely internal, symbolic, computational, and disembodied, but seek out the gross and detailed ways that language and thought are inextricably shaped by embodied action.

With this shift, symbols and thought are both seen as grounded in bodily experience, addressing the Ungrounded Symbols Impasse of the TMM. However the new treatment of mind continues to take the individual actor as the unit of cognitive analysis and continues to lack a formative role for social processes (short of second-order evolutionary constraints on the emergence of brain properties). The distributed cognition model of mind prescribes putting the social, historical, and material back into an account of mind. This allows us to see the negotiated nature of meaning, the distributed nature of knowledge, and the dynamic nature of culture. Meaning and knowledge exist in the relations among structures which are under continual revision as part of the dynamics of an evolving ecology of structures. It is these dynamics which constitute the cultural process. The methodological implication is that the empirical study of human cognition requires ethnographic description of sociohistorically situated activity. Anthropology has an important role to play in this vision of cognitive science.

The distributed cognition perspective also suggests a renewed role for cognitive theory in anthropology. In the history of anthropology, peoples of the world have typically had distinct and stable boundaries, leading researchers most often to think of culture in structural rather than dynamic terms. Culture, in this period of intellectual history, has been taken to be (in roughly chronological order) the language, the toolkit, the institutions, the knowledge, the symbols, and the meanings of historically and socially interconnected peoples. Accounts which have addressed cultural dynamics have generally been framed in terms of how *cultures* change. These accounts have typically not treated dynamics as the central property of human life, choosing instead to focus on *change* as the transformation of one distinct cultural form into another. This fact may account for the diversity in definitions of culture – each specifying what the organization of form is that undergoes change. It should be the case, in other words, that a truly processual account would accommodate the origins and evolution of all of these different kinds of forms.[5]

As the boundaries dividing peoples have become permeable and societies of larger scale and complexity more extensively studied, theory in anthropology based upon structural descriptions has bogged down. American anthropology's "symbolic" movement, which came into force in the 1970s, entailed an explicit recognition of this development. This led to researchers focusing upon events acted out in the public world of social life, taking these events to be definitive of local meaning systems and thus culture (see Geertz 1973). Unfortunately, caught up in the anti-positivist polemic of postmodernism, the offspring of this tradition have retreated en masse from the methods of science and from any treatment of the internal properties of individuals. Cognitive anthropology has also sought to reconcile structure with process – what is known with how the organization of knowledge affords cognition (see Hutchins 1980; Quinn and Holland 1987). However, much of this work – subscribing as it does to the Turing machine model of mind – inherits the three theoretical impasses discussed above. D'Andrade, in debating the symbolic movement in anthropology, argued for focusing upon individual knowledge as a research strategy for getting at the larger meaning system, or culture. Regarding what he takes to be the alternative, he says: "Although messaging, public and private, is an almost constant activity, the collecting of messages is not, I believe, the best way to start the study of culture ... the external signs, the public events, are too elliptical to serve as a good place to begin the search for organization and structure" (D'Andrade 1984:105).

While D'Andrade is correct that the messages (as structural forms) will not in and of themselves reveal the organizing principles of behavior, the communications entailed by those messages (i.e., the context-specific processing of messages) may well do so. The distributed cognition model of mind proposes that human cognition is built from the *interactions among structures* which organize behavior. There are two important implications of this proposal which bear on the current discussion. First, there is no priority given to the boundary of the individual. Interactions constituting cognition take place among things inside and things outside, among structures private and public. There is no ontological priority given to any particular medium in which structures serving cognitive functions may reside. Second, understanding both culture and cognition will require addressing the interaction itself – the "messaging" and not just the structures which are involved. In other words, for getting at the characteristic properties of cognitive systems a research strategy suggested by David Rumelhart may be more appropriately general: "Bound the system where the traffic is least."[6] In so doing, one would expect to capture the most significant processing performed by the system. Clearly, such a boundary cannot exclude events internal to individuals. On the other hand, the appropriate boundary is not guaranteed – contra the TMM – to coincide with the skins of individuals. The DCM suggests that a more inclusive system boundary, one that corresponds with what is sometimes called the "situated task world" or "activity system," will be more appropriate because it contains many different media which hold structure and constrain processes that tie such structures together into functional arrangements that participate in cognition.

The challenge which promises to reinvigorate culture theory in anthropology entails articulation of the dynamics of sociohistorically situated activity. In these activities, actors employ and generate structures and processes – interpretive procedures – which mediate the organization of behavior. The distributed cognition model of mind offers one avenue for taking up the challenge.

NOTES

1 D'Andrade (1981, 1989a), makes the suggestion that cultural knowledge is not the *data* but is, at some level in the architecture, the *programs* which direct processing, suggesting the need for an architecture significantly different from the TMM. However, a Turing machine can always load its program as data from the tape, and so divergence from the TMM is not necessarily implied by this suggestion.

2 Although Fodor and Pylyshyn claim their theory of mind is independent from the details of a Turing machine, their argument that the essential features of mind depend upon the nature of symbol processing as exemplified in a Turing machine means that they subscribe to what is called the Turing machine mind in this paper. They also explicitly acknowledge that their and other "classical models of the mind were derived from the structure of Turing and Von Neumann machines" (Fodor and Pylyshyn 1988:4).

3 Bloch (1991) begins with the same admonition offered here, but from this draws the conclusion that the proper study of culture may reside in the ethnographer's personal experience of the organization of native life. As will become clear, I believe there are much more profound and scientifically attractive implications to be drawn. Also, see Kronenfeld (2006) for a similar warning about imputing the properties of formal systems to the underlying cognitive mechanisms that use formal systems.

4 In addition to Bloch (1991), Strauss and Quinn (1997) and Shore (1991) are two other anthropological efforts to make use of the research of Rumelhart, McClelland, and others emphasizing a non-symbolic mechanism of information-processing underlying human cognition that is generally called "connectionism". Both Shore and Quinn and Strauss are primarily interested in promoting a view of cognition which permits the re-integration of

representational functions with other psychological phenomena, such as motivation and affect. Both also see the opportunity for reconciling the schism in anthropological theory generated by intellectual traditions which have focused exclusively upon either the public or the private. The current paper proposes a similar reconciliation, but differs in its fairly strict emphasis upon the representational or, more accurately, the epistemological side of cognition – which is also where connectionist research has been primarily focused within cognitive science.

5 Sperber (1985) and Atran and colleagues (2005) recognize these same objectives for anthropology and have advocated for a science based on the "epidemiology of mental representations."

6 Edwin Hutchins, personal communication.

REFERENCES

Atran, S., D. Medin, and N. Ross

2005 The Cultural Mind: Environmental Decision Making and Cultural Modeling within and across Populations. Psychological Review 112:744–776.

Beer, Randall D.

2003 The Dynamics of Active Categorical Perception in an Evolved Model Agent. Adaptive Behavior 11(4):209–243.

Bickhard, M.

1987 The Social Nature of the Functional Nature of Language. *In* Social and Functional Approaches to Language and Thought. M. Hickman, ed. Orlando, FL: Academic Press.

Bloch, M.

1991 Language, Anthropology and Cognitive Science. Man 26:183–198.

Boster, J.

1987 Introduction. Special issue, "Intracultural Variation," American Behavioral Scientist 31(2):150–162.

Boyer, P.

1994 Cognitive Constraints on Cultural Representations: Natural Ontologies and Religious Ideas. *In* Mapping the Mind. L. Hirschfeld and S. Gelman, eds. New York: Cambridge University Press.

Brooks, R.

1991 Intelligence without Representation. Artificial Intelligence 47:139–159.

Chiel, H., and R. Beer

1997 The Brain Has a Body: Adaptive Behavior Emerges from Interactions of Nervous System, Body and Environment. Trends in Neurosciences 20:553–557.

Clark, A.

1997 Being There: Putting Brain, Body and World Together Again. Cambridge, MA: MIT Press.

Damasio, A.

1994 Descartes' Error: Emotion, Reason, and the Human Brain. New York: Grosset.

D'Andrade, R.

1981 The Cultural Part of Cognition. Cognitive Science 5:179–195.

1984 Cultural Meaning Systems. *In* Culture Theory. R. Shweder and R. Levine, eds. Cambridge: Cambridge University Press.

1989a Cultural Cognition. *In* Foundations of Cognitive Science. M. Posner, ed. Cambridge, MA: MIT Press.

1989b Culturally Based Reasoning. *In* Cognition and Social Worlds. A. Gellatly, D. Rogers, and J. A. Sloboda, eds. Oxford: Clarendon.

Fauconnier, G., and M. Turner
2002 The Way We Think. New York: Basic Books.
Feigenbaum, E.
1963 The Simulation of Verbal Learning Behavior. *In* Computers and Thought. E. Feigenbaum and J. Feldman, eds. New York: McGraw-Hill.
Fetzer, J.
1992 Connectionism and Cognition: Why Fodor and Pylyshyn are Wrong. *In* Connectionism in Context. A. Clark and R. Lutz, eds. New York: Springer.
Fodor, J., and Z. Pylyshyn
1988 Connectionism and Cognitive Architecture: A Critical Analysis. In Connections and Symbols. S. Pinker and J. Mehler, eds. Cambridge, MA: MIT Press. (Repr. of special issue of Cognition.)
Freyd, J.
1983 Shareability: The Social Psychology of Epistemology. Cognitive Science 7:191–210.
1990 Natural Selection or Shareability? Behavioral and Brain Sciences 13(4):732–734. (Comment on "Natural Language and Natural Selection" by S. Pinker and P. Bloom in same issue.)
Gatewood, J.
2001 Reflections on the Nature of Cultural Distributions and the Units of Culture Problem. Cross-Cultural Research 35:227–241.
Geertz, C.
1973 The Interpretation of Cultures. New York: Basic Books.
Gibbs, R.
2006 Embodiment in Cognitive Science. New York: Cambridge University Press.
Gladwin, Thomas
1970 East Is a Big Bird: Navigation and Logic on Puluwat Atoll. Cambridge, MA: Harvard University Press.
Goodwin, C.
1994 Professional Vision. American Anthropologist 96(3):606–633.
Goodwin, C., and M. H. Goodwin
1996 Seeing as a Situated Activity: Formulating Planes. *In* Cognition and Communication at Work. Y. Engeström and D. Middleton, eds. Pp. 61–95. Cambridge: Cambridge University Press.
Haglund, J.
1985 Artificial Intelligence. Cambridge, MA: MIT Press.
Hazlehurst, B.
1994 Fishing for Cognition: An Ethnograpy of Fishing Practice in a Community on the West Coast of Sweden. Unpublished dissertation, University of California, San Diego. http://www.dcog.net/dissertation/dissertation.html, accessed October 5, 2010.
2003 The Cockpit as Multiple Activity System: A Computational Model for Understanding Situated Team Performance. International Journal of Aviation Psychology 13(1):1–22.
Hazlehurst, B., and E. Hutchins
1998 The Emergence of Propositions from the Coordination of Talk and Action in a Shared World. Special issue, K. Plunkett, ed., Language and Cognitive Processes on Connectionist Approaches to Language Development 13(2/3):373–425.
Hopcroft, J., and J. Ullman
1979 Introduction to Automata Theory, Languages, and Computation. Reading, MA: Addison-Wesley.
Hutchins, E.
1980 Culture and Inference. Cambridge, MA: Harvard University Press.
1995a Cognition in the Wild. Cambridge, MA: MIT Press.
1995b How a Cockpit Remembers Its Speed. Cognitive Science 19:265–288.

Hutchins, E., and B. Hazlehurst
1991 Learning in the Cultural Process. *In* Artificial Life II. C. Langton, C. Taylor, D. Farmer, and S. Rasmussen, eds. Redwood City, CA: Addison-Wesley.
1995 How to Invent a Shared Lexicon: The Emergence of Shared Form-Meaning Mappings in Interaction. *In* Social Intelligence and Interaction. E. Goody, ed. Cambridge: Cambridge University Press.
Hutchins, E., and L. Palen
1997 Constructing Meaning from Space, Gesture and Talk. *In* Discourse, Tools, and Reasoning: Essays on Situated Cognition. L. B. Resnick, R. Saljo, C. Pontecorvo, and B. Burge, eds. Berlin: Springer.
Johnson, M.
2007 The Meaning of the Body: Aesthetics of Human Understanding. Chicago: University of Chicago Press.
Johnson-Laird, P., and P. Wason
1977 A Theoretical Analysis of Insight into a Reasoning Task [with Postscript]. *In* Thinking: Readings in Cognitive Science. P. Johnson-Laird and P. Wason, eds. New York: Cambridge University Press.
Kirsh, D., and P. Maglio
1994 On Distinguishing Epistemic from Pragmatic Action. Cognitive Science 18(4): 513–549.
Kronenfeld, D.
2006 Formal Rules, Cognitive Representations and Learning in Language and Other Cultural Systems. Language Sciences 28:425–435.
Lakoff, G.
1987 Women, Fire, and Dangerous Things. Chicago: University Of Chicago Press.
Lakoff, G., and M. Johnson
1999 Philosophy in the Flesh. Cambridge, MA: MIT Press.
Langacker, R.
1986 The Foundations of Cognitive Grammar, vol. 1. Stanford: Stanford University Press.
Levinson, S., and P. Brown
1992 Immanual Kant among the Tenejapans. Working paper no. 11 of the Cognitive Anthropology Research Group at the Max Planck Institute for Psycholinguistics.
McClelland, J. L., D. E. Rumelhart, and PDP Research Group
1986 Parallel Distributed Processing, vol. 2: Psychological and Biological Models. Cambridge, MA: MIT Press.
Miller, G., E. Galanter, and K. Pribram
1960 Plans and the Structure of Behavior. New York: Holt, Rinehart and Winston.
Newell, A., and H. Simon
1963 GPS, a Program that Simulates Human Thought. *In* Computers and Thought. E. Feigenbaum and J. Feldman, eds. New York: McGraw-Hill.
1990[1976] Computer Science as Empirical Inquiry: Symbols and Search. *In* Foundations of Cognitive Science: The Essential Readings. J. Garfield, ed. New York: Paragon House.
Ochs, E., P. Gonzales, and S. Jacoby
1996 "When I'm down I'm in the domain state": Grammar and Graphic Representation in the Interpretive Activity of Physicists. *In* Interaction and Grammar. E. Ochs, E. Schegloff, and S. Thompson, eds. Pp. 328–369. Cambridge: Cambridge University Press.
Pinker, S.
2000 The Language Instinct: How the Mind Creates Language. New York: HarperCollins.
Pylyshyn, Z.
1990[1980] Computation and Cognition: Issues in the Foundations of Cognitive Science. *In* Foundations of Cognitive Science: The Essential Readings. J. Garfield, ed. New York: Paragon House.

Quinn, N., and D. Holland
1987 Culture and Cognition. *In* Cultural Models in Language and Thought. D. Holland and N. Quinn, eds. Cambridge: Cambridge University Press.
Rumelhart, D. E., J. L. McClelland, and PDP Research Group
1986 Parallel Distributed Processing, vol. 1: Foundations. Cambridge, MA: MIT Press.
Shore, B.
1991 Twice Born, Once Conceived: Meaning Construction and Cultural Cognition. American Anthropologist 93:9–27.
Sperber, D.
1985 Anthropology and Psychology: Towards an Epidemiology of Representations. Man 20:73–89.
Strauss, C., and N. Quinn
1997 A Cognitive Theory of Cultural Meaning. Cambridge: Cambridge University Press.
Suchman, L.
1987 Plans and Situated Actions: The Problem of Human–Machine Communication. Cambridge: Cambridge University Press.
Thompson, E., and F. J. Varela
2001 Radical Embodiment: Neural Dynamics and Consciousness. Trends in Cognitive Sciences 5(10):418–425.
Turing, A.
1950 Computing Machinery and Intelligence. Mind 59:433–460.
Wallace, A.
1961 Culture and Personality. New York: Random House.

CHAPTER 26

A Foundational Cultural Model in Polynesia: Monarchy, Democracy, and the Architecture of the Mind

Giovanni Bennardo

Introduction

On "Black Thursday," November 16, 2006, the Kingdom of Tonga witnessed streets riots that left several buildings in the center of the capital town of Nuku'alofa burnt to the ground.[1] The event was apparently motivated by demonstrators – supporters of the reform-advocating democratic movement – becoming more and more impatient with the pace of the promised parliamentary changes. Since the early 1990s, the Tongan democratic movement has been shaking the foundations of the millennium-old Tongan monarchial system by denouncing administrative corruption and demanding political and constitutional changes (Hoponoa 1992; James 1994, 2002, 2003). Fundamentally, they are advocating a larger, thus reaching majority, parliamentary representation (Tonga is a constitutional monarchy) for commoners vis-à-vis nobles and the possibility of subjecting the power of the king to the mandates of the constitution.

Were the riots then an expression of the deeply felt ("burning") desire for democratic, hence social and political, reforms by Tongans? Is this millennium-old monarchy bound to collapse within a few years? Have the intrinsic qualities of monarchial and hierarchical Tongan life been washed away by the surging wave of democratic principles? While these questions were crowding my mind, I was getting more and more acquainted with the results of my research about the mental

A Companion to Cognitive Anthropology, First Edition. Edited by David B. Kronenfeld, Giovanni Bennardo, Victor C. de Munck, and Michael D. Fischer.

representation of spatial relationships and how these were reduplicated in other domains of Tongan knowledge such as traditional religion and navigation, possession, time, kinship, and social relationships.

A foundational cultural model emerged that I called *radiality*. Thinking radially implies focusing on a point in the environment and establishing relationships out of or toward that point. As a direct consequence of this model, ego is backgrounded and other-than-ego is foregrounded. This fundamental thinking modality is not compatible with democracy, where a primary focus on ego is, first, required to be followed by choosing (typically, by voting) an other-than-ego to represent one's interests. On the contrary, the radiality model is compatible with a monarchial system, where focus has to be on an other-than-ego who rules on hereditary claims and possibly governs for the good of the collectivity.

In this chapter, I argue that the shift from monarchy to democracy in the Kingdom of Tonga will be a very long and slow process. My argument is fundamentally a cognitive argument, that is, I demonstrate that the Tongan foundational cultural model, which is rooted in the mental module of spatial relationships and called radiality, is also pervasive in other Tongan domains of knowledge. As such, it stands for a preferred modality of thinking that happens to be congruent with a monarchial and highly hierarchical society and in strident contrast to basic democratic principles. Change is always possible and sometimes desirable, but I am convinced that hidden and less evident mental processes are much slower and less quick to be adopted than technological innovations. These latter, more apparent and easier to detect, may suggest that "modernization" or better "fundamental" changes may have occurred. I believe that this is highly misleading and will try to make my case in what follows.

My Blended Approach to Cognition and Mind Architecture

There are two hypotheses about the architecture and nature of cognition that represent the foundations of my own position. The first hypothesis is Jackendoff's (1983, 1992b, 1997, 2002, 2007) *representational modularity*.[2] Conceptual structures are central to Jackendoff's architecture of cognition and the module called "spatial representation" is proposed as independent from conceptual structures. Jackendoff (1992a, 2007) also hypothesized a social cognition module (see Figure 26.1) based on cultural knowledge.[3]

The second hypothesis I consider is a *radically intensional* approach to the general architecture of cognition (Keller and Lehman 1991), in which this latter is conceived as computational (Ballim and Wilks 1991), thus generatively "abstract." Only the characteristics of the computational, or relational, spaces that make up what we call "cognition" are reiterated in each cognitive module and not the specific characteristics of the substantive content that instantiate these "abstract" relationships.[4] A computational approach to cognition can be proposed by accepting compositionality and by adopting from mathematics (e.g., algebra and geometry) the fundamental idea that the primitives of a system are a set of axioms. These axioms generate indefinitely many theorems and each theorem can establish a foundation for yet another theorem. Furthermore, theorems may share parts with other theorems in a redundant manner. The set of relational properties of any cognitive system could be, then, nothing but a theorem derived from a set or sets of other theorems.

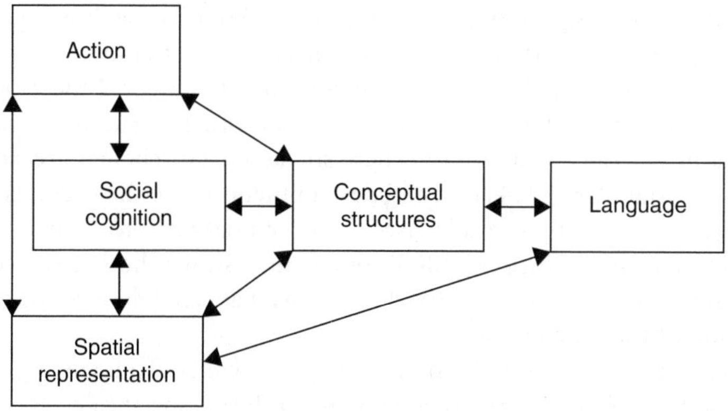

Figure 26.1 Jackendoff's (1997) architecture of cognition revised.

I blend Jackendoff's and Keller and Lehman's proposals to adopt a computational approach to cognition within a general representational modularity architecture of mind (Bennardo 2004). My intensional analyses of both English spatial prepositions and Tongan lexemes expressing spatial relationships yielded a number of axioms for a partial theory of space, that is, for a substantial part of the content of Jackendoff's spatial representation module (Bennardo 1993, 1996, 1999a, 1999b, 2000b; Lehman and Bennardo 2003).

The major axioms of this partial theory include concepts like locus, object, vector, path, verticality, and horizontality (Bennardo 2004). These concepts are used to construct frames of reference (for a similar approach, see Levinson 2003) that are part of the content of the spatial representation module (Jackendoff 1997, 2002). A frame of reference (FoR) is a set of coordinates (three intersecting axes: vertical, sagittal, and transversal) used to construct an oriented space within which spatial relationships between objects are identified. There are three major types of FoR: relative, intrinsic, and absolute (Levinson 2003; Bennardo 2004). A relative FoR is centered on a speaker and it remains centered on the speaker when the speaker moves, for example, when one says, "The ball is in front of me." An intrinsic FoR is centered on an object and it remains centered on the object when the object moves, for example, "The ball is in front of the car." An absolute FoR uses fixed points of reference, for example north, south, east, west, as in "The town is south of the river." Frames of reference, then, are considered theorems derived from the major axiomatic content of the partial theory of space.

My approach to cognition – its architecture and its computational nature – allows me to shed light on why my finding about the specific way of organizing spatial relationship in Tonga could be replicated in other domains of knowledge. The common generative computational nature of the content of cognition, knowledge, combined with the inevitable exchange pathway between the spatial representation and other cognitive modules, including the conceptual structures and social cognition modules, are the two explanatory landmarks. Since knowledge is structured in the same way, it can travel across modules. Since spatial representation knowledge interacts with conceptual structures, action, social cognition, and other modules, it can be replicated in other domains of knowledge.

The role that knowledge about space and the preferential way it is organized plays in human cognition is of paramount importance. The vast amount of research and publications on spatial cognition clearly support this statement. I mention here only three works. First, that of Lakoff (1987) on conceptual organization in which he clearly delineates a conceptual theory where spatial image-schemas are fundamental. Second, that of Mandler (2004) on child development where she suggests that spatial image-schemas are prelinguistically used and foundational to human conceptual development. Finally, Levinson (2003) poignantly shows how cross-cultural and cross-linguistic investigation of space yield findings that can illuminate our still limited understanding of the human mind.

In this chapter, I show how the preferred way in which Tongans organize spatial representations is reiterated in other mental modules, specifically, the conceptual structures module (e.g., possession, traditional religious beliefs, traditional navigation), time (i.e., temporal relationships), and the social cognition module (e.g., kinship, social relationships). Thus, I suggest that understanding any preference in the spatial representation module provides a unique and relevant entry into the preferred organization of other mental modules

Radiality in Space and Other Domains of Knowledge

At the end of my investigation of the linguistic representations of spatial relationships in Tonga (Bennardo 1996, 1999b, 2000a, 2000b), I pointed out how their lexemic distribution differed substantially from English. In fact, three spatial prepositions, seven directionals, and a good number (24) of spatial nouns constitute the linguistic means used to express spatial relationships in Tongan. This clearly contrasts with English and its more than 80 spatial prepositions (Jackendoff 1992b) used almost exclusively to do the same job. Besides, two Tongan directionals, *mai* ("toward center") and *atu* ("away from center"), are used to express movement away from and toward a specified center, mostly ego or other-than-ego.

The analyses of the linguistic representations of spatial relationships were integrated by an examination of the preferred frame or frames of reference realized while using the language to describe spatial relationships (Bennardo 1996). The findings were nuanced; a preference for the relative FoR was detected in small-scale space and a preference for the absolute FoR in large-scale space. Besides, a common use of the translation subtype of the relative FoR in both types of spaces was also found. An object A lying beyond an object B – both in front of the speaker – would be labeled as lying "in front of B," instead of "behind B" as in English. Conversely, object A is labeled "behind B" instead of "in front of B," as in English. Only two other documented cases of a similar preference exist in the literature, Hausa (Hill 1982) and Marquesan (Cablitz 2006).

Continuing my investigation, I used a number of cognitive tasks to collect information about a preference for a specific FoR in the mental representations of spatial relationships (Bennardo 1996). The results pointed unequivocally towards a preference for the absolute FoR. Since the tasks were about small-scale space, they contrasted with the preference for the relative FoR detected in the same type of space for the linguistic representations of spatial relationships. However, because of the way the

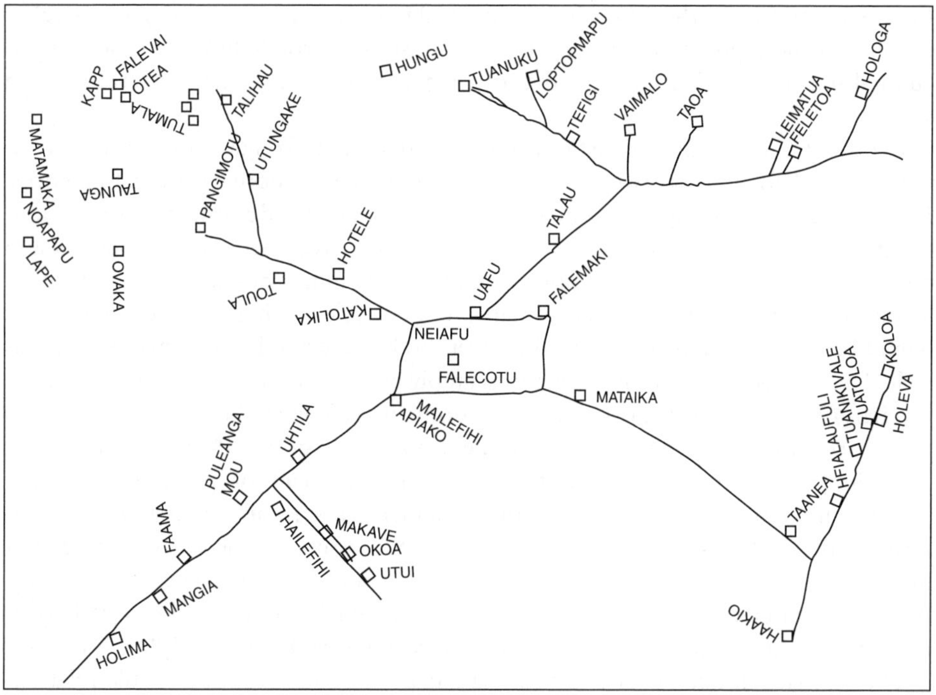

Figure 26.2 Map of the island of Vava'u by #15 (Bennardo 2002).

tasks were conceived and conducted, the results could not distinguish between subtypes of the absolute FoR. An absolute FoR can be realized by two axes (i.e., four cardinal points), one axis (e.g., seaward–landward), or by one point (i.e., centripetal and/or centrifugal movement from a center).

A clear indication of which subtype of the absolute FoR is privileged in the Tongan mind emerged from the results of a set of drawing tasks. The organization of the drawings of one's village and of one's islands, together with the strategies used demonstrated how the radial (one point) subtype of the absolute FoR is privileged by Tongans to represent geographical space. An illustrative example is provided in Figure 26.2.

Essential radiality features are shared between the translation subtype of the relative FoR and the radial subtype of the absolute FoR. They both share ego's field without having one of their own; they are both focused on an other-than-ego not-oriented object in the field of ego; they both establish spatial relationships with ego or a second object in the field of ego as toward or away from the focus object. In other words, it appears that – both when expressed linguistically and when represented mentally – spatial knowledge is organized preferentially in a radial fashion. That is, an other-than-ego point is chosen in the field of ego and relationships are established towards and away from this point.

These findings convinced me to posit radiality as a salient constitutive part of the content of the spatial representations mental module in Tonga. I also suggested that the Tongan cultural milieu – conceived as geographical, human, and behavioral places – provides the essential context for the acquisition of such a preference. This led me to inquiry about other domains of knowledge. Basically, I asked, is radiality also present in the organization of other domains of knowledge or is it restricted only to space? If radiality in the representation of spatial relationships is strictly linked to the Tongan cultural milieu, then is it possible that other domains of knowledge are affected in a similar way?

In order to answer these questions, I investigated other Tongan domains of knowledge. First, I focused on two traditional religious beliefs and navigational practices. Both represent knowledge that is neither believed nor practiced any more. Nonetheless, traditional knowledge, especially of the saliency of navigation for Polynesians and religion for any culture, is not simply erased from the mind (or collective memory) of a community in one or even more than one generation. Thus, I concluded that it would be relevant if radial organizations were to be detected in these two domains as well. The results of the two investigations amply confirmed my hypothesis: radiality is a salient organizing principle of these two domains of Tongan knowledge and it also actively contributes to the generation of behavior (Bennardo 2009:188–190).

Second, my attention fell on the ontological domain of possession because Polynesian languages express it in a dual manner. That is, all possessives have two forms with a focus on either the possessor or the possessed object. Consequently, I investigated this domain convinced that I could find some evidence for radiality. Again, the findings supported my hypothesis and radiality was found to clearly contribute to the construction and use of Tongan possessives (Bennardo 2009:191–198).

Third, it is well known that in many languages lexemes realizing spatial relationships are also used for temporal relationships. It is then apparent that I needed to investigate the ontological domain of time to see if the preference elicited for the representation of spatial relationships would also be found in the representation of temporal relationships. The Tongan preference for the use of the translation subtype of the relative FoR (Bennardo 1996) in talking about spatial relationships (i.e., space), was reported in Bender et al. (2005) as present also in the linguistic representations of temporal relationships (i.e., time). This preference relates to the hypothesized radiality since the translation subtype of the relative FoR shares fundamental characteristics with the radial subtype of the absolute FoR (see above). Thus, I concluded that radiality is replicated in the temporal domain.

Fourth, in any cultural milieu, the role of kinship is always of paramount significance. Thus, the mentioned relationship between radiality and the Tongan cultural milieu should have a similar relevance in the domain of kinship relationships. Then, in collaboration with Dwight Read, I conducted an algebraic investigation of the Tongan kinship terminology (Bennardo and Read 2007). One essential aspect of the findings is presently relevant, namely, the centrality of the sibling relation. In a descriptive terminology like American, a sibling is a compound term constructed from taking products of the Mother or Father term with the Son term (Read and Behrens 1990; Read 2005), that is, it is constructed starting from ego. In a classificatory terminology like Tongan, the sibling term is one of the atomic terms. It is from there that the terminology springs out, generates. Fundamentally, then, the working of radiality can be seen at play in the kinship terminology. An other-than-ego individual, sibling, is conceived first as the starting point of the terminology.

Thus rooted in the content of the spatial relationships module, radiality finds its way into other mental domains of knowledge. Specifically, I found evidence regarding the religious domain, the navigation domain, the possession domain, the temporal domain, and the kinship domain. It was at this juncture that I decided to explore another universally salient domain, social relationships. Besides, a hypothesis emerged that needed to be thoroughly tested. The preference for organizing knowledge radially – or radiality – that I found in the domain of spatial relationships and replicated in a number of other domains could be conceived as a foundational cultural model, that is, a fundamental cognitive molecule that participates in the generation of larger mental organizations (i.e., cultural models) in a variety of domains. Both terms, *cultural model* and *foundational cultural model*, need some clarification.

Cultural Models and Foundational Cultural Models

What is a cultural model? First and fundamentally, a cultural model is a mental model. A mental model consists of bits of knowledge organized in such a way as to facilitate storage and/or retrieval and use of that same knowledge (Craik 1943; Gentner and Stevens 1983; Johnson-Laird 1983). A comparatively similar mental organization of knowledge is also called a frame, or a script, or a schema (Bateson 1972; Minsky 1975; Abelson and Schank 1977; Rumelhart 1980; Fillmore 1982; Brewer 1984, 1987, 1999; Brewer and Nakamura 1984; Keller 1992). In Johnson-Laird's words, "A crucial feature [of mental models] is that their structure corresponds to the structure of what they represent" (1999:525). The investigation of mental models, then, is enhanced by a thorough understanding of the context (physical and human, that is, cultural) in which they are acquired and realized.

Second, a mental model becomes a cultural model when it "is intersubjectively shared by a social group" (D'Andrade 1989:809). That is, a cultural model entails that the knowledge that it organizes is shared between members of a community (Holland and Quinn 1987; Kronenfeld 1996, 2008; Shore 1996; Strauss and Quinn 1997; Quinn 2005). Third, a cultural model is used in reasoning and in planning actions, and it may motivate action as well (D'Andrade and Strauss 1992; Holland 1992). In other words, cultural models construct the mental context, that is, culture in mind, within which and out of which behavior will be generated.

Where are cultural models located in the mind? Since cultural models vary in complexity and content, they can be located in possibly any major module of the mind and domain of knowledge therein. I restrict my discussion to the partial architecture of the mind introduced in Figure 26.1. Any of the five modules – action, conceptual structures, language, social cognition, and spatial representation – can host a number of cultural models. Besides, some cultural models can span over more than one of those modules and/or domains. That is, it may be the composite result or assemblage of some of the content, that is knowledge, typically found in a number of domains and sometimes also in more than one module.

These assemblages or, better, cultural models are constructed by each individual while accumulating experiences in life. In whatever community they grow and develop, individuals share a human mind and a similar context of experience. Again then, these individually constructed models are cultural because they are very similar and highly shared. In addition, it is not a coincidence that one of the fundamental ontological concepts, space, is assigned a mental module of its own. The representation of spatial relationships plays an essential role in highly mobile living individuals such as humans.

I suggest that a cultural model located in a spatial representation module may as well be replicated in other modules and domains simply because it is generated early in mental development and is fundamental to subsequent bodily and mental experiences (see Strauss and Quinn 1997; Mandler 2004).

In other words, cultural models can be located in any of the mental modules, and they may also be generated first in ontological domains. However, since spatial representation is the only ontological domain with a clearly defined mental module, it is very likely that a cultural model, that is a foundational one, can be located in this module. The overall results of my research presented in this chapter robustly confirm and definitely support this last hypothesis.

A cultural model can exist at various levels of molarity with consequent different degrees of emergent complexity (Brewer 1987; Shore 1996; Kronenfeld 2008). There exists a type of cultural model that, while simple in its structure, is repeatedly used, perhaps because of its simplicity. Lakoff suggests and elaborates the concept of "image schema" defined as: A way of thinking about one's experience in the world derived from "relatively simple structures that constantly recur in our everyday bodily experience: CONTAINERS, PATHS, LINKS, FORCES, BALANCE, and in various orientations and relations: UP–DOWN, FRONT–BACK, PART–WHOLE, *CENTER–PERIPHERY*, etc." (1987:267, emphasis added). Holland and Quinn argue that a "thematic effect arises from the availability of a small number of *very general-purpose cultural models* that are repeatedly incorporated into other cultural models" (1987:11, emphasis added). And Shore, after introducing a variety of types of schemas, states: "*Foundational* schemas organize or link up a 'family' of related models" (1996:53, emphasis added).

I decided to combine the insights of Brewer, Lakoff, Holland, Strauss, and Shore (among others) and label my own conceptual synthesis a *foundational cultural model.* This latter is a basic and simple structure, that is, an assemblage of knowledge, that can generate other more complex models when used to merge a larger number of units of knowledge. In this chapter I suggest comparing it to a "cognitive molecule." I located one of these potential models in the spatial representation module of Tongans. They prefer to organize mentally spatial relationships by using a specific frame of reference, the radial subtype of the absolute frame of reference (see above). I found this preference replicated in a variety of other modules and domains. I called the phenomenon a foundational cultural model and labeled it *radiality.*

Radiality in Social Relationships

The finding of radiality at the conceptual roots of the Tongan kinship terminology led me to the investigation of the domain of social relationships. Kinship is fundamental to the establishment of a multitude of types of social relationships. Sometimes, in many cultures, it is kinship exclusively that provides the necessary and sufficient reason to engage in any type of social relationship. Besides, a good number of ethnographic observations had already attracted my attention to this vital aspect of the Tongan cultural milieu.[5]

Tongans position themselves socially in a distinctive way. In everyday conversations, when trying to define their position in the social hierarchy, they often make initial reference to a high-status person as a fixed point of reference. They then trace their personal position from that person or point. Similarly, in a *fono* ("official village meeting") an individual's status is indicated and determined by the "distance" – calculated in units represented by intervening individuals – from the highest-status person present, for example, the local village chief, a noble, or the king (Bott 1972; Marcus 1980). This conceptualization of social hierarchy and social relationships is reminiscent of the foundational cultural model I termed *radiality*.

A new methodology

How does one go about investigating possible mental representations of social relationships? Both linguistic and experimental data have inherent limitations. Using the former, one cannot control for the difference in dimensionality between language and cognition, that is, one dimension vs. many, respectively. Using the latter, it leaves the doubt of being circumstantial to the experimental context, that is, how can one convincingly relate the results of the experiments to behavior in real life, to what people actually do?

A way out of this methodological conundrum is provided by examples found in tasks involving the use of maps as in the research on spatial representations (see Downs and Stea 1977; Tversky 1981, 1993, 1996; Gould and White 1986[1974]; Golledge 1999; Bennardo 2002). During these tasks subjects are asked to either draw a map, follow a map to reach a place, or talk about the relationships between maps and real places. The discrepancies and/or distortions of the geographical world produced in the maps drawn, the places reached, or the speech elicited are used to hypothesize specific mental representations of spatial relationships in those individuals. Fundamentally, real maps and real places provide the parameters to discover mental representations of those maps and/or places. Subjects' performance is matched against geographical reality to obtain information-rich data about mental representations of space.

I became convinced that by finding a sufficiently equivalent substitute for geographical space in the domain of social relationships/space, I would be able to validate results obtained by means of linguistic analyses and/or experimental tasks. It is at this juncture that social network analysis came to mind. Social network analysis can provide similar accuracy about social relationships and reality as that found in maps about geographical relationships and reality (Wasserman and Faust 1994). Both maps and social networks are simply a representation of the reality to which they refer. As such, they are not exhaustive, a complete repetition of that reality. They leave something out in their representing effort. Nonetheless, they are representations that are the closest to the reality of the geographical world and of the social relationships world, respectively.

Once a social network map of the social relationships world/space has been obtained, results from linguistic and experimental data about the same world/space can be compared or, more precisely, correlated with them. This would allow one to discover those similarities, discrepancies, and/or distortions that are telling about a specific way of mentally representing significant aspects of the social world. Besides, social network analysis can be revealing regarding a preference for ego-centered or other-than-ego-centered networks, a fundamental issue for the present investigation.

What are then social network data? Social network data consist of information collected by means of questionnaires (for an example, see Burkett 1998), interviews (for an example, see Wellman and Wortley 1990), and/or structured observations (for an example, see Bernard et al. 1980, 1982; Freeman and Romney 1987) about individuals' perceived and actual frequency of interactions with other individuals. The analyses of the social network data (e.g., density, symmetry, and centrality measures) highlight the nature (e.g., star graph, circle graph), structure, and composition of these imagined and actual social interactions in public arenas (Freeman et al. 1989; Scott 1992; Wasserman and Faust 1994; McCarty 2002). Radial organizations (star graphs) or vectorial subtypes (line graphs) – always centered on an individual different from the one providing the information – can be detected. The finding of circle graphs, graphs with low and uniform measures of centrality for all members, would undermine the radiality hypothesis.

Data collected To investigate the mental representations of social relationships a variety of data was collected: ethnographic data, experimental (cognitive) data, social network data, and linguistic data. The ethnographic data collected consist of detailed information about the village of Houma which constitutes my main field site. The experimental (cognitive) data consist of a set of cognitive tasks administered to adult (aged 18+) villagers (the village mentioned above). The first task, a memory task, or free listing (see Weller and Romney 1988; Ross 2004), involved asking adult individuals to remember their co-villagers. The second task, a pile sort, involved using knowledge about social space – kinship, social relationships, and social networks – while sorting a deck of photos of all the adult co-villagers.[6] The third task, a drawing task, involved rendering one's social space in a drawing (see Bennardo 2002).

The social network data were also collected in the same field site from all the adult villagers. I employed three data collection strategies: two questionnaires, five types of interviews, and what I termed indirect observation. Since I could not observe the total interactions occurring between all villagers at any one time, I conducted repeated interviews with villagers (once a week for three weeks) about people they had interacted with during the previous day (indirect observation). The two questionnaires I administered asked questions about influence and about social support in the village. The interviews were about various types of social relationships (see below, linguistic data).

Linguistic data have typically been assigned a privileged place when inquiring into the mind, that is mental representations (Chomsky 1972; Miller and Johnson-Laird 1976; Dougherty 1985; Lakoff 1987; Pinker 1997; Olivier and Gapp 1998; Bowerman and Levinson 2001). The way in which meaning is organized and expressed linguistically is regarded as a reflection of mental organization of knowledge (see, for example, Strauss and Quinn 1997; Talmy 2000; Quinn 2005). For this reason, I conducted semi-structured interviews in which I inquired about and discussed social relationships. The interviews were all conducted in Tongan, videotaped, and transcribed in the field with the help of local assistants.

The first interviews (18) were about "personal" relationships. In other words, interviewees were asked questions about their relationships to other people in the village. The second group (18) was about the *perceived* social relationships of others. In these, interviewees were asked questions about the existence and composition of groups in their village. In the same interviews they were also asked about their knowledge and opinions about the current Tongan political situation; in particular about the monarchy-versus-democracy controversy. Basically, these interviews were about social relationships at the larger, national level.

The third group (24) was about *indirect* social relationships. That is, interviewees were asked to tell a story about something that had occurred in their village which they regarded as representative of the village life. This time, it was the type of story, the people remembered as having participated, and the relationships between these latter that represented the relevant data. The interviewees were chosen from among the clusters of villagers (six clusters with distinctly different profiles of a villager's influence over other villagers) obtained by a preliminary analysis conducted on the questions about influence.

Finally, I conducted interviews with individuals representing the top echelon of the Tongan population, such as nobles, ministers, and top government, religious, and political figures. I labeled these interviews "view from above" and they provide a necessary different point of view about the perceived social relationships at the national level.

All the interviews conducted come to a total of around 45 hours of speech production about social relationships. I analyzed this linguistic corpus with two goals in mind: first, I wanted to see if I could obtain clues toward a salient presence of radiality in the structure of the mental representations of social relationships; second, data from this corpus, such as people (e.g., heads of families, government or religious officials, and chiefs) and groups mentioned (e.g., families, extended families, and cultural groups) could be later correlated to the results of the analyses of the complete social network survey. The results of the analyses of the experimental (cognitive) tasks would also become part of this final correlation.

Partial homologies (e.g., radial and vectorial organization with other-than-ego as center or apex) between these three types of data were hypothesized as specific (e.g., "radial") mental representations of social relationships. Only a few centers may exist embedded in individuals around which and out of which social relationships are organized and represented mentally. Thus, Johnson-Laird's statement, "A crucial feature [of mental models, in our case a foundational cultural model] is that their structure corresponds to the structure of what they represent" (1999:525), would be supported.

Results of the analyses

Results from the linguistic data In order to discover if the linguistic data about social relationships pointed toward the hypothesized foundational cultural model, I ran several analyses on the texts at an increasing level of linguistic complexity. The lexical frequencies analyses were at the word level. The metaphor analyses were at the sentence level. And, finally, the discourse organization analyses were at the level of discourse, that is, stories and narratives. First, I conducted a frequency count of lexical items expressing radiality. The two lexemes focused on are two Tongan directionals, *mai* ("toward center") and *atu* ("away from center"). The results of these counts in the interviews were compared with similar counts about other types of Tongan texts (written and oral). A higher incidence of occurrence (than in discourse about other topics) of the two directionals with a specific meaning (either toward or away from other-than-ego) was hypothesized and found.

Second, the metaphors used during the interviews were recorded, counted, and classified in types (see Strauss and Quinn 1997:144 for the role of metaphors in pointing to cultural models, but see also Lakoff and Johnson 1980). The metaphor analysis reveals a Tongan model for social relationships whose core part is summarized by the following sentence: *'ofa* "love" is giving, either giving help (up-down) or giving duty and/or respect (down-up) (Bennardo 2008b:190). Fundamentally, on a background of hierarchically arranged social positions, Tongans label many of the actions that characterize social relationships as a form of *'ofa* "love" (Kavaliku 1977). The directionality of the action (from agent to recipient) is essential in determining what type of action is envisaged: help, from up to down; duty/respect, from down to up. The preferred agent for the action, as hypothesized, is an individual other-than-ego and ego is kept uninvolved as far as possible.

Third, the discourse structure or organization of the content of the stories narrated during the interviews in 2005 was highlighted (both types and frequencies). As hypothesized, I found a discourse radiality that implies narratives organized around what is termed "referential nodes." A referential node can be an actor (other-than-ego) or an event from which other actors or events are represented (Bennardo 2009:283–285).

Results from the cognitive data The results of the first task, memory list or free-listing, pointed toward a preference for the backgrounding of ego and the foregrounding of other-than-ego (Bennardo 2008a). The results of the second task, pile sort, pointed to a similar preference such as a focus on the group over the individual (Bennardo 2009:296–299). The findings of the analyses conducted on the third task, the drawing task, pointed again in the same direction, backgrounding of ego and focus on group (Bennardo 2009:300–307).

All the above findings are congruent with the general hypothesis of radiality as a foundational cultural model. Essential to radiality is the backgrounding of ego and the foregrounding of other-than-ego. The focus on a group entails that this generative process was already activated and instantiated by choosing an other-than-ego. Thus, in their own particular way, the mental representations of social relationships are fundamentally structured in a manner similar to the mental representations of spatial relationships. That is, non-ego-centered foci are used to organize the constituting elements, places, and things for space, and individuals and groups for social relationships.

Results from the social network data All the social network data collected were organized into sociometric form. To uncover the structure of the social networks we used Ucinet 6, a social network analysis application (Borgatti et al. 2002). Other programs were also used like NetDraw, Pajek (Batageli and Mrvar 1996), and SAS. The first group of analyses included measures of density, symmetry, and transitivity of the networks. The density measure tells us what percentage of the potential relations was activated by the question. Symmetry tells us the proportion of relations that were reciprocated, thus a measure of symmetric relation. And the transitivity measure reveals the extent to which groups of three villagers have at least one set of closed relations, such that if villager A is related to villager B, and villager B is related to villager C, it is also the case that villager A is related to villager C. The transitivity measure indicates the extent to which intermediaries are not important and can be thought of as highlighting a more developed hierarchical structure.

The second group of analyses included four measures of centrality. The rationale was that variations in the villagers' centrality measures would stand for a type of radiality (or star graph) for the social networks elicited. Thus, one could examine and/or test the principal hypothesis. The four measurements were: outdegree, outcloseness, betweenness, and network constraint. Outdegree represents the number of villagers each ego mentioned as someone they would be able to relate to directly (indegree represents the opposite measure, that is, the number of villagers that nominate ego as someone they could relate to directly). Outcloseness takes into account the ability of ego to extend relations throughout the network and measures how close or proximate that extended sphere of relationships is (Wasserman and Faust 1994:183–198). A higher number indicates that more villagers can be reached in fewer steps. This is a measure of the extent of the relationship across the entire network, through intermediary as well as direct links.

Betweenness is a measure of the network's dependence on the ability of a villager to link to other villagers in the network (Wasserman and Faust 1994:188–192). Betweenness measures of centrality thus describe the degree to which the network is characterized by how much the connections between villagers are dependent upon a link to a third party. Constraint is a measure of the "redundancy" in the network, of how interconnected one's alters are with one another. In establishing relationships broadly within a social group, it appears that closed, constrained network-based positions reflect closer relationships.

The results of all the analyses conducted (for details, see Bennardo and Cappell 2008) indicate that the structures representing the networks of influence in the village are possibly star graphs. Thus, the local hypothesis is supported, where the village is hierarchically organized when influence is taken into consideration. What is the relevance of these local findings within the global hypothesis of radiality? In order to answer this question, it is necessary to find what parameter(s) is(are) causing the variance that leads to the formation of the groups just described above. In other words, when villagers are answering the questions under analysis, they are shaping their answer according to specific organizing concepts. Such concepts can be revealing regarding their mental representation of social relationships. That is, they may be using individual characteristics of individuals (including themselves), such as gender, age, land ownership, income, and/or more collective features such as belonging to cultural groups like a *kāinga* ("extended family"), thus, either focusing on characteristics that ego and other-than-ego maximally share (e.g., gender, age, income), or focusing on collective entities that need to be conceived as other-than-ego (e.g., *kāinga*).

The only factor able to account for any substantial and statistically significant variation in asymmetric influence was *kāinga* membership (Bennardo and Cappell 2008). While ownership of land, cars, and income explained no substantial variation when considered individually, income does explain a portion of the variance in vote influence balance when *kāinga* is controlled for; the higher the income the greater the asymmetric voting influence of the villager. *Kāinga* membership continues to be the most important explanation of vote influence even when the resource variables are included in the same model. It is relevant then, that in an attempt to explain salient parameters used by villagers to answer questions about social networks, it became clear that an other-than-ego parameter such as *kāinga* membership was found to have a large priority over any other parameter linked to features of an individual. Such finding supports the global hypothesis of radiality.

Correlations The results from some linguistic data and some cognitive data were correlated with the results of some social network data. Two sets of linguistic data were used. The first consists of the lists of people mentioned in the first part (local level) of the "perceived" social relationships interviews. The second set consists of the lists of people obtained in the "indirect" social relationships interviews. The reason these linguistic data were selected for correlation is that both data, the linguistic and the social network, are directly related to the same social reality, the village of Houma. Besides, the narratives in the second sets were produced by a randomly selected sample of individuals from six clusters of villagers obtained by a preliminary analysis conducted on the social network questions about influence. In a similar fashion, the cognitive data chosen to be correlated with the social network data were the lists of villagers obtained by the free-listing task.

As stated above, the results of the social network analyses provide a map of the social relationships world. As with any map, it is a partial picture of the "world" represented; nonetheless, it represents a positive step toward an objective representation of that world.[7] Furthermore, people use, either consciously or unconsciously, individual and collective mental representations of that world. The linguistic and the cognitive data collected about social relationships were analyzed in an attempt to make the nature of those representations explicit.

The availability of the social network map of the social relationship world makes possible a comparison between the two sets of data. That is, centrality measures of influence, social support, and indirect observation social networks can be correlated with the results of some of the linguistic and cognitive data. The assumption is that mental representations of social relationships do participate in the construction of social networks in the social world. In other words, people's social behavior is generated by the way people think and organize their social relationships in their minds. A relevant feature regarding the nature of these mental constructions, that is radiality, is hypothesized to be reflected in the nature of people's social behavior or social networks, that is, star graph networks.

The first measure of network centrality that is correlated is the indegree, that is, the number of times an individual is nominated by other co-villagers. The indegree measure for the influence, the social support, and the indirect observation networks is correlated with the results of three other analyses. First, the results of the interviews, people mentioned in the first part (local level) of the "perceived" social relationships interviews. Second, the lists of people obtained in the "indirect" social relationships interviews. And third, the lists of villagers obtained by the free-listing.

Given the nature of the social networks presented above, I propose a number of local hypotheses. The star graph nature of influence networks should be conducive to higher correlations with the interview results. Villagers were asked after all to think of ways in which the social world of the village was structured. Questions about preferential traditional groups like *kāinga*s were asked, as well as information requested about their internal structures. Similarly, in the narrative texts, choosing a co-villager as the center of a specific episode to be reported and narrated is expected to activate a parameter like *kāinga* membership. Thus, since *kāinga* is one of the generative forces for the influence social networks, the two sets of data are expected to show similarity, hence substantial correlations. The cognitive data from the free-listing activity, which is memory-based, are also expected to correlate well. In fact, though the main parameter used to create the lists is spatial, that is, a sequence of houses in a mental scanning of the village, the organizing principle behind both data is hypothesized to be the same, radiality. Thus, both the influence social networks and the memory lists should reflect that shared structure.

Contrary to the influence networks, the tendency to obtain circle graphs for the social support networks makes it plausible that little or marginal correlations would be found between the indegree centrality measure of the influence social networks and the linguistic data, the interview and the narrative texts. The centrality measure of the independent observation social networks, instead, should correlate well with the results of the cognitive data. In fact, both required the use of memory about co-villagers, though, in a different way.

The results of the first type of correlations (Pearson) between indegree centrality measures of influence, social support, and independent observation networks with the linguistic data (interview and narrative) and the cognitive data (free-listing) are contained in Table 26.1. The picture that emerges is very nuanced, and requires a closer examination.

First, substantial correlations exist for the indegree measures of the influence networks, while the few correlations for the social support and the indirect observation networks are low if not very weak. These results are in line with the local hypotheses introduced. Second, the most positive correlations are between influence networks and interview and narrative data. Lower correlations exist between influence networks and the cognitive task, that is memory. Furthermore, the positive correlations are not replicated for question SNI1b. This question is about people who can act as intermediaries in influencing the town officer to change an assigned task and is labeled "administrative" influence by Bennardo and Cappell (2008). Third, a couple of low correlations were found between social support networks and only two of the three data sets, interview and narrative. One low correlation was found between indirect observation networks and the results of the memory cognitive task.

The results of the correlations between outdegree measures of the influence and social support networks (see Table 26.2) do not replicate those just discussed for indegree measures. No significant correlations are found. The correlation results between betweenness of the influence and social support networks (see Table 26.3) instead replicate in many respects those about indegree measures. That is, two questions (SNI2a and SNI2b) used to generate betweenness of influence networks correlate positively with interview data and to a lesser degree with narrative data. One of the two questions (SNI2a) also correlates with the data of the memory cognitive task. Two modest correlations also exist between one question (SNS1a) used to generate betweenness for social support networks and the memory cognitive task and between another question (SNS1b) and the interview data.

How do these local results relate to the larger hypothesis of radiality as a foundational cultural model? First, that features of social networks correlate with features of linguistic and cognitive representations of social relationships is remarkable in itself.

Table 26.1 Correlations of influence, support, and indirection observation (IO) indegree with interview, memory, and narrative

	Interview	*Memory*	*Narrative*	*P-value for H_0 that r = 0*
Influence indegree				
Indegree SNI1a (voting)	0.322	0.336	0.274	*0.002/0.001/0.009*
Indegree SNI1b (influence decision)	0.046	0.004	0.001	*0.666/0.970/0.990*
Indegree SNI2a (kin dispute mediator)	0.693	0.311	0.610	*<0.0001/0.003/<0.0001*
Indegree SNI2b (non-kin dispute mediator)	0.772	0.342	0.628	*<0.0001/0.001/<0.0001*
Social support indegree				
Indegree SNS1a (ask help *fakaafe*)	0.129	0.172	0.149	*0.233/0.110/0.167*
Indegree SNS1b (give help *fakaafe*)	0.185	0.172	0.150	*0.087/0.110/0.165*
Indegree SNS2a (ask help repairs)	0.102	0.123	0.232	*0.344/0.254/0.030*
Indegree SNS2b (give help repairs)	0.224	0.164	0.186	*0.037/0.128/0.084*
Indirect observation indegree				
Indegree (people mentioned)	−0.014	0.221	0.190	*0.891/0.032/0.066*

Table 26.2 Correlations of influence and support outdegree with interview, memory, and narrative

	Interview	*Memory*	*Narrative*	*P-value for H_0 that r = 0*
Influence outdegree				
Outdegree SNI1a (voting)	0.073	0.068	0.055	*0.493/0.528/0.611*
Outdegree SNI1b (influence decision)	0.143	0.028	0.050	*0.179/0.794/0.641*
Outdegree SNI2a (kin dispute mediator)	0.0176	0.181	0.081	*0.870/0.089/0.449*
Outdegree SNI2b (non-kin dispute mediator)	0.109	0.077	0.044	*0.310/0.473/0.678*
Social support outdegree				
Outdegree SNS1a (ask help *fakaafe*)	0.114	0.067	0.003	*0.293/0.537/0.976*
Outdegree SNS1b (give help *fakaafe*)	0.130	0.085	0.172	*0.228/0.432/0.110*
Outdegree SNS2a (ask help repairs)	0.156	0.063	0.002	*0.150/0.56/0.982*
Outdegree SNS2b (give help repairs)	0.030	0.0283	0.041	*0.780/0.795/0.708*

Table 26.3 Correlations of influence and support normed betweenness scores with interview, memory, and narrative

	Interview	*Memory*	*Narrative*
Influence betweenness			
NBetweenness SNI1a (voting)	0.047	0.105	–0.031
P-value for H_0 that r = 0	0.658	0.325	0.770
NBetweenness SNI1b (influence decision)	0.112	0.041	0.080
P-value for H_0 that r = 0	0.294	0.703	0.453
NBetweenness SNI2a (kin dispute mediator)	0.404	0.303	0.292
P-value for H_0 that r = 0	<0.0001	0.003	0.005
NBetweenness SNI2b (non-kin dispute mediator)	0.403	0.115	0.249
P-value for H_0 that r = 0	<0.0001	0.282	0.019
Social support betweenness			
NBetweenness SNS1a (ask help *fakaafe*)	0.059	0.248	0.113
P-value for H_0 that r = 0	0.583	0.020	0.298
NBetweenness SNS1b (give help *fakaafe*)	0.265	0.188	0.147
P-value for H_0 that r = 0	0.013	0.080	0.175
NBetweenness SNS2a (ask help repairs)	–0.091	0.185	0.059
P-value for H_0 that r = 0	0.340	0.086	0.585
NBetweenness SNS2b (give help repairs)	0.181	0.1201	0.111
P-value for H_0 that r = 0	0.093	0.266	0.307

This significant finding validates the common untested assumption that mental representations of social relationships contribute to the generation of social behavior.

Second, the three measures of centrality of networks – indegree, outdegree, and betweenness – that were correlated to the two linguistic data and to the memory cognitive data represent three different ways in which ego relates to other-than-ego in social networks. Indegree represents the number of villagers that nominate ego as someone to whom they could relate directly. Thus, it stands for an other-than-ego to ego type of relationship. Outdegree represents the number of villagers each ego mentioned as someone to whom they would be able to relate directly. Thus, it stands for an ego to other-than-ego type of relationship. Betweenness represents the network's dependence on the ability of a villager to link other villagers in the network. In other words, it describes the degree to which the network is characterized by how much the connections between villagers are dependent upon a link to a third party. Thus, it stands for an other-than-ego to other-than-ego type of relationship.

Third, one can further examine the results in two ways: (1) by looking at which networks produce the most extensive correlations, and (2) by looking at which network centrality measures correlate best. The correlation results clearly indicate that it is the influence networks that are the most extensively correlated with the two linguistic data sets and the cognitive data set. These networks are characterized by star graphs; thus, composed of central individuals toward which and out of which a number of relationships are established, in other words, a hierarchical organization or "authority ranking" (Fiske 1991). The radial nature of these influence networks seems to correlate extensively with the way in which villagers speak about and think of, that is, represent mentally, social relationships: those individuals with more influence centrality have higher levels of cognitive centrality. This result beautifully supports the global hypothesis of radiality.

The social support networks, on the other hand, do not correlate well with the other data sets. The nature of these networks is likely not star graphs but circle graphs, where equality is highlighted. It appears that collectivism (Triandis 1995) or "communal sharing" norms of equality (Fiske 1991) characterize these networks. Then, since the radiality hypothesis is about a mental organization of knowledge that may contribute to the generation of social behavior, these results open the discussion to a diversified participation of radiality to the contextual construction of one's behavior. Radiality appears to contribute to the generation of influence networks, but is set aside when social support networks are constructed. In other words, villagers realize that social support networks in their small close-knit community could be a better living (and surviving) strategy to implement than that of always complying to the hierarchical dictates reverberating onto their village from the centralized monolithic monarchy that characterizes their society. My ethnographic experience amply supports this conclusion.

The extension of the correlation between each centrality measure of the networks and the other data can be used to rank the three ways in which these three measures stand for types of relationships between ego and other-than-ego. Since the indegree is the measure that correlates more extensively (see Table 26.1), it is the relationship from other-than-ego to ego that is most salient, thus, participating in the construction of both sets of data. The betweenness measure is the one that correlates less extensively than the indegree, but more than the outdegree (see Table 26.3). Then, the relationship from other-than-ego to other-than-ego is also less salient than that from other-than-ego to ego but more salient than that from ego to other-than-ego. Finally, the outdegree measure is the one that correlates least (see Table 26.2). Thus, the relationship from ego to other-than-ego is the least salient.

To summarize, the ranking of the three relationships between ego and other-than-ego as evinced from the correlation results stands in this way: first, from other-than-ego to ego; second, from other-than-ego to other-than-ego; third, from ego to other-than-ego. The foregrounding of other-than-ego and the backgrounding of ego are constituent parts of the radiality foundational cultural model I hypothesized. The results of the correlations just introduced provide additional supporting evidence towards my global hypothesis.

Conclusion

I started this chapter by presenting a contemporary political scenario in the South Pacific, specifically, in Polynesia, the Kingdom of Tonga. A millennium-old monarchy is challenged by a recently born democratic movement. I asserted that, inspite of what a casual observer may conclude, democracy as such is contrary to the way people think about social relationships in Tonga. Thus, I suggested that the way to democracy will be a very long and slow one for this fascinating Pacific island nation. I reached this conclusion when discovering a foundational cultural model that characterizes the "Tongan mind." I called this cognitive molecule *radiality.*

I first found radiality in the spatial representation module and then found it duplicated or at least utilized in other modules and domains of knowledge such as time, possession, traditional religious belief system and navigational practices, kinship and social relationships (this latter, both in the mind and in behavior such as social networks). It will take more than the introduction of few technological wonders like cars, cell phones, and airplanes to change this way of organizing knowledge. I am not predicting that Tongans will not eventually become a democracy, only that it will be a longer journey than the fast one that characterized their adoption of modern technology. How and what they will do about the dichotomy between monarchy and democracy is up to them and to their wonderful minds.

NOTES

1 The extensive treatment of the whole research project and its results presented in this chapter appear in their full form in Bennardo 2009.
2 Foundational to this proposal, but not homologous, are Chomsky's (1972) and Fodor's (1983) modularity suggestions (Hirschfeld and Gelman 1994).
3 Talmy (2000) and Levinson (2006) made similar proposals.
4 Hirschfeld and Gelman (1994) draw a similar distinction between "module" and "domain."
5 "Relation" is another of the fundamental ontological categories, as in Aristotle and Kant.
6 I took photos, close-ups, of all the adult villagers, numbered them, printed them, and constructed a laminated deck to be safely used as many times as needed in the field.
7 "All maps are spatial analogies in the sense that they preserve some of the spatial relationships of the world they depict" (Hutchins 1995:61).

REFERENCES

Abelson, Robert, and Roger Schank
1977 Scripts, Plans, Goals, and Understanding: An Inquiry into Human Knowledge Structures. Hillsdale, NJ: Lawrence Erlbaum.

Ballim, A., and Y. Wilks
1991 Artificial Believers: The Ascription of Belief. Hillsdale, NJ: Lawrence Erlbaum.

Batagelj, Vladimir, and Andrej Mrvar
1996 Pajek: Program for Large Network Analysis. http://vlado.fmf.uni-lj.si/pub/networks/pajek/, accessed October 8, 2010.

Bateson, Gregory
1972 A Theory of Play and Fantasy. *In* Steps to an Ecology of Mind. Pp. 177–193. New York: Ballantine.

Bender, A., G. Bennardo, and S. Beller
2005 Spatial Frames of Reference for Temporal Relations: A Conceptual Analysis in English, German, and Tongan. *In* Proceedings of the 27th Annual Conference of the Cognitive Science Society. Bruno G. Bara, Lawrence Barsalou, and Monica Bucciarelli, eds. Pp. 220–225. New York: Lawrence Erlbaum.

Bennardo, G.
1993 Towards a Computational Approach to Spatial Cognition: An Investigation of Relevant Computations in the Visual System and the Linguistic System. Urbana, IL: Beckman Institute for Advanced Science and Technology.

1996 A Computational Approach to Spatial Cognition: Representing Spatial Relationships in Tongan Language and Culture. Unpublished doctoral dissertation, University of Illinois at Urbana–Champaign, Urbana, Illinois.

1999a A Conceptual Analysis of Tongan Spatial Nouns: From Grammar to Mind. Munich: LINCOM Europa.

1999b The Conceptual Content of Tongan Directionals: Mental Representations of Space in Tongan. Rongorongo Studies 9(2):39–61.

2000a A Conceptual Analysis of Tongan Spatial Nouns: From Grammar to Mind. Language of the World 12(1):1–25.

2000b Language and Space in Tonga: "The Front of the House is Where the Chief Sits!" Anthropological Linguistics 42(4):499–544.

2002 Map Drawing in Tonga, Polynesia: Accessing Mental Representations of Space. Field Methods 14(4):390–417.

2004 Linguistic Untranslatability vs. Conceptual Nesting of Frames of Reference. *In* Proceedings of the 26th Annual Conference of the Cognitive Science Society. K. Forbus, Dedre Gentner, and Terry Regier, eds. Pp. 102–107. New York: Lawrence Erlbaum.

2008a Familiar Space in Social Memory. Social Structure and Dynamics 3(1):7–23.

2008b Metaphors in Tongan Linguistic Production about Social Relationships: 'Ofa "Love" is Giving. Anthropological Linguistics 50(2):174–204.

2009 Language, Space and Social Relationships: A Foundational Cultural Model in Polynesia. Cambridge: Cambridge University Press.

Bennardo, Giovanni, and Charles Cappell

2008 Influence Structures in a Tongan Village: "Every Villager Is Not the Same!" Structure and Dynamics: eJournal of Anthropological and Related Sciences 3(1). http://repositories.cdlib.org/imbs/socdyn/sdeas/vol3/iss1/art2, accessed October 8, 2010.

Bennardo, G., and D. W. Read

2007 Cognition, Algebra, and Culture in the Tongan Kinship Terminology. Journal of Cognition and Culture 7(2):49–88.

Bernard, H. R., P. D. Killworth, and L. Sailer

1980 Informant Accuracy in Social Network Data IV: A Comparison of Clique-Level in Behavioral and Cognitive Network Data. Social Science Research 11:30–66.

1982 Informant Accuracy in Social Network Data V: An Experimental Attempt to Predict Actual Communication from Recall Data. Social Networks 2:191–218.

Borgatti, S. P., M. G. Everett, and L. C. Freeman

2002 Ucinet 6 for Windows. Cambridge, MA: Analytic Technologies.

Bott, E.

1972 Psychoanalysis and Ceremony. *In* The Interpretation of Ritual. J. S. L. Fontaine, ed. Pp. 205–237. London: Tavistock.

Bowerman, Melissa, and S. C. Levinson

2001 Language Acquisition and Conceptual Development. Cambridge: Cambridge University Press.

Brewer, W. F.

1984 The Nature and Functions of Schemas. *In* Handbook of Social Cognition, vol. 1. Pp. 119–160. Hillsdale, NJ: Lawrence Erlbaum.

1987 Schemas versus Mental Models in Human Memory. *In* Modelling Cognition. P. Morris, ed. Pp. 187–197. New York: John Wiley.

1999 Schemata. *In* The MIT Encyclopedia of the Cognitive Sciences. R. A. Wilson and F. C. Keil, eds. Pp. 729–730. Cambridge, MA: MIT Press.

Brewer, W. F., and G. V. Nakamura

1984 The Nature and Functions of Schemas. *In* Handbook of Social Cognition, vol. 1. R. S. Wyer and T. K. Srull, eds. Pp. 119–160. Hillsdale, NJ: Lawrence Erlbaum.

Burkett, Tracy Lynn
1998 Co-Sponsorship in the United States Senate: A Network Analysis of Senate Communication and Leadership, 1973–1990. Unpublished dissertation, University of South Carolina, Columbia.
Cablitz, G. H.
2006 Marquesan: A Grammar of Space. New York: Mouton de Gruyter.
Chomsky, N.
1972 Language and Mind. New York: Harcourt Brace Jovanovich.
Craik, K.
1943 The Nature of Explanation. Cambridge: Cambridge University Press.
D'Andrade, Roy G.
1989 Cultural Cognition. *In* Foundations of Cognitive Science. M. I. Posner, ed. Pp. 795–830. Cambridge, MA: MIT Press.
D'Andrade, Roy G., and Claudia Strauss, eds.
1992 Human Motives and Cultural Models. Cambridge: Cambridge University Press.
Dougherty, Janet W., ed.
1985 Directions in Cognitive Anthropology. Champaign: University of Illinois Press.
Downs, Roger M., and David Stea
1977 Maps in Minds: Reflections on Cognitive Mapping. New York: Harper and Row.
Fillmore, Charles
1982 Frame Semantics. *In* Linguistics in the Morning Calm. Linguistic Society of Korea, ed. Pp. 111–137. Seoul: Hanshin.
Fiske, Alan P.
1991 Structures of Social Life: The Four Elementary Forms of Human Relations. New York: Free Press.
Fodor, J.
1983 Modularity of Mind. Cambridge, MA: MIT Press.
Freeman, L. C., and A. K. Romney
1987 Words, Deeds, and Social Structure: A Preliminary Study of the Reliability of Informants. Human Organization 46:330–334.
Freeman, L. C., D. R. White, and A. K. Romney, eds.
1989 Research Methods in Social Network Analysis. Fairfax, VA: George Mason University Press.
Gentner, D., and A. L. Stevens, eds.
1983 Mental Models. Hillsdale, NJ: Lawrence Erlbaum.
Golledge, R. G.
1999 Wayfinding Behavior: Cognitive Mapping and Other Spatial Processes. Baltimore: Johns Hopkins University Press.
Gould, Peter, and Rodney White
1986[1974] Mental Maps. New York: Routledge.
Hill, C.
1982 Up/Down, Front/Back, Left/Right: A Contrastive Study of Hausa and English. *In* Here and There: Cross-Linguistic Studies on Deixis and Demonstration. J. Weissenborn and W. Klein, eds. Pp. 13–42. Amsterdam: Benjamins.
Hirschfeld, L. A., and Susan A. Gelman, eds.
1994 Mapping the Mind: Domain Specificity in Cognition and Culture. Cambridge: Cambridge University Press.
Holland, Dorothy
1992 How Cultural Systems Become Desire. *In* Human Motives and Cultural Models. R. D'Andrade and C. Strauss, eds. Pp. 61–89. Cambridge: Cambridge University Press.
Holland, Dorothy, and Naomi Quinn, eds.
1987 Cultural Models in Language and Thought. Cambridge: Cambridge University Press.

Hoponoa, L.

1992 Pro-Democratic Movement in Tonga: The Case of Samiuela "Akilisi Pohiva." *In* Pacific History: Papers from the 8th Pacific History Association Conference. D. Rubenstein, ed. Mangilau: University of Guam Press.

Hutchins, Edwin

1995 Cognition in the Wild. Cambridge, MA: MIT Press.

Jackendoff, R.

1983 Semantics and Cognition. Cambridge, MA: MIT Press.

1992a Is There a Faculty of Social Cognition? *In* Language of the Mind: Essays on Mental Representation. R. Jackendoff, ed. Pp. 69–82. Cambridge, MA: MIT Press.

1992b Languages of the Mind: Essays on Mental Representations. Cambridge, MA: MIT Press.

1997 The Architecture of the Language Faculty. Cambridge, MA: MIT Press.

2002 Foundations of Language: Brain, Meaning, Grammar, and Evolution. Oxford: Oxford University Press.

2007 Language, Consciousness, Culture: Essays on Mental Structure. Cambridge, MA: MIT Press.

James, K. E.

1994 Tonga's Pro-Democracy Movement. Pacific Affairs 67(2):242–263.

2002 The Recent Elections in Tonga: Democratic Supporters Win but Does Democracy Follow? Journal of Pacific History 37(3):313–322.

2003 Is There a Tongan Middle Class? Hierarchy and Protest in Contemporary Tonga. Contemporary Pacific 15(2):309–336.

Johnson-Laird, P. N.

1983 Mental Models: Towards a Cognitive Science of Language, Inference, and Consciousness. Cambridge: Cambridge University Press.

1999 Mental Models. *In* The MIT Encyclopedia of the Cognitive Sciences. R. A. Wilson and F. C. Keil, eds. Pp. 525–527. Cambridge, MA: MIT Press.

Kavaliku, Sione Langi

1977 *'Ofa*! The Treasure of Tonga. South Pacific Social Science 6:47–67.

Keller, Janet D.

1992 Schemas for Schemata. *In* New Directions in Psychological Anthropology. Theodore Schwartz, G. M. White, and Catherine A. Lutz, eds. Pp. 59–67. Cambridge: Cambridge University Press.

Keller, J. D., and F. K. Lehman

1991 Complex Concepts. Cognitive Science 15(2):271–292.

Kronenfeld, David

1996 Plastic Glasses and Church Fathers. Oxford: Oxford University Press.

2008 Cultural Models. Intercultural Pragmatics 5(1):67–74.

Lakoff, G.

1987 Women, Fire, and Dangerous Things: What Categories Reveal about the Mind. Chicago: University of Chicago Press.

Lakoff, G., and M. Johnson

1980 Metaphors We Live By. Chicago: University of Chicago Press.

Lehman, F. K., and G. Bennardo

2003 A Computational Approach to the Cognition of Space and Its Linguistic Expressions. Mathematical Anthropology and Cultural Theory 1(2):1–83. http://www.mathematicalanthropology.org/pdf/Lehman&Bennardo0603.pdf, accessed October 7, 2010.

Levinson, C. S.

2003 Space in Language and Cognition. Cambridge: Cambridge University Press.

2006 On the Human "Interaction Engine." *In* Roots of Human Sociality: Culture, Cognition, and Interaction. N. J. Enfield and S. C. Levinson, eds. Pp. 39–69. Oxford: Berg.

Mandler, J. M.
2004 The Foundations of Mind: Origins of Conceptual Thought. Oxford: Oxford University Press.
Marcus, G. E.
1980 The Nobility and the Chiefly Tradition in the Modern Kingdom of Tonga. Wellington: Polynesian Society.
McCarty, C.
2002 Measuring Structure in Personal Networks. Journal of Social Structure 3(1).
Miller, G. A., and P. N. Johnson-Laird
1976 Language and Perception. Cambridge, MA: Belknap Press of Harvard University Press.
Minsky, M.
1975 A Framework for Representing Knowledge. *In* The Psychology of Computer Vision. P. H. Winston, ed. Pp. 211–277. New York: McGraw-Hill.
Olivier, Patrick, and Klaus-Peter Gapp
1998 Representation and Processing of Spatial Expressions. Mahwah, NJ: Lawrence Erlbaum.
Pinker, S.
1997 How the Mind Works. New York: W. W. Norton.
Quinn, Naomi
2005 Finding Culture in Talk: A Collection of Methods. New York: Palgrave Macmillan.
Read, D. W.
2005 Kinship Algebra Expert System (KAES): A Software Implementation of a Cultural Theory. Social Science Computer Review 24(1):43–67.
Read, D. W., and C. A. Behrens
1990 KAES, an Expert System for the Algebraic Analysis of Kinship Terminologies. Journal of Quantitative Anthropology 2:353–393.
Ross, Norbert
2004 Culture and Cognition: Implications for Theory and Method. London: Sage.
Rumelhart, David
1980 Schemata: The Building Block of Cognition. *In* Theoretical Issues in Reading Comprehension. R. Spiro, ed. Pp. 33–58. Hillsdale, NJ: Lawrence Erlbaum.
Scott, J.
1992 Social Network Analysis. Newbury Park, CA: Sage.
Shore, Bradd
1996 Culture in Mind: Cognition, Culture, and the Problem of Meaning. Oxford: Oxford University Press.
Strauss, Claudia, and Naomi Quinn
1997 A Cognitive Theory of Cultural Meaning. Cambridge: Cambridge University Press.
Talmy, L.
2000 Toward a Cognitive Semantics: Typology and Process in Concept Structuring, vol. 2. Cambridge, MA: MIT Press.
Triandis, Harry C.
1995 Individualism and Collectivism. Boulder, CO: Westview.
Tversky, Barbara
1981 Distortions in Memory for Maps. Cognitive Psychology 13:407–433.
1993 Cognitive Maps, Cognitive Collages, and Spatial Mental Models. *In* Spatial Information Theory: A Theoretical Basis for GIS. Andrew U. Frank and Irene Campari, eds. Pp. 14–24. Berlin: Springer.
1996 Spatial Perspective in Descriptions. *In* Language and Space. P. Bloom, M. A. Peterson, L. Nadel, and M. F. Garrett, eds. Pp. 463–529. Cambridge, MA: MIT Press.

Wasserman, Stanley, and Katherine Faust
1994 Social Network Analysis: Methods and Applications. Cambridge: Cambridge University Press.
Weller, Susan C., and A. Kimball Romney
1988 Systematic Data Collection. Newbury Park, CA: Sage.
Wellman, B., and S. Wortley
1990 Different Strokes from Different Folks: Community Ties and Social Support. American Journal of Sociology 96:558–688.

CHAPTER 27

Cognitive Approaches to the Study of Romantic Love: Semantic, Cross-Cultural, and as a Process

Victor C. de Munck

In this paper I present three different cognitive approaches to the study of romantic love; each provides a different slant on what it is and how it works. The first study shows how to obtain data, and to construct and analyze cultural models of what Americans think romantic love is and how it may influence behavior. The second study compares cultural models of romantic love in the USA with those in Lithuania and relies on Bateson's concept of *framing* for the analysis of cultural differences. The third study presents a new method for discovering, testing, and analyzing prototypical and alternative cultural models, of a process – in this case courtship.

The purpose of this paper is to show the flexibility and usefulness of a cognitive approach that is scientific in theory and method. Let me quickly add that by "scientific" I don't mean that it excludes interpretivist, hermeneutic, or more generally humanitarian approaches but simply that the theory and methods for data collection and analysis are made as explicit and systematic as possible. The scientific study of culture is humanitarian in that the means to the results are publicly presented so that anyone can evaluate the strengths and weaknesses of the research. Science, to me, does not necessarily mean using questionnaires and complex mathematical or statistical formulations to collect and analyze data; rather, it means that results logically follow from the data and that the means by which the data are obtained are made explicit enough to be replicable.

A Companion to Cognitive Anthropology, First Edition. Edited by David B. Kronenfeld, Giovanni Bennardo, Victor C. de Munck, and Michael D. Fischer.

Prototype–Schema–Cultural Models Approach to Explaining What Americans Mean When They Say They are "In Love" versus "Love but Not in Love"

This study relies on three different cognitive methods: free-listing; obtaining brief commentaries on free-list data; and asking a third set of informants to pile-sort the most frequently mentioned terms in the free-list. The pile-sort procedure produces a multidimensional scaling figure which visually displays the relationship between these terms on the basis of proximate similarity. The above methods provide us with sufficient information to construct a prototypical cultural model of romantic love. Interview data are briefly presented to show how this model can be used to interpret how people describe courting relationships.

Forty Americans from a small rural town in upstate New York, and 40 from New York City were asked to respond to the free-list question, "What do you associate with romantic love?" The respondents were between 20 and 50 years of age; 44 were females and 36 males. There were no obvious differences in the responses between rural and urban New Yorkers and so I do not differentiate between the two in this chapter. Gender differences are also not differentiated in the analysis.

The initial free-list output contained 448 terms. Working with two assistants, I culled the number of items by combining responses considered synonymous. We eventually reduced the list to 160 terms. The free-list in Table 27.1 includes only those terms mentioned five or more times.

The terms in the table are organized into five clusters; the analysis of these clusters is supported with commentary data.

Cluster 1: being together. "Being together" and similar terms – "intimacy," "connection" – signal that romantic love expresses itself as a desire to spend time together. A typical commentary related to "being together" is provided by a 21-year-old woman who said, "You want to spend time with that special person and can't go too long without seeing him. He makes you feel like you are important to him." Rational explanations for why one partner can't spend time with the other can trigger concerns that he or she is not "in love" with their partner. Culturally this aspect of romantic love is expressed by a plethora of metaphors such as "one's better or other half," "feeling completed," and so on. The strength of this desire may manifest itself most forcefully when love relations are unrequited or fail.

Cluster 2: mutual. One 34-year-old male noted this relational quality of love when he said, "Love must always be mutual if it is to last; by mutual I mean that both partners express their feelings of love to each other equally." A 27-year-old woman said, "Love is when a couple is mutually responsible for each other's welfare and happiness." A 28-year-old woman said that "mutual" is the same as "supporting each other in all things, listening and caring for each other, meeting mutual expectations and being honest and then trusting each other and this strengthens the relationship."

If "friendship" and "equality" were included in this constellation, as seems reasonable, then "mutual" (for this sample) becomes a core semantic dimension (or metaphor) of the American cultural model of romantic love (see also Quinn 1992, 1996, 1997). "Mutual," "friendship," and "equality," refer to the relationship rather than a quality of the lovers. These terms shift the analysis of romantic love from the

Table 27.1 Free-list terms for "What do you associate with romantic love?" sorted by frequency

	Item	*Frequency*	*% of respondents*	*Average rank*
1	Being together	22	28	4.133
2	Mutual	21	26	4.875
3	Friendship	17	21	2.600
4	Sex	16	20	3.143
5	Gifts	15	19	3.500
6	Care	14	18	3.375
7	Excited	12	15	5.333
8	Passion	10	13	2.714
9	Connection	8	10	3.333
10	Intimacy	8	10	3.000
11	Do anything	8	10	2.750
12	Trust	7	9	2.000
13	Commitment	7	9	1.200
14	Happy	6	8	2.333
15	Content	5	6	4.000
16	Equality	5	6	4.000
17	Comfortable	5	6	5.500
18	Honest	5	6	3.000
19	Butterflies	5	6	4.000
20	Sacrifice	4	5	3.000

individual as the point of reference to the relationship itself. Couples desire that the relationship be one of equality and are probably sensitive to cues that suggest that the other partner is not responding in kind emotionally, in terms of labor, free time, and whatever other features a person considers salient in a romantic relationship. Romantic love is not only supposed to be non-hierarchical, as friendship would imply, but both parties should give in kind and equally.

Cluster 3: building a love relationship. "Care," "trust," "commitment," and "honest" signal qualities that are expected to be expressed by both partners of a relationship. One 20-year-old female said, "[my boyfriend] and I care for each other, we talk about everything." A 24-year-old female commented, "I care about my boyfriend's life and he cares about my life." A 25-year-old male said, "I've got to be able to trust her otherwise I'll be jealous and worry about who she is with. I can love someone without trust but I'll have to get out of the relationship eventually, otherwise it's too painful." A 24-year-old male said, "Without trust, there's no relationship." A 30-year-old male said, "A relationship is build on honesty and trust otherwise you got nothing to build on."

"Care" is a quality of a loving relationship, and suggests that one identifies with the other so that the beloved's success and failure, ups and downs, are felt as one's own. "Honesty" and "trust" seem to have a different function; they are not so much components or derivatives of love but a requirement for building a relationship from a feeling of love. However, these building blocks are not motivated, unless they are preceded by caring for the other.

Cluster 4: altruism. "Do anything" and "sacrifice" indicate that there is a strong altruistic component to romantic love and both imply that there are no limits, including perhaps the sacrifice of one's life, for one's beloved. Both are also claims about the strength of one's love for the beloved and do not necessarily imply that the other is willing to make the same claim, though it may be hoped for.

Cluster 5: good feelings. "Happy," "content," and "comfortable" have to do with a general psycho-physiological feeling of pleasure that results from "being together" or just being in love. These responses to the stimulus of love suggest that they are part of a positive motivational feedback loop. When they do not feel "happy" and "comfortable" then they strive to deal with whatever causes the feedback system to get out of whack so that it functions smoothly.

Overall, the above five clusters refer to "companionate love." Individually, many of these terms can refer to friend or family relationships, but taken together they do not fit, at least not comfortably, into either of these alternative categories. For instance, seldom do young adults strive to be with their parents or siblings every day most of the time simply because they want to "be together." Second, people can feel "happy," "content," and "comfortable" around family but "equality," "friendship," and "mutual" are more problematic aspects of familial relations, given the hierarchical nature of parent–child ties, and the competitive nature of sibling relationships in America. While parents may "do anything" for their children, it is unlikely and not really expected that children will "do anything" for their parents.

The two clusters of terms that definitely distinguish romantic love from friendship and family relations are "sex–passion" and "excited–butterflies." "Sex" was the fourth most frequently mentioned term (20 percent) and "passion" the eighth most frequently mentioned (13 percent). These terms suggest that sexual desire and attraction are necessary components of romantic love. When informants commented on "sex" they usually specified "making love" or how satisfying sex was in the context of love (Sternberg 1988, 2006).

"Sex" may be the most problematic of the terms above. Tennov (1979) and most love researchers have shown that people who are "in love" usually distinguish love from sex. I think sex cannot be a required or core component of romantic love because, if it is only for sex, then sex partners by definition are commensurable (i.e., interchangeable) while love relations are incommensurable (i.e., unique). Informants unanimously said that sex was "more meaningful," "more satisfying," et cetera in a love than in a non-love relationship. Love is also said by some to legitimize having sex. Third, love symbolically stamps sex as an act of monogamy and intimacy.

Typical commentaries on sex were, "I like sex [with my boyfriend] in the shower, it feels so intimate" (22-year-old woman); "sex without love is robotic, but with love it is divine" (24-year-old woman); "there needs to be some form of love before any sex starts otherwise it is just lust" (41-year-old man). I suggest that when informants talk about sex in this way they usually mean something like "passion." Passion is different than sex because it is an appraisal of a sex partner as someone who uniquely arouses you, thus again the person is incommensurable. Passion is a necessary core feature of romantic love, though it is frequently referred to as "sex." "Excited" and "butterflies" are the psycho-physiological indicators of passionate love.

From the above data and discussion we can provide a simple episodic narrative of the normative model of romantic love in America. It consists of the desire by the couple to be together, to interact as friends, and feel content with each other, while also feeling excited and passionate toward each other. In order to develop such a relationship the couple should be honest and care for each other; this increases trust and commitment. Thus romantic love involves a set of good feelings that are related to the companionate and passionate aspect of the relationship. It also involves a sense of responsibilities that are mutual and build trust. Finally, altruism is expected as a symbol that the beloved is uniquely valued and also a symbol of commitment to the relationship. This leads to the hypothesis that the more a couple evaluates their relationship to fit the above episodic description of romantic love the less they will question that they are in love and also the more satisfied they will be with their relationship.

Pile-sorts

To further explore the above cultural model, I took the top 43 terms from the free-list (leaving out "gifts" which doesn't fit), and with my assistants recruited 39 informants to conduct a pile-sort task. The pile-sort task involved asking informants to sort index cards (with a term listed on each card) into groups based on perceived similarity. Informants were asked to sort the cards into two piles and to continue dividing each pile into two piles until they were left with only two index cards per pile. From this data an "aggregate proximity matrix" of the proportion of times each term was sorted with another was produced. This matrix was used to produce a multidimensional scale (MDS) using two dimensions (0.081 stress level) (see Figure 27.1). A two-dimensional MDS provides a visual representation of the aggregate proximity matrix. Terms that are located closer to each other were sorted together more frequently than those far away, thus they can be interpreted as similar to each other in meaning.

The MDS includes terms not presented in the free-list to present a clearer more holistic picture of the pattern of relations between terms associated with romantic love. The dotted lines indicate the two dimensions – a vertical high- to low-energy dimension and a horizontal good to bad dimension. For interpretive purposes, the MDS can be divided into four quadrants: (1) a bad feeling, low-energy quadrant;

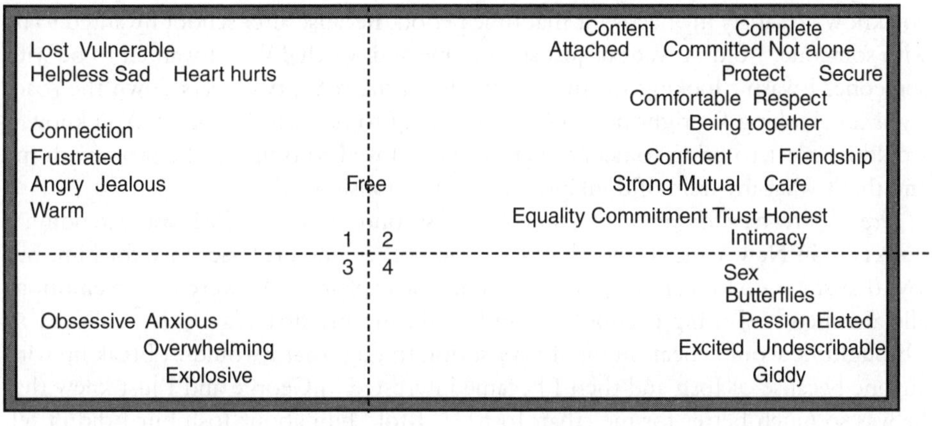

Figure 27.1 Multidimensional scale (MDS) of terms associated with romantic love (using pile-sort data) by US informants.

(2) a good feeling, low-energy quadrant; (3) a bad feeling, high-energy quadrant; and (4) a good feeling, high-energy quadrant. Quadrants 1 and 3 seem to refer to unstable and unrequited love conditions, whereas quadrants 2 and 4 refer to stable or requited love relationships. Quadrant 2 corresponds to companionate love and quadrant 4 to passionate love. The American cultural model of romantic love includes both quadrants 2 and 4, for the love relationship to be satisfying. Theoretically, one can deduce from the above MDS that a satisfying romantic love relationship consists of a positive assessment of a relationship based on features that adequately represent quadrants 2 and 4. If one wants a romantic love relationship and one's current relationship satisfies only quadrant 2 or 4 but not both, then the person will be motivated to acquire the features associated with the missing quadrant. If the strategy does not work satisfactorily, then the person will leave the relationship or, if they remain in it, either feel unsatisfied, blame themselves, or devalue the features of the lacking quadrant.

I will now briefly show how this cultural model works *in situ* by presenting interview data from only one informant about her current relationship. The data are meant to suggest how Americans use the above model to evaluate their own love relationships. This step is necessary to show that the above cultural model is feasible in that it can be used to make sense of people's behaviors in a romantic love relationship. Many more examples of both genders could be included but there is not enough space; more importantly, however, it doesn't matter how many informants one uses, only that the cultural model seems to correspond with and partially explain the reasoning and actions of a relatively typical person.

Rose was a 21-year-old female who was a junior at a New England university. I conducted four interviews with her: three within a period of three months and a fourth about a year later. I present only small slices of these interviews to illustrate the usefulness of the cultural models prototype approach.

First interview data: Rose met her boyfriend, Josh, in the 11th grade. She says, "All my friends had boyfriends and I was just sick of it; I mean I was a fat lonely person just by myself." She and Josh became a couple quickly. Rose continues, "After one month together he said he was in love with me and I thought that was just too soon, that there was no way. And I told him, there was just no way he could know enough of me to say 'I love you.' ... We stayed together every day ... I was looking for love at that moment, you know, to satisfy my needs for that time period. Because after school I wanted to be with someone, I didn't want to just sit at home and watch TV ... I wanted to be with someone. I wasn't looking for three years down the road, two years down the road; I was just looking for right now. Who am I going to bring to my prom? You know it would be great to bring someone there whom I loved to bring to the prom with me and that's what my train of thinking was of a relationship ..."

Second interview data: At the time of the second interview, Josh was attending a university in New York. They seldom see each other; she professes love for him, but says that she is no longer "in love" with him. She explains: "We were just so emotionally attached ... [in high school] ... and ... during my first year ... [in college] ... I thought he would cheat on me. I kept saying to guys that I wouldn't break up with anyone because of Josh and then I became interested in George and I just knew that he was so much better for me [than Josh] ... I told him about Josh but I didn't tell Josh about George. I thought it would naturally happen that I would get attracted to someone else. So I told Josh that I wanted to see other people because we hadn't been with other people. If he wasn't so honest and so good to me [pause] I know that he would never cheat on me ... [referring to Josh]. He just knows that we're going to get married ... I am afraid that if I do break up with him I'm not going to find someone as good as him."

Third interview data (paraphrased): Rose wanted to become "in love" with Josh again and decided to have sexual intercourse with him. Prior to this she had had sex with him only twice and both times it was protected. This time she asked him not to use a condom, nor was she on birth control. Rose said she knew it was risky, but she wanted sex with Josh to be exciting and hoped this might do the trick, that is, to make her feel "in love" with him. It didn't work. She states that she both wants to and cannot break up with Josh because she "may never find someone as good as Josh again." She blames herself for her inability to be sexually aroused, stating that she belongs to the "one per cent of women who don't enjoy sex."

Fourth interview data (excerpts): Rose is still with Josh. She says, "Marriage is a priority for me, it is *the* top priority. With marriage and stuff you just have to take on great responsibilities ... a great boyfriend is someone who could be totally spontaneous and you could have so much fun with him and he could be outgoing, humorous you know but then you ... [pause] ... he could be great in marriage too ... [pause] ... but you want to be sure that he can hold on to his responsibilities and when he has to be serious he will be serious so there is a difference, I think ... [pause] ... someone you love and who is exciting can be bad for you, like chocolates."

Josh satisfies all the conditions of quadrant 2. She did not succeed in meeting some of the states in quadrant 4. Had she attained them once or a few times she can retain them as "precious memories" (a quote from another interview with a married woman). What she has done is foreground and increase the value of features of quadrant 2 and simultaneously devalue the features of quadrant 4 to justify staying with Josh; further she also places the blame on herself rather than on Josh.

In conclusion the prototypical cultural model of romantic love is one that includes a slate of features from both quadrants 2 and 4; how these are worked out requires further study. A combined free-list, commentary, pile-sort, and interview analysis indicates that a complete prototypical cultural model of romantic love for Americans includes the following core features: mutuality, security, altruism, friendship, and passion.

Comparing Cultural Models of Romantic Love in the USA and Lithuania: Framing

The exact same methods (free-listing, commentaries, pile-sorting, and interviews) presented above were used in Lithuania. Forty Lithuanians from a small rural town, Telsiai, and 40 from Vilnius, the largest city and capital of Lithuania, were asked to respond to the free-list question "What do you associate with romantic love?" The respondents were between 20 and 40 years of age; 46 were female and 34 were males (see Figure 27.2). There were no obvious differences in the responses between rural and urban Lithuanians and so I do not differentiate between the two in this chapter. Gender differences were minor and not differentiated in the analysis of the free-list data. Working with two assistants, I culled the number of items by combining responses considered synonyms; phrases were reduced to short replies. A second free-list output

Table 27.2 Lithuanian free-list terms sorted by frequency

	Term	*Frequency*	*% of respondents*	*Average rank*
1	Being together	40	50	4.850
2	Happy	29	36	3.813
3	Walk	14	17.5	3.500
4	Emotional upsurge	14	17.5	3.786
5	Kiss	12	15.0	4.083
6	Do things together	9	11.25	4.889
7	Temporary	9	11.25	5.111
8	Sex	9	11.25	3.444
9	Attention	8	10.00	4.250
10	Love talk	8	10.00	5.375
11	Surprise	8	10.00	3.400
12	Passion	7	8.75	3.286
13	Cinema	7	8.75	2.857
14	Travel	7	8.75	4.286
15	Tender	7	8.75	3.857
16	Attachment	7	8.75	2.714
17	Holding hands	7	8.75	3.000
18	Mutual	6	7.50	4.000
19	Trust	6	7.50	1.500
20	Dream	6	7.50	7.333
21	Admire	6	7.50	3.500
22	Little presents	6	7.50	6.167
23	Honest	5	6.25	5.600
24	Not pragmatic	5	6.25	5.800
25	Candlelight dinner	5	6.25	2.800
26	Initial stage of love	5	6.25	2.800
27	Care	4	5.00	4.500
28	Physical upsurge	4	5.00	3.750
29	Strong	4	5.00	3.000
30	Longing	4	5.00	2.500
31	Self-confidence	4	5.00	6.750
32	One	4	5.00	8.750
33	Carefree	4	5.00	7.250
34	Doubt	4	5.00	10.750
35	Enduring	4	5.00	2.500
36	Flowers	4	5.00	2.750

of 180 terms was generated; below we list only those terms mentioned four or more times. Terms were translated into English by me and two assistants. To save space I have not included the Lithuanian terms here. (See Table 27.3 for a list of the key terms coming out of this discussion.)

One cannot help but notice a fundamental underlying similarity in terms and frequency counts between the free-list outputs from Lithuania and the United States: "Being together," "happy," and other terms from quadrants 2 and 4 predominate with the Lithuanian sample. But there are three important differences. Of the 80 Lithuanians not one mentioned "friendship" or those terms that associate romantic love with comfort and security. How can such core features be missing from the

Table 27.3 Key terms used to discover a prototypical courtship process

Events	*Orientation*
Developing a friendship in the relationship	Feeling like you are a part of each other's future
First kiss	Having routines in the relationship
Dating	Feeling dependent on the other person
Saying "I love you" for the first time	Taking each other for granted
Moving in together	Cooperating with one another
Having sex for the first time	Fighting
Getting married	Making a commitment
Cooperating economically	Being best friends
Meeting each other's friends	Being honest with one another
Meeting each other's family	Trusting one another
Instant attraction	Feeling insecure
Getting to know each other	Joy
Making plans together	Needing to be together
Having deep conversations	Being infatuated
Finding common interests	Feeling a physical attraction
	Feeling excited
	Feeling comfortable
	Communicating openly with one another
	Fear

free-list outputs of 80 informants who are citizens of a European country? Second, notice the much higher frequency of activities mentioned by Lithuanians compared to Americans. For the Lithuanians romantic love is not just conceptualized as a feeling state but as actions – "walk" (together), "love talk," going to the "cinema," "holding hands," "candlelight dinner." Third, Lithuanians mentioned terms suggestive of the unreality or transience of romantic love: "temporary," "initial stage of love," "dream," "not pragmatic," "doubt."

Swidler (2001) asserts that Americans hold two cultural models of romantic love – "real love" and the "myth of romantic love" – simultaneously. Both have complementary "institutional functions"; the function of the "myth of romantic love" is to give people a reason for dating and for marrying; the function of "real love" is to keep the couple together after they are married. For Swidler's American informants, the belief in romantic love is an important, if not necessary, prelude to marriage:

"When thinking about the choice of whether to marry or stay married people see love in mythic terms. Love is the choice of one right person whom one will or could marry. Therefore love is all-or-nothing, certain, exclusive, heroic, and enduring … The institutional demands of marriage continually reproduce the outlines of the mythic love story" (Swidler 2001:129).

But this was not the case with the Lithuanian informants, almost all of whom doubted the reality of romantic love, perceiving it to be a "fantasy." In lectures on my research and in all of my discussions with Lithuanians, close to 100 percent insisted that romantic love was not a serious affair, often invoking the image of "champagne bubbles." In commentaries, one 22-year-old rural female person said, with a touch of irony, "Romantic love is when both sides love each other, fulfill each other's desires, listen to romantic music, and go together for a walk. In a word – it's the love that one finds in TV soap operas. Romantic love can only exist between dreaming people." In that same, though less wry, vein a 24-year-old male noted that "Romantic love equals exaggerated feelings ... exaggerated perceptions of the other; an exaggerated estimation of closeness, physical attraction, etc." A female informant said, "Romantic love can last only one or two years but not longer."

What does it mean to assess romantic love as unreal, a fantasy? How is this related to Swidler's and my analyses of the American cultural model of romantic love, which combines friendship and passion? If something is unreal, then why does it make Lithuanian lovers (like American lovers) want to be together and feel happy in each other's presence? If one views ghosts as unreal or does not believe in supernatural beings, it is unlikely that one could love God or believe in an afterlife. Yet here we have the case that state X is conceptualized as unreal but one is nevertheless motivated to be with someone who induces that state. I think the answer is that the idea of "fantasy" does not denote a quality of romantic love but, rather "frames" the state of "being in love." Thus romantic love semantically frames a relationship that is psycho-physiologically arousing as "unreal," and there are some real benefits to doing so, particularly if the couple should break up. Second, it allows one to give in to the pleasures of romantic love without taking them too seriously. If one survives this period and remains with one's partner then one can get down to the business of developing a "real love" relationship.

Evidence to support this analysis is found in the free-list, commentary, and interview data. First, if romantic love is thought of as a fantasy, then it is unlikely to be associated with friendship, comfort, and the like, which are grounded in the developmental process of long-term "real world" relationships. Second, one other difference between Americans and Lithuanians in both free-list and commentary data was that no American (n = 160) ever waxed poetic about romantic love, but Lithuanians did. The most poetic American responses were "surreal feeling," "divine union," or "warm fuzzy feeling." In contrast, Lithuanian women and men often gave such poetic free-list and commentary responses as "wet stars," "wading in the marshes during a warm rain," " a flower's secret" (*gėlės paslaptis*), "the shadow of the moon's path on a lake as it moves to eternity"(*mėnulio tako į amžinybę šešėlis virš 'ežero*), "the tranquility of a cigarette" (*cigaretės svaigulys*), "lyrical deviations" (*lyriniai nukrypimai*), "a photo of your lover instead of a pornographic picture" (*mylimojo nuotrauka vietoje pornigrafijos*), "torturing passion" (*kankinanti aistra*), or "the opposite of a mechanical life."

If romantic love is an intense, arousing, but transient period, then a poetic response makes sense, but if it is the stuff of friendship and security, then, except for poets, it seems to serious and lacking in pizzazz to inspire ordinary folks to poetry. Of course, Americans sometimes do view romantic love as temporary and false, but this view usually stems from personal experience and is not part of a normative cultural model. As a result, the temporary nature of romantic love is perceived not as an inherent quality but as a possible consequence of romantic love. For Lithuanians, "temporary" and "fantasy" are inherent qualities of romantic love and they not only expect, but even wish for it to end, so that the relationship may progress into "real" or "mature" love. This belief in the fantasy framing of romantic love was also evident in interview material.

Ausra, a 23-year-old university student, described meeting her lover: "At the moment when I met him I liked him. He was really nice and handsome. And I couldn't believe that … how could such a handsome guy … look at me. Though not very ugly … I didn't consider myself a very special girl either … What's going on here? It must be a dream or something like that." Tania, a 32-year-old divorced civil servant describes romantic love as: "you create an ideal, you see a beautiful picture. He pays big attention to you, you like him you almost worship him … Romantic love is an upsurge of feeling [*pakilimas*], you don't feel how you walk, what you do, how you work only that person is in your head. I had such a love [after divorce] and it affected my brain very much. It is a terrible disease, I wouldn't like to experience it again … I loved him very romantically until we moved in together. Everyday life/routine [*buitis*] destroys everything, it's a terrible thing."

In an interview with a 27-year-old male, Darius, he states that "I know this for sure from my own experiences … It [romantic love] always ends … that fairytale, it always has to end: happy or unhappy, and only then do you start looking at the world realistically." Later he describes how romantic love can be choking and that the reason for the break-up of his second relationship was that the woman wanted the relationship to be more romantic. He said, "There was too much of each other; we were not teenagers who need to be together all the time. It began to suffocate. As an adult you have a big circle of friends with whom you want to spend time. Also among males, when three males are talking a woman is unnecessary … The feeling of love remains but becomes friendly not romantic."

Thus for Lithuanians "true" or "mature" love begins when romantic love ends, while for Americans true love is subsumed in romantic love by combining the latter with companionate love. This distinction is also seen in situations where couples who are in a state of romantic love break up. In the United States, such break-ups, as evident from Rose's commentary on Josh, is usually accompanied by a relatively extended period of suffering and healing, before one enters the fray again. This may also occur in Lithuania, but with the knowledge that extended suffering or depression over a break-up is not seen very sympathetically by friends and family. The individual realizes that romantic love is a fantasy, and one does not suffer over the loss of a fantasy. This is well expressed by Gita, a 27-year-old dental hygienist, who said of her previous love affair, "Last winter I was still deeply depressed over Raimis [her former lover, who left her] and there appeared a guy whom I had met two years ago. I liked him back then. He is studying to be a dentist and he is a musician: romantic, clever, a strong personality, likable … he fascinated me [*suzhavėjo*] not because he is handsome but because of his masculinity … For me a man should be a little bit more handsome than a monkey, but not much. But first of all I am fascinated by a man's masculinity. When I met this guy and we became lovers, I began to recover. He was from Kaunas. He restored me, I felt very good, I recovered, I started living again, because I fell in love. I trusted him, I did a lot of stupid things for him. I ignored all of my friends and hurt them. I devoted myself [*atsidaviau*] completely to him. Then finally when some school term started for him, some exams, I found out that he didn't care much about me [*jam ash ne tiek daug ir rupiu*]. For him, his studies, his career, are in first place. He told me he might not even stay in Kaunas and that he didn't see a future with me. Well, I became very depressed and began again to visit my friends. After him, my friends at work introduced me to someone also from the workplace. Now we are going out and I am very happy because I met him. The previous relationship that hurt me so much now is in the past, thanks to him [her new lover]."

Undoubtedly both Americans and Lithuanians suffer equally when they lose at love, but for the American the loss is conceptualized as a failure that one is, at least, partially responsible for. For Lithuanians the termination of a romantic love relationship is normatively conceptualized as typical of relations framed as "unreal" and hence should not be viewed as a reflection of personal failure.

Romantic Love as Part of a Prototypical Courtship Process

Romantic love is not just a feeling or thought state but also the essential motivational force and aspect of contemporary Euro-American courtship processes. In 2006, I began with undergraduate student Meghan Garry to develop a systematic cognitive approach to studying romantic love as part of the courtship process. We did this by asking informants, "What is the typical process by which people fall in love?" As Garry conducted her interviews she realized that "personal experience was being used … to invoke cultural prototypes" (Garry n.d.:1). We then developed a method for understanding how individuals perceived models of romantic love and applied them to their lived courtship experiences.

After ten interviews, Garry compiled two lists of the key terms elicited from coding ten interviews. The first list was of key *events* and the second of key *emotions/values/states of being*. Event terms and what we called "orientation" terms were written on different colored index cards and given to informants who were asked to construct a time line of the *typical* American courtship process using the index cards as temporal points of reference. Pieces of yarn were also given to the informants to indicate how long an emotion lasted after it entered the model. An example of a time line is shown in Figure 27.2.

Ryan Quadrel and Aaron Leo, two undergraduate students, conducted interviews in which participants were asked to construct time lines. Interviewees were also asked to explain their reasoning for their placement of the two sets of cards and the year. Time lines were photographed to provide a visual backup for the recorded interview.

Owing to space constraints only the event time lines will be discussed. Following Nick Colby's (Colby and Colby 1981; Colby 1975) work we presumed that there was a cultural grammar to the courtship process so that there was an underlying idea of how these events should be sequenced, and that there would also be significant variation

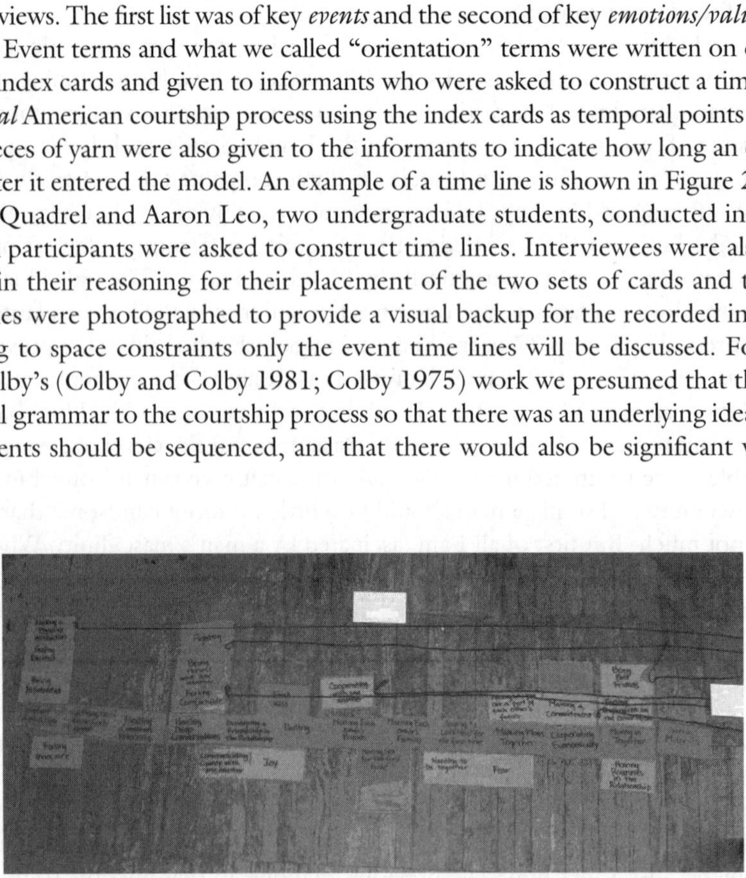

Figure 27.2 Example of constructed time line.

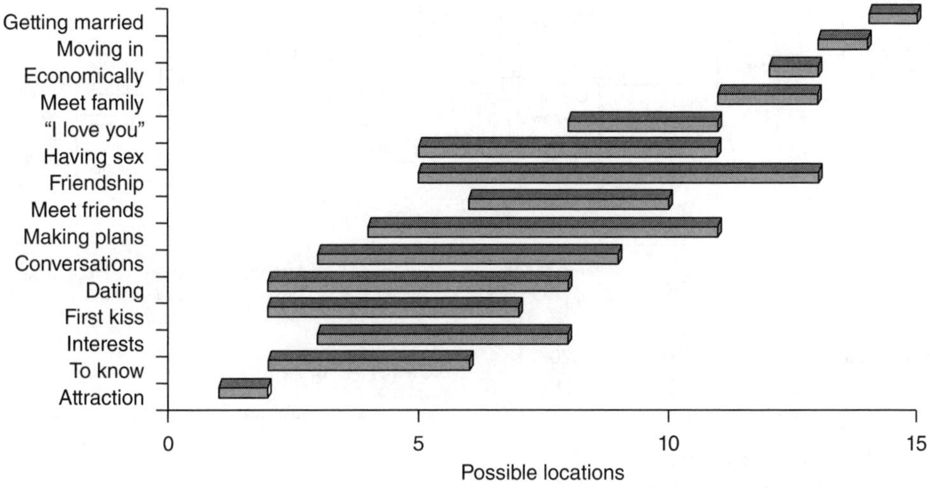

Figure 27.3 Range of events.

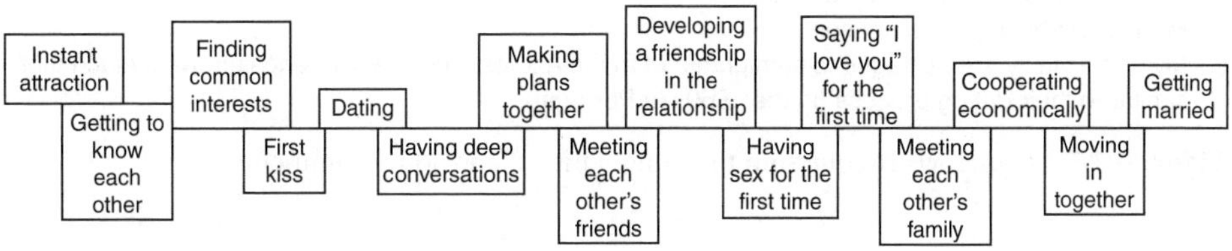

Figure 27.4 Prototypical time line (sequence 4).

between informants. For some, sex might come before marriage and for others after. However, there would be an underlying structure so that events such as "economically cooperating together" or "developing a friendship" could come only later in the sequence. Figure 27.3 shows the range of variation for all of our interviews.

We constructed a prototypical courtship process by taking the average position of each of the 15 events for the 30 people we interviewed. The prototypical courtship time line sequence is presented in Figure 27.4.

In order to test the validity of this prototypical time line, we constructed five additional time lines, some of which violated the "grammar" or range of variation that was found among our informants. Each of the six time lines is presented with survey results of their ratings on typicality below them (see Figures 27.5–27.10 for these additional time lines). Sequence 4 in Figure 27.4 is the prototype.

We compared the ratings of the six time lines and noted the key themes of each time line. These results are presented in Table 27.4.

A consensus analysis showed Factor 1 with an eigenvalue ratio of 3.0, indicating that there was agreement among the 50 informants on the ratings of the six time lines. Our sample was fairly diverse, with an age range from 20 to 56 and an average age of 28. Our prototype time line was not only confirmed as the most typical of the six time lines; even more so, informants chose it as the one that best fit their own courtship experiences. Many participants felt that sequences 2 and 6 were typical of today's

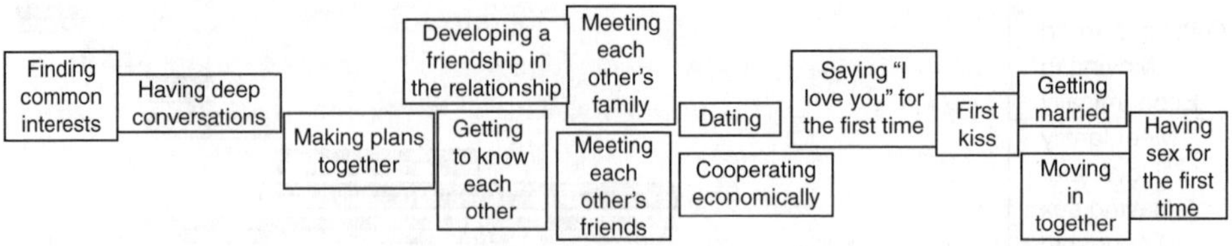

	Very unlikely	Not likely	Possible	Probable	Almost always	Rating average	Response count
Sequence 1	60.0% (30)	20.0% (10)	20.0% (10)	0.0% (0)	0.0% (0)	1.60	50

Some typical comments on sequence 1:
1 It's a silly sequence all in all.
2 There are some that might adhere to this, in more conservative cases, but most of the people I know would not.
3 Never happens.
4 This seems like a totally random order.
5 Many/most have premarital sex.
6 My wife's family are Portuguese immigrants from the Azores, and the sequence above is much more similar to their dating process (in the 1960s in Portugal).

Figure 27.5 Sequence 1: courtship time line, ratings, and some comments.

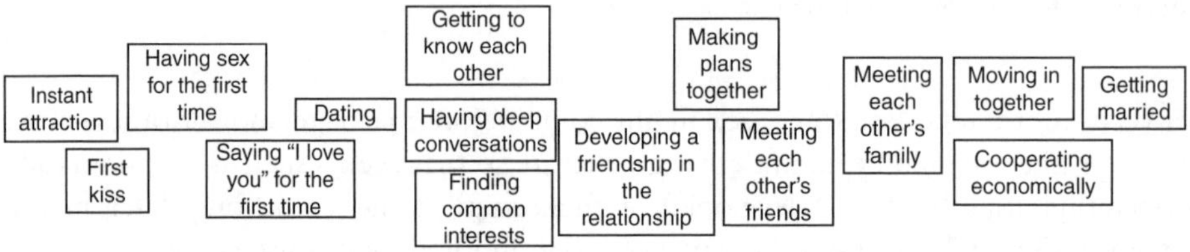

	Very unlikely	Not likely	Possible	Probable	Almost always	Rating average	Response count
Sequence 2	4.0% (2)	14.0% (7)	46.0% (23)	36.0% (18)	0.0% (0)	3.14	50

Some comments on sequence 2:
1 This is the way a lot of my peers work, not me in particular, but for a lot of people having sex comes before "I love you," and really getting to know someone.
2 In between probable and almost always.
3 Many will attempt this, but few will succeed.
4 Maybe even probable.
5 This is closer to the mark than the first example.

Figure 27.6 Sequence 2: courtship time line, ratings, and some comments.

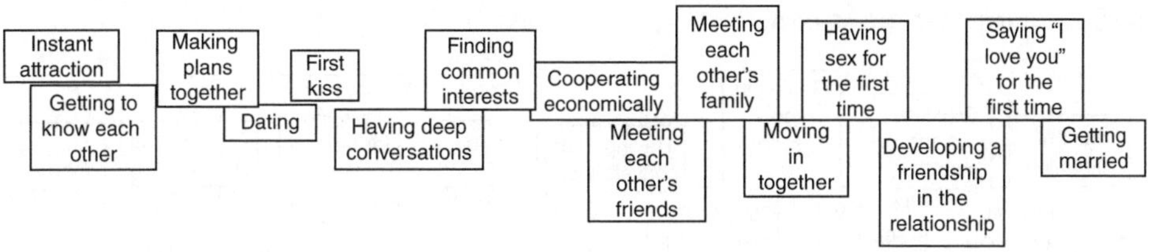

	Very unlikely	Not likely	Possible	Probable	Almost always	Rating average	Response count
Sequence 3	6.0% (3)	34.0% (17)	44.0% (22)	16.0% (8)	0.0% (0)	2.70	50

Some comments on sequence 3:

1 Having sex for the first time and saying "I love you" are too far toward the end.
2 Cooperating economically seems a little soon and developing a friendship in the relationship seems way too late. Also saying "I love you" seems to be late.
3 The placement of "cooperating economically" in the sequence I think should fall more to the right side of the sequence. I think the events "meeting friends/family," "developing friendship in the relationship," "I love you" and "having sex" would typically happen sooner in a relationship in US culture.
4 Now we're talking. Though the "I love you" is still too late in the game. While some would think cooperating economically should come later, I think it is all right where it is. This is an example of two individuals taking it slow but having a really enriching, lasting relationship.
5 How can you make plans together before having deep conversations, which help you get to know each other? Sex will happen way before this sequence in my world, possibly after deep conversations and probably before dating or planning together. Family get-togethers are a romance buzz kill. Marriage is scary. I like my solo life … what was I thinking getting involved with this guy anyway!!??
6 Who would move in with someone they haven't fucked?

Figure 27.7 Sequence 3: courtship time line, ratings, and some comments.

	Very unlikely	Not likely	Possible	Probable	Almost always	Rating average	Response count
Sequence 4	4.0% (2)	4.0% (2)	20.0% (10)	50.0% (25)	22.0% (11)	3.82	50

Some comments on sequence 4:

1 Perfect.
2 Seems to be good.
3 This situation is typical of a relationship in US culture. Many of the events in the beginning of the sequence are events which may happen very quickly in a relationship.
4 I think the "sex" poised with the "I love you" speaks volumes. It makes great sense.
5 This seems pretty reasonable, but I tend to develop a relationship or friendship earlier.
6 Saying "I love you" after "having sex for the first time." "First kiss" before "dating."
7 This one makes the most sense to me out of what I've seen so far. I'd say this is closest to my personal ideal and what I've done the most of in my life.
8 I don't think this one is that abnormal. Maybe because they are cooperating economically, but if they are moving in together and plan to get married that makes sense.
9 I feel like out of all the situations this seems the most preferred way for things to happen. I think that a relationship which developed in this manner would probably have the best chance at lasting in the long run.
10 This is the most probable of all the sequences. My only question would be if the friendship started to develop earlier.

Figure 27.8 Sequence 4 (the hypothesized prototype): courtship time line, ratings, and some comments.

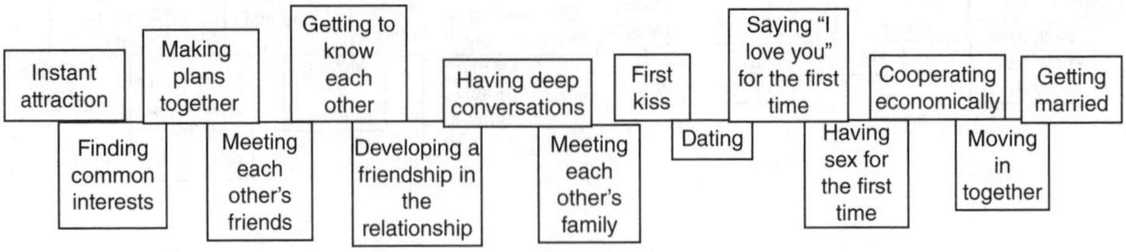

	Very unlikely	Not likely	Possible	Probable	Almost always	Rating average	Response count
Sequence 5	6.0% (3)	22.0% (11)	44.0% (22)	20.0% (10)	8.0% (4)	3.02	50

Some comments on sequence 5:

1 "Meeting family" seems a little early, and "first kiss" seems a little late.
2 The event "first kiss" I think would commonly happen sooner in a relationship than it appears in this sequence.
3 This is totally more of a friendship first kind of relationship. Though I wonder if the "attraction" came after "having deep conversation," how that would work out …
4 How would you know you love them if you haven't had the magic of sex? Maybe if you met his family you wouldn't want sex. In fact, after you meet them, you could just bolt seeing how dysfunctional they are!
5 Waiting so long to kiss, I bet he's gay.
6 "Meeting each other's families" before the "first kiss" seems highly unlikely. Also, I don't know that people generally wait until they say "I love you" to have sex for the first time.
7 Sounds good as well.
8 This seems like another sort of, traditional, slow road approach. Not common among my friends though.
9 "Sex" too late.
10 "Dating" and "first kiss" would come on earlier.
11 Move "developing a friendship" further to the right!

Figure 27.9 Sequence 5: courtship time line, ratings, and some comments.

sexualized culture. However, while informants often rated these two time lines (both of which had sex early) as "probable" they also often used hedges to distance themselves from these time lines.

Courtship time lines serve as mental maze ways which couples use to monitor the development of a relationship, to see if both are on the "same page," to negotiate and contest each other's courtship time lines if they are significantly different, and to reassure themselves or modify their behaviors if they feel they are out of whack with the time line they deem most appropriate.

Though it is clear that cultural models can affect individual behavior, it is difficult to ascertain to what degree one's behavior changes or how effective a model is in shaping behavior. Surely, the chaste model represented by time line 1 (sex after marriage) has had a strong influence throughout Victorian times as well as through most of the 20th century, at least as a normative model of the appropriate courtship sequence. It seems that a new model has taken its place, a gradual construction of friendship and comfort that ultimately leads to sexual consummation and perhaps marriage.

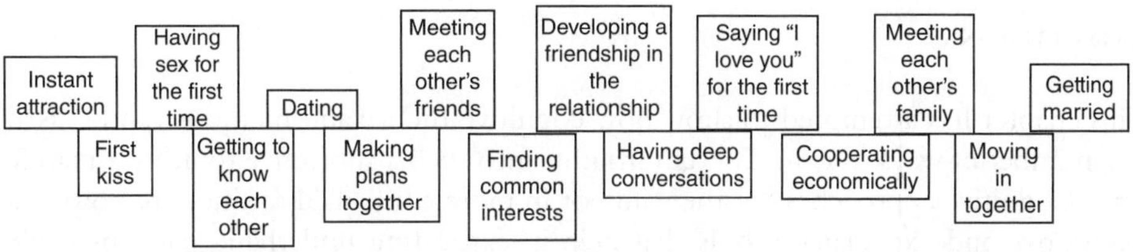

	Very unlikely	Not likely	Possible	Probable	Almost always	Rating average	Response count
Sequence 6	2.0% (1)	4.0% (2)	38.0% (19)	40.0% (20)	16.0% (8)	3.64	50

Some comments on sequence 6:

1 When people hook up so quick, it doesn't work out.
2 It sounds like a one-night stand extended.
3 This one is pretty spot on. My only thing is the "cooperating economically" (in my opinion) should be in sync with "moving in together," although I guess you do have to pool your finances a bit if you're spending lots of time with someone and buying things together before you live together.
4 I don't think this is all that atypical. Maybe they had sex too early, but a lot of Americans do.
5 "Finding common interests" seems out of place, but this could be a relationship where someone may have just wanted sex but then realized that it was more.
6 This seems to be the one where they meet at a bar and "hook up" and then decide they like each other more than they anticipated.

Figure 27.10 Sequence 6: courtship time line, ratings, and some comments.

Table 27.4 Rankings of time lines and key theme of each time line

Time line	*Title*	*Rating*	*Best fits life experience (%)*	*Cultural appropriateness*
4	Prototype	3.82	55.1	Constructed with the averages of all informants' placement of events
6	Sex early/one-night stand	3.64	26.5	"First kiss" and "sex" are the 2nd and 3rd events in the time line
2	Love/sex early	3.14	6.1	"Having sex" was the 2nd event, followed by "I love you"
5	Platonic time line	3.02	12.2	Sexual aspects, "I love you," and "dating" are reserved for the second half of the time line.
3	Commitment early	2.70	0.0	"Cooperating economically" and "moving in" occurred before "sex" and "I love you"
1	Old-fashioned/religious	1.60	0.0	"Having sex" was placed after "marriage"

Conclusions

This chapter has attempted to show how cognitive theory and methods can be used in a number of ways to gain different insights into such a subjective topic as romantic love. Cognitive approaches "in the wild" or in more controlled settings are powerful descriptive and explanatory tools that help in extricating underlying patterns while simultaneously attending to cultural diversity.

REFERENCES

Colby, Benjamin N.

1975 Cultural Grammars. Science 187:913–919.

Colby, Benjamin, and Lore M. Colby

1981 The Daykeeper: The Life and Discourse of an Ixil Diviner. Cambridge, MA: Harvard University Press.

Garry, Meghan

N.d. Describing Cultural Models of Courtship in America. Unpublished MS, SUNY New Paltz.

Quinn, Naomi

1992 The Motivational Force of Self-Understanding: Evidence from Wives' Inner Conflicts. *In* Human Motives and Cultural Models. Roy D'Andrade and Claudia Strauss, eds. Pp 90–126. Cambridge: Cambridge University Press.

1996 Culture and Contradiction: The Case of Americans Reasoning about Marriage. Ethos 24(5):391–425.

1997 Research on Shared Task Solutions. *In* A Cognitive Theory of Cultural Meaning, Claudia Strauss and Naomi Quinn, eds. Pp. 137–188. Cambridge: Cambridge University Press.

Sternberg, Robert J.

1988 The Triangle of Love. New York: Basic Books.

2006 A Duplex Theory of Love. *In* The New Psychology of Love. Robert J. Sternberg and Karen Weis, eds. Pp. 184–199. New Haven: Yale University Press.

Swidler, Ann

2001 Talk of Love: How Culture Matters. Chicago: University of Chicago Press.

Tennov, Dorothy

1979 Love and Limerence. New York: Day and Stein.

CHAPTER 28

Trouble as Part of Everyday Life: Cognitive and Sociocultural Processes in Avoiding and Responding to Illness

Linda C. Garro

As a real-world problem, illness opens onto questions of "*meaning* and the processes and transactions involved in the construction of meanings" (Bruner 1990:33). With the lens on the relationship between meaning-making and action in situated contexts, this chapter revolves around culturally informed efforts to recognize, avoid, and deal with trouble through attention to the conjoined cognitive and sociocultural processes by which individuals, perhaps in concert with or in response to others, configure what transpires in the world as illness (involving themselves or others) or carrying the potential for illness (see also Garro 1998a, 1998b, 2001, 2003, 2005). The intertwining of these processes with experiences of uncertainty and anxiety reveals the interdependence of thought and feeling.

The term *sociocultural processes* refers to socially grounded ways of learning which contribute to the way an individual thinks, feels, and acts (Garro 2003:17–18). A process-oriented approach encompasses the way past or present interactions (as active participant or observer), including those mediated through artifacts, inform knowing

A Companion to Cognitive Anthropology, First Edition. Edited by David B. Kronenfeld, Giovanni Bennardo, Victor C. de Munck, and Michael D. Fischer.

and action, underscoring the socially situated and distributed nature of cognition. In this view, culturally available interpretive frameworks are resources that are linked to and dependent on participatory involvements and cognitive engagements in specific settings.

Through remembering, culturally available interpretive frameworks come into play in situations of trouble and potential trouble. It is not uncommon for such interpretive frameworks, which may be indexed by the use of a label, to situate a present trouble in relation to what has transpired in the world and thus guide practical action geared toward the problem's resolution. And, as perhaps first discussed in Frake's (1961) study of "skin diseases" among the Subanun, evaluating illness may become a "social activity." Different perspectives may be offered by others and/or the perspective of others is actively sought. Actions taken in response to illness may have less to do with what the person afflicted (or whoever, whether individual or social unit, assumes responsibility for adopting a course of action) knows about how to deal with the case at hand than with what counsel from others she or he is willing to entertain as possibly helpful, even provisionally or tentatively.

Central to the position advanced here is narrative as a fundamental human mode of cognitive activity for understanding life in time, for "ordering experience" and "constructing reality" (Bruner 1986:11). As culturally informed perspective-taking, narrative thinking situates present illness or other trouble within a larger temporal surround, and links, however tentatively, present concerns with an account of what transpired in the past and/or with possible futures. Narrative thinking depends upon one's personal experiences and what one learns about illness and misfortune from and through others, through participating in and overhearing narratively oriented interactions, including the remembered accounts of others (see Garro 2000a, 2000b).

Although space does not permit adequate elaboration, work by Bartlett and Hallowell provides a theoretical backdrop. Bartlett, a psychologist, noted that cognitive activities are a "function of daily life, and must have developed to meet the demands of daily life" (Bartlett 1932:16). He maintained, "it is fitting to speak of every human cognitive reaction – perceiving, remembering, thinking and reasoning – as an *effort after meaning*." "Certain of the tendencies" which individuals bring to tasks or problems are "utilised" in "an effort to connect what is given with something else. Thus, the immediately present 'stands for' something not immediately present, and 'meaning' in a psychological sense, has its origin" (44–45). Always, however, the process of fitting "the new into relation to the old" is an "active process, depending directly upon the pre-formed tendencies and bias which the subject brings to his task" (85).

Bartlett adopted the notion of schemas as active organizations of past experience that mediate our ongoing cognitive transactions with the world and engage the intimately related processes of perceiving, recognizing, and remembering. He drew attention to the way "active tendencies" to "notice, retain and construct specifically along certain directions" (Bartlett 1932:255) take shape within social settings and in individual lives.

Highlighting connections between culturally informed processes of knowing and action, Hallowell offered the notion of a behavioral environment in which "assumptions about the nature of the universe, become as it were, a priori constituents in the perceptual process itself" and "structure the psychological field in which the self is prepared to act" (Hallowell 1955:84, 110). As experiential reality takes shape in relation to ontological reality, the range of what one takes to be possible and plausible, as well as what is routinely anticipated, can be understood only with reference to a specific behavioral environment. Hallowell characterized perceiving, in a way reminiscent of Bartlett, as an activity which cannot be viewed as "completely unaffected by the experience, concepts, attitudes, needs and purposes of the perceiver" (84). For Hallowell, our worlds become culturally meaningful worlds in concert with the development and attunement of orientational frameworks (schemas) for selectively attending to and organizing experience in those worlds.

Through observations and remembered accounts recorded during fieldwork in Ojibwa communities in Manitoba, Hallowell offered numerous instances revealing the entwining of Ojibwa "conceptual reality" and "*personal* experience" (Hallowell 1955:182). Included among these are situations which, "from the standpoint of an outside observer," appear to be "objectively innocuous" but from the "outlook" of the "Ojibwa self" in "its behavioral environment" arouse anxiety and fear as "a danger situation defined ... in cultural terms" (1955:88, 257, 172, 255). While Hallowell can often sound like a cultural determinist, he left "scope for variation" in how individuals interpreted the meaning of events and settled on courses of action (Hallowell 1976:391). Reading across his work offers an essentially processual view of the relation between culture and experience, individual experience as culturally informed (oriented) rather than culturally determined (see Garro 2010).

Although most of the ethnographic material presented here draws on past fieldwork in Mexico, I start with an example from Hallowell's research which provides a platform for contrasting stances on the relationship between cultural knowledge and action. As a situation of everyday trouble, it is relevant to the arguments advanced here.

Responding to Trouble: Personal Experience and Cultural Resources

This case, first published in February of 1938, concerns the "exaggerated fear reaction" of an Ojibwa man identified as W.B. in a situation which Hallowell characterized as culturally marked as potentially dangerous and anxiety-arousing. First, there is a "generalized fear" of toads (an animal "associated with evil forces") and second, "the approach of a wild animal of any sort to their camp or habitation is an ill omen" (see Hallowell 1955:252–254, 259–260).

W.B., who worked with Hallowell "more as a collaborator than interpreter," was "an excellent hunter" and seasoned outdoorsman who was also a Christian and "believed himself to be emancipated from native 'superstition'" (1955:260, 252–253). While traveling with Hallowell, W.B. noticed a toad hopping toward him in a tent. W.B. is described as "so panic stricken" that he had trouble killing the toad. Searching for others, he killed several additional toads nearby. Despite this, W.B. passed a relatively sleepless night. On following nights, W.B. took "special pains" to ensure the tent was sealed.

In illuminating W.B.'s response, Hallowell pointed to other contributing factors including an aversive childhood experience when W.B. crushed a toad that had crawled up his pants against his skin. Another was W.B.'s breaking of a cultural proscription against narrating "myths" during summer (at Hallowell's request) given the cultural expectation that this leads toads to "come and crawl up one's clothes."

Although W.B. professed not to credit this culturally plausible connection, his reactions to the toad belied his statements (in particular, the seeking out of additional toads and the securing of the tent on future nights). For Hallowell, this contradiction served to indicate that the "inner conflict" revolving around differences between Ojibwa "conceptual reality" and that of Christianity was yet another "etiological factor" (1955:253, 260).

While one could ask whether Hallowell's presence had any impact, consideration of possible additional "etiological factors" at such a distance remains speculative. Nonetheless, the material seems sufficient to comment on the notion of "internalization" – which D'Andrade defined as the "process by which cultural representations become a part of the individual; that is, become what is right and true" (1995:227) – and its relation to action. Spiro has offered a proposal delineating a hierarchy of five levels of cognitive salience with which "doctrines are acquired as personal beliefs" (1987:163–164; a version with four "levels of conviction" appears in Spiro 1997:6–9). In ascending order, the first three levels comprise learning about, understanding, and believing the doctrines (as true, correct, or right). Spiro explained the fact that "actors hold a doctrine to be true does not in itself, however, indicate that it importantly effects [*sic*] the manner in which they conduct their lives." It is at the fourth level, when "cultural doctrines are not only held to be true, but they inform the behavioral environment of social actors, serving to structure their perceptual worlds and, consequently, to *guide* their actions," that beliefs become "genuine beliefs." At the fifth, "the doctrines not only guide but they also serve to *instigate* action; they possess motivational as well as cognitive properties."

In the case involving W.B., there are several behavioral actions of interest, some occurring prior to and following the central incident. First, he knowingly broke the cultural proscription against telling myths during the summer. On subsequent evenings, he acted to ensure that toads would not penetrate the tent. Yet, W.B. also apparently recounted at least one additional myth after Hallowell's article was published (Berens 2009:172).

With regard to the initial evening, is W.B.'s immediate, and perhaps unreflective, reaction to the toad hopping toward him in the tent to be taken as revelatory of his hitherto untested "genuine belief" (that toads will trouble those who narrate myths at the wrong time of year)? Did this "genuine belief" instigate the tent-securing actions on subsequent nights, confirming the belief's position at the highest cognitive salience in Spiro's hierarchy? But then what of the subsequent narration to Hallowell of another myth? Did the "genuine belief" lose its potency to guide action? Did his self-identification as a Christian, and his earlier statements dismissing the connection between telling myths and the arrival of toads, bear no relationship to his telling of the myths to Hallowell? Was it the case that W.B.'s professed commitment to the Christian view about "native superstition" did not have a significant impact on the manner in which W.B. conducted his life?

Another way to approach these questions is to explore other ways to think about the connection between cultural knowledge and action in this situated context. Did contextual factors increase the likelihood of W.B.'s orientation to see the toad as a harbinger of more trouble to come (an "active bias" in "effort after meaning" to meet the "demands of daily life")? Given that W.B. knew about the foreshadowed penalty for telling myths in summer (the trip may have been one during which W.B. was serving as an interpreter for other individuals, including those who agreed to tell myths during the summer), and given that he had acted in a manner such that this penalty could follow (if the culturally posited connection did correspond to reality), what if the unexpected event, the sight of the toad hopping toward him in the tent, awakened W.B. to the possibility that this event evidenced the reality of this causal connection (as did the finding of additional toads nearby)?

Rather than making a genuine commitment to this version of reality as what is "right and true" (which seems to me to be entering rather murky waters), another possibility to consider is that the response to the toad involved the adoption of a "what if" perspective on reality (along with his pre-established pronounced aversion to toads). In this light, through an imaginative act (of narrative thinking) W.B. became aligned with the potential relevance of a culturally informed perspective positing a connection between the present state of affairs, his own past actions, and a possible future. Given the alternative perspectives available, the present situation was one of uncertainty. While the toad in the tent may just be an unwelcome chance visitor, if the present situation is possibly one where toads are drawn to you for a past transgression, taking steps to avoid toads crawling on you can be preferable to waiting to find out if this will happen. In this view, W.B.'s knowledge of conflicting perspectives on the nature of ontological reality provided him with cultural resources potentially useful in meeting the demands of everyday life (though they may also engender feelings of ambivalence and conflict), and the specific context heightened the likelihood that this interpretive framework entered into the response to the unexpected and troubling event. Interpretive frameworks (as schema-based constructive processes) are less like "blueprints" than resources (tools) that come into play as part of "effort after meaning" (see Garro 1998b:348 for a complementary discussion). An individual's past experiences may lead to an "outlook of the self" upon the behavioral environment in which there exist divergent interpretive possibilities for the same situation or events, even when one's actions align with one version rather than another.

Further, even when one's self-related actions never evidence any alignment with a particular construction of reality, the knowledge that others may do so provides us with resources for interpreting the actions of others and appreciating alternative perspectives that may be taken on a situation. Through participating in social life we acquire cultural resources, the interpretive tools, for appreciating the behavior of others. It is possible for interpretive frameworks to be intersubjectively understood (e.g., as Hallowell understood the situation involving W.B.) without being intersubjectively shared with respect to the interpretive salience and motivational force in everyday life contexts. And while this is not part of Spiro's model (given his stress on "personal beliefs" and action), one may also be instigated to action under the guidance of another in the absence of "genuine belief" (or even acceptance as being "true").

The next sections are based on fieldwork carried out in Pichátaro, a Purépecha (Tarascan) community in west central Mexico. I give further consideration to the role of culturally available interpretive frameworks and orientational processes in the "effort after meaning." While actions to avoid or deal with illness are situated in the present, they bear the imprint of what is remembered and concern for the future. In situations of trouble construed as illness, the associated uncertainty and anxiety can prompt the active seeking of the perspectives and care of others as well as the consideration of alternative interpretive frameworks. Potentialities for interpretation and action are emergent in situated contexts and take shape in relation to past experience, concerns about the future, and culturally available resources.

Knowing as Framework for Action: Recognizing Trouble as Illness

In contrast to the situation involving W.B., the next case is much simpler. One morning, I arose with reddened eyes accompanied by some irritation and discharge. My husband and I thought my eye was infected by a pathogen. We were mildly concerned but I did not want to leave town at that time to seek care from a physician. I visited a woman, widely considered to be knowledgeable about illness and herbal remedies, for advice. She told me I had *calor subido* ("risen heat"). Although I could not remember doing so, she informed me that my bare feet must have come in contact with the cold ground, most likely when I arose from sleeping. The normal body heat in my feet had been displaced upward leading to the symptoms in my eyes. As this problem was easily cured, she prepared a remedy to place on my feet at night. She explained that the "cool" herbs would draw the heat back down and the redness and irritation in my eyes would go away. Throughout the day, the proclivity for interpreting my bodily state as *calor subido* was evident in a number of conversations with others.

In transforming the trouble with my eyes into a potentially manageable illness ("effort after meaning"), the woman I consulted drew upon a widely known interpretive framework for making sense of the situation at hand – culturally available understandings that had proved useful in the past. Further, she evinced an inclination to see the roots of much illness as resulting from contact with hazards present in the external environment, as did the others who proffered the same diagnosis. Even more generally, in addition to *calor subido*, the conceptual workings of bodily disequilibrium, which can take different forms, underpinned many illnesses in Pichátaro.

Here, the active process of fitting the new in relation to the old involved supplementing what was given (perceived and reported experience), through establishing connections with available knowledge in the behavioral environment of those involved (or consulted). Consistent with Bartlett, remembering is integral to this meaning-construing process. Taking shape through the woman's past experience and culturally available resources, a possible fit was established which situated the present set of troublesome signs (reddened and irritated eyes) in a broader temporal context – an example of narrative as a mode of thinking. In this narrative mode, an ordered sequence of possible events is posited, relying on an occurrence in the past (bodily contact with excessive cold) and a desired future in which the illness is resolved (with the displaced heat returned to its normal location). Through inferring the way I became exposed to cold (in a way which "fits" with a likely possibility, as I, unlike many others, wore sturdy footwear), culturally available knowledge became situated knowledge applicable to the case at hand and an appropriate course of action was projected. To recognize an instance of *calor subido* is to situate its occurrence with reference to actions which were better avoided (given the likelihood of subsequent illness) as well as remedial actions to counter the disruption – there are narrative possibilities and/or expectations connected with specific illness labels. Recognizing (knowing) what type of illness this was afforded a framework for action uniting past, present, and hoped-for future.

Over the next couple of days there was no discernible improvement. Given my affirmations that I had followed treatment directives, a couple of people suggested that perhaps this wasn't *calor subido* after all and that it might be best if I were to consult a doctor given the uncertainty. By the third day, even the woman consulted seemed less confident, though she recommended continuing with her treatment. Indeed, the continued viability of the interpretive frame of *calor subido* depended upon properly prepared treatments actually having the desired effect. Thus, although there was a predisposition to perceive my reddened eyes as indicative of *calor subido*, this interpretive frame could pragmatically be put to one side to allow consideration that other possibilities, perhaps an alternative diagnosis and/or the need for treatment by a physician, could potentially be more relevant to the case at hand. Even when a culturally available interpretive frame appears to be a good fit, varying degrees of uncertainty and the potential for revision remain open.

By the fourth day, however, the visible improvement in my eyes was taken as confirmation that my condition had been appropriately identified as *calor subido*, and several times thereafter people reminisced about the time when I had *calor subido* and was successfully cured. My previous, albeit unintentional, contact with the cold ground became established fact. In addition to bearing the imprint of past effort after meaning, the remembered past may be marshaled to meet present needs. For instance, the woman who treated me reminded me of my past illness when I wanted to eat bread hot from the oven along with water; a combination commonly seen as having the potential to lead to illness due to the way one's bodily equilibrium is upset by this hot–cool mixture. Retelling this incident at that particular time highlighted the logic of cultural practice in a way that foreshadowed the possibility that my current actions could lead to future illness (another example of narrative thinking). Thus oriented to this present danger and potential future, I would bear responsibility for illness that might result from such injudicious mixing. For my part, although none of my actions involved commitment to a cultural theory of embodied disequilibrium, I was a participant insofar as I waited for the bread to cool before eating it. And it was a perspective on reality that I was able to adopt in other social situations.

Foreshadowed Possibilities and Everyday Actions

As this last example demonstrates, an illness need not be present for knowing to guide action. The threat of what could be, the foreshadowing of potential future illness in present or imminent circumstances, can be sufficient. A formal analysis of responses given in a "term frame" interview (which systematically paired illnesses and propositions and asked individuals whether the resulting statement was true) also revealed the link between knowing and action. The finding that the "structuring of illness categories tends to be congruent with how this knowledge is used in purposive action relating to illness" directed attention to "important considerations involved in actions aimed at preventing and alleviating illness" (Young and Garro 1994[1981]:13,101). These distinctions included the main ways that one's body could enter into a state of disequilibrium – through exposure to external environmental hazards, through powerful emotional experiences (both negative and positive), or diet-caused imbalances (see also Garro 2002).

The lived reality of the body's vulnerability is revealed through how individuals actively orient toward seemingly omnipresent sources of potential danger in everyday contexts. Similar to the incident involving the warm bread and cool water, there were numerous indicators that Pichatareños were concerned about and alert to everyday actions and situations with the potential to lead to illness. The external environment, in particular, was seen to contain a variety of menaces which must constantly be appraised and dealt with. At times we observed individuals looking at a cloudy sky and commenting "much illness, pure illness." Culturally available strategies to guard against the incursions of the external environment often became routine components of everyday life, of "habitus" (Bourdieu 1977). For example, many women placed small pieces of leaf on their temples to avoid "attacks" of air when leaving the warmth of a hearth, and men, hot from working in the fields, took time to "cool off" before washing. As meaningful actions, these and other routines, whether they occur at the level of conscious awareness or not, rely upon jointly cognitive and sociocultural processes.

Events or activities that bring one in contact with the cold and with water, including washing oneself, are culturally marked as requiring special care, even more so at times when one is more at risk of illness. Coming in contact with the cold is particularly dangerous when one is in an overheated state (e.g., from exertion, cooking near an open fire, arising from a warm bed). Similarly, there are many ways to guard against diet-related imbalances and times when one is considered to be particularly susceptible to internal upset (e.g., when one is in a highly emotional state and "heated up," even "normal" amounts of "cold" foods can result in illness). Situations of risk with the potential to cause illness were a recurrent feature of everyday life and the "behavioral environment" or "habitus" is one in which there is a "normative orientation" (Hallowell 1976:391) or "routine motivation" (Strauss and Quinn 1997:226) to protect against and notice possible threats and behave in a manner not to invite illness. Lapses in vigilance or deliberate infringements (e.g., with regard to what one chooses to consume) were considered one's own fault and led the illness to be judged as due to "carelessness" or "trespass," and carry the implication that the individual should know better. A similar moral freighting did not arise in cases of illness considered to have an emotional base as those experiences intense enough to lead to illness were seen to be an inevitable part of life (these include adverse events, euphoric occasions, economic travails, and interpersonal difficulties). Nonetheless, normal bodily functioning was seen to depend on a moderately steady emotional state and deviations were noteworthy.

That distinctions like these were central to illness experience in Pichátaro gains support through analyses which show that of 323 illness episodes collected, approximately 70 percent of the illness cases were ultimately ascribed to one of these three sources. Of these, external environmental dangers made up the major part at nearly 40 percent (most often "the cold" and "airs"), with around 20 percent due to dietary imbalances, and 10 percent attributable to emotional experiences.

Some other explanatory frameworks situated the origins of one person's illness in the reaction or action of another. *Mal de ojo* ("evil eye") was specific to young children and is caused by an adult seeing and then experiencing a strong emotional reaction to the child. *Mala enfermedad* ("bad illness") was caused by the intentional, malevolent, and covert actions of one person to bring about illness in another through *brujería* ("witchcraft"). However, in contrast to the explanatory frameworks revolving around threats to bodily disequilibrium, evidence was lacking for an orientation of everyday concern that another person might cause *mal de ojo* or employ *brujería*. In other words, in the cases we learned about, there was little evidence of an initial "active bias" toward these cultural resources despite their availability. Yes, preventive actions were commonly taken to ward off *mal de ojo* (such as amulets) and it was considered common sense to adopt a cautious approach when interacting with the few local individuals (variably) suspected of knowing how to cause *mala enfermedad*, but, to all appearances at least, foreshadows of potential illness did not commonly enter into everyday interactions and suspicions that an illness had its origins in another person did not typically surface early on. Active consideration of this literally interpersonal realm was reported only after earlier efforts after meaning and treatment failed to resolve the problem. In sum, less than 2 percent of the household illness cases collected were eventually judged to be instances of *mal de ojo* and none was considered to be *mala enfermedad*, although the viability of this interpretive framework received support through attestations of past cases of *mala enfermedad* in a number of these same households.

Effort After Narrative?

As noted above, to recognize or identify an illness involves applying (through remembering) culturally available knowledge to the circumstances at hand. Illness labels vary in their specificity with regard to an action-oriented cultural framework that links a current illness to the past and/or future. Some illness labels afford multiple causal attributions. For example, *anginas* ("swollen glands in the neck") referred to an illness either attributable to *calor subido* or to the repression of strong emotions ("not crying when you feel like it"). *Disentería* (dysentery – severe diarrhea in which the stool contains blood) was often associated with dietary imbalance but an emotional precipitator could loom large. Other illness labels covered a broader range of embodied manifestations. For example, the potential for many kinds of physical discomfort to be construed as resulting from emotional upset was offered by the narrative framing of *bilis*. In cases of *bilis*, the release of bile set off by emotional upset was considered capable of affecting the body in numerous and often diffuse ways. As in my case of *calor subido*, the occurrence of symptoms consistent with possible diagnoses can spark narrative thinking through a guided look backwards to causal possibilities. The extent to which experiences with the potential to bring about embodied trouble foreshadow the possibility of illness at a cognitive level is difficult to assess unless concerns are voiced, but such foreshadowings are instances of narrative thinking.

With regard to specific illnesses past, what is remembered shows how effort after meaning relies upon the intertwining of cognitive and sociocultural processes in establishing a fit between available cultural resources and personal experience. Two brief narratives of past illnesses are provided below. These narratives show how personal trouble took on a culturally recognizable narrative form and became an exemplar of a known type of illness, an instantiation that could potentially serve as a resource for the meaning-construing efforts of others (see also Garro 2001). The first is a case of *anginas* involving a somewhat more complex case of *calor subido* than my own. Initially set in motion by cold water on the girl's feet, then compounded by additional exposure to heat in the affected area while making tortillas, part of the treatment involved "cool" substances intended to drive the heat away from her throat. The second is a case of *disentería* (dysentery) which was characterized as a *bilis* and linked to the shock of significant economic loss and worry after the death of an essential farm animal:

> My sister had this last year. It lasted for three days. It came from washing her feet, and then right away coming close to the fire to make tortillas. She got better with a remedy made from roasted tomato and alcohol put on her throat. She also took some pills, and with this she got well. We've always gotten well with this.

> I've had it, two days ago – the day before yesterday and yesterday too. It came from a *sentimiento* ["sorrow"] when my ox died. I had lots of pity – I lost a lot of money. It was like a *bilis.* My wife cooked me a remedy, and with this I got well fast. There was no need to take any pills, or go to the nuns.

In these accounts, while the home treatment strategy was portrayed as following diagnosis and the diagnosis was confirmed by the cure, the sense that different treatments were possible for illnesses of these types is conveyed. Other illness labels, like *mal de ojo*, *mollera caida* (fallen fontanelle), or *mala enfermedad*, are explicit about what won't result in a cure, in addition to specifying causal precedents. None of these three illness labels was applicable to illnesses amenable to treatment by biomedically oriented practitioners and required *remedios caseros* (literally "household remedies") of the type that *curanderas* (curers) specialized in. Still others, like *sarampión* (measles), must essentially be left to run their course while the victim was kept warm and in bed at home. For most illness conditions, however, there was agreement that either *remedios caseros* or *remedios médicos* ("medical remedies" or "doctor's remedies") can be effective. Further, a physician's treatment was generally considered the most likely to bring about a cure, albeit at a much greater cost than other options.

The data from Pichátaro illuminate how the occurrence of trouble understood as illness can instigate narrative thinking – effort after meaning engages effort after narrative. The results of such efforts entered into practical action taken to redress specific instances of trouble in the future and impacted on how the past is remembered. Nonetheless, I don't want to suggest that such processes necessarily and regularly culminated in well-formed narratives that precede actions taken in response to illness. This did not occur, for example, in the case of an eight-year-old girl with mild diarrhea, lack of appetite, and general lassitude. To treat the main symptom, diarrhea, her parents initially purchased pills from a local store that had helped in the past. When her illness persisted for several weeks, the parents weren't at all sure what was going on and initially decided to take their daughter to a friend who was a *practicante* (a local unlicensed biomedically oriented practitioner who relied on *remedios médicos* – pharmaceuticals and injections). Before they did so, however, a friend's advice led them to consult a local *curandera* who, after a physical examination, diagnosed *empacho* ("blocked digestion"), thus offering a plausible interpretive scheme for the child's condition. While the diagnosis entailed that the child had eaten something in the past that had led to this condition, establishing the specific items with certainty was not stressed.

Still, the diagnosis bestows a narrative form that supports future treatment with cultural knowledge about narrative possibilities standing in, as it were, for what transpired in the past. The pragmatic need to act means that only a hazy sense of the possible past may be recruited to meet present needs. For many non-serious and moderately serious illnesses, as in the case described above, rather than an explicit initial concern with establishing that this and this must have occurred to bring about this specific illness and therefore this is what needs to be done to treat it, the task at hand was to remember what was successful in similar past instances in one's own household and to try that possibility (or possibilities) and/or seek advice from others, perhaps following recommendations made by friends or kin in light of their past experiences with similar problems.

The use of an illness label may be a reasonable guess – a loose and provisional fit between the present circumstances and a culturally available interpretive scheme – rather than a reflection of commitment to a particular explanatory scenario. Diagnoses are often proffered by others, both in informal settings and through the seeking of care from practitioners, even though the relevance (goodness of fit) may be considered confirmed only on the basis of what later transpires. This occurred in my case of *calor subido*. The causal scenario imaginatively projected by the woman who treated me was definitively established only after my symptoms disappeared.

Narrative Thinking and Care for the Future

Implicit in the preceding discussion (including the case of W.B.) is the stance that what motivates culturally informed action to avoid or respond to trouble in the present is care for the indeterminate future. Remembering may be infused with "a sense of engagement and concern for what lies ahead in the life course" (Ochs and Capps 2001:157). Through narrative thinking, effort after meaning becomes entwined with care for what may come to pass, at times orchestrating future-oriented action. As Mattingly (1998:93) elaborates: "We act in order to bring certain endings about, to realize certain futures, and to avoid others. While we may not be (often are not) successful, we act nonetheless, striving as far as we can to make some stories come true and thwart others."

Writing from a different theoretical orientation – a biocultural account of the response to illness which links anxiety, remembering, and agency – Hay (2009:12) defines anxiety as "the culturally informed emotional response to a perceived threat or fear of loss" and points out that this "kind of anxiety involves evaluating a current event relative to past events or experiences and determining whether it threatens expectations for the future." Anxiety "motivates social action" – seeking health care, remembering illness names or diagnoses, remembering treatments – because "a person becomes anxious when someone or something salient in their world is significantly threatened" (Hay 2009:20).

If trouble with one's eyes is an instance of *calor subido*, then the trouble is deemed not to be a significant threat and a solution is at hand. The prognosis for a quick recovery is favorable and treatment helps the displaced heat return to its normal location. But when illness resists initial treatment, uncertainty and care (anxiety) can motivate the exploration of other treatment options, as in the case of the 8-year-old girl with diarrhea. And, in other illness cases followed in Pichátaro, the assessment that illness symptoms have become so grave that the illness poses a potential or direct threat to life or livelihood resulted in the desire to seek out treatment with the highest likelihood of achieving a cure. In most instances, a physician's help is preferred; exceptions were those cases where circumstances warrant the narrative framing of an illness curable only through *remedios caseros*. As one individual explained, when illness turns "very grave" people go "running to the doctor because it's *más seguro* ['more certain'] there." The statement which followed, "But you have to have the money to go," made clear that whether conditions are such that the desire to consult a physician can be realized is a separate matter.

As mentioned earlier, the research in Pichátaro revolved around discovering locally shared considerations involved in reaching decisions concerning treatment and, on the basis of that information, modeling the decision-making process itself in a manner that would account for the use of different treatment alternatives during the course of illness. Since this project is discussed in detail elsewhere (Young and Garro 1994 [1981]; Garro 1998a), the comments in the next section concerning the decision-modeling approach serve primarily to situate this work in relation to the process-oriented perspective on meaning-making and action advanced here. Simply put, the two approaches offer complementary yet distinctive lenses on the dynamics of treatment actions in Pichátaro. Even when the decision model does a good job of accounting for actual treatment choices, as is the case for Pichátaro, the need remains for greater attention to the jointly cognitive and sociocultural processes through which meaning is conferred on perceived afflictions (see Mathews 1982; Garro 1998a).

Decision Models and Deciding on a Course of Action in Times of Illness

The decision model was constructed using specially designed interviews with one sample; the 323 illness cases used to evaluate the model were obtained through visits every two weeks to an independent sample of 62 randomly selected households for a period of six months.

In brief, derived from information obtained through interviews, the decision-making process can be understood with reference to two basic strategies which relate four key considerations to expected orderings of treatment use. When an illness was not serious, the general pattern was expected to be "cost-ordered," starting with alternatives that are less costly. Self-treatment was expected to be tried first, unless an appropriate home remedy was not known. If no remedy was known, or if illness continued despite home-based treatment, the ordering moved next to a *curandera* or *practicante*, depending on which was judged to be potentially more efficacious for the specific illness at hand at a specific point in time. The most expensive alternative, usually the physician, was expected to be consulted only after the less costly options had been exhausted, and *remedios médicos* were seen to offer the highest likelihood of a cure. The second strategy was structured by "probability of cure" assessments for illnesses considered grave enough to potentially threaten life. The expected ordering was to consult the preferred alternative first, which was often, but not always, a physician. Resort to other alternatives was anticipated to occur only after the preferred alternative was unsuccessful.

While economic realities were entrenched in the cost-ordered strategy, both the cost of care and the lack of transportation were real-world conditions constraining resort to physicians. Thus, when a serious illness, for which a physician's care was seen to offer the highest likelihood of cure, occurred in a household with scarce financial resources, economic limitations were expected to result in lower-cost alternatives being attempted first. The decision model formalizes these strategies and constraints by specifying the considerations which were expected to result in the use of a given treatment alternative. For example, given the combination of knowledge of an appropriate home remedy and an illness judged non-serious or moderately serious, the expected initial response was home treatment. Another illustration is the combination of a moderately serious illness for which *remedios médicos* were assessed as more likely to result in a cure than *remedios caseros*. Here the cost-ordering strategy was expected, leading to the expectation that a *practicanate* was consulted. Resort to a *practicante* was also expected in the situation of a grave illness for which *remedios médicos* were preferred but there was a lack of resources (money and/or transportation) needed in order to consult a physician.

In evaluating the extent to which the decision model accounted for treatment actions in the illness histories, evidence apart from the actual illness case histories helped to minimize subjective assessments. For example, relative wealth rankings of the case-collection households served as an independent criterion of the availability of economic means (see Young and Garro 1994[1981]:163). For families below the median wealth rank, resort to a physician was scored as an error in evaluating the decision model unless less costly practitioners were consulted first.

Overall, the decision model accounted for approximately 90 percent of treatment actions (out of a total of 444). Home treatment was overwhelmingly the most common initial response and constituted about half of the cases used to evaluate the decision model. Nonetheless, even excluding these cases, the decision model still accounted for over 80 percent of remaining cases.

These findings, along with additional analyses of the sequential patterning of treatment use, corroborate the position that impediments to consulting a physician, like the high cost of care, account for why it was mainly under fairly extreme conditions that a physician's treatment was considered at all. The social justice and applied policy implications of this research are strengthened by the formal evaluation of the decision model using illness cases obtained from a sample of households independent of those consulted in constructing the model. At the same time, a closer look at the errors in the decision model in accounting for treatment actions shows that the most frequent pattern, accounting for almost half of the total of 39 correspondence errors between the decision model and treatment actions (19 instances or 49 percent), occurred when a physician was consulted even though a less costly alternative was anticipated by the model (in all but one instance a *practicante* was the outcome expected). Remaining in the universe of the model, one could point to the shortfalls of relying on median wealth ranking as a proxy measure for the availability of financial resources to pay for a physician's care. It seems unlikely, though, that this is the full story. From the lens of a process-oriented approach to meaning-making and action, what we observed in following a number of these cases is that the anxiety and concern about a grave illness and the grimness of a projected future prompted families to somehow marshal the needed resources, perhaps through borrowing funds or assuming significant financial risk in order to consult a physician and thereby minimize the risk of negative consequences should this action be delayed.

Generally speaking, the decision model does a good job of accounting for treatment decisions because effort after meaning is integral to the model itself. But this success is often achieved through modeling situations that are culturally framed rather than through the cultural framing of the situation (see Mathews 1982; Garro 1998a). Take, for example, the common initial response of attempting home treatment. To report knowledge of a home remedy for the illness at hand is also to assert some level of knowledge about the illness. And while such home treatment can be considered a "routine" action, this cannot simply be seen as equivalent to the "motivation to enact *routine* behaviors ... a kind of automatic, unreflected-upon tendency to act as everyone else (like you) does" (Strauss and Quinn 1997:226). Rather, knowing a home remedy depends upon effort after meaning, recruiting past experience and culturally available resources (as schema-based constructive processes), to settle on, even tentatively, a sense of what kind of illness this is, how serious it is or may potentially become, and what kind of remedy might work. Thus, although initial home treatment can be considered "routine," there is still much to be learned about active meaning-conferring processes through attention to the routine. Indeed, the treatment of a particular illness can be considered routine only because some sort of fit with what is known is established.

Another example of how framed judgments are part of the decision model concern judgments with regard to the potential efficacy of *remedios caseros* or *remedios médicos*. Consider, for instance, the situation of a moderately serious illness when no one in the household knows an appropriate remedy and there is a judgment that a *curandera*, rather than a *practicante*, offers the highest likelihood of cure at this point in time. All cases conforming to these assessments are considered equivalent from the standpoint of the decision model. Thus, the decision to consult a *curandera* in a situation where an illness was diagnosed and remembered as one that a *curandera* had provided successful treatment for a family member in the past is one exemplar accounted for by the decision model. But so is the situation where there was uncertainty about the type of illness involved and whether *remedios caseros* or *remedios médicos* were better, and the decision to consult a particular *curandera* rather than a *practicante* was swayed by advice given by a friend, where the friend remembered a similar case that was treated successfully by a curer. From a process-oriented approach, these are quite different, involving distinctive processes as well as experiential realities. In the first, remembering (knowing) provided a framework for action. In the second, "effort after meaning" takes on a different cast, accompanied by ambiguity and uncertainty, and the active consideration, perhaps even seeking, of informal advice about whom to consult from others. Given limited financial resources and the illness at hand, the decision to consult a *curandera* is a provisional assessment that the *curandera* is more likely to resolve the ambiguity and uncertainty surrounding the illness, more likely to possess the knowledge and skills to identify and successfully treat the illness.

Open to the possibility that the way an illness is understood may change through time, the decision model accommodates, but is not directly concerned with, the vicissitudes of effort after meaning in navigating the uncertainty of illness in social contexts where much is often at stake. In one household with a regular source of cash income, the intermittent vomiting, diarrhea, and general restlessness of a young child was initially considered moderately serious, in part because the child was not yet old enough to talk. The parents were unsure why the child had fallen ill though they targeted a diet-related imbalance as likely. Treated with a home remedy, the illness did not abate and came to be seen as serious, leading the worried parents to hire a taxi to consult a physician. The physician confirmed the problem as diet-related. Despite the medicine prescribed and taken, the symptoms persisted. Rather than return to the same physician, the perceived failure of *remedios medicos* led to a shift toward *remedios caseros* as offering the best chance of cure. Two days after seeing the physician, the parents hastened to consult a locally renowned *curandera*. She identified the illness as *mal de ojo*, a diagnosis supported by the failure of the earlier treatments and later seen to be confirmed by the child's subsequent recovery and the mother's recollection of the interpersonal interaction deemed responsible for the illness. While the parents' quest was set in motion by anxiety, what accompanied the cessation of symptoms was a narrative account, one implicit in the curer's diagnosis but filled in with concrete details of the remembered past by the mother. Although the sequence of actions for this case conformed with the expectations of the decision model, the intertwining of effort after meaning and action is illuminated through attention to the jointly cognitive and sociocultural processes leading up to and following the framing of this and other cases as *mal de ojo*. As in other cases we recorded, the initial proclivity to construe illness in terms of bodily disequilibrium was present. Yet the viability of this cultural resource, the ontological reality of *mal de ojo*, gained strength through the testing and failing of other perspectives for this specific illness reality as well as the family's assessment that the alleviation of the illness was due to the curer's ministrations.

Concluding Remarks

Narrative possibilities inform action taken to avoid situations with the potential to lead to illness as well as efforts motivated by the pragmatic need to decide on a course of action in situations of trouble. Some of the ethnographic examples examined show how narrative possibilities and expectations are connected with illness labels, illness categories, and broader interpretive frameworks. Identifying a specific instance of trouble as a known illness can guide the remembered past and offer a framework for action. The local salience of culturally available knowledge of explanatory frameworks for illness may be revealed through an "active bias" to rely upon some sense-making frames, and to overlook others, for concrete instances of trouble and in avoiding everyday situations in which illness is narratively foreshadowed. Yet, the fit between present circumstances and a culturally available interpretive scheme may be tentative or called into question in light of what transpires. For any situation of trouble, more than one narrative frame may come under active consideration and the interpretive frame associated with a given illness may change through time. That others may know differently or may be able to resolve the ambiguity and uncertainty occasioned by trouble often motivates the seeking of advice or care from others.

In acknowledging the role played by experiences of uncertainty and anxiety in motivating culturally informed action to avoid or respond to trouble, it is important to note that distinctive kinds of uncertainty are present in the ethnographic material examined. For the cases from Pichátaro, uncertainty in illness identification, and who would be best positioned to offer a cure, did not challenge assumptions about the nature of reality. Yet, in situations where the actions taken are at odds with one's avowed stance prior to the trouble, as in case of W.B. and others not presented here from my field research in an Ojibwa community (see Garro 1998b:348; 2005:66), what was experienced was existential uncertainty about the nature of ontological reality (e.g., do toads trouble those who recount myths at the wrong time of the year?). While such cases may more clearly reveal how culturally available explanatory frameworks serve as resources informing actions taken to avoid or deal with trouble in everyday life, the diversity of examples offered attests to the broader applicability of the process-oriented approach advanced here.

D'Andrade has claimed that "any cultural theorist interested in action needs a psychological theory of internalization," although he also defined internalization (immediately preceding a discussion of Spiro's model) as "the process by which cultural representations become part of the individual; that is, become what is right and true" (D'Andrade 1995:243, 227). While I have no difficulty with the truncated statement "any cultural theorist interested in action needs a psychological theory," and see this chapter as sketching out just what that involves in avoiding and responding to trouble which comes to be construed as illness, I do not hold that "internalization," as defined above by D'Andrade, is the only lens for theorizing about culturally informed action. Here, and in earlier writings (see especially Garro 2000a, 2003, 2005), I have drawn attention to culturally available resources as offering alternative framings for endowing experience with meaning. In addition, as explored here, the limits of what one knows, of uncertainty, an appreciation or hope that others might be better positioned to know how to resolve a specific problem, underscores the need to go beyond what has become "part of the individual" in understanding action in response to trouble as part of everyday life.

REFERENCES

Bartlett, F. C.
1932 Remembering: A Study in Experimental and Social Psychology. Cambridge: Cambridge University Press.
Berens, W. B.
2009 Memories, Myths, and Dreams of an Ojibwe Leader, as told to A. I. Hallowell. J. S. H. Brown and S. E. Gray, eds. Montreal: McGill-Queen's University Press.
Bourdieu, P.
1977 Outline of a Theory of Practice. Cambridge: Cambridge University Press.
Bruner, J.
1986 Actual Minds, Possible Worlds. Cambridge, MA: Harvard University Press.
1990 Acts of Meaning. Cambridge, MA: Harvard University Press.
D'Andrade, R.
1995 The Development of Cognitive Anthropology. Cambridge: Cambridge University Press.
Frake, C. O.
1961 The Diagnosis of Disease among the Subanun of Mindanao. American Anthropologist 63:113–132.
Garro, L. C.
1990 Continuity and Change: The Interpretation of Illness in an Anishinaabe (Ojibway) Community. Culture, Medicine and Psychiatry 14:417–454.

1998a On the Rationality of Decision Making Studies: Part 1: Decision Models of Treatment Choice. Medical Anthropology Quarterly 12:319–340.

1998b On the Rationality of Decision Making Studies: Part 2: Divergent Rationalities. Medical Anthropology Quarterly 12:341–355.

2000a Cultural Knowledge as Resource in Illness Narratives: Remembering through Accounts of Illness. *In* Narrative and the Cultural Construction of Illness and Healing. C. Mattingly and L. Garro, eds. Pp. 70–87. Berkeley: University of California Press.

2000b Remembering What One Knows and the Construction of the Past: A Comparison of Cultural Consensus Theory and Cultural Schema Theory. Ethos 28:275–319.

2001 The Remembered Past in a Culturally Meaningful Life: Remembering as Cultural, Social and Cognitive Process. *In* The Psychology of Cultural Experience. H. Mathews and C. Moore, eds. Pp. 105–147. Cambridge: Cambridge University Press.

2002 Hallowell's Challenge: Explanations of Illness and Cross-Cultural Research. Anthropological Theory 2:77–97.

2003 Narrating Troubling Experiences. Transcultural Psychiatry 40:5–44.

2005 "Effort After Meaning" in Everyday Life. *In* A Companion to Psychological Anthropology: Modernity and Psychocultural Change. C. Casey and R. B. Edgerton, eds. Pp. 48–71. Malden, MA: Blackwell.

2010 By the Will of Others or by One's Own Action. *In* Toward an Anthropology of the Will. K. Murphy and C. J. Throop, eds. Pp. 69–100. Stanford: Stanford University Press.

Hallowell, A. I.

1955 Culture and Experience. Philadelphia: University of Pennsylvania Press.

1976 Contributions to Anthropology: Selected Papers of A. Irving Hallowell. Chicago: University of Chicago Press.

Hay, M. C.

2009 Anxiety, Remembering, and Agency: Biocultural Insights for Understanding Sasaks' Responses to Illness. Ethos 37:1–31.

Mathews, H.

1982 Illness Classification and Treatment Choice: Decision Making in the Medical Domain. Reviews in Anthropology 9:171–186.

Mattingly, C.

1998 Healing Dramas and Clinical Plots: The Narrative Structure of Experience. Cambridge: Cambridge University Press.

Ochs, E., and L. Capps

2001 Living Narrative: Creating Lives in Everyday Storytelling. Cambridge, MA: Harvard University Press.

Spiro, M.

1987 Collective Representations and Mental Representations in Religious Symbol Systems. *In* Culture and Human Nature: Theoretical Papers of Melford E. Spiro. B. Kilborne and L. L. Langness, eds. Pp. 161–184. Chicago: University of Chicago Press.

1997 Gender Ideology and Psychological Reality. New Haven: Yale University Press.

Strauss, C., and N. Quinn

1997 A Cognitive Theory of Cultural Meaning. Cambridge: Cambridge University Press.

Young, J. C., and L. C. Garro

1994[1981] Medical Choice in a Mexican Village. Prospect Heights, IL: Waveland.

CHAPTER 29

Using Consensus Analysis to Investigate Cultural Models of Alzheimer's Disease

Robert W. Schrauf and Madelyn Iris

This chapter demonstrates the use of *cultural consensus analysis* as a tool for assessing within- and between-group knowledge of Alzheimer's disease among African Americans, Mexican Americans, and refugees/immigrants from the Former Soviet Union. The study is grounded in the notion of *cultural models of illness* and seeks to characterize how knowledge of disease models is variably distributed across individuals.

Intermediate between professional clinicians and scientists and any individual lay person stands a larger network of people that comprises a world of daily contact, mutual influence, collective information, shared advice, and common problem-solving. It is arguable that what any one person knows about particular illness conditions is largely mediated through this local network. Thus, before and after contact with the medical establishment, people puzzle through symptoms, hazard guesses about possible diagnoses, manage treatment, and monitor their illnesses in conversation with other lay people whom they know. Some people in the group will know a great deal about particular conditions, and others will know considerably less. Practically speaking, people seek out and learn new information as the need arises. What is important is that the knowledge is available somewhere in the network. In the end, knowledge is primarily a property of groups and secondarily a property of individuals.

This group, lay knowledge comprises a *cultural model* of the illness condition. A cultural model is a series of interwoven beliefs about a particular domain, the knowledge of which is distributed through a group or network of persons, such that some individuals

A Companion to Cognitive Anthropology, First Edition. Edited by David B. Kronenfeld, Giovanni Bennardo, Victor C. de Munck, and Michael D. Fischer.

know the majority of the model, some know significant portions, and some know only part of the model. Research on explanatory models and illness cognition shows that lay people organize their knowledge about disease entities in roughly the same categories as biomedical clinicians and scientists: causes, symptoms, course, and treatment (Kleinman 1980; Skelton and Croyle 1991; Baer et al. 2004). Nevertheless, although folk or local models may overlap with biomedical models, they often form coherent networks of beliefs that differ from more than they resemble medical models.

Consensus Analysis of Illness Knowledge

Anthropologists and cognitive psychologists have developed both a theoretical model, *cultural consensus theory*, and a series of analytic methods, *consensus analysis*, for characterizing and analyzing cultural models within groups and comparing them between groups (Romney et al. 1986; Batchelder and Romney 1988; Romney and Moore 1998; Weller and Baer 2002). Consensus theory sees culture as a shared pool of local knowledge. The theory makes the assumption that culture members implicitly or explicitly agree on the series of beliefs that constitute the knowledge domain, but that even among cultural insiders there will be some who know more and some who know less (*intra*cultural variability). Further, those who know more of the domain will agree more with one another than those with less knowledge of the domain. Those with higher levels of shared agreement about the series of beliefs "know" the model better than those with lower levels of shared agreement (Weller 1987; Batchelder and Romney 1988; Weller and Mann 1997).

The prime ethnographic example is Boster's (1986) work among Aguaruna Jivaro cultivators of manioc in the Amazon Basin. Boster found that Jivaro gardeners held a common classification system for manioc plants, and also that those who agreed more with one another knew more of the classification system than those who did not. For an anthropologist (a cultural "outsider") this solves the thorny problem of reliably identifying local expertise by directing attention to people with high levels of pair-wise agreement about the domain. *Their* statements are more likely representative of the group model. More formally, consensus analysis as a method provides the means for determining (1) whether there exists a consistent series of beliefs – *a single cultural model*, (2) which beliefs are part of the model and which are not – the *culturally correct answer key*, and (3) how much each individual knows about the model – each person's *cultural competence.*

Consensus analysis in studies of health and illness

If indeed there are local cultural models of a particular diseases or illness conditions in ethnic communities, cultural consensus theory provides a way of documenting such models through a stepwise process of eliciting local, lay formulations of beliefs and then testing for agreement patterns between every pair of informants in order to find out which beliefs are central, which peripheral, and which are not part of the model.

Focus on intracultural variation As noted above, once it is established that a group possesses a unitary cultural model, competence scores can be generated for each individual. These reflect the proportion of the model that each person knows, and in effect they are measures of *intracultural* (within-group) variation. Prior studies of intracultural variation in health domains include: sexual risk perception among college students in New York (Swora 2003), malaria among the Gusii in lowland Kenya (Nyamongo 2002), diabetes among patients in Thailand (Ratanasuwan et al. 2005), post-partum hemorrhage among childbearing women in Bangladesh (Hruschka et al. 2008), physician norms and health-care decisions by older Medicare recipients in the USA (Hurwicz 1995), depression among African American older adults in the USA (Barg et al. 2006), and "folk" models of diagnostic classifications by clinical psychologists in the USA (Flanagan and Blashfield 2008).

Focus on intercultural variation Consensus analysis also facilitates cross-cultural or cross-ethnic comparison of beliefs about health and illness. Once the local beliefs of two or more populations have been elicited, these may be combined into a single instrument that is then administered across the groups. Results of the analysis show whether there is a single "core" model of a disease across the groups or whether individual groups have separate but overlapping models (or no sharing whatsoever). Typically, this is established by pooling the data and testing for consensus in the pooled data and/or by testing for significant correlation between beliefs in each pair of local models. These are studies of *intercultural variation*.

Prior cross-cultural applications of the method have addressed: breast and cervical cancer among women in El Salvador and Mexico, Chicana and Anglo women in the US, and US physicians (Chavez et al. 1995), AIDS among Guatemalans in Guatemala, Mexicans in Mexico, Mexican Americans in the USA, Puerto Ricans on the US mainland, and physicians from Mexico and the USA (Baer et al. 1999a, 2004), asthma among Guatemalans in Guatemala, Mexicans in Mexico, Mexican Americans in the USA, and Puerto Ricans on the US mainland (Pachter et al. 2002), dental pain descriptors among Americans and Mandarin-speaking Chinese patients (Moore et al. 1997), and the common cold among Guatemalans in Guatemala, Mexicans in Mexico, Mexican Americans in the USA, Puerto Ricans on the US mainland, middle-class whites, and physicians (Baer et al. 1999b, 2008).

Conventional Approaches to Investigating Lay Knowledge of Alzheimer's Disease

Cultural beliefs about Alzheimer's disease (AD) have been investigated for a number of ethnic groups in the United States, and these studies have provided valuable insights into local beliefs. A sampling of that literature is reviewed here. The consensus approach differs from these prior studies in the following ways. First, the consensus approach involves developing an item pool based on qualitative interviews with culture members, with final survey items preserving the original wordings of culture members. Contrariwise, typical survey approaches often employ items derived from scientific or clinical models of the disease. Second, the consensus approach assesses intracultural variation within each group model, and then compares group models with one another. Conventional approaches, on the other hand, often compare modal or mean responses to individual items across groups without attention to the web of beliefs within which these are intertwined.

Qualitative studies

Prior studies of knowledge of dementia among ethnic groups in the USA have followed both qualitative and quantitative methodologies. Qualitative studies, often based on open-ended or semi-structured interviews, have the strength of eliciting local cultural beliefs, but they commonly lack an assessment of within-sample variation around these beliefs. For example, in semi-structured interviews with African Americans, Chinese Americans, Hispanics, and European Americans, Dilworth-Anderson and Gibson (2002) found specific ethnic beliefs. For example, Chinese participants noted that the cultural value of filial piety eased caregivers' acceptance of the role reversal in which adult children find themselves taking care of a sometimes "childlike" parent. However, from the results presented, it is difficult to ascertain how many individuals expressed this belief and whether it was part of a coherent local model. In other words, the reader cannot assess *intra*cultural variation in beliefs and must assume (but cannot know) that there is a group model.

A second example is found in the study by Hinton et al. (2005) that reported results from semi-structured interviews with African Americans, Asian Americans, Latinos, and European Americans. Based on a previously derived typology (Levkoff et al. 1997; Hinton and Levkoff 1999), the investigators categorized respondents' beliefs into one of three models: biomedical (brain-based disorders), folk (psychosocial stress, normal aging), and "mixed." Testing for factors that would account for model choice, the authors found (via logistic regression) that minority vs. majority status and lower education (but not age) were significant predictors of having a folk or mixed model vs. a biomedical model. In this case, no formal test of whether group models exist was undertaken, and potential ethnic differences were collapsed into minority vs. majority status.

Quantitative studies

Quantitative studies are generally strong on measuring cross-group differences, but the trade-off is that groups are often tested on items drawn from scientific models of the disease instead of community beliefs. Thus, there is little insight into whether groups hold specifically ethnic models. For example, Ayalon and Areán (2004) developed a 17-item instrument with the assistance of experts in dementia and then administered the instrument to samples of European Americans, Asian Americans, Latinos, and African Americans. Omnibus differences between the groups were reported for each of the 17 items, but in planned comparisons the authors combined the minority samples for comparison with the whites. Because the analysis lumped together ethnic groups vs. whites, and because the survey items did not come from the groups themselves, the reader cannot know whether these ethnic groups have particular models of the disease that might differ from one another.

In a series of studies on race and knowledge of Alzheimer's, Connell and Roberts and colleagues (Roberts et al. 2003; Connell et al. 2009) did in fact elicit community beliefs from African Americans and whites, but the analyses concerned group differences on individual items and not whether and to what extent local cultural models actually existed. Roberts et al. (2003) developed an 82-item questionnaire from in-depth interviews and focus groups in the Atlanta area and administered the questionnaire to new samples of whites and African Americans. The authors compared percentages of items endorsed by either group. Results showed, for instance, that whites answered more knowledge items correctly than African Americans, reported a greater number of sources of information, and perceived AD as a greater threat. Interestingly, race proved to be a more potent predictor of differences in beliefs than experience with the disease (i.e. family or caregiving history).

In a more recent study, Connell et al. (2009) administered a survey to whites and African Americans with subsections on knowledge of AD, concerns about AD, beliefs about AD risk, and beliefs about treatment. Items were drawn from published tests and the previous study. Direct comparisons were made between groups at the item level, and odds ratios computed by race. They found that African Americans were more likely than whites to believe that AD can be diagnosed with a blood test; that scientists were on the brink of discovering a cure; and that age, toxins, head injury, mental illness, stress, smoking, and use of alcohol were risk factors. Again, however, it is difficult to know whether these groups differ from one another in possessing this or that particular belief, or whether there are differences in their models of the disease.

The "AD Beliefs Study"

In this present study, using the cultural consensus model, we combine the relative strengths of qualitative and quantitative studies. From the former, we take the careful elicitation of statements describing local cultural understandings of AD, and from the latter we take the systematic survey of knowledge to examine within-group heterogeneity. The study involved the administration of a questionnaire containing various cultural beliefs about Alzheimer's disease to samples of African Americans, Mexican Americans, and refugees from the Former Soviet Union (FSU) in the Chicago area. We specifically recruited Mexican Americans, as opposed to Latinos or Hispanics in general, because we were interested in examining the presence or absence of a specific cultural model. Inclusion of persons from other Spanish-speaking countries would have confounded our analyses. Refugees from the Former Soviet Union were chosen as a cultural group in order to examine a specific sub-population of what would otherwise be absorbed within the larger, undefined category of "white" Americans. The questionnaire was developed from initial open-ended interviews with key informants from each group. All respondents also completed demographics questionnaires and measures of acculturation. Our aims were to (1) test for the presence of cultural models in each group, (2) describe these models, (3) compare them across groups, and (4) identify the effect of demographic predictors, prior experience with AD, and level of acculturation on knowledge of the local models.

Interview materials

Questionnaire development Open-ended, qualitative interviews were conducted with 30 key informants, with 10 individuals carefully selected from each group according to the following criteria. Using a *reputational case selection methodology* (Miles and Huberman 1994) we sought referrals within the ethnic communities to individuals who did not necessarily have formal training in aging-related issues, but were recognized as knowledgeable about aging. To ensure ***maximum variation sampling*** (Guba and Lincoln 1989), we asked each participant to name another community expert who was known to hold different opinions from themselves. In general, these participants were middle-aged, with African Americans and FSU refugees having some college education, and Mexican Americans having high-school education. Most participants either knew someone with AD or in fact had a family member with the disease (African Americans 60 percent, Mexican Americans 80 percent, FSU refugees 40 percent). Interviews lasted approximately 60 to 90 minutes, and began with typical ethnographic "grand tour" questions (e.g., "Tell me about African American views on aging," "Tell me about Alzheimer's disease") and were followed by more focused questions on aging, memory loss, dementia, and AD (Spradley 1979; Ryan and Bernard 2003). Interviews were conducted in English (with African Americans), Spanish (with Mexican Americans, if they preferred), and Russian (with FSU refugees).

All interviews were transcribed according to conventions common in anthropology (Powers 2005). Spanish and Russian interviews were simultaneously transcribed and translated according to a multistage model (Werner 1997) and downloaded to the qualitative analysis software package Atlas.ti (Muhr 2004). Coding was both deductive and inductive. A priori codes included the larger categories of interest in the project: statements about aging, statements about memory loss, perceived causes of memory loss, statements about dementia, perceived causes of dementia, Alzheimer's disease, perceived causes of Alzheimer's disease, symptoms of Alzheimer's disease, community-specific (ethnic) beliefs about Alzheimer's. In addition, inductive coding involved *in vivo* marking of unanticipated or emergent themes (Ryan and Bernard 2003). Codes were operationalized, refined, and split or combined into families via an iterative process involving two coders (M.I. and the project director) and reviewed by two additional team members (R.W.S. and the research assistant).

Examples of coded material from these two topics may be illustrative of the process of moving from semi-structured interviews to the construction of a final survey. In the domain of *Alzheimer's disease*, the coding process resulted in 26 codes (some with further sub-codes) spread across 412 tokens. For example, comments that suggested that Alzheimer's disease is a normal part of aging were coded as "AD Normal Aging" (21 tokens), and these eventually became the survey item "Alzheimer's disease is normal for old age." Interestingly, no community expert held this opinion, but rather attributed it to others in the community. Two excerpts make this point, the first from an African American informant and the second from a Mexican informant.

Participant 101, African American
The community at large would think it's a part of normal aging. Yeah. Again, they'll call it senility or "grandma's going crazy." They do not understand normal aging versus Alzheimer's disease, they don't. So it's lumped together, unfortunately [laughs].

Participant 201, Mexican American
I believe that if you are uneducated, or don't have that much knowledge of education, that you might say that it's something that's a normal process.

As another example, the eventual survey item, "Alzheimer's disease is curable" emerged from 39 tokens in which participants mentioned "cure." The following excerpt from a Russian participant captures this theme.

> *Participant 304, Russian*
> You know people want to believe it [that AD is curable] – but no one is naive. They do … find good doctors or some cure: some new treatment or medication. Sometimes it helps. They get the medication in balance and good supportive therapy. It stabilizes the flow of disease, prevents rapid changes. Sometimes people who are used to knowing their parent in a different way – active, intelligent, sharp – try to seek the help of doctors, try to "cure" them and help them. But they know that it cannot be treated. It is common knowledge.

As we developed the final questionnaire from the material generated by these interviews and the pilot, we were particularly interested in keeping as far as possible the original wordings used by the participants themselves. After we transformed the original articulations into survey items in this way, an initial version of the final questionnaire was piloted with the same 30 individuals who had participated in the structured interviews.

For the final questionnaire, we eliminated items that were ambiguous or repetitive or for which there was no variation (either universal agreement or disagreement) in the pilot study. Finally, to construct a survey that would maximize the likelihood of detecting intercultural variation, we prioritized items that were mentioned by at least two or by all three groups, but we were careful to include items of particular cultural relevance mentioned by only one group.

The final questionnaire included a total of 81 items about Alzheimer's disease, divided into three sections: statements about AD (34 items), causes of AD (35 items), and possible treatments (12 items). All items were rewritten with yes/no answer formats, balanced across likely yes or no responses based on data from the pilot. The proportion of yes vs. no responses fell between 0.40 and 0.70 on each scale, to comply with the consensus analysis requirement that scales be constructed with roughly equal numbers of yes/no or true/false items (Weller 2007).

Demographics and experience with AD In addition to the final questionnaire, all participants were asked to provide standard demographic information (age, education, income). Self-rated proficiency in English was obtained for Spanish and Russian speakers in response to the question: "How well do you speak English? (not at all; not well; well; very well). Experience with AD was operationalized as a binary variable in response to the question: "Do you have friends or family who have received a diagnosis of AD?" (yes/no).

Measures of acculturation In general, acculturation describes the process of affirming, adapting, negotiating, modifying, and/or rejecting beliefs, customs, values, attitudes, and behaviors of the dominant culture in the context of maintaining and developing those of one's own group (Spradley 1979; Berry 1980, 2003; Ryan and Bernard 2003; for critique of the concept see Hunt et al. 2004). The process is highly situational, context-dependent, inherently longitudinal, and variable by cultural domain (Schrauf 2002). Because people come to the experience of aging with culturally conditioned expectations, it is a reasonable hypothesis that level of acculturation will shape those expectations.

African Americans completed the *African American Acculturation Scale-33* (AAAS-33). The AAAS-33 is the 33-item short form (Landrine and Klonoff 1995) of a longer 74-item version (Landrine and Klonoff 1994). The instrument is composed of ten sub-scales: Preference for Things African American (6 items), Religious Beliefs/Practices (6 items), Traditional Foods (4 items), Traditional Childhood (3 items), Superstitions (3 items), Interracial Attitudes (3 items), Falling Out (2 items), Traditional Games (2 items), Family Values (2 items), and Family Practices (2 items). The long form of the AAAS was validated on 183 participants (118 African Americans), and the correlation between short and long forms was high ($r = 0.94$). Internal reliabilities for the short form ranged from 0.81 to 0.88.

Mexican American and FSU refugees took the *Stephenson Multigroup Acculturation Scale* (SMAS; Stephenson 2000). The SMAS is a 32-item instrument that measures ethnic society immersion (ESI) and dominant society immersion (DSI) on separate sub-scales. The SMAS was initially validated on 436 ethnic Americans from 31 countries of origin ranging in age from 18 to 76. Factor analysis confirmed the two sub-scales, and coefficient alphas were 0.97 for the ESI and 0.97 for the DSI. The English instrument was translated and back-translated in Spanish and Russian. The SMAS is not appropriate for use with African Americans as it relies heavily on questions regarding use of "native language" and use of English.

Substantively, the AAAS-33 is unidimensional, wherein each item is worded so that high scores indicate greater adherence or agreement with specific African American beliefs and customs, whereas low scores reflect adherence and/or agreement with white customs and beliefs only by implication. Thus, in item articulation and design, only the ethnic society immersion scale (ESI) of the Stephenson Scale matches the African American Scale. Thus, our analyses involve direct comparisons of the AAAS-33 and the ESI (but not the DSI).

Study sites, sampling, and recruitment

It is important to note that a key assumption of consensus analysis is that there exists a single response pattern, or single set of answers to the questions asked, around which there will be some variability (Romney et al. 1986). If there are multiple, systematic patterns of response, then group members are not responding similarly to one another, and there would seem to be more than "one culture" present in the data. Given this assumption, sample sizes need not be large. The Spearman–Brown prophesy formula is used to determine sample sizes for particular levels of agreement (mean competency scores) and levels of correlation (e.g., 0.95, 0.96, 0.97, 0.98, 0.99) between estimated answers and true answers (Bayesian posterior probabilities). For a moderate level of agreement between informants (mean group cultural competence of 0.50), a sample of 29 informants has at least a 0.99 probability of correctly classifying each item as yes/no with an a posteriori probability of at least 0.95. We expected a moderate level of agreement and recruited 36 individuals in each of the three ethnic sub-samples, for a total of 108 participants. Again, this reflects the formalized relation between agreement levels, the correlation between observed and estimated answers, and the size of the sample. As agreement levels increase, the samples needed to achieve sufficient power decrease in size (Weller 1987, 2007).

Thirty-six participants were recruited from each ethnic group through community groups, ethnic organizations, and churches. To ensure a range of acculturation experience, we recruited from both ethnically homogenous and heterogeneous neighborhoods based on ethnic concentration by zip code from the 2000 Census. For African Americans, the homogenous group (n = 20) came from zip codes with 94.8–98.1 percent black residents. The core homogeneous community was located on the south side of Chicago, and has been described as a stronghold of the African American middle class (Reiff et al. 2005). For Mexican Americans, the homogenous group (n = 16) came from zip codes with 48.6–62.9 percent Hispanic residents. The core community area from which we sampled was located on the near southwest side of Chicago and is a port of entry for immigrants from Mexico. It has many Mexican-owned small businesses and is well known for its vibrant Hispanic cultural life (Reiff et al. 2005).

The heterogeneous groups for both African Americans (n = 16) and Mexican Americans (n = 22) were drawn from the same contiguous southeast Chicago community. In these zip codes Hispanics represented between 8.1 to 34.3 percent of residents and African Americans represented 38.6 to 54.6 percent, with the remaining population consisting of European Americans, particularly immigrants from eastern Europe who settled in the area to work in nearby steel mills during the 20th century.

In the case of refugees from the Former Soviet Union, ethnic concentrations by zip code were too low (range: 0.0001–0.11) to serve as indicators of acculturation, and we were forced to use self-rated proficiency in English. Prior research shows that language preference and use are uniquely predictive of acculturative adjustment (Kang 2006) and correlate positively with ethnic self-identification (Laroche et al. 1998). We created a homogenous group (n = 14) who responded "not at all" and "not well" to the question "How well do you speak English?" and a heterogenous group (n = 22) that responded "well" or "very well" to the same question. FSU refugees lived in several ethnically diverse neighborhoods in Chicago as well as in the north and northwest suburbs of the city. In some cases, these participants lived in subsidized housing that included significant proportions of Russian-speaking residents, reflecting a highly localized "mini-enclave."

Demographic information for the 108 pooled participants, as well as for each ethnic group, is found in Table 29.1. In general, half or more of the participants were female, in their early sixties, having household incomes below $30,000 per year, with no significant differences between groups on income (H = 1.07). Among Mexican Americans, 12 were born in the United States; the remainder were born in Mexico and had spent approximately one-third of their lives in the USA. FSU refugees had spent approximately a quarter of their lives in the USA and none was born in the USA.

Non-parametric ANOVA's (Kruskall–Wallis tests) and post hoc comparisons show significant differences between groups on several factors related to experience in the health field or specifically with AD. More African Americans vs. FSU refugees and Mexican Americans worked in the health field ($H = 19.99$, $p < 0.001$). More African Americans vs. FSU refugees had friends and family that worked in the health field, with no significant differences between Mexican Americans and either group ($H = 8.26$, $p < 0.05$). Finally, although the Kruskall–Wallis H-statistics suggested omnibus differences in means, post hoc multiple comparisons did not show

Table 29.1 Final survey: Demographics of sample

	African Americans	*Mexican Americans*	*Immigrants/refugees from FSU*
Gender (F/M)	27/9	24/12	21/15
Age (mean, SD)	62.3 (12.9)	63.7 (13.0)	60.4 (14.0)
Education: years (mean, SD)	12.9 (2.6)	8.6 (4.9)	14.3 (3.1)
Income < $30,000 p.a. (%)	81	86	67
Proportion of lifespan in USA	1.0	0.30[1]	0.25
Work in health field (%)	44	11	6
Friends or family work in health field (%)	72	50	39
Friends or family with Alzheimer's (%)	42	39	17
Self-identify as caregiver (%)	28	11	6
Contacted a service organization[2] (%)	25	3	0

[1] This portion represents 24 individuals who were born in Mexico. Twelve of the participants were born in the USA.

[2] "Have you ever contacted an organization or program to help get caring for an older person or to learn about Alzheimer's disease?"

differences between groups in whether participants had family members or friends with AD ($H = 6.11, p < 0.05$), whether participants self-identified as caregivers ($H = 7.56, p < 0.05$), and whether participants had contacted an outside organization for information about AD ($H = 15.94, p < 0.001$). In sum, African Americans were more likely than the other two groups to have experience in, or to know someone who had experience in, the health field, but not more likely to have direct experience of individuals with the disease.

Data analysis

Consensus analysis assesses within group knowledge as follows. Given responses by a sample of culture members on a series of beliefs (e.g., yes/no, true/false), an agreement matrix is constructed in which cells in the matrix contain the pair-wise agreement (co-variance or match coefficients) between each pair of respondents. Specifically, in the pooled data, we converted the respondent-by-item matrix (108 × 81) to a respondent-by-respondent agreement matrix (108 × 108) using the co-variance method because it is relatively insensitive to individual response biases (i.e., the tendency for an individual to favor "yes" responses to "no" responses). Similarly, with separate data from each group, we transformed the respondent-by-item matrices (36 × 108) into separate group-agreement matrices (36 × 36). These agreement matrices were then subjected to a minimum residuals factor analysis (Anthropac 4.983). In practice, the presence of a single group model is indicated by a large first factor that accounts for the majority

Table 29.2 Results of consensus analysis of beliefs about Alzheimer's disease across African American, Mexican American, and FSU samples

	African Americans	*Mexican Americans*	*Immigrants/ refugees from FSU*	*Pooled*
Ratio 1st/2nd (eigenvalue)	5.31	5.68	5.61	4.93
Variance accounted for by first factor (%)	75.4	76.8	77.7	76.1
Mean cultural competence (SD)	0.48 (0.15)	0.46 (0.17)	0.51 (0.17)	0.47 (0.16)

of the variance (agreement) between individuals (by convention, a 3:1 ratio of first to second eigenvalue is required) and a lack of negative factor loadings on the first factor. Where single within-group models emerged (which they in fact did for all groups), we used Bayesian logic to determine the "culturally correct" answers, effectively producing the "cultural answer key" to the questionnaire. In this analysis, a probabilistic confidence level is associated with each item, and we set the confidence level at $p < 0.95$.

As noted above, to characterize levels of agreement between groups, we pooled the data and used consensus analysis to test for a single model, and we used a measure of association called the free marginal kappa coefficient between each pair of group answer keys (Brennan and Prediger 1981; Randolph 2005). Kappa coefficients control for chance agreement and are appropriate for categorical data (yes, no, unclassified responses). They range from 0.0, indicating no agreement, to 1.0, indicating perfect agreement. The loadings on the first factor represent cultural competence scores, or the proportion of the model that each respondent knows. We then used demographic factors (age, education, and income), participant experience with the disease, and acculturation as predictors of competence scores in multiple regression analyses to assess *where* higher levels of competence were located in the sample(s).

Results

Cultural models of Alzheimer's disease: Intra- and intercultural variation

Consensus analysis of the data showed a single cultural model (a single set of beliefs) of Alzheimer's disease within each group. That is, the ratio of first to second eigenvalues was at or above 3:1; first factors accounted for between 75 and 78 percent of the variance in agreement; and all loadings were positive on the first factor in each analysis (Table 29.2). The mean proportion of knowledge of the cultural model was moderate for each group: African American 0.48 (SD = 0.15), Mexican American 0.46 (SD = 0.17), and FSU refugees 0.51 (SD = 0.17). Kolmogorov–Smirnov one-sample tests showed that these competence scores were normally distributed in each group.

Agreement between groups was moderately high, and we concluded that a single core model existed between groups with some variation within groups. We confirmed this shared core model in two ways: via consensus analysis of the pooled data and by calculating agreement measures between the individual group "answer keys." In the consensus analysis of the pooled data, the ratio of first to second eigenvalue was above the 3:1 requirement, accounting for 76.1 percent of the variance in agreement, with no negative factor loadings on the first factor (Table 29.2). Thus, a single cultural model existed for the pooled data. The mean competence score was 0.47, meaning that on average participants knew just under half of the common core model. Again, these scores were normally distributed.

As a second method of assessing between-group agreement, kappa coefficients were calculated for each pair of models, and these were relatively high: African American and Mexican American (kappa = 0.63), African American and FSU refugee (kappa = 0.67), and Mexican American and FSU refugee (kappa = 0.74). In sum, using both consensus analysis of the pooled data and kappa coefficients for comparing pairs of models, we found substantial sharing of one core model of Alzheimer's disease.

The intercultural core model

In the following, we summarize this core model under the three headings used to divide the questions in the questionnaire: statements, causes, and treatments. Note that numbers in parentheses following phrases or sentences represent the corresponding number of the item in the questionnaire.

Statements about Alzheimer's disease Alzheimer's is a disease (1) that affects brain cells (2) and involves cognitive decline (3). The symptoms depend on which parts of the brain are affected (33). The disease gets worse over time (9), has several stages (6), and there is no cure (4). Patients can be in the initial stages for many years (28). As a condition, it has been around a long time but used to remain more hidden in families (14). It is not normal for old age (8) and is not the same as "senility" (19). However, the disease is rarely diagnosed in people under 50 years of age (29).

Although it is important to go to the doctor as soon as possible for someone with AD (15), many doctors don't actually know about the disease (25). It cannot be diagnosed with a blood test (10). It is not true that "the only way to know for sure if someone has AD is an autopsy after death" (20).

Alzheimer's disease occurs in all ethnic and racial groups (5), and the risk is equal whether a person does physical or intellectual work (30). It is not a punishment for having lived a bad life (17), people do not get it because it's their destiny (22), and having a good family does not prevent the disease (32). However, keeping busy, like going for walks, playing games, or doing crossword puzzles helps prevent the disease (7). "Being eccentric" and "losing your mind" are inappropriate ways of talking about the disease (24, 21).

Causes of Alzheimer's disease Causes of the disease include: deterioration of the brain (42), neurological problems (49), psychiatric problems (54), and too much stress (66). However, a host of physiological conditions were excluded as causes: diabetes (37), high blood pressure (48), heart disease (50), high cholesterol (59), and chronic illnesses (62). It is not the result of medications taken for other conditions (53), nor a side effect of such medications (65). It is not the result of the following specific stressors: having a difficult life (60), a heavy work schedule (63), a monotonous life (64), loneliness (45), or the "syndrome of tiredness" (68). It is not related to lifestyle factors such as excessive use of alcohol (47), poor diet (52), or lack of exercise (56).

Treatments for Alzheimer's disease There is no cure for the disease (4). None of the following was considered effective: placement in a nursing home (71), use of herbs/roots/tonics/teas (74), alternative healers (79), gingko biloba (80), and making a bargain with God (78).

Intercultural variation around the core model

Table 29.3 lists the beliefs for which there was disagreement. Again, these are listed according to the sections of the survey in which they were found (statements, causes, and treatments). The following discussion of beliefs on which there was model variance is organized by cultural group.

The African American model The African American model included the belief that Alzheimer's disease is a mental illness (11), and that (perhaps by implication) mental activities, such as doing crossword puzzles or reading, would help with behavioral problems associated with Alzheimer's disease (31). Nevertheless, in this model Alzheimer's is clearly a disease entity, distinct from even severe age-associated memory impairment, as is evident in the denial that "When forgetfulness gets really bad, then a person has Alzheimer's disease" (12). Disease causality also confirms both the organic and possibly psychogenic nature of the disease. On the one hand, organic/physical causes include: plaques and tangles, heredity or genetics, stroke, head injury, and high concentrations of aluminum in the brain. On the other hand, psychogenic causes include: nerves or nervous breakdown (46) and experiencing strong emotions or having emotional problems (51). Finally, in terms of appropriate treatments, the model envisages medications (70), prayer (73), and going to a specialist (75).

The Mexican American model It was also true of the Mexican American model that AD is a mental illness (11), and that engaging in mental activities would help with the behavioral problems associated with the disease (31). Further, this model includes the belief that "a positive attitude slows down the process of Alzheimer's disease" (34) and that how the disease affects the individual "depends on their personality" (13). There was no consensus on whether the severity of forgetfulness equates with the disease itself (12), though old age was seen as a cause of the disease (41). Perhaps consistent with the framing of the disease as "mental illness," there was consensus that psychological trauma is a cause of the disease (67). In this regard, it is noteworthy that "plaques and tangles in the brain" (43) were not recognized as a cause. There was consensus on several behavioral treatments: socializing with the person with AD (72), distracting a person with AD from confusing thoughts (76), and changes in diet – more soy, less red meat, more vegetables (81). There was also consensus on biomedical treatments: medications (70), participating in drug trials (77), and going to a specialist (75).

The immigrant/refugee Former Soviet Union model Unlike the other models, the FSU model most clearly favored a biological framing of the disease, clearly distinct

Table 29.3 Items with disagreements across samples

Item	*African Americans*	*Mexican Americans*	*Immigrants/ refugees from FSU*	Statement
Statements about Alzheimer's disease				
11	Y[1]	Y	N	Alzheimer's disease is a mental illness.
12	N	U	N	When forgetfulness gets really bad, a person then has Alzheimer's disease.
13	N	Y	N	How Alzheimer's disease affects a person depends on their personality.
16	Y	U	Y	Doctors will often tell patients that they have dementia rather than Alzheimer's disease.
23	N	U	N	"Talking nonsense" is one way to talk about someone with Alzheimer's disease.
26	N	N	U	"Being bad in the head" is one way of talking about someone with Alzheimer's disease.
31	Y	Y	N	Mental activities, such as doing crossword puzzles or reading, can prevent behavioral problems associated with Alzheimer's disease.
34	N	Y	Y	A positive attitude slows down the process of Alzheimer's disesase.
Causes of Alzheimer's disease				
35	Y	N	N	Head injury or trauma
36	U	N	N	Depression
39	Y	U	U	Stroke
40	U	U	Y	Heredity or genetics
41	Y	Y	U	Old age
43	Y	N	Y	Plaques and tangles in the brain
46	Y	U	Y	Nerves or nervous breakdown
51	Y	N	U	Experiencing strong emotions or having emotional problems
61	Y	U	N	Mental weariness
67	U	Y	Y	Psychological trauma
Treatments of Alzheimer's disease				
70	Y	Y	Y	Medications
72	N	Y	Y	Socializing with a person that has Alzheimer's disease
73	Y	N	N	Prayer
75	Y	Y	Y	Taking the person with Alzheimer's disease to a specialist
76	N	Y	Y	Distracting a person with Alzheimer's disease from confusing thoughts
77	N	Y	Y	Participating in experimental drug trials
81	N	Y	Y	Modify diet, e.g., more soy, less red meat, more vegetables, etc.

[1] Yes/no response calculated at 0.95 level (Bayesian).

from normal aging. In this model, AD is not seen as "mental illness" (11), it is not simply the extension of severe forgetfulness (12), its effects do not depend on a person's personality (13), and mental activities will not ameliorate the behavioral effects of the disease (31). The causes are clearly biological/physical in nature: heredity and/or genetics (4), plaques and tangles (43), and high amounts of aluminum in the brain (58). However, AD may also be caused by nerves or nervous breakdown (46) or psychological trauma (67). Treatments included the same behavioral and lifestyle factors and biomedical factors as the Mexican American model (see above).

Predictors of intracultural variation

We also examined five predictors that might account for interpretable variation in cultural competence scores within each sub-sample. These were demographic factors (age, education, and income), participant experience with the disease, and acculturation. Within the Mexican American sample, younger age ($r = -0.47$, $p < 0.05$) and higher education ($r = 0.58$, $p < 0.05$) were associated with greater knowledge of the cultural model. For FSU refugees, younger age ($r = -0.50$, $p < 0.05$) and higher acculturation ($r = -0.45$, $p < 0.05$) were associated with greater knowledge of the cultural model. Among African Americans, none of the predictors was associated with variance in cultural competence scores.

Discussion

Consensus analysis answers three key questions about cultural models. (1) Does a single cultural model exist for this group of people? (2) What are the "culturally correct" beliefs that constitute the model? (3) What intracultural variation is present in the group concerning knowledge of this model? In this research, we found that African Americans, Mexican Americans, and refugees from the Former Soviet Union possessed a common core model of AD, with high levels of agreement between groups about what beliefs were central to that model. We address below how this core folk model differs from a scientific-clinical model. Analysis also revealed within-group models as well. Of interest here is the differing character of these models – their intercultural variation around the core model. Finally, it is interesting to note that the mean cultural competence scores within each model (reflecting the proportion of answers individuals knew) were moderate – ranging between 0.47 and 0.51. Why this is so requires that we revisit the differences between cultural consensus analysis of ethnic beliefs versus traditional survey approaches. The following sections take up these three themes.

The core model and how it differs from a scientific-clinical model

In many ways, the intercultural core model is largely consistent with a scientific-clinical model. Alzheimer's is seen as a brain-based disease ("deterioration of the brain"), that is associated with, but different from, "normal aging." There is no medical cure and there are no effective folk remedies. It is not particular to any one ethnic group. The disease is not associated with lifestyle issues such as abuse of alcohol, poor diet, or lack of exercise, but in fact physical and mental activity could help prevent the disease.

Nevertheless, the model reflects confusion about causes. On the one hand, the model included the belief that Alzheimer's is caused by "psychiatric problems" and "too much stress," but other specific beliefs were excluded. Alzheimer's is not caused by "having a difficult life," "having a monotonous life," or "loneliness." In contrast to the scientific-clinical model, the core cultural model included the belief that "many doctors do not know about the disease" and denied that "the only way to be sure if someone has Alzheimer's is to do an autopsy after death."

Differences between ethnic group models

One way of framing the differences between the ethnic models is whether or not AD is considered a mental illness. In this regard, the groups seem to fall on a continuum, with both Mexican American and African American models affirming that it *is* a mental illness and the FSU model denying it. At one end of the continuum, the Mexican American model frames the disease primarily in mental or psychological terms vs. physiological or neurological terms. Here, AD is seen as a mental illness, the effects of which are mediated through personality factors. Engaging in mental activities and having a positive attitude slow the progression of the disease. Whether deep forgetfulness signals the disease or is simply a consequence of aging remains questionable, and perhaps most telling, "plaques and tangles" were not recognized as a cause.

At the other end of the continuum, the Russian model denies that AD is a mental illness, and sees it as clearly distinct from deep forgetfulness. Here AD is associated with plaques and tangles, heredity and genetics, and possibly concentrations of aluminum in the brain. However, other causes include nervous breakdown or psychological trauma. The notion that AD is not a mental illness accords with the results of other studies and may have to do with higher levels of education and knowledge about the physiological causes as well as the stigmatization of mental illness during the Soviet era (Shulman and Adams 2002).

Between these two, the African American model affirms that AD is a mental illness, but allows for a range of causes: biological (plaques and tangles, heredity and genetics), physical (head injury, stroke), and psychological (nervous breakdown, emotional problems). In contrast to some previous research, the model of AD found in this sample did not simply conflate dementia with normal aging (e.g., Dilworth-Anderson and Gibson 2002; Jett 2006; Connell et al. 2009). This is not to say that all African Americans typically distinguish between AD and normal aging, but that the model of AD in the community distinguishes them. This point opens onto a discussion of the differences between consensus and survey approaches to community knowledge.

The consensus approach to ethnic beliefs versus the conventional survey approach

At an empirical level, it seems odd that on average the participants knew just less than half the models of their respective communities (African Americans, 0.48; Mexican Americans, 0.46; FSU immigrants/refugees, 0.51). At a theoretical level, we might ask how the cultural consensus approach differs from the usual survey approach to examining knowledge. Answering the former requires addressing the latter.

It is important to remember that the cultural model of the disease in a particular community does not represent what *everyone* knows, but rather what *those people who most agree with one another* know. This is because the "culturally correct" set of answers is determined by examining the pair-wise patterns of agreement on the entire set of beliefs across all group members, and then weighting the answers of participants with highest agreement. The logic is that "the correspondence between the answers of any two informants is a function of the extent to which each is correlated with the truth" (Romney et al. 1986:316). In essence, the fullest articulation of a cultural model comes from "highly agreeing individuals." At any one point in time, however, a sizable proportion of people may not know the whole model. On the ground, of course, knowledge of the experts "comes online" when people actually need the model (i.e., when community members experience AD and need help navigating the experience).

The value of a cultural model resides in the fact that most symptom recognition, lay diagnosis, help-seeking, and treatment adherence take place via collaboration within the local social network. What knowledgeable others believe is likely to have considerable influence over what an individual thinks and does. But not everyone has need of the model at all times, and therefore average group competence may well be only moderate.

By looking at interpretable variation in cultural competence (knowledge) scores, we attempted to locate *where* in the three communities these higher patterns of agreement resided. Regarding knowledge of the disease models for AD, we found that among Mexican Americans higher competence scores were found for younger and more highly educated individuals, but not necessarily those who were more highly acculturated. For FSU refugees, younger and more acculturated individuals were those who knew more of the model. In fact, however, there was little to no variation in educational levels among the FSU refugees, and this may account for our inability to detect an effect. None of our demographic, acculturation, or experience with AD factors was helpful in locating the African American model. This suggests that other factors, unmeasured by us, account for who is "in the know" among African Americans.

It is interesting to note that acculturation, for which we conducted stratified sampling, and for which we had carefully selected measures, was a factor only for FSU refugees. This may be explained by the fact that FSU refugees were a less acculturated group, at least in comparison with the Mexican Americans on the ESI scores (M_{FSU} = 58.01, SD = 7.07; M_{Mex} = 53.97; SD = 63.47; $t(70) = 2.57$, $p < 0.05$), and this may have heightened the influence of the more acculturated individuals.

This research highlights the contribution of the consensus model to the literature on illness cognition. Measuring and comparing between-group knowledge based on individual item scores cannot tell us whether a coherent local model exists. Nor can we probe local models with surveys whose items derive primarily from scientific and/or clinical accounts of the disease. Consensus analysis provides a different picture by deriving items based on community interviews and by deriving the communally "correct" answers based on high agreement across a number of items. This tells us whether there is a fund of knowledge in the social network that would be appropriately available to the group.

On a practical level, this is an important distinction. The cultural consensus model provides a more sophisticated picture of ethnic differences in knowledge about AD by taking seriously two factors. First is the notion that ethnic groups are likely to have their own disease models, which overlap, but are not coterminous, with scientific-clinical models. Second is the notion that these models are not known in their entirety by every member of the community, but are significantly represented by a portion of community members who are highly concordant with one another as to what constitutes the "correct" set of beliefs. From a public health perspective, this would suggest that programs targeted at improving knowledge of the disease and correcting misperceptions could well be more efficient if they were to target individuals in the community who are the primary carriers of the cultural models, on the assumption that these are the individuals through whom corrected information can most credibly circulate.

There are limitations in this study. First, larger samples might give a more accurate picture of mean levels of competence scores (proportion of the model known), but the large amount of variance accounted for by the first factors of the factor analyses suggest that the basic pattern of answers would not change. Second, we looked at a limited number of predictors of cultural competence (age, experience with AD, and acculturation). To provide a more accurate picture of factors predicting variability, it would help to recruit a sample stratified along other dimensions as well. This is especially true of the African American sample, for which none of the predictors that we looked at had an effect.

Conclusion

Based on cultural consensus analysis from cognitive anthropology, we have documented the existence of a core intercultural model of AD that spans the three ethnic communities of the study: African Americans, Mexican Americans, and refugees from the Former Soviet Union. However, each community possesses distinctive framings of the disease that run from an emphasis among Mexican Americans on primarily psychological or mentalistic accounts to an emphasis among FSU immigrants/refugees on primarily neurological and/or physical accounts. African Americans seem to fall between these. We argue that the consensus approach to characterizing knowledge within ethnic communities gives a more sophisticated picture of the distribution of that knowledge within these communities and the factors that might account for that distribution. In effect, we have shown that a coherent set of beliefs can be located within a knowledgeable subset of the community, while others in the community may know only portions of the model. Nevertheless, the knowledge resides in the community, and it is arguable that it comes online when needed. This approach is distinguished by the notion that illness knowledge is not primarily a property of individuals but of social groups. This suggests that health education efforts would perhaps most effectively identify and target those subsets of social groups that are already most knowledgeable about communal models.

ACKNOWLEDGMENTS

This research was supported by the Alzheimer's Association (IIRG-06-26520). Title: Beliefs about Alzheimer's Disease, Dementia, and Aging: Cultural and Social Factors.

REFERENCES

Ayalon, L., and P. A. Areán
2004 Knowledge of Alzheimer's Disease in Four Ethnic Groups. International Journal of Geriatric Psychiatry 19:51–57.
Baer, R. D., S. C. Weller, L. Pachter, R. Trotter, J. G. de Alba García, M. Glazer, R. Klein, T. Lockaby, J. Nichols, R. Parrish, B. Randall, J. Reid, S. W. Morfit, and V. Morfit
1999a Beliefs about AIDS in Five Latin American and Anglo-American Populations: The Role of the Biomedical Model. Anthropology and Medicine 6(1):13–29.
Baer, R. D., S. C. Weller, L. Pachter, R. Trotter, J. G. de Alba García, M. Glazer, R. Klein, L. Deitrick, D. F. Baker, L. F. Brown, K. Khan-Gordon, S. R. Martin, J. Nichols, and J. Ruggerio
1999b Cross-Cultural Perspectives on the Common Cold: Data from Five Populations. Human Organization 58(3):251–260.
Baer, R. D., S. C. Weller, J. G. de Alba García, and A. L. Salcedo Rocha
2004 A Comparison of Community and Physician Explanatory Models of AIDS in Mexico and the United States. Medical Anthropology Quarterly 18(1):3–22.
2008 Cross-Cultural Perspectives on Physician and Lay Models of the Common Cold. Medical Anthropology Quarterly 22(2):148–166.
Barg, F. K., R. Huss-Ashmore, M. N. Wittink, G. F. Murray, H. R. Bogner, and J. J. Gallo
2006 A Mixed-Methods Approach to Understanding Loneliness and Depression in Older Adults. Journals of Gerontology, series B, Psychological Sciences and Social Sciences 61:S329–S339.
Batchelder, William H., and A. Kimball Romney
1988 Test Theory without an Answer Key. Psychometrika 53:71–92.
Berry, John W.
1980 Acculturation as Varieties of Adaptation. *In* Acculturation: Theory, Models, and Some New Findings. A. M. Padilla, ed. Boulder, CO: Westview.
2003 Conceptual Approaches to Acculturation. *In* Acculturation: Advances in Theory, Measurement, and Applied Research. K. M. Chun, P. B. Organista, and G. Marin, eds. Washington, DC: American Psychological Association.
Boster, James S.
1986 Exchange of Varieties and Information between Aguarana Manioc Cultivators. American Anthropologist 88(2):428–436.
Brennan, R. L., and D. J. Prediger
1981 Coefficient Kappa: Some Uses, Misuses, and Alternatives. Educational and Psychological Measurement 41:687–699.
Chavez, L. R., F. A. Hubbell, J. M. McMullin, R. G. Martinez, and S. I. Mishra
1995 Structure and Meaning in Models of Breast and Cervical Cancer Risk Factors: A Comparison of Perceptions among Latinas, Anglo Women, and Physicians. Medical Anthropology Quarterly 9(1):40–74.
Connell, C. M., J. S. Roberts, S. J. McLaughlin, and D. Akinleye
2009 Racial Differences in Knowledge and Beliefs about Alzheimer's Disease. Alzheimer Disease and Associated Disorders 23(2):110–116.
Dilworth-Anderson, P., and B. E. Gibson
2002 The Cultural Influence of Values, Norms, Meanings, and Perceptions in Understanding Dementia in Ethnic Minorities. Alzheimer Disease and Associated Disorders 16(2):S56–S63.
Flanagan, E. H., and R. K. Blashfield
2008 Clinicians' Folk Taxonomies of Mental Disorders. Philosophy, Psychiatry, and Psychology 14(3):249–269.
Guba, E., and Y. Lincoln
1989 Fourth Generation Evaluation. Newbury Park, CA: Sage.

Hinton, L., W. Ladson, and Sue Levkoff
1999 Constructing Alzheimer's: Narratives of Lost Identities, Confusion and Loneliness in Old Age. Culture, Medicine, and Psychiatry 23(4):453–475.
Hinton, L., C. E. Franz, G. Yeo, and S. Levkoff
2005 Conceptions of Dementia in a Multiethnic Sample of Family Caregivers. Journal of the American Geriatrics Society 53:1405–1410.
Hruschka, D. J., L. M. Sibley, N. Kalim, and J. K. Edmonds
2008 When There is More than One Answer Key: Cultural Theories of Postpartum Hemorrhage in Matlab, Bangladesh. Field Methods 20(4):315–337.
Hunt, Linda M., Suzanne Scheider, and Brendon Comer
2004 Should "Acculturation" be a Variable in Health Research? A Critical Review of Research on US Hispanics. Social Science and Medicine 59:973–986.
Hurwicz, Margo-Lea
1995 Physicians' Norms and Health Care Decisions of Elderly Medicare Recipients. Medical Anthropology Quarterly 9(2):211–235.
Jett, K. F.
2006 Mind-Loss in the African American Community: Dementia as a Normal Part of Aging. Journal of Aging Studies 20:1–10.
Kang, Sung-Yeon
2006 Measurement of Acculturation, Scale Formats, and Language Competence. Journal of Cross-Cultural Psychology 37(6):669–693.
Kleinman, Arthur
1980 Patients and Healers in the Context of Culture: An Exploration of the Borderland between Anthropology, Medicine, and Psychiatry. Berkeley: University of California Press.
Landrine, Hope, and Elizabeth A. Klonoff
1994 The African-American Acculturation Scale: Development, Reliablity, and Validity. Journal of Black Psychology 20(2):104–127.
1995 The African-American Acculturation Scale II: Cross-Validation and Short Form. Journal of Black Psychology 21(2):124–152.
Laroche, Michel, Chankon Kim, Michael K. Hui, and Marc A. Tomiuk
1998 Test of a Non-Linear Relationship between Linguistic Acculturation and Ethnic Identification. Journal of Cross-Cultural Psychology 29(3):418–433.
Levkoff, S., W. L. Hinton, J. Simmons, M. Lam, M. Hicks, Z. Guo, J. Hillgus, R. Dunigan, B. Lui, H. Reynoso, R. Levy, S. Fung, and A. Kleinman
1997 A Qualitative Analysis of Dementia Explanatory Models. *In* Alzheimer's Disease: Biology, Diagnosis, and Therapeutics. K. Iqbal, B. Winblad, T. Nishimura, M. Takeda, and H. M. Wisnieski, eds. New York: John Wiley.
Miles, M., and A. Huberman
1994 Qualitative Data Analysis: An Expanded Sourcebook. 2nd edition. Thousand Oaks, CA: Sage.
Moore, R., I. Brodsgaard, M. L. Miller, T.-K. Mao, and S. F. Dworkin
1997 Consensus Analysis: Reliability, Validity, and Informant Accuracy in Use of American and Mandarin Chinese Pain Descriptors. Annals of Behavioral Medicine 19(3):295–300.
Muhr, T.
2004 Atlas.ti: The Knowledge Workbench 5.0. Scientific Software Development, Berlin.
Nyamongo, I. K.
2002 Assessing Intracultural Variability Statistically Using Data on Malaria Perceptions in Gusii, Kenya. Field Methods 14(2):148–160.
Pachter, L., S. C. Weller, R. D. Baer, J. G. de Alba García, R. Trotter II, M. Glazer, and R. Klein
2002 Variations in Asthma Beliefs and Practices among Mainland Puerto Ricans, Mexican-Americans, Mexicans, and Guatemalans. Journal of Asthma 39(2):119–134.

Powers, W. R.
2005 Transcription Techniques for the Spoken Word. Lanham, MD: AltaMira.
Randolph, J.
2005 Free Marginal Multirater Kappa: An Alternative to Fleiss' Fixed Marginal Multivariate Kappa. Paper read at Joensuu University Learning and Instructional Symposium, October 14–15, 2005, Joensuu, Finland.
Ratanasuwan, T., S. Indharapakdi, R. Promrerk, T. Komolviphat, and Y. Thanamai
2005 Health Belief Model about Diabetes Mellitus in Thailand: The Culture Consensus Analysis. Journal of the Medical Association of Thailand 88(5):623–631.
Reiff, J., A. Durkin-Keating, and J. Grossman
2005 Encyclopedia of Chicago. Chicago: Newberry Library.
Roberts, J. S., C. M. Connell, D. Cisewski, Y. G. Hipps, S. Demissie, and R. C. Green
2003 Differences between African Americans and Whites in Their Perceptions of Alzheimer's Disease. Alzheimer Disease and Associated Disorders 17(1):19–26.
Romney, A. K., and C. C. Moore
1998 Toward a Theory of Culture as Shared Cognitive Structures. Ethos 26(3): 314–337.
Romney, A. Kimball, Susan C. Weller, and William H. Batchelder
1986 Culture as Consensus: A Theory of Culture and Informant Accuracy. American Anthropologist 88(2):313–338.
Ryan, G. W., and H. R. Bernard
2003 Techniques to Identify Themes. Field Methods 15(1):85–109.
Schrauf, Robert W.
2002 Comparing Cultures within Subjects: A Cognitive Account of Acculturation as a Framework for Cross-Cultural Study. Anthropological Theory 2(1):101–118.
Shulman, N., and B. Adams
2002 A Comparison of Russian and British Attitudes towards Mental Health Problems in the Community. International Journal of Social Psychiatry 48(4):266–278.
Skelton, J. A., and R. T. Croyle, eds.
1991 Mental Representations in Health and Illness. New York: Springer.
Spradley, James P.
1979 The Ethnographic Interview. New York: Holt, Rinehart and Winston.
Stephenson, M.
2000 Development and Validation of the Stephenson Multigroup Acculturation Scale (SMAS). Psychological Assessment 12(1):77–88.
Swora, M. G.
2003 Using Cultural Consensus Analysis to Study Sexual Risk Perception: A Report on a Pilot Study. Culture, Health, and Sexuality 5(4):339–352.
Weller, S.
1987 Shared Knowledge, Intracultural Variation, and Knowledge Aggregation. American Behavioral Scientist 31(2):178–193.
2007 Cultural Consensus Theory: Applications and Frequently Asked Questions. Field Methods 19(4):339–368.
Weller, S., and R. D. Baer
2002 Measuring Within- and Between-Group Agreement: Identifying the Proportion of Shared and Unique Beliefs across Samples. Field Methods 14(1):6–25.
Weller, S., and N. C. Mann
1997 Assessing Rater Performance without a "Gold Standard" Using Consensus Theory. Medical Decision Making 17(1):71–79.
Werner, O.
1997 Short Take 21: Multistage Translation. Cultural Anthropology Methods 9(1):10–11.

Afterword
One Cognitive View of Culture

David B. Kronenfeld

Introduction

I want to lay out a picture of how collective knowledge systems work and how they differ from individual knowledge.[1] By "knowledge" I mean not just the usual kind of intellectual knowledge that the term often betokens. I mean, as well, the knowledge we have of how to act in some situation, given one or another goal. I mean our knowledge of what are reasonable or possible goals, our knowledge of how to interpret the actions of those around us, our understanding of the goals and values that are likely to be guiding the actions of others, and our understanding of the implications of someone's choice of one or another course of action. Included also are the values that one's society recognizes, the ways those are generally interpreted, and how or under what conditions they are likely to be flouted. That is, I am talking about knowledge that may be consciously or unconsciously held, that makes up a cultural system, and that guides a social system.

Involved here is a theoretical conception of "culture" and of what it does for us that makes it worth having. That worth has to do with enabling collective action that is based on varyingly complex divisions of labor. It is the participation in shared cultural knowledge systems (including behavior, values, goals, etc.) that defines social entities. Culture, thus, is constitutive of society. At the same time, as we shall see, it is the interaction patterns of social entities that produce shared cultural knowledge. Society, thus, is equally constitutive of culture.

Since cultural and linguistic systems entail a variety of subcultural or dialectical sub-systems – in some number of which we each participate – questions arise. How do we learn the productive systems with their productive variants? How do we keep

A Companion to Cognitive Anthropology, First Edition. Edited by David B. Kronenfeld, Giovanni Bennardo, Victor C. de Munck, and Michael D. Fischer.

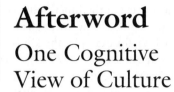

the variants and their essential interrelatedness straight in our minds? How does synchronic flexibility of application lead to diachronic change?

I address some basic aspects of the functioning of both language and culture. I am concerned with concepts – not simply vocabulary but also action concepts and conceptual structures – such as, for example, the kinds of regularities and understandings captured by Schank and Abelson's (1977) restaurant scenarios (see below). The approach I lay out applies to collective cognitive structures in general – including the pragmatic knowledge systems of various sorts that make up culture. These latter systems are differentially distributed, such that different individual members of the relevant community have varying mixes of overlapping and contrasting knowledge, and no single person knows it all.

I am not directly addressing the relationship between language and culture here (though I have addressed it elsewhere – see Kronenfeld 1996, 2000), but I do want to offer an observation that may prove useful. As I see it, culture – in contrast to language – is not a single coherent system, but rather a congeries of varyingly autonomous and varyingly complex component systems – Lowie's "thing of shreds and patches."[2] I want to emphasize that culture is not monolithic; pieces from different cultures are often mixed and matched. Language, then, can be seen as a much more coherent and complex system that either contrasts with culture or forms a major component of it.

Not all parts of what follows are new, and some even are old hat; what is important is how they all, together, form a package.

Collective – Differentially Distributed – Cognitive Structures

Going back at least to Durkheim and Saussure we have been aware of the idea of "collective representations" – knowledge systems that are properties of groups or communities, and thus shared among members of relevant groups. These collective systems include both linguistic and cultural knowledge. As treated by Durkheim and Saussure, these systems represented "emergent properties" of the relevant groups, in the sense that they were not seen as simply individual knowledge writ large. While sometimes dismissed as mystical, these asserted systems were empirical, and lived in the individual representations of collective group knowledge that members of the relevant groups formed, based on their interactions with other members of the group. These emergent systems thus represented a kind of social distillation of the regularities that characterized interactions within each of the various communities in which individuals participated. This distillation had to produce productive systems, since the actual specific content was too variegated and situationally relevant to allow any simple rote learning. Groups were perceived as supra-individual entities, and knowledge, behavior, values, et cetera were seen as characterizing these groups. These emergent systems differed from related individual knowledge, because the process of their formation, organization, and transmission filtered out the idiosyncrasies of individual knowledge, including the idiosyncrasies of each of our representations of other individuals.

Such systems have sometimes been considered to be merely epiphenomenal – that is, to have no actual direct existence, but only the appearance of such existence insofar as they are the by-products of a collection of individuals with similar minds confronting similar situations in similar contexts. The problem with this view is, first, that we, as natives, talk about and rely upon language and culture as if they actually exist, and exist externally to us as individuals. Second, our individual understandings of these shared systems are quite consistent across individuals – more so than are our senses of our own individual patterns. That is, we not only have highly shared senses of the collective patterns, but also are each capable of describing how we ourselves deviate or are a bit idiosyncratic. Part of my evidence for this distinction between the individual and the individually known collective is our awareness of personal linguistic usages that we each have and know we have which are not part of the normal everyday language of our community – that is English for me.[3] Similarly, many informants of mine have noted that there exist "rules" for kinds of cousins in English without themselves knowing these rules, and sometimes these informants actually know one or the other rule system, but don't themselves use it.

My claim is that culture and language are technically epiphenomenal (and thus, in any strong sense – from an external analytic point of view – non-existent), but that we each as individuals ("native" participants in an analyzed community) rely upon them as if they actually exist. It is the combination of shared experiences by shared minds in shared contexts (spoken of above) and interactive and communicative interdependence that keeps these individual representations close enough to one another to function as single systems distributed across many individuals. "Close enough" is a function of a variety of collective and interactive factors, including density of interaction, interdependence, focus, logical or emotional relevance, relation to goals, and so forth. What makes my position different from the "culture and language are merely epiphenomenal" position described above is my claim that we, as native participants, have a strong innate disposition to see collectivities as if they were super-organic entities (that is, if you will, to anthropomorphize them) and to ascribe to these entities the properties that we see as associated with the given group of people. However, we – again, as native participants – do *not ever* see ourselves (from a first-person perspective) as being intrinsically part of any such super-organic collectivity.

Traditionally, holders of the view that culture is "real" have dealt with the problem of the relationship between the individual and the collectivity by seeing a child's socialization or enculturation as a process by which basic cultural structures and propositions were "internalized" – inserted deeply into the individual psyche. The problem with this approach is the cultural analog of code-switching between languages. We all seem capable of learning some variety of cultural systems and of switching between them as events require. And we seem capable of learning such systems well past any period of childhood socialization (even if the quality and completeness of such later learning depends on various factors, including the effort expended and the degree to which specific differences of the newer system from the initial childhood system are actually focused on). Thus, such cultural knowledge seems unlikely to be deeply embedded in anyone's psyche or to be deeply constitutive of anyone's inner "self" (whatever such a "self" might turn out to be).

These collective knowledge systems are learned, but usually not explicitly taught. That is, they are inferred by learners from their observation of and interaction with members of the relevant communities. The learning is not any careful logical induction, but is a matter of looking for some pattern, leaping to some generalization about it, and applying that generalization. If the application works, great; if not, then another one gets leapt to. Thus the learning is constrained by the communicative and interactional patterns of the group.

From the beginning, the learning is not memorization but consists of trial pattern generalizations (codable as "rules" by external analysts, but not learned or applied in such a form); the learning always applies to an open class of cases, rather than only narrowly to the cases on which it is based. What is being learned is a pattern which is ascribed to the members of some group. What ties the pattern to the given group is repeated use by members of the group and it is the line between users and non-users of the pattern that defines the relevant group. It takes an adequate frequency of use by group members to get the pattern recognized and learned in the first place. The extent of the pattern and its internal structure depend on how both it and parts of it get used within the group – and on what it has (or doesn't have) in common with the usage of members of related groups (either the super-ordinate groups that include the group in question or neighboring groups that contrast with it).

The pattern learned, then, is based on experienced usage, and as usage changes – whether through changes in technology or in social organization or fashion or whatever – the experienced pattern and the generalizations drawn from that experience by new learners change. For example, we can consider changes in the reference of the word "calculator." A century ago it was simply the agentive form of "calculate" – "a person who performs calculations"; this meaning is still seen in dictionaries from the 1950s. Presently, of course, the word refers primarily to the small (personal) digital electronic device that performs various mathematical calculations. Similarly, the word "corn" used to mean grain in general, but now (in American English) refers primarily to *Zea mays.* And finally, the kin term applied in English to close friends has shifted from the "cousin" (or "cuz") of Elizabethan times to our present "brother" or "sister." I note that such shared semantic references are not necessarily slavishly or literally followed but can be made use of in creative and nuanced ways; that is, they can be played against (as in ironic usage), utilized for their tonal implications (as in using kinterms for religious leaders), and so forth, as long as context and presumed shared knowledge seem adequate to produce understanding.

The constraint on creativity is what successfully communicates. My wife is a poet. Poetry – at least to some degree – depends on establishing some kind of pattern or rhythm of sound or meaning, and then playing off that pattern in some way that adds meaning and focus. Too regular a pattern produces boredom (or doggerel), while too little pattern can come across as ordinary prose or white noise. The problem is that the pattern constraint varies across individuals. Thus, early in our marriage, the poetic patterns that struck her as live and stimulating often came across to me as white noise – my expectations ("ear," if you will) were not educated enough to recognize the patterns that she heard. Conversely, it was often the case that poetry which I liked struck her as boring and dull (if, mostly, not quite doggerel) – a pattern had to be pretty heavy before I reliably picked up on it!

Semantics and Pragmatics

In a general sense semantics and pragmatics together make up what we commonly speak of as "meaning" in language. Of the two, semantics deals specifically and narrowly with linguistic meaning, while pragmatics refers to broader senses of meaning.

Semantics breaks up into syntactic meaning and lexical or word meaning. For this discussion I focus on lexical meaning.

In general usage, pragmatic meaning is understood as whatever meaning is left over when one finishes one's consideration of semantic meaning. If one has an actual, specific semantic theory, then the line between semantics and pragmatics can be a sharp one, but if one has no theory or is simply considering the range of semantic meanings that different scholars variously offer, then the line is necessarily muddy. In *Plastic Glasses and Church Fathers* (1996) I have offered a specific semantic theory, and thus have suggested a clear division between semantics and pragmatics. In addition, in *Culture, Society, and Cognition* (2008b) I have offered an independent case for what pragmatic meaning might be seen as and what different tasks semantics and pragmatics each accomplish.

In my theory semantics has to do with the Saussurean (and ethnoscience) relations of contrast and inclusion – X as opposed to what Y? What other Xs are similarly opposed to Y; is there a cover term, Z, for those Xs? What is the difference between X_1 and X_2? What other Xs differ from one another in the same way as X_1 vs. X_2? And so forth. These are the kind of relationships that were picked up in linguistic anthropology by componential analysis and by much work on folk taxonomic systems. For instance, in the domain of furniture, semantics is concerned with: How do dining chairs differ from recliners? How do chairs differ from tables, and dining tables from end tables?

Pragmatics, in this view, has to do with how conceptual entities fit together in systems. Dining chairs are commonly used with dining tables, under which their seats fit, in a dining room, while recliners and end tables both go in living rooms or dens, sometimes next to each other. Dining chairs tend to have a straight back and a relatively hard seat and back, while recliners have softer seats and backs.

In kinship the feature differences between uncle and cousin – generation and lineality – are semantic. In contrast, the genealogical relationship between them – the fact that, in English, the child of an uncle is a cousin (as is the child of a cousin) – is pragmatic. In kinship the basic determination of what kinterm category a person belongs in is based on pragmatic relations, but the knowledge that speakers use to reason about attributes of kinfolk or about the extension of kinterms to non-kin is based on semantic features. Kinship terms have been much analyzed from both perspectives (see Kronenfeld 2009).

The semantics of language seems isolatable from the rest of culture, but the kinds of knowledge on which our pragmatic sense of word meanings can be based potentially reach seamlessly into any facet of culture. What we mean when we speak of someone as a "brother" depends not only on sameness of sex and similarity of relative age between that person and a real brother, but also on the cultural situation of use – whether the speaker is referring to a fellow participant in a religious or political meeting, or talking about a tight chum, or speaking of a monk. What we mean also depends on the conclusions that are to be understood from the use of the term – for example, committed general support of the group endeavor, or strong identification with a friend, or a ritualized expression of religious respect. Some of these distinctions are marked linguistically (*my* brother vs. *a* brother) but others are not; in general, there is no substitute for cultural knowledge – even if some knowledge, like much (though certainly not all) of how kin behave to one another, is pretty common across all cultures, while other knowledge – such as theories of the origin of the universe – can be quite variable across cultures.

"Culture" as Shared Differentially Distributed Pragmatic Knowledge

Communal – differentially shared – pragmatic knowledge consists of everything we need to know of the socially constructed or coded world in order to participate in linguistic and other interactions; it is hard to see what else "culture" *could* consist of – if "culture" refers to the knowledge that enables us to behave appropriately in one or another particular community (and to produce the artifacts associated with that culture). Yes, the range of pragmatic knowledge required for the understanding of any particular communication or interaction falls far short of the totality of culture. But it seems impossible to draw any hard line separating out any particular section of culture which clearly will *never* be relevant to any communication. Similarly, it also seems hard to separate the pragmatic meaning of communicative systems (such as language, proxemics, gesture, and so forth) and from the pragmatics of any kind of interactively based collective action.

The Requirements of Flexibility

The requirements of flexibility across novel situations (all situations are always novel in some way) mean that these shared cognitive systems cannot be learned as memorized lists of actions (or items) but have to be learned (individually reconstructed by each new learner) as productive systems which members of pertinent communities can use to reason to new applications. This productive applicability is what is sometimes spoken of as "generative capacity." Many such systems, including some of the most basic (such as those of natural language and of everyday culture), have to be simple enough for a three-year-old to learn the basics of, and for an average pre-teen to have reasonable competence in.

The requirements of productivity and ease of learning both demand systems that are simple for new learners to infer and provide a biased transmission filter that moves systems – across successive learners – toward such simplicity. Studies of initial learning of new systems should then provide important insights into underlying patterns and allow us to explore what in normal usage accounts for the patterns that learners pick out as basic. It should be similarly instructive to see how complexity and subtlety then get added in. I know that such research itself is old and common; I only want to emphasize the relevance of such research on learning to our understanding of the systems themselves and to suggest an analytic angle from which research on the learning of systems might be approached or interpreted.

The Role Culture Plays in Regard to Society and Social Living

There exist at least two not unrelated roles that culture plays for society. First, it provides the particulars that enable us to recognize other members of any given social system and distinguish them from non-members. Second, it provides the conceptual overhead that enables the division of labor in society, especially the attendant levels of cooperation that are required for that division.

The first role of culture for society – its provision of what it is that enables us to recognize other members of any given social unit – is crucial, and constitutive, for society. A society – whether an independent social unit or a sub-unit of some larger unit – is an emergent collective entity. That is, it is not just an incidental collection of people, but it is a unit – a group that exhibits some activity as a unit; a given unit can be split, in turn, into categories as well as into sub-groups. The way in which we recognize other members of social units that we belong to, or members of other connected units, is via the reliance of these people on some shared knowledge that enables them to behave jointly in some coherent manner.

The second role of culture for society – its provision of the conceptual overhead that enables the division of labor in society – can be seen in a consideration of the idea in computer science of getting a bunch of little computers linked together so that they perform like – "simulate," if you will – a supercomputer. The computing problem crucially involves the social distribution of knowledge; the problem is to divide up the overall computational task into sub-tasks and then allocate these sub-tasks in an efficient manner such that each little computer is working efficiently and coordinating its input needs and output results effectively in real time with computers that are providing its input and to which it is providing input. Additionally, the system has to be flexible enough to continue functioning even when some particular computer breaks down or takes unexpectedly long on a task. "Master–slave" structures were tried by programming engineers, in which some central computer allocated tasks to the others. But something significant always screwed up. Even dynamic interactive versions of the master–slave approach did not work – no programmer was smart enough (and no one computer had adequate data) to anticipate all problems that might arise and how they might be solved. So the analytic solution that emerged was one in which the little computers *negotiated* their coordination between themselves – what is called parallel distributed processing. But this solution required that the computers each have some knowledge about the overall task and how their particular sub-tasks related to it; different computers needed different levels of knowledge, depending on how much coordination (vs. simple calculation) they were doing. This solution also required that neighboring computers have varyingly overlapping knowledge, so that one could fill in for another if that other went out of commission or just got bogged down unexpectedly in some task. And the computers had to "converse" enough among themselves to monitor the status of relevant tasks being executed by neighbors. It was a division of labor that was built on a plan, with default operations, but in which a myriad of details were continually being negotiated on the fly.

People are not computers. But the problems involved in the simulation of a supercomputer are also crucial for the organization and structure of society. The kind of knowledge-based division of labor that I am speaking of can be seen in the prosaic activity of house-building in the USA. Functional roles include structural engineer, contractor, carpenter, plumber, electrician, cement guy, wallboard guy, wood-floor installer, tile guy, roofer, heating and air-conditioning guy, stucco guy, and so forth. Often, especially on a job as small as the room that we recently added to our house, one person will fill several of these roles. There are no firm rules about such overlapping roles. The contractor is central. Contractors generally have to have basic knowledge of carpentry, plumbing, cement work, roofing, and wiring, and to be capable of doing at least simple work in these areas. In home construction contractors will often but not always have started as carpenters, and so take on the carpentry role. But they can come from other areas, such as appliance installation or cabinetry. The actual role overlap on any particular job by any particular person depends in part on which skills the given person happens to have picked up over past jobs, and in part on the cost and scheduling problems associated with bringing in a specialist. The more complicated the particular instance is, the more likely it is that a specialist will be brought in. Some of the relevant knowledge comes from classes, but much of it comes from apprenticeship or from working with specialist friends on joint jobs, and much is inarticulately learned – that is, not learned through language and not easily expressed by its holder in language. What we have in this example is a distributed knowledge structure in which no one participant has complete knowledge of the component tasks and in which the details of who does what – how and when – have to be continually negotiated on the job in real time.[4]

The Role Social Groups Play in Culture

The knowledge that makes up culture is learned but, for the most part without its being actively taught. We pick it up from our experience with people around us. As we pick up patterns of behavior and other information we begin to notice that some people do some things one way while other people do related things another way – and we begin the process of learning and sorting out the various groups in which we participate or which we otherwise encounter. Thus, the social groups which we encounter structure our learning of culture and of the various subcultures that make up our cultural universe. Cultural content and cultural differences come with no predetermined tags or categorizations; our cultural knowledge comes out of social interactions and our understanding (and construction) of cultural differences comes out of that same experience. The mutual constitutivity of culture and society applies not just to them as inclusive framing units, but also to all of the particular subcultural and subsocietal entities in which we participate or which we encounter.

We each belong to, for example, occupational groups, neighborhoods, political groups, ecological groups, religious groups, and so forth. Some of these are tight, formally defined groups, while others are looser ones consisting of people with whom we more incidentally interact, but with whom we share views and a recognized stake. Each of these groups comes with its own presuppositions about what matters, what is good or bad, how one goes about accomplishing relevant ends, who matters, and so forth – all of which is pragmatic cultural information.

The social perspective on culture has a long history, starting with Durkheim's work and continuing more recently through Dan Sperber's (1996) epidemiological approach to culture up to Douglas White's current sophisticated use of network theory (Chapter 18, this volume). I have done no network-based research myself, but do want to underscore the potential importance of network properties to our understanding of cultural systems. That is, culture is something that we, in some sense, "catch" from others, and the more we can find out about the conditions which facilitate or inhibit its transmission, and about the patterns produced by these factors, the better will be our understanding of this and other shared cognitive systems.

Our Social Universe is Made Up of a Multiplicity of Overlapping Social Groups

There are several consequences of this multiplicity and overlap. First, all individuals – each of us – do much "code-switching" between different subcultural (and dialectical) groups even if not between full-blown cultures (or languages). That is, we move from a neighborhood community to a workplace one, often with a different way of talking and different conversational and interactive presuppositions. The driving personality that it takes to get ahead at work might, for instance, not be attractive in interactions with one's neighbors. And the passionate advocacy which might drive one's participation in political groups entails a different persona than that easy-going and friendly persona one's neighbors know. The point is that these various settings, including our own individual roles and personae in them, are socially constructed collective entities. I don't mean that we don't also each have our own individual characteristics that run consistently through our participation in these various settings, but that the behavior and knowledge we exhibit in each setting is a combination of the individual and the collective.

A second consequence of our membership in multiple overlapping groups is that no one of us is a pure (privileged or intrinsic) exemplar of any such group! That is, the old and classic anthropological goal of finding and working with the ideal informant, one who had the privileged position of knowing all of the "true" culture, is impossible. Such a person does not and cannot exist. The culture itself, like Saussure's *langue*, is the collective system of which all participating individuals know, and the content of which they each know varying amounts. *Each* of these individuals has a representation of each collectivity they participate in or know of as an entity outside themselves – even the ones with which they most closely identify.

Thus, a third consequence of our membership in multiple overlapping groups is that all social groups are made up *totally* and *only* of what can be seen as heterogeneous collections of outsiders looking in, even if some groups are more heterogeneous than others and even if some members are further outside than others. These members also, at the same time, each belong to other groups, sometimes contrasting – or even actively opposed – ones. For example, in the fairly homogeneous "Bible Belt" southern Appalachian community that I spent my high school years in, moonshiners (illegal whiskey distillers, sellers, and often consumers) participated actively in fundamentalist churches that damned the evils of alcohol. I heartily participated in religious and secular youth groups that held sometimes contradictory goals or values. And I could go on. My point here is that even in a small, relatively isolated, and homogeneous rural community in a traditional backwater, the kind of code-switching that I am talking about took place, and that even here groups (including the most basic ones) were made up completely of people who were not simply *of* the group. The collectivities each had a consistent reality that transcended the particular individuals who happened to be making it up at any given moment.

As an analogy, think of a wave coming in toward shore and think of the molecules of water that make it up. The wave is real and dynamically moving. The molecules are also real and dynamically moving. But no *one* molecule is intrinsic to the wave or moves for long with it. Each molecule moves in a more or less circular or oval pattern in a given place; each gets drawn into the wave as the wave passes by, extending or compressing its ambit to fit the passing wave, *but* the complete wave is made up *totally* and *only* of such molecules. The movement of the wave is an emergent phenomenon much like the emergent phenomena that we call language, culture, and society.[5]

Prototype Extension: The Basis of the Application of Shared Concepts to the Experienced and Imagined World

In 1996 I proposed that semantic reference – what in the world words refer to – is in general a two-level system involving the contrast between primary prototypic referents and more peripheral extended referents.[6] My approach derived from early work by Berlin and Kay (1969) on color terms by Lounsbury (1964a, 1964b) on kinterms, and by Berlin (1972, and see 1992) on ethnobiological terms.[7] I now want quickly to sketch out my theory of semantic reference. I want to suggest that this prototype extension approach applies to the reference of concepts in general, and not only to the referential semantics of words, and thus to culture as well as to language.

Whether one looks at perception (say, of colors, or of plant or animal variations), or at actions, or at artifact classifications (e.g., of tools), it is clear that we are able to distinguish many more variants than we have separate words to label. A big part of the word "semantics" concerns how we are able to use old words for new things or for new variants of old things. The means for dealing with variability and novelty seem to involve a two-tier system of reference: words are both tied tightly to prototypic referents, and extended productively from those prototypes on a variety of bases to a range of other referents. Prototypic referents are the referents that normally and cleanly fulfill the functional tasks whose frequency in conversation produces and maintains the terminological categories in the language; they satisfy what are felt to be the essential properties of the word category. "Cleanly" refers both to the cleanness with which the given referent fulfills the relevant functional task and to the cleanness with which a prospective prototype fits into the pattern of contrasts within the paradigm of prototypes of contrasting terms. Thus, the prototype is not simply the most common referent, but is the one that best exemplifies the functions of the term's referent. Prototypic referents have variously been spoken of in the literature as "kernel," "focal," "real," and "core" referents.

Within the prototype's domain, extension can be based on similarity of denotative form, or of connotative function, or of both. Outside that domain, figurative extension relates the semantic opposition within the source domain to the perceptual or experiential oppositions of the target domain, and then extends the particular term from the source domain that either best distinguishes the target entity or that comes closest to putting the desired interpretation on it. Figurative extension to a given target thus involves a two-stage process – picking the desired source domain (given one's communicative goals) and then picking the best category within that domain.

The process of semantic extension relates to the Saussurean semantic task of distinguishing the referents of one term from the referents of another – that is, finding relations of contrast and inclusion. But, beyond such narrowly semantic concerns, our use of words depends on additional, shared pragmatic knowledge, including the functional importance of actions, items, or qualities which lead to these prototypic referents getting their own terms, and including the functional relations that exist between the members of a contrast set (hammers and nails, legs and feet, running and walking, fathers and mothers, loving and liking, and so forth).

Our individual pragmatic knowledge is not necessarily shared. We each have rich individual experiences and the cognitive structuring that pertains to them, whether coded linguistically or not. When we do anything with other people, including talking(!), it is necessary to interrelate our separate cognitive structures; and when we routinely do something with a variety of others we will tend to develop some standardized way of doing it – where "standardized" refers to categories of actions, items, acceptable results, and so forth. These shared action plans emerge as cultural models. Language gets involved only when we need to communicate verbally, and then only with regard to those aspects of the action plan that need to be talked about or coded in memory.

From my perspective, all words imply referents (even if, as with unicorns, the referents are sometimes only hypothetical) and all words imply some sort of focal or prototypic situation that involves semantic contrasts and pragmatic functional relations. At the same time, we also have much shared knowledge that we do not have explicit terms for. Some of this knowledge can be paraphrastically described, some has first to be raised to consciousness before it can be talked about, and some may well be beyond words (for example, the coordination involved in paddling a two-person canoe). In my theory, then, language is a socially constructed tool. It is a tool that can be exceedingly helpful (and even important) to thought, but in no sense does it form the basis for individual thought, and it need not provide the basis for much of the shared or coordinated thought that makes up culture.

In my prototype extension approach to semantics a distinctive feature semantic analysis applies to the prototypic referents of contrasting terms, but not necessarily to extended referents. Similarly, what philosophers have spoken of as "essential" attributes of a term's reference necessarily apply only to prototypic referents. Prototypic referents are default referents in the sense of being presumed in the absence of any specific information to the contrary. Their default status is reflected in informant answers to questions such as "Describe an X," "Tell me about your X," or "How do you X?" where X is the term in question. Verbs, nouns, adjectives, and other content words all have prototypic referents.

In many cases extended referents may be labeled by either of the contrasting terms that bracket them, depending on the relevant context and communicative goals. For instance, in classroom experiments, "Get me the red shirt" elicits the reddest shirt among the population from which the choice is being made, similarly for "Get me the orange shirt." By changing the make-up of the set of objects that form the context of selection, I can structure things such that both questions elicit the same shirt. But this shifting categorization will not be possible with shirts that are prototypically red or orange.

Depending on the category in question and on its definitional basis, some referents can be "real" referents without being *the* "real" referent. Thus, in Fanti, one's mother's sister is really a "mother" of ego, but is not ego's "real mother." This contrasts with a close family friend of one's mother's age who, in Fanti, can be called "mother" in courtesy or honorific usage, but is not really a "mother" of ego.

Cultural Knowledge Systems

I turn now to cultural knowledge systems. Chapter 5 of this volume contains a discussion of the variety of such systems, of what they do, and of how they work. Here I want to mention only two of these kinds of shared differentially distributed cognitive structures that are particularly germane to my present discussion

The first, *cultural conceptual systems* (CCS) are reference structures defining how systems of terms referring to entities in the world go together. The second, *cultural models of action* (CMA) are models of how to act in given situations.

The distinction between cultural conceptual systems and action was made clear years ago by Frake (1961) in his article on Subanun disease, where he showed how knowledge of the Subanun classification of diseases and of the diagnostic criteria for each was not sufficient to predict a specific actual diagnosis. This was partly because of problems associated with the concrete interpretation or recognition of an instance of something like "severe redness." It was also because diagnostic decisions often took account, where criteria were ambiguous, of the consequences of alternative diagnoses – and of who preferred which outcome for what reason. The specificity of diagnoses could also vary according to interpersonal factors that pushed in one or another direction – for example, as in the difference between answering a "what is this?" query with "eczema" or with "a skin rash."

In the use of kinterms (a CCS) similar application issues arise. What alternatives do the rules of the formal system and the nature of relevant genealogical links provide? For English, "the nature of genealogical links" refers to genealogical distance and to the presence or absence of alternative paths connecting the given pair of possible kinfolk. When does one feel tied to the correct formal system versus being free to use some alternative, less formal system? As an example, take the case of a person who is technically a child's "cousin" but who is the child's mother's age and whom the child frequently interacts with – and whom the child might call or address as "aunt." Similarly, an "aunt" of one's own age is likely to be treated (and addressed) more as a cousin.

CMA include not just action models themselves, but also the implications of alternative actions, and the effects of relevant social variation (such as gender, class, subculture, etc.) – as well as variation in personal and cultural values, personal dispositions, and so forth. Such models have been an important recent research interest of mine.

CMA provide a kind of "kit-bag" of scenarios keyed to kinds of understandings or goals that individuals bring to any given situation. The choice is driven by a variety of factors and can depend on such things as the credibility with which one can play relevant roles, the alternative outcomes different choices lead to, the degree of similarity of the application situation to the prototypic situation for the given cultural model, and so forth. Nothing guarantees that the different individuals involved in a given situation will all be working off the same CMA, but they will have to mutually adjust (or negotiate) their separate models in order to ensure the desired degree of mutual interpretability and interactive reciprocity.

CMA are not learned directly as models (from any kind of central repository – since none such exists), but are inferred anew by each of us from what we see and experience with those around us. But what we see and experience are never the models themselves – any more than the speech acts we experience are directly equivalent to *langue*. In both cases we infer the "code" from our experience of messages. Therefore, the exact form of the code that we infer depends directly on what parts of it are sufficiently saliently and repetitively present in our world of experience for us to pull out the regularities on which we will base our construction of the code behind them. Thus systematic and repeated novelties in speech or cultural behavior in one generation will be learned by the next generation as part of the givens of *langue* or culture.

In sum, action is always by individuals, and individuals are always adapting cultural forms to fit their needs. Individuals use CMA as devices to enable effective interaction with other individuals in the various communities to which they belong. Most of these models come from their past experience, but new groups and new situations always require some creativity, and interactive creations which catch on and are repeated from the basis of new or adapted cultural models. They can (and often do) exhibit nuanced variations across groups to which we all belong – whether the groups be formal or informal, long-lived or evanescent, imposed or voluntary, and so forth.

Flexibility and Variability

The flexibility and variability that we find among individual representations of collective knowledge structures are important to the functional adaptation of these structures to the needs of their holders. Since, at a sufficiently detailed level, each learner gets exposed to a somewhat different sample of instances (within the context of any given social group), she or he may infer a slightly different individual representation of the presumed collective system. Such variation works as long as the behavior and expectations thereby produced are not too discordant. This looseness is part of what enables linguistic drift and what enables language and culture to track changing technology and social forms.

As an example consider the focal or prototypic example of a writing "pen." In the contemporary world, and for my students as well as my own children, that prototype is a kind of ball-point pen. But for me it is a little different. When I learned the word "pen" ball-points were either non-existent or rare, and for a while after their introduction they were messy to use. Fountain pens were the dominant type. By the time I was in high school the ball-points were becoming common, but without their present variety and sophistication, and fountain pens were still felt to produce a better and better-controlled line. So, for me the prototypic pen was a fountain pen, and it still is. Communication still works fine because, for me, ball-points are a common basic type of pen, while my students and children recognize fountain pens as a slightly archaic type (compared, say, to deeply archaic quills). Additionally, I might note that for a while it seemed that felt-tips might enter the fray, but, while still around, they never became dominant – perhaps because they dried out too quickly.

The constraints of intergenerational communication and effective intergenerational cooperation are important factors in keeping most words or other collective concepts from changing too rapidly. "Most" is my hedge for the occasional situation where some people (normally the kids) push change that is deep enough and rapid enough to lose outsiders (for example, parents who have not yet picked up texting).[8]

CONCLUSION

Basically, I am making an argument about culture – what it is and what it does. The subject is an old one in anthropology, and one which has mostly been dealt with via one or another simple abstraction that claimed everything while saying not much. For much of my professional life I had assumed that "culture" had no technical meaning, but was merely used to speak of whatever one or another anthropologist happened to study. The abstractions – for example, the 162 definitions compiled by Kroeber and Kluckhohn from the statements of a range of anthropologists – were often neither silly nor wrong, but so unworked out as to seem meaningless. The complexity of what I have talked of in this chapter, but have not had the time to go into in any detail, follows from an attempt to seriously work through the conceptions that have been offered for culture and the claims that have been made about it. I came to realize that, whatever we choose to call it, something complex and systematic has to be doing the organizing and coordinating that has been credited to culture. And then I began to try to work through the specifics of what culture might be doing, and how. The progression of topics that I have offered all seem to me essential if we are to understand how what we speak of as culture could have the scope and effects that we ascribe to it.

NOTES

1 This Afterword is adapted from a paper presented at the 34th International Laud Symposium, Landau, Germany, March 15–18, 2010, and a version of that paper is to be published in a volume of papers from the symposium. Significant portions of that paper were taken from Kronenfeld 2008a.

2 Lowie's (1920:441) phrase goes back through Gilbert and Sullivan's *Mikado* to Shakespeare's "a king of shreds and patches" in *Hamlet*!

3 Here I am not referring to the kind of "correct English" that I, like many other Americans, was taught in school, but to the sense we gain of the ordinary language of the community around us.

4 Contrary to what some people might think, the structural engineer (or architect) does not know it all either – cannot anticipate it all and lacks knowledge of many of the tricks of the trade that get used on the job.

5 The idea behind this example was suggested to me by Bateson's (1958[1938]) treatment of the relationship between the individual and the collective in *Naven*.

6 "In general" means normally for natural language, but certainly there exist technical terms that do not work this way.

7 Aspects of Berlin and Kay's work were picked up on and expanded by Eleanor Rosch in psychology.

8 Initial learning contexts seem important because in the normal course of events it is the initial learning situation (what's learned, where it's learned, and how it's organized) that produces our basic mental framework for any given conceptual domain, and subsequent learning is adapted to that framework. I think this is generally true across linguistic and cultural constructions (including, for the former, phonology, grammar, and semantic reference). As an illustration I would like to offer a case from my own personal pragmatic experience.

When I was young I read a book in play form called *Vinland the Good* that treated the voyages to North America of Leif Ericson and his crew. That book not only told me where exactly the Vikings went but what they said to each other on the way! At best the book's historical fiction contained a generous dollop of pure guesswork. But, since it was the first thing I ever encountered about Viking North America (or, for that matter, Viking voyages at all), it provided the basic structuring knowledge of the Vikings that still, to this day, guides my intuitions – even though I'm a good enough academic to know intellectually that its guesses were often quite iffy and sometimes probably simply wrong. I am not absolutely locked into that particular intuitive understanding, but it would take a sustained interaction with better material plus some important stake in getting it right to override the effects of that early learning.

REFERENCES

Bateson, Gregory
1958[1938] Naven. Palo Alto, CA: Stanford University Press.
Berlin, O. Brent
1972 Speculations on the Growth of Ethnobotanical Nomenclature. Language in Society 1:51–86.
1992 Ethnobiological Classification. Princeton: Princeton University Press.
Berlin, O. Brent, and Paul Kay
1969 Basic Color Terms. Berkeley: University of California Press.
Frake, Charles O.
1961 The Diagnosis of Disease among the Subanun of Mindanao. American Anthropologist 93:113–132.
Kronenfeld, David B.
1996 Plastic Glasses and Church Fathers: Semantic Extension from the Ethnoscience Tradition. Oxford Studies in Anthropological Linguistics. New York: Oxford University Press.
2000 Language and Thought: Collective Tools for Individual Use. *In* Explorations in Linguistic Relativity. Martin Pütz and Marjolijn H. Verspoor, eds. Pp. 197–223. Amsterdam: John Benjamins.
2008a Cultural Models. Intercultural Pragmatics 5(1):67–74.
2008b Culture, Society, and Cognition: Collective Goals, Values, Action, and Knowledge. Berlin: Mouton de Gruyter.
2009 Fanti Kinship and the Analysis of Kinship Terminologies. Urbana: University of Illinois Press.
Lounsbury, Floyd L.
1964a The Structural Analysis of Kinship Semantics. *In* Proceedings of the Ninth International Congress of Linguists. Horace G. Lunt, ed. Pp. 1073–1093. The Hague: Mouton. *Repr. in* Cognitive Anthropology. Stephen A. Tyler, ed. Pp. 193–211. New York: Holt, Rinehart and Winston, 1969.
1964b A Formal Account of the Crow- and Omaha-Type Kinship Terminologies. *In* Explorations in Cultural Anthropology. Ward H. Goodenough, ed. Pp. 351–393. New York: McGraw-Hill. *Repr. in* Cognitive Anthropology. Stephen A. Tyler, ed. Pp. 212–255. New York: Holt, Rinehart and Winston, 1969.
Lowie, Robert
1920 Primitive Society. New York: Boni and Liveright.
Schank, Roger, and R. P. Abelson
1977 Scripts, Plans, Goals and Understanding: An Inquiry into Human Knowledge Structures. Hillsdale, NJ: Lawrence Erlbaum.
Sperber, Dan
1996 Explaining Culture: A Naturalistic Approach. Malden, MA: Blackwell.

Index

A Companion to Cognitive Anthropology, First Edition. Edited by David B. Kronenfeld, Giovanni Bennardo, Victor C. de Munck, and Michael D. Fischer.